COLONIAL AMERICA
ESSAYS IN POLITICS AND
SOCIAL DEVELOPMENT

COLONIAL AMERICA
ESSAYS IN POLITICS AND SOCIAL DEVELOPMENT

edited by   STANLEY N. KATZ
University of Chicago

Boston   LB   LITTLE, BROWN AND COMPANY

For
Viola Florence Barnes

Preface

This volume of essays is designed as supplementary reading for the colonial history survey course, although I hope instructors may find it useful in social history courses and graduate proseminars in colonial history. The essays are reprinted in full, with all charts and footnotes.

The essays are distributed over the full time period covered in the colonial course, but no essays on the Revolutionary era are included, since the Revolution is generally given a semester to itself and requires a more intensive selection than could be included in this volume. I have not reprinted essays on "European background" or "comparative colonization," although I am fully persuaded of their place in American history, since both fields are now so extensive that it is impossible to represent them fairly in a volume of this sort.

The colonial period is currently the subject of some of the most exciting substantive and methodological work in American history, and it seems important to me to convey a sense of the new discoveries and techniques to students. My selection is also slightly weighted in favor of the eighteenth century, since it has been my experience that paperback monographs for the earlier century are more readily available.

The essays are mostly concerned with colonial socio-political development. In justification I will plead only that this seems to me the most promising area of recent research, and it is the area in which I am most interested. The essays are, in addition, mostly by younger scholars, although no slight is intended to established historians. Rather, I assume that instructors will assign works by leading scholars in addition to these articles. The book is intended to do no more than to make a series of provocative and enlightening essays accessible to undergraduates and to provide a selection of readings out of which the instructor can choose those that suit his own lectures and reading list.

Contents

I ORIGINS OF COLONIAL SOCIETY: THE SEVENTEENTH CENTURY

II POLITICS AND THE IMPERIAL RELATIONSHIP

III COLONIAL POLITICS AND SOCIETY: THE EIGHTEENTH CENTURY

IV AMERICANS IN THE EIGHTEENTH CENTURY

COLONIAL AMERICA
ESSAYS IN POLITICS AND
SOCIAL DEVELOPMENT

ORIGINS OF COLONIAL SOCIETY: THE SEVENTEENTH CENTURY

I

From Organization to Society: Virginia in the Seventeenth Century

SIGMUND DIAMOND

Most historians have considered the great English trading companies which sponsored North American colonial ventures as encumbrances to successful settlement. From this point of view both the Virginia Company and the Massachusetts Bay Company were legal and economic hindrances to colonial initiative in creating permanent communities in the New World. The historical sociologist Sigmund Diamond suggests, however, a radically different interpretation of the founding of Virginia. He argues that the idea of an independent American society was the unintended consequence of Virginia Company policy.

The primary obstacle to the Company's commercial design in Virginia was a shortage of trained manpower, since the Indian population could not be satisfactorily exploited. The promoters responded to this problem by furnishing incentives to emigration and long-term employment. They attempted to regulate the enterprise and to maintain deferential relations between their supervisors and the workers by imposing a quasi-military organization upon the colony; but the need for increasing numbers of laborers finally prompted the company to offer additional incentives of land, spouses, and representative political institutions which had the effect of subverting the commercial organization originally envisioned. The result was that by 1619 a society had been created which had an integrity of its own, and which was no longer suited to the aims of the company.

Diamond challenges historians of colonization to look beyond the immediate concerns and ambitions of the settlers. He attempts to demonstrate that particular examples of historical change are governed by the general rules of social change which form the subject matter of sociology. This search for generalization in history is one of the themes binding the essays in this volume together.

Fad and fashion play their roles in the world of scholarship as elsewhere, and often products of the intellect may assume the quaint air of artifacts for no better reason than that, with the passage of time, they are made obsolete by the appearance of new, if not necessarily better, models. But in scholarship, if not in manufacturing, novelty is a virtue that has limits; and even old ideas and interests may be resurrected if they demonstrate the existence of problems or give promise of solving problems for which more recent ideas have proved inadequate. So it is that historical sociology, though conceded to be one of the roots from which the discipline itself emerged, has, in this country at least, suffered from the competition of more stylish fashions. And so it is, too, that there is increasing evidence today that historical sociology, so long an outmoded form of inquiry, is once again commending itself as an important subject of research. What follows is, frankly, an attempt to aid in the rehabilitation of historical sociology, not by exhortation, but, it is hoped, by a persuasive demonstration that questions of considerable importance for sociological theory may be raised when problems are examined in historical perspective. Our interest in this essay is in the utilization of certain aspects of the history of Virginia in the early seventeenth century to suggest significant questions concerning the creation of new statuses and the circumstances under which the character of an organization may be so altered as to be transmuted into something which is not, properly speaking, an organization at all but a society.

I

It must be conceded at the outset that the group we have selected for study was pathetically small. In 1607, when the Virginia Company established a settlement at Jamestown, its population numbered 105; and in 1624, when the crown revoked the charter of the Company, the population of Virginia amounted to just over 1,200, despite the fact that the Company had sent more than 5,000 emigrants during that seventeen-year period.[1] But, just as a limited duration of time is no necessary detriment to a study of this kind, because there are periods of history when the rate of change is accelerated, so, too, the limited size of the group affords no accurate measure of the importance of the enterprise. Judged in terms of its outcome, its importance is self-evident. But, judged even

Reprinted by permission from Sigmund Diamond, "From Organization to Society; Virginia in the Seventeenth Century," *American Journal of Sociology*, LXIII (1958), 457–475.

[1] Philip Alexander Bruce, *Social Life of Virginia in the Seventeenth Century* (Richmond, 1907), pp. 15, 17–18; "The Virginia Census, 1624–25," *Virginia Magazine of History and Biography*, VII (1899–1900), 364–67; Edward Channing, *A History of the United States* (New York and London, 1905–25), I, 204–5.

in terms of the criteria of importance imposed by contemporaries, the verdict must be the same. The articles on the Virginia settlement in the *Kölnische Zeitung* and the *Mercure françoise;* the running series of reports from the Venetian ambassadors in London to the Doge and Senate; the letters from Jesuit priests in England to the Propaganda Fide in Rome and the newsletters from Venice and Antwerp in the Vatican archives; the continuing stream of dispatches from Spanish ambassadors to King Philip III, pressing him to attack Jamestown, advising him of the latest decisions of the Virginia Company, and relating their efforts to recruit English spies; and the existence in the royal archives at Simancas of a description of the layout of Jamestown and the earliest known map of the town, the work of an Irish spy in the service of Spain [2] – all this is eloquent testimony of the position of Virginia in the international relations of the seventeenth century and of the concern felt in the capitals of Europe in the Virginia Company's undertaking. Nor was the expression of this concern merely verbal. In August, 1613, when the population of Virginia barely exceeded 200, the settlement at Jamestown had a decidedly cosmopolitan cast, for it contained eighteen prisoners – fifteen Frenchmen, including two Jesuits and several members of the nobility; a Spanish spy, Don Diego de Molina; a renegade Englishman in the pay of Spain; and an Indian princess, Pocahontas.[3]

At the May Day, 1699, exercises at the College of William and Mary, one of the student orators – who must have been a sophomore – exclaimed:

> Methinks we see already that happy time when we shall surpass the Asiaticians in civility, the Jews in religion, the Greeks in philosophy, the Egyptians in geometry, the Phoenicians in arithmetic, and the Chaldeans in astrology. O happy Virginia.[4]

We may be intrigued by the ingenuousness of the student, but we are interested in the statement as evidence of the fact that in 1699 – and for some time earlier – Virginia was a society and Virginians were nothing if not ebullient about its prospects. For it had not always been so.

[2] See, e.g., Alexander Brown, *The Genesis of the United States* (Boston and New York, 1897), I, 142, 180, n. 1, 244–45, 393–99; II, 595–96, 738, 741; *Calendar of State Papers and Manuscripts Relating to English Affairs . . . in the Archives and Collections of Venice . . .* , Vol. XI, Nos. 52, 466, 794, 821; Carl Russell Fish (ed.), *Guide to the Materials for American History in Roman and Other Italian Archives* (Washington, 1911), pp. 150 ff.; Henry Chandlee Forman, *Jamestown and St. Mary's* (Baltimore, 1938), pp. 37, 38; Alexander Brown, *The First Republic in America* (New York and Boston, 1898), pp. 48, 50, 51–52, 62, 79–80, 121, 123, 125, 152, 160, 184–85, 218–19.

[3] Brown, *Genesis*, II, 700–706.

[4] Quoted in Louis B. Wright, *The First Gentlemen of Virginia* (San Marino, 1940), p. 109.

⌈At its inception — and for a number of years thereafter — it had been a formal organization,⌉ and, if the joyous outburst of the student reflects its character at a later date, its earlier character is better revealed by the instructions given by the Virginia Company to Sir Thomas Gates on the eve of his departure for Jamestown in May, 1609:

> You must devide yor people into tennes twenties & so upwards, to every necessary worke a competent nomber, over every one of wch you must appointe some man of Care & skill in that worke to oversee them and to take dayly accounte of their laboures, and you must ordayne y^t every overseer of such a nomber of workemen Deliver once a weeke an accounte of the wholle comitted to his Charge . . . you shall doe best to lett them eate together at reasonable howers in some publique place beinge messed by six or five to a messe, in wch you must see there bee equality and sufficient that so they may come and retourne to their worke without any delay and have no cause to complain of measure or to excuse their idleness uppon ye dressinge or want of diet. You may well allowe them three howers in a somers day and two in the winter, and shall call them together by Ringinge of a Bell and by the same warne them againe to worke.[5]

And, if in later years "O happy Virginia" could be a spontaneous outcry of its citizens, it could not have been earlier. Testifying in 1625 about conditions under the administration of Sir Thomas Dale in 1614–16, Mrs. Perry, one of the fortunates who survived more than a few years in the first quarter-century of Virginia's history, revealed that

> in the time of Sr: Thomas Dales Government An leyden and June Wright and other women were appoynted to make shirts for the Colony servants and had six nelds full of silke threed allowed for making of a shirte, wch yf they did not p'forme, They had noe allowance of Dyott, and because theire threed naught and would not sewe, they tooke owt a ravell of ye lower p^{te} of ye shirte to make an end of ye worke, and others y^t had threed of thiere owne made it up wth that, Soe the shirts of those wch had raveled owt proved shorter than the next, for wch fact the said An leyden and June Wright were whipt, And An leyden beinge then wth childe (the same night thereof miscarried).[6]

Our first inquiry, then, must be into the characteristics of the original settlement at Jamestown — characteristics which changed so markedly during the course of the next quarter-century.

---

[5] Susan Myra Kingsbury (ed.), *Records of the Virginia Company* (Washington, 1906–35), III, 21.

[6] "Minutes of the Council and General Court," *Virginia Magazine of History and Biography*, XXIII (1915), 138.

[Virginia was not established as a colony to take its place among the territories governed by the British crown; it was not a state, and, properly speaking, it was not a political unit at all. It was property, the property of the Virginia Company of London, and it was established to return a profit to the stockholders of that company.] Under the political and economic conditions of seventeenth-century England, speculators in overseas expansion could count on no support from the government except verbal encouragement and some legal protection — and sometimes precious little of these. [Under the circumstances, therefore, colonization had to be undertaken as a private business venture, and the first charge imposed on the property was the return on the shareholder's investment. Traditionally, this episode has been dealt with primarily in terms of the motivation of participants — did they come to establish religious freedom, to seek a haven for the politically persecuted, or to found a "First Republic"? — and it is true that those who joined the Virginia enterprise did so for many reasons.] Some, like Richard Norwood, were footloose and fancy-free after having completed their apprenticeships. Robert Evelin wrote his mother that he was "going to the sea, a long and dangerous voyage with other men, to make me able to pay my debts, and to restore my decayed estate again . . . and I beseech you, if I do die, that you would be good unto my poor wife and children, which God knows, I shall leave very poor and very mean, if my friends be not good unto them." In its promotional literature the Virginia Company took advantage of this broad spectrum of motives and cast its net wide to snare the purses and bodies of all sorts and conditions of persons in support of a venture in which

> . . . profite doth with pleasure joyne,
> and bids each chearefull heart,
> To this high praysed enterprise,
> performe a Christian part.[7]

[But, from the point of view of the managers of the enterprise, recruitment was perceived less as a problem of motivation than of achieving an organizational form through which the resources and energies of the participants could be mobilized. The basic objectives of the promoters in establishing a plantation in Virginia are quite clear: to exploit the mineral resources which they were certain were there; to search for that elusive will-o'-the-wisp — a water route to the Pacific through North America — and to monopolize whatever local trade existed and whatever

---

[7] Wesley Frank Craven and Walter B. Hayward, *The Journal of Richard Norwood, Surveyor of Bermuda* (New York, 1945); Brown, *Genesis*, I, 442; "London's Lotterie," *William and Mary Quarterly*, V (3d ser., 1948), 259–64.

oriental trade would be developed with the opening-up of the northwest passage]

The organizational form adopted for the venture was not created by the promoters; the roots of the joint-stock company, though it was still subject to considerable experimentation, lay deeply imbedded in English history. Nor were the proprietors themselves totally without experience in the establishment of plantations or unaware of the experience of others. Sir Thomas Smythe, a leader of the Virginia enterprise, was one of the merchant princes of London, a governor of the East India Company, the Muscovy Company, and many others. And they had before them the experience — which was, as we shall see, not entirely an un-mixed blessing — of the colonizing efforts of Sir Walter Raleigh and Sir Humphrey Gilbert, of the trading posts established by the great commercial companies, of Spain and Portugal, and of the founding of plantations in Ireland.[8]

[What they established was a business organization; and, though the form of that organization was changed at various times during the Company's history, those changes were at all times dictated by the need to make business pay,] which, in the words of Sir Edwin Sandys, one of the two great leaders of the Company, was "that whereon all men's eyes were fixed." [9] Its problems were those of any business orginization. It sold shares, begged contributions, and organized lotteries to raise the necessary funds; it was concerned to recruit a proper labor force; it had to cope with the problem of adequate supervision and administration so as to maintain its authority; and it engaged in a full-scale advertising campaign to sell to potential adventurers and planters the glories of a land where the "horses are also more beautiful, and fuller of courage. And such is the extraordinarie fertility of that Soyle, that the Does of their Deere yeelde Two Fawnes at a birth, and sometimes three." And it was confronted with the petty harassments of cajoling those whose good will was needed for the success of the organization. "Talking with the King," wrote the Earl of Southampton to Sir Robert Cecil, "by chance I told him of the Virginia Squirrills which they say will fly, whereof there are now divers brought into England, and hee presently and very earnestly asked me if none of them was provided for him. . . .

---

[8] Herbert Levi Osgood, *The American Colonies in the Seventeenth Century* (New York and London, 1904, 1907), I, 32–34; II, 30–32; Philip Alexander Bruce, *Economic History of Virginia in the Seventeenth Century* (New York and London, 1896), I, 3–4.

[9] Wesley Frank Craven, *Dissolution of the Virginia Company* (New York, 1932), p. 24. For an account of the structure of the Company see William Robert Scott, *The Constitution and Finance of English, Scottish and Irish Joint-Stock Companies to 1720* (Cambridge, 1910), II, 247–59, 266–88.

I would not have troubled you with this but that you know so well how he is affected by these toyes." [10]

[But though the Company's plans were eminently rational, its grand design suffered from a fatal flaw: reality was far different from what the Company expected. Its model had been the East India Company, and its dream had been to reproduce the Spanish looting of a continent; but conditions in Virginia were not those of India or Mexico and Peru.] "It was the Spaniards good hap," wrote Captain John Smith later in the history of the Virginia Company,

> to happen in those parts where were infinite numbers of people, whoe had manured the ground with that providence that it afforded victuall at all times; and time had brought them to that perfection they had the use of gold and silver, and the most of such commodities as their countries affoorded; so that what the Spaniard got was only the spoile and pillage of those countries people, and not the labours of their owne hands. But had those fruitfull Countries been as Salvage, as barbarous, as ill-peopled, as little planted laboured and manured, as Virginia; their proper labours, it is likely would have produced as small profit as ours. . . .
>
> But we chanced in a land, even as God made it. . . . When ere wee could bring to recompence our paines, defray our charges, and satisfie our adventurers; wee were to discover the country, subdue the people, bring them to be tractable civil and industrious, and teach them trades that the fruits of their labours might make us recompence, or plant such colonies of our owne that must first make provision how to live of themselves ere they can bring to perfection the commodities of the countrie.[11]

But though the error in conception made by the leaders of the Virginia Company was, from their viewpoint, a grievous one, it is also thoroughly understandable. [It is true that the late sixteenth and early seventeenth century was a period of rapid expansion in the organization of trading companies; no less than thirty-four were chartered during that time. But the significant point is that the Virginia Company was the eighteenth to be founded, and, of the previous seventeen, whose experience could be taken as models, all dealt with countries within the European seas, with settled communities along the African coast, or with the advanced

---

[10] A Declaration of the State of the Colonie and Affairs in Virginia (London, 1620), in Peter Force (ed.), Tracts and Other Papers, Relating . . . to the . . . Colonies in North America (Washington, 1836–46), III, 5; Brown, Genesis, I, 357.

[11] John Smith, Description of Virginia and Proceedings of the Colonie (Oxford, 1612), in Lyon Gardiner Tyler (ed.), Narratives of Early Virginia (New York, 1907), p. 178.

societies of Asia. For them, the problem was to exploit the already existing labor force of a settled society.[12] For the Virginia Company, the
problem — and it is in this that the crucial difference lies — was to recruit
a labor force.]

It must be understood, therefore, that, in conformity with its objectives
and organizational form, the establishment planted by the Virginia
Company at Jamestown was a private estate, which, in the absence of
an amenable local labor force, was worked on the basis of imported
labor. Basic policies were laid down in London by the General Court of
the Company, the body of those who had purchased the £12. 10s. shares
or who had been admitted for favors in the Company's behalf; the
management and direction of affairs were intrusted to agents of the
shareholders; and the supervision of those whose labor in Virginia was
necessary for the attainment of the Company's objectives was placed in
the hands of officials appointed in London.

Under the circumstances there were many potent inducements to
English investors to purchase the Company's £12. 10s. shares, a price,
incidentally, which was the Company's estimate of the cost of transporting a settler to Virginia. Under the charter of 1606 they were guaranteed
that after a five-year period, during which the settlers in Virginia would
be supported by a stream of supplies sent at Company expense, the profits
gained through trade and the discovery of minerals would be divided
among the investors in proportion to the number of shares they held,
and grants of land would be made to them on the same basis. [But what
were to be the inducements to become the labor force of a company
trading post?]

[It should be noted at once that the English imitated the Spaniards in
attempting to mobilize native labor. For the Company the key to the
integration of the Indians into the labor force was in the ease with
which, it was anticipated, they could be converted to Christianity and
thereby won over as well to the secular values of Europeans. To them
would accrue spiritual benefits; the Company, already blessed with those,
would receive something more substantial.] As a certain "Maister Captaine
Chester" put it:

> The land full rich, the people easilie wonne,
> Whose gaines shalbe the knowledge of our faith
> And ours such ritches as the country hath.[13]

[12] Susan Myra Kingsbury, "A Comparison of the Virginia Company with the
Other English Trading Companies of the Sixteenth and Seventeenth Centuries,"
Annual Report of the American Historical Association for the year 1906 (Wash-
ington, 1907), pp. 162–63.

[13] Quoted in Keith Glenn, "Captain John Smith and the Indians," *Virginia
Magazine of History and Biography*, LII (1944), 231, n. 12.

But though the Company succeeded for a time in extracting some tribute from the local tribal chiefs in the form of goods and weekly labor services, the Indians proved unwilling to accept the Company's spiritual and secular offerings. Long before the Indian uprising of 1622 gave an excuse to the settlers to engage in a campaign of extermination, it was clear that the Virginia Company would be forced to import its own labor force.[14]

Between 1607 and 1609, when its charter was changed, the Virginia Company sent over 300 persons to Jamestown. They were a disparate crew of adventurers and roughnecks, imbued with the hope that after a short period in Virginia they would return home with their fortunes in their purses. The social composition of the original labor force, the tasks they were expected to perform, and the nature of the settlement they were expected to establish can all be inferred from the passenger lists of the first expedition and the three subsequent supplies that were sent out by the Company before its charter was modified in 1609. The original expedition numbered 105 persons, of whom we have the names of 67. Of these 67, 29 were listed as gentlemen and 6 were named to the local council; the rest were listed by occupation – 1 preacher, 4 carpenters, 12 laborers, 1 surgeon, 1 blacksmith, 1 sailor, 1 barber, 2 bricklayers, 1 mason, 1 tailor, 1 drummer, and 4 boys – and 2 were unidentified. In the three succeeding supplies, the rather high proportion of gentlemen was not substantially reduced, nor did the range of occupations alter significantly. Seventy-three of the 120 persons in the first supply of 1608 can be identified. In this group, gentlemen exceeded laborers 28 to 21. The remainder was made up of an odd assortment of craftsmen, including jewelers, refiners, and goldsmiths – bespeaking the expectations of the Company – apothecaries, tailors, blacksmiths, and – mute testimony to the fact that gentlemen must be gentlemen whether in the wilds of Virginia or a London drawing room – a perfumer. In brief, the two most striking characteristics of this original labor force are the presence of so high a proportion of gentlemen and the absence of any occupations indicative of an intention to establish a settled agricultural community.[15]

From the point of view of the promoters of the Virginia enterprise, these men were not citizens of a colony; they were the occupants of a status in – to use an anachronistic term – the Company's table of organization, and the status was that of workman. Such other qualities or attributes that they possessed might have been of importance when they

[14] Wesley Frank Craven, "Indian Policy in Early Virginia," *William and Mary Quarterly*, I (3d ser., 1944), 65–82.

[15] John Smith, *Description of Virginia*, in Tyler (ed.), *op. cit.*, pp. 125–26, 140–41, 159–60; Thomas Jefferson Wertenbaker, *Patrician and Plebeian in Virginia* (Charlottesville, 1910), pp. 5–9; Bruce, *Social Life*, pp. 39–43.

were in London, Norwich, or Bristol, but what counted in Virginia was that they should accept the directions of their superiors and that they should be willing to work.

[Even under the best of circumstances, the problem of maintaining discipline and authority would have been crucial to the success of the Company. But these were hardly the best of circumstances, for the very social composition of the original labor force intensified what in any case would have been a grievously difficult problem.] In the long intervals between arrival of supplies under the direction of the Company's admiral, Christopher Newport, conditions in Jamestown bordered on anarchy; men were beaten by their officers, plots were hatched to escape the country, and insubordination was rampant. The Company's administrative methods, characterized by the utmost laxness, could not cope with the situation. "I likewise as occasion moved me," wrote President Wingfield, discussing the supplies in Virginia, "spent them in trade or by guift amongst the Indians. So likewise did Captain Newport take of them . . . what he thought good, without any noate of his hand mentioning the certainty; and disposed of them as was fitt for him. Of these likewise I could make no accompt." Nor did the high percentage of aristocrats help matters. Unused to the heavy work of axing timber, they cursed so much at their blisters that the president of the council ordered that at the end of the day's work a can of cold water be poured down the sleeve of each offender for every curse he had uttered. To Captain John Smith, the problem was the presence of too many gentlemen: "For some small number of adventrous Gentlemen . . . nothing were more requisite; but to have more to wait and play than worke, or more commanders and officers than industrious labourers was not so necessarie. For in Virginia, a plaine Souldier that can use a Pickaxe and spade, is better than five Knights." [16]

Clearly, even if the mortality figures had been less gruesome than they were — in July, 1609, between 80 and 100 were alive of the 320 who had been sent since 1607 [17] — qualitative considerations alone would have dictated a change in the composition of the labor force. For the Company the situation was brought to a head with the realization that there were to be no quick returns from metals and trade and that profits would have to be made through the exploitation of agricultural resources.

[Never did the Company rely fundamentally on the recruitment of involuntary labor, but so desperate were its labor requirements and so

---

[16] The quotations are in Osgood, *op. cit.*, I, 46–47; Smith, *Generall Historie*, in Tyler (ed.), *op. cit.*, pp. 331–32; John Smith, *The Proceedings of the English Colonie in Virginia* (Oxford, 1612), in the A. G. Bradley edition of Edward Arber (ed.), *Travels and Works of Captain John Smith* (Edinburgh, 1919), I, 149. See also Osgood, *op. cit.*, I, 50, 54–55; Bruce, *Economic History*, I, 197.

[17] Channing, *op. cit.*, I, 204.

necessary was it to keep the good will of those authorities who favored
the transportation of undesirables that it felt compelled to resort to
forced labor.]

As early as 1609, a letter from Lisbon revealed that the Portuguese
were transporting fifteen hundred children over the age of ten to the
East Indies and suggested that the same be done in the case of Virginia.
Shortly thereafter the Privy Council notified the mayor of London that
the plagues of the city were due mainly to the presence of so many poor
persons and recommended that a fund be raised, with the help of the
commercial companies, to send as many of these as possible to Virginia.
The Virginia Company promptly gave an estimate of the expenses involved and of the terms that would be offered to the emigrants; but,
though a large sum of money was raised, no persons were actually transported at that time. In 1617, however, the City of London raised £500
to pay the cost of shipping one hundred children to Virginia, where they
were to be apprenticed until the age of twenty-one, thereafter to be fee-
simple owners of fifty acres of land each. So delighted were the Company
and the Virginia planters that they continued the practice, but it is evident that not all the children were equally pleased by the future arranged
for them. In January, 1620, Sandys wrote to Sir Robert Naunton, the
king's principal secretary, that "it falleth out that among those children,
sundry being ill-disposed, and fitter for any remote place than for this Citie,
declare their unwillingness to goe to Virginia: of whom the Citie is
especially desirous to be disburdened; and in Virginia under severe
Masters they may be brought to goodness." Since the City could not
deliver and the Company could not transport "theis persons against
their wills," Sandys appealed to the Privy Council for the necessary authority. It was quickly given.[Exact figures cannot be determined, but,
before the demise of the Company in 1624, additional shipments of
children had been delivered to Virginia, and it is evident that several
hundred must have been involved.[18]]

Concerning the shipment of convicts and rogues and vagabonds the
information is scanty. Some convicts were certainly in Virginia before
1624, though we do not know how many; but the Virginia Company
was antagonistic to the importation of such persons, and, in any case,
convict-dumping on a large scale did not become a characteristic of the
colonial scene until the second half of the seventeenth century.[19] So, too,

---

[18] *Calendar of State Papers, East Indies, 1571–1616*, No. 432; Brown, *Genesis*,
I, 252–54; E. Ribton-Turner, *A History of Vagrants and Vagrancy* (London,
1887), 141; Kingsbury (ed.), *Records*, I, 304–6, 270, 359; III, 259; *Acts of the
Privy Council of England, Colonial Series*, Vol. I, No. 42; Abbot Emerson Smith,
Colonists in Bondage (Chapel Hill, 1947), pp. 147–49; Richard B. Morris, *Gov-
ernment and Labor in Early America* (New York, 1946), p. 385.

[19] A. E. Smith, *op. cit.*, pp. 94–95; Morris, *op. cit.*, p. 323.

was the Company antagonistic to the importation of rogues, possibly
because, unlike the case of the London children, it was forced to assume
the cost of transportation. It engaged in the practice under pressure
from King James I. For one group of fifty boys sent out in 1619, the
Company expected to receive £500 in tobacco from the planters to whom
they were indentured; but as late as October, 1622, it had received only
£275.15.6, and Governor Yeardley was told that the planters "should be
caused to make satisfaccon for the 224^{li}4:6:wch is remayninge due unto
the Companie this yeare in good leafe Tobacco." That still others were
sent is certain; the Court Book of Bridewell Hospital records that in
1620 Ellen Boulter was "brought in by the Marshall for a Vagrant, that
will not be ruled by her father or her friends," to be kept at her father's
charges to go to Virginia.[20]

[But throughout its history the Company was dependent upon the
recruitment of voluntary labor, and especially was this true when it
realized that profits would have to be made from agricultural staples and
not minerals. The change in objective not only emphasized the necessity
of recruiting a larger labor supply but required that it be qualitatively
different from the earlier one, for now that the glitter of gold was
vanishing the Company needed not soldiers of fortune but sober workmen who would be able to extract from the land the food supplies
necessary for their own support and the staples whose export would
produce profit for the shareholders.[21] But what could the Company offer
as sufficient inducement to motivate large numbers of persons to come
to Virginia, especially when — as the evidence indicates — enthusiasm
for emigration from England was confined to the wealthy, who themselves were hardly likely to exchange the comforts of life in England for
the dangers of life in Virginia? [22] The difficulties the Company faced in
this respect were exacerbated by the whispering campaign started by
settlers who had already returned from Virginia. "Some few of those unruly youths sent thither," said a Virginia Company broadside in 1609,

> (being of most leaued and bad condition) and such as no ground
> can hold for want of good direction there, were suffered by stealth
> to get aboard the ships returning thence, and are come for England
> againe, giving out in all places where they come (to colour their
> owne misbehaviours, and the cause of their returne with some pre-
> tence) most vile and scandalous reports, both of the Country itselfe,
> and of the Cariage of the business there.[23]

[20] Kingsbury (ed.), *Records*, I, 520, II, 108; A. E. Smith, *op. cit.*, pp. 139–40.
[21] Craven, *Virginia Company*, pp. 29–33; Scott, *op. cit.*, II, 250–52; Philip
Alexander Bruce, *Institutional History of Virginia in the Seventeenth Century*
(New York and London, 1910), II, 237–41.
[22] A. E. Smith, *op. cit.*, pp. 44–46.
[23] Brown, *Genesis*, I, 355.

The Company now determined to be discriminating in the selection
of settlers:

> And for that former experience hath too clearly taught, how muche
> and manie waies it hurtheth to suffer Parents to disburden them-
> selves of lascivious sonnes, masters of bad servants and wives of ill
> husbands, and so to dogge the business with such an idle crue, as
> did thrust themselves in the last voiage, that will rather starve for
> hunger, than lay their hands to labor.[24]

It was conceded that some "base and disordered men" might inveigle
themselves into the body of settlers, but they could not do too much harm,
for, as the Reverend William Crashaw said on the departure of Governor
de la Warr to Virginia, "the basest and worst men trained up in a severe
discipline, sharp lawes, a hard life, and much labour, do prove good
members of a Commonwealth. . . . The very excrements, of a full and
swelling state . . . wanting pleasures, and subject to some pinching
miseries," will become "good and worthie instruments." [25]
[Clearly, if prospective settlers in Virginia faced "severe discipline, sharp
lawes, a hard life, and much labour," substantial concessions would have
to be offered to induce them to emigrate.] The status the Company was
asking them to accept was that of servant, employee of the Company,
but it was one thing to create a position and quite another to get men to
fill it. [Since perpetual servitude was obviously no inducement, the Company was required to limit the period of service and to make other concessions. Every settler over the age of ten, whether he paid his own way or
was shipped at Company expense, was promised one share of stock in the
Company, with potential dividends from the profits of trade and a land
grant to be made at the time of the first division after seven years. Every
"extraordinarie" man — such as "Divines, Governors, Ministers of State
and Justice, Knights, Gentlemen, Physitions" or such as were "of worth
for special services" — was given additional shares according to the value
of his person] The Company expected, in return for assuming all the costs
of maintaining the plantation and providing supplies to the emigrants,
that each settler would work at tasks assigned him under the direction of
Company-appointed officers. For a period of seven years, all supplies
were to be distributed through the Company store, all exports were to be
shipped through the Company magazine, and all land was to be held

---

[24] *Ibid.*, I, 356.
[25] *A Sermon Preached in London before the Right Honourable Lord la warre,
Lord governor and Captaine Generall of Virginia* (London, 1610), quoted in
Perry Miller, "Religion and Society in the Early Literature: The Religious Impulse in the Founding of Virginia," *William and Mary Quarterly*, VI (3d ed.,
1949), 31; Brown, *Genesis*, I, 364.

by the Company.[26] [In effect, the Company created the status of land-owner in order to induce persons to accept the status of non-landowner; it was asking emigrants to accept the present burdens of membership in a lower status in anticipation of the future benefits they would receive up-on promotion to a higher status. From the point of view of the structure of an organization, this was simply automatic progression — promotion to a higher position in the table of organization after a limited tenure in a lower position. From the point of view of a society, however, this was a guaranty of social mobility, and, as we shall see, it seriously compromised the Company's ability to secure its organizational objectives.]

That the Company expected the combination of limited servitude and potential landownership to solve its labor problem is quite clear; sufficient numbers of workmen would be induced to emigrate to Virginia and, having arrived, would be motivated to do the work that was essential to the Company's success. Virginia planter and London adventurer were to be united in a single relationship. Do not discourage the planters, the London stockholders were admonished, "in growing religious, nor in gathering riches, two especiall bonds (whether severed or cojoined) to keepe them in obedience, the one for conscience sake, the other for fear of losing what they have gotten." How the planter's concern for his own interests was to benefit the Company was quite clear. "The Planters," wrote Alderman Johnson, "will be in such hope to have their owne shares and habitations in those lands, which they have so husbanded, that it will cause contending and emulation among them, which shall bring foorth the most profitable and beneficiall fruites for their ioynt stock." [27]

[But land for the settlers and profits for the stockholders were affairs of the future, and both were dependent upon the skill and speed with which the planters could be molded into an efficient labor force. It was of the utmost importance, therefore, that the Company establish its authority in Virginia and maintain discipline, and for the achievement of these purposes the Company was not content to rely simply on the self-discipline it hoped would be the byproduct of the effort to obtain profits. The first step was taken with the issuance of the new charter of 1609] During its first three years in Virginia, the Company felt, "experi-

---

[26] James Curtis Ballagh, *White Servitude in the Colony of Virginia* ("Johns Hopkins University Studies in Historical and Political Science, 13th Series," Vols. VII–VIII [Baltimore, 1895]), pp. 15–17; Craven, *Virginia Company*, pp. 29–33; Craven, *Southern Colonies*, pp. 85–90; A. E. Smith, *op. cit.*, pp. 8–10; Kingsbury, "Comparison," *op. cit.*, pp. 163–69.

[27] *The New Life of Virginea . . . Being the Second Part of Nova Britannia* (London, 1612), in Force (ed.), *op. cit.*, I, 17–18; *Nova Britannia*, in Force (ed.), *op. cit.*, I, 26.

ence of error in the equality of Governors, and some out-rages, and follies committed by them, had a little shaken so tender a body." To avoid the evils of divided authority, "we did resolve and obtain, to renew our Letters Pattents, and to procure to ourselves, such ample and large priviledges and powers by which we were at liberty to reforme and correct those already discovered, and to prevent such as in the future might threaten us . . . under the conduct of one able and absolute Governor." [28] But changes in the formal structure of authority were not sufficient.

[Religion, too, was counted upon to do its part in maintaining order. Doctrinal conflict was minimized from the start by the ban on Catholics, but what really distinguishes the role of religion under the Virginia Company was its conscious utilization for disciplinary purposes.] No less an authority on colonization than Richard Hakluyt had pointed to the advisability of taking along "one or two preachers that God may be honoured, the people instructed, mutinies better avoided, and obedience the better used." [29] The Company was quick to take the hint. Religion was used to screen prospective planters before their arrival in Virginia, and it was used to discipline them after their arrival. "We have thought it convenient to pronounce," stated the Company in a broadside of 1609, "that . . . we will receive no man that cannot bring or render some good testimony of his religion to God." [30] And during the time that Sir Thomas Dale's code of laws was sovereign in Virginia — from May, 1610, to April, 1619 — the settlers were marched to church twice each day to pray for relief from dissension and for the showering of blessings upon the shareholders:

> O Lord . . . defend us from the delusion of the devil, the malice of the heathen, the invasions of our enemies, & mutinies & dissentions of our own people. . . . Thou has moved . . . the hearts of so many of our nation to assist . . . with meanes and provision, and with their holy praiers . . . and for that portion of their substance which they willingly offer for thy honour & service in this action, recompence it to them and theirs, and reward it seven fold into their bosomes, with better blessinges.[31]

[In a society of ranks and orders, deference is owed to certain persons by virtue of their social position, and the Company attempted to maximize the potentiality for discipline in such an arrangement by appoint-

[28] A *True and Sincere Declaration* (London, 1609), in Brown, *Genesis*, I, 352.
[29] Quoted in Craven, *Southern Colonies*, p. 64.
[30] Appendix to A *True and Sincere Declaration*, in Brown, *Genesis*, I, 352.
[31] *For the Colony in Virginea Britannia, Lawes Divine, Morall and Martiall, &c* (London, 1612), in Force (ed.), *op. cit.*, III, 68.

ing to leading posts in Virginia those persons to whom obedience was
due because of their high status.] Insofar as it was possible, the Company
selected only persons of high birth to be governor; when it was not possible, as in the case of Governor Yeardley, it quickly, and it seems surrep-
titiously, secured for him a knighthood.[32] And at all times the governors
were urged to surround themselves with the pomp and circumstance of
high office, the better to impress the governed. "You shall for the more
regard and respect of yor place," read the Company's instructions to Sir
Thomas Gates,

> to beget reverence to yor authority, and to refresh their mindes that
> obey the gravity of those lawes under wch they were borne at yor
> discrecon use such formes and Ensignes of government as by our
> letters Pattents wee are enabled to grant unto you, as also the at-
> tendance of a guarde uppon your pson.[33]

[Ultimately, however, the Company relied upon a military regimen and
upon the imposition of force to obtain labor discipline.] Governor de la
Warr had been instructed that his men were to be divided into groups
and placed under the charge of officers "to be exercised and trayned up
in Martiall manner and warlike Discipline." [34] Settlers were forbidden to
return to England without permission, and their letters were sealed and
sent first to the Company in London before being forwarded.[35] But
the full code of military discipline was not worked out until the arrival in
Jamestown of Captain Thomas Dale, marshal of the colony, who had
been granted a leave of absence from his post in the Netherlands army
at the behest of the Company. Dale supplemented the usual list of
religious offenses and crimes against the state and the person with a
series of enactments designed to protect the Company's interests. Slander
against the Company, its officers, or any of its publications; unauthorized
trading with the Indians; escaping to the Indians; theft; and killing of
any domestic animal without consent; false accounting by any keeper of
supplies — all were punishable by service in the galleys or death. Failure
to keep regular hours of work subjected the offender to the pain of being
forced to lie neck and heels together all night for the first offense, whipping for the second, and one year's service in the galleys for the third.[36]

Moreover, Dale created a military rank for every person in Virginia
and specified the duties of each in such a way as to provide us with

[32] Kingsbury (ed.), *Records*, III, 216–19.
[33] *Ibid.*, p. 15.
[34] *Ibid.*, p. 27.
[35] *Ibid.*, p. 22.
[36] For the full text of the code see *For the Colony in Virginea Britannia. Lawes Divine, Morall and Martiall &c* (London, 1612), in Force (ed.), *op. cit.*, Vol. III.

important clues into the nature of labor discipline and what was expected to provide the motivation to work.

> Because we are not onely to exercise the duty of a Souldier, but that of the husbandman, and that in time of the vacancie of our watch and ward wee are not to live idly, therefore the Captaine . . . shall . . . demand . . . what service, worke, and businesse he hath in charge, from the Governor . . . in which worke the Captaine himselfe shall do exceeding worthily to take paines and labour, that his Souldiers seeing his industry and carefulnesse, may with more cheerfulnesse love him, and bee incouraged to the performance of the like.

Of the corporal:

> His duty is to provide that none of his Squadron, be absent, when the drumme shall call to any labour, or worke, or at what time soever they shall be commanded thereunto for the service of the Collonie, in the performance of which said workes he is to be an example of the rest of his Squadron by his owne labouring therein . . . that thereby giving incoraging to his superior officers he may be held by them worthy of a higher place.

Of the private soldier:

> He shall continue at his worke until the drumme beat, and . . . be conducted into the church to heare divine service, after which he may repayre to his house or lodging to prepare for his dinner, and to repose him until the drumme beate shall call him forth againe in the afternoone . . . the Generall having understanding of his promptitude and diligence may conferre upon him, and call him into place of preferment and command.[37]

[What is so striking about Dale's Code is the way in which it stripped from people all attributes save the one that really counted in the relationship which the Company sought to impose on them — their status in the organization. Behavior was expected to conform to a set of prescriptions the major characteristic of which was that the rights and obligations of persons depended on their position within the organization. In this respect, the contrast between Dale's Code and the first set of laws the settlers were able to enact for themselves at the General Assembly of 1619 is startling. For then, considerations other than status within an organization were fundamental:]

> All persons whatsoever upon the Sabaoth days shall frequente divine service and sermons both forenoon and afternoone. . . . And everyone that shall transgresse this lawe shall forfeicte three shillinges a

---

[37] For the Colony in Virginea Britannia, in Force (ed.), op. cit., III, 44, 55, 61–62.

time to the use of the churche. . . . But if a servant in this case
shall wilfully neglecte his Mr's commande he shall suffer bodily
punishment.

Or consider the following petition drafted by the Assembly:

> . . . that the antient Planters . . . suche as before Sir T. Dales'
> depart were come hither . . . maye have their second, third and
> more divisions successively in as lardge and free manner as any other
> Planter. Also that they wilbe pleased to allowe to the male children,
> of them and of all others begotten in Virginia, being the onely
> hope of a posterity, a single share a piece.[38]

[For the planters in Virginia, considerations of length of residence and
of varying degrees of freedom now affected the rights and obligations of
persons. No longer could relations be determined exclusively by the
positions persons held within a single system – the organization of the
Company. By 1619 Virginia was becoming a society, in which behavior
was in some way determined by the totality of positions each person held
in a network of sometimes complementary, sometimes contradictory,
relationships. The key to this transformation from organization to society lies in the concessions the Company was forced to offer to induce
persons to accept positions in the organizational relationship; for those
concessions so multiplied the number of statuses and so altered the
status of persons that a system of relationships was created where only
one had existed before]
[The fact is that the reforms the Company instituted in 1609 were not
sufficient either to swell the supply of labor migrating to Virginia or to
motivate the planters who were there to work with the will the Company
expected] The Company had hoped that by its reforms it would be able
to obtain not "idle and wicked persons; such as shame, or fear compels
into this action [but] fit and industrious [persons], honest sufficient
Artificers." [39] Yet so unproductive were they that as late as 1616 John
Rolfe could indicate to Sir Robert Rich that what had been was still
the Company's most serious problem. Our greatest want, he wrote, is
"good and sufficient men as well of birth and quality to command,
soldiers to marche, discover and defend the country from invasion,
artificers, labourers, and husbandmen." [40] And so dissatisfied had the
settlers become with their situation that, in a letter smuggled to the
Spanish ambassador in London with the connivance of English sailors,
Don Diego de Molina, the prisoner in Jamestown, reported that "a good
many have gone to the Indians . . . and others have gone out to sea . . .

---

[38] Kingsbury (ed.), *Records*, III, 173, 160.
[39] Appendix to *A True and Sincere Declaration* (1609), in Brown, *Genesis*, I,
352; Virginia Company broadside of 1610, in Brown, *Genesis*, I, 439.
[40] Quoted in Charles M. Andrews, *The Colonial Period of American History*
(New Haven, 1934–38), I, 113–14.

and those who remain do so by force and are anxious to see a fleet come from Spain to release them from this misery." [41] The hope that Don Diego attributed to the colonists was, no doubt, the wish of a patriotic Spaniard; but it is nevertheless true that some settlers did flee to the Indians, that the Company did succeed in obtaining authority to deport to Virginia those settlers who had escaped back to England, and that Coles and Kitchins, who had been Don Diego's guards, were executed in 1614 for organizing a plot to escape to Florida.[42]

[Nor did the concessions granted to superior colonists in 1614, including a kind of modified right to private property and some relief from the obligation to work on the Company lands, suffice to solve the labor problem.[43] For the simple fact was, as Captain John Smith wrote, that "no man will go from hence to have less liberty there then here." [44] [The Company, determined in 1619 to make a final effort to create of Virginia the profitable investment it had always hoped it would be, took his advice to heart. Though it was faced with declining financial resources, with internal bickering, and with increasing evidence that the king was losing patience with its meager achievement, the Company decided to pin its hopes on a quick return. The key to profits, it felt, lay in raising the value of the Company lands through increasing population and in diversifying products through the importation of labor skilled in many trades. The success of the effort, obviously, rested upon the strength of the additional inducements that could be offered to both investors and potential emigrants.[45]

[As always, one of the principal devices used by the Company to attract labor and to increase productivity was that of easing the terms on which land could be acquired. The effect of the reform was to create within the Company a new group of statuses differentiated from one another in terms of the amount of property attached to each or the length of time required to obtain land on the part of those who were not yet entitled to it:]

1. "Ancient planters" who had come to Virginia at their own cost before 1616 received 100 acres per share in perpetuity rent-free.

2. "Ancient planters" who had come to Virginia at Company expense received 100 acres at an annual rent of 2s. after the com-

[41] Brown, *Genesis*, II, 648–49.

[42] Morris, *op. cit.*, pp. 169–71.

[43] Ballagh, *op. cit.*, pp. 22–23; Osgood, *op. cit.*, I, 75–77; Bruce, *Economic History*, I, 212–15; Craven, *Southern Colonies*, pp. 116–17; A. E. Smith, *op. cit.*, pp. 10–11.

[44] Quoted in Miller, "Religion and Society," *op. cit.*, p. 37.

[45] Craven, *Virginia Company, passim*, but esp. pp. 168–71; Craven, *Southern Colonies*, pp. 145–47; Scott, *op. cit.*, II, 266–88; Susan Myra Kingsbury. *An Introduction to the Records of the Virginia Company of London* (Washington, 1905), pp. 34–35, 40–41, 94–95.

pletion of their seven-year period of servitude on the Company's land.

3. All persons who came to Virginia after 1616 at their own expense received 50 acres at an annual rent of 1s.

4. All persons who came to Virginia after 1616 at Company expense were to receive 50 acres after having worked on the Company's land for seven years, during which time half their produce belonged to the Company and half to themselves.

5. All tradesmen received a house and 4 acres of land so long as they plied their trades.

6. All persons who paid for the transportation of emigrants received 50 acres per person.

7. Company officers not only were entitled to their regular land grants but were supported by the labor of tenants-at-halves on large tracts of land reserved by the Company for that purpose.[46]

8. Indentured servants, whose transportation was paid by the Company or by private associations of investors and who were then sold to planters on their arrival in Virginia, were entitled to "freedom dues" — including a land grant — on the expiration of their servitude.[47]

Nor was this all. [Determined to improve the morale of the colonists and, eventually, to relieve the Company of the burdensome cost of transporting labor from England, Sandys also began in 1620 to ship women to Virginia to become wives of the planters. There had been marriages in Virginia before, of course, but the supply of single women, restricted to the few female servants of married couples, was far smaller than the demand. Now, however, the Company organized the shipment of women on a business basis, forming a separate joint-stock company for the purpose.] Though the women were, in any case, to be paid for by the planters at the rate of 120 pounds of the best leaf tobacco per person and though the Company conceded that it was dubious as to its authority to control marriages — "for the libertie of Mariadge we dare not infrindg" — it nevertheless discriminated between classes of planters in the bestowal of the women. "And though we are desireous that mariadge be free according to the law of nature," the Company wrote to the Governor and Council of Virginia, "yett would we not have these maids deceived and married to servants, but only to such freemen or tenants as have meanes to maintaine them." [48]

---

[46] "Instructions to Governor Yeardley, 1618," *Virginia Magazine of History and Biography*, II (1894–95), 161–62; Bruce, *Economic History*, I, 226–33, 511–14; Ballagh, *op. cit.*, pp. 25–28, 31; Craven, *Virginia Company*, pp. 50–57; Craven, *Southern Colonies*, pp. 127–29.

[47] A. E. Smith, *op. cit.*, pp. 11–17; Ballagh, *op. cit.*, pp. 28–30; Bruce, *Economic History*, II, 41–48; Morris, *op. cit.*, p. 395.

[48] Kingsbury (ed.), *Records*, III, 115, 493–94, 505.

Finally, in a radical departure from previous policy, the Company limited the scope of martial law and ordered Governor Yeardley to convene an assembly of elected representatives from each district in Virginia. The Company did not intend to diminish its own authority, for the Governor was given the right to veto all enactments of the Assembly, and the General Court of the Company in London retained the right to disallow its decisions. Rather was it the Company's hope that the degree of acceptance of its program would be increased if it had the added sanction of approval by representatives of the planters themselves.[49]

In a sense, the Company's reforms succeeded too well. Lured by the new prospects in Virginia, about 4,800 emigrants departed from England between November, 1619, and February, 1625, nearly twice as many as had gone during the entire period from 1607 to 1619.[50] But, while the Company's propaganda could refer blandly to "each man having the shares of Land due to him" and to "the laudable forme of Justice and government," [51] actual conditions in Virginia were quite different. Goodman Jackson "much marviled that you would send me a servant to the Companie," young Richard Freethorne wrote to his parents:

> He saith I had beene better knocked on the head, and Indeede so I fynde it now to my great greefe and miserie, and saith, that if you love me you will redeeme me suddenlie, for wch I doe Intreate and begg. . . . I thought no head had beene able to hold so much water as hath and doth daylie flow from mine eyes. . . . But this is Certaine I never felt the want of ffather and mother till now, but now deare freinds full well I knowe and rue it although it were too late before I knew it.

"To write of all crosses and miseries wch have befallen us at this tyme we are not able," said Samuel Sharp. "So the truth is," Edward Hill wrote to his brother, "we lyve in the fearefullest age that ever Christians lived in." [52]

Though Company policy was not responsible for all the suffering endured by the settlers, it was responsible for intensifying their sense of

---

[49] Thomas Jefferson Wertenbaker, *Virginia under the Stuarts* (Princeton, 1914), pp. 38–39; Craven, *Virginia Company*, pp. 70–80; Craven, *Southern Colonies*, pp. 127–29; "Proceedings of the First Assembly in Virginia, Held July 30, 1619," in *Colonial Records of Virginia* (Richmond, 1874).

[50] Samuel H. Yonge, "The Site of Old 'James Towne,' 1607–1698," *Virginia Magazine of History and Biography*, XI (1903–4), 399–400.

[51] *A Declaration of the State of the Colony* (1620), in Force (ed.), *op. cit.*, III, 5–6.

[52] Kingsbury (ed.), *Records*, IV, 59, 61–62, 239, 234; see also *ibid.*, pp. 41–42, 232, 235–36.

deprivation by having promised too much.] "My Master Atkins hath sould me," Henry Brigg wrote to his brother, Thomas:

> If you remember he tould me that for my Diett the worst day in the weeke should be better then the Sonday, & also he swore unto you that I should never serve any man but himselfe: And he also tould us that there they paled out their groundes from Deare & Hoggs. But in stead of them we pale out oʳ Enemyes.

"If the Company would allow to each man a pound of butter and a pounde of Chese weekely," wrote a planter to Sir John Worsenholme,

> they would find more comfort therin then by all the Deere, Fish & Fowle is so talked of in England of wᶜh I can assure yoᵘ yoʳ poore servants have nott had since their cominge into the Contrey so much as the sent.

"I am pswaded," George Thorp wrote to John Smyth of Nibley,

> that more doe die of the disease of theire minde then of theire body by having this country victualls over-praised unto them in England & by not knowing, they shall drinke water here.[53]

[No doubt the chasm between expectation and reality contributed to the planters' alienation from the organizational relationship into which they had been lured by the Company's promises. But that relationship was affected even more by the development of a network of relations that followed inevitably from the inducements to get men into the Company.]

[At one time in Virginia, the single relationship that existed between persons rested upon the positions they occupied in the Company's table of organization. As a result of the efforts made by the Company to get persons to accept that relationship, however, each person in Virginia had become the occupant of several statuses, for now there were rich and poor in Virginia, landowners and renters, masters and servants, old residents and newcomers, married and single, men and women; and the simultaneous possession of these statuses involved the holder in a network of relationships, some congruent and some incompatible, with his organizational relationship.]

Once the men in Virginia had been bachelors who lived in Company-provided barracks. Now they lived in private houses with their families, and, though the Company attempted to make use of the new relationship by penalizing each "Master of a family" for certain crimes committed by those under his authority [54] — hoping thereby that the master

---

[53] *Ibid.*, pp. 235–36, 312–32; III, 417; see also *ibid.*, III, 456.
[54] Proclamation of Governor Wyatt, June, 1622, in Kingsbury (ed.), *Records*, III, 659.

would use his authority to suppress crime — it can hardly be doubted that its action involved the head of the family in a conflict of loyalties.

Once all persons had been equal before Company law, and penalties had been inflicted solely in accordance with the nature of the offense. Now, the General Assembly found that "persones of qualitie" were "not fitt to undergoe corporall punishment." [55]

Once length of residence was irrelevant in determining the obligations of persons to the Company. Now, however, it was enacted that all "ye olde planters, y^t were heere before, or cam in at ye laste cominge of Sr. Tho: Gates they and theire posteritie shalbe exempted from theire psonall service to ye warres, and any publique charge (Churche dewties excepted)." [56]

Once Virginians had been governed administratively through a chain of command originating in the Company's General Court. Now an authentic political system existed, and the members of the Assembly demanded the same right to disallow orders of the General Court that the Court had with respect to the Assembly.

Once all land had been owned by the Company. Now much of it was owned by private persons, and even more had been promised to them, and the opportunities for the creation of private fortunes involved the planters in a new relationship with the Company. No longer was the planter willing to have his tobacco exported through the Company at a fixed price, when, as a free landowner, he might strike his own bargain with the purchaser. No longer was the planter willing, at a time when labor meant profit, for the Company to commandeer his servants. Even officers of the Company, expected to administer its program in Virginia, saw the chance to subvert it to their own purposes; "The servants you allow them, or such as they hire," Captain John Smith told the Company, "they plant on their private Lands, not upon that belongeth to their office, which crop alwaies exceeds yours." Indeed, it became increasingly difficult to get planters to accept Company positions:

> Sr George is taken up with his private. . . . Capt. Hamor is miserablie poore and necessities will inforce him to shift. . . . Capt: Mathews intends wholie his Cropp, and will rather hazard the payment of forfeictures, then performe our Injunctions. . . . Mr Blanie is now married in Virginia, and when he hath discharged your trust in the Magazine wilbee a Planter amongst us. . . . And I would you could persuade some of qualities and worth to come out.[57]

[55] Act of March, 1623/24 (*ibid.*, IV, 584).

[56] Act of March, 1623/24 (*ibid.*, IV, 582).

[57] *Ibid.*, IV, 564, 581; Smith, *Generall Historie*, in Tyler (ed.), *op. cit.*, p. 356; George Sandys to John Ferrar, April 11, 1623, in Kingsbury (ed.), *Records*, IV, 110–11.

⎰The increase in private wealth tended to subordinate status in the
Company to status in a different relationship among the planters.⎱ The
muster roll of early 1625 shows 48 families bearing various titles of
distinction, most of which had been earned in Virginia. They alone held
266 of the approximately 487 white servants in Virginia, 20 of the 23
Negro servants, and 1 of the 2 Indian servants.[58] These were the families
at the apex of Virginia society, determined to uphold their rights as over
against other persons and sometimes going beyond their rights. Acting
through the General Assembly, they insisted upon scrupulous enforcement of contracts of servitude, forbade servants to trade with the Indians,
and, so as not to lose their labor, regulated the right of their servants to
marry. Nor, as the chronic complaints bear witness, were they loath to
keep their servants beyond the required time.[59] That aspect of the relationship between master and servant was eloquently revealed in a petition
to the Governor by Jane Dickenson in 1624:

> [She] most humblie sheweth that whereas her late husband Ralph
> Dickenson Came ov^r into this Country fower Yeares since, obliged
> to Nicholas Hide deceased for ye tearme of seaven yeares, hee only
> to have for himselfe & yor petitioner ye one halfe of his labors, her
> said husband being slaine in the bloudy Masacre, & her selfe Caried
> away wth the Cruell salvages, amongst them Enduring much misery
> for teen monthes. At the Expiration it pleased God so to dispose the
> hartes of the Indians, y^t for a small ransome yor petitioner wth
> divers others should be realeased, In Consideration that Doctor Potts
> laid out two pounds of beades for her releasement, hee alleageth yor
> petitioner is linked to his servitude wth a towefold Chaine the one
> for her late husbandes obligation & thother for her ransome, of both
> wch shee hopeth that in Conscience shee ought to be discharged, of
> ye first by her widdowhood, of the second by the law of nations,
> Considering shee hath already served teen monthes, two much for
> two pound of beades.
>   The pmises notwthstanding Dr Pott refuseth to sett yor peticioner
> at liberty, threatning to make her serve him the uttermost day,
> unless she pcure him 150^{li} waight of Tobacco, she therefore most
> humbly desireth, that you^u wilbe pleased to take w^t Course shalbe
> thought just for her releasement fro' his servitude, Considering that
> it much differeth not from her slavery wth the Indians.[60]

But that was only one aspect of the relationship.⎰Conditions in Virginia were now more fluid than they had been, and persons of low estate

[58] The figures are derived from the muster rolls in John Camden Hotten, *The
Original Lists of Persons of Quality; Emigrants, Religious Exiles . . . Who
Went from Great Britain to the American Plantations, 1600–1700* (London,
1874).
[59] A. E. Smith, *op. cit.*, pp. 226–29; Kingsbury (ed.), *Records*, IV, 128–30.
[60] Kingsbury (ed.), *Records*, IV, 473.

might also rise.] Secretary of State John Pory wrote Sir Dudley Carleton that "our cowekeeper here of James citty on Sundays goes accowtered all in freshe flaminge silke; and a wife of one that in England had professed the black arte, not of a scholler, but of a collier of Croydon, wears her rought bever hatt with a faire perle hat band." The Company was opposed to such unseemly displays of wealth on the part of persons of low estate,[61] but it could not prevent them.

[The ultimate stage in the transition of Virginia from organization to society was reached when the settlers came to feel that the new relationships in which they were now involved were of greater importance than the Company relationship, when their statuses outside the organization came largely to dictate their behavior. For at that point they were no longer willing to accept the legitimacy of their organizational superiors.] William Weldon warned Sir Edwin Sandys that the planters who now had land were grumbling at Company policy:

> I acquainted them wth my restraint of plantinge Tobacco wch is a thinge so distastefull to them that they will wth no patience indure to heare of it bitterly Complayninge that they have no other meanes to furnish themselves with aparell for the insuinge yere but are likely as they say (and for aught I Can see) to be starved if they be debarred of it.[62]

From general discontent it was but a short step to ridicule of Company officials and outright refusal to accept a Company assignment. Wrote planter William Capps to John Ferrar:

> The old smoker our (I know not how to terme him but) Governor, so good so careful mild, Religious, just, honest that I protest I thinke God hath sent him in mercie for good to us, he undergoeth all your cares & ours and I feare not but god will bless him in all his pceedings but who must be th'Instrument to make all this whole againe? Why Capps: all voyces can sett him forth about the business: But who must pay him his hyre? The Contrey is poore and the Companie is poore and Cappes is poore already, & poorer he will be if he follow this course.

Like other men, planter Capps believed that "Charity first beginnes at home," and he divorced his own interest from that of the Company:

> I will forsweare ever bending my mind for publique good, and betake me to my own profit with some halfe a score men of my owne and lie rootinge in the earthe like a hog, and reckon Tobacco ad unguem by hundrethes, and quarters.[63]

---

[61] Pory to Carleton, September 30, 1619, in Tyler (ed.), *op. cit.*, p. 285; Kingsbury (ed.), *Records*, III,.469.

[62] Kingsbury (ed.), *Records*, III, 263.

[63] *Ibid.*, IV, 38–39.

[That the Company could no longer expect to command obedience was clear, for even its officers in Virginia perceived themselves as having a set of interests distinct from those of their London superiors and turned their backs to their authority] "Such is the disposicon of those who glorie in their wisdomes," wrote George Sandys, the treasurer in Virginia, to his brother, Sir Miles,

> that they will rather Justifye and proceed in their Errors than to suffer a supposed disgrace by reforming them. . . . Who clere themselves by the wrongings of others; objecting unto us their Instructions, whereof manie are infeasible and the most inconvenient, for to say the truth they know nothing of Virginia.

"Such an Antipathy is there between theyr vast Comands and oʳ grumbling Obedience," Sir Francis Wyatt wrote to his father:

> Mingling matters of honor and profitt often overthrow both. They expect great retournes to pay the Companies debt. . . . For me I have not a third part of my men to inable me to either. . . . I often wish little Mʳ Farrar here, that to his zeale he would add knowledge of this Contrey.[64]

In 1607 there had been no "Contrey," only the Virginia Company. It was the Company's fate to have created a country and to have destroyed itself in the process. More than a century later, James Otis wrote bitterly: "Those who judge of the reciprocal rights that subsist between a supreme and subordinate state of dominion, by no higher rules than are applied to a corporation of button-makers, will never have a very comprehensive view of them." [65] His comment was intended as an observation on contemporary political affairs, but we can detect in it a verdict on the past as well.

[The Company had been faced with the problems of motivating its members to work for the ends which it was created to achieve and, at the same time, of maintaining the discipline that was essential for its organizational integrity. The solution it adopted for the first problem made it impossible to solve the second; and the burden of achieving order and discipline now became the responsibility not of an organization but of a society]

Among the papers in the Sackville collection is a document entitled "A Form of Policy for Virginia," written when it was already apparent

[64] *Ibid.*, pp. 71, 237; see also *ibid.*, pp. 455–57.
[65] *The Rights of the British Colonies asserted and proved* (Boston, 1764), in Samuel Eliot Morison (ed.), *Sources and Documents Illustrating the American Revolution* . . . (2d ed.; Oxford, 1929), p. 8.

that the Company had failed. The proposal was never adopted, but it is significant nonetheless, for, as Professor Fernand Braudel reminds us,

> victorious events come about as a result of many possibilities, often contradictory, among which life finally has made its choice. For one possibility which actually is realized innumerable others have been drowned. These are the ones which have left little trace for the historians. And yet it is necessary to give them their place because the losing movements are forces which have at every moment affected the final outcome.[66]

The significance of the document, drafted as a royal proclamation, lies in its awareness of the problems of motivation and order, in its realization that they could no longer be solved by instructions handed down through a chain of command, and in its conscious application of particular social inventions to solve them:

> Wee . . . knowinge that the perfection and happinesse of a commonwealth, lyeth . . . first and principally in the government, consisting in the mutuall duties of commandeing and obeyeing, next in the possessing thinges plentifully, necessarie for the life of man, doe professe that . . . we intend wholely the good of our subjects . . . endeavouringe to cause both England and Virginea, to endowe each other with their benefittes and profitts that thereby layeing aside force and our coactive power, we may by our justice and bountie marrye and combinde those our provinces to us and our soveraigntye in naturall love and obedience.

[The problem of order was solved by the meticulous enumeration of every social status that was to exist in Virginia, with a specification of the rights and obligations that inhered in each. The problem of motivation was solved by the granting of both economic rewards and social privileges to each status and by the opportunity given to move from one to another:]

> The meanest servant that goeth (God soe blessing him and his endeavours, that hee can purchase and [an] estate in England or compasse to carrie over or drawe over with him of his friends and adherences the number of 300 men) he may become a lord patriot which is the greatest place the commonwealth canne beare.

The problem of consensus was solved through devices to enhance the mutual affection of persons in these statuses:

> To the end that love may be mayntayned, and that theise degrees may not estrange the upper orders from the lower, we wish that

---

[66] Quoted in Paul F. Lazarsfeld, "Public Opinion and the Classical Tradition," *Public Opinion Quarterly*, XXI, No. 1 (Spring, 1957), 53.

the heires and eldest sonnes of the upper orders may marrie with
the daughters of the lower orders. . . . And that the daughters of
the upper orders being heires may marrye with the sonnes of the
lower orders, makeing choice of the most vertuous . . . that all
degrees may bee thereby bound togeather in the bonds of love that
none may bee scorned but the scorner. To this end alsoe, although
we would not have you imitate the Irish in their wilde and barbarous maners, yet we will commend one custome of theires unto
you, which is that the poorer sort sueing to gett the nurseing of the
children of the lordes and gentrie, and breedeinge upp in their
minorities as their owne, this breedinge . . . doth begett anoether
nature in them to love their foster children and brethren, as if they
were naturally bread of the same parentes.

Written in the margin of the document, by whom we do not know, is
a lengthy commentary. Concerning the importance of status and order,
the following is written: "This maintenance of theire degrees will im-
moveably fixe the frame of the collonie." Concerning the importance
of mobility and motivation, the following is written: "Soe framinge the
government that it shall give all men both liberty and meanes of
riseinge to the greatest places and honours therein, whereby they will
receave such content that they will all strive to maintaine it in the same
forme we shall now settle it." [67]

Shakespeare had written:

> Take but degree away, untune that string
> And hark, what discord follows.

[The author of the document agreed. He rested his hopes for stability
on the attachment of each person to a position in which recognized
rights and responsibilities inhered. What he did not realize is what may
be learned from the history of the Virginia Company — that each man
is attached to many positions, that each position involves him in a
separate relationship that imposes its own necessities, and that his behavior is the product of all the positions he holds and, because he has a
memory, of all the positions he once held.]

II

The generalizations that emerge from our study are of two kinds: those
directly tied to the events of the time and place that we have analyzed
and those of a more abstract kind that derive from the analysis of these
historical particulars but can be stated in such a way as to be of more
general applicability.

There seems little room for doubt about some of the conclusions we

[67] Kingsbury (ed.), *Records*, IV, 411, 417, 424–25, 416, 419.

have drawn: [that the character of seventeenth-century North American society was shaped decisively by the fact that, in contrast to the situation in Latin America, the creation of the society was accomplished through the recruitment of a voluntary labor force; that higher statuses in that society were created as a result of the need to induce persons to accept positions in lower statuses; and that the behavior of persons in that society was determined not only by opportunities for advancement, as Whiggish interpreters of our history would have us believe, but, as well, by the fact that these opportunities were less than people had been led to expect.]

With respect to more general hypotheses, it may be suggested that the mechanism by which the change from organization to society was accomplished lay in the very effort to apply the blueprint that was intended to govern the relations between persons, for this so multiplied the number of statuses persons held, and therefore the relationships in which they were involved, as to alter their behavior in a decisive fashion.

The testing of these hypotheses, of course, would involve the examination of still other consciously selected historical situations for the purpose of comparison — the experience of the British in establishing other colonies in North America and in coping with a totally different problem in India, of the French in Canada and the Spanish in South America, of the reasons for the difference between the blueprint in accordance with which utopian communities were planned and the outcome of their establishment, and the like. Herein lies the design for a research in historical sociology.

Understanding
the Puritans

DAVID D. HALL

For the past two generations, the history of seventeenth-century New England has been written in terms of "Puritanism." Samuel Eliot Morison, Perry Miller, Edmund S. Morgan, and others have treated Puritanism as a monolithic, Americanized intellectual structure which determined the social and political behavior of the early colonists. In the past ten years, however, scholars have begun to stress the secular and English aspects of early American society. At the same time, historians in the United States and in England have developed a more highly sophisticated understanding of the nature of reformed religion in the sixteenth and seventeenth centuries.

David Hall's essay is an attempt to redefine the meaning of Puritanism in its colonial context. He tries to answer, from the intellectual historian's point of view, the traditional question: What was the meaning of American Puritanism? He argues that we must disengage ourselves from the static, American-centered, and rather idiosyncratic model of Perry Miller's The New England Mind: The Seventeenth Century (Cambridge, Mass., 1939). Puritanism is, he thinks, best understood as part of the European Reformation which lasted until the pressures of pietism, the Enlightenment, and Anglican particularism brought it to an effective end at the close of the seventeenth century.

Hall attempts to strike a balance between the view that Puritanism was a precisely articulated intellectual structure and the contention that it can only be described vaguely as a socio-intellectual "thrust." He finds it a church and faith of opposites: formal and experiential, static and dynamic, spiritualistic and church-oriented. He believes we can identify three or four key theological ideas, and he admits that at its core Puritanism was peculiarly concerned with redemption and the conversion experience, but he concludes that this was "the eschatological dynamic" which provided a link between faith and church. Above all, Hall contends, we must try to see Puritanism as an organic whole and as an example of the very gradual transformation of European culture in the New World. Can you reconcile this account with the behaviorally oriented analysis presented in the three essays by Philip Greven and John Demos?

"How does one define Puritanism?" This question, the first sentence of Alan Simpson's *Puritanism in Old and New England*, is one to which the answers in recent years have grown increasingly complex and contradictory.[1] Thirty years ago there was no doubt about the answer; the

© 1970 by David D. Hall. Reprinted from *The State of American History* (Chicago, 1970), ed. Herbert Bass.

[1] I am indebted to John Eusden of Williams College and Sacvan Bercovitch of the University of California, San Diego, for comments that enlarged my view of the subject.

scholarship of Morison and Haller, and, towering over both, the massive symmetry of Perry Miller's *The New England Mind,* gave compelling definition to the subject.[2] But climates of opinion change, and with them the historian's angle of perception. What Perry Miller had to say now has the ring of the 1930's, for the period in which he wrote saw the old myth that the Puritan hated life still strong upon us. If Miller's great achievement was to free us from that myth, the question remains as to the proper understanding of Puritanism. To describe the differences of opinion between Miller and his critics is one purpose of this essay.[3] But its deeper task is to identify the problems that every student of the Puritans must inevitably confront, the problems of interpretation and methodology that always seem to turn up in dealing with this subject.[4]

Abraham Lincoln once said that slavery was "somehow" the cause of the Civil War. Historians of Puritanism know likewise that the history of the movement was somehow related to the contemporary culture and social structure. [Puritanism had social sources and social conse-

[2] Samuel Eliot Morison, *The Puritan Pronaos* (New York, 1936); William Haller, *The Rise of Puritanism* (New York, 1938); Perry Miller, *The New England Mind: The Seventeenth Century* (Cambridge, Mass., 1939). Miller's contributions in the 1930's also included many of the essays in *Errand into the Wilderness* (Cambridge, Mass., 1956), as well as the anthology *The Puritans* (New York, 1938), co-edited with Thomas Johnson.

[3] It falls beyond the limits of this essay to describe the intersection of Puritan scholarship in America with the search for a "usable past" in which Americans have engaged in the twentieth century. A good beginning on the history of this search, including information on changing views of the Puritans, is Richard Ruland, *The Reinterpretation of American Literature* (Cambridge, Mass., 1967).

[4] There have been several other published essays of a similar nature: Edmund S. Morgan, "The Historians of Early New England," in Ray Billington, ed., *The Reinterpretation of Early American History* (San Marino, Calif., 1966); Richard Schlatter, "The Puritan Strain," in John Higham, ed., *The Reconstruction of American History* (New York, 1962); Sidney James, introduction, *The New England Puritans* (New York, 1968). Since this essay is based on the assumption that American Puritanism is broadly continuous with Puritanism in England, it may be pertinent to note the differences of approach between British and American scholarship. When American historians investigate the period of Puritan history before 1630, on the whole they are seeking the origins of ideas and institutions found in New England. This purpose entails several consequences, one of them the postulating of ideal types (like "nonseparating congregationalism") which presumably the colonists imported, another an emphasis on intellectual history, and a third a principle of selection in reading pre-1630 material, namely those writers who were most cited in New England. Much of British scholarship — and this includes Americans writing on English history — is concerned with the social and political consequences of Puritanism, especially the relationship between the movement and the English Revolution, or else with its local and institutional history. In this scholarship the variety and fluidity of opinion is often allowed to obscure the fundamental stance of the Puritan.

quences; were historians to define precisely which groups supported (and dissented from) the Puritan program, as well as the movement's consequences for the broader culture, they would move closer to an understanding of its nature. One of their tasks, then, is to determine how Puritanism was socially functional.

A second problem arises out of the close relationship between Puritanism and two other religious movements, the Reformed tradition and Pietism. Heir of the first and parent of the second, Puritanism at the onset of its history depended for ideas on Reformed Protestantism, and at the close faded into Pietism. John Eusden has suggested that Puritanism may be understood as an "evangelical Calvinism," a term that links it both to the sixteenth-century world of Calvin and to the eighteenth-century world of the Pietists.[5] If Eusden's suggestion is correct, historians must also be able to distinguish between Puritanism and these other movements. At the same time their task is to fix the time span within which Puritanism played out its course; to give dates to a movement is, perforce, to make a statement about its origins and legacy. A periodization of Puritanism and an inventory of its distinctive (or shared) religious ideas are two sides of the same problem: to mark off the historical and intellectual boundaries of the movement.

A third problem is to construct a definition that includes the range of Puritan types. Here I agree with Alan Simpson, who insists on viewing the broad spectrum from presbyterians to Quakers as one continuous whole. He is right in criticizing historians who legitimize too narrow a slice of this spectrum, and he is right also in asking if there is not something fundamental in the nature of Puritanism that made it dynamic and expansive.[6] The history of the movement offers innumerable examples of the Puritan as a man in motion, a man possessed by a peculiar restlessness, a man who may attack the idea of a gathered church while still a minister in England, yet form such a group within his English parish and publicly defend the practice once he reached America. These inconsistencies, and more besides, mark the career of John Cotton, and the life histories of countless other Puritans were fashioned in the same erratic manner.

We need a definition of Puritanism which takes account of this restlessness, and if dissatisfaction with the scholarship of the 1930's is on the rise, the reason is largely its failure to meet such a test. It fails this test in one obvious way. Together with the denominational historians, Perry Miller assumed that denominational categories could be imposed upon

[5] William Ames, *The Marrow of Theology*, translated and edited by John Eusden (Boston, 1968), p. 19.

[6] Alan Simpson, *Puritanism in Old and New England*, paperback ed. (Chicago, 1961), pp. 1–2.

Puritan conceptions of the church.] But can we call the New England
Puritans "congregationalists" with a capital C when the actual working-
out of their church order was so confused and contradictory? Or can we
call Thomas Cartwright a "presbyterian" with a capital P when his conception of the church involved recognizably "congregational" elements?
More recent studies, in recognition of these ambiguities, have moved
away from the categories of denominational history, substituting in their
place an emphasis upon the "continuity of experience" which united all
Puritans.[8] The result may be a certain loss of clarity, but the new scholarship at least has the virtue of restoring the dynamic quality of Puritanism
to the center of any definition.]

The scholarship of the 1930's minimized the restlessness within Puritanism because of another assumption. In Perry Miller's view, "Puritanism was not only a religious creed, it was a philosophy and a metaphysic;
it was an organization of man's whole life, emotional and intellectual."
The structure of *The New England Mind* imposed a coherence upon
Puritanism which Miller described as the reconciliation of "piety" and
"intellect." To define the movement in these terms was explicitly to
rule out any spiritualists as un-Puritan; it was to cut off the spectrum
short of the Quakers and Antinomians. Here again, recent scholarship
points toward a more inclusive definition. [In place of the intellectual
commitments Miller saw as crucial, Alan Simpson would put the terms
"experience" and "thrust," intending by them a particular type of religious experience which unleashed the zeal of the Puritan saint.[9] The

[7] Though Miller distinguished between "separating" and "nonseparating"
congregationalists, thereby departing from earlier explanations of the genesis
of Massachusetts congregationalism, he left unchallenged the premise of denominational scholarship (as represented by Williston Walker and Henry
Martyn Dexter) that the thread of congregationalism could be unraveled from
the tapestry of Puritanism. The most important critique of Miller, careful to
distinguish true congregationalism from its "prehistory," is Geoffrey Nuttall,
Visible Saints, The Congregational Way, 1640–1660 (Oxford, 1957), though
I would press Nuttall's critique of denominational history further than he does.
See also Robert Paul, ed., *An Apologeticall Narration* (Philadelphia, 1963), pp.
57–66, and the scholarship cited therein.

[8] Simpson, *Puritanism in Old and New England*, p. 2. In a footnote, Simpson cites A. S. P. Woodhouse, *Puritanism and Liberty* (London, 1938), p.
xxxvii: "It is unnecessary to posit a unity in all Puritan thought; it is sufficient to
recognize a continuity."

[9] Simpson, *Puritanism in Old and New England*, chap. 1. Earlier, William
Haller had criticized denominational historians for their "historical piety," and
called for an inclusive definition of Puritanism structured around the figure of
the preacher: "The disagreements that rendered Puritans into presbyterians,
independents, separatists, and baptists were in the long run not so significant as
the qualities of character, of mind and imagination, which kept them all alike
Puritans." *The Rise of Puritanism*, paperback ed. (New York, 1957), p. 17.
Earlier still, William York Tindall had insisted upon "the essential identity of

value of these terms must not obscure their weaknesses; though they permit the Quakers to reenter the fold as authentic Puritans, their meaning seems inherently subjective,[10] and they may act to exclude the array of distinctions that Miller so successfully identified as woven into the texture of Puritanism.

[An adequate definition of the Puritan movement must therefore seek to unite the experiential dimension with the formal structure of the Puritan intellect. It must locate the movement within a particular time period, and with reference to the Reformed tradition and Pietism. It must identify the bond between the social sources of the movement and its history, between its rhetoric and its social consequences.]

How close do we stand to such a definition? The literature that deals with the relationship between John Calvin and the Puritans is both extensive and contradictory, and for these reasons affords an opportunity to begin the task of evaluation. All historians agree that Puritanism belongs within the family of Reformed churches.[11] Yet the family resemblance has not prevented many historians from detecting differences between the two — differences, broadly speaking, of two kinds, philosophical and theological. The philosophical loom especially large in Perry Miller's account. "In defining the intellectual character of the New England Puritans," he declared in 1938, "we must always exercise caution about calling them Calvinists. John Calvin's metaphysics were still Aristotelian and scholastic; New Englanders had thrown aside much of the philosophy which is implied at every point in Calvin's theology, and had taken up a system of which the implications were quite different." These differences were due largely to the Puritans' acceptance of Peter Ramus, a French educator and logician; because the New Englanders were Ramists, Miller argued, they had emancipated themselves from Aristotle and scholasticism. More profoundly, Calvin was a nominalist who asserted the doctrine of an "arbitrary" God wholly unconditioned and determinis-

---

the radical sects in both nature and purpose." *John Bunyan, Mechanick Preacher* (New York, 1934), p. 5. See also James F. Maclear, " 'The Heart of New England Rent': The Mystical Element in Early Puritan History," *Mississippi Valley Historical Review*, XLII (1956), 621–656.

10 Cf. the remark by Richard T. Vann — "This 'thrust' — whatever that means" — in his review essay of Michael Walzer, *Revolution of the Saints*, in *History and Theory*, VII (1968), 108.

11 Much can be learned about Puritanism from general histories of the Reformed tradition, among which are John T. McNeill, *The History and Character of Calvinism* (New York, 1954); James L. Ainslie, *The Doctrine of Ministerial Order in the Reformed Churches of the Sixteenth and Seventeenth Centuries* (Edinburgh, 1940); Geddes MacGregor, *Corpus Christi: The Nature of the Church According to the Reformed Tradition* (London, 1959).

tic in His actions; Puritans (at least those in New England) imposed limitations on the will of God and order upon the universe.[12]

More recent scholarship suggests, on the other hand, that the philosophical differences between Calvin and the Puritans were not very great. The essential continuity between the two was partly a matter of their common reliance upon the nominalistic distinction between *potentia absoluta* and *potentia ordinata*. Sharing the same confidence in the order of the world, they shared also the scholastic definition of man as a rational animal. Both agreed that God respected the nature of man in the process of redemption. Both agreed that in the "order of nature" (another concept taken over from scholasticism) man's will was free in such a way that he voluntarily obeyed the laws of God. And if the comparison stands between the Puritans and the continental theologians commonly known as Reformed scholastics, the continuities in philosophy and metaphysics are still more striking.[13]

But what of Peter Ramus? The road to an understanding of his significance for the Puritans is littered with obstacles, some of them placed there by Perry Miller. *The New England Mind* contains the suggestion that Ramus, a victim of the St. Bartholomew's Day massacre, "died equally for the cause of logic" and for the cause of Protestantism. In a manner characteristic of his approach to intellectual history, Miller framed the difference between Ramus and Aristotle as one between mortal enemies: those who murdered Ramus must have been disciples of Aristotle. For the New England Puritans to read Ramist texts thus amounted to a declaration of war; it was a decision, declared Miller, that entailed enormous consequences.[14] But no war between Aristotelians and Ramists was ever fought in New England, or even on the continent. The curriculum at Harvard College depended on textbooks written by a

[12] Miller, *The Puritans*, pp. 32–33, 24; Miller, *The New England Mind*, pp. 92–97, 157, 194–195. One of the problems with his argument is to agree on a meaning of "scholasticism." The Puritans frequently denounced the "School-men," as Miller pointed out; but he also warned against taking their denunciations at "face value." On the one hand he thus asserted that the Puritans "revolted" against scholasticism, while on the other he perceived that they accepted "scholastic premises in physics and astronomy, the scholastic theory of the four elements or the four causes," and much else besides. Miller, *The Puritans*, pp. 25–26; *The New England Mind*, pp. 100–102.

[13] Francois Wendel, *Calvin: The Origins and Development of His Religious Thought* (New York, 1963), pp. 127 ff, 179; Eusden, ed., *The Marrow of Theology*, pp. 51–52; Heinrich Heppe, *Reformed Dogmatics* (London, 1950), pp. 144, 155, 159, 167; David D. Hall, ed., *The Antinomian Controversy, 1636–1638: A Documentary History* (Middletown, Conn., 1968), see "Cause" and "Order" under index. More precise study is needed of the place such scholastic terms had in the Puritan mind.

[14] Miller, *The New England Mind*, pp. 117–120.

group of continental Reformed scholastics — Alsted, Keckermann, Heereboord, Burgersdicius — who blended Ramist and scholastic elements into an eclectic whole.[15] The second president of Harvard, Charles Chauncy, was hostile to Ramus, but he was never martyred on this account. To drain the ferocity from the mortal combat between Aristotelian and Ramist is, admittedly, to lessen the drama of the Puritan mind. But the truth seems to be that Ramist method, though practiced in New England, did not serve in any major way to divide the Puritans from the Reformed tradition. Nor did their reading in Ramus provide the New England Puritans with a metaphysic, the congregational church order, and a "plain style" of preaching, as Miller argued; all of these have other sources that far outweigh Ramus in importance.[16]

[As for the second category of difference, there is general agreement among many historians that Puritanism has a different theological outlook from Calvinism.] Comparison of the Puritans with John Calvin easily turns up some divergences: Calvin retained a sense of the real presence in his understanding of the Lord's Supper, while most Puritans followed Zwingli in adopting a memorialist view; Calvin's doctrine of assurance excluded the evidence of "works," evidence which many Puritans thought legitimate.[17] In broader terms, Thomas Torrance has contrasted Calvin's Christocentric focus to the anthropocentric orientation

[15] Samuel Eliot Morison, *Harvard College in the Seventeenth Century* (Cambridge, Mass., 1936), I, 157–159, 191–192. Miller drew heavily upon these same writers in reconstructing the Puritan mind — the statements and extended quotation on page 264 are from Zanchy and Ursinus, and the quotation bridging pages 287–288 is from Zanchy — to an extent that the text does not reveal, though he also was explicit in recognizing the importance of these Protestant scholastics. *The New England Mind*, pp. 102–105; the citations above are drawn from the annotated copy in the Harvard Library. The fullest study of Keckermann, Heereboord, and Burgersdicius in the educational setting of the late sixteenth and early seventeenth centuries is Paul Dibon, *L'Enseignement Philosophique dans les Universités Néerlandaises à L'Epoque Pré-Cartésienne (1575–1650)* (Paris, 1954). Dibon argues (pp. 10, 133, and throughout) against reading the philosophical instruction of the period as a battle between Aristotelianism and Ramism; instead he perceives "une tendence *concilatrice*" in the logic teaching: "Il ne s'agit pas tant d'opposer Ramus à Aristote que de compléter celui-ci par celui-là" (p. 133).

[16] Miller, *The New England Mind*, chaps. 5, 6, 11, and 12. On the rhetoric of the Puritans, cf. J. W. Blench, *Preaching in England in the Late Fifteenth and Sixteenth Centuries* (New York, 1964), and Wilbur S. Howell, *Logic and Rhetoric in England, 1500–1700* (New York, 1961).

[17] Wilhelm Niesel, *The Theology of Calvin* (London, 1956), pp. 170–171, cites Calvin's disapproval of the "practical syllogism" and his carefully hedged exegesis of 2 Peter 1.10, a text William Perkins placed on the title page of a treatise dealing with assurance, and which the "legal" preachers in New England invoked repeatedly during the Antinomian controversy, together with the "practical syllogism." Perkins, *Works* (London, 1608–1631), I, 419; Hall, *The Antinomian Controversy*, pp. 58, 237.

of the Puritans. [And Perry Miller declared that the New England Puritans fashioned the covenant theology in order to escape from the rigors of "strict Calvinism." [18]

No idea of Miller's has gained greater currency, or been more widely attacked. Counter-interpretations of the covenant theology have generally succeeded in establishing two points. One is that the covenantal idiom figured in the Reformed tradition long before it appeared among the Puritans whom Miller cited. Certain of these studies suggest, in other words, that the Puritans in resorting to the idiom were not particularly novel or illegitimate by Reformed standards. The second point is that the idea of a covenant, though apparently implying a voluntary, contractual relationship between God and man, was not intended by the Puritans as a means of bringing God more within man's reach, but rather to accomplish other ends — to provide a rationale for the sacraments, or a basis for their doctrine of assurance.[19]

In spite of all this scholarship we still lack a clear understanding of the covenant theology, and on the larger question of the theological differences between Calvin and the Puritans the confusion is just as great. The time has come, I believe, to reconsider the terms of the question, for we seem to be dealing with a question *mal posée*, so posed as to lead to answers which are never satisfactory. [The essential error has been to postulate a "strict" orthodoxy, a "pure" Calvinism, defined in terms of John Calvin and the *Institutes of the Christian Religion*. Once the name of Calvin becomes synonymous with "orthodoxy," certain deadly consequences ensue: the concept presumes a static system of ideas, so that

---

[18] Thomas Torrance, *The School of Faith* (New York, 1959); Torrance, "Justification: Its Radical Nature and Place in Reformed Doctrine and Life," *Scottish Journal of Theology*, XIII (1960), 225–246; Miller, *Errand into the Wilderness*, pp. 51–53, an argument repeated in *The New England Mind*.

[19] Leonard J. Trinterud, "The Origins of Puritanism," *Church History*, XX (1951), 37–57; Jens G. Moller, "The Beginnings of Puritan Covenant Theology," *Journal of Ecclesiastical History*, XIV (1963), 46–67; Everett H. Emerson, "Calvin and the Covenant Theology," *Church History*, XXV (1956), 136–144; Emerson, "Thomas Hooker: The Puritan as Theologian," *Anglican Theological Review*, XLIX (1967), 190–203; John von Rohr, "Covenant and Assurance in Early English Puritanism," *Church History*, XXXIV (1965), 195–203; C. J. Sommerville, "Conversion *versus* the Early Puritan Covenant of Grace," *Journal of Presbyterian History*, XLIV (1966), 178–197; J. A. Ross MacKenzie, "The Covenant Theology — A Review Article," *Journal of Presbyterian History*, XLIV (1966), 198–204. Also of importance are E. R. Daniel, "Reconciliation, Covenant and Election: A Study in the Theology of John Donne," *Anglican Theological Review*, XLVIII (1966), 14–30; Richard L. Greaves, "John Bunyan and Covenant Theology in the Seventeenth Century," *Church History*, XXXVI (1967), 151–169, which clarifies three different uses of the covenantal idiom; and Norman Pettit, *The Heart Prepared* (New Haven, 1966), pp. 217–221.

change of any kind — any variation, no matter how slight — is taken as evidence of declining rigor and faith] Perry Miller fell into this trap, and so have many others.[20] [But we have been warned against it by the post-Millerian scholarship on the covenant theology: on the one hand this scholarship suggests that the strict orthodoxy of the pure Calvin must not be interpreted so narrowly as to exclude the idiom of the covenant, and on the other, that the Puritans who invoked the idiom did not thereby fall from the heights of orthodoxy. These warnings must be extended. In particular, the differences between Puritans and continental Reformed theology must not be measured solely in terms of Calvin. Reformed theology [21] was a system of thought elaborated and defended in varying ways by many persons in the sixteenth century.] Several of these Reformed theologians — Beza, Piscator, Zanchy, Bullinger, Pareus — figure more often than Calvin in the religious thought of seventeenth-century New England.[22] To overlook these intermediary figures, in any case, is to risk overlooking the complexities of the Reformed tradition, and consequently the materials for proving the continuity between this tradition and the Puritans. In fact, once these Calvinists, and not Calvin, are brought into the comparison, the continuities far outweigh the differences.

Let me cite some recent scholarship in support of this assertion. One of

[20] In describing Calvin's theology, Miller relied as much upon tone as upon specific doctrines. Both the tone and content of his "Calvin" are suggested by the following citations: Calvinism was "the relatively simple dogmatism of its founder"; "pure Calvinism"; "the absolute dogmatism of original Calvinism"; "primitive Calvinism"; "the doctrine of divine determinism"; "the inexorable logic of Calvin"; "Calvinism pictured man as lifeless clay in the potter's hand." Miller, *Errand into the Wilderness*, pp. 53, 69, 84; Miller, *Nature's Nation* (Cambridge, Mass., 1967), pp. 50, 53–54. The point is not only that Miller relied upon a stage-figure Calvin (the same Calvin, ironically, which V. L. Parrington depicted in *Main Currents of American Thought*) but that he played off the ideas of the New England Puritans against this false stereotype, thereby producing a divergence of views. Had Miller's understanding of Calvin been closer to the truth, the divergence would not have seemed so important. For other critiques of Miller's view of Calvin, see Pettit, *The Heart Prepared*, p. 40n, and Conrad Cherry, *The Theology of Jonathan Edwards*, paperback ed. (New York, 1966), pp. 2–6 and *passim*.

[21] "Reformed" is a better term than "Calvinist," precisely for the reason that it avoids the unnecessary connotations of direct discipleship. "Calvinist" is, in any event, an overused and much abused term. Cf. Basil Hall, "Calvin Against the Calvinists," *Proceedings* of the Huguenot Society of London, XX (1958–1964), 284–301.

[22] Miller himself called attention to these theologians: *The New England Mind*, pp. 92–93. John Norton's annotations in *The Orthodox Evangelist* (London, 1657), and John Cotton's references in the debates during the Antinomian controversy (cf. Hall, *The Antinomian Controversy, 1636–1638*) provide other leads to the colonists' indebtedness to Reformed scholasticism.

the more notable contributions of the past decade to our understanding of Puritanism is Norman Pettit's *The Heart Prepared*, a history of the doctrine of "preparation for salvation" as invoked (or rejected) by Reformed theologians from Calvin to Stoddard. Pettit's approach is significantly different from that of Miller, who argued that the Puritans in New England developed the idea as a means of extending social control over the entire population. Miller set the doctrine within a functional context, Pettit within a scriptural one, for he begins by showing how Scripture itself establishes the problem of reconciling man's initiative with God's. Thereafter the focus is upon a continuity of speculation which begins with Calvin and moves on through English to American Puritanism. In this fashion Pettit locates the New England appropriation of the doctrine firmly within the broad context of Reformed theology.[23]

Recent scholarship on William Perkins provides further evidence of continuity between Puritanism and the Reformed tradition on the continent. Perkins was a key link between Reformed scholasticism and English Puritanism. He drew freely on the writings of continental theologians for ideas and even actual texts; included in his collected works were translations (or adaptations) of treatises by Beza and Zanchy. At the same time his own writings were widely reprinted on the continent, where his reputation was nearly as considerable as in England. It is not surprising, therefore, that the Dutchman Jacobus Arminius should have challenged Perkins on the doctrine of predestination, thereby precipitating the debate that led eventually to the synod of Dort.[24] Such evidence of connections between Puritanism and Reformed theology could be multiplied many times over, and all of it goes to suggest that the two were essentially congruent, if not identical.[25]

Yet we need not rely on external evidence to demonstrate the congruence. Calvin, his successors on the continent, and the Puritans all shared a theological outlook founded on a common understanding of God. The God they defined was the sovereign creator of the world, a creator who stood aloof from His handiwork. Calvinist and Puritan alike asserted the radical separation of grace and nature, declaring that an ever-free and independent God stood over and above "the created world of man and nature." Both went on to describe God in terms of His will, and for both

[23] Norman Pettit, *The Heart Prepared*; Miller, " 'Preparation for Salvation' in Seventeenth-Century New England," in *Nature's Nation*.

[24] I. Breward, "The Significance of William Perkins," *Journal of Religious History*, IV (1966–1967), 113–128.

[25] The career of William Ames is a case in point: cf. Eusden, introduction to Ames, *Marrow of Theology*, and Karl Reuter, *William Ames: The Leading Theologian in the Awakening of Reformed Pietism*, trans. D. Horton (Cambridge, Mass., 1965).

the action of the Holy Spirit in restoring fallen man to the state of grace was the focus of "divinity." Both Calvinist and Puritan saw God as ceaselessly at work bending the course of human history toward the goal of the kingdom.[26]

It was this eschatological understanding of God which gave the Reformed tradition (including Puritanism) its special cast. To put the matter broadly, all Calvinists were imbued with a certain kind of historical consciousness. All of them understood reality as dynamic, not static. All of them looked forward to the coming of the new order, and the urge to hasten on the kingdom was what lay behind their programs of communal discipline. The same historical consciousness may account for the prominence of the decree of election in their thought. As they interpreted the doctrine of predestination, it was a statement of God's promise to enter into and renew a fallen world. The doctrine offered men the assurance that "God has willed and is acting in his power to restore and justify them through his love." Restated in this fashion, the doctrine took on an eschatological significance, for it linked the election of the saints with the coming of the kingdom.[27]

Elsewhere the activist, historical orientation of Reformed divinity was reflected in the great interest Calvin and the Puritans expressed in the Holy Spirit and in the Atonement, rather than the Incarnation; in their use of the covenant theology,[28] and in their fascination with "method." William Perkins provided readers of his works with a fold-out chart marking off the stages of salvation. This chart was actually a form of history, for when the Puritan wrote his spiritual autobiography, he ordered his life according to the spatial and dynamic plan that Perkins had outlined. The methodizing of the *ordo salutis*, the elaboration of the

[26] David Little, "Max Weber Revisited: The 'Protestant Ethic' and the Puritan Experience of Order," *Harvard Theological Review*, LIX (1966), 422; Eusden, ed., Ames, *Marrow of Theology*, pp. 21–23, 77–78.

[27] A major work spelling out in detail the "relation of eschatology to the life of the Church" in the theology of Calvin and Bucer is Thomas Torrance, *Kingdom and Church* (Edinburgh, 1956). There is a growing literature on millennarian thought among the Puritans, much of it originating in studies of typology and aesthetics. Cf. Bercovitch, "Typology in Puritan New England: The Williams-Cotton Controversy Reassessed," *American Quarterly*, XIX (1967), 166–190; Jesper Rosenmeier, "Veritas: The Sealing of the Promise," *Harvard Library Bulletin*, XVI (1968), 26–37; Joy B. Gilsdorf, "The Puritan Apocalypse: New England Eschatology in the Seventeenth Century," Unpublished Ph.D. Dissertation (Yale University, 1964); Le Roy Edwin Froom, *The Prophetic Faith of Our Fathers* (Washington, D.C., 1946), III.

[28] Charles S. McCoy, "Johannes Cocceius: Federal Theologian," *Scottish Journal of Theology*, XVI (1963), 352–370; and Eusden, introduction, Ames, *Marrow of Theology*.

"morphology of conversion," the development of a "plain style" of preaching that was deliberately "practical" — these aspects of seventeenth-century Puritanism emerged from an eschatological consciousness which the Puritans shared with the Reformed tradition.[29]

If it is important in understanding the Puritans to recognize their alliance with the international Reformed tradition, certain differences between the two must also be noted. Like members of a family, the national churches within the Reformed tradition resembled one another but also varied in detail, for each adapted a common idiom to particular circumstances. The special character of Puritanism arose from the refusal of Elizabeth I to allow certain changes in the structure and worship of the Church of England, changes favored by many English Protestants but especially by a group which gained the name of "Puritans." Denied a hearing by the Queen, these Puritans turned to Parliament and to the population at large for support, at the same time sharpening their indictment of the Church beyond what Calvin would have said. By the 1570's they were declaring that the bishops of the Church — the persons charged with suppressing them — were unlawful, which was to say that their office had no warrant in the word of God. Calvin had never been so explicit, nor did he make the validity of the Church depend on the exercise of discipline, as many Puritans maintained. It was Calvin, to be sure, who taught the Puritans their legalism, but the political situation in which they found themselves encouraged the development of this legalism beyond the point where he had stopped. Similarly, the Puritans inherited a bias against Catholic sacerdotalism, a bias intensified in England in the heat of struggle against the "popish remnants" in the Church. And because the Puritans could not rely on bishops or civil magistrates to enforce the moral code they taught, the preachers in the movement directed their attention increasingly to the individual conscience, encouraging the practice of pietistic self-scrutiny.[30]

This final tendency is one to which many historians have pointed as the crucial difference between the Reformed tradition (or Calvin) and the Puritans. When more is known of the Reformed scholastics from whom the Puritans borrowed so deeply, this "piety" may not

[29] The chart precedes page 11 in Perkins, *Works*, I. The fullest study of how Puritans methodized the spiritual life remains Haller, *The Rise of Puritanism*; the phrase "morphology of conversion" is taken from Edmund S. Morgan, *Visible Saints: The History of a Puritan Idea* (New York, 1963). On Puritan rhetoric as eschatological, see Larzer Ziff, *The Career of John Cotton* (Princeton, 1962), chap. 5.

[30] George Yule, "Theological Developments in Elizabethan Puritanism," *Journal of Ecclesiastical History*, I (1960–1961), 21–23; Patrick Collinson, *The Elizabethan Puritan Movement* (London, 1967).

seem so original.[31] Nor was it taught in the same way by every preacher.[32] Throughout the history of the movement, Puritans debated a wide range of religious issues, many of them arising out of the tension between this pietistic bias and Reformed sacramentalism, others out of the complexities of methodizing the *ordo salutis*. What was the normative experience of conversion, an awakening by degrees or some compressed reaction? [33] How was man's striving for grace and his cleansing under the Law to be accommodated with the gospel promise of grace without conditions? What were the role and nature of the means of grace — the ministry and the sacraments — in a system in which the elect were predestinated to salvation? These questions arose in part because most Puritans, as heirs of the Reformed tradition, held on to the sacraments and an objective understanding of the ministry. To be sure, they held on to both in an attenuated form; their heightened interest in the workings of the Holy Spirit left little room for a high doctrine of the sacraments or a sacerdotal view of the ministry. The logic of their spiritism was such, moreover, that amidst the turmoil of the seventeenth century some Puritans would overthrow the sacraments and ministry altogether.[34] Perhaps it could be

[31] Pettit, *The Heart Prepared*, p. 6. In his comments on this paper John Eusden sketched a number of sub-traditions within Reformed theology, one of which included William Ames and the Puritans in New England. These "covenant of grace" theologians, as Eusden calls them, are the subject of an extended study he is making.

[32] Charles H. and Katherine George, *The Protestant Mind of the English Reformation* (Princeton, 1961), argue that Puritan and Anglican shared the same religious attitudes. Although this conclusion is disputable — John H. F. New, *Anglican and Puritan* (Stanford, Calif., 1966), argues the case for their difference — it serves as a worthwhile reminder that the meaning of the terms Puritan and Anglican was relative and changing. Just as the line between the two in England was a fluid one, so the relationship of the Puritans to Calvin varied from one period to another, from William Perkins, say, to John Bunyan. Methodologically the problem is to abstract an ideal type while doing justice to variety.

[33] The tendency among modern historians has been to single out the most tormented accounts of the conversion experience and make of them the normative pattern. Alan Simpson, who bases his interpretation upon such accounts, also noted that "Puritans acknowledge the possibility that the saint might have grown into his condition without any recollection of a violent rebirth. But it was sufficiently unusual for it to be a matter of anxiety to some of the godly that they could not date their conversion." *Puritanism in Old and New England*, p. 115. The problem loomed larger for the Puritans than Simpson allows; there was a continuous debate among Puritans and their descendants, stretching from Richard Greenham and Perkins down to Horace Bushnell and Harriet Beecher Stowe, over the normative pattern of the spiritual life.

[34] The logic of spiritism is explained in Maclear, " 'The Heart of New England Rent': The Mystical Element in Early Puritan History," and in Geoffrey Nuttall, *The Holy Spirit in Puritan Faith and Experience* (Oxford, 1946). The contradictions within Puritanism have been variously described by Nuttall, Maclear, Morgan, Miller, Sommerville, Pettit, and others, but agreement would be general

said that Puritans finally divided on these issues according to their view of history and the world. Millennarian Puritans saw the world as in process of renewal, and discounted all existing structures; others saw it in legalistic and static terms as composed of ordained institutions and fixed forms, and spoke of the millennium as far off.

[The political situation of the Puritans had one further consequence. Resentful of the Church's imperfection, yet believing that schism was a sin, Puritans found themselves caught in a dilemma from which flowed much of their restlessness.[35] The same dilemma was a cause of the fragmentation of the movement into sects, a process that began in the late sixteenth century with the emergence of the separatists. By one set of Reformed standards the separatists were perfectly legitimate in demanding freedom for the church to cleanse itself; by another they were schismatics who carried their legalism too far. The emergence of the separatists is thus a perfect measure of how the English situation acted to confuse the meaning and application of Reformed ideas.[36]

It is in this context, moreover, that denominational categories become inadequate; too abstract and rigid, they sever the Puritan sects from their dynamic and fluid relationship with the Reformed tradition. [Denominational categories conceal the fact that all Puritans, whether "presbyterian" or "congregationalist" or some other group, held four propositions in common: the revitalization of the laymen's role, including greater privileges in the government of the church; the purification of church membership; the assignment of the power of the keys to each parish or congregation; and the separation of church and state so as to give the church effective responsibility for discipline.] Many historians would add a fifth proposition to this list: the assertion that the nature of the church must conform to the will of God.[37] But the Biblicism of the Puritans is less important in explaining their ecclesiology than the emphasis they

---

on the proposition that Puritan sacramentalism, together with a "preparationist" approach to the spiritual life, clashed with Puritan spiritism, together with a "conversionist" mentality. Pettit has noted the connections between the doctrine of preparation and sacramental views, *The Heart Prepared*, pp. 117–124, 134–136. The problem is a legacy from the Reformed tradition, as John Baillie indicates in *Baptism and Conversion* (London, 1964).

[35] Collinson, *The Elizabethan Puritan Movement*, p. 132.

[36] Morgan, *Visible Saints*, cites the separatist Henry Barrow's explicit denunciation of Calvin, an action forced upon Barrow by the contradictions in which he was enmeshed.

[37] Paul, *An Apologeticall Narration*, pp. 123–125; Miller, *The Puritans*, pp. 41–55. Sacvan Bercovitch writes, ". . . the connection between eschatology and historiography — one which relies heavily on scriptural exegesis and prediction — should make us hesitate to render tribute to the things of the Spirit *at the expense* of giving due emphasis to the settlers' profound 'Biblicism.' "

placed upon the Holy Spirit. [The essential impulse within the movement was to relate the church to the intervention of the Spirit, to understand the community of the saints as a type of the kingdom. In this they were not unique] Calvin himself looked upon the church in two ways, as an institution ordained by God to exist upon earth, and as the realm of the Spirit, a realm in which "the original order of creation" had been restored.[38] Inheriting both views, the Puritans were driven to identify the first with the Church of England, and so to emphasize the second. But the issue of keeping the two in balance was inherent within the Reformed tradition.

[There is another reason for discarding denominational categories. Puritanism began as a movement within the Church of England at the time of the Elizabethan religious settlement of 1559. From that time until the accession of William III, most Puritans thought of themselves as members of the Church, not as founders of new churches. It was only when the religious settlement under William denied the legitimacy of this claim that the connections between English Puritans and the Church were finally severed. On this side of the Atlantic, the new charter of 1691 and the events associated with it mark a similar end to the affiliation] Thereafter, any colonist who claimed membership or ministerial orders within the Church would have to renounce his current status and formally rejoin the mother body.[39]

The historic association of Puritanism with the Church of England is a means of giving dates to the movement, a periodization which other evidence sustains. The decade of the 1690's saw Reformed scholasticism giving way under the impact of the Enlightenment, leaving eighteenth-century Reformed theologians to work out a new alliance between philos-

---

[38] Benjamin C. Milner, Jr., "Calvin's Doctrine of the Church," *Harvard Theological Review*, LVIII (1965), 458; Little, "Max Weber Revisited: The 'Protestant Ethnic' and the Puritan Experience of Order," p. 423. The problem that Calvin passed on to the Puritans was described by Ernst Troeltsch in these terms: ". . . how could a 'holy community' composed of sterling Christians, whose faith was a matter of profound personal conviction, and whose lives were controlled by an exalted and austere ideal, be at the same time a Church which would provide a spiritual home for the masses of the population?" *The Social Teaching of the Christian Churches* (Glencoe, Ill.; 1949), II, 659. See also Geoffrey Nuttall, "The Early Congregational Conception of the Church," *Transactions of the Congregational Historical Society*, XIV, 197–204, and George H. Williams, *The Radical Reformation* (Philadelphia, 1962), pp. 581n, 787–788.

[39] It could, of course, be argued that the significant break came in 1640 or 1662, the date of the act excluding nonconformists from the Church and declaring their orders illegitimate. The most important studies that seek to transcend denominational categories are Collinson, *The Elizabethan Puritan Movement*, and Morgan, *Visible Saints*, a carefully measured reply to Perry Miller, *Orthodoxy in Massachusetts* (Cambridge, Mass., 1933).

ophy and religion.[40] On the whole, however, Pietists were content to abandon philosophy and science, just as they abandoned the theocratic vision of a holy commonwealth which inspired Calvin and the Puritans. What passed from Puritanism to Pietism was the assertion that religion fundamentally involved the affective self, the heart, rather than the reason.[41]

An adequate definition of Puritanism must incorporate this periodization of the movement, and go on from there to recognize the essential continuity between Calvinists and Puritans. An adequate definition must allow for the adaptation of Reformed ideas to England, a process that eventually resulted in the splintering of the movement into many sects. Despite this splintering, an adequate definition must recognize the wholeness of Puritan history. What gave substance to the movement was a certain inventory of ideas — the separation of grace and nature, an understanding of God and man as active forces, an eschatology. And what linked the Puritan program for reform of the church to Puritan descriptions of the spiritual life was the common motif of renewal. Edmund S. Morgan has seen the Puritan as caught in the dilemma of remaining pure while living in the world. Such a posture was forced upon the Puritan by the dynamic relationship between this world and the next. He knew himself to be at mid-point between these worlds, and his striving for self-discipline, his endless self-scrutiny, was directed toward the end of winning freedom from the world and entrance to the kingdom.[42]

There still remains to be answered, finally, the problem of the relationship between Puritanism and culture. What we know for sure is very little. The extensive scholarship of Christopher Hill has shown that class, status, and occupation have something to do with Puritanism, but Hill himself would surely agree that they are not sufficient as analytical categories.[43] It seems likely that the social sources of Puritanism will eventu-

---

[40] Perry Miller, *Jonathan Edwards* (New York, 1949), describes Edwards' labors in this regard. The collapse of scholasticism occurred more rapidly in England than in America; rational theology was making inroads among English presbyterians in the 1690's, and the dissenting academies were ahead of their time in teaching the new logic and the new sciences. The situation in New England with respect to the academic curriculum is described in Edmund S. Morgan, *The Gentle Puritan* (New Haven, 1962), chap. 3, and in Perry Miller, *The New England Mind: From Colony to Province* (Cambridge, Mass., 1953). On the English side, Olive M. Griffiths, *Religion and Learning: A Study in English Presbyterian Thought from the Bartholomew Ejections (1662) to the Foundation of the Unitarian Movement* (Cambridge, 1935) is valuable.

[41] The emergence of Pietism is described in Reuter, *William Ames*, and in F. Ernest Stoeffler, *The Rise of Evangelical Pietism* (Leyden, 1965).

[42] Morgan, *The Puritan Dilemma* (Boston, 1958).

[43] Perhaps the best of Hill's many surveys is *Society and Puritanism in Pre-Revolutionary England* (New York, 1964).

ally be described in terms of personality structure (and thus of family structure), life style, generations, and negative reference groups, but exact information is wanting on all of these for both England and America. It is possible to declare with more certainty that the dynamics of Puritanism in England bear a direct relationship to its status as an out-group remote from the center of power; the greater this distance, the more intense became the urge to free the church from the world and hasten on the coming kingdom.[44]

The millennarian fervor which runs through Puritanism may provide the best clue to the social function of the movement. Puritanism, it seems, furnished certain Englishmen with a new identity as members of a special group. All English Protestants believed that the history of the Christian church revealed God's favoring providence toward England. And Christian history also taught that God's people must fight a cruel and bloody war against Anti-Christ and all his minions.[45] The Puritans were able to appropriate this rhetoric and apply it to their cause for two reasons: they were most outspoken in attacking Catholicism, and their outgroup status lent itself to a sense of persecution. The identity of the Puritan as saint in covenant with God was reinforced by the idea that history was moving rapidly toward the coming of the kingdom. The prophetic stance of the Puritan teachers grew out of an historical perspective which saw the task of reformation as increasingly urgent, lest the final day prove a day of judgment. Those who responded to this preaching, those Englishmen who in life style withdrew from the "world" and set their hearts upon the kingdom, established a new identity for themselves as the Lord's free people.

From this identity flowed the Puritan understanding of the church as a voluntary, gathered congregation. From it came also the Puritan theory of community, the vision of a social order (to quote John Winthrop) "knit together" in a "bond of love." The immigration to New

44 "The fertilized ground [for the word as preached by Puritans] was the ground which for one reason or another was out of sympathy with official policy." A list of out-groups, together with a brief critique of Hill's position, is in Simpson, *Puritanism in Old and New England*, pp. 11–12. In the 1930's there were attempts to link left-wing Puritanism (measured theologically) with lower social and economic groups; cf. Tindall, *John Bunyan, Mechanick Preacher*.

As for the social consequences of Puritanism, recent studies suggest that the movement worked to create a new kind of personality — Michael Walzer's radical saint, or, more correctly, David Little's self-disciplining activist. Walzer, *Revolution of the Saints: A Study in the Origins of Radical Politics* (Cambridge, Mass., 1965); Little, *Religion, Order and Law*, paperback ed. (New York, 1969). Walzer's study should be read in the light of two extended reviews, both indicating difficulties with his interpretation: Little, "Max Weber Revisited," and Richard T. Vann, *History and Theory*, VII (1968), 102–114.

45 William Haller, *Foxe's Book of Martyrs and the Elect Nation* (London, 1967).

England can equally be counted as a consequence of this millennarianism. In the late 1620's events in England and abroad convinced many Puritans that the final day was close at hand. New England loomed before them both as refuge and as paradise, the wilderness which they could make into the kingdom. Not only did the chiliastic zeal of certain Puritans precipitate their immigration; it also inspired the congregationalism that emerged in New England in the 1630's — the strict limits on church membership, the more democratic church structure.[46]

Whether the colonists were exceptional in their chiliasm is not clear. [In their general vision of the kingdom, and in their activist drive, they stood as one with the entire Puritan movement, sharing in a historical consciousness that originated with Calvin and Bucer. Any understanding of Puritanism in America must ignore artificial boundaries and distinctions and build instead upon the continuities that linked England and America.] On this matter of continuities, American scholarship has far to go in working out the relationships between institutional forms, and even ideas.[47]

Does this mean there is nothing distinctive about American Puritanism, nothing American historians can study without going back to Perkins or Calvin? There is not as much as many would assert, but there is something. [We can speak of the Americanizing of Puritan ideas just as historians of the Revolutionary period speak of the Americanizing of Whig ideas. The analogy is nearly exact;] the colonists imported the radical Whig ideology from abroad, and we can only understand what they are saying by reference to the English sources. Yet there is a difference, for although the ideas seem the same on both sides of the Atlantic, the pattern of culture in America had departed from the English model in ways that affected the meaning and consequences of these ideas.[48] So also in the seventeenth century, the Reformed tradition took on a new significance in the "free air of a new world." [Here Puritanism became the majority point of view, and preachers who had whetted their fiery preaching on targets that the Church of England had to offer underwent an agonizing adjustment to a new life style. Here the ideal of a gathered church had strange consequences, and here the alliance between church

[46] Cf. Gilsdorf, "The Puritan Apocalypse."

[47] Harvard College, which Morison located within the broad context of Western humanism, needs to be studied in the context of Reformed educational practices; one of the major characteristics of Reformed Protestantism in the sixteenth century was the founding of schools for training ministers. New England political history needs to be studied in light of the "holy commonwealth" literature, both continental and English.

[48] Oscar and Mary Handlin, "James Burgh and American Revolutionary Theory," *Proceedings* of the Massachusetts Historical Society, LXXIII, 38–57; Bernard Bailyn, *The Ideological Origins of the American Revolution* (Cambridge, Mass., 1967).

and state gave the "New England Way" its notoriety.[49] The future of Puritan studies in America, a future that seems without limit, lies in articulating these differences, as well as the continuities, between Old World and New.]

[49] The bibliography of relevant studies is too immense to be listed here. An interesting overview is Darrett B. Rutman, "The Mirror of Puritan Authority," in G. A. Billias, ed., *Law and Authority in Colonial America* (Barre, Mass., 1965). The accommodation of Puritanism to the "wilderness" is the theme of *From Colony to Province*, the second volume of Miller's *The New England Mind*. The first describes a static system of ideas (hedging on whether they were held only in New England or also abroad), the second the meaning and consequence of these ideas in America. *From Colony to Province* is open to many criticisms; still, it offers an amazing number of insights into the nature of New England history. A fair estimate of Miller is not easy to achieve, and although I have joined in the "ritual patricidal totem feast" (to borrow Bercovitch's phrase), I share his feeling that *The New England Mind* continues to supply "the best overview we have of American Puritanism."

Hingham, Massachusetts, 1631–1661: An East Anglian Oligarchy in the New World

JOHN J. WATERS

How American is America? In one form or another, generations of historians of the United States have asked this question, and it is fair to say that most have concluded that "American" and "the Americans" have been unique from the days of the earliest settlements. They have explained the creation of distinctive societies in the New World in several ways, ranging from the environmentalism of Frederick Jackson Turner's frontier thesis to the historical sociology of Sigmund Diamond. They have less frequently suggested that the cultural continuities which survived in the ocean crossing were more significant than the differences which appeared in America.

John Waters uses the techniques of local history to demon-

strate how the settlers of a town in New England organized themselves and behaved very much as they had in their homeland. He shows that <u>Hingham, Massachusetts, was populated by colonists from two very different parts of England, that these men and women retained their traditional English local characteristics, and that the early history of the town is the story of the conflict of specific old world values.</u> *Not until* <u>1660 did the second generation of East Anglian and West Countrymen in Hingham consolidate in defense of their local and class interests against the threats of provincial interference and town diversity.</u>

Waters employs a genealogical approach to local history, tracing the history of each person in order to assess the roles of individuals and families in the history of Hingham. His method is similar to Sumner Chilton Powell's in Puritan Village *(Middletown, Conn., 1963), although his results are quite different. Compare Waters's analysis with the more social scientific approach of the essays on Andover and Plymouth. Are there advantages in traditional historical methodology?*

Until fairly recently the study of early New England towns reflected the "germ theory" approach of nineteenth-century historical scholarship. Such distinguished historians as Herbert Baxter Adams, Edward Channing, and Charles McLean Andrews sought the origins of those "virile little commonwealths" in the teutonic woods, the Anglo-Saxon villages, or the towns of Elizabethan England.[1] Contemporary historians, while using these studies for information, generally reject their quest for primeval archetypes. For the present-day student, settlement and immigration involve different kinds of questions. [He wants to know why these immigrants came to New England. Were they established members of the English social structure or displaced yeomen looking for a second chance? How did these "planters," coming as they did from different parts of England, with different attitudes on politics and religion, and with diverse customs, adjust to each other? How did the institutions they brought with them change in the New World?]

The detailed investigations of Andover and Sudbury by Philip Greven

© 1968 by the Regents of the University of California. Reprinted from the *Journal of Social History*, Vol. I, No. 4, pp. 351–370, by permission of The Regents.

[1] See Herbert B. Adams, *The Germanic Origin of New England Towns* (Baltimore, 1882), pp. 8–9, for the initial statement of the "germ" thesis. The controversy itself received detailed treatment in A. S. Eisenstadt, *Charles McLean Andrews* (New York, 1956), pp. 11–20.

and Sumner Chilton Powell give two partial answers to these questions; this study of Hingham offers a third analysis. Greven in his essay on Andover points out that its first settlers conceived of their town as a "replica of an English village . . . in which all of the inhabitants dwelt side by side and tilled their lands in small plots adjacent to those of their neighbors in the general fields." Within a generation, however, this community-centered ideal had been transformed by the sheer abundance of available land into an individually oriented farming area.[2] Sumner Chilton Powell, by focusing his attention on the English backgrounds of Sudbury's settlers, sees a diversity of farming and leadership patterns tempered by the American experience. Sudbury's first generation found its aims and ideals opposed by the new.[3] Both Andover and Sudbury underwent real change within the lives of their founders. They show marked contrast to the much more conservative town of Hingham which successfully preserved many features of traditional English life in the Massachusetts wilderness.

The internal life of Bear Cove, or what became Hingham Plantation, was dominated for its first generation by a rivalry between its first settlers from the English "West Country," who arrived between 1631 and 1634, and the subsequent immigrants from East Anglia, who came between 1633 and 1640.[4] These two groups are broadly representative of almost 40 per cent of the "Great Emigration."[5] Their contrasting values led

[2] Philip J. Greven, Jr., "Old Patterns in the New World: The Distribution of Land in 17th Century Andover," Essex Institute, *Historical Collections*, CI (1965), 147–48.

[3] Sumner Chilton Powell, *Puritan Village, The Formation of a New England Town* (Middletown, 1963), pp. xvii–xx, 139–146.

[4] For Bear Cove identifications I have used Andrew H. Ward's "First Settlers of Hingham," *New England Historical and Genealogical Register*, II (1848), 250–251, at the same time correcting this list with the names of church members as recorded in Peter Hobart's "Diary," Massachusetts Historical Society (MHS), and those of land owners as recorded in the *History of Hingham*, George Lincoln, ed., 4 vols. (Hingham, 1893), II, III, hereafter cited as *HH*. English parish identifications follow the works of C. E. Banks and *Extracts from the Minutes of Daniel Cushing of Hingham with a Photograph of His Manuscript*, H. A. Whitney, comp. (1865), hereafter cited as Cushing Manuscript.

These sources indicate that the settlers of Hingham up to 1640 numbered one hundred and thirty-one families of which ninety may be identified by parish and county (70 per cent of the total). Fifty-two families were from East Anglia, with forty-five from Norfolk alone, constituting in all 40 per cent of the immigration. The West Country supplied eighteen families, or 15 per cent of the Bear Cove total.

[5] The four counties of Cornwall, Devon, Dorset, and Somerset, which make up the West Country, accounted for almost fifteen per cent of New England settlers. Suffolk, Essex, and Norfolk, the East Anglian complex, supplied twenty-five per cent of the immigrants. See C. E. Banks, *Topographical Dictionary of 2885 English Emigrants to New England, 1620–1650* (Baltimore, 1937), pp. 15, 19, 37, 147, and 166, 54, 124, and the same author's *Planters of the Commonwealth* (Boston, 1930), pp. 13–15.

to ethnic, political, and theological conflicts. These differences illuminate Hingham's constitutional challenges to both the political and religious norms of John Winthrop's Massachusetts. Its 1645 militia dispute involved a direct attack upon the role of the "Assistants" in that Puritan Commonwealth, while its support of Dr. Child's *Petition* showed its opposition to the "Congregational" religious policy. Hingham's East Anglians took their values from their experiences in old Hingham. They came with an established ruling class and a church policy that was clearly Presbyterian. Once in Bear Cove they had to fight first the West Countrymen and then the Massachusetts authorities before their East Anglian pattern could triumph. This is one of the reasons why the new Hingham resisted change and insisted upon the retention of traditional ways. Yet within a generation the rivalry of West Countrymen and East Anglian ceased to be important. It was replaced by class interest. West Countrymen and East Anglian had joined together in an upper class oligarchy intent upon perpetuation of its way of life.

The original "planters" of Bear Cove came from England's West Country. Their land differed in both soil and husbandry from East Anglia. In Devon and Dorset tilling the land stood for a way of life yet to be changed by the loom. Those towns that faced the sea, such as Plymouth, Weymouth, and Barnstaple, combined the working of both the sea and land. In the ancient city of Glastonbury in Somerset, the people took the new Puritan ethos lightly. They raised the May pole, evoking with it merriment and the primitive rites of spring. Pretty girls cast their spells, drunkards crowded its streets, and the barber plied his trade on the Sabbath. The 1620 episcopal visitation of St. John the Baptist Church found it without the "booke of sermons and a bible of the last translation." The records indicate little discontent with the ways of the old church,[6] The West Country sent at least eighteen families to the new town in Massachusetts, the majority of whom sailed from Bristol Port on the *Lyon*, which made four recorded voyages to the Bay Colony between 1630 and 1632.[7]

Typical of these West Countrymen was John Otis. In 1631 he was nearly fifty years of age and came with his wife and five children. Although born in Glastonbury, he had moved with his family in 1621 to

---

[6] The analysis of the Glastonbury social scene is based on Bath and Wells' "Visitation Act Books," 1617 and 1620, D/D/Ca 206, 220, Somerset Record Office, Taunton, England. For Barnstaple see entries under 1622, 1628, and 1631 in "Exeter Episcopal Visitation," CCXVII–CCXVIII, Exeter Diocesan Record Office, Exeter. Thomas Wainwright, the editor of *Barnstaple Parish Register of Baptisms* . . . (Exeter, 1903), observed that such ancient liturgical practices as the ban on the solemnization of marriages during Lent, as well as the retention of common Christian names, were retained throughout this period.

[7] While these lists are fragmentary, what information exists is summarized in C. E. Banks, *Planters of the Commonwealth*, pp. 85–86.

Barnstaple in Devon. His father had been sufficiently stationed at death to have his will proved in the Consistorial Court at Wells in 1611. And John was prosperous enough to pay the heavy cost of migrating to Massachusetts, which came to at least £30.[8] Yet the Otis family was neither the wealthiest nor the most important of the West Country families that came to Bear Cove. The richest would certainly be the Andrews, who along with the Cades repaid the subsidy to King James in 1624.[9] Thomas Andrews, a patriarch in his fifties, must have thought it understandable that his son Joseph should be the town's first clerk, a selectman, and for a brief time representative to the General Court.[10]

Then there was Mr. William Walton from Seaton Parish. He was a product of Emmanuel College, the cradle of Puritanism at Cambridge University. It is more than likely that Mr. Walton knew Peter Hobart, also a Cambridge man, who came to Bear Cove as its first pastor.[11] The shipwright James Cade, a Devon man, held lands in Northam Parish. By rural standards this was a wealthy family. In New England Cade utilized the full regnal citation ". . . Lord Charles by the grace of God King of England," a formula distasteful to the majority of the settlers of the Bay Colony, who used the simpler "Caroli Angliae &c." [12] Cade was no rebel. His position as the second son must have been a major factor in his reasons for migrating. The gentleman and rich planter George Strange was his attorney. At Bear Cove they were John Otis's neighbors, as was another West Countryman, Thomas Loring, who became the first deacon and held the license "to sell wine & strong

---

[8] The will of "Richard Ottis" of Glastonbury, November 29, 1611, proved at the Consistorial Court at Wells, exists in transcript in the Somerset Record Office, Taunton. John Otis's birth date follows his deposition in the Massachusetts Archives, XXXIX, 9, Boston. For transportation costs see *Records of the Governor and Company of the Massachusetts Bay* . . . , N. B. Shurtleff *et al.*, eds., 5 vols. (Boston, 1853–54), I, 66, hereafter cited as *MBR*.

Most historians have followed William Tudor's supposition that John Otis "came from Hingham, in Norfolk, England, June, 1635, in Company with the Rev. Peter Hobart," *Life of James Otis* (Boston, 1823), p. 496. But Hobart's party did not arrive at Bear Cove until September, whereas John Otis's early presence in Hingham may be seen in his June 1635 "Proprietors Grants of Land . . . John Ottis . . . for a planting lott four acres of land lying upon Weariall hill," *Liber I*, Hingham Records, Hingham, Massachusetts.

[9] "*Taxacio Tertii subsidii Trium* . . . *Jacobo Regi*," (1624), 102/463, Public Record Office, London, England.

[10] *HH*, II, 10–11; Solomon Lincoln, "Appendix," in *History of the Town of Hingham* (Hingham, 1827), pp. 162–163.

[11] *HH*, II, 335; III, 274.

[12] James Cade, conveyance, 4 Dec. 1638, in Thomas Lechford, *Note-Book* . . . (Cambridge, 1885), pp. 42–44; C. H. Pope, *Pioneers of Massachusetts* (Boston, 1900), p. 87; Henry F. Waters, "Genealogical Gleanings in England," *New England Historical and Genealogical Register*, L (1896), 505, *ibid.*, LXVIII (1914), 61.

Water." [13] These families are hardly underprivileged. Along with the
Strongs, Phippenys, and Betscombes, they were people of record, literate,
property owners, and careful husbanders of the soil. Probably the key
element in their migration was a desire for greater estates and profits
than England offered them. However, these West Country settlers were
not to remain alone to fulfill their dreams.

West Country

In June of 1633 the *Elizabeth Bonaventure* arrived at Boston from the
East Anglian County of Norfolk. It brought to the Bay Colony sixty-
three-year-old Edmund Hobart and his family, with their servant Henry
Gibbs, as well as the Jacobs and Chubocks. Late that summer this advance guard from old Hingham in Norfolk settled at Bear Cove. They
were heralds of a new wave of immigrants that would profoundly change
the political and social makeup of that New England town.[14]

In contrast to the general agrarian backgrounds of the West Countrymen, these East Anglians from Norfolk, Essex, and Suffolk, represented
an area famous for its weaving industries, although the trade itself had
been in the grips of depression since the twenties. The land they left
was as flat as fine fustian, while the Norfolk Broads periodically suffered
from "innundations of water." In fact, it was just such a flood that
provided the needed pretext for the citizens of Norwich when they
failed to furnish Charles I with £3,000 of ship money in 1635. East
Anglia meant dissent in both religion and politics.[15] This region, so very
much like Holland, had received heavy influxes of Dutch weavers, whose
separatist activities, together with those of the native Puritans, were
thorns in the side of at least three High Church bishops. The most
famous of those shepherds was the Anglo-Catholic Bishop Matthew
Wren. It was his practice to elevate the "consecrated host" and as
Master of Peterhouse, Cambridge, he had restored the use of Latin in
the Divine Service. "Uniformity in doctrine and Uniformity in discipline" — his own words indicated what he wanted. Presbyterian Hingham would feel the wrath of his visitation.[16] Wren offered an early
economic interpretation for this Puritan migration: ". . . the chiefest
Cause of their Departure, was the small Wages which was given to the
poor Workmen, whereby the Work-masters grew rich." [17] In justice to
the bishop it should be noted that this explanation, with its critique of

13 *MBR*, I, 221; *HH*, III, 27.

14 C. E. Banks, *Planters of the Commonwealth*, 102–3; Cushing Manuscript.

15 William Page, ed., *Victoria History of the County of Norfolk* (London,
1906), II, 505–506; Wallace Notestein, *The English People on the Eve of
Colonization, 1603–1630* (New York, 1954), pp. 153–154, and petition in
Calendar of State Papers, Domestic, 1625–1649, 521.

16 [Anon], *Wrens Anatomy* (London, 1641), pp. 3, 12; Louis C. Cornish,
"The Settlement of Hingham," in *Hingham* (1911), pp. 38–39.

17 "*The most humble answer of Matthew Wren . . . to the Articles of Impeachment . . . ,*" in Sir Christopher Wren, *Parentalia* (London, 1750), p. 101.

the Puritan "Work-masters," was his reply to those parliamentarians who charged that it was his seeking after "Uniformity" that drove the godly out of Norfolk.[18] Actually, either an economic interpretation or a theory of migration based upon religious persecution *per se*, is an inadequate explanation for this particular flight to the Bay Colony.

The key element that brought the Norfolk planters to Bear Cove is to be found in their historical awareness of themselves as a self-existing Puritan community. These emigrants had shared since 1615 a set of religious experiences that had alienated them from the traditional poles of English life as symbolized in King and Church. They separated from the English nation when they saw their identity as a godly people threatened by the integrating policies of Charles I and Archbishop William Laud. The men of Hingham did not come to Bear Cove as individual settlers, but rather as members of a conscious community of God's people. Their migration followed an observable plan of three parts. The first is Edmund Hobart's landing party in 1633, seeking a place of settlement; next, a continuing wave of friends, relatives, and enthusiasts, which lasted until 1637; and finally in 1638, the flight of the "visible" church.

The coming of the Hobarts as an advance guard in 1633 laid the groundwork for at least seven subsequent shiploads of human freight. In 1634 the *Elizabeth Dorcas* contributed the recently widowed Mrs. Bosworth and her five children. Her husband, as he had sensed death's approach before the voyage would end, requested to be "carried on deck that he might see Canaan, the promised land." [19] His was the religious intensity of ancient Israel. Such a people would not be without a gathered church, as the West Country settlers had been since they settled the Cove. Fortunately, the Hobarts had a candidate for pastor in their son Peter. He had been guided along the path of Puritan righteousness by Robert Peck, the pastor of old Hingham, who was himself a graduate of St. Catherine's and Magdalene at Cambridge. The religious vocation of Peter Hobart, which took him to Queen's and Magdalene, represented a real social advance for his family. Hobart received priest's orders in 1627 and then settled down to the life of a non-conforming curate at Haverhill in Norfolk.[20] That he differed from the views of the Anglican Church is clear. No records exist, however, to substantiate Cotton Mather's belief that it was the "cloud of prelatical impositions and persecutions" that determined his flight to America.[21] A less nebulous reason was the promptings of his relatives to join them in New

[18] *Articles of Impeachment, of the Commons . . . Against Matthew Wren, Doctor in Divinitie, late Bishop of Norwich* . . . (London, 1641), art. 13, p. 9.

[19] *HH*, II, 86–87.

[20] J. Venn *et al.*, *Alumni Cantabrigienses* . . . (Cambridge, 1922), Pt. I, II, 423.

[21] Cotton Mather, *Magnalia Christi Americana* (London, 1704), III, xxvii, 4.

England. And as new Hingham's pastor, Peter Hobart would now be his own master. This was a real consideration for a man of his strong-willed nature.

The arrival of Peter Hobart in 1635 gains perspective when it is combined with the friends and neighbors from Haverhill and old Hingham who accompanied him. These East Anglians included Mr. Anthony Cooper, who came with his wife and four children, and four servants, as well as the less stationed Farrows and Larges. They had come over on the *Hopewell*, the *Defence*, and the *Elizabeth* (all of London), and were followed in 1637 by the *Increase* and the *Mary Anne*. But the most important ship to sail since the *Lyon* transported John Otis and the other West Countrymen in the early 1630's was the East Anglian *Diligent*, which arrived in August of 1638.[22]

The coming of the *Diligent* marked the final chapter in an affair which stretched back to 1615. In that year Robert Peck, the pastor of St. Andrew's in Hingham, was convicted of non-conformity. The established church did not look favorably upon his teaching parishioners "not to kneel when they came to Church" and that "it was Superstition to bow down at the Name of Jesus." Pastor Peck carefully organized such like-minded souls. Under the pretense of catechising and psalm singing this inner parish group held conventicles. In 1622 he was caught in the act with twenty-two of his neighbors, some of whom defiantly told Bishop Harsnett that there was "no Difference between an Alehouse and the Church, till the Preacher be in the Pulpit." While the bishop extracted a public "*I confess my Errors*" from Peck, the degree of penitence must have been small indeed. Peck gave his account of this "persecution" to influential friends in neighboring Norwich, who then proceeded to enlist Sir Edward Coke to present their petition against the bishop in the House of Commons. Harsnett found himself accused of simony, persecution, idolatry, and popery.[23]

Robert Peck is an interesting example of the combination of religiosity and precocious political awareness found in the Puritan cause. He was the third in a direct line of priests who had never favored the royal authority. He intended to resist any concept of the church that did not agree with his own Presbyterian insights, and he did this successfully for almost twenty years.[24] Such a policy of defiance rested upon con-

[22] C. E. Banks, *Planters of the Commonwealth*, pp. 139–140, 144–145, 167–170, 174–176; Cushing Manuscript.

[23] For the introduction of the petition, see *Journals of the House of Commons*, I, 699, while the petition itself, together with Bishop Harsnett's answer, is in the *Journals of the House of Lords*, III, 388–390.

[24] Wren in the *Parentalia*, p. 95, lists Peck's earlier difficulties. Additional information is in the Norwich Consignation Book, 1629, and Norwich Visitation, Deanery of Hingham, 1633, in Norfolk and Norwich Public Record Office, Central Library, Norwich, Norfolk.

sensus within St. Andrew's, the sympathy of well-placed Puritan supporters, the inefficiency of the established church, and finally a set of
compromises on the part of Peck with the required church rituals. This
last element was the most vulnerable point in the system. It was the
opening gambit that Matthew Wren, appointed Bishop of Norwich in
1635, utilized. It had become traditional for Puritan parishes to arrange
for two kinds of bell ringings, one for readings from the *Book of Common Prayer*, and another, "when there were both Prayers to be read, and
a Sermon preached." [25] Presumably, the Puritan faithful attended only
the latter. Wren did away with this device and with the assistance of
his able chancellor Clement Corbett, charged Peck with "contumacious
disobedience to the orders and ceremonies of the Church." [26] The bishop
did not think kindly of Peck's digging a ditch in the east end of the
chancel and placing in it the communion table that he had been ordered
to set up. Pastor Peck was deprived of his living, but his former parishioners showed their feelings by paying him "their tithes." [27] When the
new vicar excommunicated two of Peck's supporters for these "factious"
activities, they sued the curate for that act in the Puritan controlled
"Court of Arches." Archbishop Laud squelched that attempt at what he
considered Puritan subversion.[28]

Chancellor Corbett continued the hunt after that "old Fox" Peck.
Although deprived of his parish, Robert Peck ministered in secret to his
flock, much in the same manner as had his grandfather, who in the days
of the Catholic Queen Mary preached the gospel "in woods and forrest
places." [29] Corbett now used the threat of action from the Court of
High Commission to rid Hingham of that very difficult rebel. It was
with a sense of accomplishment that the chancellor reported to Bishop
Wren in March of 1638 that Robert Peck *"parat se ad fugam in novam
Angliam,"* taking with him his rebellious friends.[30] Near one hundred
persons and twenty servants sailed with Peck for what had been Bear

[25] *Articles of Impeachment* . . . , art. 9, p. 7.

[26] Corbett to Wren, May 3, 1637, Tanner Mss, LXVIII, 7, Bodleian Library,
Oxford University, Oxford.

[27] *Idem*, April 29, 1637, *ibid.*, LXVIII, 7.

[28] "The humble petition of Edward Agas" to Archbishop Laud, Hingham,
Feb. 14, 1637/38, State Papers Domestic, Charles I, 16/382, no. 14, Public
Record Office. Laud replied, "I shall not suffer my Court to be made an Instrument to trouble any man for doing his duty or informing his Ordinary." The
suit against Agas is another example of the Puritan genius for nullifying governmental action against their cause by their control of the local process, in this case
the Court of Arches. This time it was opposed by a forceful metropolitan and
king, who utilized the prerogative to stop hostile proceedings in the Court of
Arches.

[29] Peck Family Pedigree, Tanner Mss, CLXXX, 24–25.

[30] Corbett to Wren, March 9, 1637/38, *ibid.*, LXVIII, 11.

Cove and was now known as Hingham in Massachusetts. Those left behind in old Hingham sadly noted in their petition to the House of Commons that ". . . most of the able Inhabitants have forsaken their dwellings & have gone severall ways for their peace & quiett & the town is now left and like to be in misery by reason of the meanness of the [remaining] Inhabitants." [31]

This description of the distressed state of Norfolk's Hingham is no empty complaint. In the space of six years it had witnessed the decamping of more than forty families, which included the better part of the local wealth. It did not include the titled gentry, nor is there a single name from the 1633 poor relief roll of Hingham Parish.[32] Heading the list of these settlers were Master Robert Peck with his wife, two children, and two servants, and his brother Mr. Joseph Peck, with a family of four, and five servants. Joseph Peck brought with him the family plate, silver drinking cups, and his banqueting linens.[33] There was also Mr. Henry Smiths from Derbyshire, but related to the Smiths of Hingham, with a family of six, and five servants, as well as the elder Hobart's son-in-law John Beals, with a family of eight, and two servants. These were the substantial citizenry of East Anglia. And along with these families of distinction came Samuel Lincoln, weaver, and great great grandfather of the sixteenth president of the United States; Thomas Lincoln, cooper; Henry Chamberlain, blacksmith; Henry Rust, glover; as well as felt makers, carpenters, wheelwrights, and a host of other occupations essential to the well-being of a community.[34]

[The emigration of the Presbyterian parishioners of St. Andrew's is unique in that its reconstruction in Massachusetts perpetuated the norms of old Hingham. It came as a formed body. It was not caused by economic distress, although the depressed state of the East Anglian weaving industry undoubtedly lessened the reasons for remaining in England.]The policies of Norfolk's Anglo-Catholic bishops can not be held as the first cause either, for the faithful from Hingham and its neighboring parishes started their peculiar flight in 1633, long before Matthew Wren occupied the Norwich See in November of 1635. At most, that bishop may be charged with the final push that propelled the remaining segment of Hingham's Puritan community to depart. They were willing to go into the "Wilderness" because they had seen the signs of Anti-Christ. As John Winthrop noted, the Church of England ignored the Romish

---

[31] Petition to the House of Commons, Hingham, c. 1640, *ibid.*, CCXX, 54–56.

[32] "Norwich Rate Book, 1633/34," in Walter Rye, *History of the Parish of Heigham* (Norwich, 1917), pp. 193–194.

[33] Cushing Manuscript; Joseph Peck, will, March 3, 1663/64, Wills, II (pt. ii), 11, Old Colony Records, Plymouth, Massachusetts.

[34] HH, II, 21, 38, 150, 396, 428, 461, III, 3, 20, 113, 141, 142, 164, 330.

enemy while it persecuted godly Puritan divines because of "poynts of ceremonies." Meanwhile "multitudes of papistes" roamed the realm. The dealings of Charles I with Parliament signified that the day of judgment could not be far away. The "Saints" awaited a "general distruction" that would overwhelm the reformed churches of Europe.[35] It was this mental unrest, this uneasiness of conscience, combined with an expectation of the Second Coming of Christ, that set the stage for the East Anglian migration to New England.[36] The men from Hingham sought a land where they could forever praise Christ the Lord, their only "god and king," in their particular way.

The continual movement of these East Anglians to Bear Cove during the middle and late 1630's is documented by changes both within and without this plantation. Indicative of the coming direction of things was the renaming of the town as Hingham in 1635, shortly after the Massachusetts General Court accorded municipal recognition. As a legal part of the body politic it was required to maintain a church, enforce law, have a militia unit, while on the provincial level it had to pay taxes and send its representatives to the General Court. Considering that the town had been founded by West Country settlers, and that they constituted the better part of the electorate until 1639, it was only natural that they supplied the first slate of town officers. Joseph Andrews of Devon was the town clerk and constable, and a representative in 1636, 1637, and 1638. Andrews used his influence to obtain the local liquor franchise for his neighbor Thomas Loring. Anthony Eames, a Somerset man, led Hingham's seven man militia requisition during the Pequod Indian difficulties in 1637. He was also the town's representative to the General Court in 1637 and 1638. Mr. Joseph Hull, likewise from Somerset, completed this list by serving as the other representative in 1638.[37]

The year 1639 saw the displacement of the West Countrymen by the East Anglians. From that year until the Otises left Hingham in 1661, the representatives would all be men from East Anglia, save for a single exception in 1643. This should not be interpreted as a planned policy of excluding the West Country planters. Rather it reflects a changing

[35] John Winthrop, "Common Greuances Groaninge for Reformation," c. 1624, and "Reasons to be considered for iustifieinge the undertakers of the intended Plantation in New England . . . ," in *Winthrop Paper*, A. B. Forbes, ed., 5 vols. (Boston, 1929–1947), I, 295, 303–305, II, III.

[36] See G. F. Nuttall, *Visible Saints* (Oxford, 1957), pp. 144–149, for the usually over-looked eschatological factors.

[37] Hingham Town Records, I, 28, Hingham, Mass.; *MBR*, I, 221; Solomon Lincoln, "Appendix," in *History of Hingham*, pp. 162–163. The single Hingham exception was Anthony Eames, who served his last term at the 1643 March Court. The two non-Hingham men, Mr. John Blackledge, formerly of London, and Jeremiah Houchin, formerly of Harleston in Norfolk, acted as surrogates for the East Anglians.

population ratio based upon the continuing influx of settlers from Nor-folk and the surrounding areas. The arrival of the *Diligent* in 1638, with more than a hundred East Anglians, meant that numerical superior-ity rested in the hands of the elders from old Hingham. And due to the community effort of resisting the ecclesiastical policies of the Norwich bishops for better than twenty years, <u>these immigrants came with a sense of purpose and cohesiveness.</u> What could be more natural than for neighbors and relatives to elect their own to the provincial posts — espe-cially when they were Pecks, Hobarts, Allens, Jacobs, and Beales, the very families that had held positions of leadership in the old country!

While this influx had its repercussions in the more distant halls of the Bay Colony's General Court, its effects were most obvious in the twelfth "Church of Christ" gathered at Hingham. Its pastor, Peter Hobart, belonged to the Presbyterian wing of the Puritan reform move-ment. He held that the pastor, who ministered and instructed (unless there was a teacher who then instructed while the minister dispensed the sacraments), and the two deacons and elders constituted a ruling presbytery. Once these officials had received the "gifts" of office, they formed a council over the church. In Governor Winthrop's unflattering portrait, this was a system in which Pastor Hobart "did manage all affairs without the church's advice." [38] With the coming of Master Peck from old Hingham in 1638, the church divided the ministry by ordaining him as "teacher." These two strong-willed men, who had opposed episcopal interference in England, would be just as willing to challenge the "Con-gregational" way of the Massachusetts puritans. While that way had started in flux and without a clear-cut policy of separatism from the Church of England, by 1634 it stood for churches "governed by Pastors, Teachers ruling Elders and Deacons" in which the "power lies in the wholl Congregation, and not in the Presbitrye further then for order and precedencye." [39] This was a position directly opposite to the beliefs of Masters Hobart and Peck, and their adherents from Norfolk.[40]

[Unlike the Boston churches, which by 1640 included less than half the capital's population, the Hingham church encompassed virtually the entire town's one hundred and forty families.[41] There was thus an identity between townsmen and church members that gave to the pastor a role of unquestioned authority.] The Rev. Peter Hobart was the highest paid official in his community, receiving £70 to 100 *per annum* from the

Church membership

[38] *Winthrop's Journal*, J. K. Hosmer, ed., 2 vols. (New York, 1908), II, 244.
[39] John Winthrop to Nathaniel Rich, Boston, May 22, 1634, *Winthrop, Papers*, III, 167,
[40] For a perceptive account of early church polity in the Bay Colony, see Darrett B. Rutman, *Winthrop's Boston* (Chapel Hill, 1965), pp. 18–19.
[41] Rutman, p. 144; the Hingham estimate is based upon a comparison of baptisms in Peter Hobart's "Diary," MHS, and land owners in *HH*, II, III.

town, in addition to special land grants.[42] The many bequests from the faithful testify to the general approval of his society to this status.[43] As pastor, Hobart was in a key position to aid both his family and his adherents. The former, headed by his illiterate father Edmund and his brother Joshua, sought to dominate the political life of Hingham, while the latter sought to reconstruct their traditional way of life. The church presbytery mirrored these aspirations. Peter Hobart was its pastor, Robert Peck its teacher, and by 1641 the deaconships also passed into the hands of East Anglian supporters.[44]

The control of both the two-man Hingham delegation to the General Court and the presbytery by the East Anglians resulted in new judicial and political appointments favorable to their party. Following their election as deputies in 1639, Edmund Hobart, the pastor's father, and Joseph Peck, the teacher's brother, were nominated along with Anthony Eames, as the three commissioners for small causes. This office gave any two of them power to decide at their discretion all legal suits in Hingham in which the damage was under twenty shillings.[45] The deputies then used their positions to award the liquor franchise to neighbors from old Hingham. Of equal import, the three men appointed by the General Court to evaluate property for the province tax came from their adherents, as did the constable elected in 1640.[46] The only important colony office still held by any of the first settlers from the West Country was the militia lieutenancy. With that execption, the East Anglians controlled all major positions of status and profit.

On the town level, the change was equally obvious as may be seen from the personnel which formed the rate-makers, land division, and townsmen committees. In 1637 and 1638 the land grant and rate committees had achieved a kind of parity between West Countrymen and East Anglians. The "great lots division" committee was controlled by the West Countrymen who held five out of the seven places. However, Anthony Eames was the only representative of the West Country settlers on the rate committee. The remaining eight members, headed by the elder Edmund Hobart, as well as Nicholas Jacob, Samuel Ward,

[42] Hingham Town Records, I, 3–28, 107, 118, 121, and also "Copy of a Record from the Great Book," Jan. 17 1669/70, Suffolk Court Files, 10; 16 (#948). At £100 Hobart was one of the highest salaried men in the Bay Colony, see J. B. Felt, *Ecclesiastical History of New England* (Boston, 1855–1862), II, 3, 160.

[43] Bozoun Allen's bequest of £10 is the largest on record, no. 123, although the widow's mite of Margaret Johnson, which came to £5, is by no means unusual. Suffolk Register of Probate, III, 181, Boston.

[44] Peter Hobart, Jan. 29, 1640/41, "Diary," MHS.

[45] MBR, I, 255, 259; George Lee Haskins, *Law and Authority in Early Massachusetts* (New York, 1960), p. 34.

[46] MBR, I, 258, 295, 299, 302.

and Thomas Underwood, were symptomatic of things to come. East Anglians or their mercantile friends would dominate the committees. By 1644 they held absolute majorities on these three major committees — although the West Country sector could always muster up at least one representative on each committee.[47] By and large, West Country representation meant Anthony Eames and John Otis. The main support of Eames came from his leadership in the militia. He had a team of oxen that he would rent out — certainly an asset in a farming community.[48] Eames also had joined the select circle of Hingham men who pooled their capital to erect a town mill.[49]

The case of John Otis is somewhat different, for he was essentially a farmer. Presumably his knowledge of the local land was excellent. He was almost always a standing member of the divisions committee, and his testimony on boundaries was cited in more than one court case. Otis might be considered the spokesman for the old-timers from Devon. While this could explain his two elections to the rates committee, he must have had the respect of the majority of his neighbors, for he was sent to Boston as a grand juror in 1640, receiving six shillings for this service from the "Country." And in 1647 he was elected as one of the nine men in charge of the town. He also served on the church seating committee with Anthony James and Nicholas Jacob, which in its own way symbolized the coming together of this society.[50] The inventory of John's estate shows that he had £20 at loan in small sums to various townsmen.[51] As one's vote in the town was a public act before all men these unpaid debts were in one respect political obligations. They undoubtedly increased Otis's influence in Hingham.

Oddly enough, it would be a marriage in the Otis family that raised the first constitutional challenge to "Congregational" rule in the Massachusetts Bay Company. In 1641 John Otis's daughter Margaret presented her husband Thomas Burton, former "clarke of the prothonataries office," with a daughter, Hannah. Burton remained within the Church of England, although inclined to the Presbyterian viewpoint.[52] In Massachusetts he had not taken the covenant in any of its churches as that act would have made him an "Independent" or separatist. As he was not a member

---

[47] Based upon analyses of thirteen committees, 1637 to 1647, in Hingham Town Records, I, 28, 38, 46, 58, 70, 81, 82, 83, 97, 98–104.

[48] Petition of Anthony Eames, c. 1640, in Thomas Lechford, *Note-Book*, pp. 405–406.

[49] Undertakers, June 1643, Massachusetts Archives, LIX, 8.

[50] Hingham Town Records, I, 38, 58, 81, 86, 100, 104; Massachusetts Archives, XXXIX, 11.

[51] Otis Inventory, July 28, 1657, Suffolk Register of Probate, III, 100.

[52] George L. Kittredge, "Dr. Robert Child the Remonstrant," Colonial Society of Massachusetts, *Publications*, XXI (1920), 24.

of the Hingham Church, "master *Hubbard* Pastor, [and] master *Peck* Teacher" refused to "baptise old Ottis grandchildren [*sic*], an ancient member of their own Church." [53] Otis must have attempted to gain church standing for his grandchild through his own membership and failed. In this instance the Hingham Church followed congregational usage, which limited the sacraments to the "Visible Saints" and their children.[54] This must have been a very difficult decision on the part of the pastor and teacher, who sympathized with Burton's position. Pastor Hobart soon either changed his mind or decided to follow his conscience. He baptized Hannah Otis Burton, although this extension of congregational membership to a grandchild violated the current doctrinal norms.[55] It would exacerbate relations with Boston. This is the background of the third article of Robert Child's *Petition*, countersigned by Thomas Burton, which protested against this exclusive baptismal policy which denied that sacrament to the children of Anglicans.[56] In the eyes of Congregational Massachusetts neither Burton nor Hobart were orthodox. If there were any doubts on this, the Hingham militia controversy removed them.

This dispute involved Anthony Eames, the experienced militia leader and the outstanding West Countryman in Hingham, who alone of the "first" planters had retained his official position in Hingham. In 1640 he had threatened "to looke out for himselfe elsewhere" if he did not receive a larger grant of land. However, Eames did not move — unlike several of his friends — perhaps because he expected promotion to captain. That militia post would bring with it an honorarium in the form of a special land grant. And land alone could supply the lack of employment for his oxen, which had led him earlier to think of going elsewhere.[57] In the spring of 1645 Eames was elected to the captaincy. Un-

[53] Thomas Lechford, "Plain Dealings: or Newes from New England," in Massachusetts Historical Society, *Collections*, 3rd ser., III (1833), 93.

[54] For the significance of this see Edmund S. Morgan, *Visible Saints* (Ithaca, 1963), pp. 121–122, and Perry Miller, *Orthodoxy in Massachusetts, 1630–1650* (Cambridge, 1933), pp. 206–211.

[55] As John Davenport and William Hooke put the case in A *Catechisme Containing the Chief Heads of Christian Religion* (London, 1659), p. 33, ". . . if Infants should have this right in their Grand-fathers, &c. where shall we stop or stay? shall it be extended to a thousand generations? as some misapply the promise in the second Commandement."

[56] Major John Childe, *New England's Jonas Cast up at London* (London, 1647), pp. 12–13, as in Peter Force, *Tracts* (Washington, 1847), IV, iii, and "A Declaration of the General Court . . . 1646," in *Hutchinson Papers*, I, 239, Prince Society, *Publications* (1865).

[57] In the period under study slightly less than half of the original West Countrymen moved elsewhere and slightly more than one-quarter of the East Anglian contingent followed suit. If these figures are compared with Kenneth A. Lockridge's "The Population of Dedham, Massachusetts, 1636–1736," *Economic History Review*, 2nd ser., XIX (1966), 321–323, which shows a 25 to 40 per

fortunately, shortly after this election Eames committed some indiscretion which offended "the greater part of the town." The militia band then held another election and gave the office to the wealthy Norfolk man and "very good friend" of Peter Hobart, Mr. Bozoun Allen. The Boston magistrates, who were the governor's assistants in the Bay Colony and had the right of confirmation, refused to sanction this change until the General Court should meet. All in Hingham were charged to keep their former places. The supporters of Allen now called a training day for the militia. When Eames showed up and told them of the magistrates' position, they accused him of lying and refused to drill under him. The end result was a defection of two-thirds of the band to Allen, while the *de jure* leader Eames, now minus the militia, found himself denounced in church with Pastor Hobart moving for his excommunication.[58]

In the minds of the Bay Colony magistrates, this had become a "slighting of authority" which must be corrected if the commonwealth was not to degenerate into a "mere democracy." John Winthrop called the Hobarts to Boston to answer for their insubordination, whereupon far from expressing sorrow, they rejected his argument and charged him with exceeding his authority.[59] As the deputy governor himself admitted, "many of the deputies were of opinion that the magistrates exercised too much power, and that the people's liberty was thereby in danger." [60] It was precisely this fear that the Hobarts exploited. They introduced a petition, signed by more than eighty of their Hingham supporters, which "complained of their liberties infringed" and asked the deputies for redress.[61] This brilliant maneuver gained the support of fifteen out of thirty-one representatives at its high tide; the issue paralyzed the central government for three months. Finally, doubting deputies were won over to Winthrop's position and fined the Hobarts and their petitioning adherents from the "train band." [62] The Hinghamites had no intention of paying their fines. They were led by their pastor, who intimidated the marshal by "questioning the authority of his warrant because it was not in the king's name." Considering the East Anglian's past observances

---

cent change in Dedham's early decades, then Hingham's extraordinary stability becomes evident, even for the West Countrymen. [The real point is that three-quarters of Hingham's East Anglian contingent stayed put. The East Anglian rejection of mobility was the major factor for the continuation of old Hingham ways and new Hingham's ruling oligarchy.]

[58] *Winthrop's Journal*, II, 229–231. The quote on Allen is in Peter Hobart's "Diary," Sept. 14, 1652 entry, MHS.

[59] *Winthrop's Journal*, II, 231, 235; Winthrop [Memoranda of Occurrences, 1643–1647], in Belknap Papers, MHS.

[60] *Winthrop's Journal*, II, 235.

[61] May 14, 1645, *MBR*, II, 97.

[62] *Winthrop's Journal*, II, 239; *MBR*, III, 19–26.

of the royal writs one might be tempted to doubt Peter Hobart's sincerity — but it struck home at Winthrop and his associates, who had altered the Bay Company's oath so as to remove all reference to the king. Hobart's constitutional point was that "Government here was not more than a Corporation in England" and its action against him and the men of Hingham was not "agreeable to the laws of England." [63] Following the trend of events in 1646 this was the opportune time for a congregation organized along the Presbyterian lines to appeal to England.

It is now that the Hobarts allied themselves with Dr. Robert Child and his petitioners, amongst whom was Thomas Burton — John Otis's son-in-law — who had seen his child initially denied baptism by Peter Hobart in 1641. This petition also declared that the Bay Corporation was but a chartered company and did not have a legal right to govern or to pass laws that infringed the "Naturall rights" of "freeborne subjects of the English nation" (which as a modern critic notes anticipates Locke's position by almost fifty years).[64] The General Court recognized behind this defense of "civil liberty" a plot to weaken the autonomy of the Colony and subject it to English authority. It ordered a day of fast and humiliation so as to implore God's assistance against those *"that seeke to undermyne ye libertyes of Gods people here."* Pastor Peter Hobart refused to comply, holding that his parishioners "would not fast against Dr. Child and against themselves." [65] Doubtlessly Perry Miller is correct in interpreting the *Child Petition* as a planned maneuver "to arouse the then Presbyterian Parliament against the Congregational power" but this does not account for the internal difficulties within Hingham.[66]

While Pastor Peter Hobart, his brother Joshua and their friend Bozoun Allen, posed now as the defenders of home rule, as well as championing the Presbyterian viewpoint, the militia dispute in fact reflected the long smoldering regional and political differences within their town. It has not been possible to locate the eighty-one signatures on the Hingham petition against Captain Eames, but we do have a list of the nine ringleaders, who were fined from £1 to £20, as well as a petition from five of the rank and file, who claimed their "poverty" prevented them from paying their smaller fines. The leaders were the four Hobarts — Edmund, Joshua, Thomas, and the Rev. Peter — Bozoun Allen, Daniel Cushing, William Hersey, and John Towers, all from old Hingham, and Edmound Gold, from Kent, as was his servant John Winchester; the

[63] *MBR*, II, 99, 264–65. Peter Hobart's remarks on the Bay Colony are in *New England's Jonas* . . . , p. 6.

[64] *New England's Jonas* . . . , pp. 9–10; Loren Baritz, *City on a Hill* (New York, 1964), p. 41.

[65] Kittredge, 36.

[66] *The New England Mind: The Seventeenth Century* (New York, 1939), p. 454.

four remaining petitioners were all East Anglians.[67] It is significant that there is not a single West Countryman on either list. The split in the militia unit reflected the regional origins of the Bear Cove planters. Eames of Dorset versus Allen of Norfolk is the West Country against East Anglia. No documents exist to show where John Otis, Sr. stood in this fray, or for that matter his son, who was twenty-five and doubtlessly an active member of the train band. But if in 1646 Otis wanted an excuse to stand clear he had it when his house "burnt to the ground." [68] John Winthrop recorded that fire in his *Journal*, part of his compilation of examples showing the "special providence of God, pointing out his displeasure against some profane persons, who took part with Dr. Child, etc.; against the government and churches here." [69]

[The Massachusetts General Court's solution to this militia leadership squabble was to impose officers from neighboring towns to take charge of the band. This brought about a closing of ranks within Hingham.] By November the two former disputants, Bozoun Allen and Anthony Eames, were back at their milling undertaking.[70] Obviously the desideratum was to regain control of the band and, where dispute and defiance had failed, humility might succeed. In 1648 the "Humble Petions of the Souldiours of Hingham" were submitted to the General Court thanking this honored body for many undeserved favors that they had received ". . . from the Lord, or you his instruments" and requesting the privilege "which we take to be our due, to chouse our owne offesors." They were allowed to elect the lieutenant and ensign, and these posts went to none other than Bozoun Allen and Joshua Hobart.[71] It was not till 1651 that they had authority to elect the captain. This time Bozoun Allen received his coveted prize, and upon his retirement the following year, the post went to Joshua Hobart, thereby completing that family's monopoly of local offices. But the Boston magistrates, determined not to increase the Hobart influence, refused their consent in 1660 to Joshua's application as Hingham's official notary.[72]

[67] *MBR*, II, 113, 164. The court, after examining the petition, correctly held that some of the men "are of good ability." However, for the servant class, if they "will make an open acknowledgment of their offence, upon some lecture day, at Boston," their fines would be remitted. What the magistrates wanted above all was the acknowledgment of error.

[68] Peter Hobart, March 15, 1645/46, "Diary," MHS.

[69] *Winthrop's Journal*, II, 264, 321.

[70] Nov. 17, 1645, Massachusetts Archives, LIX, 8, as well as both signing a local petition, Mass. Archives, CXII, 17.

[71] Mass. Archives, LXVII, 42; *MBR*, II, 252.

[72] Upon the request that "Capt. Hubbard be empowered to give oath in all Civil Causes according to Law in Hingham" which would have made him the official notary, the legend is recorded, "Consented not by the Magistrates," Oct. 25, 1660, Mass. Archives, CXII, 129a.

By 1650 Hingham had obtained a broad degree of stability. Life as it existed in countless English towns continued its daily pace. Although agriculture constituted the major activity of the inhabitants, there are a handful of extant documents which show that Hingham supplied boards, masts, planks, and small boats for the Boston market.[73] This society could afford such amenities as a fine glass of wine served in silver beakers.[74] It also had carefully arranged marriages in the Elizabethan tradition, for the second generation was now coming into its own. The marriage of John Otis, Jr., to Mary, the daughter of Nicholas Jacob, formerly of old Hingham, is fairly typical, with Otis, Sr. turning over his extensive properties as of 10 May 1649 in "consideration of Tenn pownds p. ann°" and the father-in-law turning over meadow lands to the newlyweds, as well as providing a bequest in his will.[75] This is but one example of how well-to-do Hingham families married each other regardless of their parents' different English backgrounds and past disagreements over policy.

Differences would continue to exist, but on other grounds than West Country against East Anglia. In fact, the Hobarts by their engrossing of local honors helped to bring about a new alignment within the town. Joshua Hobart as militia captain in 1654–55 recieved a grant of 300 acres, which was followed in March by a town vote exempting him "from paying any Rates for the public charge of the town" while he held the office of captain.[76] This did not sit well with such leading citizens and ratepayers as Nathaniel Baker, John Jacob, the two John Tuckers, Joseph Jones, Henry Chamberlain, William Hersey, who had been fined £10 for signing the Hobart petition during the militia dispute, and John Otis, Jr. In 1661 these land-holders moved unsuccessfully to change the exemption at the Janurary 1st town meeting.[77] [No longer are the Hingham lists restricted to West Country men or East Anglians. This protest was a combined attack against Joshua Hobart's special status, with the second generation united by interests and not ethnic diversity.] In its own way, this symbolized Hingham's coming of age.

[By 1660 Hingham witnessed the disappearance of old-country differences as a major factor in its community life.] The daughter of Anthony

---

[73] *Aspinwall Notarial Records* (Boston, 1903), pp. 100, 124, 233–34; Thomas Lechford, *Note-Book*, p. 304; *Winthrop's Journal*, II, 321–22.

[74] See "Inventory of Debts," Estate of Capt. Allen, Suffolk Court Files, 16:31 (#1389), Boston — a key document for occupational classifications within Hingham.

[75] John Otis, Sr. to John Otis, Jr., conveyance, recorded May 23, 1655, in *Suffolk Deeds*, II (1883), 161–62; Nicholas Jacob, will, May 18, 1657, No. 161, Suffolk Register of Probate, and deposition of Ralph Woodward, Mass. Archives, XXXIX, 9.

[76] Hingham Town Records, I, 125.

[77] Hingham Town Records, I, 131.

Eames married John Jacob, Thomas Loring Jr. married Hannah Jacob, and John Otis II took Mary Jacob as his wife. This confirms Crevecoeur's "melting pot" concept of the American as a "new man." However, these are all upper class marriages tending toward the consolidation of position and influence within a small group. Crevecoeur's upwardly mobile "new man" is a stranger in Hingham. For those who follow Frederick Jackson Turner's thesis on the primacy of the evironment in the American experience, Hingham exemplifies the retention of old-world forms and values in the wilderness. Its people might meet in the church and mix on the commons, but this did not mean that all could be elected within this community, or that the yeoman's daughter married the village laborer. Its founders were patriarchs. It gave office to its elders, not its youth. Hingham recognized merit; it insisted upon performance from those in office; it believed in hierarchy; and it nurtured an early American oligarchy. Was Hingham unique in this respect or did other towns follow their old-world paths? The resolution of this question is a challenge to the social historian for additional research into the neglected field of local history in New England's formative period.

Notes on Life
in Plymouth Colony

JOHN DEMOS

Historians have pictured local communities in the seventeenth-century New England colonies as pious, hierarchical, and unchanging. They were run, we have been told, by an interlocking elite of religious and political leaders, and they were organized in a tightly controlled patriarchal fashion. Land, like authority, was carefully doled out so as not to diminish either the binding sense of community or the manipulative power of the elite.

John Demos argues that, if Plymouth Colony is at all typical, this traditional conception of the static religious community is quite misleading. In Plymouth, land changed hands rapidly, men frequently moved from one dwelling place to another, and the community very quickly became dispersed and loosely organized. Furthermore, family groups were not dominant in this process of rapid social change; on the contrary, individual activity dominated in an extremely mobile society.

Demos uses demographic techniques to demonstrate some of the salient characteristics of the Plymouth population: size of family, life expectancy, patterns of marriage. He shows how it is possible to move from apparently lifeless statistics to novel insights into patterns of courtship and marriage, family structure, and child rearing. Demos's training in sociological technique enables him to reexamine evidence that traditional historians have neglected or misinterpreted and to exploit new types of historical source material.

Our traditional picture of the earliest New England communities is essentially a still life. By emphasizing the themes of steadfast piety, the practice of the old-fashioned virtues, measured forms of civil government, and a closely-ordered social life, it suggests a placid, almost static kind of existence. We take for granted the moral and religious aims which inspired the founding of many of these communities; and we accept the assumption of the colonists themselves, that success in these aims depended on maintaining a high degree of compactness and closeness of settlement.

Yet, in the case of the Plymouth Colony at least, this picture is seriously misleading. It has served to obscure certain striking elements of movement and change — indeed, a kind of fluidity that is commonly associated with a much later phase of our national history. Individuals frequently transferred their residence from one house, or one town, to another. Land titles changed hands with astonishing rapidity. Families were rearranged by a wide variety of circumstances.[1]

These tendencies can be traced back to the first years of the settlement

Reprinted by permission from John Demos, "Notes on Life in Plymouth Colony," *William and Mary Quarterly*, 3d Ser., XXII (1965), 264–286.

[1] Such conclusions, and the observations which follow, are based upon an examination of several sorts of records. Town and church records have been useful for determining certain vital statistics such as dates of birth, marriages, and deaths. Nathaniel B. Shurtleff and David Pulsifer, eds., *Records of the Colony of New Plymouth, in New England* (Boston, 1855–61), offers a broad picture of laws and law-breaking, and, less directly, of deeper social and economic forces at work in 17th-century Plymouth. Numerous genealogical studies provide many relevant dates and places, and are obviously indispensable for establishing family relationships. Land deeds reveal much about the economic and geographic layout of the colony; there are also other deeds relating to such things as marriage and apprenticeship. Finally, of particular importance are the wills, perhaps the prime source of information about family and community organization.

at Plymouth. Some of the original townspeople began to take up lots across the river in Duxbury even before 1630; among them were such prominent figures as John Alden, Myles Standish, Jonathan Brewster, and Thomas Prence. The process was accelerated by the arrival to the north of the settlers at Massachusetts Bay. An important new market for cattle and corn was thereby opened up, and the compact town of Plymouth was not large enough to meet the demand for increased production.[2] But the profits to be made from farming were probably not the only, or even the major, stimulus to expansion. The land beckoned because it was empty; the colonists were excited simply by the prospect of ownership for its own sake.

In any case, by the mid-1630's this pattern of geographical expansion had become well established. In 1636 the town of Scituate was officially incorporated and began to send its own representatives to the General Court. Duxbury achieved a similar status the following year; and by 1646 seven other new towns had been established. The direction of the earliest expansion was north and south along the coast; then a westerly thrust began, which led to the founding of such towns as Taunton, Rehoboth, Bridgewater, and Middleborough, all well inland. Still other groups of people pushed on to Cape Cod; indeed, in the early 1640's there was a move to abandon the original settlement at Plymouth altogether and relocate the town on the outer cape. This proposal was finally defeated after much discussion in the meetings of the freemen, but some families went anyway, on their own, and founded the town of Eastham. By 1691, the year that Plymouth ended its independent existence and joined with Massachusetts Bay, it contained no less than twenty-one recognized townships, and many smaller communities as well.[3]

This steady dispersion of settlement caused considerable anxiety to some of the leaders of the colony, and sporadic efforts were made to keep it under control. On several occasions when new land was parceled out, the General Court directed that it be used only for actual settlement by the grantees themselves.[4] Also, the Court critized the unrestrained way

[2] See William Bradford, *Of Plymouth Plantation, 1620–1647*, ed. Samuel E. Morison (New York, 1952), 252–253.

[3] Plymouth, 1620; Scituate, 1636; Duxbury, 1637; Barnstable, 1639; Sandwich, 1639; Taunton, 1639; Yarmouth, 1639; Marshfield, 1641; Rehoboth, 1645; Eastham, 1646; Bridgewater, 1656; Dartmouth, 1664; Swansea, 1667; Middleborough, 1669; Edgartown, 1671; Tisbury, 1671; Little Compton, 1682; Freetown, 1683; Rochester, 1686; Falmouth, 1686; Nantucket, 1687.

[4] See the terms of the grant to Charles Chauncey, John Atwood, and Thomas Cushman at Mattapoisett, in *Plym. Col. Recs.*, II, 9. Also Bradford, *Of Plymouth Plantation*, ed. Morison, 253–254, where another kind of attempt to control expansion is described: "Special lands were granted at a place general called Green's Harbor" to "special persons that would promise to live at Plymouth, and likely to

in which lands were distributed by the freemen in certain of the newer townships. Grants were no longer confined to upright, religious-minded settlers. Towns accepted, with no questions asked, almost anyone who proposed to move in. Such was the charge leveled against the people of Sandwich, for example, in 1639. A similar situation seems to have prevailed in Yarmouth, for in 1640 the Court specifically directed the town elders there to require of each new arrival a "certificate from the places whence they come . . . of their religious and honest carriage." [5]

William Bradford was one of those to whom the process of dispersion came as a great disappointment; it runs through much of his famous history of Plymouth as a kind of tragic refrain. "This I fear will be the ruin of New England, at least of the churches of God there," he wrote at one point, "and will provoke the Lord's displeasure against them." When the plan for moving the town to Eastham was debated, Bradford, and others of like mind, discerned the real motive behind the proposal: "Some were still for staying together in this place, alleging men might here live if they would be content with their condition, and that it was not for want or necessity so much that they removed as for the enriching of themselves." Finally, near the end of his work, with more and more of the original stock moving away, Bradford described Plymouth as being "like an ancient mother grown old and forsaken of her children, though not in their affections yet in regard of their bodily presence and personal helpfulness; her ancient members being most of them worn away by death, and these of later time being like children translated into other families, and she like a widow left only to trust in God. Thus, she that had made many rich became herself poor." [6] He could hardly have chosen a better metaphor. It is extremely telling as a literary device, and — more than that — is highly suggestive from a historical standpoint. It describes an experience that must have been quite real, and quite painful, for many Plymouth settlers. The whole process of expansion had as one of its chief effects the scattering of families, to an extent probably inconceivable in the Old World communities from which the colonists had come. This was particularly hard upon elderly people; their anxiety that they should be properly cared for in their old age is readily apparent in the wills they wrote. The flow of men into new areas was inexorable, but it took a pro-

---

be helpful to the church or commonwealth and so [to] tie the lands to Plymouth as farms for the same; and there they might keep their cattle and tillage by some servants and retain their dwellings here." No sooner was the plan put into effect, however, than its beneficiaries demanded permission to move directly onto their new farms. "Alas," concludes Bradford, "this remedy proved worse than the disease."

[5] *Plym. Col. Recs.*, I, 131, 142.
[6] Bradford, *Of Plymouth Plantation*, ed. Morison, 254, 333–334.

found psychological toll, even among those who were most willingly a part of it.

Nearly every category of person – young and old, rich and poor, immigrant and old settler – was involved in the expansion of the Plymouth community. The careers of the four Winslow brothers who arrived at various times during the early years of the colony may be regarded as more or less typical.[7] Kenelm Winslow came from England to Plymouth in 1629 and moved to Marshfield in 1641; Edward came in 1620 from Leyden and returned to England in 1646; John went from England to Leyden, to Plymouth, and in 1656 to Boston; and Josiah Winslow arrived in Plymouth from England in 1631, moved to Scituate in 1637, and then went from there to Marshfield. Although two of the sons of Kenelm Winslow remained in Marshfield on land that he bequeathed to them, another son moved to Yarmouth and the fourth one moved three times, to Swansea in 1666, to Rochester in 1678, and to Freetown in 1685. And third-generation Winslows could be found scattered among many different towns of Massachusetts and in other colonies as well. Nor did William Bradford's strong convictions on the matter of expansion prevent his own children from leaving Plymouth. His daughter married a Boston man; two sons moved to the neighboring settlement of Kingston; and a third led a large Bradford migration, mostly third generation, to Connecticut.[8]

The movers were often young men, but not invariably so. Indeed there were many who moved in middle age and with a large family. Experience Mitchell and William Bassett, both of whom arrived in the early 1620's, were among the original proprietors – and residents – of three different towns. After several years in Plymouth they resettled in Duxbury (each one, by this time, with a wife and young children), and in the 1650's they went to Bridgewater.

For the most part, removals were arranged and carried out by individuals; they were not affairs of large groups and elaborate organization. Family ties were sometimes a factor, as in the case of the Connecticut Bradfords, but even here the pattern was rather loose. It was usually a matter of one man moving to a new community, and then several other members of his family following, separately and later on.

An obvious concomitant of such general mobility was a rapid rate of turnover in the ownership of land. In this connection the land deeds and proprietary lists that survive from the period become an important source. For example, there are two lists of proprietors for the town of Bridge-

[7] See David-Parsons Holton, *Winslow Memorial* . . . , I (New York, 1877).
[8] See Ruth Gardiner Hall, *Descendants of Governor William Bradford* (Ann Arbor, 1951).

water, one made in 1645 at the time of its incorporation, and the other in 1682 when additional grants of land were being debated.[9] Of the fifty-six names on the first list only twelve reappear thirty-seven years later. To the latter group should be added five sons of original proprietors who had died in the meantime, making a grand total of seventeen men who retained their interest in Bridgewater. But this means that thirty-nine relinquished their holdings altogether, fully 70 per cent of the initial group. It is probable that some of them never lived in Bridgewater at all, acquiring rights there only in order to sell.

This pattern of land turnover is further exemplified by the varied transactions of certain individuals, as noted in the *Colony Records*. Samuel Eddy, a good case in point, came to Plymouth in 1630 as a young man of twenty-two. In the next fifty years he was involved in at least eighteen transactions for land and housing.[10] Presumably there were still more, of which no record remains, as in some cases we find him selling lands not previously identified as being in his possession. At least three times he seemed to have moved his residence within Plymouth (selling one house in order to buy another), and as an old man he left the town altogether and went to Swansea in the western part of the colony. Two of his sons had already settled there, and he probably wished to be near them. A third son had gone to Martha's Vineyard; and a fourth, who seems to have been particularly restless, moved from Plymouth to Sandwich, to Middleborough, back to Plymouth, back to Middleborough, back to Plymouth, to Taunton, and back once more to Middleborough, over a period of some forty years.

Seven of Samuel Eddy's land transactions seem to have been directly connected with his changes of residence; the rest were for the purpose of enlarging his estate, or for profit. Eddy, incidently, was a tailor by trade and not a rich man; most of the business in which he engaged was for relatively small amounts of land and money. The profit motive was equally clear in the dealings of many other Plymouth residents. Perhaps one more example will suffice. In June 1639 John Barnes bought four acres of meadowland from John Winslow for eight pounds and a month later resold them to Robert Hicks for nine pounds, fifteen shillings. Soon afterwards he made a similar deal in which he bought a parcel of land for twelve pounds and sold it within a few months for eighteen.[11]

It would be interesting to know more about the lives of these people,

---

[9] "A Description of Bridgewater, 1818," in Massachusetts Historical Society, *Collections*, 2d Ser., VII (Boston, 1826), 137–176.

[10] Byron B. Horton, *The Ancestors and Descendants of Zachariah Eddy of Warren, Pa.* (Rutland, Vt., 1930), 29–31.

[11] *Plym. Col. Recs.*, XII, 45, 64–65, 69.

and the lives of their ancestors, before their migration to America. Perhaps there was more mobility among inhabitants of the English countryside than is commonly supposed.[12] Perhaps the first colonists at Plymouth were conditioned for change by their prior attempt to establish themselves in Holland. It is hard to say. In any case, the settlers were doubtless predisposed to conceive of wealth in terms of land, and the circumstances of Plymouth, where currency was so scarce and land so plentiful, probably strengthened this instinct. It is clear from the wills they left that their desire to possess and to expand was usually satisfied. Even a man of relatively moderate means usually had several plots of land to deed away, and wealthy ones had as many as twelve, fifteen, or even twenty.[13] In some cases these holdings were located in a number of different townships — showing that their owners could not always have thought in terms of actual settlement at the time of acquisition.

It would be interesting to know how many people lived in Plymouth Colony during these years. Three scholars have offered guesses based on varying kinds of evidence.[14] Their findings do not agree, but suggest, when averaged together, that the total number of Plymouth residents was probably around 300 in 1630, and did not exceed 1,000 before the early 1640's. It had passed 3,000 by 1660, 5,000 by 1675, and by the time the colony had merged with Massachusetts probably stood somewhere between 12,000 and 15,000. The rate of growth, if not spectacular, was steady and fairly sharp; the population seems to have doubled about every fifteen years.

This growth was due, in part, to immigration but perhaps even more to certain characteristics of the people within the colony itself. For example, the popular impression today that colonial families were extremely large finds the strongest possible confirmation in the case of Plymouth. A sample of some ninety families about whom there is fairly reliable information, suggests that there was an average of seven to eight children per family who actually grew to adulthood. The number of live births was undoubtedly higher, although exactly how much higher we cannot

family size

[12] For recent works directed to this point, see E. E. Rich, "The Population of Elizabethan England," *Economic History Review*, 2d Ser., II (1949–50), 247–265; and Peter Laslett and John Harrison, "Clayworth and Coggenhoe," in H. E. Bell and R. L. Ollard, eds., *Historical Essays, 1600–1750, Presented to David Ogg* (London, 1963), 157–184.

[13] See, for example, the wills of Samuel Fuller (Barnstable, 1683) and Thomas Cushman (Plymouth, 1690) in *Mayflower Descendant*, II (1900), 237–241; IV (1902), 37–42.

[14] See Richard LeBaron Bowen, *Early Rehoboth* . . . , I (Rehoboth, 1945), 15–24; Joseph B. Feet, "Population of Plymouth Colony," in American Statistical Association, *Collections*, I, Pt. ii (Boston, 1845), 143–144; and Bradford, *Of Plymouth Plantation*, ed. Morison, xi.

be sure because no trace exists today of many who died in infancy and early childhood.[15]

Even allowing for the obvious likelihood that errors in the figures for the number born are somewhat greater than in the figures for those who grew to maturity, the rate of infant mortality in Plymouth seems to have been relatively low. In the case of a few families for which there are unusually complete records, only about one in five children seems to have died before the age of twenty-one. Furthermore, births in the sample come for the most part at roughly two-year intervals[16] with relatively few "gaps" which might indicate a baby who did not survive. All things considered, it appears that the rate of infant and child mortality in Plymouth was no more than 25 per cent[17] — less than half the rate in many parts of the world today.

[These figures seem to indicate a suprising standard of health and physical vigor among Plymouth residents, and a study of their longevity — the average life expectancy in the colony — confirms this impression] [Tables

[15] Various attempts to subject evidence to quantitative analysis have been an important part of my "method," such as it is. It is not possible to achieve anything approaching total accuracy in these computations; the sources simply are not that exact. I have not knowingly employed doubtful figures, but probably a small portion of those that I have used are incorrect. In certain cases I have accepted an approximate date (e.g. 1671, when it might as well be 1670 or 1672), but only where it would not prejudice the over-all result. In general, the numerical data that I shall present should be regarded as suggestive rather than conclusive in any sense. Above all, I have sought to keep my focus on individual lives and to build up my story from there. The people about whom I have assembled information total roughly 2,000. (It is very difficult even to estimate the total number of people who lived in Plymouth Colony between 1620–91, but it was probably between 25,000 and 50,000.) Only a part of these could be employed in the treatment of any particular question, since the data for most individuals are not complete. But a sample of several hundred should still be enough at least to outline certain general patterns.

With respect to the data on family size (Table 1), I have used only families in which both parents lived at least to age 50, or else if one parent died, the other quickly remarried. That is, in all these families there were parents who lived up to and past, the prime years for childbearing.

[16] This spacing is quite interesting in itself, for it immediately raises questions as to how Plymouth parents avoided having even higher numbers of children. Probably the mothers nursed their babies for at least one year, but — contrary to popular belief — there is no proved biological impediment in this to further conception. Since effective contraceptive methods are a fairly recent development, it seems likely that Plymouth couples simply eschewed sexual contact over long periods of time. In many less advanced cultures of the world today there are taboos on sexual relations between husband and wife for one year or more following the birth of a child. It is just possible that a similar custom prevailed in Plymouth.

[17] It is impossible to estimate what proportion of these were infants (less than one year old) and what proportion were young children, for in most cases the records say only "died young."

Size of Families in Plymouth

TABLE 1

	Average number of children born	Average number lived to age 21
Sixteen First-Generation Families	7.8	7.2
Forty-seven Second-Generation Families	8.6	7.5
Thirty-three Third-Generation Families	9.3	7.9

2 and 3] are based on a sample of more than six hundred people, who lived at least to the age of twenty-one and for whom the age at death was ascertainable.

The figures in 2 are really astonishingly high. Indeed, in the case of the men, they compare quite favorably with what obtains in this country today. (The life expectancy of an American male of twenty-one is now a fraction over seventy, and for a female of the same age, is approximately seventy-six.) It is at least possible that some selective bias, built into the data, may have distorted the results. For example, as between two men one of whom died at thirty and the other at ninety, it is more likely that the latter should leave some traces for the genealogist and historian to follow up. Still, I do not believe that this has been a serious problem in the above sample. A good part of the information on longevity has come from a few especially well-preserved graveyards in the Plymouth area, and presumably these offer a fairly random selection of the adults in the community. Moreover, those families for which information is relatively complete — where we know the age at death of all the members — present a picture not very different from that of the total sample. And even if

Life Expectancy in Plymouth

TABLES 2 AND 3

TABLE 2

(The figures in the left-hand column are the control points, i.e., a 21-year-old man might expect to live to age 69.2, a 30-year-old to 70.0, and so forth.)

Age	Men	Women
21	69.2	62.4
30	70.0	64.7
40	71.2	69.7
50	73.7	73.4
60	76.3	76.8
70	79.9	80.7
80	85.1	86.7

TABLE 3

(The figures in columns two and three represent the percentages of the men and women in the sample who died between the ages indicated in column one.)

Age group	Men (percentages)	Women (percentages)
22–29	1.6	5.9
30–39	3.6	12.0
40–49	7.8	12.0
50–59	10.2	10.9
60–69	18.0	14.9
70–79	30.5	20.7
80–89	22.4	16.0
90 or over	5.9	7.6

we do follow for a certain inflation of the figures, the outcome is still striking.

The difference in the results for men and women is mainly due to the dangers attendant on childbirth. A young woman's life expectancy was seven years less than a man's, whereas today, with childbirth hazards virtually eliminated by modern medicine, it is six years longer. The second table shows that 30 per cent of the women and only 12 per cent of the men in the sample died between ages twenty and fifty, the normal years of child bearing. If a woman survived these middle years, her prospects for long life became at least as good as those of a man, and indeed a little better. A majority of those who lived to a really very old age (ninety or more) seem to have been women.

The records which reveal this pattern of growth and dispersion in the colony of Plymouth also provide much information about courtship, marriage, and family life. [Courtships were usually initiated by the young people themselves, but as a relationship progressed toward something more permanent, the parents became directly involved.] In fact, a requirement of parental consent was written into the colony's laws on marriage: "If any shall make any motion of marriage to any mans daughter . . . not having first obtayned leave and consent of the parents or masters so to doe [he] shall be punished either by fine or corporall punishment or both, at the discretion of the bench and according to the nature of the offence." [18] The attitude of parents toward a proposed match depended on

18 *Plym. Col. Recs.*, XI, 29, 108, 190. Occasionally there were prosecutions under this statute, the most notorious of which involved Elizabeth Prence, the daughter of a governor of the colony, and Arthur Howland, Jr., who belonged to another of Plymouth's leading families. Many of the Howlands had become

a variety of spiritual and material considerations. Speaking very generally, it was desirable that both parties be of good moral and religious character. Beyond that, the couple would hopefully have enough land and possessions, given to them by both sets of parents, to establish a reasonably secure household.

But in a community as fluid as Plymouth it is unlikely that parental control over courtship and marriage could have been fully preserved. A few surviving pieces of evidence suggest that it was possibly quite an issue. In 1692 the widow Abigail Young died without leaving a will. The court moved to settle her estate on the basis of her intentions as revealed in several conversations held before her death. Two sons, Robert and Henry, were the prime candidates for the inheritance. Witnesses testified that "when shee dyed [she said] shee would Leave all the estate that shee had with Henry, if Robert had that gierl that there was a discourse about: but if he had her not I understand that the estate should be devided betwix them." A third son, Nathaniel, confirmed this. "My mother young," he reported, "told me that if Robert had that gierl which there was a talke about shee would not give him a peny." [19]

The first official step toward marriage was normally the betrothal or "pre-contract" — a ceremony before two witnesses at which the couple exchanged formal promises to wed in due time. A period of several weeks or months followed, during which these intentions were "published." A betrothed couple was considered to have a special status, not married but no longer unmarried either. They were required to be completely loyal each to the other; the adultery laws treated them no differently from husbands and wives. Sexual contact between them was forbidden; but the penalty for it was only a quarter of what was prescribed for single people.[20] It may be that this actually encouraged premarital relations among betrothed couples because of its implication that fornication was much less reprehensible in their case than otherwise.[21] The Court records show sixty-five convictions for misconduct of this kind, over a forty-five

---

Quakers, young Arthur among them; the Governor, on the other hand, was firmly opposed to this new and "foreign" religious movement. Twice he brought Howland before the General Court for having "disorderly and unrighteously endeavored to obtain the affections of Mistress Elizabeth Prence." But the story had a happy ending: after seven young years the Governor relented, and the couple were finally married in the spring of 1668. *Ibid.*, IV, 140, 158–159. For another case of this kind, see *ibid.*, III, 5.

[19] *Mayflower Descendant*, XV (1913), 79–80.
[20] *Plym. Col. Recs.*, XI, 172.
[21] This point is argued at greater length in George Elliott Howard, *A History of Matrimonial Institutions . . .* , II (Chicago, 1904), 169–200. Howard's discussion of marriage customs in colonial New England is, in general, quite helpful.

year period. (Note that this total comprises only those who were *caught*, and whose cases were recorded.) In some instances members of the most prominent families were involved: for example, Peregrine White, Thomas Delano, and Thomas Cushman, Jr. Occasionally the basis for conviction was the arrival of a child less than nine months after the wedding ceremony. Perhaps innocent couples were sometimes punished under this system; but the number of "early" babies was, in any event, extremely high.[22]

Once the betrothal was formalized, considerable thought had to be given to the economic future of the couple. In all but the poorest families each child could expect to receive from its parents a "portion" — a certain quantity of property or money with which to make an independent start in life. In most cases this occurred at the time of marriage, and its purpose was everywhere the same. A man was to use it to "be for himself" (in the graphic little phrase of the time); a woman would transfer it to her husband for the greater good of the household which they were starting together. To make special provision for the possibility that he might die while his children were still young, a man usually directed in his will that his "overseers" hold part of his estate intact to be distributed later as portions, at the appropriate time.

There was no set formula governing the actual substance of these portions. More often than not, however, a male child was given land, cattle, tools, and a house or a promise of help in the building of a house; a woman, for her part, usually received movable property, such as furniture or clothing and money. Occasionally the terms of these bequests were officially recorded in a "deed of gift"; [23] more often they seem to have been arranged informally. Most parents hoped to have accumulated sufficient property by the time their children came of age to make these gifts without suffering undue hardship. Some had to buy land specifically for this purpose; [24] others petitioned the Court "to accommodate them for theire posterities," i.e., to give them a free grant.[25] It appears that fathers sometimes retained the title to the lands which they gave as portions: there are many Plymouth wills which direct that a son shall in-

[22] For example, a random sampling of fourth-generation Bradfords turned up nine couples whose first child arrived within eight months of their wedding and all but two of these within six months. Also, it appears that Thomas Cushman's first baby was not only conceived, but actually born, before his marriage.

[23] As on the occasion of the marriage of Jacob Cook and Damaris Hopkins in 1646. *Mayflower Descendant*, II, 27–28.

[24] In 1653, for instance, John Brown of Rehoboth bought land from Capt. Thomas Willet, which he immediately deeded over to his sons, John and James. *Ibid.*, IV, 84.

[25] *Plym. Col. Recs.*, III, 164.

herit "the land wherein he now dwells," or use words to this effect.[26]
Perhaps this practice served to maintain some degree of parental authority beyond the years of childhood.

It is widely supposed that people married early in the colonial period.
For Plymouth, however — and I suspect for most other communities of
that time — this impression cannot be sustained. Indeed, the average age
of both men and women at the time of their first marriage was considerably higher then than it is today — and quite possibly has never been
exceeded at any subsequent point in our history.

[Table 4] is largely self-explanatory. Only one point requires additional
comment: the steady, if unspectacular, narrowing of the age gap between the sexes at the time of marriage. At the start this gap averaged
six and one-half years; by the end it was verging on two. Men were
marrying earlier and women later. During the early years of the colony
there was certainly a shortage of women; spinsters were a rarity, and
marriageable girls, of whatever charm and property, must have received
plenty of offers. At some point, however, new factors began to come into
play, and this imbalance in the sex ratio was gradually corrected. Above

	Born before 1600	Born 1600–25	Born 1625–50	Born 1650–75	Born 1675–1700
TABLE 4	*First Marriages in Plymouth* *				
Mean age of men at time of 1st marriage	27.0	27.0	26.1	25.4	24.6
Mean age of women at time of 1st marriage	— †	20.6	20.2	21.3	22.3
Percentage of men married at age 23 or over	25%	18%	25%	26%	38%
Percentage of men married at age 30 or over	44%	23%	27%	18%	14%
Percentage of women married at age 25 or over	— †	9%	10%	20%	28%

* Based on a sample of some 650 men and women.
† Insufficient data for women born before 1600.

[26] See, for examples, the wills of John Thompson and Ephraim Tinkham, *Mayflower Descendant*, IV, 22–29, 122–125.

all, the process of expansion removed substantial numbers of young men from the areas that had been settled first, and by the end of the century some towns may well have held a surplus of females. Wherever women outnumbered men, there were some who did not find husbands until relatively late and at least a few who never married at all. Conversely, the men had a larger and larger group to choose from and tended to marry somewhat earlier. By 1700 there were occasional marriages in which the woman was older than her husband, and for the first time the number of spinsters had become noticeable. The earliest official count of males and females in Plymouth that still survives comes from a census taken for all Massachusetts in 1765. At that time all of the eastern counties showed a substantial majority of women over men; the reverse was true for the western counties. In the towns which formerly belonged to Plymouth Colony the figures were 53.2 per cent female as against 46.8 per cent male. It is my guess that this surplus began as much as a century earlier.[27]

Marriage was conceived to be the normal estate for adults in colonial New England. When one spouse died, the other usually remarried within a year or two. Most were in their thirties and forties at the time of their remarriage, but some were much older. Robert Cushman, Jr., for instance, took a new wife at eighty! This pattern affected a very considerable portion of the community, as [Table 5] shows.

Generally speaking, the property of husband and wife was not merged in a second marriage to the extent customary for a first one. The main reason for this, of course, was to preserve the claims of the children by the first marriage to a just inheritance. In fact, wills were always framed with this point in mind. Often the bulk of a man's estate was transmitted at his death directly to his children, or if to his wife, only until she married again. The part that remained to herself alone was usually

[27] See J. H. Benton, Jr., *Early Census Making in Massachusetts, 1643–1765* . . . (Boston, 1905). The dimensions of the problem, for Plymouth, can be further refined. The findings in the 1765 census are divided into two parts: people under 16, and people 16 and over. The 53.2 to 46.8 ratio, quoted above, is for the 16-and-over group. But, as almost all males remained single until age 21, a more significant ratio would be one for only those males and females who were 21 or over. We can assume, from a breakdown of other parts of the census, that the 16–21 grouping composed about 10 per cent of the total over 16. We also know from the census that the ratio of males under 16 to females under 16 was 51.2 males to 48.8 females. If this ratio of 51.2 to 48.8 is projected to the 16–21 age group for the purpose of eliminating those under 21 from the final ratio, we discover that the ratio of men 21 or older to women 21 or older becomes approximately 53.8 to 46.2. This means that for one out of every seven girls there was no man, at least in her own home area. In a few individual towns the situation was worse — as high as one in four.

	Men		Women	
Number of Marriages	Over 50	Over 70	Over 50	Over 70
1	60%	55%	74%	69%
2	34%	36%	25%	30%
3	6%	8%	1%	1%
4	— †	.5%	—	—
5	— †	.5%	—	—
Total married more than once	40%	45%	26%	31%

TABLE 5   *Rates of Remarriage in Plymouth Colony* *

* The figures for men and women are separate, and in each case there is a percentage for all those who lived to be fifty or more, and another for those who lived to be seventy or more. The sample, comprising over seven hundred people, does not include anyone who died before the age of fifty.
† Less than one half of one per cent.

one third of the estate, and sometimes less. Widows in Plymouth did not control a large amount of property.

When a marriage between a widow and widower was planned it was customary to make an explicit agreement as to terms. The man pledged a certain sum to his (new) wife in the event of his death, but it was often only a token amount, much less than the "thirds" that a first wife might expect. The woman, for her part, retained the right of "sole disposition" of any property she might possess; it never became part of her husband's estate.[28]

A widow's children were placed in a doubtful position when their mother remarried. Sometimes the new husband agreed to take them into his household, but more often they were placed elsewhere. Occasionally the first husband had anticipated this problem before his death. Anthony Besse's will provided that should his widow remarry, "the five bigest [children] to bee put forth and theire Cattle with them according to the Descretion of the overseers." Another father,

> Lawrance Lichfeild lying on his Death bedd sent for John Allin and Ann his wife and Desired to give and bequeath unto them his

[28] See, for example, the agreement between Ephraim Morton and Mary Harlow, widow. *Mayflower Descendant*, XVII (1915), 49. There were, admittedly, some exceptions to the pattern. When William Sherman died in 1680, he left six small children and no will. His widow remarried soon afterwards. When her new husband agreed to provide for the children, the courts ordered Sherman's estate made over to him, because of the obvious expenses he would have to meet. *Ibid.*, IV, 171 ff.

youngest son Josias Lichfeild if they would accept of him and take him as theire Child; then they Desired to know how long they should have him and the said Lawrance said for ever; but the mother of the child was not willing then; but in a short time after willingly Concented to her husbands will in the thinge; if the said John and Ann would take the child for theire adopted Child; whereunto they Assented . . . [The boy too] being asked by his owne mother . . . if hee Did Concent and Chuse to live with the said John and Ann as hitherto by the space of about nine years hee had Done; Willingly answered yea.

No doubt the boy was deeply attached to the Allens after having lived with them for so long. The agreement, then, imposed no particular hardship on anyone involved; it simply continued, and formalized, a previous arrangement.[29]

If children did remain with their mother after her remarriage, their stepfather was not supposed to exercise normal parental authority over them. Although at the time of his marriage to the widow, Mary Foster, Jonathan Morey contracted to "bring up" her son Benjamin at his own expense, he also agreed not to interfere in any future plans for binding the boy out. A fairly common solution to the problem of stepchildren was to keep them with their mother for a few years and then as they grew older to "put them out." Ultimate responsibility for such children passed to some persons specially designated in their father's will — often to his overseers, occasionally to his own parents. When Jacob Mitchell and his wife were killed by Indians at Rehoboth in 1675, their small children went to live with Mitchell's father in Bridgewater. John Brown of Swansea wrote in his will: "Conserning all my five Children I Doe wholly leave them all to the ordering and Disposeing of my owne father . . . for him to bring them up not once questioning but that his love and Care for them wilbee as it hath bine for my selfe." Brown's wife survived him, and the children probably remained in her day-to-day care, or else were "bound out"; but over-all direction of their lives was henceforth in the hands of their grandfather.[30]

It has been widely assumed that the "extended family" was characteristic of Western society everywhere until at least the eighteenth century, and that the change to our own "nuclear" pattern came only with the Industrial Revolution.[31] The term "extended family" in its strict

[29] *Ibid.*, XIV (1912), 152; XII (1910), 134.

[30] *Ibid.*, XIV, 15–16; XXI (1919), 185; XVIII (1916), 14–15.

[31] However, a few very recent studies have thrown some doubt on this idea. See Laslett and Harrison, "Clayworth and Coggenhoe," for evidence implying very small families indeed in rural English villages of the late 17th century.

sense means a household consisting of several couples, related as siblings or cousins, and their children, and perhaps their children's children. This pattern, of course, still prevails in many parts of the world. Its most striking results are a diffusion of affections and authority within the whole, or extended, family, and a sharing of economic responsibilities. The term is also applied, somewhat more loosely, to situations where the various family members do not form one household in the sense of living "under one roof" but still live close together and share loyalties and responsibilities which go beyond their own offspring or parents.

In colonial Plymouth, there were no extended families at all, in the sense of "under one roof." The wills show, beyond any doubt, that married brothers and sisters never lived together in the same house. As soon as a young man became betrothed, plans were made for the building, or purchase, of his own house. For example, when Joseph Buckland of Rehoboth married his father promised "to build the said Joseph a Convenient house for his Comfortable liveing with three score of acrees of land ajoyning to it." [32] Some young men moved out of the family even before marrying, either to join in the expansion toward the interior or simply to "be for themselves" while remaining nearby. Girls stayed with their parents until they found a husband, but never beyond that time. I know of only one case in which there is documentary evidence suggesting that two couples shared a house, and it is truly the exception that proves the rule. The will of Thomas Bliss (Plymouth, 1647) contained this clause: "I give unto my soon Jonathan my house and home lot Conditionally that hee shall give unto my sonninlaw Thomas Willmore his lot which hee now hath and allso the one half of my broken up ground for two yeares and shall healp him to build him an house and let him peacably and quietly live in the house with him untell they shall bee able to set up an house for him." [33]

In a true extended family the death of the father, or even of both parents, causes no radical change in living arrangements. The widow or the children, or both, continue their lives much as before, and the functions of the deceased are assumed by other relatives (uncles or cousins or grandparents). When a man died in Plymouth, however, his household usually broke up. If the children were still young, some might remain with their mother, but others were likely to be placed in new families. If the children were adult, the "homestead" was given to a certain designated one of them, who was then obliged to pay to each

---

[32] *Mayflower Descendant*, XVI (1914), 82. When Thomas Little of Taunton died leaving two teenage sons, his will directed that £10 be paid to each toward the building of houses "when they shall have occasion." *Ibid.*, IV, 162.
[33] *Ibid.*, VIII (1906), 85.

of his brothers and sisters an amount equivalent to some fair proportion of the property's value.[34]

An unusually wealthy man in Plymouth Colony, and especially one who participated directly in the founding of new towns, could accumulate enough land to provide his sons with lots near or adjoining his own. Wills and land deeds show, for example, that John Washburn divided up his very large estate in Bridgewater with three sons, and that John Turner did the same kind of thing in Scituate.[35] This sort of arrangement comes as close to being an extended family as anything found in and around Plymouth — and it is not very close at all. There is no evidence of shared economic activity, no mention in the wills of profits or crops to be divided up. Moreover, in both the Washburn and the Turner families there were other sons who do not seem to have remained nearby.

[Among those who were less wealthy, the drive to expand and to increase their property proved more powerful than the bonds which might have held families together. Children left, when they came of age, to take up new holdings several towns and many miles away. The process of dispersion was, in fact, sometimes encouraged by the very system of portions described earlier. Often a father simply had no land to spare in the immediate vicinity of his own farm. He might, however, own property in one, or two, or three, of the newer townships; and this was what he passed on to his children] The will of William Bradford, Jr., shows that he had sons living in Connecticut (on land which he had given them); and he made additional bequests, to his youngest children, in Plymouth and Duxbury. Similarly, when Benjamin Bartlett died he left his children a wide variety of lots in Duxbury, Middleborough, Little Compton, and Rochester.[36] In some cases the recipients may have sold these gifts soon afterwards, but at least as often they went to make their homes on them.

What we would most like to know is something of the effect of this dispersion on a whole range of more intimate aspects of family life. A court case at Plymouth in 1679 throws some light on such matters. An elderly man named Samuel Ryder had just died and left his whole estate to two sons, Benjamin and John. A third son, Joseph, had been left nothing. What made this especially hard was the fact that Joseph had already built a house on a piece of land belonging to his father and had expected to receive title to it in the father's will. The Court approached the problem by taking a number of depositions from friends and family.

---

[34] See, for example, the will of David Linnell (Barnstable, 1688), *ibid.*, X (1908), 100–101.

[35] *Ibid.*, XV, 248–253; V (1903), 41–46.

[36] *Ibid.*, IV, 143–147; VI (1904), 44–49.

Elizabeth Mathews was called first and gave the following testimony: "I being att the Raising of Joseph Riyders house; Joseph Ryders Mother Came into the house Joseph then lived in and Cryed and wrong her hands fearing that Joseph would Goe away; Josephs Mother then said that if you would beleive a woman beleive mee that youer father saith that you shall never be Molested; and you shall Never be Molested." Samuel Mathews verified this report and supplied additional details: "In the Morning before wee Raised the house old Goodman Ryder Joseph Ryders father Came out and marked out the Ground with his stick; and bid the said Joseph sett his house where it Now stands . . . the occation of the womans Lamenting as above said was fearing her son would Goe away; for shee said if hee went shee would Goe too." [37]

There are several striking things about this episode: the mother's distress at the thought that her son might leave (even to the point of suggesting that she would follow him); the hint of hostility between father and son; the threat to go away used by the son as a means of forcing a gift from his father; and the implication that parents could, and did, use gifts of land to induce their children to stay nearby. Evidence bearing directly on the human dimension of life in Plymouth is extremely hard to come by, but something like the Ryder case does offer a glimpse of the enormous strain that the whole pattern of geographic mobility must have placed upon family ties and sanctions.

Land and property represented one advantage still possessed by most parents when they wished to rearrange their own lives and the lives of their children. They tried to use it in a variety of ways. Bequests to children were often hedged by a requirement of good behavior: "I give [my estate to] my two sonnes Daniell and Samuell [ages 15 and 17] upon this proviso that they bee Obedient unto theire mother and carrye themselves as they ought . . . but if the one or both live otherwise then they ought and undewtyfully and unquietly with theire Mother . . . then hee that soe carryeth himselfe shall Disinherit himselfe of his parte of this land." Another legacy, this one to a daughter, was made conditional on her "pleas[ing] her mother in her match." In still another case a man left his widow to judge their child's behavior and reward him accordingly from out of his estate. And the reasoning behind this was made explicit: "I would have the boy beholding to my wife; and not my wife to the boy." [38] Sometimes portions were shaped in the same way. One of the rare letters that survives from seventeenth-century Plymouth describes

---

[37] *Ibid.*, XI (1909), 50–53. In this context to "molest" means to make trouble about the ownership of something.

[38] Will of Thomas Hicks (Scituate, 1652), will of Samuel Newman (Rehoboth, 1661), and depositions concerning the estate of John Allen (Scituate, 1662), *ibid.*, XI, 160; XV, 234–236; XVII, 218.

a father bestowing upon his son "the full of his porshon except upon his sons better behaver [he] should desarve more." [39]

[It is likely, then, that rewards in the form of property were held out as an inducement to all sorts of "better behavior." But this was especially true in regard to the care of elderly couples and widows.] Virtually every man who left a widow directed in his will that she be looked after by one of their children, and made a large bequest contingent thereupon. Usually the family homestead went to a particular child, with one room or more reserved for the widow. Often the instructions were spelled out in great detail: She would have full rights to the use of the "garden" and "orchard"; yearly payments of a certain specified amount must be made to her, wood must be brought to her door in wintertime, her cows milked, etc.[40]

Some men made arrangements of this kind even before their deaths. John and Deborah Hurd of Barnstable, for example, deeded "all that our hom sted" to their daughter and son-in-law in exchange for "the whole and sole Care and charge of us . . . for and during the tarm of our Natural Lives." And Robert Sprout of Middleborough gave his farm to his sons Ebenezer and James, on condition that they "pay yearly for my support . . . the sum of forty pounds to that child which I live with and provides for me and looks after me." [41] These conditions are nailed down so tightly in so many wills (and similar deeds) that it is tempting to infer some particular anxiety behind them.[42] It clearly was the general custom for aged parents to live with one of their children who would provide the care and support they needed. Probably in the majority of cases this was managed without too much difficulty; but in a society as fluid as Plymouth there must have been some elderly fathers and mothers who were more or less neglected. One recalls Bradford's vivid image of the "ancient mother, grown old and forsaken of her children, though not in their affections, yet in regard of their bodily presence and personal helpfulness."

[Although one set of parents with their own children always formed the core of a Plymouth household, this nuclear pattern was, as we have seen, sometimes modified by the inclusion of one or more aged grandparents. It was often further modified by servants and apprentices, who lived in the houses of their masters.] Among such people were at least a

[39] Benjamin Brewster to Daniel Wetherell, date not known, *ibid.*, II, 113.

[40] See, for examples, the wills of Thomas King, Sr., of Scituate and of Robert Hicks of Plymouth, *ibid.*, XXXI (1933), 101; VIII, 144–146.

[41] *Ibid.*, XVI, 219; VI, 9–10.

[42] One eldest son who inherited his father's homestead complained that the conditions attached to the bequest, especially with regard to his father's widow, were such as to make him virtually "a servant for life." *Ibid.*, XII, 106.

few Negroes and Indians whose service was normally for life.[43] The vast majority, however, were young boys and girls, "bound out" for a specified term of years. Some of them were orphans but many others had both parents living. Often, in fact, the parents had made all the arrangements and signed a formal contract with the couple whom their child served. In 1660 "An agreement appointed to bee Recorded" stated that "Richard Berry of yarmouth with his wifes Concent; and other friends; hath given unto Gorge Crispe of Eastham and his; wife theire son Samuell Berry; to bee att the ordering and Disposing of the said Gorge and his wife as if hee were theire owne Child, untill hee shall accomplish the age of twenty one yeares; and in the meane time to provide for the said Samuell in all thinges as theire owne Child; and afterwards if hee live to marry or to goe away from them; to Doe for him as if hee were theire own Child." [44] It is noteworthy that the Crispes took full responsibility for young Samuel — even to the point of promising him a portion. This is, then, a virtual deed of adoption.

No age was indicated for Samuel Berry, but it is clear from other cases that the children involved were often very young. John Smith and his wife gave their four-year-old son to Thomas Whitney "to have the full and sole disposing of him . . . without annoyance or disturbance from the said John Smith or Bennit his wife." [45] Samuel Eddy arranged apprenticeships for three of his sons, at ages six, seven, and nine. Two of them went to the same man, Mr. John Brown of Rehoboth. Upon reaching maturity, they both received property from Brown, and, in addition, were given modest portions by their father. It appears from this that Eddy continued to take a direct interest in his children even after they had left his household.

The most difficult question these arrangements raise is, what purpose lay behind them? No answer that would serve in all cases suggests itself. In some, poverty was obviously a factor. For example, Samuel Eddy, in the apprenticeship papers for his sons, pleaded his "many children" and "many wants." On the other hand, George Soule of Duxbury bound out his daughter to John Winslow, and Soule was a wealthy man. In certain cases, learning a trade was mentioned, but in a perfunctory manner. When young Benjamin Savory was bound out to Jonathan Shaw in 1653, the papers directed that he be taught "whatsoever trad[e] the said Jonathan Shaw can Doe." Something must have gone amiss with this arrangement, because four years later the child was placed with still

---

[43] The inventory of the property of John Gorham of Yarmouth in 1675 included the item "1 Negro man." *Ibid.*, IV, 156. For similar treatment of Indian servants, see the wills of Samuel Fuller and Anthony Snow, *ibid.*, II, 237–241; V, 1–5.

[44] *Ibid.*, XV, 34.

[45] *Plym. Col. Recs.*, XII, 181–182.

another family. The terms were only slightly less vague: his new master, Stephen Bryant, was to "teach him in learning that is to say to read and write and to Instruct him in husbandry." [46]

Another possible motive was to improve a child's educational opportunities. Instruction in reading and writing was often included among the conditions of the contract, as in the case of Benjamin Savory above. Finally, Edmund Morgan has suggested in his *The Puritan Family* that "Puritan parents did not trust themselves with their own children . . . and were afraid of spoiling them by too great affection"; [47] it was for this reason, he argues, that so many children were placed in families other than their own. It is an interesting thought, but there is simply no explicit proof for it. At least Morgan found none, and I have had no better luck with the materials for Plymouth.

The household of Samuel Fuller seems to have been about as varied as any in Plymouth, and is worth mentioning in this connection. When Fuller died in 1633 it included nine people, six of whom were not of his own immediate family. There were, beside himself, his wife, and his son, a nephew, two servants, a ward, and two "additional children." The last of these had been sent to him for education, from families in Charlestown and Sagos. The ward was the daughter of a close friend who had died some years before. Meanwhile, Fuller's own daughter was living with "goodwife Wallen." Fuller was obliged to leave instructions about all these people in his will.[48] His daughter was to continue where she was for the time being. The children from Charlestown and Sagos should be returned to their former homes. The ward was committed to his brother-in-law, and passed thereby into her third family. Fuller's son should continue to live in the "homestead" and one day would inherit it; but the same brother-in-law was to take charge of his education. Fuller's wife would have the day-to-day care of the youth until she died or remarried. She would also take charge of the servants for the remainder of their contracted term.

Fuller's household was hardly typical, however. A close reading of hundreds of Plymouth wills has turned up no other family as complicated as this one. In many there were one or two people not of the immediate family — aged grandparents, servants, wards, or additional children — but rarely more. The basic unit remained one set of parents and their children or stepchildren, living apart from all other relatives.

[Clearly children in seventeenth-century Plymouth often found themselves growing up in a household other than that of their parents. The records are so scattered that it is impossible to calculate how many this category actually included. It must, however, have been a considerable number; my own guess is somewhere between a third and a half of all

[46] *Mayflower Descendant*, II, 30; V, 90; XII, 133.
[47] Edmund S. Morgan, *The Puritan Family* . . . (Boston, 1956), 38.
[48] *Mayflower Descendant*, I (1899), 24–28.

the children. This figure does not seem too high when it is remembered that one in three of the parents in the colony married twice or more, and that some children were placed in new homes even when their own father and mother were living.]

The impact of these situations on the children cannot be proved — only imagined. But a hint of what they could mean comes to us in the story of a rather sad little episode, which by a lucky chance has been preserved in the *Colony Records*. Christian (Penn) Eaton and Francis Billington, widow and widower, were married in Plymouth in 1635. Christian's son, Benjamin Eaton, was "put forth" into another family immediately thereafter. The couple began to have children of their own: first, Elizabeth, and then, Joseph — both of whom were also placed in other families. But little Joseph apparently did not take to this arrangement very well, for in 1643 the Court was obliged to issue the following order:

> Whereas Joseph, the sonn of Francis Billington . . . was . . . placed with John Cooke the younger, and hath since beene inveagled, and did oft departe his said masters service, the Court, upon longe heareing of all that can be said or alleadged by his parents, doth order and appoynt that the said Joseph shalbe returned to his said master againe immediately, and shall so remaine with him during his terme and that if either the said Francis, or Christian, his wyfe, do receive him, if he shall againe depart from his said master without his lycence, that the said Francis, and Christian, his wyfe, shalbe sett in the stocks . . . as often as he or shee shall so receive him, untill the Court shall take a further course with them.[49]

Joseph Billington was five years old.

[49] *Plym. Col. Recs.*, II, 58–59.

Family Structure in Seventeenth-Century Andover, Massachusetts

PHILIP J. GREVEN, JR.

Philip Greven is another of the newly prominent demographic historians of colonial America. He applies the same quantitative and conceptual analysis to the study of life in

> *Andover that Demos does in regard to Plymouth, and yet his results are sharply divergent. [Greven's Andover was a very static community in which children married late, lived close to the homes of their parents, and were quite mature before they owned farms of their own. It was a patriarchal society in which first generation males held onto control of their families, lands, and town government, and in which continuity was fostered by a self-conscious system of arranged marriages. There seems to have been little immigration into Andover or emigration from the town.]*
>
> *"Family structure" is a relatively novel concept in historical analysis, but Greven uses it to show how sociological categories can provide fresh historical insights. His implicit contention is that until we understand precisely how men behaved, we shall not be able to find out why they acted as they did. His essay attempts to demonstrate how very broad conclusions can be drawn from masses of very minute bits of evidence, however, and he suggests that many questions about the New England town remain unanswered. One obvious problem is why Andover should have been so different from Plymouth. Might the answers lay outside the scope of demographic inquiry?*

Surprisingly little is known at present about family life and family structure in the seventeenth-century American colonies. The generalizations about colonial family life embedded in textbooks are seldom the result of studies of the extant source materials, which historians until recently have tended to ignore.[1] Genealogists long have been using records preserved in county archives, town halls, churches, and graveyards as well as personal documents to compile detailed information on successive generations of early American families. In addition to the work of local genealogists, many communities possess probate records and deeds for the colonial period. A study of these last testaments and deeds together with the vital statistics of family genealogies can provide the answers to such questions as how many children people had, how long people lived, at what ages did they marry, how much control did

Reprinted by permission from Philip J. Greven, "Family Structure in Seventeenth-Century Andover, Massachusetts," *William and Mary Quarterly*, 3d Ser., XXIII (1966), 234–256. A revised version of this article is included in Philip J. Greven, *Four Generations: Population, Land and Family in Colonial Andover, Massachusetts* (Ithaca, 1970).

[1] Two notable exceptions to this generalization are Edmund S. Morgan, *The Puritan Family . . .* (Boston, 1956), and John Demos, "Notes on Life in Plymouth Colony," *William and Mary Quarterly*, 3d Ser., XXII (1965), 264–286.

fathers have over their children, and to what extent and under what conditions did children remain in their parents' community. The answers to such questions enable an historian to reconstruct to some extent the basic characteristics of family life for specific families in specific communities. This essay is a study of a single seventeenth-century New England town, Andover, Massachusetts, during the lifetimes of its first and second generations — the pioneers who carved the community out of the wilderness, and their children who settled upon the lands which their fathers had acquired. A consideration of their births, marriages, and deaths, together with the disposition of land and property within the town from one generation to the next reveals some of the most important aspects of family life and family structure in early Andover.

The development of a particular type of family structure in seventeenth-century Andover was dependent in part upon the economic development of the community during the same period. Andover, settled by a group of about eighteen men during the early 1640's and incorporated in 1646, was patterned at the outset after the English open field villages familiar to many of the early settlers. The inhabitants resided on house lots adjacent to each other in the village center, with their individual holdings of land being distributed in small plots within two large fields beyond the village center. House lots ranged in size from four to twenty acres, and subsequent divisions of land within the town were proportionate to the size of the house lots. By the early 1660's, about forty-two men had arrived to settle in Andover, of whom thirty-six became permanent residents. During the first decade and a half, four major divisions of the arable land in the town were granted. The first two divisions established two open fields, in which land was granted to the inhabitants on the basis of one acre of land for each acre of house lot. The third division, which provided four acres of land for each acre of house lot, evidently did not form another open field, but was scattered about the town. The fourth and final division of land during the seventeenth century occurred in 1662, and gave land to the householders at the rate of twenty acres for each acre of their house lots. Each householder thus obtained a minimum division allotment of about eighty acres and a maximum allotment of about four hundred acres. Cumulatively, these four successive divisions of town land, together with additional divisions of meadow and swampland, provided each of the inhabitants with at least one hundred acres of land for farming, and as much as six hundred acres. During the years following these substantial grants of land, many of the families in the town removed their habitations from the house lots in the town center onto their distant, and extensive, farm lands, thus altering the character of the community through the establishment of independent family farms and scattered residences. By the 1680's, more than half the families in Andover lived outside the original center of the town on their own ample farms. The

[transformation of the earlier open field village effectively recast the basis for family life within the community.²]

An examination of the number of children whose births are recorded in the Andover town records between 1651 and 1699 reveals a steady increase in the number of children being born throughout the period. (See Table 1.³) Between 1651 and 1654, 28 births are recorded, followed by 32 between 1655 and 1659, 43 between 1660 and 1664, 44 between 1665 and 1669, 78 between 1670 and 1674, and 90 between 1675 and 1679. After 1680, the figures rise to more than one hundred births every five years. The entire picture of population growth in Andover, however, cannot be formed from a study of the town records alone since these records do not reflect the pattern of generations within the town. Looked at from the point of view of the births of the children of the first generation of settlers who arrived in Andover between the first settlement in the mid-1640's and 1660, a very different picture emerges, hidden within the entries of the town records and genealogies.⁴ The majority of the second-

TABLE 1					*The Number of Sons and Daughters Living at the Age of 21 in Twenty-nine First-Generation Families*						
Sons	0	1	2	3	4	5	6	7	8	9	10
Families	1	2	7	1	6	6	3	3	0	0	0
Daughters	0	1	2	3	4	5	6	7	8	9	10
Families	0	2	7	6	11	2	0	0	0	1	0

² For a full discussion of the transformation of 17th-century Andover, see my article, "Old Patterns in the New World: The Distribution of Land in 17th Century Andover," *Essex Institute Historical Collections*, CI (April 1965),133–148. See also the study of Sudbury, Mass., in Sumner Chilton Powell, *Puritan Village: The Formation of a New England Town* (Middletown, Conn., 1963).

³ The figures in Table 1 were compiled from the first MS book of Andover vital records. A Record of Births, Deaths, and Marriages, Begun 1651 Ended 1700, located in the vault of the Town Clerk's office, Town Hall, Andover, Mass. For a suggestive comparison of population growth in a small village, see W. G. Hoskins, "The Population of an English Village, 1086–1801: A Study of Wigston Magna," *Provincial England: Essays in Social and Economic History* (London, 1963), 195–200.

⁴ The most important collection of unpublished genealogies of early Andover families are the typed MSS of Charlotte Helen Abbott, which are located in the Memorial Library, Andover. The two vols. of *Vital Records of Andover, Massachusetts, to the End of the Year 1849* (Topsfield, Mass., 1912) provide an invaluable and exceptionally reliable reference for vital statistics of births, marriages, and deaths.

generation children were born during the two decades of the 1650's and the 1660's. The births of 159 second-generation children were distributed in decades as follows: 10 were born during the 1630's, either in England or in the towns along the Massachusetts coast where their parents first settled; 28 were born during the 1640's; 49 were born during the 1650's; 43 were born during the 1660's; declining to 21 during the 1670's, and falling to only 8 during the 1680's. Because of this pattern of births, the second generation of Andover children, born largely during the 1650's and the 1660's, would mature during the late 1670's and the 1680's. [Many of the developments of the second half of the seventeenth century in Andover, both within the town itself and within the families residing there, were the result of the problems posed by a maturing second generation.]

From the records which remain, it is not possible to determine the size of the first-generation family with complete accuracy, since a number of children were undoubtedly stillborn, or died almost immediately after birth without ever being recorded in the town records. It is possible, however, to determine the number of children surviving childhood and adolescence with considerable accuracy, in part because of the greater likelihood of their names being recorded among the children born in the town, and in part because other records, such as church records, marriage records, tax lists, and wills, also note their presence. Evidence from all of these sources indicates that the families of Andover's first settlers were large, even without taking into account the numbers of children who may have been born but died unrecorded. An examination of the families of twenty-nine men who settled in Andover between 1645 and 1660 reveals that a total of 247 children are known to have been born to these particular families. Of these 247 children whose births may be ascertained, thirty-nine, or 15.7 per cent, are known to have died before reaching the age of 21 years.[5] A total of 208 children or 84.3 per cent of the number of children known to be born thus reached the age of 21 years, having survived the hazards both of infancy and of adolescence. [This suggests that the number of deaths among children and adolescents during the middle of the seventeenth century in Andover was lower than might have been expected.]

In terms of their actual sizes, the twenty-nine first-generation families varied considerably, as one might expect. Eleven of these twenty-nine families had between 0 and 3 sons who survived to the age of 21 years;

[5] While this figure is low, it should not be discounted entirely. Thomas Jefferson Wertenbaker, *The First Americans, 1607–1690* (New York, 1929), 185–186, found that, "Of the eight hundred and eight children of Harvard graduates for the years from 1658 to 1690, one hundred and sixty-two died before maturity. This gives a recorded child mortality among this selected group of *twenty* per cent." Italics added.

twelve families had either 4 or 5 sons surviving, and six families had either 6 or 7 sons living to be 21. Eighteen of these families thus had four or more sons to provide with land or a trade when they reached maturity and wished to marry, a fact of considerable significance in terms of the development of family life in Andover during the years prior to 1690. Fewer of these twenty-nine families had large numbers of daughters. Fifteen families had between 0 and 3 daughters who reached adulthood, eleven families had 4 daughters surviving, and three families had 5 or more daughters reaching the age of 21. In terms of the total number of their children born and surviving to the age of 21 or more, four of these twenty-nine first-generation families had between 2 and 4 children (13.8 per cent), eleven families had between 5 and 7 children (37.9 per cent), and fourteen families had between 8 and 11 children (48.3 per cent). Well over half of the first-generation families thus had 6 or more children who are known to have survived adolescence and to have reached the age of 21. The average number of children known to have been born to these twenty-nine first-generation families was 8.5, with an average of 7.2 children in these families being known to have reached the age of 21 years.[6] The size of the family, and particularly the number of sons who survived adolescence, was a matter of great importance in terms of the problems which would arise later over the settlement of the second generation upon land in Andover and the division of the estates of the first generation among their surviving children. The development of a particular type of family structure within Andover during the first two generations depended in part upon the number of children born and surviving in particular families.

Longevity was a second factor of considerable importance in the development of the family in Andover. For the first forty years following the settlement of the town in 1645, relatively few deaths were recorded among the inhabitants of the town. Unlike Boston, which evidently suffered from smallpox epidemics throughout the seventeenth century, there is no evidence to suggest the presence of smallpox or other epidemical diseases in Andover prior to 1690. With relatively few people, many of whom by the 1670's were scattered about the town upon their own farms, Andover appears to have been a remarkably healthy community during its early years. Lacking virulent epidemics, the principal

---

[6] Comparative figures for the size of families in other rural New England villages are very rare. Wertenbaker, *First Americans*, 182–185, suggested that families were extremely large, with 10 to 20 children being common, but his data for Hingham, Mass., where he found that 105 women had "five or more children," with a total of 818 children "giving an average of 7.8 for each family," is in line with the data for Andover. The figures for seventeenth-century Plymouth are also remarkably similar. See Demos, "Notes on Life in Plymouth Colony," 270–271.

hazards to health and to life were birth, accidents, non-epidemical diseases, and Indians. Death, consequently, visited relatively few of Andover's inhabitants during the first four decades following its settlement. This is evident in the fact that the first generation of Andover's settlers was very long lived. Prior to 1680, only five of the original settlers who came to Andover before 1660 and established permanent residence there had died; in 1690, fifteen of the first settlers (more than half of the original group) were still alive, forty-five years after the establishment of their town. The age at death of thirty men who settled in Andover prior to 1660 can be determined with a relative degree of accuracy. Their average age at the time of their deaths was 71.8 years. Six of the thirty settlers died while in their fifties, 11 in their sixties, 3 in their seventies, 6 in their eighties, 3 in their nineties, and 1 at the advanced age of 106 years.[7] The longevity of the first-generation fathers was to have great influence on the lives of their children, for the authority of the first generation was maintained far longer than would have been possible if death had struck them down at an early age. The second generation, in turn, was almost as long lived as the first generation had been. The average age of 138 second-generation men at the time of their deaths was 65.2 years, and the average age of sixty-six second-generation women at the time of their deaths was 64.0 years. (See Table 2.[8]) Of the 138 second-generation men who reached the age of 21 years and whose life-span is known, only twenty-five or 18.1 per cent, died between the ages of 20 and 49. Forty-two (30.3 per cent) of these 138 men died between the ages of 50 and 69; seventy-one (51.6 per cent) died after reaching the age of 70. Twenty-five second-generation men died in their eighties,

---

[7] The town of Hingham, according to the evidence in Wertenbaker, *First Americans*, 181–186, was remarkably similar to Andover, since the life expectancy of its inhabitants during the 17th century was very high. "Of the eight hundred and twenty-seven persons mentioned as belonging to this period [17th century] and whose length of life is recorded, one hundred and five reached the age of eighty or over, nineteen lived to be ninety or over and three . . . attained the century mark."

[8] Since the size of the sample for the age of women at the time of their death is only half that of the sample for men, the average age of 64.0 may not be too reliable. However, the evidence for Hingham does suggest that the figures for Andover ought not to be dismissed too lightly. "The average life of the married women of Hingham during the seventeenth century," Wertenbaker noted, "seems to have been 61.4 years." He also found that for their 818 children, the average age at the time of death was 65.5 years. "These figures," he added, "apply to one little town only, and cannot be accepted as conclusive for conditions throughout the colonies, yet they permit of the strong presumption that much which has been written concerning the short expectation of life for women of large families is based upon insufficient evidence." *Ibid.*, 184. The observation remains cogent. For the longevity of Plymouth's settlers, see Demos, "Notes on Life in Plymouth Colony," 271.

Second-Generation
TABLE 2   *Ages at Death*

	Males		Females	
Ages	Numbers	Percentages	Numbers	Percentages
20–29	10	7.3	4	6.1
30–39	9	6.5	4	6.1
40–49	6	4.3	6	9.1
50–59	16	11.5	10	15.2
60–69	26	18.8	13	19.7
70–79	42	30.4	16	24.2
80–89	25	18.1	8	12.1
90–99	4	3.1	5	7.5
Total	138	100.0%	66	100.0%

and four died in their nineties. Longevity was characteristic of men living in seventeenth-century Andover.

The age of marriage often provides significant clues to circumstances affecting family life and to patterns of family relationships which might otherwise remain elusive.[9] Since marriages throughout the seventeenth century and the early part of the eighteenth century were rarely fortuitous, parental authority and concern, family interests, and economic considerations played into the decisions determining when particular men and women could and would marry for the first time. And during the seventeenth century in Andover, factors such as these frequently dictated delays of appreciable duration before young men, especially, might marry. The age of marriage both of men and of women in the second generation proved to be much higher than most historians hitherto have suspected.[10]

Traditionally in America women have married younger than men, and this was generally true for the second generation in Andover. Although the assertion is sometimes made that daughters of colonial families

[9] The most sophisticated analyses of marriage ages and their relationship to the social structure, family life, and economic conditions of various communities have been made by sociologists. Two exceptionally useful models are the studies of two contemporary English villages by W. M. Williams: *Gosforth: The Sociology of an English Village* (Glencoe, Ill., 1956), esp. pp. 45–49, and *A West Country Village, Ashworthy: Family, Kinship, and Land* (London, 1963), esp. pp. 85–91. Another useful study is Conrad M. Arensberg and Solon T. Kimball, *Family and Community in Ireland* (Cambridge, Mass., 1940). For the fullest statistical and historiographical account of marriage ages in the United States, see Thomas P. Monahan, *The Pattern of Age at Marriage in the United States*, 2 vols. (Philadelphia, 1951).

[10] In Plymouth colony during the seventeenth century, the age of marriage also was higher than expected. See Demos, "Notes on Life in Plymouth Colony," 275. For a discussion of various historians' views on marriage ages during the colonial period, see Monahan, *Pattern of Age at Marriage*, I, 99–104.

			Second-Generation Female Marriage Ages

TABLE 3

Age	Numbers	Percentages	
Under 21	22	33.3	24 & under = 69.7%
21–24	24	36.4	25 & over = 30.3%
25–29	14	21.2	29 & under = 90.9%
30–34	4	6.1	30 & over = 9.1%
35–39	1	1.5	
40 & over	1	1.5	
			Average age = 22.8 years
	66	100.0%	

frequently married while in their early teens, the average age of sixty-six second-generation daughters of Andover families at the time of their first marriage was 22.8 years. (See Table 3.) Only two girls are known to have married at 14 years, none at 15, and two more at 16. Four married at the age of 17, with a total of twenty-two of the sixty-six girls marrying before attaining the age of 21 years (33.3 per cent). The largest percentage of women married between the ages of 21 and 24, with twenty-four or 36.4 per cent being married during these years, making a total of 69.7 per cent of the second-generation daughters married before reaching the age of 25. Between the ages of 25 and 29 years, fourteen women (21.2 per cent) married, with six others marrying at the age of 30 or more (9.1 per cent). Relatively few second-generation women thus married before the age of 17, and nearly 70 per cent married before the age of 25. They were not as young in most instances as one might have expected if very early marriages had prevailed, but they were relatively young nonetheless.

The age of marriage for second-generation men reveals a very different picture, for instead of marrying young, as they so often are said to have done, they frequently married quite late. (See Table 4.) The average age

			Second-Generation Male Marriage Ages

TABLE 4

Age	Numbers	Percentages	
Under 21	4	4.3	24 & under = 39.4%
21–24	33	35.1	25 & over = 60.6%
25–29	34	36.2	29 & under = 75.6%
30–34	16	17.2	30 & over = 24.4%
35–39	4	4.3	
40 & over	3	2.9	
			Average age = 27.1 years
	94	100.0%	

for ninety-four second-generation sons of Andover families at the time of their first marriages was 27.1 years. No son is known to have married before the age of 18, and only one actually married then. None of the ninety-four second-generation men whose marriage ages could be determined married at the age of 19, and only three married at the age of 20. The contrast with the marriages of the women of the same generation is evident, since only 4.3 per cent of the men married before the age of 21 compared to 33.3 per cent of the women. The majority of second-generation men married while in their twenties, with thirty-three of the ninety-four men marrying between the ages of 21 and 24 (35.1 per cent), and thirty-four men marrying between the ages of 25 and 29 (36.2 per cent). Nearly one quarter of the second-generation men married at the age of 30 or later, however, since twenty-three men or 24.4 per cent delayed their marriages until after their thirtieth year. In sharp contrast with the women of this generation, an appreciable majority of the second-generation men married at the age of 25 or more, with 60.6 per cent marrying after that age. This tendency to delay marriages by men until after the age of 25, with the average age being about 27 years, proved to be characteristic of male marriage ages in Andover throughout the seventeenth century.

[Averages can sometimes obscure significant variations in patterns of behavior, and it is worth noting that in the second generation the age at which particular sons might marry depended in part upon which son was being married. Eldest sons tended to marry earlier than younger sons in many families, which suggests variations in their roles within their families, and differences in the attitudes of their fathers towards them compared to their younger brothers.] For twenty-six eldest second-generation sons, the average age at their first marriage was 25.6 years. Second sons in the family often met with greater difficulties and married at an average age of 27.5 years, roughly two years later than their elder brothers. Youngest sons tended to marry later still, with the average of twenty-two youngest sons being 27.9 years. In their marriages as in their inheritances, eldest sons often proved to be favored by their families; and family interests and paternal wishes were major factors in deciding which son should marry and when. More often than not, a son's marriage depended upon the willingness of his father to allow it and the ability of his father to provide the means for the couple's economic independence. Until a second-generation son had been given the means to support a wife — which in Andover during the seventeenth century generally meant land — marriage was virtually impossible.

Marriage negotiations between the parents of couples proposing marriage and the frequent agreement by the father of a suitor to provide a house and land for the settlement of his son and new bride are familiar facts.[11] But the significance of this seventeenth-century custom is much greater than is sometimes realized. It generally meant that the marriages of the second generation were dependent upon their fathers' willingness to let them leave their families and to establish themselves in separate households elsewhere. The late age at which so many sons married during this period indicates that the majority of first-generation parents were unwilling to see their sons married and settled in their own families until long after they had passed the age of 21. The usual age of adulthood, marked by marriage and the establishment of another family, was often 24 or later. Since 60 per cent of the second-generation sons were 25 or over at the time of their marriage and nearly one quarter of them were 30 or over, one wonders what made the first generation so reluctant to part with its sons?

At least part of the answer seems to lie in the fact that Andover was largely a farming community during the seventeenth century, structured, by the time that the second generation was maturing, around the family farm which stood isolated from its neighbors and which functioned independently. The family farm required all the labor it could obtain from its own members, and the sons evidently were expected to assist their fathers on their family farms as long as their fathers felt that it was necessary for them to provide their labor. In return for this essential, but prolonged, contribution to their family's economic security, the sons must have been promised land by their fathers when they married, established their own families, and wished to begin their own farms. But this meant that the sons were fully dependent upon their fathers as long as they remained at home. Even if they wanted to leave, they still needed paternal assistance and money in order to purchase land elsewhere. The delayed marriages of second-generation men thus indicate their prolonged attachment to their families, and the continuation of paternal authority over second-generation sons until they had reached their mid-twenties, at least. In effect, it appears, the maturity of this generation was appreciably later than has been supected hitherto. The psychological consequences of this prolonged dependence of sons are difficult to assess, but they must have been significant.

Even more significant of the type of family relationships emerging with

---

[11] See especially Morgan, *Puritan Family*, 39–44. For one example of marriage negotiations in Andover during this period, see the agreement between widow Hannah Osgood of Andover and Samuel Archard, Sr., of Salem, about 1660 in the *Records and Files of the Quarterly Courts of Essex County, Massachusetts* (Salem, 1912–21), III, 463, cited hereafter as *Essex Quarterly Court*. Also see the negotiations of Simon Bradstreet of Andover and Nathaniel Wade of Ipswich, *New England Historical and Genealogical Register*, XIII, 204, quoted in Morgan, *Puritan Family*, 41.

the maturing of the second generation than their late age of marriage i the fact that paternal authority over sons did not cease with marriage. Ir this community, at least, paternal authority was exercised by the first gen eration not only prior to their sons' marriages, while the second genera tion continued to reside under the same roof with their parents and t work on the family farm, and not only at the time of marriage, whei fathers generally provided the economic means for their sons' establish ment in separate households, but also *after* marriage, by the further step of the father's withholding legal control of the land from the sons wh had settled upon it.[12] The majority of first-generation fathers continue to own the land which they settled their sons upon from the time th older men received it from the town to the day of their deaths. All o the first-generation fathers were willing to allow their sons to build house upon their land, and to live apart from the paternal house after thei marriage, but few were willing to permit their sons to become fully ir dependent as long as they were still alive. By withholding deeds to th land which they had settled their sons upon, and which presumabl would be theirs to inherit someday, the first generation successfully as sured the continuity of their authority over their families long after thei sons had become adults and had gained a nominal independence.[13] Sinc the second generation, with a few exceptions, lacked clear legal titles t the land which they lived upon and farmed, they were prohibited fron selling the land which their fathers had settled them upon, or fron alienating the land in any other way without the consent of their fathers who continued to own it. Being unable to sell the land which they ex

[12] Similar delays in the handing over of control of the land from one generatior to the next are discussed by W. M. Williams in his study of Ashworthy, *Wes Country Village*, 84–98. Williams noted (p. 91) that "the length of time whick the transference of control takes is broadly a reflection of the degree of patri archalism within the family: the more authoritarian the father, the longer the son has to wait to become master."

[13] The use of inheritances as a covert threat by the older generation to control the younger generation is revealed only occasionally in their wills, but must have been a factor in their authority over their sons. One suggestive example of a threat to cut off children from their anticipated inheritances is to be found in the will of George Abbot, Sr., who died in 1681, about 64 years old. Prior to his death, his two eldest sons and one daughter had married, leaving at home five unmarried sons and two unmarried daughters with his widow after his death. Abbot left his entire estate to his wife except for the land which he had already given to his eldest son. At her death, he instructed, his wife was to divide the estate with the advice of her sons and friends, and all the children, except the eldest, who had already received a double portion, were to be treated equally unless "by their disobedient carige" towards her "there be rasen to cut them short." Widow Abbot thus had an effective means for controlling her children, the oldest of whom was 24 in 1681. George Abbot, MS will, Dec. 12, 1681, Probate File 43, Probate Record Office, Registry of Deeds and Probate Court Building Salem, Mass.

pected to inherit, second-generation sons could not even depart from Andover without their fathers' consent, since few had sufficient capital of their own with which to purchase land for themselves outside of Andover. The family thus was held together not only by settling sons upon family land in Andover, but also by refusing to relinquish control of the land until long after the second generation had established its nominal independence following their marriages and the establishment of separate households. In a majority of cases, the dependence of the second-generation sons continued until the deaths of their fathers. And most of the first generation of settlers was very long lived.

The first generations' reluctance to hand over the control of their property to their second-generation sons is evident in their actions.[14] Only three first-generation fathers divided their land among all of their sons before their deaths and gave them deeds of gift for their portions of the paternal estate. All three, however, waited until late in their lives to give their sons legal title to their portions of the family lands. Eleven first-generation fathers settled all of their sons upon their family estates in Andover, but gave a deed of gift for the land to only one of their sons; the rest of their sons had to await their fathers' deaths before inheriting the land which they had been settled upon. Ten of the settlers retained the title to all of their land until their deaths, handing over control to their sons only by means of their last wills and testaments. For the great majority of the second generation, inheritances constituted the principal means of transferring the ownership of land from one generation to the next.[15] The use of partible inheritances in Andover is evident in the

[14] For deeds of gift of first-generation Andover fathers to their second-generation sons, see the following deeds, located in the MSS volumes of Essex Deeds, Registry of Deeds and Probate Court Building, Salem, Mass.: Richard Barker, v. 29, pp. 115–116; Hannah Dane (widow of George Abbot), v. 94, pp. 140–141; Edmund Faulkner, v. 39, p. 250; John Frye, v. 9, pp. 287–288; Nicholas Holt, v. 6, pp. 722–723, 814–821; v. 7, pp. 292–296; v. 9, p. 12; v. 32, pp. 130–131; v. 34, pp. 255–256; Henry Ingalls, v. 14, pp. 40–41; John Lovejoy, v. 33, pp. 40–41.

[15] The intimate relationship between inheritance patterns and family structure has been noted and examined by several historians and numerous sociologists. George C. Homans, in his study of *English Villagers of the Thirteenth Century* (New York, 1960), 26, pointed out that "differences in customs of inheritance are sensitive signs of differences in traditional types of family organization." See Homans' discussions of inheritance in England, chs. VIII and IX. H. J. Habakkuk, in his article, "Family Structure and Economic Change in Nineteenth-Century Europe," *The Journal of Economic History*, XV (1955), 4, wrote that "inheritance systems exerted an influence on the structure of the family, that is, on the size of the family, on the relations of parents to children and between the children . . . ." Very little, however, has been written about the role of inheritance in American life, or of its impact upon the development of the American family. One of the few observers to perceive the importance and im-

division of the estates of the first generation.[16] Twenty-one of twenty-two first-generation families which had two or more sons divided all of their land among all of their surviving sons. Out of seventy-seven sons who were alive at the time their fathers either wrote their wills or gave them deeds to the land, seventy-two sons received some land from their fathers. Out of a total of sixty-six sons whose inheritances can be determined from their fathers' wills, sixty-one or 92.4 per cent received land from their fathers' estates in Andover. Often the land bequeathed to them by will was already in their possession, but without legal conveyances having been given. Thus although the great majority of second-generation sons were settled upon their fathers' lands while their fathers were still alive, few actually owned the land which they lived upon until after their fathers' deaths. With their inheritances came ownership; and with ownership came independence. Many waited a long time.

The characteristic delays in the handing over of control of the land from the first to the second generation may be illustrated by the lives and actions of several Andover families. Like most of the men who wrested their farms and their community from the wilderness, William Ballard was reluctant to part with the control over his land. When Ballard died intestate in 1689, aged about 72 years, his three sons, Joseph, William, and John, agreed to divide their father's estate among themselves "as Equally as they could." [17] They also agreed to give their elderly mother, Grace Ballard, a room in their father's house and to care for her as long as

---

pact of inheritance customs upon American family life was the shrewd visitor, Alexis de Tocqueville. See, for instance, his discussion of partible inheritance in *Democracy in America*, ed. Phillips Bradley (New York, 1956), I, 47–51.

[16] For further details, see the following wills: George Abbot, Probate File 43; Andrew Allen, Probate File 370; John Aslett, *Essex Quarterly Court*, IV, 409; William Ballard, Administration of Estate, Probate Record, Old Series, Book 4, vol. 304, pp. 388–389; Richard Barker, Probate File 1708; Samuel Blanchard, Probate File 2612; William Blunt, Probate File 2658; Thomas Chandler, Probate File 4974; William Chandler, Probate File 4979; Rev. Francis Dane, Probate File 7086; John Farnum, Probate File 9244; Thomas Farnum, Probate File 9254; Edmund Faulkner, Probate File 9305; Andrew Foster, Probate Record, Old Series, Book 2, vol. 302, pp. 136–137 (photostat copy); John Frye, Probate File 10301; Henry Ingalls, Probate File 14505; John Lovejoy, Probate File 17068; John Marston, Probate File 17847; Joseph Parker, *Essex Quarterly Court*, VII, 142–144; Andrew Peters, Probate File 21550; Daniel Poor, Probate Record, vol. 302, pp. 196–197; John Russ, Probate File 24365; John Stevens, *Essex Quarterly Court*, II, 414–416; and Walter Wright, Probate File 30733. The Probate Files of manuscript wills, inventories, and administrations of estates, and the bound Probate Records, are located in the Probate Record Office, Registry of Deeds and Probate Court Building, Salem, Mass.

[17] MS Articles of Agreement, Oct. 23, 1689, Probate Records, Old Series, Book 4, vol. 304, pp. 388–389 (photostat copy). For genealogical details of the Ballard family, see Abbott's Ballard genealogy, typed MSS, in the Memorial Library, Andover.

she remained a widow, thus adhering voluntarily to a common practice for the provision of the widow. The eldest son, Joseph, had married in 1665/6, almost certainly a rather young man, whereas his two brothers did not marry until the early 1680's, when their father was in his mid-sixties. William, Jr., must have been well over 30 by then, and John was 28. Both Joseph and William received as part of their division of their father's estate in Andover the land where their houses already stood, as well as more than 75 acres of land apiece. The youngest son, John, got all the housing, land, and meadow "his father lived upon except the land and meadow his father gave William Blunt upon the marriage with his daughter," which had taken place in 1668. It is unclear whether John lived with his wife and their four children in the same house as his parents, but there is a strong likelihood that this was the case in view of his assuming control of it after his father's death. His two older brothers had been given land to build upon by their father before his death, but no deeds of gift had been granted to them, thus preventing their full independence so long as he remained alive. Their family remained closely knit both by their establishment of residences near their paternal home on family land and by the prolonged control by William Ballard over the land he had received as one of the first settlers in Andover. It was a pattern repeated in many families.

There were variations, however, such as those exemplified by the Holt family, one of the most prominent in Andover during the seventeenth century. Nicholas Holt, originally a tanner by trade, had settled in New-bury, Massachusetts, for nearly a decade before joining the group of men planting the new town of Andover during the 1640's. Once established in the wilderness community, Holt ranked third among the householders, with an estate which eventually included at least 400 acres of land in Andover as a result of successive divisions of the common land.[18] At some time prior to 1675, he removed his family from the village, where all the original house lots had been located, and built a dwelling house on his third division of land. Although a small portion of his land still lay to the north and west of the old village center, the greatest part of his estate lay in a reasonably compact farm south of his new house. Holt owned no land outside of Andover, and he acquired very little besides the original division grants from the town. It was upon this land that he eventually settled all his sons. In 1662, however, when Nicholas Holt received the fourth division grant of 300 acres from the town, his eldest son, Samuel, was 21 years old, and his three other sons were 18, 15, and 11. The fifth

---

[18] For Nicholas Holt's land grants in Andover, see the MS volume, A Record of Town Roads and Town Bounds, 18–19, located in the vault of the Town Clerk's office, Andover, Mass. For genealogical information on the Holt family, see Daniel S. Durrie, A *Genealogical History of the Holt Family in the United States* . . . (Albany, N.Y., 1864), 9–16.

son was yet unborn. His four sons were thus still adolescents, and at ages at which they could provide the physical labor needed to cultivate the land already cleared about the house, and to clear and break up the land which their father had just received. The family probably provided most of the labor, since there is no evidence to indicate that servants or hired laborers were numerous in Andover at the time. With the exception of two daughters who married in the late 1650's, the Holt family remained together on their farm until 1669, when the two oldest sons and the eldest daughter married.

By 1669, when Holt's eldest son, Samuel, finally married at the age of 28, the only possible means of obtaining land to settle upon from the town was to purchase one of the twenty-acre lots which were offered for sale. House-lot grants with accommodation land had long since been abandoned by the town, and Samuel's marriage and independence therefore depended upon his father's willingness to provide him with sufficient land to build upon and to farm for himself. Evidently his father had proved unwilling for many years, but when Samuel did at last marry, he was allowed to build a house for himself and his wife upon his father's "Three-score Acres of upland," known otherwise as his third division.[19] Soon afterwards, his second brother, Henry, married and also was given land to build upon in the third division. Neither Samuel nor Henry was given a deed to his land by their father at the time he settled upon it. Their marriages and their establishment of separate households left their three younger brothers still living with their aging father and step-mother. Five years passed before the next son married. James, the fourth of the five sons, married in 1675, at the age of 24, whereupon he, too, was provided with a part of his father's farm to build a house upon.[20] The third son, Nicholas, Jr., continued to live with his father, waiting until 1680 to marry at the late age of 32. His willingness to delay even a token independence so long suggests that personal factors must have played an important part in his continued assistance to his father, who was then about 77 years old.[21] John Holt, the youngest of the sons, married at the age of 21, shortly before his father's death.

For Nicholas Holt's four oldest sons, full economic independence was delayed for many years. Although all had withdrawn from their father's house and had established separate residences of their own, they nonetheless were settled upon their father's land not too far distant from their family homestead, and none had yet been given a legal title to the land where he lived. Until Nicholas Holt was willing to give his sons deeds of gift for the lands where he had allowed them to build and to farm, he

[19] Essex Deeds, v. 32, p. 130.
[20] *Ibid.*, v. 7, pp. 292–296.
[21] See *ibid.*, v. 6, pp. 814–815.

retained all legal rights to his estate and could still dispose of it in any way he chose. Without his consent, therefore, none of his sons could sell or mortgage the land where he lived since none of them owned it. In the Holt family, paternal authority rested upon firm economic foundations, a situation characteristic of the majority of Andover families of this period and these two generations.

Eventually, Nicholas Holt decided to relinquish his control over his Andover property by giving to his sons, after many years, legal titles to the lands which they lived upon. In a deed of gift, dated February 14, 1680/1, he conveyed to his eldest son, Samuel, who had been married almost twelve years, one half of his third division land, "the Said land on which the said Samuels House now Stands," which had the land of his brother, Henry, adjoining on the west, as well as an additional 130 acres of upland from the fourth division of land, several parcels of meadow, and all privileges accompanying these grants of land.[22] In return for this gift, Samuel, then forty years old, promised to pay his father for his maintenance so long as his "naturall life Shall Continue," the sum of twenty shillings a year. Ten months later, December 15, 1681, Nicholas Holt conveyed almost exactly the same amount of land to his second son, Henry, and also obligated him to pay twenty shillings yearly for his maintenance.[23] Prior to this gift, Nicholas had given his fourth son, James, his portion, which consisted of one-third part of "my farme" including "the land where his house now stands," some upland, a third of the great meadow, and other small parcels. In return, James promised to pay his father three pounds a year for life (three times the sum his two elder brothers were to pay), and to pay his mother-in-law forty shillings a year when she should become a widow.[24] The farm which James received was shared by his two other brothers, Nicholas and John, as well. Nicholas, in a deed of June 16, 1682, received "one third part of the farme where he now dwells," some meadow, and, most importantly, his father's own dwelling house, including the cellar, orchard, and barn, which constituted the principal homestead and house of Nicholas Holt, Sr.[25] In "consideration of this my fathers gift . . . to me his sone," Nicholas, Junior, wrote, "I doe promise and engage to pay yearly" the sum of three pounds for his father's maintenance. Thus Nicholas, Junior, in return for his labors and sacrifices as a son who stayed with his father until the age of 32, received not only a share in the family farm equal to that of his two younger brothers, but in addition received the paternal house and homestead. The youngest of the five Holt sons, John, was the only one to receive his inheritance from his father by deed prior to his marriage. On June 19, 1685, Nicholas Holt,

22 *Ibid.*, v. 32, pp. 130–131.
23 *Ibid.*, v. 34, pp. 255–256.
24 *Ibid.*, v. 7, pp. 292–296.
25 *Ibid.*, v. 6, pp. 814–816.

Sr., at the age of 83, gave his "Lovinge" son a parcel of land lying on the easterly side of "my now Dwelling house," some meadow, and fifteen acres of upland "as yett unlaid out." [26] One month later, John married, having already built himself a house upon the land which his father promised to give him. Unlike his older brothers, John Holt thus gained his complete independence as an exceptionally young man. His brothers, however, still were not completely free from obligations to their father since each had agreed to the yearly payment of money to their father in return for full ownership of their farms. Not until Nicholas Holt's death at the end of January 1685/6 could his sons consider themselves fully independent of their aged father. He must have died content in the knowledge that all of his sons had been established on farms fashioned out of his own ample estate in Andover, all enjoying as a result of his patriarchal hand the rewards of his venture into the wilderness.[27]

Some Andover families were less reluctant than Nicholas Holt to let their sons marry early and to establish separate households, although the control of the land in most instances still rested in the father's hands. The Lovejoy family, with seven sons, enabled the four oldest sons to marry at the ages of 22 and 23. John Lovejoy, Sr., who originally emigrated from England as a young indentured servant, acquired a seven-acre house lot after his settlement in Andover during the mid-1640's, and eventually possessed an estate of over 200 acres in the town.[28] At his death in 1690, at the age of 68, he left an estate worth a total of £327.11.6, with housing and land valued at £260.00.0, a substantial sum at the time.[29] Although he himself had waited until the age of 29 to marry, his sons married earlier. His eldest son, John, Jr., married on March 23, 1677/8, aged 22, and built a house and began to raise crops on land which his father gave him for that purpose. He did not receive a deed of gift for his land, however; his inventory, taken in 1680 after his premature death, showed his major possessions to consist of "one house and a crope of corn" worth only twenty pounds. His entire estate, both real and personal, was valued at only £45.15.0, and was encumbered with £29.14.7 in debts.[30] Three years later, on April 6, 1683, the land which he had farmed without owning

---

[26] *Ibid.*, v. 9, p. 12.

[27] For an example of a first-generation father who gave a deed of gift to his eldest son only, letting his five younger sons inherit their land, see the MS will of Richard Barker, dated Apr. 27, 1688, Probate File 1708. The deed to his eldest son is found in the Essex Deeds, v. 29, pp. 115–116. All of Barker's sons married late (27, 31, 35, 28, 28, and 25), and all but the eldest continued to be under the control of their father during his long life.

[28] For John Lovejoy's Andover land grants, see the MS volume, A Record of Town Roads and Town Bounds, 96–98.

[29] See John Lovejoy's MS inventory in Probate File 17068.

[30] For the inventory of the estate of John Lovejoy, Jr., see *Essex Quarterly Court*, VIII, 56.

was given to his three-year-old son by his father, John Lovejoy, Sr. In a deed of gift, the elder Lovejoy gave his grandson, as a token of the love and affection he felt for his deceased son, the land which John, Junior, had had, consisting of fifty acres of upland, a piece of meadow, and a small parcel of another meadow, all of which lay in Andover.[31] Of the surviving Lovejoy sons only the second, William, received a deed of gift from the elder Lovejoy for the land which he had given them.[32] The others had to await their inheritances to come into full possession of their land. In his will dated September 1, 1690, shortly before his death, Lovejoy distributed his estate among his five surviving sons: Christopher received thirty acres together with other unstated amounts of land, and Nathaniel received the land which his father had originally intended to give to his brother, Benjamin, who had been killed in 1689. Benjamin was 25 years old and unmarried at the time of his death, and left an estate worth only £1.02.8, his wages as a soldier.[33] Without their father's land, sons were penniless. The youngest of the Lovejoy sons, Ebenezer, received his father's homestead, with the house and lands, in return for fulfilling his father's wish that his mother should "be made comfortable while she Continues in this world." [34] His mother inherited the east end of the house, and elaborate provisions in the will ensured her comfort. With all the surviving sons settled upon their father's land in Andover, with the residence of the widow in the son's house, and with the fact that only one of the sons actually received a deed for his land during their father's life-time, the Lovejoys also epitomized some of the principal characteristics of family life in seventeenth-century Andover.

Exceptions to the general pattern of prolonged paternal control over sons were rare. The actions taken by Edmund Faulkner to settle his eldest son in Andover are instructive precisely because they were so exceptional. The first sign that Faulkner was planning ahead for his son came with his

[31] Essex Deeds, v. 33, pp. 40–41.

[32] This deed from John Lovejoy, Sr., to his son, William, is not recorded in the Essex Deeds at the Registry of Deeds, Salem, Mass. The deed, however, is mentioned in his will, Probate File 17068, wherein he bequeathed to William the lands which he already had conveyed to his son by deed. It was customary for such deeds to be mentioned in wills, since they usually represented much or all of a son's portion of a father's estate.

[33] For the inventory to Benjamin Lovejoy's estate, see the Probate File 17048.

[34] *Ibid.*, 17068. Provision for the widow was customary, and is to be found in all the wills of first-generation settlers who left their wives still alive. Generally, the son who inherited the paternal homestead was obligated to fulfill most of the necessary services for his mother, usually including the provision of firewood and other essentials of daily living. Provision also was made in most instances for the mother to reside in one or two rooms of the paternal house, or to have one end of the house, sometimes with a garden attached. Accommodations thus were written into wills to ensure that the mother would be cared for in her old age and would retain legal grounds for demanding such provisions.

purchase of a twenty-acre lot from the town at the annual town meeting of March 22, 1669/70.[35] He was the only first-generation settler to purchase such a lot, all of the other purchasers being either second-generation sons or newcomers, and it was evident that he did not buy it for himself since he already had a six-acre house lot and more than one hundred acres of land in Andover.[36] The town voted that "in case the said Edmond shall at any time put such to live upon it as the town shall approve, or have no just matter against them, he is to be admitted to be a townsman." The eldest of his two sons, Francis, was then a youth of about nineteen years. Five years later, January 4, 1674/5, Francis was admitted as a townsman of Andover "upon the account of the land he now enjoyeth," almost certainly his father's twenty acres.[37] The following October, aged about 24, Francis married the minister's daughter. A year and a half later, in a deed dated February 1, 1676/7, Edmund Faulkner freely gave his eldest son "one halfe of my Living here at home" to be "Equally Divided between us both." [38] Francis was to pay the town rates on his half, and was to have half the barn, half the orchard, and half the land about his father's house, and both he and his father were to divide the meadows. Significantly, Edmund added that "all my Sixscore acres over Shawshinne river I wholly give unto him," thus handing over, at the relatively young age of 52, most of his upland and half of the remainder of his estate to his eldest son. The control of most of his estate thereby was transferred legally and completely from the first to the second generation. Edmund's second and youngest son, John, was still unmarried at the time Francis received his gift, and waited until 1682 before marrying at the age of 28. Eventually he received some land by his father's will, but his inheritance was small compared to his brother's. Edmund Faulkner's eagerness to hand over the control of his estate to his eldest son is notable for its rarity and accentuates the fact that almost none of his friends and neighbors chose to do likewise.[39] It is just possible that Faulkner, himself a younger son of an English gentry family, sought to preserve most of his Andover

[35] Andover, MS volume of Ancient Town Records, located in the Town Clerk's office, Andover.

[36] For Edmund Faulkner's land grants in Andover, see the MS Record of Town Roads and Town Bounds, 52–53.

[37] Town meeting of Jan. 4, 1674/5, Andover, Ancient Town Records.

[38] Essex Deeds, v. 39, p. 250. Only one other instance of the co-partnership of father and son is to be found in the wills of seventeenth-century Andover, but not among the men who founded the town. See the MS will of Andrew Peters, Probate File 21550.

[39] The only instance of impartible inheritance, or primogeniture, to be found in the first generation of Andover's settlers occurred within the first decade of its settlement, before the extensive land grants of 1662 had been voted by the town. See John Osgood's will, dated Apr. 12, 1650, in *Essex Quarterly Court*, I, 239. Osgood left his entire Andover estate to the eldest of his two sons.

estate intact by giving it to his eldest son. If so, it would only emphasize his distinctiveness from his neighbors. For the great majority of the first-generation settlers in Andover, partible inheritances and delayed control by the first generation over the land were the rule. Faulkner was the exception which proved it.

Embedded in the reconstructions of particular family histories is a general pattern of family structure unlike any which are known or suspected to have existed either in England or its American colonies during the seventeenth century. It is evident that the family structure which developed during the lifetimes of the first two generations in Andover cannot be classified satisfactorily according to any of the more recent definitions applied to types of family life in the seventeenth century. It was not simply a "patrilineal group of extended kinship gathered into a single household," [40] nor was it simply a "nuclear independent family, that is man, wife, and children living apart from relatives." [41] The characteristic family structure which emerged in Andover with the maturing of the second generation during the 1670's and 1680's was a combination of both the classical extended family and the nuclear family. This distinctive form of family structure is best described as a *modified extended family* — defined as a kinship group of two or more generations living within a single community in which the dependence of the children upon their parents continues after the children have married and are living under a separate roof. This family structure is a *modified* extended family because all members of the family are not "gathered into a single household," but it is still an *extended* family because the newly created conjugal unit of husband and wife live in separate households in close proximity to their

[40] Bernard Bailyn, *Education in the Forming of American Society: Needs and Opportunities for Study* (Chapel Hill, 1960), 15–16. "Besides children, who often remained in the home well into maturity," Bailyn adds, the family "included a wide range of other dependents: nieces and nephews, cousins, and, except for families at the lowest rung of society, servants in filial discipline. In the Elizabethan family the conjugal unit was only the nucleus of a broad kinship community whose outer edges merged almost imperceptibly into the society at large." For further discussions of the extended family in England, see Peter Laslett, "The Gentry of Kent in 1640," *Cambridge Historical Journal*, IX (1948), 148–164; and Peter Laslett's introduction to his edition of *Patriarcha and Other Political Works of Sir Robert Filmer* (Oxford, 1949), esp. 22–26.

[41] Peter Laslett and John Harrison, "Clayworth and Cogenhoe," in H. E. Bell and R. L. Ollard, eds., *Historical Essays, 1660–1750, Presented to David Ogg* (London, 1963), 168. See also H. J. Habakkuk, "Population Growth and Economic Development," in *Lectures on Economic Development* (Istanbul, 1958), 23, who asserts that "from very early in European history, the social unit was the nuclear family — the husband and wife and their children — as opposed to the extended family or kinship group." See also Robin M. Williams, Jr., *American Society: A Sociological Interpretation*, 2d ed. rev. (New York, 1963), 50–57. For a contrasting interpretation of family structure in other 17th-century New England towns, see Demos, "Notes on Life in Plymouth Colony," 279–280.

parents and siblings and continue to be economically dependent in some respects upon their parents. And because of the continuing dependence of the second generation upon their first-generation fathers, who continued to own most of the family land throughout the better part of their lives, the family in seventeenth-century Andover was *patriarchal* as well. The men who first settled the town long remained the dominant figures both in their families and their community. It was their decisions and their actions which produced the family characteristic of seventeenth-century Andover.]

[One of the most significant consequences of the development of the modified extended family characteristic of Andover during this period was the fact that remarkably few second-generation sons moved away from their families and their community] More than four fifths of the second-generation sons lived their entire lives in the town which their fathers had wrested from the wilderness.[42] The first generation evidently was intent upon guaranteeing the future of the community and of their families within it through the settlement of all of their sons upon the lands originally granted to them by the town. [Since it was quite true that the second generation could not expect to acquire as much land by staying in Andover as their fathers had by undergoing the perils of founding a new town on the frontier, it is quite possible that their reluctance to hand over the control of the land to their sons when young is not only a reflection of their patriarchalism, justified both by custom and by theology, but also of the fact that they could not be sure that their sons would stay, given a free choice.] Through a series of delays, however, particularly those involving marriages and economic independence, the second generation continued to be closely tied to their paternal families. By keeping their sons in positions of prolonged dependence, the first generation successfully managed to keep them in Andover during those years in which their youth and energy might have led them to seek their fortunes elsewhere. Later generations achieved their independence earlier and moved more. It remains to be seen to what extent the family life characteristic of seventeenth-century Andover was the exception or the rule in the American colonies.

---

[42] Out of a total of 103 second generation sons whose residences are known, only seventeen or 16.5 per cent, departed from Andover. Five left before 1690, and twelve left after 1690. The majority of families in 17th-century Andover remained closely knit and remarkably immobile.

Underlying Themes in the Witchcraft of Seventeenth-Century New England

JOHN DEMOS

No episode in our colonial past has captivated the American imagination more than the outbreak of witchcraft in Salem in 1692. Nevertheless, several leading historians of New England have concluded that it was not an event of great historical consequence. Perhaps the difficulty has been that most commentators have restricted themselves to asking who was to blame for the executions. It is unlikely that we shall find an objective answer to such a question, however, and Demos directs our attention to a more important problem: Why should witchcraft have caused such a stir? The advantage of this strategy is that it relates the study of witchcraft to the fundamental elements of personality and social structure.

Demos argues that witchcraft has been resistant to historical inquiry because historians have been overly cautious in their conceptual analysis. He tries to show how the techniques of anthropology and psychoanalysis are better suited to deal with the external and irrational elements of witchcraft. Basically, his argument is that neither New England society nor the seventeenth-century personality provided satisfactory outlets for man's aggressive tendencies. From this point of view, the Salem incident is not so much an isolated tragedy as an indication of a pervasive psycho-social disturbance. What have traditionally been taken to be examples of individual eccentricity can be seen as evidence of the inability of individuals and society to cope with widespread human difficulties. Are there other aspects of colonial life which might be similarly reinterpreted? Conversely, might there be an equally plausible explanation for group conflict based on the relationship of land distribution to family structure?

It is faintly embarrassing for a historian to summon his colleagues to still another consideration of early New England witchcraft. Here, surely, is a topic which previous generations of writers have sufficiently worked, indeed overworked. Samuel Eliot Morison once commented that the Salem witch-hunt was, after all, "but a small incident in the history of a great superstition"; and Perry Miller noted that with only minor qualifications "the intellectual history of New England can be written as though no such thing ever happened. It had no effect on the ecclesiastical or political situation, it does not figure in the institutional or ideological development." [1] Popular interest in the subject is, then, badly out of proportion to its actual historical significance, and perhaps the sane course for the future would be silence.

This assessment seems, on the face of it, eminently sound. Witchcraft was not an important matter from the standpoint of the larger historical process; it exerted only limited influence on the unfolding sequence of events in colonial New England. Moreover, the literature on the subject *does* seem to have reached a point of diminishing returns. Details of fact have been endlessly canvassed, and the main outlines of the story — particularly the story of Salem — are well and widely known.

There is, to be sure, continuing debate over one set of issues: the roles played by the various persons most directly involved. Indeed the historiography of Salem can be viewed, in large measure, as an unending effort to *judge* the participants — and above all, to affix blame. A number of verdicts have been fashionable at one time or another. Thus, the ministers were really the people at fault; or Cotton Mather in particular; or the whole culture of Puritanism; or the core-group of "afflicted girls" (if their "fits" are construed as conscious fraud).[2] The most recent and in some ways most sophisticated study of the Salem trials plunges right into

---

This article appeared in a slightly revised form in the *American Historical Review*, LXXV (1970), 1311–1326.

An earlier version of this paper was presented at the meetings of the Organization of American Historians in April, 1967. I am grateful to the following for comments and criticism at various stages along the way: Robert Middlekauff, Mary Maples Dunn, Robert I. Rotberg, Raphael Demos, Dorothy Lee, Robert A. LeVine, the members of the Group for Applied Psychoanalysis, and — most especially — David Hackett Fischer and Virginia Demos.

[1] S. E. Morison, *The Intellectual Life of Colonial New England* (Ithaca, 1956), 264; Perry Miller, *The New England Mind: From Colony to Province* (Boston, 1961), 191.

[2] Examples of these varying interpretations may be found in Charles W. Upham, *Salem Witchcraft* (Boston, 1867); Winfield S. Nevins, *Witchcraft in Salem Village* (Salem, 1916); John Fiske, *New France and New England* (Boston and New York, 1902); W. F. Poole, "Witchcraft in Boston," in *The Memorial History of Boston*, ed. Justin Winsor (Boston, 1881); Marion L. Starkey, *The Devil in Massachusetts* (Boston, 1950); S. E. Morison, *The Intellectual Life of Colonial New England* (Ithaca, 1956), 259 ff.

the middle of the same controversy — and with yet another conclusion. Not the girls, not the clergy, not Puritanism, but the accused witches themselves are now the chief culprits. For "witchcraft actually did exist and was widely practiced in seventeenth century New England"; and women like Goody Glover, Bridget Bishop, and Mammy Redd were "in all probability" guilty as charged.[3]

Clearly these questions can still generate lively interest, but are they the most fruitful, the most important questions to raise about witchcraft? Will such a debate ever be finally settled? Are its partisan terms and moral tone appropriate to historical scholarship? And if, with Morison and Miller, we agree that witchcraft does not loom large as historians usually measure events, what significance remains for the old arguments about personal credit and blame? The outlook, on all counts, seems discouraging.

But this situation is not a hopeless one if only we are willing to look beyond the limits of our own discipline. There is, in particular, a substantial body of interesting and relevant work by anthropologists. Many recent studies of "primitive" societies contain chapters about witchcraft, and there are several entire monographs on the subject.[4] The approach they follow differs strikingly from anything in the historical literature. Broadly speaking, the anthropological work is far more analytic, striving always to *use* materials on witchcraft as a set of clues or "symptoms." The subject is important not in its own right, but as a means of exploring certain larger questions about the society and the individuals directly concerned. Thus witchcraft throws light on social structure, or the organization of families, or the inner dynamics of personality. The substance of such investigation is, of course, highly variable from one culture to another, but the framework, the informing purposes are roughly the same. To apply this framework and these purposes to historical materials is not inherently difficult. The data may be inadequate in a given case, but the analytic categories themselves are designed for any society, whether simple or complex, Western or non-Western, past or contemporary.

Consider, by way of illustration, the strategy proposed for the main body of this essay. The whole enterprise turns on a set of complex relationships between the alleged witches and their victims. The former group includes (for these purposes) all the persons accused of practicing witch-

---

[3] Chadwick Hansen, *Witchcraft at Salem* (New York, 1969). See especially x, 22 ff., 64 ff., 226–27.

[4] Those I have found particularly helpful in developing my own approach toward New England witchcraft are the following: Clyde Kluckhohn, *Navajo Witchcraft* (Boston, 1967); E. E. Evans-Pritchard, *Witchcraft, Oracles, and Magic Among the Azande* (Oxford, 1937); M. G. Marwick, *Sorcery in its Social Setting* (Manchester, 1965); *Witchcraft and Sorcery in East Africa*, ed. John Middleton and E. H. Winter (London, 1963); Beatrice B. Whiting, *Paiute Sorcery* (New York, 1950).

craft; and from henceforth let them be called, simply, "witches." [5] The category of victims, on the other hand, comprises everyone who claimed to have suffered from witchcraft. But note, too, an important distinction between different *kinds* of victims. As every schoolchild knows, some of them experienced "fits" — bizarre seizures that, in the language of modern psychiatry, closely approximate the clinical picture for hysteria. These people may be called "accusers," since their sufferings and their accusations seem to have carried the greatest weight in generating formal proceedings against witches. A second, much larger group of victims includes people who attributed to witchcraft some particular misfortune they had suffered: most typically, an injury or illness, the sudden death of domestic animals, the loss of personal property, or repeated failure in important day-to-day activities like farming, fishing, and hunting. This type of evidence was of secondary importance in actual trials of witches and was usually brought forward after the accusers had pressed their own more damaging charges. For people testifying to such experiences, therefore, the short-hand term "witnesses" seems reasonably appropriate.

Witches, accusers, and witnesses: here, then, are the three basic categories of participants in witchcraft proceedings. But just who were they? And how did their lives intersect with one another? And, most important, what attributes were generally characteristic of each group? These will be the organizing questions in the pages that follow. They will, however, demand answers of two distinct kinds, one that corresponds roughly to actual circumstances in the lives of the persons involved, and another which treats imaginary (or "irrational") materials. In short, the questions will point towards two most fundamental levels of human experience — external and internal, objective and subjective, social and psychological, define them as you will.

Consider, for example, the specific case of the witches. It is important to discover, if at all possible, their age, marital status, socio-economic position, visible personality traits, and so forth. And it is equally important to examine the chief characteristics *attributed* to witches by others (flying about at night, for instance, and transforming themselves into animals). In short, we can construct a picture of witches in fact and in fantasy; and we can make comparable efforts with accusers and witnesses as well. Analysis directed to the level of fact or "external reality" helps to locate certain points of tension or conflict in the social structure of a community. The fantasy-picture, on the other hand, reveals more directly the

[5] This usage is purely a matter of convenience and is not meant to convey any judgment as to whether such people actually tried to perform acts of witchcraft. Chadwick Hansen claims to show, from trial records, which of the accused women were indeed "guilty"; but in my opinion his argument is not convincing. The testimony that "proves" guilt in one instance seems quite similar to other testimony brought against women whom Hansen regards as innocent. There may indeed have been "practicing witches" in colonial New England, but the surviving evidence does not decide the issue one way or another.

psychological dimension of life, the inner preoccupations, anxieties, and conflicts of individual members of that community.]

An outline such as this looks deceptively simple — even, perhaps, easy to put into practice. In fact, it demands an unusual degree of caution, from writer and reader alike. The approach is explicitly cross-disciplinary, reaching out to anthropology for a strategy, and to psychology for theory. There is, of course, nothing new about the *idea* of a working relationship between history and the behavioral sciences. It is more than ten years since William Langer's famous summons to his colleagues, to consider this as their "next assignment." [6] But the record of actual output is still very meager. Hence all such efforts remain quite experimental — designed more to stimulate discussion than to prove a definitive case.

There is a final point about context and the larger purposes of this form of inquiry. Historians have traditionally worked with purposeful, conscious events, "restricting themselves," in Langer's words, "to recorded fact and to strictly rational motivation." [7] They have not necessarily wished to exclude non-rational, or irrational behavior; but it has mainly worked out that way in practice. Surely in our own post-Freudian era there is both need and opportunity to develop a more balanced picture. It is to these long-range ends that further study of witchcraft should be dedicated. For witchcraft is, if nothing else, an open window on the irrational.

The first witchcraft trial of which any record survives occurred at Windsor, Connecticut, in 1647,[8] and during the remainder of the century the total of cases ran to nearly 100. Thirty-eight people were executed as witches during this span of time; and a few more, though convicted, managed somehow to escape the death penalty. There was, of course, a variety of other outcomes as well: full dress trials resulting in acquittal, hung juries, convictions reversed on appeal, "complaints" filed but not followed up. Finally, no doubt, there were many unrecorded episodes touching on witchcraft, episodes of private suspicion or public gossip that never eventuated in legal action at all.[9]

This long series of witchcraft cases needs emphasis lest the Salem outbreak completely dominate our field of vision. Salem differed radically

[6] William L. Langer, "The Next Assignment" [*American Historical Review,* LXIII (Jan. 1958), 283–304], in *Psychoanalysis and History,* ed. Bruce Mazlish (Englewood Cliffs, N.J., 1963).

[7] *Ibid.,* 90.

[8] See John M. Taylor, *The Witchcraft Delusion in Colonial Connecticut* (New York, 1908), 145 ff.

[9] Some of these episodes are mentioned, in passing, among the records of witchcraft cases that came before the court. See, for example, the references to Besse Sewall and the widow Marshfield, in the depositions of the Parsons case, published in Samuel G. Drake, *Annals of Witchcraft in New England* (Boston, 1869), 218–57. It is clear, too, that many convicted witches had been the objects of widespread suspicion and gossip for years before they were brought to trial.

from previous episodes in sheer scope; it developed a degree of self-rein-forcing momentum present in no other instance. But it was very similar in many qualitative aspects: the types of people concerned, the nature of the charges, the fits, and so forth. Indeed, from an analytic standpoint, *all* these cases can be regarded as roughly equivalent and interchangeable. They are pieces of a single, larger phenomenon: a "system" of witchcraft belief that was generally prevalent in early New England. The evidence for such a system, must, of course, be drawn from a variety of cases in order to produce representative conclusions. For most questions this is quite feasible: there is more evidence from a greater range of cases than can ever be presented in a single study.

Yet in one particular matter the advantages of concentrating on Salem are overwhelming. It affords a unique opportunity to portray the demog-raphy of witchcraft, to establish a kind of profile for each of the three basic categories of people involved in witchcraft, in terms of sex, age, and marital status. Thus the statistical tables that follow derive entirely from detailed work on the Salem materials.[10] The earlier cases do not yield the breadth of data necessary for this type of quantitative investiga-tion. They do, however, provide many fragments of evidence that are generally consistent with the Salem picture.

There is at least minimal information about 165 people accused as witches during the entire period of the Salem outbreak.[11] (See Tables 1, 2, and 3.) These figures point to an important general conclusion: the witches were predominantly married or widowed women, between the ages of forty-one and sixty. The exceptions add up to a considerable num-ber; but, significantly, most of them belonged to the *families* of middle-aged, female witches. Virtually all the young persons in the group can be identified as the children of previously suspected women, and most of the men as their husbands. In fact this pattern conformed to an assumption then widely prevalent that the transmission of witchcraft would naturally follow the lines of family or of close friendship. An official statement from the government of Connecticut included among the "grounds for Examination of a Witch" the following:

> If ye party suspected be ye son or daughter the servt or familiar
> friend; neer Neighbor or old Companion of a Knowne or Convicted
> witch this alsoe a presumton for witchcraft is an art yt may be
> learned & Convayd from man to man & oft it falleth out yt a witch
> dying leaveth som of ye aforesd. heirs of her witchcraft.[12]

---

[10] These findings are based largely on materials in the vital records of Salem and the surrounding towns.

[11] In some cases the information is not complete — hence the variation in the size of sample among the different tables. Still the total for each table is large enough to lend overall credence to the results.

[12] An early copy of this statement (undated) is in the Ann Mary Brown Memorial Collection, Brown University.

TABLE 1

Sex	Total
Male	42
Female	120
Total	162

TABLE 2

Marital Status	Male	Female	Total
Single	8	29	37
Married	15	61	76
Widowed	1	20	21
Total	24	110	134

TABLE 3

Age	Male	Female	Total
Under 20	6	18	24
21–30	3	7	10
31–40	3	8	11
41–50	6	18	24
51–60	5	23	28
61–70	4	8	12
Over 70	3	6	9
Total	30	88	118

In short, young witches and male witches belonged to a kind of derivative category. They were not the prime targets in these situations; they were, in a literal sense, rendered suspect by association. The deepest suspicions, the most intense anxieties, remained fixed on middle-aged women.

Thirty-four persons experienced fits of one sort or another during the Salem trials and qualify thereby as accusers. (See Tables 4, 5, and 6.)

TABLE 4

Sex	Total
Male	5
Female	29
Total	34

TABLE 5

Marital Status	Male	Female	Total
Single	5	23	28
Married	0	6	6
Widowed	0	0	0
Total	5	29	34

TABLE 6

Age	Male	Female	Total
Under 11	0	1	1
11–15	1	7	8
16–20	1	13	14
21–25	0	1	1
26–30	0	1	1
Over 30	0	4	4
Total	2	27	29

Here again the sample shows a powerful cluster. The vast majority of the accusers were single girls between eleven and twenty years old. The exceptions in this case (two boys, three males of undetermined age, four adult women) are rather difficult to explain, for there is little evidence about any of them. By and large, however, they played only a minor role in the trials. [Perhaps the matter can be left this way: the core group of accusers was entirely composed of adolescent girls, but the inner conflicts so manifest in their fits found an echo in at least a few persons of other ages or of the opposite sex.]

Eighty-four persons came forward as "witnesses" at one time or another during the Salem trials. (See Tables 7, 8, and 9.) Here the results seem relatively inconclusive. Three-fourths of the witnesses were men, but a close examination of the trial records suggests a simple reason for this: men were more likely in seventeenth-century New England, to take an active part in legal proceedings of any type. When a husband and wife were victimized together by some sort of witchcraft, the former would normally come forward to testify. As to the ages of the witnesses, there is a fairly broad distribution between twenty and sixty years. [Probably, then, this category reflects the generalized belief in witchcraft among all elements of the community in a way that makes it qualitatively different from the groupings of witches and accusers.]

There is much more to ask about "external realities" in the lives of such people, particularly with regard to their social and economic position.

TABLE 7

Sex	Total
Male	63
Female	21
Total	84

TABLE 8

Marital Status	Male	Female	Total
Single	11	3	14
Married	39	16	55
Widowed	3	1	4
Total	53	20	73

TABLE 9

Age	Male	Female	Total
Under 20	3	2	5
21–30	13	4	17
31–40	14	6	20
41–50	18	7	25
51–60	11	1	12
61–70	2	1	3
Over 70	2	0	2
Total	63	21	84

Unfortunately, however, the evidence is somewhat limited here, and permits only a few impressionistic observations. It seems clear that many witches came from the lower levels of the social structure; but there were too many exceptions to regard this as a really significant pattern. The first three accused at Salem were Tituba, a Negro slave, Sarah Good, the wife of a poor laborer, and Sarah Osbourne, who possessed a very considerable estate.[13] Elizabeth Godman, tried at New Haven in 1653, seems to have been poor and perhaps a beggar [14]; but Nathaniel and Rebecca Greensmith, who were convicted and executed at Hartford eight years later, were quite well-to-do.[15] And "Mistress" Ann Hibbens, executed at Boston in 1656, was the widow of a wealthy merchant and former magistrate of the Bay Colony.[16]

What appears to have been common to nearly all these people, irrespective of their economic position, was some kind of personal eccentricity, some deviant or even criminal behavior that had long since marked them out as suspect. Some of them had previously been tried for theft or battery or slander.[17] Others were known for their interest in dubious activities like fortune-telling or certain kinds of folk-healing.[18] The "witch

[13] The proceedings against these three defendants are included in the typescript volumes, *Salem Witchcraft, 1692*, compiled from the original records by the Works Progress Administration in 1938. These volumes, an absolutely invaluable source, are on file in the Essex County Courthouse, Salem.

[14] See *Records of the Colony of New Haven*, ed. C. J. Hoadly (Hartford, 1858), II, 29–36, 151–52, and *New Haven Town Records 1649–1662*, ed. Franklin B. Dexter (New Haven, 1917), I, 249–52, 256–57.

[15] Some original records from this trial are in the Willys Papers, Connecticut State Library, Hartford. For good short accounts see Increase Mather, *An Essay for the Recording of Illustrious Providences*, in *Narratives of the Witchcraft Cases*, ed. G. L. Burr (New York, 1914), 18–21, and a letter from John Whiting to Increase Mather, Dec. 10, 1682, entitled "An account of a Remarkable passage of Divine providence that happened in Hartford, in the yeare of our Lord 1662," in *Massachusetts Historical Society Collections*, 4th Ser., VIII (Boston, 1868), 466–69.

[16] See *Records of Massachusetts Bay*, ed. Nathaniel B. Shurtleff (Boston, 1854), IV, Pt. I, 269; William Hubbard, *A General History of New England* (Boston, 1848), 574; Thomas Hutchinson, *The History of the Colony and Province of Massachusetts Bay*, ed. Lawrence S. Mayo (Cambridge, Mass., 1936), I, 160–61.

[17] For example, Giles Corey, executed as one of the Salem witches, had been before the courts several times, charged with such offenses as theft and battery. Mary Parsons of Springfield was convicted of slander not long before her trial for witchcraft.

[18] For example, Katherine Harrison, prosecuted for witchcraft at Weathersfield, Connecticut, in 1668, was reported to have been given to fortune-telling; and a group of ministers called to advise the court in her case contended that such activity did "argue familiarity with the Devil." See John M. Taylor, *The Witchcraft Delusion in Colonial Connecticut* (New York, 1908), 56–58. Evidence of the same kind was offered against Samuel Wardwell of Andover, Massa-

Glover" of Boston, on whom Cotton Mather reports at some length, was Irish and Catholic, and spoke Gaelic; and a Dutch family in Hartford came under suspicion at the time the Greensmiths were tried.[19]

More generally, many of the accused seem to have been unusually irascible and contentious in their personal relations. Years before her conviction for witchcraft Mrs. Hibbens had obtained a reputation for "natural crabbedness of . . . temper"; indeed she had been excommunicated by the Boston church in 1640, following a long and acrimonious ecclesiastical trial. William Hubbard, whose *General History of New England* was published in 1680, cited her case to make the general point that "persons of hard favor and turbulent passions are apt to be condemned by the common people as witches, upon very slight grounds." In the trial of Mercy Desborough, at Fairfield, Connecticut, in 1692, the court received numerous reports of her quarrelsome behavior. She had, for example, told one neighbor "yt shee would make him bare as a bird's tale," and to another she had repeatedly said "many hard words." Goodwife Clawson, tried at the same time, was confronted with testimony such as the following:

> Abigail Wescot saith that as shee was going along the street goody Clason came out to her and they had some words together and goody Clason took up stones and threw at her: and at another time as shee went along the street before sd Clasons dore goody Clason caled to mee and asked me what was in my Chamber last Sabbath day night; and I doe afirme that I was not there that night: and at another time as I was in her sone Steephens house being neere her one hous shee folowed me in and contended with me becase I did not com into her hous caling of me proud slut what — are you proud of your fine cloths and you love to be mistres but you neuer shal be and several other provoking speeches.[20]

---

chusetts, in 1692. See the proceedings in his case in the typescript volumes by the Works Progress Administration, *Salem Witchcraft, 1692,* in the Essex County Courthouse, Salem. Margaret Jones, convicted and executed at Boston in 1648, was involved in "practicing physic." See John Winthrop's *Journal,* ed. J. K. Hosmer (New York, 1908), II, 344–45. Elizabeth Morse, prosecuted at Newbury, Massachusetts, in 1679, was alleged to have possessed certain occult powers to heal the sick. See the depositions published in Drake, *Annals of Witchcraft,* 258–96.

[19] Cotton Mather, *Memorable Providences, Relating to Witchcraft and Possessions,* in *Narratives,* ed. Burr, 103–06; Increase Mather, *An Essay, ibid.,* 18.

[20] Hutchinson, *History of the Colony and Province of Massachusetts Bay,* ed. Mayo, I, 160; Hubbard, *General History of New England,* 574. There is a verbatim account of the church proceedings against Mrs. Hibbens in the journal of Robert Keayne, in the Massachusetts Historical Society, Boston. I am grateful to Anita Rutman for lending me her transcription of this nearly illegible document. Manuscript deposition, trial of Mercy Desborough, Willys Papers; manuscript deposition, trial of Elizabeth Clawson, Willys Papers.

The case of Mary and Hugh Parsons, tried at Springfield in 1651 affords a further look at some of these same questions. There is, for example, the record of a tax-rating taken at Springfield in 1646, which shows the land-holdings of most of the principals in the witchcraft prosecutions of five years later. When the list is arranged according to wealth, Parsons falls near the middle (twenty-fourth out of forty-two), and those who testified against him come from the top, middle, *and* bottom. This outcome tends to confirm the general point that economic position is not, for present purposes, a significant datum. What seems, on the basis of the actual testimonies at the trial, to have been much more important is the whole dimension of eccentric and anti-social behavior. Mary Parsons was very nearly insane. She succumbed repeatedly to periods of massive depression; and during the witchcraft investigations she began by testifying against her husband, and ended by convicting herself of the murder of their infant child. Hugh Parsons was a sawyer and brickmaker by trade, and there are indications that in performing these services he was sometimes suspected of charging extortionate rates.[21] But what may have weighed most heavily against him was his propensity for prolonged and bitter quarreling; many examples of his "threatening speeches" were reported in court.

One other aspect of this particular episode is worth noting: namely, the apparent influence of spatial proximity. When the names of Parsons and his "victims" are checked against a map of Springfield in this period, it becomes very clear that the latter were mostly his nearest neighbors. In fact, nearly all the people who took a direct part in the trial came from the southern half of the town. No other witchcraft episode yields such a detailed picture in this respect, but many separate pieces of evidence suggest that neighborhood antagonism was usually an aggravating factor.[22]

We can summarize the major characteristics of this — the "external" — side of New England witchcraft as follows. First, the witches themselves were chiefly women of middle age, and their accusers were girls of about one full generation younger. This may reflect the kind of situation which anthropologists would call a "structural conflict" — that is, some focus of tension created by the specific ways in which a community arranges the lives of its individual members. In a broad sense it is quite probable that

---

[21] The tax list is published in Henry Burt, *The First Century of the History of Springfield* (Springfield, Mass., 1898), I, 190–91; a long set of depositions from the Parsons case is published in Drake, *Annals of Witchcraft*, 219–56; see especially 224–28, 242. Mary Parsons herself offered some testimony reflecting her husband's inordinate desire "for Luker and Gaine."

[22] See Burt, *First Century of the History of Springfield*, I, for just such a map; see Increase Mather, *An Essay*, in *Narratives*, ed. Burr, 18 ff., on the case of the Greensmiths. Also Richard Chamberlain, *Lithobolia, ibid.*, 61, on the case of Hannah Jones at Great Island, New Hampshire, in 1682.

adolescent girls in early New England were particularly subject to the control of older women, and this may well have given rise to a powerful underlying resentment. By contrast, the situation must have been less difficult for boys, since their work often took them out of the household and their behavior generally was less restricted.

There are, moreover, direct intimations of generational conflict in the witchcraft records themselves. Consider a little speech flung out by one of the afflicted girls during a fit and meticulously taken down by Cotton Mather. The words are addressed to the "spectre" of a witch, with whom the girl has been having a heated argument:

> What's that? Must the younger Women, do yee say, hearken to the Elder? — They must be another Sort of Elder Women than You then! they must not bee Elder Witches, I am sure. Pray, do you for once Hearken to mee. — What a dreadful Sight are You! An Old Woman, an Old Servant of the Divel! [23]

Second, it seems notable that most witches were deviant persons — eccentric or conspicuously anti-social or both. This suggests very clearly the impact of witchcraft belief as a form of control in the social ordering of New England communities. Here indeed is one of the most widely found social functions of witchcraft; its importance has been documented for many societies all over the world.[24] The process operates in a fairly straightforward way on any individual who contemplates actions of which the community disapproves. He knows that if he goes ahead, he will make himself more vulnerable either to a direct attack by witchcraft or to the charge that he is himself a witch. Such knowledge is a powerful inducement to self-constraint.

What can be said of our third basic conclusion, that witchcraft charges particularly involved neighbors? Very briefly, it must be fitted with other aspects of the social setting in these early New England communities. That there was a great deal of contentiousness among these people is suggested by innumerable court cases from the period, dealing with disputes about land, lost cattle, trespass, debt, and so forth. Most men seem to have felt that the New World offered them a unique opportunity to increase their properties,[25] and this may have served to heighten competi-

---

[23] See Cotton Mather, A *Brand Pluck'd Out of the Burning*, in *Narratives*, ed. Burr, 270.

[24] See, for example, Whiting, *Paiute Sorcery*; Evans-Pritchard, *Witchcraft, Oracles, and Magic Among the Azande*, 117 ff.; and *Witchcraft and Sorcery in East Africa*, ed. Middleton and Winter.

[25] For material bearing on the growth of these acquisitive tendencies, see Philip J. Greven, Jr., "Old Patterns in the New World: The Distribution of Land in 17th Century Andover," *Essex Institute Historical Collections*, CI (April, 1965), 133–48; and John Demos, "Notes on Life in Plymouth Colony,"

tive feelings and pressures. On the other hand, cooperation was still the norm in many areas of life – not only in local government, but for a variety of agricultural tasks as well. In such ambivalent circumstances it is hardly surprising that relations between close neighbors were often tense or downright abrasive.

"In all the Witchcraft which now Grievously Vexes us, I know not whether any thing be more Unaccountable, than the Trick which the Witches have, to render themselves and their Tools Invisible." [26] Thus wrote Cotton Mather in 1692; and three centuries later it is still the "invisible" part of witchcraft that holds a special fascination. Time has greatly altered the language for such phenomena – "shapes" and "spectres" have become "hallucinations"; "enchantments" are now a form of "suggestion"; the Devil himself seems a fantasy – and there is a corresponding change of meanings. Yet here was something truly remarkable, a kind of irreducible core of the entire range of witchcraft phenomena. And how much of it remains "unaccountable"? To ask the question is to face directly the other side of our subject: witchcraft viewed as psychic process, as a function of "internal reality."

These phrases are obvious signposts on the road from history to psychology, and they suggest the need for another brief comment on method. Ordinarily, the biggest obstacles to a joining of history and psychology are practical ones, involving severe limitations of historical data. Yet for witchcraft the situation is, on just these grounds, uniquely promising. Even a casual look at writings like Cotton Mather's *Memorable Providences* or Samuel Willard's *A briefe account*,[27] discloses material so rich in psychological detail as to be nearly the equivalent of clinical case reports. The court records on witchcraft are also remarkably full in this respect. The clergy, the judges, all the leaders whose positions carried special responsibility for combatting witchcraft, regarded publicity as a most important weapon. Witchcraft would yield to careful study and the written exchange of information. Both Mather and Willard received "afflicted girls" into their own homes and recorded "possession" behavior over long periods of time.

Of course, a wealth of evidence does not by itself win the case for a

---

William and Mary Quarterly, 3d Ser., XXII (Apr. 1965), 264–86. It is possible that the voluntary mechanism of colonization had selected unusually aggressive and competitive persons at the outset.

[26] Cotton Mather, *The Wonders of the Invisible World*, in *Narratives*, ed. Burr, 246.

[27] Cotton Mather, *Memorable Providences*, in *Narratives*, ed. Burr, 93–143; Samuel Willard, *A briefe account of a strange & unusuall Providence of God befallen to Elizabeth Knap of Groton*, in Samuel A. Green, *Groton in the Witchcraft Times* (Groton, Mass., 1883), 7–21.

psychological approach to witchcraft. Further problems remain, problems of language, for example, and of validation.[28] There is, moreover, the very basic problem of selecting from among a variety of *different* theoretical models. Psychology is not a monolith, and every "psycho-historian" must declare a preference. In opting for psycho-analytic theory (as in the following pages), he performs, in part, an act of faith — faith that this theory provides deeper, fuller insights into human behavior than any other. In the long run the merit of such choices will probably be measured on pragmatic grounds. Does the interpretation "work"? Does it serve to explain materials which would otherwise lie inert? Is it consistent with different evidence in related subject-areas?

If, then, the proof lies in the doing, let us turn back to the New England witches and especially to their "Trick . . . to render themselves and their tools Invisible." What was the character of these spectral witches? What qualities were attributed to them by the culture at large? First and definitely foremost in the minds of most New Englanders was the idea that witches gave free rein to a whole gamut of hostile and aggressive feelings. In fact most witchcraft episodes began after some sort of actual quarrel. The fits of Mercy Short (reported by Cotton Mather) followed an abusive encounter with the convicted witch Sarah Good. The witch Glover was thought to have attacked Martha Goodwin after an argument about some missing clothes.[29] Many such examples could be accumulated here, but the central message seems immediately obvious: never antagonize witches, for they will invariably strike back hard. Their compulsion to attack was, of course, most dramatically visible in the fits experienced by some of their victims. These fits were treated as tortures imposed directly and in every detail, by witches or by the Devil himself. It is also significant that witches often assumed the shape of animals in order to carry out their attacks. Animals, presumably, are not subject to constraints of either an internal or external kind; their aggressive impulses are immediately translated into action.

Another important facet of the lives of witches was their activity in company with each other. In part, this consisted of long and earnest conferences on plans to overthrow the kingdom of God and replace it with the reign of the Devil. Often, however, these meetings merged with "feasts" — the witches' main form of self-indulgence. Details are a bit thin here, but it is clear that the focus was on eating and drinking. The usual beverage was wine or beer (occasionally described as bearing a sus-

---

[28] The best group of essays dealing with such issues is in *Psychoanalysis and History*, ed. Mazlish. See also the interesting statement in Alexander L. George and Juliette L. George, *Woodrow Wilson and Colonel House* (New York, 1964), v–xiv.

[29] See Cotton Mather, *A Brand Pluck'd Out of the Burning*, in *Narratives*, ed. Burr, 259–60, and *Memorable Providences*, *ibid.*, 100.

picious resemblance to blood); and the food was bread or meat. It is also worth noting what did *not* happen on these occasions. There were a few reports of dancing and "sport," but very little of the wild excitements associated with witch revels in continental Europe. Most striking of all is the absence of allusions to sex; there is no nakedness, no promiscuity, no obscene contact with the Devil. This seems to provide strong support for the general proposition that the psychological conflicts underlying the belief in witchcraft in early New England had much more to do with aggressive impulses than with libidinal ones.

The persons who acted as accusers also merit the closest possible attention, for the descriptions of what they suffered in their fits are perhaps the most revealing of all source materials for present purposes. They experienced, in the first place, severe pressures to go over to the Devil's side themselves. Witches approached them again and again, mixing threats and bribes in an effort to break down their Christian loyalties. Thus Elizabeth Knapp, bewitched at Groton, Massachusetts, in 1671, was alternately tortured and plied with offers of "money, silkes, fine cloaths, ease from labor"; in 1692 Ann Foster of Andover confessed to being won over by a general promise of "prosperity"; and in the same year Andrew Carrier accepted the lure of "a house and land in Andover." The same pattern appears most vividly in Cotton Mather's record of another of Mercy Short's confrontations with a spectral witch:

> "Fine promises!" she says, "You'l bestow an Husband upon mee, if I'l bee your Servant. An Husband! What? A Divel! I shall then bee finely fitted with an Husband: . . . Fine Clothes! What? Such as Your Friend Sarah Good had, who hardly had Rags to cover her! . . . Never Dy! What? Is my Life in Your Hands? No, if it had, You had killed mee long before this Time! — What's that? — So you can! — Do it then, if You can. Come, I dare you: Here, I challenge You to do it. Kill mee if you can." [30]

Some of these promises attributed to the Devil touch the most basic human concerns (such as death), and others reflect the special preoccupations of adolescent girls (such as future husbands). All of them imply a kind of covetousness generally consistent with the pattern of neighborhood conflict and tension mentioned earlier.

But the fits express other themes more powerfully still; and once again problems of aggression seem to occupy the central place. The seizures themselves have the essential character of attacks: in one sense, physical

---

[30] Willard, *A briefe account*, in *Groton in the Witchcraft Times*, ed. Green, 8; deposition by Ann Foster, case of Ann Foster, deposition by Andrew Carrier, case of Mary Lacy, Jr., in Works Progress Administration, *Salem Witchcraft, 1692*; Cotton Mather, *A Brand Pluck'd Out of the Burning*, in *Narratives*, ed. Burr, 269.

attacks by the witches on the persons of the accusers; and, in another sense, verbal attacks by the accusers on the reputations and indeed the very lives of the witches. This points directly toward one of the most important inner processes involved in the witchcraft, the process that psychologists call "projection" and define roughly as follows: "Projection is escape from repressed conflict by attributing . . . emotional drives to the external world." [31] In short, the dynamic core of belief in witchcraft in early New England was the difficulty experienced by many individuals in finding ways to handle their own aggressive impulses. Such impulses were not readily acceptable in terms of their culture and upbringing; but witchcraft accusations did provide one approved means of resolving the problem. Aggression was in this manner denied in the self and attributed directly to others. The accuser says, in effect, "I am not attacking you; you are attacking me!" In reality, however, the accuser *is* attacking the witch, and in an extremely dangerous fashion too. Thus witchcraft enables him to have it both ways: the impulse is denied and gratified at the same time.

And yet, too, the situation has another side, for the seizures of the afflicted children also permitted them to engage in a considerable amount of direct aggression. Of course, they were not held personally responsible; it was always the fault of the Devil at work inside them. Sometimes these impulses were aimed against the most important — and obvious — figures of authority. A child in a fit might act in a very disobedient way towards his parents, or revile the clergy who came to pray for his recovery.[32] The Reverend Willard of Groton, who ministered to Elizabeth Knapp during the time of her most severe fits, noted that the Devil "urged upon her constant temptations to murder her p'rents, her neighbors, our children . . . and even to make away with herselfe & once she was going to drowne herselfe in ye well." The attacking impulses were quite random here, so much so that even suicide seemed a possibility. Cotton Mather reports a slight variant on this type of behavior in connection with the fits of Martha Goodwin. She would, he writes, "fetch very terrible Blowes with her Fist, and Kicks with her Foot at the man that prayed; but still . . . her Fist and Foot would alwaies recoil, when they came within a few hairs breadths of him just as if Rebounding against a Wall." [33] This little paradigm of aggression attempted, and then at the last moment inhibited,

[31] This is the definition suggested by Clyde Kluckhohn in his own exemplary monograph, *Navajo Witchcraft*, 239, n. 37.

[32] See, for example, the descriptions of the Goodwin children during the time of their affliction, in Cotton Mather, *Memorable Providences*, in *Narratives*, ed. Burr, 109 ff., 119.

[33] Willard, *A briefe account*, in *Groton in the Witchcraft Times*, ed. Green, 9; Cotton Mather, *Memorable Providences*, in *Narratives*, ed. Burr, 108, 120.

expresses perfectly the severe inner conflict that many of these people were acting out.

One last, extremely pervasive theme in the witchcraft data is more difficult to handle without having direct recourse to clinical models; and the summary word for it is "orality." It is helpful to recall at this point the importance of "feasts" in the standard imaginary picture of the witches, but the experience of the accusers speaks even more powerfully to the same point. The evidence is of several kinds. First, the character of the "tortures" inflicted by the witches was most often described in terms of biting, pinching, pricking; and, in a psychiatric sense, these modes of attack all have an oral foundation. The pattern showed up with great vividness, for example, in the trial of George Burroughs:

> It was Remarkable that whereas Biting was one of the ways which the Witches used for the vexing of the Sufferers, when they cry'd out of G.B. biting them, the print of the Teeth would be seen on the Flesh of the Complainers, and just such a sett of Teeth as G.B.'s would then appear upon them, which could be distinguished from those of some other mens.[34]

Second, the accusers repeatedly charged that they could see the witches suckling certain animal "familiars." The following testimony by one of the Salem girls, in reference to an unidentified witch, was quite typical: "She had two little things like young cats and she put them to her brest and suckled them they had no hair on them and had ears like a man." People assumed that witches were specially equipped for these purposes and searched their bodies for the evidence. In 1656 the constable of Salisbury, New Hampshire, deposed in the case of Eunice Cole,

> That being about to stripp [her] to bee whipt (by the judgment of the Court att Salisbury) lookeing upon hir brests under one of hir brests (I thinke hir left brest) I saw a blew thing like unto a teate hanging downeward about three quarters of an inche longe not very thick, and haveing a great suspition in my mind about it (she being suspected for a witche) desiered the Court to sende some women to looke of it.

The court accepted this proposal and appointed a committee of three women to administer to Goodwife Cole the standard form of examination. Their report made no mention of a "teate" under her breast, but noted instead "a place in her leg which was proveable wher she Had bin sucktt by Imps or the like." The women also stated "thatt they Heard

[34] Cotton Mather, *Wonders of the Invisible World*, in *Narratives*, ed. Burr, 216–17.

the whining of puppies or such like under Her Coats as though they had a desire to sucke." [35]

[Third, many of the accusers underwent serious eating disturbances during and after their fits.] "Long fastings" were frequently imposed on them. Cotton Mather writes of one such episode in his account of the bewitching of Margaret Rule: "Tho she had a very eager Hunger upon her Stomach, yet if any refreshment were brought unto her, her teeth would be set, and she would be thrown into many Miseries." But also she would "sometimes have her Jaws forcibly pulled open, whereupon something invisible would be poured down her throat. . . . She cried out of it as of Scalding Brimstone poured into her." [36] These descriptions and others like them would repay a much more detailed analysis than can be offered here, but the general point should be obvious. Among all the zones of the body, the mouth seems to have been charged with a special kind of importance for victims of witchcraft.

In closing, it may be appropriate to offer a few suggestions of a more theoretical nature. The reason for doing so is to indicate both the way in which an interpretation of New England witchcraft might be attempted and t^he kind of conclusions one can hope to draw from the witchcraft materials about the culture at large. But this is meant only as the most tentative beginning of a new approach to such questions.

Consider, first, an interesting set of findings included by two anthropologists as part of a broad survey of child-rearing practices in over fifty cultures around the world. They report that witchcraft belief is powerfully correlated with the training a society imposes on young children in regard to the control of aggressive impulses.[37] That is, wherever this training is severe and restrictive, there is a strong likelihood that the culture will make much of witchcraft. [The correlation seems to suggest that aggression, if forcibly suppressed, will seek indirect outlets of the sort that witchcraft belief provides. Unfortunately, there is relatively little concrete evidence about child-rearing practices in early New England; but it seems at least consistent with what is known of Puritan culture generally to imagine that quite a harsh attitude would have been taken towards any substantial show of aggression in the young.[38]]

[35] Deposition by Susannah Sheldon, case of Philip English, in Works Progress Administration, *Salem Witchcraft, 1692*; manuscript deposition by Richard Ormsbey, case of Eunice Cole, in *Massachusetts Archives*, Vol. 135, 3; manuscript record, case of Eunice Cole, *ibid.*, 13.

[36] Cotton Mather, *Memorable Providences*, in *Narratives*, ed. Burr, 131.

[37] John W. M. Whiting and Irvin L. Child, *Child Training and Personality* (New Haven, 1953), Chap. 12.

[38] John Robinson, the pastor of the original "Pilgrim" congregation, wrote as follows in an essay "Children and Their Education": "Surely there is in all children . . . a stubbornness, and stoutness of mind arising from natural pride,

The concept of "projection" has been sufficiently discussed already; but now it may be useful to speak also of the allied notion of "displacement." Only very few cases of witchcraft accusations occurred between members of the same family. But, as noted previously, the typical pattern involved adolescent girls accusing middle-aged women. It seems plausible, at least from a clinical standpoint, to think that this pattern masked deep problems stemming ultimately from the relationship of mother and daughter. Perhaps, then, the afflicted girls were both projecting their aggression and diverting or "displacing" it from its real target. Considered from this perspective, displacement represents another form of avoidance or denial; and so the charges of the accusers may be seen as a kind of double defense against the actual conflicts.

But how to locate the *source* of these conflicts is a more difficult and frankly speculative kind of issue. Indeed it leads farther and farther from the usual canons of historical explanation; the proof, such as it is, must come by way of parallels to certain findings of recent psychological research and, above all, to a great mass of clinical data. More specifically, it is to psychoanalytic theory that one may turn for insights of an especially useful sort.

Actually, the historical record does provide one more strong clue with the prominence it gives to oral themes and anxieties. This suggests that the disturbances which culminated in charges of witchcraft must be traced to the earliest phase of personality development. It would be very convenient to have some shred of information to insert here about breast-feeding practices among the early New Englanders. Possibly their methods of weaning were highly traumatic; but hard evidence does not exist, and there is simply no way to be sure.[39] What does seem plausible — if,

---

which must be broken and beaten down. . . . Children should not know, if it could be kept from them, that they have a will in their own: neither should these words be heard from them, save by way of consent, 'I will' or 'I will not.' " Robinson, *Works* (Boston, 1851), I, 246–47. This point of view would not appear to leave much room for the free expression of aggressive impulses, but of course it tells us nothing certain about actual practice in Puritan families.

[39] However, we can determine with some confidence the usual time of weaning. Since lactation normally creates an impediment to a new conception, and since the average interval between births in New England families was approximately two years, it seems likely that most infants were weaned between the ages of twelve and fifteen months. The nursing process would therefore overlap the arrival of baby teeth (and accompanying biting wishes); and this might well give rise to considerable tension between mother and child. I have found only one direct reference to weaning in all the documentary evidence from seventeenth-century New England, an entry in the Journal of John Hull: "1659, 11th of 2d. My daughter Hannah was taken from her mother's breast, and through the favor of God, weaned without any trouble; only about fifteen days after, she did not eat her meat well." American Antiquarian Society, *Transactions*, III (Boston, 1857) 49. Hannah Hull was born on February 14, 1658, making her thirteen

once again, we accept the psychoanalytic model – is that many New England children were faced with some unspecified but extremely difficult psychic tasks in the first year or so of life. The outcome was that their aggressive drives were tied especially closely to the oral mode, and driven underground.[40] Then, years later, in accordance with changes normal for adolescence, instinctual energies of all types were greatly augmented; and this tended, as it so often does, to reactivate the earliest conflicts.[41] (The process is what Freud called, in a vivid phrase, "the return of the repressed.") But these conflicts were no easier to deal with in adolescence than they had been earlier; hence the need for the twin defenses of projection and displacement.[42]

One final problem must be recognized. The conflicts on which this discussion has focussed were, of course, most vividly expressed in the fits of the accusers. But the vast majority of people in early New England – subjected, one assumes, to roughly similar influences as children – managed to get through to adulthood without experiencing fits. Does this pose any serious difficulties for the above interpretations? The question can be argued to a negative conclusion, in at least two different but complementary ways. First, the materials on witchcraft, and in particular on the fits of the accusers, span a considerable length of time in New England's early history. When taken all together, they strongly suggest that aggression and orality were more or less constant themes in the pathology of the period. Second, even in the far less bizarre testimonies of the witnesses – that

---

months and four weeks on the day of the above entry. Was it perhaps unusual for Puritan infants to be "weaned without any trouble"? Also, does it not seem that in this case the process was quite abrupt – that is, accomplished entirely at one point in time? (Generally speaking, this is more traumatic for an infant than gradual weaning.) For a longer discussion of infancy in Puritan New England see John Demos, *A Little Commonwealth: Family-Life in Plymouth Colony* (New York, 1970), Chap. 8.

[40] I have found the work of Melanie Klein on the origins of psychic conflict in infancy to be particularly helpful. See *The Psycho-Analysis of Children* (London, 1932) and the papers collected in her *Contributions to Psycho-Analysis* (London, 1950). See also Joan Riviere, "On the Genesis of Psychical Conflict in Earliest Infancy," in Melanie Klein, *et al.*, *Developments in Psycho-Analysis* (London, 1952), 37–66.

[41] See Peter Blos, *On Adolescence* (New York, 1962). This (basically psychoanalytic) study provides a wealth of case materials and some very shrewd interpretations, which seem to bear strongly on certain of the phenomena connected with early New England witchcraft.

[42] It is no coincidence that projection was so important among the defenses employed by the afflicted girls in their efforts to combat their own aggressive drives. For projection is the earliest of all defenses, and indeed it takes shape under the influence of the oral phase. On this point see Sigmund Freud, "Negation," *The Standard Edition of Sigmund Freud*, ed. J. Strachey (London, 1960), XIX, 237, and Paula Heimann, "Certain Functions of Introjection and Projection in Early Infancy," Klein *et al.*, *Developments in Psycho-Analysis*, 122–68.

category which has been taken to represent the community at large — the same sort of focus appears. Above all, it is significant that the specific complaints of the accusers were so completely credible to so many others around them. The accusers, then, can be viewed as those individuals who were somehow especially sensitive to the problems created by their environment; they were the ones who were pushed over the line, so to speak, into serious illness. But their behavior clearly struck an answering chord in a much larger group of people. In this sense, nearly everyone in seventeenth-century New England was at some level an accuser.

POLITICS AND THE IMPERIAL RELATIONSHIP

II

Politics and
Social Structure
in Virginia

BERNARD BAILYN

Colonial political history has traditionally been studied from an institutional viewpoint. The powers of governors, the role of councils, and the rise of representative assemblies have preoccupied historians who assumed that colonial political systems were sufficient unto themselves, and that their development demonstrated the steady growth of democracy in America.

In the following essay, however, Bernard Bailyn defines "politics" very broadly. He argues that there existed in the seventeenth century a correspondence between state and society, and that there was, consequently, a virtual identity betweeen colonial political and social leadership. Bailyn accordingly surveys the history of politics in Virginia to show that patterns of leadership in the highest level of society changed several times in the course of the seventeenth century, and that, in response, the structure of politics also changed. He suggests that colonial Virginia's major political upheaval, Bacon's Rebellion, was in reality the birthpang of a new ruling elite, the climax to the emergence of a new social structure.

The factors that shape the contours of political life thus become, for Bailyn, family structure, provisions for the inheritance of wealth, and the labor system, rather than the prerogatives of the governor and the assembly's power of the purse.

By the end of the seventeenth century the American colonists faced an array of disturbing problems in the conduct of public affairs. Settlers from England and Holland, reconstructing familiar institutions on American shores, had become participants in what would appear to have been a wave of civil disobedience. Constituted authority was confronted with repeated challenges. Indeed, a veritable anarchy seems to have prevailed

Reprinted by permission from J. M. Smith, ed., *Seventeenth-Century America* (Chapel Hill; University of North Carolina Press for the Institute of Early American History and Culture, Williamsburg, Va., 1959), 90–115.

at the center of colonial society, erupting in a series of insurrections that began as early as 1635 with the "thrusting out" of Governor Harvey in Virginia. Culpeper's Rebellion in Carolina, the Protestant Association in Maryland, Bacon's Rebellion in Virginia, Leisler's seizure of power in New York, the resistance to and finally the overthrow of Andros in New England — every colony was affected.

These outbursts were not merely isolated local affairs. Although their immediate causes were rooted in the particular circumstances of the separate colonies, they nevertheless had common characteristics. They were, in fact, symptomatic of a profound disorganization of European society in its American setting. Seen in a broad view, they reveal a new configuration of forces which shaped the origins of American politics.

In a letter written from Virginia in 1632, George Sandys, the resident treasurer, reported despondently on the character and condition of the leading settlers. Some of the councilors were "no more then Ciphers," he wrote; others were "miserablie poore"; and the few substantial planters lived apart, taking no responsibility for public concerns. There was, in fact, among all those "worthie the mencioninge" only one person deserving of full approval. Lieutenant William Peirce "refuses no labour, nor sticks at anie expences that may aduantage the publique." Indeed, Sandys added, Peirce was "of a Capacitie that is not to bee expected in a man of his breedinge." [1]

The afterthought was penetrating. It cut below the usual complaints of the time that many of the settlers were lazy malcontents hardly to be preferred to the Italian glassworkers, than whom, Sandys wrote, "a more damned crew hell never vomited." [2] What lay behind Sandys' remark was not so much that wretched specimens were arriving in the shipments of servants nor even that the quality of public leadership was declining but that the social foundations of political power were being strangely altered.

All of the settlers in whatever colony presumed a fundamental relationship between social structure and political authority. Drawing on a common medieval heritage, continuing to conceive of society as a hierarchical unit, its parts justly and naturally separated into inferior and superior levels, they assumed that superiority was indivisible; there was not one hierarchy for political matters, another for social purposes. John Winthrop's famous explanation of God's intent that "in all times some must be rich some poore, some highe and eminent in power and dignitie;

[1] Sandys to John Ferrar, April 11, 1623, Susan M. Kingsbury, ed., *The Records of the Virginia Company of London* (4 vols.; Washington, D.C., 1906–35), IV, 110–11.
[2] Sandys to "Mr. Farrer," March 1622/23, *ibid.*, 23.

others meane and in subieccion" could not have been more carefully
worded. Riches, dignity, and power were properly placed in apposition;
they pertained to the same individuals.[3]

So closely related were social leadership and political leadership that
experience if not theory justified an identification between state and society. To the average English colonist the state was not an abstraction
existing above men's lives, justifying itself in its own terms, taking occasional human embodiment. However glorified in monarchy, the state in
ordinary form was indistinguishable from a more general social authority;
it was woven into the texture of everyday life. It was the same squire or
manorial lord who in his various capacities collated to the benefice, set
the rents, and enforced the statutes of Parliament and the royal decrees.
Nothing could have been more alien to the settlers than the idea that
competition for political leadership should be open to all levels of society
or that obscure social origins or technical skills should be considered valuable qualifications for office. The proper response to new technical demands on public servants was not to give power to the skilled but to give
skills to the powerful.[4] The English gentry and landed aristocracy remained politically adaptable and hence politically competent, assuming
when necessary new public functions, eliminating the need for a professional state bureaucracy. By their amateur competence they made possible a continuing identification between political and social authority.

In the first years of settlement no one had reason to expect that this
characteristic of public life would fail to transfer itself to the colonies.
For at least a decade and a half after its founding there had been in the
Jamestown settlement a small group of leaders drawn from the higher
echelons of English society. Besides well-born soldiers of fortune like
George Percy, son of the Earl of Northumberland, there were among
them four sons of the West family — children of Lord de la Warr and
his wife, a second cousin of Queen Elizabeth. In Virginia the West
brothers held appropriately high positions; three of them served as governors.[5] Christopher Davison, the colony's secretary, was the son of Queen
Elizabeth's secretary, William Davison, M.P. and Privy Councilor.[6] The
troublesome John Martin, of Martin's Brandon, was the son of Sir

[3] John Winthrop, "Modell of Christian Charity," *Winthrop Papers* (5 vols.;
Boston, 1929–47), II, 282.

[4] Cf. J. H. Hexter, "The Education of the Aristocracy in the Renaissance,"
Jour. of Modern Hist., 22 (1950), 1–20.

[5] *Dictionary of National Biography*, 1908–9 edn. (New York), XV, 836–37;
Annie L. Jester and Martha W. Hiden, comps. and eds., *Adventurers of Purse
and Person: Virginia 1607–1625* ([Princeton, N.J.], 1956), 349–50.

[6] *D.N.B.*, V, 632; Richard B. Davis, *George Sandys: Poet-Adventurer* (London,
1955), 112–13n.

Richard Martin, twice Lord Mayor of London, and also the brother-in-law of Sir Julius Caesar, Master of the Rolls and Privy Councilor.[7] Sir Francis and Haute Wyatt were sons of substantial Kent gentry and grandsons of the Sir Thomas Wyatt who led the rebellion of 1554 against Queen Mary.[8] George Sandys' father was the Archbishop of York; of his three older brothers, all knights and M.P.'s, two were eminent country gentlemen, and the third, Edwin, of Virginia Company fame, was a man of great influence in the city.[9] George Thorpe was a former M.P. and Gentleman of the Privy Chamber.[10]

More impressive than such positions and relationships was the cultural level represented. For until the very end of the Company period, Virginia remained to the literary and scientific an exotic attraction, its settlement an important moment in Christian history.[11] Its original magnetism for those in touch with intellectual currents affected the early immigration. Of the twenty councilors of 1621, eight had been educated at Oxford, Cambridge, or the Inns of Court. Davison, like Martin trained in the law, was a poet in a family of poets. Thorpe was a "student of Indian views on religion and astronomy." Francis Wyatt wrote verses and was something of a student of political theory. Alexander Whitaker, M.A., author of *Good Newes from Virginia*, was the worthy heir "of a good part of the learning of his renowned father," the master of St. John's College and Regius Professor of Divinity at Cambridge. John Pory, known to history mainly as the speaker of the first representative assembly in America, was a Master of Arts, "protege and disciple of Hakluyt," diplomat, scholar, and traveler, whose writings from and about America have a rightful place in literary history. Above all there was George Sandys, "poet, traveller, and scholar," a member of Lord Falkland's literary circle; while in Jamestown he continued as a matter of course to work on his notable translation of Ovid's *Metamorphoses*.[12]

There was, in other words, during the first years of settlement a direct transference to Virginia of the upper levels of the English social hierarchy as well as of the lower. If the great majority of the settlers were recruited from the yeoman class and below, there was nevertheless a reason-

[7] Alexander Brown, *Genesis of the United States* (Boston, 1890), II, 943–44.
[8] Jester and Hiden, comps., *Adventurers*, 372; *D.N.B.*, XXI, 1092–93, 1102–4.
[9] Davis, *Sandys*, Chap. I.
[10] Brown, *Genesis*, II, 1031.
[11] Perry Miller, *Errand into the Wilderness* (Cambridge, Mass., 1956), 99–140; Howard Mumford Jones, *The Literature of Virginia in the Seventeenth Century* (*Memoirs of the American Academy of Arts and Sciences*, XIX, Part 2, Boston, 1946), 3–7.
[12] Davis, *Sandys*, especially 190–92; Harry C. Porter, "Alexander Whitaker," *Wm. and Mary Qtly.*, 3rd ser., 14 (1957), 336; Jones, *Literature of Virginia*, 14n, 5–6, 26–28.

able representation from those upper groups acknowledged to be the rightful rulers of society.

It is a fact of some importance, however, that this governing elite did not survive a single generation, at least in its original form. By the thirties their number had declined to insignificance. Percy, for example, left in 1612. Whitaker drowned in 1617. Sandys and Francis Wyatt arrived only in 1621, but their enthusiasm cooled quickly; they were both gone by 1626. Of the Wests, only John was alive and resident in the colony a decade after the collapse of the Company. Davison, who returned to England in 1622 after only a year's stay, was sent back in 1623 but died within a year of his return. Thorpe was one of the six councilors slain in the massacre of 1622. Pory left for England in 1622; his return as investigating commissioner in 1624 was temporary, lasting only a few months. And the cantankerous Martin graced the Virginia scene by his absence after 1625; he is last heard from in the early 1630's petitioning for release from a London debtor's prison.[13]

To be sure, a few representatives of important English families, like John West and Edmund Scarborough, remained. There were also one or two additions from the same social level.[14] But there were few indeed of such individuals, and the basis of their authority had changed. The group of gentlemen and illuminati that had dominated the scene during the Company era had been dispersed. Their disappearance created a political void which was filled soon enough, but from a different area of recruitment, from below, from the toughest and most fortunate of the surviving planters whose eminence by the end of the thirties had very little to do with the transplantation of social status.[15]

[13] Davis, *Sandys*, 195–97, 112–13n; Jester and Hiden, comps., *Adventurers*, 350–51; Brown, *Genesis*, II, 1031, 970; *Va. Mag. of Hist. and Biog.*, 54 (1946), 60–61; Jones, *Literature of Virginia*, 14n.

[14] Scarborough was a well-educated younger son of an armigerous Norfolk family. Among the additions were Charles Harmar (who died in 1640), nephew of the warden of Winchester College and brother of the Greek Reader, later the Greek Professor, at Oxford; and Nathaniel Littleton, whose father was Chief Justice of North Wales, two of whose brothers were Fellows of All Souls and a third Chief Justice of Common Pleas and Lord Keeper of the Great Seal. Susie M. Ames, ed., *County Court Records of Accomack-Northampton, Virginia, 1632–1640* (Washington, D.C., 1954), xxvii, xxix–xxx, xxxv.

[15] The difficulty of maintaining in Virginia the traditional relationship between social and political authority became in 1620 the basis of an attack by a group of "ancient planters," including Francis West, on the newly appointed governor, Sir George Yeardley. Although Yeardley had been knighted two years earlier in an effort to enhance his personal authority, the petitioners argued that his lack of eminence was discouraging settlement. "Great Actions," they wrote, "are carryed wth best successe by such Comanders who haue personall Aucthoritye & greatness answerable to the Action, Sithence itt is nott easye to swaye a vulgar and seruile Nature by vulgar & seruile Spiritts." Leadership should devolve on commanders

The position of the new leaders rested on their ability to wring material gain from the wilderness. Some, like Samuel Mathews, started with large initial advantages,[16] but more typical were George Menefie and John Utie, who began as independent landowners by right of transporting themselves and only one or two servants. Abraham Wood, famous for his explorations and like Menefie and Utie the future possessor of large estates and important offices, appears first as a servant boy on Mathews' plantation. Adam Thoroughgood, the son of a country vicar, also started in Virginia as a servant, aged fourteen. William Spencer is first recorded as a yeoman farmer without servants.[17]

Such men as these — Spencer, Wood, Menefie, Utie, Mathews — were the most important figures in Virginia politics up to the Restoration, engrossing large tracts of land, dominating the Council, unseating Sir John Harvey from the governorship. But in no traditional sense were they a ruling class. They lacked the attributes of social authority, and their political dominance was a continuous achievement. Only with the greatest difficulty, if at all, could distinction be expressed in a genteel style of life, for existence in this generation was necessarily crude. Mathews may have created a flourishing estate and Menefie had splendid fruit gardens, but the great tracts of land such men claimed were almost entirely raw wilderness. They had risen to their positions, with few exceptions, by brute labor and shrewd manipulation; they had personally shared the burdens of settlement. They succeeded not because of, but despite, whatever gentility they may have had. William Claiborne may have been educated at the Middle Temple; Peirce could not sign his name; but what counted was their common capacity to survive and flourish in frontier settlements.[18] They

---

whose "Eminence or Nobillitye" is such that "euerye man subordinate is ready to yeild a willing submission wthowt contempt or repyning." The ordinary settlers, they said, would not obey the same authority "conferrd vpon a meane man . . . no bettar than selected owt of their owne Ranke." If, therefore, the Company hoped to attract and hold colonists, especially of "the bettar sorte," it should select as leaders in Virginia "some eythar Noble or little lesse in Honor or Dower . . . to maintayne & hold vp the dignitye of so Great and good a cawse." Kingsbury, ed., *Records of the Virginia Company,* III, 231–32.

16 For Mathews' twenty-three servants and his "Denbigh" plantation, described in 1649 as a self-sufficient village, see John C. Hotten, ed., *Original List of Persons of Quality* . . . (London, 1874), 233–34; Jester and Hiden, comps., *Adventurers,* 244–45; *A Perfect Description of Virginia* . . . , in Peter Force, comp., *Tracts and Other Papers Relating Principally to the Origin, Settlement, and Progress of the Colonies in North America* (4 vols., Washington, D.C., 1836–46), II, no. 8. 14–15.

17 Jester and Hiden, comps., *Adventurers,* 248–49, 321, 329, 339–40; Hotten, ed., *Persons of Quality,* 226, 237, 233, 253, 228; Clarence W. Alvord and Lee Bidgood, *The First Explorations of the Trans-Alleghany Region* . . . *1650–1674* (Cleveland, 1912), 34 ff.

18 *Wm. and Mary Qtly.,* 2nd ser., 19 (1939), 475n; Davis, *Sandys,* 158n.

were tough, unsentimental, quick-tempered, crudely ambitious men concerned with profits and increased landholdings, not the grace of life.
They roared curses, drank exuberantly, and gambled (at least according
to deVries) for their servants when other commodities were lacking.[19]
If the worst of Governor Harvey's offenses had been to knock out the
teeth of an offending councilor with a cudgel, as he did on one occasion,
no one would have questioned his right to the governorship.[20] Rank had
its privileges, and these men were the first to claim them, but rank itself
was unstable and the lines of class or status were fluid. There was no
insulation for even the most elevated from the rude impact of frontier
life.

As in style of life so in politics, these leaders of the first permanently
settled generation did not re-create the characteristics of a stable gentry.
They had had little opportunity to acquire the sense of public responsibility that rests on deep identification with the land and its people. They
performed in some manner the duties expected of leaders, but often public office was found simply burdensome. Reports such as Sandys' that
Yeardley, the councilor and former governor, was wholly absorbed in his
private affairs and scarcely glanced at public matters and that Mathews
"will rather hazard the payment of fforfeitures then performe our Injunctions" were echoed by Harvey throughout his tenure of office. Charles
Harmar, justice of the peace on the Eastern Shore, attended the court
once in eight years, and Claiborne's record was only slightly better. Attendance to public duties had to be specifically enjoined, and privileges
were of necessity accorded provincial officeholders. The members of the
Council were particularly favored by the gift of tax exemption.[21]

The private interests of this group, which had assumed control of
public office by virtue not of inherited status but of newly achieved and
strenuously maintained economic eminence, were pursued with little in-

[19] Ames, ed., *Accomack-Northampton Recs.*, xxxiv, xxxix–xl; Susie M. Ames,
Studies of the Virginia Eastern Shore in the Seventeenth Century (Richmond,
Va., 1940), 181, 183. DeVries wrote of his astonishment at seeing servants
gambled away: "I told them that I had never seen such work in Turk or Bar-
barian, and that it was not becoming Christians." David P. deVries., *Short Historical . . . Notes of several Voyages . . .* (Hoorn, 1655), reprinted in the
New York Hist. Soc., *Collections*, 2nd ser., 3 (1857), 36, 125.

[20] Harvey readily confessed to the deed, offering as an official justification the
fact that it had all taken place outside the Council chamber, and anyhow the
fellow had "assailed him with ill language." *The Aspinwall Papers*, Mass. Hist.
Soc., *Collections*, 4th ser., 9 (1871), 133n.

[21] Kingsbury, ed., *Records of the Virginia Company*, IV, 110–11; *Va. Mag. of
Hist. and Biog.*, 8 (1900–1), 30; Ames, ed., *Accomack-Northampton Recs.*, xxv,
xxix; William W. Hening, ed., *The Statutes-at-Large . . . of Virginia* (1619–
1792) (New York, 1823), I, 350, 454; Philip A. Bruce, *Institutional History of
Virginia in the Seventeenth Century* (2 vols.; New York, 1910), II, Chaps. XV,
XXIX.

terference from the traditional restraints imposed on a responsible ruling class. Engaged in an effort to establish themselves in the land, they sought as specific ends: autonomous local jurisdiction, an aggressive expansion of settlement and trading enterprises, unrestricted access to land, and, at every stage, the legal endorsement of acquisitions. Most of the major public events for thirty years after the dissolution of the Company — and especially the overthrow of Harvey — were incidents in the pursuit of these goals.

From his first appearance in Virginia, Sir John Harvey threatened the interests of this emerging planter group. While still in England he had identified himself with the faction that had successfully sought the collapse of the Company, and thus his mere presence in Virginia was a threat to the legal basis of land grants made under the Company's charter. His demands for the return as public property of goods that had once belonged to the Company specifically jeopardized the planters' holdings. His insistence that the governorship was more than a mere chairmanship of the Council tended to undermine local autonomy. His conservative Indian policy not only weakened the settlers' hand in what already seemed an irreconcilable enmity with the natives but also restricted the expansion of settlement. His opposition to Claiborne's claim to Kent Island threatened to kill off the lucrative Chesapeake Bay trade, and his attempt to ban the Dutch ships from the colony endangered commerce more generally. His support of the official policy of economic diversification, together with his endorsement of the English schemes of tobacco monopoly, alienated him finally and completely from the Council group.[22]

Within a few months of his assuming the governorship, Harvey wrote home with indignation of the "waywardness and oppositions" of the councilors and condemned them for factiously seeking "rather for their owne endes then either seekinge the generall good or doinge right to particular men." Before a year was out the antagonisms had become so intense that a formal peace treaty had to be drawn up between Harvey and the Council. But both sides were adamant, and conflict was inescapable. It exploded in 1635 amid comic opera scenes of "extreame coller and passion" complete with dark references to Richard the Third and musketeers "running with their peices presented." The conclusion was Harvey's enraged arrest of George Menefie "of suspicion of Treason to his Majestie"; Utie's response, "And wee the like to you sir"; and the governor's forced return to England.[23]

Behind these richly heroic "passings and repassings to and fro" lies not

[22] The charges and countercharges are summarized, together with supporting documents, in the profuse footnotes of *Aspinwall Papers*, 131–52.

[23] *Va. Mag. of Hist. and Biog.*, 8 (1900–1), 30, 43–45; I (1893–94), 418, 419, 427, 420.

a victory of democracy or representative institutions or anything of the sort. Democracy, in fact, was identified in the Virginians' minds with the "popular and tumultuary government" that had prevailed in the old Company's quarter courts, and they wanted none of it; the Assembly as a representative institution was neither greatly sought after nor hotly resisted.[24] The victory of 1635 was that of resolute leaders of settlement stubbornly fighting for individual establishment. With the reappointment of Sir Francis Wyatt as governor, their victory was assured and in the Commonwealth period it was completely realized. By 1658, when Mathews was elected governor, effective interference from outside had disappeared and the supreme authority had been assumed by an Assembly which was in effect a league of local magnates secure in their control of county institutions.[25]

One might at that point have projected the situation forward into a picture of dominant county families dating from the 1620's and 1630's, growing in identification with the land and people, ruling with increasing responsibility from increasingly eminent positions. But such a projection would be false. The fact is that with a few notable exceptions like the Scarboroughs and the Wormeleys, these struggling planters of the first generation failed to perpetuate their leadership into the second generation. Such families as the Woods, the Uties, the Mathews, and the Peirces faded from dominant positions of authority after the deaths of their founders. To some extent this was the result of the general insecurity of life that created odds against the physical survival in the male line of any given family. But even if male heirs had remained in these families after the death of the first generation, undisputed eminence would not. For a new emigration had begun in the forties, continuing for close to thirty years, from which was drawn a new ruling group that had greater possibilities for permanent dominance than Harvey's opponents had had. These newcomers absorbed and subordinated the older group, forming the basis of the most celebrated oligarchy in American history.

Most of Virginia's great eighteenth-century names, such as Bland, Burwell, Byrd, Carter, Digges, Ludwell, and Mason, appear in the colony for the first time within ten years either side of 1655. These progenitors of the eighteenth-century aristocracy arrived in remarkably similar cir-

---

[24] *Ibid.*, I (1893–94), 418; Hening, ed., *Va. Stat. at L.*, I, 232–33. For a balanced statement of the importance attached by contemporaries to Virginia's representative Assembly, see Wesley Frank Craven, *Dissolution of the Virginia Company* (New York, 1932), 71 ff., 330 ff. Cf. Charles M. Andrews, *The Colonial Period of American History* (4 vols.; New Haven, Conn., 1934–38), I, 181 ff., and Davis, " 'Liberalism' in the Virginia Company and Colony," *Sandys*, Appendix G.

[25] Wesley Frank Craven, *The Southern Colonies in the Seventeenth Century, 1607–1689* (Baton Rouge, La., 1949), 288–94.

cumstances. The most important of these immigrants were younger sons of substantial families well connected in London business and governmental circles and long associated with Virginia; family claims to land in the colony or inherited shares of the original Company stock were now brought forward as a basis for establishment in the New World.

Thus the Bland family interests in Virginia date from a 1618 investment in the Virginia Company by the London merchant John Bland, supplemented in 1622 by another in Martin's Hundred. The merchant never touched foot in America, but three of his sons did come to Virginia in the forties and fifties to exploit these investments. The Burwell fortunes derive from the early subscription to the Company of Edward Burwell, which was inherited in the late forties by his son, Lewis I. The first William Byrd arrived about 1670 to assume the Virginia properties of his mother's family, the Steggs, which dated back to the early days of the Company. The Digges's interests in Virginia stem from the original investments of Sir Dudley Digges and two of his sons in the Company, but it was a third son, Edward, who emigrated in 1650 and established the American branch of the family. Similarly, the Masons had been financially interested in Virginia thirty-two years before 1652, when the first immigrant of that family appeared in the colony. The Culpeper clan, whose private affairs enclose much of the history of the South in the second half of the seventeenth century, was first represented in Virginia by Thomas Culpeper, who arrived in 1649; but the family interests in Virginia had been established a full generation earlier. Thomas' father, uncle, and cousin had all been members of the original Virginia Company and their shares had descended in the family. Even Governor Berkeley fits the pattern. There is no mystery about his sudden exchange in 1642 of the life of a dilettante courtier for that of a colonial administrator and estate manager. He was a younger son without prospects, and his family's interests in Virginia, dating from investments in the Company made twenty years earlier, as well as his appointment held out the promise of an independent establishment in America.[26]

Claims on the colony such as these were only one, though the most important, of a variety of forms of capital that might provide the basis for secure family fortunes. One might simply bring over enough of a merchant family's resources to begin immediately building up an imposing

---

[26] Nell M. Nugent, *Cavaliers and Pioneers* (Richmond, Va., 1934), I, 160; Jester and Hiden, comps., *Adventurers*, 97, 108, 154–55, 288; Louis B. Wright, *The First Gentlemen of Virginia* (San Marino, Calif., 1940), 312–13; *Va. Mag. of Hist. and Biog.*, 35 (1927), 227–28; Helen Hill, *George Mason, Constitutionalist* (Cambridge, Mass., 1938), 3–4; Fairfax Harrison, "A Key Chart of the . . . Culpepers . . . ," *Va. Mag. of Hist. and Biog.*, 33 (1925), f. 113, 339, 344; *D.N.B.*, II, 368; Kingsbury, ed., *Records of the Virginia Company*, II, 75, 90, 391.

estate, as, presumably, did that ambitious draper's son, William Fitzhugh. The benefits that accrued from such advantages were quickly translated into landholdings in the development of which these settlers were favored by the chronology of their arrival. For though they extended the area of cultivation in developing their landholdings, they were not obliged to initiate settlement. They fell heirs to large areas of the tidewater region that had already been brought under cultivation. "Westover" was not the creation of William Byrd; it had originally been part of the De la Warr estate, passing, with improvements, to Captain Thomas Pawlett, thence to Theodorick Bland, and finally to Byrd. Lewis Burwell inherited not only his father's land, but also the developed estate of his stepfather, Wingate. Some of the Carters' lands may be traced back through John Utie to a John Jefferson, who left Virginia as early as 1628. Abraham Wood's entire Fort Henry property ended in the hands of the Jones family. The Blands' estate in Charles City County, which later became the Harrisons' "Berkeley" plantation, was cleared for settlement in 1619 by servants of the "particular" plantation of Berkeley's Hundred.[27]

Favored thus by circumstance, a small group within the second generation migration moved toward setting itself off in a permanent way as a ruling landed gentry. That they succeeded was due not only to their material advantages but also to the force of their motivation. For these individuals were in social origins just close enough to establishment in gentility to feel the pangs of deprivation most acutely. It is not the totally but the partially dispossessed who build up the most propulsive aspirations, and behind the zestful lunging at propriety and status of a William Fitzhugh lay not the narcotic yearnings of the disinherited but the pent-up ambitions of the gentleman manqué. These were neither hard-handed pioneers nor dilettante romantics, but ambitious younger sons of middle-class families who knew well enough what gentility was and sought it as specific objective.[28]

The establishment of this group was rapid. Within a decade of their arrival they could claim, together with a fortunate few of the first generation, a marked social eminence and full political authority at the county level. But their rise was not uniform. Indeed, by the seventies a new circumstance had introduced an effective principle of social differentiation among the colony's leaders. A hierarchy of position within the newly risen gentry was created by the Restoration government's efforts to extend its control more effectively over its mercantile empire. Demanding of its colonial executives and their advisors closer supervision over the external aspects of the economy, it offered a measure of patronage necessary for

[27] Wright, *First Gentlemen*, 155 ff.; Jester and Hiden, comps., *Adventurers*, 98, 108, 339–41, 363–64, 97, 99.

[28] Fitzhugh's letters, scattered through the *Va. Mag. of Hist. and Biog.*, I–VI, cannot be equalled as sources for the motivation of this group.

enforcement. Public offices dealing with matters that profoundly affected the basis of economic life — tax collection, customs regulation, and the bestowal of land grants — fell within the gift of the governor and tended to form an inner circle of privilege. One can note in Berkeley's administration the growing importance of this barrier of officialdom. Around its privileges there formed the "Green Spring" faction, named after Berkeley's plantation near Jamestown, a group bound to the governor not by royalist sympathies so much as by ties of kinship and patronage.

Thus Colonel Henry Norwood, related to Berkeley by a "near affinity in blood," was given the treasurership of the colony in 1650, which he held for more than two decades. During this time Thomas Ludwell, a cousin and Somerset neighbor of the governor, was secretary of state, in which post he was succeeded in 1678 by his brother Philip, who shortly thereafter married Berkeley's widow. This Lady Berkeley, it should be noted, was the daughter of Thomas Culpeper, the immigrant of 1649 and a cousin of Thomas Lord Culpeper who became governor in 1680. Immediately after her marriage to Berkeley, her brother Alexander requested and received from the governor the nomination to the surveyor-generalship of Virginia, a post he filled for twenty-three years while resident in England, appointing as successive deputies the brothers Ludwell, to whom by 1680 he was twice related by marriage. Lady Berkeley was also related through her mother to William Byrd's wife, a fact that explains much about Byrd's prolific office-holding.[29]

[29] Colonel [Henry] Norwood, A *Voyage to Virginia* (1649), in Force, ed., *Tracts*, III, 49, 50; *Va. Mag. of Hist. and Biog.*, 33 (1925), 5, 8; Harrison, "Key Chart," *ibid.*, 351–55, 348; *Wm. and Mary Qtly.*, 1st ser., 19 (1910–11), 209–10. It was after Culpeper's appointment to the governorship that Byrd was elevated to the Council and acquired the auditor- and receiver-generalships. William G. and Mary N. Stanard, comps., *The Colonial Virginia Register* (Albany, N.Y., 1902), 22–23.

The Berkeley-Norwood connection may be followed out in other directions. Thus the Colonel Francis Moryson mentioned by Norwood as his friend and traveling companion and whom he introduced to the governor was given command of the fort at Point Comfort upon his arrival in 1649, replacing his brother, Major Richard Moryson, whose son Charles was given the same post in the 1660's. Francis, who found the command of the fort "profitable to him," was elevated by Berkeley to the Council and temporarily to the deputy-governorship, "wherein he got a competent estate"; he finally returned to England in the position of colony agent. Norwood, *Voyage*, 50; *Va. Mag. of Hist. and Biog.*, 9 (1900–1), 122–23; Ella Lonn, *The Colonial Agents of the Southern Colonies* (Chapel Hill, 1945), 21 ff.

The inner kinship core of the group enclosed the major provincial positions mentioned above. But the wider reaches of the clique extended over the Council, the collectorships, and the naval offices as well as mnior positions within the influence of the governor. On these posts and their holders, see Stanard and Stanard, comps., *Va. Register*, 38–40; Bruce, *Institutional History*, II, Chaps. XXXVIII–XLII. On the limitations of the gubernatorial influence after 1660, see Craven, *Southern Colonies*, 293.

The growing distinctiveness of provincial officialdom within the landed gentry may also be traced in the transformation of the Council. Originally, this body had been expected to comprise the entire effective government, central and local; councilors were to serve, individually or in committees, as local magistrates. But the spread of settlement upset this expectation, and at the same time as the local offices were falling into the hands of autonomous local powers representing leading county families, the Council, appointed by the governor and hence associated with official patronage, increasingly realized the separate, lucrative privileges available to it.[30]

As the distinction between local and central authority became clear, the county magistrates sought their own distinct voice in the management of the colony, and they found it in developing the possibilities of burgess representation. In the beginning there was no House of Burgesses; representation from the burghs and hundreds was conceived of not as a branch of government separate from the Council but as a periodic supplement to it.[31] Until the fifties the burgesses, meeting in the Assemblies with the councilors, felt little need to form themselves into a separate house, for until that decade there was little evidence of a conflict of interests between the two groups. But when, after the Restoration, the privileged status of the Council became unmistakable and the county magnates found control of the increasingly important provincial administration preempted by this body, the burgess part of the Assembly took on a new meaning in contrast to that of the Council. Burgess representation now became vital to the county leaders if they were to share in any consistent way in affairs larger than those of the counties. They looked to the franchise, hitherto broad not by design but by neglect, introducing qualifications that would ensure their control of the Assembly. Their interest in provincial government could no longer be expressed in the conglomerate Assembly, and at least by 1663 the House of Burgesses began to meet separately as a distinct body voicing interests potentially in conflict with those of the Council.[32]

Thus by the eighth decade the ruling class in Virginia was broadly based on leading county families and dominated at the provincial level by a privileged officialdom. But this social and political structure was too new, too lacking in the sanctions of time and custom, its leaders too close to humbler origins and as yet too undistinguished in style of life, to be accepted without a struggle. A period of adjustment was necessary, of which Bacon's Rebellion was the climactic episode.

Bacon's Rebellion began as an unauthorized frontier war against the

[30] Craven, *Southern Colonies*, 167–69; 270, 288; Bruce, *Institutional History*, II, Chap. XV.

[31] For the Assembly as "the other Counsell," see the "Ordinance and Constitution" of 1621 in Kingsbury, ed., *Records of the Virginia Company*, III, 483–84.

[32] Andrews, *Colonial Period*, I, 184–85; Craven, *Southern Colonies*, 289 ff.

Indians and ended as an upheaval that threatened the entire basis of social and political authority. Its immediate causes have to do with race relations and settlement policy, but behind these issues lay deeper elements related to resistance against the maturing shape of a new social order. These elements explain the dimensions the conflict reached.

There was, first, resistance by substantial planters to the privileges and policies of the inner provincial clique led by Berkeley and composed of those directly dependent on his patronage. These dissidents, among whom were the leaders of the Rebellion, represented neither the downtrodden masses nor a principle of opposition to privilege as such. Their discontent stemmed to a large extent from their own exclusion from privileges they sought. Most often their grievances were based on personal rebuffs they had received as they reached for entry into provincial officialdom. Thus — to speak of the leaders of the Rebellion — Giles Bland arrived in Virginia in 1671 to take over the agency of his late uncle in the management of his father's extensive landholdings, assuming at the same time the lucrative position of customs collector which he had obtained in London. But, amid angry cries of *"pittyfull fellow, puppy* and *Sonn of a Whore,"* he fell out first with Berkeley's cousin and favorite, Thomas Ludwell, and finally with the governor himself; for his "Barbarous and Insolent Behaviors" Bland was fined, arrested, and finally removed from the collectorship.[33] Of the two "chiefe Incendiarys," William Drummond and Richard Lawrence, the former had been quarreling with Berkeley since 1664, first over land claims in Carolina, then over a contract for building a fort near James City, and repeatedly over lesser issues in the General Court; Lawrence "some Years before . . . had been partially treated at Law, for a considerable Estate on behalfe of a Corrupt favorite." Giles Brent, for his depredations against the Indians in violation of official policy, had not only been severely fined but barred from public office.[34] Bacon himself could not have appeared under more favorable circumstances. A cousin both of Lady Berkeley and of the councilor Nathaniel Bacon, Sr., and by general agreement "a Gent:man of a Liberall education" if of a somewhat tarnished reputation, he had quickly staked out land for himself and had been elevated, for reasons "best known to the Governour," to the Council. But being "of a most imperious and dangerous hidden Pride of heart . . . very ambitious and arrogant," he wanted more, and quickly. His alienation from and violent opposition

[33] Jester and Hiden, comps., *Adventurers,* 98–99; R. H. McIlwaine, ed., *Minutes of the Council and General Court . . . 1622–1632, 1670–1676* (Richmond, Va., 1924), 399, 423.

[34] Charles M. Andrews, ed., *Narratives of the Insurrections, 1675–1690* (New York, 1915), 96, 27; Wilcomb E. Washburn, "The Humble Petition of Sarah Drummond," *Wm. and Mary Qtly.,* 3rd ser., 13 (1956), 368–69; H. R. McIlwaine, ed., *Journals of the House of Burgesses of Virginia 1659/60–1693* (Richmond, Va., 1914), 14.

to Berkeley were wound in among the animosities created by the Indian problem and were further complicated by his own unstable personality; they were related also to the fact that Berkeley finally turned down the secret offer Bacon and Byrd made in 1675 for the purchase from the governor of a monopoly of the Indian trade.[35]

These specific disputes have a more general aspect. It was three decades since Berkeley had assumed the governorship and begun rallying a favored group, and it was over a decade since the Restoration had given this group unconfined sway over the provincial government. In those years much of the choice tidewater land as well as the choice offices had been spoken for, and the tendency of the highly placed was to hold firm. Berkeley's Indian policy — one of stabilizing the borders between Indians and whites and protecting the natives from depredation by land-hungry settlers — although a sincere attempt to deal with an extremely difficult problem, was also conservative, favoring the established. Newcomers like Bacon and Bland and particularly landholders on the frontiers felt victimized by a stabilization of the situation or by a controlled expansion that maintained on an extended basis the existing power structure. They were logically drawn to aggressive positions. In an atmosphere charged with violence, their interests constituted a challenge to provincial authority. Bacon's primary appeal in his "Manifesto" played up the threat of this challenge:

> Let us trace these men in Authority and Favour to whose hands the dispensation of the Countries wealth has been commited; let us observe the sudden Rise of their Estates [compared] with the Quality in wch they first entered this Country. . . . And lett us see wither their extractions and Education have not bin vile, And by what pretence of learning and vertue they could [enter] soe soon into Imployments of so great Trust and consequence, let us . . . see what spounges have suckt up the Publique Treasure and wither it hath not bin privately contrived away by unworthy Favourites and juggling Parasites whose tottering Fortunes have bin repaired and supported at the Publique chardg.

Such a threat to the basis of authority was not lost on Berkeley or his followers. Bacon's merits, a contemporary wrote, "thretned an eclips to there riseing gloryes. . . . (if he should continue in the Governours

[35] Wilcomb E. Washburn, *The Governor and the Rebel, A History of Bacon's Rebellion in Virginia* (Chapel Hill, 1957), 17–19; Andrews, ed., *Narratives*, 74, 110. For the offer to buy the monopoly and Berkeley's initial interest in it, see Bacon to Berkeley, September 18, 1675, and William and Frances Berkeley to Bacon, September 21, 1675, Coventry Papers, Longleat Library of the Marquises of Bath, LXXVII, 6, 8 (microfilm copy, Library of Congress); for the refusal, see *Aspinwall Papers*, 166. Mr. Washburn, who first called attention to these Bacon letters at Longleat, is editing them for publication by the Virginia Historical Society.

favour) of Seniours they might becom juniours, while there younger Brother . . . might steale away that blessing, which they accounted there owne by birthright." [36]

But these challengers were themselves challenged, for another main element in the upheaval was the discontent among the ordinary settlers at the local privileges of the same newly risen county magnates who assailed the privileges of the Green Spring faction. The specific Charles City County grievances were directed as much at the locally dominant family, the Hills, as they were at Berkeley and his clique. Similarly, Surry County complained of its county court's highhanded and secretive manner of levying taxes on "the poore people" and of setting the sheriffs' and clerks' fees; they petitioned for the removal of these abuses and for the right to elect the vestry and to limit the tenure of the sheriffs. At all levels the Rebellion challenged the stability of newly secured authority.[37]

It is this double aspect of discontent behind the violence of the Rebellion that explains the legislation passed in June, 1676, by the so-called "Bacon's Assembly." At first glance these laws seem difficult to interpret because they express disparate if not contradictory interests. But they yield readily to analysis if they are seen not as the reforms of a single group but as efforts to express the desires of two levels of discontent with the way the political and social hierarchy was becoming stabilized. On the one hand, the laws include measures designed by the numerically predominant ordinary settlers throughout the colony as protests against the recently acquired superiority of the leading county families. These were popular protests and they relate not to provincial affairs but to the situation within the local areas of jurisdiction. Thus the statute restricting the franchise to freeholders was repealed; freemen were given the right to elect the parish vestrymen; and the county courts were supplemented by elected freemen to serve with the regularly appointed county magistrates.

On the other hand, there was a large number of measures expressing the dissatisfactions not so much of the ordinary planter but of the local leaders against the prerogatives recently acquired by the provincial elite, prerogatives linked to officialdom and centered in the Council. Thus the law barring office-holding to newcomers of less than three years' residence struck at the arbitrary elevation of the governor's favorites, including Bacon; and the acts forbidding councilors to join the county courts, outlawing the governor's appointment of sheriffs and tax collectors, and nullifying tax exemption for councilors all voiced objections of the local chieftains to privileges enjoyed by others. From both levels there was objection to profiteering in public office.[38]

[36] Craven, *Southern Colonies*, 362–73; *Va. Mag. of Hist. and Biog.*, 1 (1893–94), 56–57; Andrews, ed., *Narratives*, 53.

[37] *Va. Mag. of Hist. and Biog.*, 3 (1895–96), 132 ff. (esp. 142–46), 239–52, 341–49; IV, 1–15; II, 172.

[38] Hening, ed., *Va. Stat. at L.*, II, 341–65.

Thus the wave of rebellion broke and spread. But why did it subside? One might have expected that the momentary flood would have become a steady tide, its rhythms governed by a fixed political constellation. But in fact it did not; stable political alignments did not result. The conclusion to this controversy was characteristic of all the insurrections. The attempted purges and counterpurges by the leaders of the two sides were followed by a rapid submerging of factional identity. Occasional references were later made to the episode, and there were individuals who found an interest in keeping its memory alive. Also, the specific grievances behind certain of the attempted legal reforms of 1676 were later revived. But of stable parties or factions around these issues there were none.

It was not merely that in the late years of the century no more than in the early was there to be found a justification for permanently organized political opposition or party machinery, that persistent, organized dissent was still indistinguishable from sedition; more important was the fact that at the end of the century as in 1630 there was agreement that some must be "highe and eminent in power and dignitie; others meane and in subieccion." [39] Protests and upheaval had resulted from the discomforts of discovering who was, in fact, which, and what the particular consequences of "power and dignitie" were.

But by the end of the century the most difficult period of adjustment had passed and there was an acceptance of the fact that certain families were distinguished from others in riches, in dignity, and in access to political authority. The establishment of these families marks the emergence of Virginia's colonial aristocracy.

It was a remarkable governing group. Its members were soberly responsible, alive to the implications of power; they performed their public obligations with notable skill.[40] Indeed, the glare of their accomplishments is so bright as occasionally to blind us to the conditions that limited them. As a ruling class the Virginian aristocracy of the eighteenth century was unlike other contemporary nobilities or aristocracies, including the English. The differences, bound up with the special characteristics of the society it ruled, had become clear at the turn of the seventeenth century.

Certain of these characteristics are elusive, difficult to grasp and analyze. The leaders of early eighteenth-century Virginia were, for example, in a particular sense, cultural provincials. They were provincial not in the way of Polish *szlachta* isolated on their estate by poverty and impassable

---

[39] Thus the Burgesses, proposing in 1706 that the vestries be made elective, did not dispute the Council's assertion that the "men of Note & Estates" should have authority and assured them that the people would voluntarily elect the "best" men in the parish. H. R. McIlwaine, ed., *Legislative Journals of the Council of Colonial Virginia* (Richmond, Va., 1918–19), I, 468.

[40] Charles S. Sydnor, *Gentlemen Freeholders: Political Practices in Washington's Virginia* (Chapel Hill, 1952), Chaps. I, VI–IX.

roads, nor in the way of sunken *seigneurs* grown rustic and oldfashioned in lonely Norman chateaux. The Virginians were far from uninformed or unaware of the greater world; they were in fact deeply and continuously involved in the cultural life of the Atlantic community. But they knew themselves to be provincials in the sense that their culture was not self-contained; its sources and superior expressions were to be found elsewhere than in their own land. They must seek it from afar; it must be acquired, and once acquired be maintained according to standards externally imposed, in the creation of which they had not participated. The most cultivated of them read much, purposefully, with a diligence the opposite of that essential requisite of aristocracy, uncontending ease. William Byrd's diary with its daily records of stints of study is a stolid testimonial to the virtues of regularity and effort in maintaining standards of civilization set abroad.[41]

In more evident ways also the Virginia planters were denied an uncontending ease of life. They were not *rentiers*. Tenancy, when it appeared late in the colonial period, was useful to the landowners mainly as a cheap way of improving lands held in reserve for future development. The Virginia aristocrat was an active manager of his estate, drawn continuously into the most intimate contacts with the soil and its cultivation. This circumstance limited his ease, one might even say bound him to the soil, but it also strengthened his identity with the land and its problems and saved him from the temptation to create of his privileges an artificial world of self-indulgence.[42]

But more important in distinguishing the emerging aristocracy of Virginia from other contemporary social and political elites were two very specific circumstances. The first concerns the relationship between the integrity of the family unit and the descent of real property. "The English political family," Sir Lewis Namier writes with particular reference to the eighteenth-century aristocracy,

> is a compound of "blood," name, and estate, this last . . . being the most important of the three. . . . The name is a weighty symbol, but liable to variations. . . . the estate . . . is, in the long run, the most potent factor in securing continuity through identification. . . . Primogeniture and entails psychically preserve the family in that they tend to fix its position through the successive generations, and thereby favour conscious identification.

[41] Albert Goodwin, ed., *The European Nobility in the Eighteenth Century* (London, 1953), *passim*; John Clive and Bernard Bailyn, "England's Cultural Provinces: Scotland and America," *Wm. and Mary Qtly.*, 3rd ser., 9 (1954), 200–13; Louis B. Wright and Marion Tinling, eds., *The Secret Diary of William Byrd of Westover 1709–1712* (Richmond, Va., 1941).

[42] Willard F. Bliss, "The Rise of Tenancy in Virginia," *Va. Mag. of Hist. and Biog.*, 58 (1950), 427 ff.; Louis B. Wright, *Cultural Life of the American Colonies, 1607–1763* (New York, 1957), 5–11.

The descent of landed estates in eighteenth-century England was controlled by the complicated device known as the strict settlement which provided that the heir at his marriage received the estate as a life tenant, entailing its descent to his unborn eldest son and specifying the limitations of the encumbrances upon the land that might be made in behalf of his daughters and younger sons.[43]

It was the strict settlement, in which in the eighteenth century perhaps half the land of England was bound, that provided continuity over generations for the landed aristocracy. This permanent identification of the family with a specific estate and with the status and offices that pertained to it was achieved at the cost of sacrificing the young sons. It was a single stem of the family only that retained its superiority; it alone controlled the material basis for political dominance.

This basic condition of aristocratic governance in England was never present in the American colonies, and not for lack of familiarity with legal forms. The economic necessity that had prompted the widespread adoption of the strict settlement in England was absent in the colonies. Land was cheap and easily available, the more so as one rose on the social and political ladder. There was no need to deprive the younger sons or even daughters of landed inheritances in order to keep the original family estate intact. Provision could be made for endowing each of them with plantations, and they in turn could provide similarly for their children. Moreover, to confine the stem family's fortune to a single plot of land, however extensive, was in the Virginia economy to condemn it to swift decline. Since the land was quickly worn out and since it was cheaper to acquire new land than to rejuvenate the worked soil by careful husbandry, geographical mobility, not stability, was the key to prosperity. Finally, since land was only as valuable as the labor available to work it, a great estate was worth passing intact from generation to generation only if it had annexed to it a sufficient population of slaves. Yet this condition imposed severe rigidities in a plantation's economy — for a labor force bound to a particular plot was immobilized — besides creating bewildering confusions in law.

The result, evident before the end of the seventeenth century, was a particular relationship between the family and the descent of property. There was in the beginning no intent on the part of the Virginians to alter the traditional forms; the continued vitality of the ancient statutes specifying primogeniture in certain cases was assumed.[44] The first clear

[43] Lewis B. Namier, *England in the Age of the American Revolution* (London, 1930), 22–23; H. J. Habakkuk, "Marriage Settlements in the Eighteenth Century," Royal Hist. Soc., *Transactions*, 4th ser., 32 (1950), 15–30.

[44] Clarence R. Keim, Influence of Primogeniture and Entail in the Development of Virginia (unpublished Ph.D. dissertation, University of Chicago, 1926), Chap. I.

indication of a new trend came in the third quarter of the century, when the leading gentry, rapidly accumulating large estates, faced for the first time the problem of the transfer of property. The result was the subdivision of the great holdings and the multiplication of smaller plots while the net amount of land held by the leading families continued to rise.[45]

This trend continued. Primogeniture neither at the end of the seventeenth century nor after prevailed in Virginia. It was never popular even among the most heavily endowed of the tidewater families. The most common form of bequest was a grant to the eldest son of the undivided home plantation and gifts of other tracts outside the home county to the younger sons and daughters. Thus by his will of 1686 Robert Beverley, Sr., bequeathed to his eldest son, Peter, all his land in Gloucester County lying between "Chiescake" and "Hoccadey's" creeks (an unspecified acreage); to Robert, the second son, another portion of the Gloucester lands amounting to 920 acres; to Harry, 1,600 acres in Rappahannock County; to John, 3,000 acres in the same county; to William, two plantations in Middlesex County; to Thomas, 3,000 acres in Rappahannock and New Kent counties; to his wife, three plantations including those "whereon I now live" for use during her lifetime, after which they were to descend to his daughter Catherine, who was also to receive £200 sterling; to his daughter Mary, £150 sterling; to "the childe that my wife goeth with, be it male or female," all the rest of his real property; and the residue of his personal property was "to be divided and disposed in equall part & portion betwix my wife and children." Among the bequests of Ralph Wormeley, Jr., in 1700 was an estate of 1,500 acres to his daughter Judith as well as separate plantations to his two sons.

Entail proved no more popular than primogeniture. Only a small minority of estates, even in the tidewater region, were ever entailed. In fact, despite the extension of developed land in the course of the eighteenth century, more tidewater estates were docked of entails than were newly entailed.[46]

Every indication points to continuous and increasing difficulty in reproducing even pale replicas of the strict settlement. In 1705 a law was passed requiring a special act of the Assembly to break an entail; the law stood, but between 1711 and 1776 no fewer than 125 such private acts

---

[45] E.g., Ames, *Eastern Shore*, 29–32.

[46] Keim, Primogeniture and Entail, 44 ff., 113–14. Keim found that only 1 of a sample of 72 wills in Westmoreland (1653–72) contained provisions for entailing; by 1756–61 the proportions had risen to 14 out of 39, but these entails covered only small parts of the total estates. Typical of his other tidewater samples are Middlesex, 1698–1703, 16 out of 65, and 1759–72, 7 out of 48; Henrico, 1677–87, 2 out of 29, and no increase for the later periods. The piedmont samples show even smaller proportions; *ibid.*, 54–62. The Beverley will is printed in *Va. Mag. of Hist. and Biog.*, 3 (1895–96), 47–51; on Wormeley, see *ibid.*, 36 (1928), 101.

were passed, and in 1734 estates of under £200 were exempted from the
law altogether. The labor problem alone was an insuperable barrier to
perpetuating the traditional forms. A statute of 1727, clarifying the confused legislation of earlier years, had attempted to ensure a labor force on
entailed land by classifying slaves as real property and permitting them to
be bound together with land into bequests. But by 1748 this stipulation
had resulted in such bewildering "doubts, variety of opinions, and confusions" that it was repealed. The repeal was disallowed in London, and
in the course of a defense of its action the Assembly made vividly clear
the utter impracticality of entailment in Virginia's economy. Slaves, the
Assembly explained, were essential to the success of a plantation, but
"slaves could not be kept on the lands to which they were annexed without manifest prejudice to the tenant in tail. . . . often the tenant was
the proprietor of fee simple land much fitter for cultivation than his in-
tailed lands, where he could work his slaves to a much greater advantage."
On the other hand, if a plantation owner did send entailed slaves where
they might be employed most economically the result was equally disastrous:

> the frequent removing and settling them on other lands in other
> counties and parts of the colony far distant from the county court
> where the deeds or wills which annexed them were recorded and
> the intail lands lay; the confusion occasioned by their mixture with
> fee simple slaves of the same name and sex and belonging to the
> same owner; the uncertainty of distinguishing one from another
> after several generations, no register of their genealogy being kept
> and none of them having surnames, were great mischiefs to pur-
> chasers, strangers, and creditors, who were often unavoidably de-
> ceived in their purchases and hindered in the recovery of their just
> debts. It also lessened the credit of the country; it being dangerous
> for the merchants of Great Britain to trust possessors of many
> slaves for fear the slaves might be intailed.[47]

A mobile labor force free from legal entanglements and a rapid turnover of lands, not a permanent hereditary estate, were prerequisites of
family prosperity. This condition greatly influenced social and political
life. Since younger sons and even daughters inherited extensive landed
properties, equal often to those of the eldest son, concentration of authority in the stem family was precluded. Third generation collateral descen-

[47] Hening, ed., *Va. Stat. at L.*, III, 320, IV, 399–400, 222 ff., V, 441–42n
(quoted). In 1765 the legal rigors of entailment were permanently relaxed by a
law permitting the leasing of entailed land for up to three lives, a move made
necessary, the Assembly said, because "many large tracts of entailed lands remain
uncultivated, the owners not having slaves to work them. . . ." *Ibid.*, VIII, 183.
For a striking example of the difficulties of maintaining entailed lands, see *ibid.*,
VI, 297–99; Keim, Primogeniture and Entail, 108.

dants of the original immigrant were as important in their own right as the eldest son's eldest son. Great clans like the Carters and the Lees, though they may have acknowledged a central family seat, were scattered throughout the province on estates of equal influence. The four male Carters of the third generation were identified by contemporaries by the names of their separate estates, and, indistinguishable in style of life, they had an equal access to political power.[48]

Since material wealth was the basis of the status which made one eligible for public office, there was a notable diffusion of political influence throughout a broadening group of leading families. No one son was predestined to represent the family interest in politics, but as many as birth and temperament might provide. In the 1750's there were no fewer than seven Lees of the same generation sitting together in the Virginia Assembly; in the Burgesses they spoke for five separate counties. To the eldest, Philip Ludwell Lee, they conceded a certain social superiority that made it natural for him to sit in the Council. But he did not speak alone for the family; by virtue of inheritance he had no unique authority over his brothers and cousins.

The leveling at the top of the social and political hierarchy, creating an evenness of status and influence, was intensified by continuous intermarriage within the group. The unpruned branches of these flourishing family trees, growing freely, met and intertwined until by the Revolution the aristocracy appeared to be one great tangled cousinry.[49]

As political power became increasingly diffused throughout the upper stratum of society, the Council, still at the end of the seventeenth century a repository of unique privileges, lost its effective superiority. Increasingly through the successive decades its authority had to be exerted through alignments with the Burgesses — alignments made easier as well as more necessary by the criss-crossing network of kinship that united the two houses. Increasingly the Council's distinctions became social and ceremonial.[50]

The contours of Virginia's political hierarchy were also affected by a second main conditioning element, besides the manner of descent of family property. Not only was the structure unusually level and broad at the top, but it was incomplete in itself. Its apex, the ultimate source of legal decision and control, lay in the quite different society of England, amid the distant embroilments of London, the court, and Parliament. The levers of control in that realm were for the most part hidden from

---

[48] Louis Morton, *Robert Carter of Nomini Hall* (Williamsburg, 1941), 11.

[49] Burton J. Hendrick, *The Lees of Virginia* (Boston, 1935), 97.

[50] Percy S. Flippin, *The Royal Government in Virginia, 1624–1775* (New York, 1919), 166–67, 169; Herbert L. Osgood, *The American Colonies in the Eighteenth Century* (4 vols.; New York, 1924–25), IV, 231–32.

the planters; yet the powers that ruled this remote region could impose an arbitrary authority directly into the midst of Virginia's affairs.

One consequence was the introduction of instabilities in the tenure and transfer of the highest offices. Tenure could be arbitrarily interrupted, and the transfer to kin of such positions at death or resignation — uncertain in any case because of the diffusion of family authority — could be quite difficult or even impossible. Thus William Byrd II returned from England at the death of his father in 1704 to take over the family properties, but though he was the sole heir he did not automatically or completely succeed to the elder Byrd's provincial offices. He did, indeed, become auditor of Virginia after his father, but only because he had carefully arranged for the succession while still in London; his father's Council seat went to someone else, and it took three years of patient maneuvering through his main London contact, Micajah Jerry, to secure another; he never did take over the receivership. Even such a power as "King" Carter, the reputed owner at his death of 300,000 acres and 1,000 slaves, was rebuffed by the resident deputy governor and had to deploy forces in England in order to transfer a Virginia naval office post from one of his sons to another. There was family continuity in public office, but at the highest level it was uncertain, the result of place-hunting rather than of the absolute prerogative of birth.[51]

Instability resulted not only from the difficulty of securing and transferring high appointive positions but also and more immediately from the presence in Virginia of total strangers to the scene, particularly governors and their deputies, armed with extensive jurisdiction and powers of enforcement. The dangers of this element in public life became clear only after Berkeley's return to England in 1677, for after thirty-five years of residence in the colony Sir William had become a leader in the land independent of his royal authority. But Howard, Andros, and Nicholson were governors with full legal powers but with at best only slight connections with local society. In them, social leadership and political leadership had ceased to be identical.

In the generation that followed Berkeley's departure, this separation between the two spheres created the bitterest of political controversies. Firmly entrenched behind their control of the colony's government, the leading families battled with every weapon available to reduce the power of the executives and thus to eliminate what appeared to be an external and arbitrary authority. Repeated complaints by the governors of the intractable opposition of a league of local oligarchs marked the Virginians' success. Efforts by the executives to discipline the indigenous leaders

---

[51] John S. Bassett, ed., *The Writings of "Colonel William Byrd of Westover in Virginia Esqr"* (New York, 1901), *xlviii–ix*; Morton, *Carter*, 28n.

could only be mildly successful. Patronage was a useful weapon, but its effectiveness diminished steadily, ground down between a resistant Assembly and an office-hungry bureaucracy in England. The possibility of exploiting divisions among the resident powers also declined as kinship lines bound the leading families closer together and as group interests became clearer with the passage of time. No faction built around the gubernatorial power could survive independently; ultimately its adherents would fall away and it would weaken. It was a clear logic of the situation that led the same individuals who had promoted Nicholson as a replacement for Andros to work against him once he assumed office.[52]

Stability could be reached only by the complete identification of external and internal authority through permanent commitment by the appointees to local interests. Commissary Blair's extraordinary success in Virginia politics was based not only on his excellent connections in England but also on his marriage into the Harrison family, which gave him the support of an influential kinship faction. There was more than hurt pride and thwarted affection behind Nicholson's reported insane rage at being spurned by the highly marriageable Lucy Burwell; and later the astute Spotswood, for all his success in imposing official policy, fully quieted the controversies of his administration only by succumbing completely and joining as a resident Virginia landowner the powers aligned against him.[53]

But there was more involved than instability and conflict in the discontinuity between social and political organization at the topmost level. The state itself had changed its meaning. To a Virginia planter of the early eighteenth century the highest public authority was no longer merely one expression of a general social authority. It had become something abstract, external to his life and society, and ultimate power whose purposes were obscure, whose direction could neither be consistently influenced nor accurately plotted, and whose human embodiments were alien and antagonistic.

The native gentry of the early eighteenth century had neither the need nor the ability to fashion a new political theory to comprehend their

[52] For the classic outcry against "the party of Malecontents," see Spotswood's letter to the Board of Trade, March 25, 1719, in R. A. Brock, ed., *The Official Letters of Alexander Spotswood* (Richmond, Va., 1882–85), II, 308 ff.; cf. 285. On patronage, see Flippin, *Royal Government*, 208–214; Leonard W. Labaree, *Royal Government in America* (New Haven, Conn., 1930), 102; Worthington C. Ford, "A Sketch of Sir Francis Nicholson," *Mag. of Amer. Hist.*, 29 (1893), 508–12.

[53] Peter Laslett, "John Locke . . . ," *Wm. and Mary Qtly.*, 3rd ser., 14 (1957), 398; Daniel E. Motley, *Life of Commissary James Blair* . . . (Baltimore, 1901), 10, 43 ff.; William S. Perry, ed., *Historical Collections Relating to the . . . Church* ([Hartford], 1870–78), I, 69, 72–73, 88, 90, 102, 135; Leonidas Dodson, *Alexander Spotswood* (Philadelphia, 1932), 251 ff.

experience, but their successors would find in the writings of John Locke on state and society not merely a reasonable theoretical position but a statement of self-evident fact.

I have spoken exclusively of Virginia, but though the histories of each of the colonies in the seventeenth century are different, they exhibit common characteristics. These features one might least have expected to find present in Virginia, and their presence there is, consequently, most worth indicating.

In all of the colonies the original transference of an ordered European society was succeeded by the rise to authority of resident settlers whose influence was rooted in their ability to deal with the problems of life in wilderness settlements. These individuals attempted to stabilize their positions, but in each case they were challenged by others arriving after the initial settlements, seeking to exploit certain advantages of position, wealth, or influence. These newcomers, securing after the Restoration governmental appointments in the colonies and drawn together by personal ties, especially those of kinship and patronage, came to constitute colonial officialdom. This group introduced a new principle of social organization; it also gave rise to new instabilities in a society in which the traditional forms of authority were already being subjected to severe pressures. By the eighth decade of the seventeenth century the social basis of public life had become uncertain and insecure, its stability delicate and sensitive to disturbance. Indian warfare, personal quarrels, and particularly the temporary confusion in external control caused by the Glorious Revolution became the occasions for violent challenges to constituted authority.

By the end of the century a degree of harmony had been achieved, but the divergence between political and social leadership at the topmost level created an area of permanent conflict. The political and social structures that emerged were by European standards strangely shaped. Everywhere as the bonds of empire drew tighter the meaning of the state was changing. Herein lay the origins of a new political system.

Equality and Empire:
The New York Charter
of Libertyes, 1683

DAVID S. LOVEJOY

New York did not finally come under English control until after 1674, when the Duke of York reestablished his proprietary authority in the colony after its brief recapture by the Dutch. In order to understand the development of New York, it is useful to compare the circumstances under which Virginia and Massachusetts Bay were settled with the very different conditions of colonial settlement in the last half of the seventeenth century. The Restoration colonies were founded by proprietors rather than joint-stock companies, they were established after it had become quite clear that there was a future for English communities on the North American continent, they came into existence at the same time as the Navigation System, and they responded to the pressures of already existing colonies.

David Lovejoy examines the remarkable political potential of the Restoration province of New York. He shows how the New England political heritage of the Long Islanders combined with the property interests of most leading New Yorkers and their precocious constitutional instincts to produce a powerful demand for representative government in this least developed of seventeenth-century American political systems. The Charter of Libertyes, according to Lovejoy's analysis, was both a shrewd mixture of local political and economic self-interest and an intuition of the ultimate equalitarian logic of English imperial relations. It failed of enactment because of English politics, but it provides an inkling of underlying American colonial political aspirations which first surfaced in New York.

The troublesome question is why such a document should have appeared in New York rather than Massachusetts Bay, essentially self-governing since 1630, or Virginia, whose first elected legislature met in 1619. Are there grounds to think that Lovejoy has read the values of the American Revolution back into the seventeenth century? Would alternative interpretations analyze the Charter of Libertyes more nearly as a document of its own time?

Historians of colonial America have given over a good deal of space to the course of events between the founding of the colonies and the American Revolution. Through them we have learned much about how colonies were settled and developed and how they were expected to fit the demands of the emerging British Empire. What historians have found difficult to determine is how American colonists felt about themselves as British subjects outside the realm, and what they believed was the colonies' role within the empire. Such an inquiry is, of course, less difficult for the eighteenth century, particularly for the period just before the American Revolution. Events at that time at last forced the colonists to come to terms with the idea of empire and to set limits upon it and upon the power of Parliament in accordance with their own needs and historic assumptions. In the seventeenth century, colonial society was less mature, less stable, and less reflective about itself and its relationship to the Mother Country. No single momentous event like the Revolution united or crystallized colonial thought around definite political or constitutional theories. Rather, each colony went its way, influenced by its own peculiar political, economic, and religious circumstances on the one hand, and by the emerging, yet fitful, colonial policy on the other. At the same time, the English government had not yet determined precisely what the colonists' role was in the larger scheme. Crown, Parliament, and ministry after the Restoration had only begun to decide how their general conclusions about empire ought to be implemented.

Despite the unsettledness of the connection between colonies and Mother country, certain events affecting individual colonies did produce in the seventeenth century reactions which help the historian determine what went on in the minds of the people, who they thought they were, and how they believed they stood in relation to England. A unique situation obtained in the colony of New York after the English conquest in 1664, and the New York colonists' response to it explains something about the colonial mind and gives a clue to what a particular group of American colonists had concluded about the imperial relationship.

I

On October 17, 1683, eighteen deputies from the settled areas of New York convened on Manhattan Island for a meeting of an assembly. They came from the city at the tip of Manhattan, down the Hudson River from Albany and Schenectady, from Long Island, Pemaquid in Maine, and the islands in the Atlantic now belonging to Massachusetts. After electing a speaker they drafted a charter or constitution, which described a structure

Reprinted by permission from David S. Lovejoy, "Equality and Empire: The New York Charter of Libertyes, 1683," *William and Mary Quarterly*, 3d Ser., XXI (1964), 493–515.

of government and defined certain individual, civil, and political rights for the people who lived there. What was the significance of this assembly and in particular the charter it drafted? What does the charter tell us about these colonists' understanding of their rights within an emerging British Empire?

First of all, this was the first official legislature to meet in the colony of New York. Virginia was settled in 1607 and its first legislature met within twelve years. Massachusetts had enjoyed a legislature from the outset, Maryland almost from the start. But not New York which the Dutch had settled as early as the 1620's and the English had conquered in 1664. Under the Dutch, four successive directors had administered the colony, including Peter Minuit and Peter Stuyvesant, first and last. Each ruled with a council and no assembly. Government was arbitrary over a heterogeneous population of Dutch, Germans, Swedes, and a number of English from Massachusetts and Connecticut who settled on Long Island.

New Netherlands came to be a thorn in the side of good mercantilists in England and hungry colonists in America, both of whom saw their trade threatened, furs siphoned off to Holland, and expansion of New England blocked by foreigners at New Amsterdam and Fort Orange (Albany). After the Restoration of Charles II in 1660, broader and better defined ideas of imperial trade emerged in the minds of the English King, ministry, and Parliament. One of the early imperial schemes of the Restoration government was the conquest of New Netherlands. After Stuyvesant reluctantly surrendered his settlements to the English Royal Commissioners in 1664, Charles II gave the colony to his younger brother, James, Duke of York, to govern as he pleased. James's pleasure was to rule New York through a governor and council.

The Duke's grant was a fat one. It initially included all of New Netherlands, Long Island, half of Connecticut, several islands off the coast of Massachusetts, part of what is now Maine, and all of what is now New Jersey. But the Duke's proprietary was different; unlike the proprietary of Maryland, and later proprietaries of the Carolinas, the Jerseys, and Pennsylvania, it had no representative assembly. There were sevearl reasons for the omission. First, the Dutch had never had a legislature, and they were a large segment of the population. Secondly, and probably more important as things turned out, Stuart monarchs were suspicious of elected legislatures since they had never had any great luck with them in England, and James in particular thought them a nuisance. New Yorkers had to be satisfied with what were known as the Duke's Laws, a New England code arbitrarily adapted to proprietary circumstances. Richard Nicolls, a member of the Royal Commission charged with the conquest of New Netherlands and the Duke's first governor, ordered a convention in 1665 at Hempstead, Long Island, where elected representatives from the settled areas close by accepted, not without some protest, the colony's first set of laws. One cannot call this meeting an assembly, for it met only to approve the laws and then did not meet again. The Duke's Laws went into effect immediately, and the governor and council ruled with an appointed Court of Assizes to dispense justice. In 1665 the proprietary colony of New York was underway.[1]

II

Between 1665 and 1683 a good deal of protest arose against the handling of New York affairs. The lack of an assembly was a primary grievance. Most of the protests originated on Long Island where New Englanders were concentrated. Their arguments were based first on Governor Nicolls's promise — supposedly made at the time of submission to the Commissioners — "of equall (if not greater) freedomes and immunityes then any of his Majesties colonyes in New England." To transplanted New Englanders, rights equal to or greater than those of other Yankee colonists must mean at the very least protection from arbitrary government by establishment of a representative assembly with the sole power to enact laws and levy taxes upon them. The Court of Assizes later denied that Nicolls made such a promise and informed Long Islanders that nothing was "required of them but obedience and submission to the Lawes of the Government." [2] A more vigorous protest complained that the inhabitants were "inslaved under an Arbitrary Power," and that Nicolls exercised more authority "than the King himselfe can do." The governor labeled this slander and high treason and reminded the colonists that the English Civil War, the "Late Rebellion," began "with the selfe same steps and pretences." [3]

Besides petitions and high words, protests also took other forms. In 1666 two constables in Southold, opposed to the arbitrary method of taxation, refused to do their duty, and the sheriff issued a warrant to levy fines upon them. In the same town there was outright refusal by several

[1] See *The Colonial Laws of New York from the Year 1664 to the Revolution* . . . , I (Albany, 1894), 1–71. Southold's deputies came to the convention armed with instructions from their town meeting which demanded that no taxes be raised from them without their consent "in a general court meeting," but no regard was paid. Edmund B. O'Callaghan, *Origin of Legislative Assemblies in the State of New York* . . . (Albany, 1861), 9. O'Callaghan's study appears also as "Historical Introduction," in *Journal of the Legislative Council of the Colony of New-York* [1691–1743] (Albany, 1861), iii–xxvii.

[2] O'Callaghan, *Origin of Legislative Assemblies*, 5–11; E. B. O'Callaghan and B. Fernow, eds., *Documents Relative to the Colonial History of the State of New-York* (Albany, 1853–87), XIV, 632.

[3] Richard Nicolls to John Underhill, May 7, 1666, *Documents of N.Y.*, XIV, 580.

people to pay their rates, even by some of the overseers who had agreed to the making of them. Petitions and protests got the Long Islanders nowhere, and they were branded "ill mynded people who take delight to breed disturbances and to infuse ill principles into the myndes of his Majesties good Subjects." [4]

In 1670, after Francis Lovelace had replaced Nicolls as governor, he and the council levied a new tax upon the inhabitants over and above the usual to defray the expenses of repairing Fort James on Manhattan. Huntington town meeting led the way and denounced the tax because it deprived people of the "liberties of english men." Besides, the meeting complained, the people of Huntington were busy with their own problems and would receive no benefit from a fort in New York City any-way. Jamaica people called the tax contrary to the "Laws of the nation" and doubted that the governor's commission permitted it. Already they were paying a penny in the pound to support the government; if the governor and council demanded money for the fort, they reasoned, they could also demand "what ills we know not tell thear be no end." [5] Flushing and Hempstead, along with Jamaica, held several town meetings and drew up resolves protesting the governor's demands. These resolutions eventually reached the governor and council, who pronounced them scandalous, illegal, and seditious, demanded that they be "publiquely burned," and ordered that the "principall contrivers thereof be inquired into." [6]

During the Third Dutch War, 1672–74, the Dutch recaptured New York, and agitation, at least against the Proprietor's governor, ceased for a time. Re-establishment of Dutch rule, however, did not stop the settlers of East Hampton, South Hampton, and Southhold from petitioning King Charles about grievances sustained from both English and Dutch governments. What they objected to was interference with their whale fishery, first by "heavy taxes" under the English, higher than those in New England, without allowing them "any deputies in court," and then by arbitrary laws imposed upon them by the Dutch. The eastern Long Islanders claimed they had purchased their land thirty years earlier and that the land rightly belonged under the Connecticut patent from where most of them had come. If they could not be governed by Connecticut, they suggested the King might make them a "free corporation," a very unlikely

[4] The Governors Commission to Thomas Delavall Esquire Mr. Mathias Nicolls Secr. and Mr. Isaack Bedlow, etc., Mar. 9, 1671, in Victor H. Paltsits, ed., *Minutes of the Executive Council of the Province of New York* (Albany, 1910), II, 524–525; *Documents of N.Y.*, XIV, 578, 582, 584.

[5] Charles R. Street, ed., *Huntington Town Records* . . . (Huntington, 1887–89), I, 163–164; Josephine C. Frost, ed., *Records of the Town of Jamaica, Long Island, New York, 1656–1751* (Brooklyn, 1914), I, 47–48.

[6] *Documents of N.Y.*, XIV, 646; *Min. of Exec. Council*, II, 485–487.

possibility to say the least. The petition got as far as the Lords of Trade and doubtless died there.[7]

In the Treaty of Westminster which ended the war, the Dutch agreed to return New York to the English, and James dispatched Major Edmund Andros as governor to serve as his link with the colony. Agitation for an assembly continued. Andros gave the colonists no encouragement, but he did report to the Duke that taxes and customs might come easier if the colonists had a part to play in the way they were levied. The Duke, of course, wanted New York to pay its own way. He also wanted income from his colony, through revenue from customs duties. After all, what was a proprietary colony for if not to profit its proprietor? James considered Andros's suggestions and agreed that the colonists' desire for an assembly was "in imitacon of their neighbor Colonies"; but he refused to go along with Andros's suggestion. Instead James commended Andros for discouraging any idea of an assembly.

James gave several reasons for his refusal. It was outside Andros's instructions to grant an assembly, he said. There was no argument there. Redress against grievances was easily come by under the Duke's Laws as they existed; all the governor and council had to do was to rule according to the laws already set down. What is more, wrote the Duke to Andros, the Court of Assizes doubtless contained the same people who would be elected to an assembly anyway. Assemblies without proper restrictions "would be of dangerous consequence" and apt to "assume to themselves many priviledges which prove destructive to, or very oft disturbe, the peace of the government wherein they are allowed." Probably the Duke could have made no statements more clearly revealing his insensitivity to, and misunderstanding of, the colonists' sentiments and attitude toward government. A final remark did suggest that if Andros still believed an assembly would help, the Duke would consider proposals the governor might make.[8]

A specific incident in 1680 brought the whole issue to a head and indicated that opposition to arbitrary government was not confined to testy transplanted New Englanders. As one might expect, it was a money problem which precipitated this sharp turn in the history of the colony of New York. The Duke's customs rates and duties on trade ran for three-year periods, and the rates levied in 1677, out of which came the support for government, expired in November 1680. But just before the date of expiration, the Duke recalled Governor Andros to London to answer several charges, including one against the governor's handling of

[7] W. Noel Sainsbury and others, eds., *Calendar of State Papers, Colonial Series, America and West Indies* (London, 1860–), *1669–1674*, #875, #875 I, pp. 380–381.

[8] Duke of York to Andros, Apr. 6, 1675, and Jan. 28, 1676, in *Documents of N.Y.*, III, 230, 235.

the revenue. Andros embarked for home without renewing the customs duties — leaving Lieutenant Anthony Brockholls in his place as deputy. When Collector William Dyer attempted to collect the customs, the merchants balked. Ships entered and cleared without paying rates. The council met but took no steps to continue the laws. Brockholls stood by helpless, watching the government's sanction crumble.[9]

Collector Dyer bore the brunt of the people's pent up anger. They claimed that his attempt to collect the expired customs and the use of soldiers to assist him were violations of Magna Carta, the Petition of Right, several other statutes, and the honor and peace of the "King that now is." For maliciously exercising such "Regall Power," a grand jury formally charged him with being a "false Traytour" to the King and with subverting the "known Ancient and Fundamentall Lawes of the Realme of England." Once in court to reply to the charges, Dyer challenged the jurisdiction of the Assizes, claiming that both he and the court had commissions from the same source, James, Duke of York, and therefore the court could not try him. The court, fearing trouble with the Duke, agreed not to pursue the case but instead sent the collector to England where he might be proceeded against as the Crown directed. In London after the prosecutor failed to appear, the charges were dropped, and Dyer was advanced in his Majesty's service.[10]

William Dyer's trial in New York got a number of people excited. The lack of power to collect the customs and Dyer's attempt to do so without authority intensified demands for an assembly. The outspoken discontent made it clear that if the Duke wanted money, he would have to allow a legislature. Long Islanders no longer fought the battle alone; evidence of bad feeling among the people was widespread. The colony's Grand Jury, which had indicted Dyer, petitioned the Court of Assizes and summarized the protests of a good many when it complained of the insupportable burden which was thrust upon them all. In a very revealing document, the Grand Jury explained that the burden could only be removed "by sitting us upon Equall Ground with our fellow Brethren and

---

[9] *Documents of N.Y.*, III, 221–223; Duke of York to Andros and Sir John Werden to Andros, May 24, 1680, *ibid.*, 283–284; O'Callaghan, *Origin of Legislative Assemblies*, 12–13.

[10] Proceedings against Mr. Dyer, Collector of the Port of New-York, and The Bill found against Capt. William Dyre, in *Documents of N.Y.*, III, 288–289 and *n*; The Bill or Accusacon against Capt. William Dyre found by the Grand Jury, in "Proceedings of the General Court of Assizes Held in the City of New York October 6, 1680, to October 6, 1682," in New-York Historical Society, *Collections*, XLV (New York, 1913), 11; Proceedings of the Court of Assizes, July 1, 1681, in *Cal. St. Papers, Col.*, *1681–1685*, p. 81; John West, Clerk of Assizes, to [Sir Leoline Jenkins], July 1, 1681, *ibid.*; Order of the Privy Council, Sept. 14, 1681, and Report of Sir John Churchill to the Commissioners of the Duke of York's revenue, Nov. 28, 1683, *ibid.*, pp. 115, 555.

subjects of the Realme of England In our Neighboring Plantacons." The only way to do this, of course, was to place the government in the hands of a governor, council, and assembly elected by the freeholders. Only by this means could New Yorkers enjoy the good and wholesome laws of the realm. In a burst of eloquence the Grand Jury proclaimed: "Thereby wee may Bud Blossom and bring forth the fruites of a Prosperous and flourishing Government for want of which wee have Been (and yett are) in a most wythering and Decaying Condicon. . . ." [11]

The Grand Jury begged the Court of Assizes — which, if not a representative body, at least included settlers from several areas — to carry their case directly to the Duke and strongly urged sending a petition, which the Court agreed to do immediately. The Assizes's petition to James complained of "inexpressible burdens" and of the "arbitrary and absolute power" over the people which exacted revenue against their will. Even more forcefully than the Grand Jury, it hammered home the idea that English subjects, no matter where they lived, were equal as far as rights and treatment from government were concerned. Under present conditions as colonists they were "esteemed as nothing" and had "become a reproach" to their neighbors in the King's other colonies who, unlike New Yorkers, flourished under the protection of the King's "unparalleled form and method of government." What was practicable at home and in other colonies, that is, an "assembly of the people," was the "undoubted birthright" of all the King's subjects.[12]

Another incident occurred which pointed to similar conclusions about government. At Albany Collector Robert Livingston took John De Lavall to court in August 1681 for refusing to pay an excise on 510 gallons of rum he had unloaded and sold. At his trial De Lavall turned the court up-side-down by directing to it several searching questions. By what right did Livingston collect the excise, and, if by order of the governor, when did the King, Lords, and Commons give such power to the governor to levy taxes? If the excise was lawful, in what law could it be found? Not bound by the limits of a customs case, De Lavall asked, too, whether he and other colonists were considered "free born subjects of the king?" If not, he asked, "during which king's reign and by which act passed during such king's reign we were made otherwise than free?" These were touchy questions, and the red-faced court found it expedient to refer the case to the "supreme authorities" at New York.[13]

With the customs uncollected, government in New York seemed to be grinding to a halt; the colony was losing its income needed for its sup-

[11] N.-Y. Hist. Soc., *Colls.*, XLV, 14–15.

[12] *Ibid.*; John Romeyn Brodhead, *History of the State of New York*, II (New York, 1871), 658.

[13] A. J. F. Van Laer, ed., *Minutes of the Court of Albany, Rensselaerswyck and Schenectady, 1680–1685*, III (Albany, 1932), 153–155.

port to say nothing of the money needed to pay what it owed to the Duke. Brockholls wrote to Andros in London describing how the merchants took advantage of the courts which were too frightened to carry out the deputy's orders. "Here it was Never worse," he declared, a government "wholly over thrown and in the Greatest Confusion and Disorder Possible." [14]

To add to Brockholls's worries, the Lord Island towns grew increasingly restless. Several town meetings elected deputies and sent them to an extralegal convention at Huntington in late September 1681 where they consulted about their "Just liberties" and dispatched a petition to the deputy governor and Court of Assizes.[15] Brockholls and his court rejected the petition, reprimanded those who presented it, and sent them home with a warning to "Remaine in Quiett." The town meeting of Oyster Bay was not put off by such treatment and defiantly answered the court: "When the five men which ware the Representatives off longisland have Satisfacktion wee are willing to make payment of whatt Is Justly due as to the publick." [16]

Sometime before Dyer's unsuccessful attempt to collect the customs, Matthias Nicolls, secretary of the governor's council, sailed home to England to have a talk with the Duke. Nicolls was an old settler, having come to New York in 1664, and a very busy officeholder. What his mission was is not clear, but once in England he followed James to Scotland and doubtless explained to him just what the colony's financial problem was. In view of the circumstances in New York, he may very well have pled directly for an assembly.[17]

There can be no doubt that James changed his mind about a New York legislature for financial reasons. The government's recent failure to collect the Duke's customs was the second blow to his revenue within the space of a year or two. Even after James had in 1680 given over East and West New Jersey to proprietors, Berkeley and Carteret, New York had continued to levy customs duties on her neighbors' trade for revenue purposes. The New Jersey people complained, and James, in a surprise move, requested a legal opinion about his customs rights in New Jersey from Sir William Jones, former attorney general, prominent Whig lawyer,

[14] *Documents of N.Y.*, III, 289n.

[15] Benjamin D. Hicks, ed., *Records of the Towns of North and South Hempstead, Long Island, N.Y.* (Jamaica, 1896–1904), I, 385–386; John Cox, Jr., ed., *Oyster Bay Town Records* (New York, 1916–40), I, 245–246; Street, ed., *Huntington Town Recs.*, I, 315.

[16] N.-Y. Hist. Soc., *Colls.*, XLV, 17, 25; Cox, ed., *Oyster Bay Town Records*, I, 247.

[17] Wait Winthrop to Fitz-John Winthrop, Dec. 19, 1681, in Massachusetts Historical Society, *Collections*, 5th Ser., VIII (Boston, 1882), 424; Brodhead, *Hist. of N.Y.*, II, 335–336.

and a new member of Parliament in 1680. Shortly after Jones replied that James had no legal right to the customs of New Jersey, the Duke released fully both colonies to their proprietors. The loss to New York was estimated to be about one third of its trade, with, of course, a consequent sharp decline in its revenue. This was not the worst of it. Jones's opinion cast great doubt, even among the Duke's commissioners, upon James's right to charge customs at all, even in New York. And, what is more, if he continued to do so, whether legally or illegally, he would likely drive his colonists across the river to New Jersey where they would be free of his jurisdiction and his taxes.[18] It was doubtless these brute facts and maybe Matthias Nicolls's persuasive arguments which helped convince the Duke that the only way to make New York worth his time and effort was to grant an assembly, on condition, of course, that the people there agreed to support the government and to pay off the arrears accumulated since the disturbances began. His intent, he wrote to Brockholls, was to establish a government with all the "advantages and priviledges" which other American plantations enjoy, and "in all other things as nere as may be agreable to the laws of England." He may or may not have been believed when he added: "I seeke the common good and protection of that countrey and the increase of their trade, before my advantages to myselfe in the matter."[19]

[18] Sir John Werden to Sir Allen Apsley, Aug. 8, 1681, in *Documents of N.Y.*, III, 291; Mayor of New York to Werden, n.d., *ibid.*, 361. William Blathwayt to Lord Culpeper, Aug. 26, 1680, William Blathwayt Papers, XVII, Colonial Williamsburg, Inc., Williamsburg, Va. (microfilm, Wisconsin State Historical Society Library, Madison). For Sir William Jones's opinion, see George Chalmers, *Political Annals of the Present United Colonies* . . . (London, 1789), 619, 626; and Chalmers, *An Introduction to the History of the Revolt of the American Colonies* . . . (Boston, 1845), I, 150. Extract of a Letter from the Mayor of New York, dated the 13th May 1685, in William Hand Browne, ed., *Archives of Maryland*, V (Baltimore, 1887), 444–445. Why James should neglect his own legal advisers and ask for an opinion from Sir William Jones, ardent Whig and a leader in the drive to exclude James from the throne, is not altogether clear. For a partial explanation, see John E. Pomfret, *The Province of West New Jersey, 1609–1702* . . . (Princeton, 1956), 111–112, and *The Province of East New Jersey, 1609–1702* . . . (Princeton, 1962), 121–123. See also Mrs. Schuyler Van Rensselaer, *History of the City of New York in the Seventeenth Century* (New York, 1909), II, 203. Sir William Jones's stand against taxation without representation made him a champion among American colonists. See his opinion as attorney general respecting Virginia's attempt in 1675 to secure from Charles II a charter which would guarantee Virginians the right to tax themselves, in John Burk, *The History of Virginia* . . . , II (Petersburg, Va., 1822), Appendix, xl–xli. See also Cotton Mather, *Magnalia Christi Americana* . . . (Hartford, 1820), I, 162.

[19] Duke of York to Brockholls, Mar. 28, 1682, in *Documents of N.Y.*, III, 317–318; Werden to Brockholls, Feb. 11, 1682, in *Cal. St. Papers, Col., 1681–1685*, p. 197.

III

James's new governor, Colonel Thomas Dongan, a Catholic, arrived in New York in August 1683 carrying instructions to call an assembly.[20] Dongan had not been off the boat very long before the people of East-hampton, probably unaware of the governor's intent, cornered him with a petition, citing fully all the arguments in favor of a colonial legislature. The arrangement made in 1664 between them and Richard Nicolls, they claimed, was a "compact" which they alone had fulfilled. They stressed what Long Islanders had tirelessly repeated: a wish for status equal to that of subjects in other colonies, claiming that their unequal condition deprived them of a fundamental privilege of the "English Nation." In short order the governor issued writs for an election of representatives.[21]

On October 17, 1683, less than two months after Dongan arrived, the first meeting of the New York assembly took place at Fort James. Long Islanders sent six deputies — two from each riding; New York City with Haerlem, four; Esopus (now Kingston) and Albany (including Rensel-laerswyck), two each; Staten Island, Schenectady, Pemaquid, and the islands, each one. Eighteen in all, they were elected, directly or indirectly, by the freeholders, although in New York City, Pemaquid, and Sche-nectady the sheriffs "appointed" the freeholders who in turn elected representatives. As to who these men were, one can be reasonably sure of the identity of only about half of them.[22] Probably a majority were origi-nally Dutch and not English.[23] Yet the Charter of Libertyes is very much an English document, which strongly suggests that the six Long Islanders and the few other Englishmen present took the lead over their Dutch colleagues in the task before them. Far better known than the names of of the members is what they accomplished, for the result speaks for itself.

Of primary importance was the Charter of Libertyes and Priviledges which the members drafted as a frame of government protecting in no

---

[20] *Documents of N.Y.*, III, 331–334.

[21] Easthampton petition is found in Benjamin F. Thompson, *History of Long Island* . . . , 3d ed. (New York, 1918), III, 637–640; O'Callaghan, *Origin of Representative Assemblies*, 14–17.

[22] For the various methods of electing representatives see the writs issued by Dongan in O'Callaghan, *Origin of Representative Assemblies*, 16–17. For names of some of the delegates see Marius Schoonmaker, *The History of Kingston, New York* . . . (New York, 1888), 75; Van Rensselaer, *Hist. of City of New York*, II, 259; J. W. Thornton, "Ancient Pemaquid: an Historical Review," in Maine Historical Society, *Collections*, V (Portland, 1857), 263–264; A.J.F. Van Laer, ed., *Correspondence of Maria Van Rensselaer, 1669–1689* (Albany, 1935), 127; and Edgar A. Werner, *Civil List and Constitutional History of the Colony and State of New York* . . . (Albany, 1889), 67.

[23] John West to William Penn, Oct. 16, 1683, in Samuel Hazard, ed., *Pennsylvania Archives*, Ser. 1, I (Philadelphia, 1852), 80.

uncertain terms the colonists' individual liberties, the right of property, and the right to consent to their laws and taxes. Even a quick reading of the Charter impresses one with the colonists' desire to guarantee for themselves rights English subjects anywhere ought to enjoy. Secondly, the very statement of these rights implied strongly that they had not enjoyed them under the Duke — that they, in fact, had been governed arbitrarily, setting them apart from his Majesty's subjects elsewhere.

First of all, the Charter set up a frame or structure, as the preamble stated, for the "better Establishing the Government of this province of New Yorke and that Justice and Right may be Equally done to all persons within the same." [24] Supreme legislative authority, under the King and the Duke of York, was to reside forever in "a Governor, Councell, and the people mett in Generall Assembly." Executive authority was lodged in a governor and council who were to rule "according to the Lawes." The Charter rescaled representation in the assembly by county, varying it from four deputies allowed from the city and county of New York to two from all other counties except Albany which might send three. Again the Charter explicitly stated that once these representatives met with the governor and council, they would forever be "the Supreame and only Legislative power under his Royall Highnesse." Bills approved by the legislature were to become laws and remain in force until vetoed by the Duke or repealed.

The framers of the Charter went out of their way to provide for the protection of individual liberties. The right to vote for representatives was guaranteed to the freeholders and freemen of any corporation, and the Charter defined a freeholder as anyone so understood according to the laws of England — a clear case of equality there. The article guaranteeing liberty of person, one of the most fundamental rights of Englishmen, came directly from Magna Carta, II, 39 and 40: "THAT Noe freeman shall be taken and imprisoned or be disseized of his Freehold or Libertye or Free Customes or be outlawed or Exiled or any other wayes destroyed nor shall be passed upon adjudged or condemned But by the Lawfull Judgment of his peers and by the Law of this province." From the Petition of Right of 1628 came a paragraph protecting New Yorkers from taxation without representation. Another defended property rights and smacked generally of both Magna Carta and the Petition of Right. Other fundamental rights, such as trial by jury, no excessive bail, and guarantees against quartering troops in private homes in peacetime, were included — every one of which protected the colonists from arbitrary treatment and suggested that under the previous government they had been apprehensive of such rights.

Besides personal and property rights, the legislators wrote into the

[24] The Charter can be found in *Colonial Laws of N.Y.*, I, 111–116.

Charter provisions for a number of parliamentary privileges for their legislature, which would have allowed a remarkable degree of legislative independence and fortified it against encroachment from either Duke or governor. Triennial meetings were guaranteed, a right Parliament in England had had trouble securing only a few years earlier and then not honored by the Crown. Representatives were empowered to appoint times of their meeting and to adjourn from time to time and assemble again as they pleased. They were to be sole judges of the qualifications of their own members and could purge their house as they saw fit. Also assembly members and at least three servants each were to be protected from arrest going to and from and during their sessions. It is clear the New Yorkers thought of their legislature as a little Parliament and intended by such privileges to maintain its power, dignity, and prestige.

The longest section in the Charter was devoted to religion, and well it might be since New York contained a heterogeneous population, each part of which maintained its own church. Long Island was predominantly Puritan and Congregational. The Calvinist churches of the Dutch appeared throughout most of the colony, particularly in New York and Albany. A number of Germans, Swedes, and other Europeans supported churches of their own. The Duke's official party was divided between Catholics (Dongan and a few others) and the more numerous Anglicans. Considerable time was probably spent by the drafters in agreeing upon a religious policy. The Long Islanders may well have been a little stiff-necked about the whole thing, and although they went along with liberty of conscience for Christians, which was, of course, a practical necessity as it had been earlier, they saw to it that the Charter confirmed the supported churches in their Long Island towns as long as two thirds of each town meeting approved. Moreover, they got written into the Charter power to compel the minor third of each town to contribute to the church's support. Liberty of conscience for Christians, yes, but as far as the English towns of Long Island were concerned, the public worship of God would continue under majority control, and the ministers' salaries would come out of taxes as was the custom in New England. All other Christian churches within the colony the Charter confirmed generally allowing them to continue their privileges.

The Charter of Libertyes is strong evidence that a number of New Yorkers had a definite idea of the kind of government colonists three thousand miles from the realm ought to enjoy. But the very liberal aspects of the Charter might lead one to believe that political and constitutional principles were *all* the framers had in mind when they drafted it. It would be wrong to assume that the New Yorkers had inquired into their unequal condition in the empire and drafted a charter to correct it only from a dispassionate love of principle. New Yorkers were made aware of these inequalities by conditions which, they believed, affected their peculiar interests, for such inequalities frequently cost them money, deprived them of economic opportunities they believed they were entitled to, or discriminated against them by denying them rights which other English subjects enjoyed. That New Yorkers should express their discontent about these inequalities in political and constitutional terms is what one would expect. This is the way political and constitutional principles usually evolve or are developed] It must be remembered that English liberties protected property and economic opportunity as well as civil and human rights. Members of the assembly owned property, or they would not have been elected, and they represented people who owned property, people who could not otherwise have voted for them.

New York colonists were well aware that the power to tax is the power to control property, and the Charter placed this power in the hands of the new legislature. But even this guarantee, it seems, was not sufficient for colonists whose property heretofore had been subject to the whim of a proprietor. Before the Duke ever saw the Charter, the lower house had expanded the "Libertyes" of the constitution and tightened the representatives' grip on the taxing power. On the same day the Charter was agreed to, the assembly worded the first revenue act in a style which echoed the House of Commons' similar business. It was the "Representatives" of the province of New York, with the advice and consent of the governor and council, which gave and granted to the Duke the "dutyes and Customes hereafter Specified." [25] Although the Charter granted control over taxes to the legislature as a whole — governor, council, and deputies — the lower house, the freeholders' representatives, at the very outset, asserted the right to originate money bills, just as did the House of Commons.

Each settled area of the colony had its peculiar demands, and no doubt these were seriously considered by the deputies and councilmen who drafted the Charter and enacted laws under it. That the six Long Islanders looked to their own interests and found votes to support them is already evident in the Charter's confirmation of religious privileges. Even better proof of Long Island influence was the new legislature's immediate repeal of a law which had annually taxed Long Islanders' property to defray public charges. The reason given for repeal was that "provision is otherwise made" for the colony's income, and the provision, of course, was the new revenue law which taxed through customs and excise.[26] The shift of part of the burden of taxation from Long Islanders' real estate to the colony's trade certainly suggests that their interest was well served by the assembly.

No doubt there were differences of opinion among those who fash-

[25] *Ibid.*, 116–117.
[26] *Ibid.*, 124. See J. M. Neil, Long Island, 1640–1691: the Defeat of Town Autonomy (unpubl. M.A. thesis, University of Wisconsin, 1963), 95.

ioned the Charter, and debates over its drafting must have reflected several definite points of view. But it must be remembered that it was acceptable to the council as well as the representatives of the freeholders. And Dongan's council was an appointed body containing six individuals whose careers in government hardly demonstrated a devotion to the rights of Englishmen and government by consent. Four of the six, including Brockholls and Dongan, continued in office from 1686 to 1688, after the business of the Charter was forgotten; and, when New York joined the Dominion of New England, Edmund Andros appointed to his council five of the six, again including Brockholls.[27] It was against the likes of these, men who willingly accepted arbitrary roles as rulers of New York under both Dongan and Andros, that Jacob Leisler revolted in 1689 in an attempt, among other things, to break the oligarchy and distribute the privileges of office and monopoly more widely, particularly to his own group.[28] Two years later, when royal Governor Henry Sloughter settled the colony's government after Leisler's Rebellion, he recommended three of the original six and one of the representatives of the 1683 assembly for seats on his council as persons of "approved Loyalty and Integrity," which, in light of the times, meant men who could be trusted to act with the royal government.[29]

The assembly which drafted the Charter *elected* Matthias Nicolls, now back from his mission to Scotland, its speaker. Nicolls, a trained lawyer and very able public servant, was a prerogative man who had come to the colony in 1664 as secretary to the Royal Commission and supposedly helped to draft the Duke's Laws the next year. He had been hand-in-glove with Governors Nicolls, Lovelace, and Andros; in 1680 he was both secretary of the council and a member of the Court of Assizes. He headed Dongan's council in 1686 but died before Andros drew New York into the Dominion. Owing to his close relationship with the proprietary government and his score or more years in vital offices, Nicolls was doubtless the most influential member of the legislature of 1683 next to Dongan. It is probable that he was more responsible than any other individual for the form the Charter took.[30]

[27] O'Callaghan, *Origin of Legislative Assemblies*, 17; Werner, *Civil List*, 363–364; *Documents of N.Y.*, III, 543.

[28] For a recent interpretation of Leisler's Rebellion, see Lawrence H. Leder, *Robert Livingston, 1654–1728, and the Politics of Colonial New York* (Chapel Hill, 1961), chap. 4.

[29] Werner, *Civil List*, 363–364; N.-Y. Hist. Soc., *Colls.*, XLV, 9; Sloughter to the Earl of Nottingham, Mar. 27, 1691, in *Documents of N.Y.*, III, 756.

[30] For pertinent information about Matthias Nicolls, see Thompson, *Hist. of Long Island*, III, 334–335; Brodhead, *Hist. of N.Y.*, II, 335–336; Leonard W. Labaree in *DAB* s.v. "Nicolls, Matthias"; Samuel Maverick to the Earl of Clarendon, Sept. 1, 1663, in N.-Y. Hist. Soc., *Colls.*, II (New York, 1870), 57, and *Colls.*, XLV, 3; *Minutes of the Common Council of the City of New York*

John Spragge, who served on Dongan's and later Andros's Dominion council, was appointed clerk of the assembly which drafted the Charter, and during the year the Duke commissioned him secretary of the colony.[31] The failure of Dongan himself to veto the Charter (for reasons to be discussed later) is even surer evidence that those who controlled the government of New York had their own reasons for co-operation.

⎣If such men as these were happy with the Charter, men who were firm supporters of any government, regardless of its principles, it must have been for reasons closely related to their own interests. Or to put it another way: if the Duke of York had decided upon representative government for New York, albeit as a last resort to secure its financial support, then that government ought to represent the interests of those who held positions of power. These men would mold the Charter in such a way that their particular needs might be reflected in the government the Charter established. While the new legislature afforded New York colonists treatment equal to what they believed other colonists and Englishmen at home enjoyed, at the same time it gave a smaller group of insiders a splendid opportunity to conduct the affairs of New York for their own good. The rights of Englishmen and colonial self-interest were peas of the same pod⎦ But the whole scheme would mean little if the Duke failed to go along.

IV

The first step was to get the Charter past Governor Dongan who, as proprietary governor, was responsible for the Duke's interests. Fortunately, this proved to be no problem, and the reason may be that one of the first laws passed by the new legislature presented Dongan with a handsome sum of money, equal to a penny in the pound on all real and personal property belonging to freeholders and inhabitants.[32] Stephen Van Cort-

---

(New York, 1905), I, 4, 19, 48–49, 66, VIII, 149; Richard B. Morris, ed., *Select Cases of the Mayor's Court of New York City, 1674–1784* (Washington, 1935), 50; Secretary Nicolls to Colonel Nicolls, Dec. 31, 1669, in *Documents of N.Y.,* III, 186; Governor Dongan's Report on the State of the Province, *ibid.,* 417; Van Laer, ed., *Min. of Court of Albany,* III, 27; and Charles M. Andrews, *The Colonial Period of American History,* III (New Haven, 1937), 116, 117. Andrews asserts that Nicolls was largely responsible for drafting the Charter of Libertyes. For a different view, see Van Rensselaer, *Hist. of City of New York,* II, 263–264; and Charles B. Moore, "Laws of 1683 – Old Records and Old Politics," *New York Genealogical and Biographical Record,* XVIII (1887), 61. Rosalie Fellows Bailey, *The Nicoll Family and Islip Grange . . .* (New York, 1940), 9.

[31] Werner, *Civil List,* 363–364; *Documents of N.Y.,* III, 543; Commission from the Duke of York appointing John Spragge Secretary of New York, Jan. 27, 1683, in *Cal. St. Papers, Col., 1681–1685,* p. 378.

[32] *Colonial Laws of N.Y.,* I, 137–138; *Min. of Common Council of N.Y.C.,* I, 102. See again J. M. Neil, *Long Island, 1640–1691,* pp. 94–96.

landt of the council, who informally represented the huge Van Rensselaer estate in the new legislature, suggested that his constituents not oppose the move "as it is for the governor," implying that they could not afford to offend Dongan at this juncture since the Van Rensselaers were seeking at that very time his confirmation of a land claim.[33] The gift to Dongan was probably not considered outright bribery by the colonists but rather a "suitable returne" for the "many great favours" conferred upon them by the governor. Following Dongan's approval, the Charter of Libertyes was published at the City Hall on the last day of October 1683 in the presence of the governor, council, and representatives, the "Inhabitants having notice by sound of Trumpet." [34]

The second step was to obtain the Duke's approval. The Duke had agreed to grant an assembly if the colony would contribute the necessary financial support for the government and make up the arrears. At its first session the assembly levied ample taxes to carry the government's charges, but in doing so it stated that the revenue act was in consideration of the gracious favors extended to the colonists by the Duke — the favors included, of course, his future confirmation of the Charter already drafted, which, they claimed, restored their rights.[35] For granting an assembly the Duke received a sufficient revenue; for granting a sufficient revenue the New Yorkers hoped to secure approval of their very liberal Charter which put control of government in the hands of their legislature. There was a good deal of risk in this transaction on the assembly's part, but Dongan's immediate acceptance of the whole business was certainly encouraging.

Once the Charter became effective and the revenue assured, the scene shifted from the Duke's colony in America to Lond and the English court. After James's commissioners, who handled his colonial business, made a few suggested amendments respecting customs, James, in October 1684, one year after the drafting of the Charter, signed and sealed it and sent it to the Auditor to be registered with orders to dispatch it to New York.[36]

But this was as far as it got. Suddenly the Charter of Libertyes ran up against obstacles in England the New York colonists had neither knowledge of nor means to combat.

---

[33] Stephanus Van Cortlandt to Maria Van Rensselaer, Nov. 2, 1683, in Van Laer, ed., *Correspondence of Maria Van Rensselaer*, 132. See also pp. 7, 127.

[34] *Colonial Laws of N.Y.*, I, 137–138; *Min. of Common Council of N.Y.C.*, I, 99.

[35] *Colonial Laws of N.Y.*, I, 116–117.

[36] Sir John Werden to Dongan, Mar. 10, 1684, in *Documents of N.Y.*, III, 341; Duke of York to Dongan, Aug. 26, 1684, in *Cal. St. Papers, Col., 1681–1685*, p. 679; Memorandum, Oct. 4, 1684, *ibid.*, p. 695; *The Historical Magazine*, VI (1862), 233.

The final years of Charles II's reign, punctuated by the Exclusion Crisis, intrigue, and several tangled plots, left him bitter and inclined to reaction, even revenge, against Whigs, dissenters, and corporation charters, particularly that of the City of London, whose juries had thwarted his will. In the last three years of his life Charles surrounded himself with an inner group of favorites — Lords Sunderland, Godolphin, Jeffreys, and above all Lady Portsmouth — who, along with M. Paul Barillon, the French minister, had the King's ear. This knot of advisers, often called the "French party," helped Charles steer an arbitrary course which resulted in more stringent policies toward the major issues of the 1680's. Charles died before the new plans jelled, but sufficient momentum was generated and strongly felt in the destruction of the London charter and in the sharp turn in the direction of colonial policy.[37]

[In November and December 1684, three months before the King's death, Charles and the Privy Council did some very serious thinking about the colonies in America. In fact, steps toward reorganization of the colonies had commenced several years earlier with an attack upon the Massachusetts Bay Charter which was finally revoked in October 1684. In order to bring other colonial governments more closely under control of the King, Charles began actions against Maryland, the Carolinas, both New Jerseys, and Delaware; and James even agreed to surrender proprietary New York to the Crown.[38]]

A major question before the King and Council, once the way was clear to consolidate New England under one head, was what kind of government it ought to have. Should the colonists retain their legislative assemblies, or should they be told what laws they might have by a governor and council as New Yorkers had been told since 1664? Discussion of this question in the Privy Council explains a great deal about the Stuart concept of empire and how Charles and James thought colonists ought to be governed.

It was Lord Halifax who brought the issue to a head when he spoke very pointedly in defense of colonial assemblies at a Privy Council meeting in early December which both Charles and James attended. M. Barillon got wind of the whole business — he may have attended the Council meeting — and reported to Louis XIV Halifax's argument. It was unques-

---

[37] David Ogg, *England in the Reign of Charles II* (Oxford, 1934), II, chap. 17; J. P. Kenyon, *Robert Spencer, Earl of Sunderland, 1641–1702* (London, 1958), chap. 3; *Bishop Burnet's History of His Own Time* . . . (London, 1857), 390–391.

[38] For the attack upon the charter and proprietary colonies, see Philip S. Haffenden, "The Crown and the Colonial Charters, 1675–1688," *William and Mary Quarterly*, 3d Ser., XV (1958), 297–311, 452–466; *Cal. St. Papers, Col., 1681–1685*, passim; Blathwayt Papers, I, IV, and particularly Blathwayt to Governor Effingham, Dec. 9, 1684, in XIV.

tionable, said Halifax, that "the same laws under which they live in England ought to be established in a country inhabited by Englishmen." He lectured the Council at length with a variety of reasons why "an absolute government is neither so happy no so stable as that which is tempered by laws and sets bounds to the authority of the prince." He ended his appeal with the plain declaration "that he could never like to live under a King who should have it in his power to take at pleasure the money out of his pocket." But Halifax was opposed by all who heard him, especially Lord Jeffreys, who replied that when it came to a question of the King's prerogative "whoso capitulateth rebelleth" — that the very attempt to define the function of the sovereign was equivalent to revolution. Ignoring Halifax's appeal, the Privy Council resolved that a governor and council alone should rule New England, "accountable only to his Britannic Majesty." Halifax paid for his boldness, for the Duke of York used the occasion to undermine Charles's confidence in Halifax by arguing that it was dangerous to share secrets of government with a man so critical of the King's prerogative. M. Barrillon reported to Louis that Lady Portsmouth and Sunderland were pleased with Halifax's defeat, and that both agreed their plans, which aimed at eliminating Halifax and persuading the King to assert his prerogative, were going nicely.[39]

The thinking of Charles, James, and the Privy Council about colonial government in late 1684 was certainly inimical to the kind of charter New Yorkers had drafted for themselves. Despite James's agreement to it in October, the Charter had not yet been returned to New York. Moreover, it would not be. Charles died in February 1685 and James, who had even stronger convictions about the prerogative, succeeded him as king.

In the meantime the Lords of Trade had decided to submit the New York Charter to scrutiny, doubtless persuaded to it by the abrupt change in colonial policy and probably by James himself. The re-appraisal resulted in what the scrutinizers called "Observations," and these clearly pointed out to all who read or heard them the true nature of the Charter: that it granted to New Yorkers rights and privileges not just equal to those enjoyed by English subjects in other colonies but doubtless greater than any other colonists enjoyed. The observers agreed that under the Charter, inhabitants of New York would be actually governed according to the laws of England, not merely as close to them as their colonial conditions might permit. This was a "Priviledge" not granted to any of the King's colonists in America. Further, the words of the Charter lodging the supreme legislative authority in the governor, council, and the "People" met

[39] Barrillon to Louis XIV, Dec. 7, 1684, in Charles James Fox, *A History of the Early Part of the Reign of James the Second* . . . (London, 1808), Appendix, vii–ix; Louis XIV to Barrillon, Dec. 13, 1684, *ibid.*, ix; H. C. Foxcroft, *The Life and Letters of Sir George Saville, Bart., First Marquis of Halifax &C.* . . . (London, 1898), I, 427–429.

in general assembly, represented an innovation and were found in no other colonial constitution or charter. The observers pointed out several other differences. The governor was much too dependent upon the council, more so than any other governor in America — which may help to explain the New York council's willingness to approve the Charter. It was true that the King was supposed to call Parliament in England at least once every three years, but to require that the legislature of New York have triennial meetings would be to put a greater obligation on the government than "ever agreed to in any other Plantation." Moreover, such a privilege had been rejected in other places "notwithstanding a Revenue offered to induce it" — a revealing admission at least. Since the governor, council, and representatives under the Charter were the supreme and only legislative power of New York, the observers asked, would not such power seriously "abridge the Acts of Parliament that may be made concerning New York?" Doubtless the New Yorkers would have agreed that this was precisely the case.[40]

[The New York Charter, the government it established, and the differences between them and what existed in other colonies were fully and finally discussed at a meeting of the Lords of Trade on March 3, 1685, with James II, the Earl of Sunderland, and Lord Godolphin all present. The conclusion reached was simple and to the point: "His Majesty doth not think fitt to confirm the same."] The government of New York, it was agreed, would "be assimilated to the Constitution that shall be agreed on for New England, to which it is adjoining." [41] Two days later James II wrote to Dongan announcing his accession to the throne and that New York was now a royal colony attached to the Crown. He ordered Dongan to hold the line as it was and to follow former instructions. Tell my subjects, he wrote, that the colony and its affairs are now committed to his Privy Council and they "may shortly expect such a gracious and suitable return by the settlement of fitting privileges and confirmation of their rights as shall bee found most expedient for Our service and the welfare of Our said Province." [42] More than a year later the colonists learned just what James meant, for in May 1686 he wrote fresh instructions to Governor Dongan declaring the New York Charter "disallowed . . . Repealed, determined and made void." The governor and council, however, were to continue the duties and impositions which were levied under the Charter until they decided otherwise upon taxes sufficient to support the government. In addition, all other laws passed by New Yorkers under the

[40] Journal of Lords of Trade and Plantations, Feb. 28, 1685, in *Cal. State Papers, Col.*, 1685–1688, p. 7. For the Observations upon the Charter of the Province of New-York, dated Mar. 3, 1685, see *Documents of N.Y.*, III, 357–359.

[41] *Documents of N.Y.*, III, 354, 357.

[42] *Ibid.*, 360–361.

short-lived government were to remain in force as long as they were not contrary to the governor's instructions.[43] The colonial assembly met in October 1685, but Dongan found "weighty and important Reasons" for proroguing it to the next year. In September 1686 repeal of the Charter was read to the governor's council, not to the whole legislature, along with Dongan's new commission and instructions. The Charter assembly never met again.[44]

Whether New Yorkers believed they had been tricked is not known. Certainly it must have appeared to some that the Duke permitted an assembly so that it might vote funds on its own terms; and once it had done so, he abolished the legislature and retained the tax laws. But probably the Duke was not quite so bold-facedly disingenuous. The New York Charter ran up against sharp Stuart reaction to Whiggism and republicanism which had its certain effect on imperial policy. In fact, the Charter was scrutinized for the last time at a crucial turning point in colonial policy which hinged on revocation of the Massachusetts Bay Charter and the decision to unite New England under one government. Begun by Charles, the new policy was strenuously pursued by James once on the throne, and the result was the Dominion of New England to which New York was added in 1688. With these plans materializing in London, no wonder James lost sympathy for the New York Charter which granted his colonists a status not only equal to that of other colonists but surely even more advantageous. What is more, if the Lords of Trade accurately understood the Charter, it gave to New Yorkers the same laws Englishmen enjoyed. And all of this was to become fact at the very time the Crown had decided to rule over half of the American colonies with little or no regard for the rights of Englishmen, let alone Englishmen's laws. The Dominion of New England under Andros proved that colonists enjoyed only the rights a Stuart king wished to give them, and despite the efforts of New Yorkers, these did not include representative government.

It is clear that New York colonists, at least those who drafted the Charter and approved of it, were vitally interested in the rights of Englishmen as they defined them, and the use of Magna Carta and the Petition of Right was proof that they knew them pretty well. New Yorkers demanded rights equal to what they believed other colonists enjoyed and saw no reason why these should not be equal at the same time to those of Englishmen at home. Although they were colonists of a proprietary government, they made it known that they did not regard themselves subordinate or inferior to his Majesty's other subjects anywhere. Their

[43] Instructions, *ibid.*, 370; James II's Commission to Dongan, *ibid.*, 378.
[44] *Min. of Common Council of N.Y.C.*, I, 166–167, 180; Minutes of Council of New York, Sept. 14, 1686, in *Cal. St. Papers, Col., 1685–1688*, p. 242.

concept of empire demonstrated a strong belief in equality among its members as far as government, rights, and opportunities were concerned. And the idea of equality they hoped to fix with a permanent charter which would guarantee it to them. This was a bold interpretation of empire in 1683, particularly in view of the fact that the Crown, Parliament, and Proprietor were only beginning to decide what rights colonists ought to have, and what they decided was a far cry from what New Yorkers assumed to be true.

In the eighteenth century most provincial asemblies in defense of self-interest and colonial rights steadily encroached upon the prerogative of the Crown and usurped authority from the King's governors. When in the 1760's Parliament and King challenged these assumptions, Americans were forced to define their ideas and concluded that, as equal members of the Empire, they ought to enjoy equal rights with Englishmen. Ahead of their time, seventeenth-century New Yorkers tried in one fell-swoop to do the same thing and set themselves up with the rights of Englishmen protected through a fundamental law of their own making. Most Americans did not fully contemplate for almost another century an empire so firmly based upon the idea of equality.

The House of Lords, Edward Randolph, and the Navigation Act of 1696

MICHAEL G. HALL

It is probably misleading to speak of a British empire during the colonial period. The colonies were begun as private or commercial ventures and the English government was very slow to assert its authority in America, so that a central administrative system for colonial affairs developed in a gradual and inefficient manner. The difficulty was that Englishmen had neither a theory of empire nor constitutional arrangements suitable to imperial government, they viewed the colonies primarily in terms of their economic value to Great Britain, and they seldom paused to consider the colonies as a separate problem.

In so far as there was an imperial system, it was structured by the Navigation Acts, which defined the economic relationship of the American possessions to the homeland. The Navigation Acts have sometimes been treated as though they formed a unified, rational scheme of commercial imperialism, but it is one of the virtues of Michael Hall's essay on the Act of 1696 to show that it was the outcome of a much more complex political process. While it was in part a response to English merchant complaints about colonial trade, it was even more immediately the product of Scottish competition, the personal lobbying of a single royal official, and the constitutional aggressiveness of the post-Revolutionary House of Lords. As is true of modern legislation, the act was both more and less than the sum of the interests which combined to make it law.

Hall's essay raises a number of interesting questions for colonial historians. What was the impact of English mercantile opinion upon colonial policy? To what extent was imperial administration influenced by constitutional considerations, and how far was it simply the product of domestic politics? Could American intervention influence the course of imperial decision-making? Above all, the essay forces us to keep England in mind when thinking about the colonies.

The constitutional form of England's colonial empire grew hesitantly, almost imperceptibly, during most of the seventeenth century. Like the English constitution itself, relationships between colonies and crown were defined over many years and in divers ways: by royal charter, judicial decision, administrative order, and by Act of Parliament. Towards the close of the century this process of definition accelerated. In 1696–97 the last of the Navigation Acts together with subsequent administrative orders implemented a policy of strict, centralized control. Edward Randolph, general factotum for the crown in America, was responsible for much in the new policy. But it was the English House of Lords which gave authority to and indeed initiated many of the changes, all of them at the colonies' expense.

Every English colony on the North American mainland save one had had its beginning as a private enterprise. Even by 1695 only two out of a dozen were wholly governed by the crown, and those two at such distance as to make effective control from England dubious at best. The rest

Reprinted by permission from Michael G. Hall, "The House of Lords, Edward Randolph, and the Navigation Act of 1696," *William and Mary Quarterly*, 3d Ser., XIV (1957), 494–515.

were private colonies, existing by authority of royal charters. Several charters had been issued to "proprietors," giving them ownership of the land and the right to govern. Others were given to the corporate bodies of colonists themselves. In neither case, proprietary or corporate, were the charters uniform, and a keen particularism existed throughout the settled areas of North America. The chartered colonies considered themselves to varying degrees independent of the king's governments in England.

Ever since the Stuart Restoration in 1660 London had been experimenting in ways to organize these overseas settlements. By 1672 canons governing economic relations between England and the colonies had been formulated in the Navigation Acts, 1660–72. It was soon evident, however, that without political control in America, the elaborate economic regulations would be difficult, if not impossible, to enforce. Hence the Dominion of New England (1686–1689), an experiment which put the independent chartered colonies under direct royal government. This experiment came to a disastrous end when the colonists revolted in 1689. By 1695 those men in London who were responsible for the management of England's empire were more than ever anxious to devise efficient colonial administration. Back from the plantations at this time came Edward Randolph, a man unsurpassed in knowledge of the colonial scene and untiring in his efforts to promote the authority of the crown.

Randolph sailed from Maryland with the tobacco fleet in the summer of 1695. He had been surveyor general of customs in America since 1691. Before that, as collector of His Majesty's customs in New England, he had encountered every local resistance short of brute force. In the four years since 1691, when he toured all the coastline from Maine to Virginia, Randolph had continued to meet with evasions and frustrations whenever he tried to enforce the Navigation Acts. Aside from a full catalogue of tricks to smuggle goods, he found that many customs collectors were dishonest, that local juries would not convict for the crown, and that all too often colonial governors were indifferent, if not opposed, to strict enforcement. It was to correct these things that Randolph had sailed for England.

On October 16, 1695, Randolph submitted to the Customs House in London an important paper: "An Account of severall things whereby illegal Trade is encouraged in Virginia Maryland and Pensilvania, together with Methods for prevention thereof." [1] Here in detail — but without the scope or literary charm of some of his earlier papers — are Ran-

---

[1] *Edward Randolph; including his Letters and Official Papers . . .* , ed. Robert Noxon Toppan and Alfred T. S. Goodrick (Boston, 1898–1909), V, 117–124. A list of illegal traders accompanied the report. *Calendar of State Papers, Colonial, 1693–1696* (London, 1903), 2237; *Manuscripts of the House of Lords, 1695–1697*, N. S. (London, 1903), II, 446. It was probably the same as a list submitted later to the Board of Trade, July 31, 1696. *Randolph Letters*, V, 139–140.

dolph's observations on misconduct in that most important of all trades, tobacco. He described under twelve heads what dodges were used to evade the Navigation Acts. Typically he included names and cases, for Randolph was a stickler for precision. It was typical too that his suggested remedies — in twelve corresponding paragraphs — also dealt in fine detail, recommending specific fines and prison terms. Randolph was a blunt man. In his first observation on illegal trading he criticized his colleagues in the customs service for "ignorance, remissness or connivance." This paragraph was suppressed by the customs commissioners when they prepared copies of Randolph's paper in the winter of 1695–96, so the official version of the October 16 paper contained only eleven items on misconduct and eleven remedies.[2] At first Randolph's paper lay at the Customs House; not until William and Mary's third Parliament began to inquire into the state of the nation did its subject become matter for national debate.

It was appropriate that after the Glorious Revolution Parliament should become the scene of many decisions on colonial affairs. That revolution had ushered in Whiggery, a new age of the constitutional monarch, and above all a businesslike attention to the nation's commerce. To be sure, William III proved a haughty champion of royal prerogative and remained in several instances the final arbiter of colonial policy. But now for the first time the Lords and Commons entered fully into the government of the colonies, and it was before Parliament, especially the House of Lords, that Randolph appeared in his most influential role.

To understand Parliament's concern, we must recall briefly the curious position of England's domestic and foreign business. Between the Restoration and the Revolution, England had experienced a magnificent prosperity. Particularly had foreign commerce grown steadily.[3] These happy circumstances were reversed in 1689 by the outbreak of war with France. The issue, for England's trade, lay in control of the seas. Victory there could for a time have gone to France as easily as to England. Not until success at La Hogue made up the damage done at Beachy Head were England and the Netherlands together superior to the French in fighting vessels. After La Hogue, France concentrated on destroying England's ocean commerce, and the English navy found it impossible to provide adequate convoy protection. In one estimate 3000 English merchantmen had fallen to French privateers before the end of 1692.[4] Gains in foreign trade made since the Restoration were wiped out. Yet at the same time

[2] House of Lords MSS, II, 449–451.

[3] William R. Scott, The Constitution and Finance of English, Scottish and Irish Joint-Stock Companies to 1720 (Cambridge, Eng., 1910–12), I, 317. In twenty-five years indices of national wealth are shown to have increased 25 per cent, of national savings 100 per cent, and of foreign trade 50 per cent.

[4] Ibid., I, 328. For colonial losses see House of Lords MSS, II, 64.

England's domestic economy flourished. Because shipping lay fettered through the length of the war, an important outlet for capital investment was pinched off, dammed up until 1697, while swelling capital funds looked in vain for a safe overseas outlet.

English merchants protested, and not only against the insufficiency of naval protection. They continued as before to charge that the Navigation Acts were poorly enforced; that smugglers easily avoided English customs and ruined legitimate trade. The outports of Bristol and Liverpool petitioned Parliament.[5] The Customs House received evidence of habitual violations. The great London merchant Micajah Perry explained how he and others found colonial bills of exchange being returned via tobacco ships discharging at Glasgow, a port expressly forbidden to colonial tobacco. The Customs House declared in 1694 a revenue loss of £50,000 from such illegal trade.[6] In 1697 Francis Nicholson sent from Maryland a list of 115 vessels which had posted bond to sail direct to England but which had not troubled or been able to return proof of having done so.[7]

To cap it all, halfway through 1695 the Scots threatened to break into England's colonial monopoly. Added to a long and growing animosity between the two countries, nothing more exacerbated the English merchants. A group of entrepreneurs in England and Scotland organized a trading company with intentions of establishing a factory at Darien on the isthmus between North and South America. For the new enterprise the Scottish government would waive import duties on colonial goods. Once these staples were landed in Scotland, they were sure to move south into England and there undersell colonial staples which had paid the heavy English customs. This open threat of regular competition touched off a storm of protest which in its first gust forced the crown to outlaw participation by Englishmen in the Darien Company.

The pressure of war, the prevalence of illegal trading, the Scottish proposal, all combined to focus Parliament's interest on the empire. Thus it was when Parliament convened in the winter of 1695 the House of Lords turned at once to the Darien Company and to the condition of colonial trade in general. In the early weeks of December representatives of the English trading companies, of the Customs House, and of the English subscribers to the Darien Company were questioned by the Lords. After several hearings the customs commissioners were directed to bring to the House of Lords a written statement of ways to meet the threat of a Scottish factory in America.[8]

[5] *Proceedings and Debates of the British Parliaments respecting North America*, ed. Leo F. Stock (Washington, 1924–41), II, 104, 106, 107–108. For the extent of Scottish interloping see *House of Lords MSS*, II, 464.

[6] Stock, *Debates*, II, 110–112.

[7] *Cal. State Papers, Col., 1696–1697* (London, 1904), 864 v.

[8] *House of Lords MSS*, II, 3–5.

Edward Randolph foresaw, or more likely was privately informed, which way the wind would blow. He prepared his own proposals for preventing a Scottish colony and submitted them on December 7, 1695, to the customs commissioners.[9] Completely rational and utterly unrealistic, Randolph's proposals outlined a sweeping reorganization of the colonies. He argued from the premise that the proprietary and corporate colonies might provide a site for the proposed Scottish factory. We have today no evidence that this was a real danger. On the other hand, we do know that Randolph, after twenty years of colonial service, was convinced that the quasi-independent charter colonies would never become loyal members of England's colonial empire. It seems clear that Randolph hoped to use "this time of danger" to rush through the abolition of corporate and proprietary colonies.

Randolph's plan was that South Carolina and the Bahama Islands be made a single crown colony; North Carolina should be put under the government of Virginia; the southern counties on Delaware Bay, then disputed between Penn and Baltimore, should be placed under the royal government in Maryland; West Jersey should be added to Pennsylvania ("and an active governor there appointed"); East Jersey and Connecticut added to New York; and Rhode Island merged with Massachusetts. Thus the hodgepodge of colonial jurisdictions would be rationalized and all put in order. The great bays of the American coast — Pamlico Sound, Chesapeake Bay, the Delaware, Hudson, and Narragansett Bays — would each be incorporated under one colonial government, and with the one exception of Pennsylvania each government would be headed by a royal governor. All this under guise of forestalling a Scottish trading factory.

The commissioners of customs did not adopt Randolph's sweeping program. They believed — correctly — that existing laws were sufficient to prevent Scottish interloping, if only the colonial governors and customs officers could enforce them. The one new approach hinted at by the commissioners in their report to the Lords was special encouragement for the trades most likely to meet with Scottish competition.[10] (This was also the position taken by the Jamaica sugar merchants, who were seeking in Parliament a reduction of English customs on sugar.[11]) By ignoring Randolph's proposals in their own report to the Lords the commissioners also ignored the one issue which Randolph considered at the root of England's colonial problems — the semi-independent status of proprietary and corporate colonies.

[9] *Randolph Letters,* VII, 474–477.

[10] Customs commissioners to Lords, Dec. 12, 1695, *House of Lords MSS,* II, 17.

[11] Jamaica merchants to Lords, Dec. 13, 1695, *ibid.,* II, 20.

Nevertheless, when the Lords reopened debate on December 20, they did turn to the proprietary colonies.[12] It would appear that Randolph had managed to circumvent the commissioners and make his point directly through friends in Parliament. The Lords decided that "the Commissioners of the Customs [shall] . . . give an account, whether . . . there be a sufficient power in Carolina, Maryland, Pennsylvania and other plantations where there are proprietors to collect the king's duty. . . ." [13]

The commissioners reported back to the House of Lords early in January 1696 and now explained in some detail the administrative measures they had taken to bring the proprietary and corporate colonies into line. The commissioners had to admit that in these colonies the Navigation Acts were not well enforced. They went on to say — after being reprimanded by the Lords for negligence — that they had prepared a bill to reinforce the existing acts.[14] This bill was to become the Navigation Act of 1696. The Lords broke off their inquiry into the proprietaries at this point. They were to return to it in just one year, as we shall see.

Meanwhile, the scene shifts to the privy council. As they had done before, and indeed as they were expected to do, the commissioners of customs referred major decisions of policy to higher authority. They now proposed that both of Randolph's memorials — those of October 16 and December 7 — should be laid before the privy council. In this winter of 1695–96 the old Lords of Trade were moribund, the new Board of Trade not yet established. Consequently Randolph's papers were sent to the King in Council and from there referred to a committee of the whole council.[15] This committee met during the winter months of 1695–96, and although the expiring Lords of Trade continued in existence until spring, Randolph's important business was with the new committee. After reading Randolph's two papers, this committee ordered the commissioners to give an opinion of them in writing, article by article.[16]

With the paper Randolph had submitted on October 16 the commissioners were in emphatic agreement. As we have seen, they did strike out the first item of complaint, that which criticized colonial customs personnel, but only for political reasons; in the next few years many changes in colonial personnel were in fact made. Of the eleven remaining items the commissioners had this to say: "Upon our first perusal of these heads . . . we saw the necessity of obtaining a new Act, and such as might reach

---

[12] *House of Lords MSS*, II, 6.

[13] *Journals of the House of Lords* (n.p., n.d.), XV, 619.

[14] *House of Lords MSS*, II, 7.

[15] Order of the Lords of a committee of the whole council, Jan. 13, 1696, *House of Lords MSS*, II, 445; customs commissioners to same, Jan. 17, 1696, *ibid.*, II, 451; Randolph to same, Jan. 31, 1696, *Randolph Letters*, V, 124–125.

[16] *House of Lords MSS*, II, 445–446.

several of the mischiefs and defects which are complained of, and which could not be cured but by law. . . ." [17] The commissioners specified nine of Randolph's complaints which deserved action. The substance of these complaints were even now, they reported, incorporated into a bill to be presented to Parliament.

The memorial submitted by Randolph on December 7, however, was given a far different appraisal. It was in this paper that Randolph had proposed reorganizing the colonies around the great bays and doing away with all but one of the proprietary colonies. The commissioners agreed that Randolph had "well considered the situation" from a geographical view point. They balked, however, at overriding the legal rights of the proprietors. They did not think it a critical issue in any event, and repeated the argument that the proprietary and corporate colonies were just as bound by English law as were the royal colonies.[18] The privy council committee, would not take these opinions at face value but itself investigated points on which the commissioners disagreed with Randolph. On the main issue, however, the council concluded — like the customs commissioners — that the wholesale reorganization of proprietary and corporate colonies would be too radical a step.[19]

Meanwhile, the customs commissioners had prepared a bill for Parliament. William Penn wrote years later that the bill had been written solely by Randolph and James Chadwick, one of the customs commissioners.[20] This may have been an exaggeration born of Penn's dislike equally of the law and of Randolph. Yet the sense of Penn's remark, emphasizing Randolph's role, is surely accurate. One other man, William Blathwayt, may have been influential in writing the bill. Blathwayt was at this time secretary to the Lords of Trade. For years he had been ubiquitous in colonial administration, and he was Randolph's intimate in official matters. Blathwayt's name, however, is strangely absent from the records dealing with the bill.[21] Although the House of Commons gave permission to Chadwick and Blathwayt together to introduce the bill, it was brought in by Chadwick alone.[22]

The first reading of the bill in Commons came on January 27, 1696,

---

[17] *Ibid.*, II, 452.

[18] *Ibid.*, II, 453–454.

[19] Report of the committee of the whole council with references and replies, Jan. 28–Feb. 7, 1696, *House of Lords MSS*, II, 454–456.

[20] Penn to Robert Harley, [c. 1701], Historical Manuscripts Commission, *Fifteenth Report, Appendix, Part IV* (London, 1897): *The Manuscripts of His Grace the Duke of Portland*, IV, 31.

[21] Jacobsen's assignment to this period of Randolph's letter to Blathwayt, *Randolph Letters*, VII, 503–505, is the result of misdating. Gertrude A. Jacobsen, *William Blathwayt, a Late Seventeenth Century English Administrator* (New Haven, 1932), pp. 297, n. 2; 335. The letter was written in Feb. 1697.

[22] Stock, *Debates*, II, 155.

the second reading on February 12.[23] We do not know whether or not Randolph testified during debate in Commons, for which no committee records have survived. After debate and amendments both in committee and on the floor, the bill was sent on March 19 to the House of Lords.[24]

There events moved more rapidly. The first and second readings were accomplished by March 20, and committee debate began on March 24. Randolph had been summoned to attend at 11:00 A.M., and he stood at the bar that day and again on the twenty-seventh. Further amendments were made by both houses, and on April 13 they concurred in the final form of the act: An Act for Preventing Frauds, and Regulating Abuses in the Plantation Trade, 7 & 8 William III, c. 22. It was the last of the Navigation Acts and the longest statute, bar one, to be enacted that session.[25]

The statute itself was by and large a regulatory measure, designed to perfect the machinery of colonial administration. To this end it put to rights some ambiguities in the language of earlier acts, emphasized the colonial governors' responsibility for their enforcement, and established new penalties and administrative rules. As far as these went, the Act for Preventing Frauds added nothing to the earlier commercial laws that was new in principle. But the act did in fact make very important changes of a constitutional nature. Certain provisions of the new law struck so closely at the government of the colonies as to alter fundamentally their relationship to the crown.

By far the most important of these changes was the decision to establish vice-admiralty courts in the American colonies and to give them jurisdiction over penal clauses in the Navigation Acts. The Act for Preventing Frauds did no more than allow, explicitly, such a jurisdiction. It did not enact the establishment of the courts. Nevertheless, the speed and thoroughness with which courts were set up leaves no doubt that establishment as well as jurisdiction was intended by the authors. This provision of the act cannot be considered merely as a tightening of existing regulations. It entailed — as charter colonies were quick to recognize — a dramatic revision of the powers to govern as granted in the colonial charters; it was a victory of prerogative courts over common law; it was a signal instance when an English form of government was intentionally ignored and a novel form invented for colonial practice.

Vice-admiralty courts were inferior branches of the High Court of Admiralty at London.[26] They were prerogative courts, following neither

[23] *Ibid.*, II, 155, 159.

[24] *Ibid.*, II, 159, 166, 167.

[25] *Ibid.*, II, 168–169, 170–173; *The Statutes at Large*, ed. Danby Pickering (Cambridge, Eng., 1762–1807), IX, 428–437.

[26] The best introductions to colonial vice-admiralty courts are Helen J. Crump, *Colonial Admiralty Jurisdiction in the Seventeenth Century* (London, 1931),

common-law procedure nor common-law precedent. A vice-admiralty court consisted of a judge, register, and marshal. It gave judgments without jury, proceeded *in rem* — that is, against the vessel or goods instead of the master or owner — and took testimony in writing rather than orally. Furthermore, it functioned throughout the year and not in certain term times. These procedures were particularly suited to maritime cases, where the parties concerned were often transients and where delays in judgment caused unusual hardship.

Jurisdiction of vice-admiralty courts was over civil actions arising at sea or in rivers and harbors — salvage, damage, wage, desertion, and the like. Vice-admiralty courts did not, ordinarily, have jurisdiction over prizes, piracy, or the Navigation Acts. But the American colonies posed extraordinary problems, and extraordinary measures were taken to meet them. Admiralty courts in existence in America before 1696 had been created largely to deal with prizes. "But for the accidence of a period of naval war [1650–70] and the need for courts which could condemn prizes, the enforcement of the navigation acts might have been entrusted to the Exchequer rather than to the admiralty courts." [27] Jurisdiction over piracy was given to the colonial courts by statute in 1698. What concerns us here is the extension in 1696 of admiralty-court jurisdiction in the colonies to include the Navigation Acts.

This jurisdiction in England belonged to the Court of Exchequer, to which any officer connected with the crown revenues was entitled to bring his actions. Like the vice-admiralty courts, the Court of Exchequer proceeded *in rem*, and by written deposition.[28] Francis Nicholson, governor of Maryland, knew English usage and desired a court of exchequer in his colony.[29] In New England the hostility of local courts had greatly hampered Randolph's work. At first he urged the formation of vice-admiralty courts; then after his close association with Nicholson during 1692–95, he too began to recommend a colonial exchequer court. This he did in his proposals of October 16.[30] In commenting on this to the privy council, the commissioners of customs neither supported nor discouraged the idea.[31] It is worth noting that at the time the commissioners drafted their bill for Parliament, they also spoke of exchequer and not admiralty courts.

---

and Charles M. Andrews, "Vice-Admiralty Courts in the Colonies," *Records of the Vice-Admiralty Court of Rhode Island, 1716–1752*, ed. Dorothy S. Towle, American Legal Records, Vol. III (Washington, 1936).

[27] Crump, *Admiralty Jurisdiction*, p. 94.

[28] Lawrence A. Harper, *The English Navigation Laws* (New York, 1939), pp. 110–111.

[29] Nicholson to Lords of Trade, Mar. 18, 1696, *Cal. State Papers, Col., 1693–1696*, 2303.

[30] *House of Lords MSS*, II, 450.

[31] *Ibid.*, II, 452.

The decision to use vice-admiralty courts in America for violations of the Navigation Acts was made by the House of Lords. Section 7 of the printed law reads: "All the penalties and forfeitures before mentioned, not in this act particularly disposed of, shall . . . be recovered in any of his Majesty's courts at Westminster, *or in the Kingdom of Ireland, or in the court of admiralty held in his Majesty's plantations respectively, where such offence shall be committed, at the pleasure of the officer or informer. . . .*" [32] These were the words on which the unprecedented enlargement of admiralty jurisdiction was based. For this reason they deserve as close a scrutiny as possible.

The pertinent words, those italicized, were certainly added to the bill by amendment in the House of Lords, as appears in the list of amendments concurred in by the Commons.[33] Two questions remain: who proposed the clause? and did the Lords understand that it would be made the basis for establishing new colonial courts? Evidence that the words were proposed by Edward Randolph exists in the official minutes of the committee debate: "Mr. Randolph was called in and asked if he had prepared a Clause for a Court of Admiralty. He says it is provided in the Act of Charles II. He proposes words to be inserted in the bill. The words annexed in a separate Schedule at line 5 of #vi are substituted for 'in any of the said Colonies or Plantations.' " [34]

The words appearing in the "separate Schedule" are those italicized in the above quotation from the statute. Are they also the words Randolph proposed "to be inserted in the bill"? Likely they are, since the two entries in the minutes run as they do. But the minutes are not conclusive on the point, and it is quite possible that one of the Lords and not Randolph contributed the amendment.

On the more important question, I think there can be no doubt that the Lords were fully aware of the significance of this clause. They must have discussed colonial admiralty courts earlier, or they would not have asked Randolph "if he had prepared a Clause for a Court of Admiralty." I think what was meant was a clause establishing colonial admiralty courts by statute, and I think Randolph had been asked to consider such a move, and that others — very probably the customs commissioners — had advised against such a statutory enactment. Admiralty courts were, after all, prerogative courts, not to be set up (or pulled down) by Parliament. But the important goal was achieved by giving the admiralty courts (such as were or might be established) jurisdiction over the Navigation Acts.

A second clause of the new act was even more directly constitutional in

---

[32] *Statutes*, IX, 432, italics mine. References to colonial admiralty courts in sections 2 and 3 can only be interpreted as referring to prize cases alone.

[33] Stock, *Debates*, II, 172.

[34] *House of Lords MSS*, II, 234.

character. The act stated that when governors were appointed by proprietors or elected in corporate colonies, those governors must be approved by the king before taking office.[35] This was a sharp limitation of the rights granted in the colonial charters. No such proposal had been suggested by Randolph in his October 16 memorandum. But in 1698 he wrote to Blathwayt, "It was with great difficulty that the Act . . . was obtained: One principall end thereof was to bring the governments of the Proprietys to a dependence on the Crown: by their governors being first allowed and approved by His Majesty's Order in Council to be such. . . ."[36] This clause, like that about admiralty courts, was added to the bill by the House of Lords, apparently on its own initiative.[37]

In both cases can be seen the over-all direction which the House of Lords intended to give colonial policy. There are other provisions of a similar nature which were also written into the bill by the Lords. Section 11 gave the Treasury authority to locate as many officers as it wished in "any of the islands, tracts of land or proprieties. . . ." Section 18 established a central registry of all ships whatever entitled to trade among the colonies.[38] In each case we see the House of Lords taking the initiative to strengthen the prerogative branch of government at the colonies' expense. It is interesting to note that these decisions were made in the short interim between the demise of the Lords of Trade and the creation of the Board of Trade.

Once the Act for Preventing Frauds was passed, Randolph played a vital part in executing it. The Board of Trade, also, played an increasingly important part. The Board of Trade was created in May 1696 to replace the Committee for Trade and Plantations — the old "Lords of Trade" — which had kept supervision over colonial affairs since 1675. The origin of the new board and the jockeying between crown and Parliament for control over it is a topic unto itself.[39] It will be enough here to point out that Randolph had powerful friends on the board. Its president was the Earl of Bridgewater; William Blathwayt was appointed a working member. Both were long-standing and vigorous supporters of Randolph.[40]

[35] *Statutes*, IX, 435, sec. 16.

[36] Aug. 25, 1698, *Randolph Letters*, VII, 536.

[37] *House of Lords MSS*, II, 234; Stock, *Debates*, II, 172.

[38] *House of Lords MSS*, II, 234; Stock, *Debates*, II, 172; *Statutes*, IX, 433, 435–436.

[39] See Charles M. Andrews, *The Colonial Period of American History* (New Haven, 1934–38), IV, 274–290; R. M. Lees, "Parliament and the Proposal for a Council of Trade, 1695–6," *English Historical Review*, LIV (Jan. 1939), 38–66; Peter Laslett, "John Locke, the Great Recoinage, and the Origins of the Board of Trade: 1695–1698," *William and Mary Quarterly*, 3d Ser., XIV (July 1957), 370–402.

[40] For Bridgewater's connection with Randolph see Bridgewater to Secretary Sir Leoline Jenkins, July 19 and 29, 1680, *Calendar of State Papers, Domestic*,

The date July 17, 1696, is the starting point from which to follow much of what was done to carry out the provisions of the Act. Edward Randolph sent an undated paper to the customs commissioners: "Proposals . . . for the more effectual putting in execution the Act for Preventing Frauds . . . ."[41] It contained five short paragraphs: 1) that governors in proprietary colonies be qualified according to the new law; 2) that "fit persons be appointed to be Governors of Carolina and Pennsylvania"; 3) that commissions under the great seal "be directed to divers persons" to administer the new oaths to governors of colonies; 4) "that there be appointed a Judge, a Register, a Marshall of the Courts of Admiralty, and an Atturney Generall, in all the colonyes . . ."; and 5) that untrustworthy customs officers be removed.

Randolph was one of those men who acquire power and influence because they are forever pushing to get things done, regardless of whether or not it is strictly their job to do so. Randolph's "Proposals" are a case in point. From them began the working of administrative machinery that sooner or later resulted in the realization of several parts of the new law. On July 17 the customs commissioners made the Treasury Lords a "presentment" of Randolph's suggestions, or at least of those parts which the commissioners approved.[42] The presentment contained drafts of commissions for administering the governors' oaths, each commission to be directed to several men in the respective colonies. However, commissions were prepared only for royal colonies. Probably it was thought best not to swear the proprietary governors until they had been approved by the King. But Randolph objected so violently that by mid-August both the Board of Trade and the customs commissioners acquiesced in his view. Subsequently seventeen groups of men were given commissions to administer the new oath to every colonial governor, irrespective of status. Randolph was named on each commission.[43]

We need not trace through a labyrinth of interdepartmental reference all the preliminaries to erecting admiralty courts in the colonies. The Board of Trade, the customs commissioners, the Lords of the Admiralty, and the Attorney General of England were all involved, while final decisions rested with the King or, when he was out of the country, with his

---

Jan. 1, 1679–Aug. 31, 1680 (London, 1915), pp. 563, 578. Root names Bridgewater as being among the most active members of the old Lords of Trade. Winfred T. Root, "Lords of Trade and Plantations, 1675–1696," *American Historical Review*, XXIII (Oct. 1917), 25.

[41] *Randolph Letters*, V, 135–136; *House of Lords MSS*, II, 419.

[42] *House of Lords MSS*, II, 411, 422–525.

[43] Randolph to Board of Trade, July 31, 1696, *Randolph Letters*, V, 137; Board of Trade Minutes, Aug. 3, 1696, *Cal. State Papers, Col.*, 1696–1697, 126; Board of Trade to Lords Chief Justices, Aug. 12, 1696, *ibid.*, 140; *Calendar of Treasury Books* (London, 1933), XI, 296–298.

vicars, the Lords Chief Justices. In laying out the court districts the Board of Trade followed Randolph's earlier suggestions of realigning colonial governments around the great coastal bays. Randolph was relied on to pick men for the court officers — judge, register, and marshal. Several of his lists survive.[44]

An unforeseen difficulty was inherent in the plan to constitute colonial admiralty courts. At home in England the administration of justice was under the crown: "The common law courts were royal courts and the judges of these courts were royal justices." [45] In the American colonies, particularly in the semi-independent ones, judicial systems were in the hands of the colonial governments and were designed to implement colonial, not English, laws. In effect, the charter colonies did not provide machinery for the judicial enforcement of English laws, except where the laws had been adopted by the colony. The admiralty courts, which were intended to remedy this in part, amounted to an additional judicial system. But in establishing a second and parallel system of courts it was necessary to create an attorney general's office for the management of crown causes.

Randolph wanted the crown to exercise outright the appointment of colonial attorneys general.[46] The commissioners of customs did not at once follow this lead. They recommended instead that the Admiralty appoint the regular court officials, and that other men "may be nominated and recommended by the King to the respective Governors to be employed as Attorneys-General for the prosecution of bonds, trying of seizures, and other matters relating to the Crown." [47]

Randolph, nevertheless, went right ahead. He included names for attorneys general in his lists of admiralty-court officers to be appointed. These men were to replace attorneys general already in the colonies. As late as August 10, 1696, there was no objection from the Board of Trade.[48] Someone, however, must have accused Randolph of overstepping his bounds, for on August 25 he brought in a defensive statement in which he rehearsed in detail the inadequacies of colonial attorneys general, showing how several of them could not be relied on to prosecute crown causes. "'Tis my only designe," Randolph protested, "in this, and all other my publick Services, that his Majesties Interest and the Acts of Trade, may be inviolably Maintained . . . ." [49] He convinced the board

[44] *Randolph Letters*, V, 136–138; VII, 500–501.

[45] W. S. Holdworth, *A History of English Law*, 3d ed. (Boston, 1922), I, 194.

[46] Randolph to customs commissioners, n.d., *Randolph Letters*, V, 135.

[47] Customs commissioners to Treasury, July 17, 1696, *House of Lords MSS*, II, 425.

[48] Board of Trade Journal, Aug. 7, 1696, *Cal. State Papers, Col., 1696–1697*, 131. Randolph to Board of Trade, Aug. 10, 1696, *Randolph Letters*, V, 138.

[49] Randolph to Board of Trade, *Randolph Letters*, V, 140–144.

that the attorneys general in Virginia, Maryland, Pennsylvania, and Massachusetts were untrustworthy. In the words of the board itself, "We are also humbly of Opinion that the forenamed persons are not fit to be His Majesty's Atturnys Generall, however fitt they may be judged by the Proprietors. . . . And that it may be expedient for His Majesty's Service that the Persons following whom the said Mr. Edward Randolph represents as duly qualified may be Constituted His Majesty's Atturnys Generall for the respective Colonys. . . ." [50]

The question of whether the crown could appoint attorneys general in the charter colonies continued to be debated for months. It was put to Sir John Trevor, Attorney General of England. Only at his instigation were the proprietors and colonial agents notified of what was afoot.[51] There were immediate protests from the proprietors, including such men as the Earl of Craven, Lord Ashley, William Penn, and Sir Thomas Lane, Lord Mayor of London in 1693 and president of the West New Jersey Society.[52] Trevor's opinion, delivered on December 4, 1696, was that the king could appoint "advocates general" to prosecute crown causes in admiralty courts (but presumably not appoint attorneys general). This was a compromise which the Board of Trade accepted.[53] It meant, of course, that crown causes not falling within the new admiralty jurisdiction would still be at the mercy of a possibly hostile colonial attorney general.

Randolph and the customs commissioners made a last effort, in March 1697, to have the crown appoint attorneys general: "It is humbly proposed for his Majesty's Service That the same person be the Attorney General for his Majesty in all pleas of the Crowne, And also the Advocate in the Courts of Admiralty to Try seizures . . . for Breach of the Acts of Trade. . . ." Randolph again proposed men for royal appointment.[54] The Board of Trade hoped to adopt this arrangement in 1699 in respect to New York: "the Attorney General [should officiate] as Advocate General . . . not only in New York, but also in the neighboring colonies. . . ." [55] Elsewhere the attorney general assumed *ad hoc* the role of advocate general. On the whole, however, throughout the eighteenth century no systematic arrangement was reached, and the situation

[50] Board of Trade to Lords Chief Justices, Sept. 7, 1696, *ibid.*, VII, 494.

[51] Order in Council, Sept. 10, 1696, *ibid.*, VII, 493, n. 477; summons to colonial proprietors, Oct. 13, 1696, *ibid.*, V, 145–146.

[52] Proprietors to king and to Board of Trade, n.d., *ibid.*, V, 146–150; Randolph memorandum, Oct. 19, 1696, Ellesmere MS. 9593, Henry E. Huntington Library.

[53] Board of Trade to king, Dec. 17, 1696, *House of Lords MSS*, II, 427–428.

[54] Secretary of Customs House to Board of Trade, Mar. 3, 1696, *Randolph Letters*, V, 163.

[55] Board of Trade to king, Dec. 14, 1699, *Documents relative to the Colonial History of the State of New York . . .*, ed. E. B. O'Callaghan, Vol. IV (Albany, 1854), p. 599.

varied from one colony to the next.[56] Randolph at any rate failed to achieve his principle that the crown should appoint the chief legal officer in every colony.

This discussion of a dualism in judicial systems has already outrun the events of 1696–97. The Board of Trade faltered in the end at overriding protests by the proprietors, many of whom were men of great power. Although recommending establishment of admiralty courts, the board passed to the King responsibility for taking the final step.[57] The whole issue of courts, as it had been developed over the summer of 1696, rested with the King in Council when in February 1697 the House of Lords returned to a consideration of colonial affairs. It is a remarkable fact that Parliament, which had taken so little interest in the colonies heretofore, should now turn about and devote so much time to them. In this respect, it was the House of Lords and not the Commons which showed such noticeable interest. A committee of the Lords was appointed February 10, 1697, to consider the trade of the kingdom: for five weeks it centered its attention on the colonies and especially on those proprietary and charter colonies which had attained a degree of independence from royal control.

Although we know a good deal about the work of the Lord's committee, we know little of its membership. Nearly one hundred men were assigned to it, but five were a quorum. The Earl of Rochester was chairman at all meetings. (He had been in the chair part of the time when the Act for Preventing Frauds was in committee.) The only other active member who can be identified was Charles Gerard, second Earl of Macclesfield, an unsavory character with apparently only slight interest in the colonies.[58] The vigor of this committee, whoever its members, gives it an important place in the development of England's policy.

The committee's first step was to continue the interrogation of the customs commissioners which had been dropped the previous year. Among other matters the commissioners were asked if they wished to supplement the Act for Preventing Frauds, implying that the Lords were ready to make that statute even more drastic. Secondly the committee ordered the Board of Trade to report on its activities over the summer and asked "if they have observed their commission does not contain sufficient power. . . ."[59] This latter remark is reminiscent of debates the previous winter, when Parliament would have commissioned a board of trade if

[56] Carl Ubbelohde, "The Vice-Admiralty Court of Royal North Carolina 1729–1759," *North Carolina Historical Review*, XXXI (Oct. 1954), 522, and "The Vice-Admiralty Courts of British North America, 1763–1776," unpublished manuscript.

[57] Board of Trade to king, Dec. 17, 1696, *House of Lords MSS*, II, 428.

[58] Macclesfield to Board of Trade, Dec. 9, 1696, *Cal. State Papers, Col., 1696–1697*, 477; J. M. Rigg in *DNB* s.v. "Charles Gerard."

[59] Committee Minutes, Feb. 11, 1697, *House of Lords MSS*, II, 410.

the King had not. The present committee of Lords was interested to make sure the King's board had effective power.

Thus on its opening day the committee made clear what direction its inquiries were to take. At its second sitting the committee called in Edward Randolph, and so made doubly clear its position, for no one could well mistake the character of Randolph's advice. Randolph brought in a copy of the same paper of July 17, 1696, which had started the summer's work on admiralty courts and other clauses of the new law. From this point the Lord's committee reviewed that work and assembled a large number of the pertinent documents.

What was in several ways the most important single document was "a list of all the Proprietors of Plantations that are independent of the government of his Majesty." The Lords ordered Randolph to bring in such a list, and he did so on February 20.[60] The paper was modeled on one or two earlier reports which he had presented to the customs commissioners and to the Board of Trade.[61] In each version Randolph sketched the character of the government in every proprietary or corporate colony from the Bahama Islands to New Hampshire. He did so with a wealth of detail, not only about the present governors but also in many cases about their predecessors and chief lieutenants. The case against each charter government was damning. One must remember in assessing the influence of the report, however, that none of the colonies had had an opportunity to make rebuttal.[62]

Randolph foresaw that if charter governments did not enforce the commercial laws with the same stringency as royal governments, the inhabitants of royal colonies would be forever uneasy under the yoke and envious of their more fortunate neighbors.[63] This situation did indeed develop in a few years, when Bellomont cracked down on malpractices in New York, while New Jersey across the river enjoyed practical freedom from government regulation.[64] But it was not until the final version of his "list of Proprietors" that Randolph drew the ultimate conclusion: "that a Clause be brought in to invest the government of all the Proprieties in his Majesty. . . ." [65]

This proposal was discussed by the Lords on February 20, 1697, and

[60] Committee Minutes, *ibid.*, II, 411–412.

[61] Randolph to customs commissioners, Aug. 17, 1696, *Cal. State Papers, Col.*, *1696–1697*, 149 i; same to same, Nov. 10, 1696, *Randolph Letters*, V, 151–160.

[62] Randolph to House of Lords Committee, Feb. 20, 1697, *House of Lords MSS*, II, 440–444.

[63] Randolph to customs commissioners, Nov. 10, 1696, *Randolph Letters*, V, 153.

[64] Randolph to Sir Benjamin Bathurst, May 12, 1698, *ibid.*, V, 182; Randolph to William Popple, Sept. 12, 1698, *ibid.*, V, 192; Randolph to Blathwayt, Sept. 12, 1698, *ibid.*, VII, 547.

[65] *House of Lords MSS*, II, 444.

later that same day Randolph described the scene to Blathwayt. "I laid before their Lordships the map shewing all the proprietyes as they lye from South to North. They were very intent, and the Earl of Mackelsfeild could not forbeare his opinion that they ought all to be . . . taken into the Kings possession: and others were of the like opinion." "I did offer the proposall in writing," Randolph continued, "about having the Governments in the proprietyes to be invested in the Crown. Some of the Lords presently agreed to have a clause to that purpose. But others agree that their Titles (such as they bee) should be well looked into, not by the Atturney Generall, because he with Mr. Serjeant Ward reported upon it, but by one more of the judges. . . ." And he signed it, "Labouring hard for a new modell of the proprietys Governments . . . your obliged humble servant, Ed. Randolph." [66]

That letter to Blathwayt sets the scene. Confiscation of charter privileges was at stake. The Lords were determined to bring the charter colonies to obedience, and that quickly. What is puzzling is why they picked on Pennsylvania almost to the exclusion of other colonies. They did, indeed, ask the proprietors of Carolina and the Bahamas to appear before the committee. Only the Earl of Bath out of that titled company presented himself, and the committee was as mild as milk with him.[67] William Penn, on the other hand, was treated with asperity, quizzed and threatened for weeks.

Randolph, I am sure, did not lead the committee to a consideration of Pennsylvania, although once this line of investigation was begun he became the principal informant. The evidence in this instance as elsewhere shows that the direction of the investigation came from within the committee, and that Randolph played a considerable role because his approach to colonial matters was in harmony with that of the Lords. There is some indication that Pennsylvania was singled out because of the dispute over the status of the southern counties — Sussex, Kent, and Newcastle on Delaware Bay — and also because of the troubles in Pennsylvania which had caused the colony to be put under Governor Fletcher's administration from 1692–94.[68] The present investigation was concerned entirely with Pennsylvania's obedience to the Navigation Acts.

Whatever the motives behind it, the committee's examination of William Penn soon took on the aspect of a trial at law. Randolph acted as prosecuting attorney. He charged that the government of Pennsylvania ignored illegal trade. He called witnesses: two previous surveyors general; Thomas Meech, master of the customs picket boat; James Walliam, the collector at Newcastle; and a customs agent who had been watching

[66] *Randolph Letters*, VII, 503–505.
[67] Committee Minutes, Feb. 22, 1697, *House of Lords MSS*, II, 412.
[68] Committee Minutes, Feb. 15–16, 1697, *ibid.*, II, 411.

in Scotland for illegal shipments of tobacco. Randolph was supported by further evidence from both the Board of Trade and the customs commissioners. Penn too named witnesses, but there is no indication that they testified.[69] It would, perhaps, be impossible to say now which man had more right on his side, Penn or Randolph. There can be no question of which way the committee decided. On March 4 they asked Penn "what objections he can make to putting the government of the Proprietor's Plantations into the King's hands." And the clerk wrote down the reply: "it will ruin him and his family." [70]

In the end Pennsylvania escaped confiscation. But the reprimand was severe and the future ominous. The Earl of Rochester told Penn the committee thought proprietors should receive the same instructions as did royal governors. "If there be further complaint against the Proprietors after this," Penn was warned, "the Parliament may possibly take another course in this matter, which will be less pleasing to them." [71] By this date, March 11, 1697, the Lords had considered appropriating the charter governments to the crown — and had stayed their hand. The decision taken in regard to Pennsylvania was applied to the other charter colonies.

Between Penn and Randolph there was every ground for animosity. The whole proceeding must have done much to destroy Penn's enthusiasm for his colonial experiment. During the hearings he had asked permission to bring charges against Randolph for his immoderate accusations, but nowhere is there evidence that he did so. Penn wrote to him in October 1697:

> Warminghurst
>
> I shall not fail to oblige Colonel Markham [Penn's deputy governor] to use his authority to right the interest of the crown in all respects, and if thou expectest my letter besides, thou shallt have it. But to be very plain, I do expect another sort of correspondence, and that those which have been instruments of raising this smoke against my province will quench that fire which feeds it: or I must fling away my scabbard and openly detect and impeach too: and I neither fear my matter, nor my interest too back it. For that a man and his family and his friends should be smothered in a dust malice has raised . . . is scandalous. And I expect, if we are to live good friends, that thou wilt here as well as there do thy utmost to lay these things before thou goest . . . .
>
> [signed] Will Penn.[72]

[69] Minutes of the committee hearings are in *House of Lords MSS*, II, 410–414; papers brought in by Penn and Randolph are in *ibid.*, II, 456–472, 488–503; Penn's witnesses are named in Stock, *Debates*, II, 198.

[70] Committee Minutes, Mar. 4, 1697, *House of Lords MSS*, II, 413.

[71] Committee Minutes, Mar. 11, 1697, *ibid.*, II, 414.

[72] Penn to Randolph, Oct. 16, 1697, Ellesmere MS. 9592, Huntington Library.

The report from Rochester's committee was approved by the House of Lords and drawn up as an address to the King on March 18. It spoke of the illegal practices in America, and "particularly, that the [Act for Preventing Frauds] . . . hath been greatly obstructed . . . by the non-compliance of some of the proprietors . . . as also by the remissness or connivance of your Majesty's own governors." The Lords recommended to the King a strongly worded admonition to be sent to every colony.[73] Never before had Parliament intervened so forcibly in the administration of the empire; never again would it hesitate to do so.

On April 22, 1697, these letters went out to the colonies over the King's signature: to the governors and companies of Rhode Island and Connecticut threatening forfeiture of their charters; to the royal governors of Virginia, Maryland, Jamaica, the Leeward Islands, Barbados, and Bermuda, threatening removal from office; to the proprietors of East and West Jersey threatening "marks of highest displeasure"; and to William Penn threatening forfeiture of his patent.[74]

These letters brought an end to the House of Lords inquiry in the spring of 1697. To some, like Randolph, the letters were a reprieve, a reprieve which they would do all they could to shorten. Meanwhile, there was the Act for Preventing Frauds to be carried out. The new law had put the colonial customs service on the same legal footing as that given the English service by a law of 1662. An administrative step of considerable importance was made in conjunction with this change, when the colonial customs staff was put on the English exchequer. An establishment of twenty-seven men, exclusive of Randolph, was planned at a cost of £1525.[75] In addition a new set of instructions to customs officers was prepared, more than twice the length of the old instructions.[76]

Randolph was to supervise the change in personnel. The customs commissioners informed the House of Lords in February 1697:

> . . . in regard it has been thought necessary to form a new establishment of officers, to be settled in Virginia and other his Majesty's Plantations on the Continent and the Bahama Islands, for the better putting in execution the several laws relating to the Plantations, which officers (in regard there could not be that reasonable confidence in persons of interest and residence upon the place as in persons disinterested in and unrelated to the place) have been for the most part chosen from hence, and will be therefore new and unexperienced in the Plantations, it may be therefore necessary forthwith to despatch Mr. Randolph with them to the Plantations,

---

[73] Stock, *Debates*, II, 205.

[74] *Cal. State Papers, Col., 1696–1697*, 958–961.

[75] Treasury to customs commissioners, Nov. 20, 1696, *Cal. Treasury Books*, XI, 312–313.

[76] *House of Lords MSS*, II, 472–481.

who is the General Surveyor of that whole business, to dispose and settle them in their respective places. . . .[77]

With this as his major job Randolph carried also a host of additional duties: the governors' oaths, instructions about the new courts, a commission to investigate the sale of prizes. Underlying all, he was to continue as the eyes and ears of the crown. The Board of Trade wanted him to write home "whatever [he] shall judge proper," and the commissioners provided a long list of places to visit and chores to be done. After many delays Edward Randolph sailed from Cowes on November 8, 1697, having achieved more in two years that he could well have expected. His success is not hard to understand. He had come to England at a time of crisis, armed with a seemingly inexhaustible fund of information. But even more important, he had come to England with a transcendent program — that His Majesty's government should assume as much as possible the government of the colonies.

The customs commissioners, the privy council, and the new Board of Trade all favored such a program. But the House of Lords led them all. The Lords made over the Act for Preventing Frauds into a law of major constitutional importance, and the Lords carried forward the attack on independent colonies. They contributed more to the character of colonial policy at this time than any other group.

[77] *House of Lords MSS*, II, 445.

III

COLONIAL
POLITICS AND
SOCIETY: THE
EIGHTEENTH
CENTURY

The Evolution of Massachusetts Town Government, 1640 to 1740

AND ALAN KREIDER

The study of local history has begun to change our notions of how New Englanders governed themselves. Historians have now begun to push beyond the earlier conceptions of the town as a Germanic inheritance or as a little frontier democracy by inquiring closely into the actual operation of town government. While they have not yet agreed on a model, they have recognized some previously unnoticed problems.

Kenneth Lockridge and Alan Kreider suggest that[there was no single form of government in the Massachusetts towns. On the contrary, there was probably a dramatic change within each town as the town meeting first delegated authority to a smaller group of selectmen, and then had to recover its power. This evolutionary process, the authors argue, corresponded to the deaths of the leading settlers and the broadening of political participation, facilitating controversy in the town. Thus, it was not until about 1740 that the town meeting actually served the purpose that has traditionally been allocated to it as a forum for conflicting local interests.]

This interpretation suggests an institutional analogy to the political maturity which scholars have noticed in the eighteenth-century colonies. It also demonstrates the value of a flexible approach to institutional history, in which political forms constantly change in relation to the society they serve. But the Lockridge-Kreider explanation is not the only one possible, as you will see in the essay by Michael Zuckerman.

No historian has yet attempted a careful study of how New England town government actually operated as it evolved. To be sure, several studies — notably those of Anne Bush MacLear and George Lee Haskins

Reprinted by permission from Kenneth A. Lockridge and Alan Kreider, "The Evolution of Massachusetts Town Government, 1640 to 1740," *William and Mary Quarterly*, 3d Ser., XXIII (1966), 549–574.

— stand out by virtue of the clarity of their analysis and the perceptive ness of their use of town records.[1] But MacLear and Haskins do not venture very far beyond 1660, by which time the basic institutional structure of the town was complete. The workings of town government during the succeeding years, down to the American Revolution, have not yet been examined.

The work which comes closest to performing this task, John F. Sly's *Town Government in Massachusetts* (Cambridge, Mass., 1930), sketches certain general trends over a period of three hundred years. But Sly's study is wanting in careful analysis. He concentrates his attention upon the continuity of external forms [2] and completely overlooks the possibility of striking shifts of political power beneath the surface similarities during the lengthy period between the first settlements and the Revolution. His failure to take into account the tendency of established political institutions to gain and lose power, to win and surrender initiative with the passage of time, is particularly unfortunate in that Sidney and Beatrice Webb had supplied a model for just such an investigation as early as 1906. In that year was published the first volume of their monumental study of *English Local Government* . . . , subtitled *The Parish and the County*.[3] The government of the English parish, with its "town meetings" and "select vestrymen," paralleled to a very large degree that of the New England town both in name and in function.[4] Within this framework, so remarkably like that described by MacLear, Haskins and Sly, the Webbs noted the operation of two opposite tendencies. In some parishes the administration of such matters as poor relief, common pastures, and church support was "practically by common consent" of the meeting, guided by its elected vestrymen. In many others, perhaps in the majority of parishes, "uncontrollable parish officers" became a self-perpetuating oligarchy and effectively denied the townsmen their traditional voice in local affairs. These conflicting trends existed side by side from the late seventeenth century to the early nineteenth.[5]

The implications are obvious. Was the much vaunted mechanism of the New England town meeting likewise subject to oligarchical tendencies? If so, when did the town meeting as we are wont to think of it — vigorous, alert, and a bit cantankerous — come into existence? What a close

---

[1] Anne Bush MacLear, *Early New England Towns: A Comparative Study of Their Development* (New York, 1908); George Lee Haskins, *Law and Authority in Early Massachusetts* (New York, 1960). In addition, Sumner Chilton Powell, *Puritan Village* (Middletown, 1963), and Darrett Rutman, *Winthrop's Boston* (Chapel Hill, 1965), reveal a great deal about the workings of town government before 1660.

[2] See esp. p. 93.

[3] (New York, 1906).

[4] Webb and Webb, *Parish and County*, 39 and *n.*, 41.

[5] *Ibid.*, 42–43, 173 ff.

study of the records of Dedham and Watertown, Massachusetts,[6] indicates is that, in the "middle period" of colonial history, the locus of effective political power in these two towns shifted from one body – the board of selectmen – to another – the town meeting – and that the locus of power remained firmly with the meeting thereafter. The shift took place, for the most part, between 1680 and 1720, a little earlier in Watertown, a little later in Dedham. The interesting questions of how and why this change took place remain to be discussed.

The town meeting was the original and protean vessel of local authority. The founding fathers of Dedham and Watertown are recorded to have assembled to deal with local problems even before the General Court moved in March 1635 to define and approve the power of the town as a body.[7] Beginning "whereas particular towns have many things which concern only themselves," the General Court provided that the town (or, its resident freemen acting collectively) should have the power to dispose of its own lands, make bylaws not repugnant to the laws established by the General Court, and "to choose their own particular officers [such] as constables, surveyors for the highways and the like." Hereafter it was clear who constituted the town meeting and what was its competence. And it was a very broad competence as it then stood, with its "bylaws . . . not repugnant" and "own particular officers . . . and the like." [8] Such clauses were broad, open-ended mandates for the town meetings to manage local business.

But even as it received this sanction, the town meeting had begun to call into being its companion and potential competitor in local government, the board of selectmen. On August 23, 1634, the freemen of Watertown agreed "that there shall be chosen three persons to be [blank] the ordering of the civil affairs in the town." [9] Such an action had no precedent in the law of the colony, but it had one evident English precedent in the select vestry. A similar step was taken by Dedham in 1639 because "it hath been found by long experience that the general meeting of so many men in one [blank] of the common affairs thereof, have wasted much time to no small damage and business is thereby nothing furthered."

[6] Don Gleason Hill, ed., *Dedham Records*, III-V (Dedham, 1892–99); Julius Tuttle, ed., *Dedham Records*, VI (Dedham, 1936); *Watertown Records*, I-II (Watertown, 1894–1900), III–IV (Boston, 1904–06).

[7] 1635 petition, *Dedham Recs.*, III, 1; Aug. 23, 1634, *Watertown Recs.*, I. These and all subsequent dates are old style. In some cases, pages will be cited in place of dates because the entry by date is unclear or is duplicated on another page.

[8] *Records of the Governor and Company of the Massachusetts Bay in New England*, I (Boston, 1853), 172.

[9] Aug. 23, 1634, *Watertown Recs.*, I. The number of selectmen fluctuated widely until fixed permanently at 7 in 1647.

In order to avoid such inconvenience in the future, the Dedham meeting selected seven men and gave them "full power to contrive, execute and perform all the business of this our whole town." [10]

Other towns also appointed selectmen. In the Body of Liberties of 1641,[11] the colony recognized the new institution. The General Court did more, for it proceeded to delegate to the selectmen of each town numerous duties, among them the power to lay out highways, supervise education, judge certain cases, and to exercise social control.[12] At the same time, both in Watertown and in Dedham, the selectmen confidently assumed broad powers, made bylaws on their own authority, and authorized expenditures independently of the meeting. It was immediately evident that this was a vital institution. A body this strong could easily have gone the way of the select vestries as noted by the Webbs, from independent action to independent control.

And, in fact, through most of the seventeenth century the town meetings of Watertown and of Dedham were no more than the equals of the boards of selectmen, and were in some ways definitely subordinate. The townsmen met infrequently, twice a year in Dedham and two or three times a year in neighboring Watertown. (See Appendix, Tables 1, 2.) At these infrequent meetings, the business transacted was largely routine in nature. Town elections, the remuneration of the minister and schoolmaster, minor adjustments in town bylaws — these occupied the attention of the meeting. The town *could* consider anything it chose, even the question of the power of the selectmen, which Dedham reaffirmed several times in the early years.[13] But generally, the town each year picked an experienced group of "respected friends" to be selectmen, and seemed glad to leave most of the difficult decisions to them. In 1676, for example, Watertown asked its selectmen to agree with a schoolmaster "as cheap as they can" and in 1679 instructed them to promulgate some bylaws which would mitigate "the disorderliness of cattle and swine and the multitude of sheep in the town." [14] Dedham often "referred to the selectmen" so that they might "prepare and ripen the answer" to a difficult matter.[15]

The key to the disparity in power between the town meeting and the board of selectmen before 1680 lies in the question of initiative. In theory the town could take any action. It had to approve all actions of the selectmen and could turn any or all selectmen out of office at the annual election. In reality, however, the town meeting only rarely ini-

---

[10] *Dedham Recs.*, III, 53.

[11] William H. Whitmore, ed., A *Bibliographical Sketch of the Laws of the Massachusetts Colony From 1630 to 1686* (Boston, 1890), 49.

[12] *Recs. of Mass. Bay*, II, 4, 6–9, 163, 180.

[13] Dec. 31, 1639, Jan. 1, 1649, Jan. 4, 1657, *Dedham Recs.*, III.

[14] Nov. 6, 1676, Nov. 3, 1679, *Watertown Recs.*, I.

[15] *Dedham Recs.*, III, 192.

tiated major legislation or voted out groups of experienced selectmen.[16]
Never once did either town disapprove an action of the selectmen. In
short, the town meeting existed largely as a passive veto power.]

Only in contrast to the activity of the selectmen can the relative pas-
sivity of the town meetings in these villages be appreciated. In every
sphere of political activity — legislative, appointive, financial, judicial, and
administrative — the selectmen were equal or superior to the meeting. In
every one of these fields the essence of their superiority lay in their possession of the initiative. The board of selectmen met formally from five to
ten times a year, and indications are that the selectmen met informally
still more often. The volume of business transacted at each formal meeting consistently exceeded the volume of business done by the town meeting. Thus, the selectmen not only met more often than the town, but also
handled a total volume of business far in excess of that handled by the
town. The sheer weight of their experience in public business gave the
selectmen an advantage over the town. And, because of its smallness (3 to
11 men), the board of selectmen could act with greater dispatch than
could the general meeting. The General Court implicitly recognized the
board's effectiveness by addressing itself specifically to the selectmen in
its delegation of power to the towns.[17]

[If initiative was the essence of leadership, the essence of initiative, in
Dedham at least, was an agenda of urgent business to be considered by
the town, an agenda which was prepared exclusively by the selectmen before each town meeting.] It was not unusual for the procedure to run as
follows: "an order being presented [to the town meeting as part of the
agenda] *already drawn by the selectmen* . . . being put to vote it was
voted in the affirmative, *confirming the same for a town order.*" [18] In both
towns, moreover, the selectmen are found deciding entirely on their own
when to call all extraordinary (non-electoral) meetings of the town.[19]

The selectmen of the two towns also exercised a good measure of
initiative in legislative matters. They promulgated a number of important
bylaws entirely without prior consultation with or subsequent approval
by the town meeting. These might range from laws governing the control
of livestock or the maintenance of fences to systems of enforcing the collection of the minister's salary.[20] The Dedham selectmen of 1647 unilater-

[16] The Dedham elections of 1657 and 1660 saw sudden turnovers, but neither
seems to have been the result of a direct power struggle between the town and
selectmen as such. Jan. 4, 1657, *ibid.*; Jan. 1660, *ibid.*, IV.

[17] See n. 12.

[18] Jan. 1, 1666, *Dedham Recs.*, IV (emphasis added). See also Dec. 31, 1663,
and Dec. 28, 1666, *ibid.*, for typical agendas.

[19] For examples, Oct. 21, 1661, July 12, 1672, *ibid.*; and Dec. 30, 1679,
Watertown Recs., I.

[20] See May 5, 1657, Apr. 10, 1669, Mar. 26, 1650, *Watertown Recs.*, I; Mar.
1, 1641, *Dedham Recs.*, III.

ally enacted a broad statute on the discovery and control of mines within the town's boundaries.[21] Numerous other ordinances which were approved by the town meeting were initially drafted and presented by the selectmen.

Certain appointive powers fell to the selectmen in the middle seventeenth century. Tithingmen, fenceviewers, and sealers of weights and measures were customarily chosen by the executive board.[22] More significantly, the selectmen in both towns chose numerous temporary committees to look into specific matters and, in some cases, to take independent action.[23] Although the town itself elected selectmen and surveyors of highways, usually approved the schoolmaster, and from time to time appointed woodreeves or hogreeves,[24] it seldom created the informal committees so often employed by the selectmen.

The selectmen also shared the power of the purse with the towns. The selectmen in Dedham and their appointees in Watertown performed the sensitive task of assessing the taxes due from each man.[25] In Watertown, in 1660, although the town had already granted a town rate of £40, the selectmen "upon the appearance of more debts and other charges . . . saw cause to grant a rate of fifty pounds" without reference to the town! In 1674 the town voted that the selectmen should make a rate "according as they shall find the town debts to amount unto." The following year the town voted no tax at all, but the Watertown selectmen proceeded to instruct two of their number to make out the rate as if they had been authorized to do so.[26] In Dedham, the financial power lay almost entirely with the selectmen. The town did not authorize rates at all throughout most of the seventeenth century, leaving it to Dedham's selctmen to decide the town's needs and to levy taxes. Once in a long while the accounts of the selectmen for a given year would be brought up for approval; but this was done by the meeting on the spur of the moment and no dissatisfaction was at any time indicated.[27]

The greatest day-to-day power of the selectmen lay in the exercise of administrative and judicial functions. Laws, appointments, and taxes were matters which came up perhaps once or twice a year, while the administration of land, wood, and livestock regulations and the maintenance of social control were constant and continuing, and touched many lives.

[21] *Dedham Recs.*, III, 119.

[22] Feb. 14, 1652, Jan. 5, 1679, *Watertown Recs.*, I; Mar. 4, 1677, *Dedham Recs.*, IV; Aug. 29, 1683, *ibid.*, V.

[23] For just one example, May 14, 1685, *Dedham Recs.*, V.

[24] See any Jan. meetings in the two towns' *Records* before 1685. Town elections were shifted from Jan. to Mar. in 1692.

[25] Nov. 30, 1685, *Dedham Recs.*, V, or any other tax list; Nov. 29, 1664, Dec. 1, 1674, *Watertown Recs.*, I.

[26] Feb. 14, 1659, Nov. 2, 1674, Nov. 4, 23, 1675, *Watertown Recs.*, I.

[27] Jan. 3, 1652, *Dedham Recs.*, III.

These matters the town meeting treated only incidentally, in passing, after the business of elections and other major issues was finished. The meetings of the selectmen, on the other hand, were concerned with small requests, judgments, and inquiries — in all of which their decisions prevailed without reference to the body of the town. Selectmen decided the guilt or innocence of men presented for allowing their livestock to run loose and damage crops, or of individuals whose inadequate fences had allowed beasts free access to the fields.[28] Questions of the locations of highways as well as of private ways of access to land came up frequently. These entailed difficult questions of property rights — the rights of one individual versus another — customarily decided by the selectmen.[29] As timber was conserved by both towns (in the case of Dedham, sometimes on orders passed by the selectmen themselves), townsmen who took wood from the public land had to gain the prior approval of the selectmen or risk a fine.[30] The town mills of Dedham were treated as public utilities: the selectmen let the franchises, specified the terms of operation, and adjusted differences over the water rights between mills, observing, "For the care of the town is, and must needs be, that both mills now in town be duly accommodated and encouraged." [31]

In each town, it was through their powers of social control that the selectmen most affected individual lives. The care of the poor, the warning out of vagabonds, and the supervision and employment of the idle were responsibilities taken very seriously, particularly by the selectmen of Watertown. "Agreed (in reference to the well-ordering of the inhabitants of Watertown) that the selectmen should divide themselves and take a survey of the several families, and take notice as of the wants of some poor families, as likewise of their improvement of their times both concerning their souls as of their bodies. . . ." [32] Part and parcel of this supervision was a concern for education. Typically, the selectmen of Watertown would agree "that they would go two and two together to go through the town to examine how children are taught to read and instructed in the grounds of religion and the capital laws." Whether the cause was a lack of firewood or the negligence of parents, the selectmen sought out every impediment to education and acted to eliminate it.[33] In early Watertown social control was a many-faceted attempt to assure an element of real uni-

[28] July 6, 1677, *Watertown Recs.*, I, offers a particularly clear case of the personal conflicts involved in such matters.
[29] Mar. 24, 1669, Sept. 22, 1668, *ibid.*; *Dedham Recs.*, III, 150–151.
[30] Feb. 23, 1650, *Dedham Recs.*, III; Feb. 27, 1668, *ibid.*, IV; Nov. 29, Dec. 13, 1670, *Watertown Recs.*, I; Apr. 10, 1674, *Dedham Recs.*, III.
[31] Nov. 29, 1664, Apr. 18, 1668, *Dedham Recs.*, IV.
[32] Jan. 8, 1660, *Watertown Recs.*, I. See also July 21, 1671, for an example of a warning out of town.
[33] Dec. 12, 1665, Nov. 29, 1670, *ibid.*

formity in a community which was theoretically an organic whole. As the agents of uniformity, the selectmen often became involved in the private lives of their fellow townsmen.

The Dedham selectmen were less energetic in their exercise of social control. Instead, they enjoyed a prerogative not always shared by their counterparts in Watertown: the power to grant or refuse hundreds of requests for parcels of land. When Francis Chickering wanted title to a little triangle of waste land "for the shortening or straightening his fence at Rock Meadow," it was the selectmen who granted his request. Nor were the requests always for mere "convenience grants": areas up to fifty acres were disposed of by the selectmen acting independently. Within the broad limits set by the proprietors, these few men could provide or withhold land, the source of life and wealth in an agricultural village.[34]

More powers, more small decisions that lay in the hands of the town executive, could easily be cited. But it should be evident enough from the foregoing that the selectmen were the most active and often the most creative political element in these towns prior to the late seventeenth century. True, the theoretical strength of the town meeting was greater, the meeting did exercise its power on some major issues and the selectmen enjoyed their position largely because the town found a strong executive useful. But whatever the theoretical power of the town meeting and for whatever reasons it deferred to the town executive, the substance of power lay with the selectmen.

Yet a vigorous town meeting of the classic mold emerged in Watertown and in Dedham as the seventeenth century wore on and the eighteenth began. The decided shift in power this represented is not easy to trace. There occurred no major constitutional crises which precipitated wholesale or grudging transfers of traditional prerogatives from one body to the other. On the contrary, overt conflict between the two bodies continued to be rare. Possibly this is because the selectmen were ultimately the creatures of the town meeting. Elected annually, the selectmen lacked formal sanctions of law with which to defend themselves or institutionalize their powers. Whatever the reason, the transfer was gradual, extending over a period of thirty or forty years, and came about largely through changes in procedure. Most of the changes were in themselves small and seemingly unimportant. But, taken together, they constituted a major change in the way these towns were governed. The town meetings slowly came alive, came to assume the management of town government in a way unheard of in the 1660's. The story of the transfer of political power in Watertown and in Dedham is in large measure the story of the rising creativity and assertiveness of the town meeting.

The most immediately apparent change was the increase in the number

---

[34] *Dedham Recs.*, III, 201; Dec. 28, 1664, *ibid.*, IV.

of town meetings after 1680.[35] In the three preceding decades the average number of meetings per year was two in Dedham and slightly under two and one half in Watertown. In some years there would be but one meeting, and rarely were there more than four. By the 1690's both towns were meeting three or four times annually in primary sessions, and four to eight times a year if meetings called by adjournment from the previous session (a device seldom employed before this) are included. The selectmen still called some of these meetings, but others the town itself called before it adjourned. The record makes it quite obvious that the town called these additional meetings because the volume of business brought before the town, both by the town and by the selectmen, had become too great to be dealt with in a single day. At the same time that the amount of business transacted by the town at each session was growing and the number of sessions was increasing, the meetings of the selectmen became increasingly brief and uneventful. The selectmen of Dedham met no less often, and in Watertown still more often, and in both towns they continued to be responsible for the co-ordination of the growing number of routine concerns of a maturing society; but the discretionary powers which they had formerly exercised fell to the newly active town meeting.

In striking contrast to the situation prior to 1680, there is not one instance recorded during the next sixty years of the framing of town bylaws by the selectmen of Watertown. The record of their compatriots in Dedham is nearly as barren. By and large, the town itself made such few new ordinances as were required. It still accepted proposals from the selectmen, but, in Watertown at least, the town meeting now freely exercised its veto on the proposals of its executive.[36]

The power of appointment also fell largely to the towns after 1690. The town meeting of Dedham, which for decades had elected only selectmen, surveyors of highways, and some of the miscellaneous regulatory officers such as field drivers, began after 1692 to fill offices formerly filled by the selectmen (i.e., tithingmen, fenceviewers, and the sealer of weights and measures). The Dedham meeting now also began for the first time to elect constables and a treasurer. Each year the town provided explicitly that the selectmen should act as "assessors for the present year" only, thus assuming a new and close control over this important function. Similar developments took place in Watertown at the same time.[37]

---

[35] In Dedham, the date is closer to 1690. See Tables 1 and 2 for the discussion which follows.

[36] May 4, 1719, *Watertown Recs.*, II; Mar. 7, 1736, *ibid.*, III.

[37] Mar. 1, 1707, Mar. 7, 16, 1708, *Dedham Recs.*, VI; Mar. 21, 1693, July 17, 1694, *Watertown Recs.*, II. Both towns were responding to a new act of the General Court, discussed below. *The Acts and Resolves . . . of the Province of Massachusetts Bay . . .* (Boston, 1869–1922), I, 166.

An even more important officer that both towns soon began to elect was the moderator of the meeting. Each had now and then chosen a moderator for a particular meeting before 1690. From 1690 to 1715 Watertown had regularly employed a respected townsman as chairman of the meeting, but it was always the selectmen who appointed him.[38] In 1711 and 1714, however, Dedham's town meeting on its own initiative elected a moderator, and in 1715 an Act of the General Court required that all town meetings elect a moderator as the initial item of business at every session.[39] Thereafter each town regularly selected a special officer to guide the business of its meeting, no longer leaving leadership entirely to the selectmen as seems to have been the case in the past. This development is roughly comparable to that of a colonial Assembly which, having formerly met under the leadership of the governor's Council, begins to meet separately under its own speaker.

These changes are mere preludes to the alterations that took place in the handling of that *sine qua non* of political power, money. In the early 1680's the Watertown meeting assumed direct control over the levying of taxes and the appropriation of the proceeds. It retained this control thereafter, each year entering its will somewhat as follows: "Granted by the inhabitants that there shall be a rate made of seventy pounds to pay the town debts and the remainder to go towards mending the way at Stony Brook." [40] In Dedham, "the town by vote have granted a rate for defraying charges" became the usual form after 1692, while the selectmen each year declared "this day a rate is made by virtue of an act of the town at their general meeting." [41] Nor did the towns automatically make the appropriations requested by the selectmen. In 1723 and again in 1727, Watertown refused to appropriate certain funds which the selectmen wished to expend on "unseen or extraordinary charges." [42] The meeting in Dedham in 1730 was no more co-operative: "It was proposed to the town whether they would do anything towards the building of a schoolhouse in any part of the town. It was passed in the negative. Also proposed to the town whether they would grant twenty pounds for defraying other charges arising in the town. It passed in the negative." [43] Together with the town's control of appropriation went a close scrutiny of the expenditures made by the constables and selectmen. For Watertown, this meant an increasing skepticism in individual cases, such as a refusal to pay the expenses of a poor woman whose care the selectmen on their own initiative had as-

[38] An exception is Oct. 2, 1694, when the town replaced the selectmen's nominee with a man of its own choice. *Watertown Recs.*, II.

[39] Mar. 3, 1711, Mar. 8, 1714, *Dedham Recs.*, VI; *Acts and Resolves*, II, 30.

[40] Nov. 3, 1684, *Watertown Recs.*, II.

[41] Mar. 5, 1693, Dec. 30, 1695, *Dedham Recs.*, V.

[42] Dec. 16, 1723, Jan. 13, 1726, *Watertown Recs.*, II.

[43] May 11, 1730, *Dedham Recs.*, VI.

signed to one of their own number.[44] Dedham went beyond this and established a formal committee for the audit of selectmen's accounts. Occasionally before 1726 and regularly thereafter, "it was proposed to the town whether it be their mind to choose a committee to examine all the accounts between the town treasurer and the town. Voted in the affirmative, and the committee is Amos Fisher, Senior, Sargeant John Ellis, and Captain Jeremiah Fisher." [45] The members of this audit committee, as of a majority of all such committees, were not selectmen. This was a regular, independent body responsible directly to the town. Appointed before approval of the accounts was due, it had ample time in which to pry and quibble to ensure that not a shilling had been wasted.

A number of those administrative matters which involved favors for individual townsmen, or which in some way directly affected them, were transferred from the jurisdiction of the selectmen to that of the town meeting. The right to grant "liberties" to hang gates on town roads and to extend fences into the highways, cases involving public property in general, decisions on ways, the details of assessments on property — these the town no longer entrusted to the selectmen as a matter of course.[46] In Dedham, management of such momentous issues as the expansion of the meetinghouse, the splitting off of part of the town, and the trust of public bills of credit was no longer left to the selectmen, but was taken over in detail by the town as a whole.[47] That the meeting should begin to occupy itself with so many matters implies a marked degree of self-confidence on its part, or, conversely, a lack of confidence in the board of selectmen.

Yet a town executive of some kind was still necessary. If it had been true back in 1639 that business was "nothing furthered" by having the town meeting handle all the problems of the community, it was all the more true in the populous villages of the 1700's. For the increasingly busy town meetings, a solution was found in the appointment of *ad hoc* committees to investigate or resolve specific matters for the town meeting.[48] These committees, ephemeral boards of "selected men," bypassed the selectmen. Unlike the true selectmen who were elected once a year and could consider any issue, the committees were chosen as needed and were restricted to a single function. Through the use of this device the town meeting came to be a sort of political amoeba, shooting out functional pseudopods as it chose. The town also delegated administrative details to its precincts — legal subdivisions within the town with autonomous control over religious and some financial matters. Before 1738, Watertown

[44] May 26, Dec. 22, Jan. 16, 1729, Dec. 6, 1731, *Watertown Recs.*, III.
[45] May 13, 1718, *Dedham Recs.*, VI.
[46] For examples see Nov. 28, 1681, Feb. 24, 1692, Mar. 28, 1698, Feb. 12, 1699, Oct. 23, 1704, Mar. 3, 1711, Mar. 4, 1722, *Watertown Recs.*, II; Feb. 12, 1710, *Dedham Recs.*, VI; and Mar. 7, 1697, *ibid.*, V.
[47] Mar. 10, 1700, *Dedham Recs.*, V; Feb. 12, 1710, Dec. 27, 1721, *ibid.*, VI.
[48] For examples, see Feb. 12, Mar. 12, 1710, *ibid.*, III.

and Dedham had each been divided into several precincts,[49] each of which had its own clerk and assessors [50] as well as militia and church officers. A good many of the routine tasks of taxation and church support fell to these bodies.

With all this increased activity went a new spirit in the town meeting, a spirit of action, of pride, and of contentiousness. "The town voted" this, "the town ordered" that, "the town" saw fit to appoint, to authorize, to decide all matters. This phrase "the town" recurs throughout the records of both towns as if part of a secular liturgy. Perhaps the best expression of the new spirit of the town meetings may be seen in matters which were purely political — elections and votes.

The age of "unanimous concurrence" was, for Watertown, clearly over by 1690. Votes were now occasionally so close as to require a division. Tallies were disputed in 1713 and again in 1729, and in each case the townsmen were asked to file out on either side of the meetinghouse in order to register their pros and cons in an indisputable fashion.[51] (In the latter case, the shrewd moderator waited until all present had gone outside and immediately announced that the majority were for adjournment.) For the first time, as a result of such disputes, both towns were forced to appeal to higher authority to settle local issues.[52]

For the first time, too, the records betray an emphasis on suffrage qualifications. After a hotly contested sectional fight for the election of selectmen, a Watertown petition of 1695 complained that twenty-nine unqualified inhabitants had voted for the winners.[53] "Great heat of spirit and party zeal, . . . great jars and contentions and animosity" were aroused by precisely the same sort of contest in Dedham some thirty-two years later, when another petition by the losers complained "that many [who] voted in said meeting were not qualified." [54]

[Less sensational, but more significant in cumulative impact, was a trend which lay beneath all local elections from the most disputed to the most calm. This was a marked increase in the rate of turnover of selectmen.] Before the 1680's the typical board of selectmen in Watertown had a collective total of nearly fifty years' experience as selectmen. This dropped to less than thirty years' experience in the following decade. What was happening in both towns was that the average selectman first elected to the office in the later period served in his lifetime fewer terms than had his

---

[49] *Dedham Recs.*, VI, 371 ff; Mar. 16, 1697, *Watertown Recs.*, II; *Acts and Resolves*, IX, 272; X, 48–49.

[50] Mar. 12, 1731, *Watertown Recs.*, IV; Nov. 7, 1730, *Dedham Recs.*, VI.

[51] June 8, 1713, *Watertown Recs.*, II; Mar. 3, 1728, *ibid.*, III.

[52] For examples, see Watertown petition of 1695, Mass. Archives, State House, Boston, CXIII, 270; Apr. 4, 1704, Miscellaneous Bound MSS, Mass. Hist. Soc., Boston; and Apr. 17, 1704, *Dedham Recs.*, V.

[53] Watertown petition of 1695.

[54] Oct. 30, 1727, Diary of the Rev. Samuel Dexter, Dedham Hist. Soc.; Mar. 18, 1727, *Dedham Recs.*, VI.

counterpart of earlier decades. (See Table 1 and 2.) The towns were calling on each man to serve less often and, as a result, were calling upon more individuals to serve as selectmen at one time or another. The towns after the 1680's faced boards of selectmen who lacked the immense accumulation of experience of the earlier boards.

Control over the agenda of town meetings was one of the few major powers that the selectmen retained. A provincial law of 1715 required that the townsmen limit their considerations to those proposals contained in a full and detailed "warrant," or agenda, prepared before each meeting by the selectmen. Ten or more freeholders could by petition force the selectmen to enter a proposal on the agenda,[55] but a petition with ten signatures called for a special effort on the part of an ordinary townsman. In effect, the initiative was put squarely in the hands of the selectmen. Yet, in their new confidence, the meetings of both towns found ways to undermine the selectmen's initiative. Watertown did not hesitate to vote down proposal after proposal in the warrants, while Dedham found a more clever (and typically legalistic) way out: the last proposal in the warrant was entered as "to do other business that may concern the town," which neatly placed the initiative back in the hands of the meeting![56]

As the selectmen lost the initiative to the towns, their meetings became ever more routine. They authorized day-to-day expenditures, warned out strangers, executed the orders of the town on specific cases, saw to the relief of the poor, and, in Dedham, were much occupied with the tedious business of assessing the various taxes. The occasions of social control declined and nearly disappeared through the years, and in Dedham the granting of land-favors became the function of special meetings of the proprietors of the town land. The numbers of poor and of strangers were on the rise in both towns, so that there was still plenty of business in this area.[57] It would, in fact, be wrong to belittle either the usefulness or the power of the eighteenth-century selectmen. They remained the major executive of the town, were still experienced and respected men. In their control over the warrants for town meetings the selectmen possessed a way of exercising a discreet leadership over town opinion and action. But power as effective control, power as initiative, was no longer theirs.

Anyone reading the records of these two towns can not but be struck, on the one hand, with the increasing vitality and authority of the towns

[55] *Acts and Resolves*, II, 30 ff.

[56] Jan. 16, 1729, *Watertown Recs.*, III; Aug. 11, 1727, *Dedham Recs.*, VI.

[57] An analysis of the occasions of poor relief and of the warnings out of strangers in the records of the two towns reveals a marked and persistant increase of both occasions in both towns after 1690. One of the authors is presently completing a paper which maintains that these statistics are typical and that they reflect a general social change in the old agricultural villages of eastern Mass. For background on this, and for authority on general statements regarding Dedham society, see Kenneth A. Lockridge, Dedham, 1636–1736: The Anatomy of a Puritan Utopia (unpubl. Ph.D. diss., Princeton University, 1965).

between 1680 and 1720 and, on the other hand, with the declining prestige and power of the selectmen during the same years. To read through the records of Dedham or Watertown in the 1660's is to gain a vivid sense of the leadership exercised by such men as Captain Mason and John Coolidge, selectmen of Watertown, or of Daniel Fisher or Timothy Dwight, selectmen of Dedham. Men such as these assembled often to look into all the pressing concerns of their communities, and dealt with assurance with the needs and transgressions of their fellow men. But if one turns to the records of the 1730's, one finds a very different state of affairs. To be sure, the framework is the same, as is the language used and a fair amount of the business conducted by each body. Yet it soon becomes evident that the town, anonymous, collective thing that it is, has acquired a forceful personality of its own. Here in the town meetings is where decisions are thrashed out. The selectmen, heirs of Mason, Coolidge, Fisher, and Dwight, execute their duties with intelligence, but missing are the feelings of energy and strength engendered by the records of their predecessors of the previous century.

If it may be accepted that the locus of political power in Dedham and in Watertown shifted in this manner and at this time, there arises the intriguing question of why it should have done so. Although it has not yet been established that these two towns were typical, they *were* both moderately large, well-established towns near the center of population and of cultural activity in the colony. This fact, and the fact that the peculiarities which they manifest are sharply defined and potentially significant, impels a closer look into their histories for the ultimate causes of events. [Though the framework of town government in Dedham and Watertown changed little between 1640 and 1740, there were some legal changes which may well have had an effect on the political center of gravity in the towns.] The provincial charter of 1691, and the laws which implemented it,[58] altered the suffrage both on the provincial and on the local level by reducing the qualifications required for the exercise of those rights. The qualifications for voting in the election of local officers and for having a voice in town decisions had, since 1670, been 80 pounds of taxable estate,[59] and now became only 20 pounds. This extension of the franchise within the towns, coming when it did, would seem at first to be a contributing cause to the growth of the town meeting's power.

The Dedham tax lists do reveal that, if both the 1670 and the later suffrage requirements were enforced, the effect of the post-1691 reduction

[58] See *Acts and Resolves,* I, 2–20.

[59] This law was not, however, to apply to men who had already qualified for the local suffrage. For a concise view of the suffrage legislation, see B. Katherine Brown, "Freemanship in Puritan Massachusetts," *American Historical Review,* LIX (1954), 865–883. Some of Mrs. Brown's interpretations should not be considered final.

from 80 to 20 pounds of taxable estate would have been to increase the eligible town voters from under 40 per cent to over 90 per cent of all adult males on the lists. But the difficulty about this is that from 1648 to 1670, a period of twenty-two years, the legal qualification required for town suffrage was never above 20 pounds, and the local suffrage in Dedham was then well over 90 per cent.[60] Yet Dedham's town meeting did not move toward greater control in those twenty-two years, nor did Watertown's. If a broad local suffrage had no effect before 1670, why should one assume that its resumption after 1691 was instrumental in improving the position of the meeting?

Moreover, it is just possible that the twenty-year period of higher local suffrage requirements (1670–90) is a fiction. The records of neither town give any grounds for assuming that the 80-pound qualification of 1670 — or any qualification at all, for that matter — was rigidly enforced. Dedham was not specific in those years, as she was after 1691, as to whether meetings were restricted to qualified persons. Watertown, in 1680, tacitly suspended the law of 1670, providing instead that "all householders should have the liberty to vote in the choosing of selectmen and other officers . . . and also to vote in matters of a prudential nature." [61] Everything considered, it seems very unlikely that the changes in the legal suffrage made after 1691 were at the heart of the new strength of the town meeting. A wide town suffrage was very probably the normal and continuing state of affairs, broken only in the years 1670–91 and possibly not even then.

Other statutes passed in the post-1691 period unquestionably did increase the power of the town meeting. The great "Act for the Regulation of Townships" of November 18, 1692, affirmed that the final authority on bylaws lay with the town meeting alone. It also provided that every town must hold general elections twice a year, once to elect local officers and once to elect provincial officers, thereby establishing two meetings a year as an absolute minimum for every town. Two years later an act of the General Court transferred the privilege of electing tithingmen and, more important, assessors, from the selectmen to the town at large. Finally, the act of 1715 already referred to gave the town meetings the right to elect their own moderators.[62]

Yet, in Watertown and to a lesser extent in Dedham, the trend to increased town power was well under way when the first of the acts on town government began to take effect in 1693. It is most likely that the law

[60] See *Dedham Recs.* and Lockridge, Dedham. Lists of eligible voters in Dedham are in *Dedham Recs.*, III, 190, and Dec. 28, 1666, *ibid.*, IV. No such lists are available for Watertown.

[61] Nov. 1, 1680, *Watertown Recs.*, II. Householder suffrage would have run from 60 to 80 per cent of the adult males in both Dedham and Watertown.

[62] *Acts and Resolves*, I, 65–66, 166; *ibid.*, II, 30.

followed and reflected, rather than inspired, the change.] By the time the "Act for the Regulating of Townships" directed that the town meeting have sole authority over town bylaws, it had been over ten years since Watertown's selectmen had ventured to enact bylaws for the town. The town meeting was entitled by the act of 1715 to elect its own moderator, but Dedham's meeting had already begun this practice on its own.

[Thus, the emergence of the town meeting as the locus of power in these villages of eighteenth-century Massachusetts cannot readily be explained in terms of legal innovations.] It would be convenient to follow the present trend of historical analysis and announce, instead, that a profound alteration in the structure of village society underlay the transfer of political power in the two Massachusetts towns. Unfortunately, a careful reading of the sources — of town records, colony records, wills, and inventories in the county courthouses — provides no basis for any such conclusion.[63]

The social character of the selectmen differed greatly between Dedham and Watertown. In Dedham, decade after decade, the selectmen almost without exception were in the most wealthy 20 per cent of the town. Often, a majority of a particular board would be found in the top 10 per cent. In Watertown, on the other hand, wills and inventories reveal that the selectmen were drawn from the upper 60 per cent in wealth, indicating a much broader range of choice.[64] Such men as John Bigelow and John Hammond, though quite wealthy, served as Watertown selectmen only three and five terms, respectively, while John Sherman and Thomas Flagg, neither above average affluence and the latter actually rather poor, served twenty-three and ten terms each.[65]

But, while this raises interesting questions as to the difference in social "styles" between the communities, it does not affect the main point of continuity. [In both towns the evidence is that the relative economic position of the selectmen as a group did not change, that it remained the same in 1680–1740 as it had been in 1640–80. No oligarchy of wealthy men was replaced by a less wealthy group of leaders. Each town continued to pick for its selectmen the same type of man, a man about forty-five years old when first elected and with many years of experience in other local offices behind him.] Family was always a factor; there were usually one or two of the men on any given board who were the immediate descendants of earlier, once-prominent selectmen. But before 1740, no tight

[63] Because of the absence of tax lists (except for one in 1730) for Watertown, evidence for this is much sparser there than in the case of Dedham. See the analysis of the first two generations of Dedham townsmen (1636–1710) in chs. v–vii of Lockridge's Dedham.

[64] Middlesex County Probate Records; Watertown Tax List, Constable Perry's Watch, Feb. 6, 1730, in Mass. Hist. Soc.

[65] Henry Bond, *Genealogies of the Families . . . of Watertown, Massachusetts* (Boston, 1855), I, 270; Middlesex Co. Probate Recs., 1716, 20338, 7789.

web of marriage and "connection" ever dominated the office. On the other hand, [the tendency in the eighteenth century to elect men for fewer terms and consequently to select more individuals for the duty did not progress anywhere near the point of a thoroughgoing, democratic rotation of the office among a large body of men.]

Without the tax lists which do so much to confirm other indications of social structure, little can be said of the general character of Watertown society. Dedham is not such an unknown quantity and it can be said with considerable assurance that [there is no indication that Dedham's social character changed very much after 1680. There was certainly no trend to a more equalitarian distribution of wealth or to a less respectful attitude toward titles. Nor was there a trend to increased social or geographical mobility. The signs of change which do crop up came after 1710 and point to a slightly less equalitarian society, if anything]

If not legal change or social change, what then could have caused the town meetings to grasp new powers and attain such self-confidence? The answer seems to lie in a sort of evolutionary process which might be labelled the "natural history" of the town. The active town meeting seems to be the result of an organic development which, for Watertown and Dedham, reached a critical stage in the 1680–1720 period.

In each town there was an "old guard," a group of men who had assumed the leadership of the community shortly after its foundation and retained it for many years thereafter. [In the years between 1670 and 1685, a number of the most influential of these leaders either died or retired from public life.] Of the first generation of leaders in Watertown, twenty-five men lived to serve as selectmen after 1660. Ten of these served for no less than ten terms each. Three, Hugh Mason, John Sherman and Thomas Hastings, were most remarkable. Mason was first elected in 1638, and served twenty-eight terms; Sherman began his career in 1636, was a member of the third panel of selectmen in the town's history, and was reelected twenty-one times; Hastings, like Mason, was first elected in 1638 and he served twenty terms in all. These three men, together with others like John Coolidge who were less dominant but still important, represented a pool of leaders upon which the town drew for many, many years. The weight of their influence is best reflected in the board elected in 1680.[66] Seven men with a total of 74 years of experience made up that board.

Mason was last elected in 1677 and died in 1679; [67] when their election was disputed in 1681, Hastings and Coolidge refused to serve again as selectmen; [68] others died in the 1670's. Taken together, these events removed the old leaders of Watertown from the scene within a relatively brief time. Fairly abruptly in the late 1670's and early 1680's, a new gen-

[66] Nov. 1, 1680, *Watertown Recs.*, II.
[67] *Ibid.*, I, 132, and p. 45 in section on Births, Marriages and Deaths.
[68] Nov. 1, 1680, Nov. 7, Mar. 31, 1681, Nov. 6, 27, 1682, *ibid.*, II.

eration was called to take over the reins of local government. The new men, raised in the shadow of the first generation, were relatively inexperienced. The men elected in 1681 had but twenty-five years of cumulative service in the office — one third of the experience of the previous board. It is probable that these younger and less experienced men who were recruited to fill the gaps left by death and retirement were viewed with less deferential respect than were their predecessors. Never again did Watertown elect a group of such great age and experience as that of 1680; the typical board of the years 1681–1740 had but half the experience of its earlier counterpart.

The giants among the early leaders of Dedham were Daniel Fisher, who served thirty-two terms as selectman beginning in 1650, Eleazer Lusher, who served twenty-nine terms beginning in 1639, Timothy Dwight, who served twenty-six terms after 1645, and Joshua Fisher, who served twenty-three terms from 1649.[69] As in neighboring Watertown, there were also lesser men who served as selectmen relatively often. Peter Woodward, for example, served sixteen terms beginning in 1643. And, again as in Watertown, most of the early leaders departed from the scene within a short space of time. Woodward last served in 1670; Lusher and Joshua Fisher last served and died in 1672; Daniel Fisher died in 1683; Dwight, though he served three scattered terms later in his very long life, ended the major part of his career in 1681, after a string of nine consecutive terms.[70]

In Dedham, however, this changing of the guard did not immediately signal a decline in the influence of the board of selectmen or an increase in the activity of the town meeting. Part of the explanation for this may lie in the pattern of the careers of the secondary members of the broad "first generation" of selectmen, those who served under and with the four early giants of local politics. Between 1639 and 1641, four men, Francis Chickering, John Dwight, John Hayward, and John Kingsbury, began careers as selectmen averaging thirteen terms apiece. Within the five years 1655–60, all four retired or died. Succeeding these men in the 1660's were seven others, Henry Wright, Richard Ellis, John Aldis, Daniel Pond, Edward Richards, Thomas Metcalf, and Thomas Fuller, who served on the average twelve terms apiece and who largely left public life between 1675 and 1690. These seven represent a second generation, or really a half-generation, of leaders. They began their service when Lusher, the Fishers, Dwight, and Woodward were in full career. Trained under the original leaders and serving with them, most of these seven men lived on and were active for a decade after the death of their seniors.

---

[69] Fisher was speaker of the House of Deputies, 1680–82, and an Assistant, 1683; Luther was an Assistant 1662–72. *Dedham Recs.*, IV, 288.

[70] See the indexes to *Dedham Recs.*, III–VI; and *Early Records of the Town of Dedham*, I, entitled Births, Marriages and Deaths, 1635–1845 (Dedham, 1886).

Thus it was not until after 1690 that the selectmen of Dedham lost their firm grip on local affairs and the town meeting began to display the energy of its counterpart in Watertown. But the Dedham meeting acted with an unprecedented burst of power once it did make its move. For some unknown reason doubtless associated with the turmoil in the colony as a whole, the meeting of 1689 not only ousted every selectman elected at the preceding election in 1687 but it also (with one exception) never again elected any of them or any other man who had been elected to the post of selectman at any time before 1680! [71] The townsmen totally and permanently repudiated the entire existing leadership of the town, among the most prominent of whom were some of the seven men listed above.

With the passing of the old leaders, there went as well one of the important ingredients of their success in dominating the towns. The early years of communal life in both towns saw a marked stress on concensus. Having just been founded in a new land whose government lacked ultimate authority and whose church was struggling to control several varieties of heresy, Dedham and Watertown sought to create a sense of communal love, of mutual responsibility among their members. Only in the 1670's does the emphasis on communal spirit slacken perceptibly and not until the 1690's may it be said to have disappeared.[72] Part of the nature of the early leadership was not simply power, not simply frequent re-elections, but a whole way of thought. In the lifetimes of these men a sense of community was the touchstone of policy. Mediation, compromise, a "loving spirit" — these largely passed away with the great men of local politics. It is no wonder that a certain amount of respect for the chief office of the town seems to have gone with them.

Time brought to Watertown and to Dedham changes other than the passing of the selectmen who had dominated town affairs for a generation. Certain inevitable developments, remarkably similar in each town, led to crises of two definite types, both of which called for controversial decisions from the town meeting. If in explaining the shift in power one side of the coin is the departure of the early leaders of the towns, the other is the stirring of town-meeting activity by the necessities of finding ministers to fill the pulpit and of resolving sectional conflicts within the towns.

Forty years of ministerial stability in Watertown were ended in 1685 with the death of the town's long-time pastor, John Sherman. The town meeting was to bestir itself with increasing frequency during the next dec-

[71] *Dedham Recs.*, V, 203. See also p. 199.

[72] Many examples come to mind, all derived from a careful reading of the records of the towns. The most vivid example of the original emphasis on a loving spirit is the town covenant of Dedham, written in 1635 and signed by each man as he became a townsman. *Dedham Recs.*, III, 2–3.

ade in the frustratingly difficult task of finding a replacement. Dedham's John Allin, another of those great old men of the community, served as its minister from the foundation of the local church in 1637 until his death in 1671. For two years after Allin's death, town and congregation fruitlessly sought a minister. Having found one, they were again presented with the problem when he in turn died in 1685. This time it was more than seven years until a replacement could be found. In these interims between ministers, church support and the ministry demanded more attention than before or after. The selectmen could not make independent decisions in such critical matters, and the towns enjoyed more perfect control than in other affairs.

But the overriding crisis which came to occupy the attention of both towns was that of sectional conflict. Watertown first experienced an acute attack of the problem in 1692, when the question arose of where to erect a new meetinghouse. Petitions by the townsmen to central authorities, heated debate in the town meetings and attempted arbitrations by committees of the General Court ensued, but all failed to prevent the *de facto* division of Watertown into two hostile congregations in 1697.[73] Not until 1738, after much bickering, petitioning, and ill will, was the new precinct granted independent status as the town of Waltham.[74] From the beginning until the end what had been most at issue was control of the meeting – since this brought with it control of town policy and the right to separate from the town at will. Between 1692 and 1738 the number of issues decided by contested votes increased, and the General Court was likely to receive petitions from the losing party. Samuel Sewall described one of these occasions in his diary: "Three of Watertown came to me and gave an account of their town meeting which was Wednesday last, but could do nothing: so adjourned to the 28th instant and then chose selectmen. Though the farmers voted with the east end; yet the middle out-voted them and have chosen selectmen to their mind, and Capt. Garfield town clerk instead of Capt. Prout, who has endeavored much to obstruct their proceedings about the new meetinghouse. Parties were so combined on either side that 'twas a continued duel in each, one to one, and four score and odd votes apiece." [75]

Dedham's sectional battle reached a peak in 1726–29. From 1703 on, the number of occasions on which a majority of the incumbent selectmen were turned out of office increased. In 1703–04 there was an openly disputed election which involved appeal to the county court.[76] What was

[73] Samuel Sewall, "Diary," in Mass. Hist. Soc., *Collections*, 5th Ser., V (Boston, 1878), 460–61, describes the tragicomic split.

[74] *Acts and Resolves*, X, 48–49; XII, 450.

[75] Sewall, "Diary," 400–401.

[76] Apr. 17, 1704, *Dedham Recs.*, V; Apr. 4, 1704, Miscellaneous Bound MSS, Mass. Hist. Soc.

at issue here is uncertain, but there may be some connection with the later petitions for separation "as Towns or precincts" presented in 1721 by the inhabitants of two peripheral areas of the town.[77] The petitioners of 1704 had complained to the county court that the meeting was "not legally warned," which is a complaint one would expect outlying areas to make. In any event, by 1726 the "outsiders" had elected a board of selectmen entirely from the parts of town which had petitioned in 1721 for separation. The losers of 1726 subsequently charged the winners with diluting the suffrage in order to carry the meeting.[78] This was probably the truth. Tax lists of the 1730's and 1740's in the Dedham Town Clerk's Office reveal that the outlying areas were substantially less wealthy than the middle of the town, and these areas would have profited from evading the property qualifications for voting. Two years later two new precincts were created in Dedham and the outsiders' control of the town was relinquished, but the issues remained alive in the congregation and in the town meeting for some time after.

[In the long period of ostensible concensus prior to the 1680's, political controversy in Dedham and in Watertown had usually been submerged or nonexistent. It was during the era of the first ministerial vacancies and sectional rivalries that town meeting politics was created. The number of issues having ramifications which affected a wide number of townsmen multiplied. A simple delegation of powers to the selectmen was no longer satisfactory, nor was a perfunctory yes-or-no answer by the town sufficient to resolve the new issues.] It had mattered relatively little to most people who the local cowherd should be. But it mattered very much whose sermons they must endure, Sabbath after Sabbath, year after year; it mattered very much whether the town was to be one town or two, whether the schoolhouse would be located conveniently for one man's children and not for those of another. Consequently, [the town meeting, composed of ordinary inhabitants whose personal interests were at stake in the issues confronting the town, arose to deal more decisively in town affairs than it had in times of placid concensus. Together with the end of the political influence of the first generation, this reaction to events does a great deal to explain the new style in town politics.]

Population growth may have served to stimulate town meeting activity in ways other than contributing to sectional cleavages and conflicts. Dedham's population doubled between 1670 and 1710, while that of Watertown grew substantially.[79] Given the same or an improved standard of living, the effect of such growth would have been to increase the abso-

[77] Mar. 6, 1721, *Dedham Recs.*, VI.

[78] See Lockridge, Dedham; and *Dedham Recs.*, VI, 1726–29.

[79] E. B. Greene and V. D. Harrington, *American Population before the Federal Census of 1790* (New York, 1932), 19–46; and the analysis of the historical demography of Dedham in Lockridge, Dedham, ch. v.

lute number of men of comfortable wealth and social standing, and this certainly was the case in Dedham. In 1670, for instance, the wealthiest 10 per cent of men in Dedham amounted to nine individuals. By 1700 the figure is thirteen men and by 1730, twenty-two.[80] Some of these men must have desired a consistent and substantial voice in town affairs and, perhaps, a chance to make a local reputation as a prelude to a career in the General Court. But, whether in 1670, or in 1700, or in 1730, there were no more than seven selectmen's offices to be filled. Political expression was limited by this fact. Efforts to get around it may have strengthened the town meeting. For, as two distinguished historians have speculated,[81] growth and social development throughout America may have created in this period an indigenous and expanding elite whose quest for some form of political expression lay behind the series of rebellions and revolutions that racked the colonies between 1676 and 1690. Might not the same consequence of growth have prevailed on the local level? That is, might not an increasing number of men of substance have found the old power base of the town, resting as it did upon seven men, too narrow? Such men would have come to view the town meeting and its *ad hoc* committees as an alternative path to the political expression which they naturally felt they deserved. They would have tended to make the meeting the vital arena of town politics.

In Dedham and in Watertown, then, the town meeting as we like to think of it was not at all an automatic result of the law which gave it existence. It had to evolve, slowly, over a period of a century and more. Not until 1690 could one begin to say that it positively held sway over the selectmen. Certain definite events helped it to emerge as the essential body of town government, to assert itself in the various spheres of local power. Among these was the law itself, but of considerably greater significance were the passing away of the first generation of leaders, the emergence of difficult problems relating to the ministry and sections, and the growth of population.

Most of these explanations are plausible enough, based on the evidence at hand. So plausible, in fact, that one cannot but wish to know whether Dedham and Watertown were typical. Who can say what practical powers the town meetings enjoyed in the many other villages of the New England countryside? It is quite possible that, in some towns, the selectmen did acquire a touch of the character of the more powerful of the select vestries in England. In other towns, even in those founded at an early date, the town meeting may always have possessed the initiative. Yet

---

[80] *Dedham Recs.*, IV, 202–203; V, 275–276; VI, 310–316.
[81] C. L. Ver Steeg, *The Formative Years, 1607–1763* (New York, 1964), 129 ff. Ver Steeg's discussion owes much to Bernard Bailyn, "Politics and Social Structure in Virginia," in James M. Smith, ed., *Seventeenth-Century America: Essays in Colonial History* (Chapel Hill, 1959), 90–115.

many towns must have experienced much the same sort and sequence of problems as were experienced by Dedham and Watertown in the years of their growth and development; and it is beyond all doubt unjustifiable to asume that from the beginning all towns governed themselves according to one idyllic pattern, as in a pastoral poem.

[APPENDIX]

TABLE 1   *Watertown*

	1660's	1670's	1680's	1690's	1700's	1710's	1720's	1730's
Av. no. of town meetings per yr. (incl. sessions by adjournment)	2.5	2.4	5.4	7.2	5.1	4.6	3.9	4.7
Av. no. of formal selectmen's meetings per yr.	4.9	6.6	7.7	14.1	9.8	13.5	11.7	13.1
Av. yrs. of cumulative experience as selectmen when elected (per yr.)	53	44.5	28.6	28.2	23.2	29.9	36.5	19.7
Ad hoc committees per decade appointed by town meeting	3	1	15	21	21	17	15	21

TABLE 2   *Dedham*

	1636–1689	1689–1736
Av. no. of town meetings per yr. (not incl. sessions by adjournment)	2	3.5
Av. no. of formal selectmen's meetings per yr.	11	11
Av. per cent of selectmen elected each yr. serving above 7 terms during their careers	43	24
Av. no. of terms served by selectmen first elected	7.6	4.75
Av. no. of ad hoc committees appointed per decade by the town meeting	5	17

The Social Context of Democracy in Massachusetts

MICHAEL ZUCKERMAN

Michael Zuckerman attempts to characterize political behavior in eighteenth-century Massachusetts by relating politics to social organization. [He argues that colonial authority was largely delegated to towns and that the towns operated by consensus rather than by the resolution of conflict. Since the legal powers of towns were not great, agreement on fundamental issues was a prerequisite of the maintenance of order. Successful consensual politics required a virtual homogeneity of interest among the inhabitants and forced the towns rigidly to exclude potential dissidents of all sorts. It was only through strict limitations on the possibility of disagreement that the towns were able to operate within what was formally a "democratic" political system.]

Zuckerman's reinterpretation of the social context of New England politics necessitates reevaluation of some of our traditional assumptions about colonial political behavior in the eighteenth century. In particular, he denies that the recent demonstration of the broad scope of the electoral franchise proves anything about the nature of popular participation in government. The right to vote can be assessed only in conjunction with the meaning of voting in the political process, and if elections were not choices between alternative policies, many historians have badly misunderstood public life in provincial Massachusetts.

Zuckerman seems to imply that town government was always consensual, and he does not come to grips with the argument that the town meeting underwent an important evolution during the seventeenth century. Is it possible that Massachusetts politics underwent a transition from the free conflict of interests to a consensual basis? If Zuckerman's theory about the town meeting can be extended to the General Court, do we need an entirely different explanation for legislative behavior in the middle and southern colonies?

For at least a decade now, a debate has passed through these pages on the extent of democracy in the old New England town. It began, of course, with Robert E. Brown, and it did not begin badly: Brown's work was a breath of fresh air in a stale discussion, substituting statistics for cynicism and adding figures to filiopietism. But what was begun decently has degenerated since, and findings that should have provoked larger questions have only produced quibbles and counter-quibbles over methodology and quantification. The discussion has not been entirely futile — few would now maintain the old claim that the franchise was very closely confined in provincial Massachusetts — but neither has its apparent potential been realized. We are, ultimately, as far from agreement as we ever were about whether eighteenth-century Massachusetts was democratic. Somehow, the discussion has stalled at the starting point; a promising avenue of inquiry has not developed beyond its initial promise.

Perhaps a part of that failure was implicit in Brown's initial formulation of the problem; but one man cannot do everything, and Brown did advance our consideration of the New England town as far as any one man ever has. If he did not answer, or even ask, all the questions which might have been raised, other students could have done so. Brown's work made that possible. But since *Middle-Class Democracy and the Revolution in Massachusetts* (Ithaca, 1955) no comparable advances have been made. Indeed, the discussion seems to have stopped conceptually where Brown stopped, and one is forced to wonder not merely whether the right questions are being asked but whether any significant questions at all are being asked, other than those of how better to compute voting percentages. Certainly the terms of the debate have been, and are, inadequate to its resolution. Most obviously, figures on the franchise simply cannot serve to establish democracy. In our own time we have seen too many travesties on universal suffrage in too many non-democratic regimes to continue to take seriously in and of itself such an abstract calculus. Yet on both sides the discussion of New England town-meeting democracy has often assumed that the franchise is a satisfactory index of democracy, and the recourse to the seeming solidity of the voting statistics has depended, if only implicitly, upon that dubious premise.

Even those few critics who have challenged the contention that the issue of eighteenth-century democracy could be settled by counting heads have generally acquiesced in the far more fundamental assumption that in one way or another the issue of the eighteenth century was what the Browns have declared it to be: "democracy or aristocracy?" But democracy and aristocracy are probably false alternatives in any case for provin-

Reprinted by permission from Michael Zuckerman, "The Social Context of Democracy in Massachusetts," *William and Mary Quarterly*, 3d Ser., XXV (1968), 523–544.

cial Massachusetts; and in this case they are surely so, because they have been made initial tools of inquiry instead of end terms.

Of course, the Browns have hardly been alone in their strategy of frontal assault. On the contrary, it is indicative of how thoroughly their work established the contours of subsequent study that others have also rushed right into the issue of democracy without even a pause to ponder whether that issue was quite so readily accessible. [Yet it would be admitted on most sides that democracy was hardly a value of such supreme salience to the men of provincial Massachusetts that it governed their conscious motives and aspirations; nor, after all, did it provide the framework for social structure in the towns of the province. In application to such a society, then, a concept such as democracy must always be recognized for just that: a concept of our own devising. It is not a datum that can be directly apprehended in all its immediacy; it is an abstraction — a rather elevated abstraction — which represents a covering judgment of the general tenor or tendency of social relations and institutions.] As such, it can carry its own assurance of validity only if it proceeds out of, rather than precedes, analysis of the society to which it is applied. To rip it out of its social context is to risk exactly the disembodied discussion of democracy we have witnessed over the past decade.

If we would study democracy in provincial Massachusetts, we cannot plunge headlong into that issue without sacrificing the context which conferred meaning on whatever degree of democracy did exist. Since democracy was incidental to the prime purposes of provincial society, we must first confront that society. [Democracy, to the extent that it existed, was no isolated element in the organization of the political community, and problems of political participation and inclusion cannot be considered apart from the entire question of the nature of the provincial community. Even if most men in eighteenth-century Massachusetts could vote, that is only the beginning, not the end, of inquiry. What, then, was the *function* of a widely extended suffrage, and what was the function of voting itself in the conduct of the community? Who specifically was admitted to the franchise, and who was denied that privilege, and on what grounds? For ultimately, if we are to understand the towns that made the Revolution in Massachusetts, we must find out not only *whether* most men could vote but also *why*.]

It is particularly imperative that we place provincial democracy in its social context because nothing else can plausibly account for its development. The founders of the settlement at Massachusetts Bay came with neither an inclusive ethos nor any larger notions of middle-class democracy. In 1630 a band of true believers had entered upon the wilderness, possessed of a conviction of absolute and invincible righteousness. Their leaders, in that first generation, proudly proclaimed that they "abhorred democracy," and, as Perry Miller maintained, "theirs was not an idle boast." [1] The spirit of the founders was set firmly against inclusion, with the very meaning of the migration dependent for many on an extension of the sphere of ecclesiastical exclusivity. The right of every church to keep out the unworthy was precisely the point of the Congregationalists' difference with the established church, and it was a right which could not be realized in England.[2] Yet, without any English prodding and within about a decade of the first settlements, the original ideals of exclusion had begun to break down at the local level. Until 1692 the colonial suffrage extended only to freemen, but by that time non-freemen had been voting in town affairs for almost half a century.[3] The ability of the settlers to sustain suffrage restrictions at the colonial level so long after they were abandoned in the towns not only indicates the incomplete coincidence of intellectual currents and local conduct in early New England but also contradicts any contention that the pressures for democratic participation derived from Puritan theology or thought. The New England Puritans were pressed to the popularization of political authority only in grudging adjustment to the exigencies of their situation.

Their situation, quite simply, was one that left them stripped of any *other* sanctions than those of the group. The sea passage had cut the new settlement off from the full force of traditional authority, so that even the maintenance of law and order had to be managed in the absence of any customarily accepted agencies for its establishment or enforcement. Furthermore, as the seventeenth century waned and settlement dispersed, the preservation of public order devolved increasingly upon the local community. What was reluctantly admitted in the seventeenth century was openly acknowledged in the eighteenth, after the arrival of the new charter: the public peace could not be entrusted to Boston, but would have to be separately secured in each town in the province. And though this devolution of effective authority to the local level resolved other difficulties, it only aggravated the problem of order, because the towns even more than the central government were without institutions and authorities sanctioned by tradition. Moreover, the towns had relatively limited instruments of enforcement, and they were demonstrably loath to use the coercive power they did possess.[4]

---

[1] Perry Miller, *Orthodoxy in Massachusetts* (Boston, 1959), 37.

[2] Edmund S. Morgan, *Visible Saints* (New York, 1963), esp. 10–12, 21.

[3] The first break occurred in 1641 when the Body of Liberties made all men free to attend town meetings; an enactment of 1647 allowed them to vote. On the other hand, some restrictions on non-freemen did remain. See Joel Parker, "The Origin, Organization, and Influence of the Towns of New England," Massachusetts Historical Society, *Proceedings*, IX (Boston, 1866), 46.

[4] Difficulties of enforcement are not easy to demonstrate in a few sentences, but they can be suggested, perhaps, by the ease of mob mobilization and by the extensive evasion of the office of constable, especially by the middling and upper classes of the community, which was both symptomatic of and contributory to

[Nonetheless, order was obtained in the eighteenth-century town, and it was obtained by concord far more than by compulsion. Consensus governed the communities of provincial Massachusetts, and harmony and homogeneity were the regular — and required — realities of local life. Effective action necessitated a public opinion approaching if not attaining unanimity, and public policy was accordingly bent toward securing such unanimity. The result was, to be sure, a kind of government by common consent, but government by consent in eighteenth-century Massachusetts did not imply democracy in any more modern sense because it required far more than mere majoritarianism. Such majoritarianism implied a minority, and the towns could no more condone a competing minority by their norms and values than they could have constrained it by their police power. Neither conflict, dissent, nor any other structured pluralism ever obtained legitimacy in the towns of the Bay before the Revolution.[5]

[Thus, authority found another form in provincial Massachusetts. Its instrument was the town meeting, which was no mere forum but the essential element in the delicate equipoise of peace and propriety which governed the New England town. In the absence of any satisfactory means of traditional or institutional coercion, the recalcitrant could not be compelled to adhere to the common course of action. Therefore, the common course of action had to be so shaped as to leave none recalcitrant — that was the vital function of the New England town meeting. To oversimplify perhaps, the town meeting solved the problem of enforcement by evading it. The meeting gave institutional expression to the imperatives of peace. In the meetings consensus was reached, and individual consent and group opinion were placed in the service of social conformity.] There the men of the province established their agreements on policies and places, and there they legitimized those agreements so

---

the structural weakness of the constabulary. There was, in other words, a formal legal system in the province without an autonomous instrument for its own enforcement. A more elaborate development of the general theme is in Michael Zuckerman, The Massachusetts Town in the Eighteenth Century (unpubl. Ph.D. diss., Harvard University, 1967), esp. 118–126.

[5] The import of the argument sketched here and developed below must be understood. No full-scale defense of the consensus hypothesis will be attempted here, nor would one be possible in such a piece as this: an examination of such a narrow matter as electoral eligibility can hardly *prove* a set of propositions about so substantial a subject as the social organization of the New England town. A full-scale defense of the hypothesis assumed here is found in Zuckerman, Massachusetts Town in the Eighteenth Century. What is in fact claimed here is, first, that this hypothesis in particular does illuminate many aspects of political "democracy" in the Massachusetts town of the eighteenth century and, second, that whatever failings may be found in this particular hypothesis, *some* kind of hypothesis is surely necessary to ground the discussion of democracy in the colony and establish it in a social context.

that subsequent deviation from those accords became socially illegitimate and personally immoral as well, meaning as it did the violation of a covenant or the breaking of a promise. In the town meetings men talked of politics, but ultimately they sought to establish moral community.

In the context of such a community, the significance of an extended franchise becomes quite clear: governance by concord and concurrence required inclusiveness. In communities in which effective enforcement depended on the moral binding of decisions upon the men who made them, it was essential that most men be parties to such decisions. Not the principled notions of the New Englanders but the stern necessities of enforcement sustained town-meeting democracy in Massachusetts. The politics of consensus made a degree of democracy functional, even made it a functional imperative. Men were allowed to vote not out of any overweening attachment to democratic principles *per se* but simply because a wide canvass was convenient, if not indeed critical, in consolidating a consensus in the community.

Under this incentive to inclusion, most towns did set their suffrage almost as liberally as Brown claimed. To seek the social context of the suffrage, then, necessitates no major quarrel with Brown's figures on franchise democracy; what it may provide is an explanation for them. It also offers the possibility of accounting for more than just the figures. As soon as we see that the high degree of participation permitted in the politics of the provincial town was not an isolated phenomenon but rather an integral aspect of the conduct of the community, we are in a position to go beyond a disembodied study of electoral eligibility and a simple celebration of middle-class democracy in Massachusetts. We are in a position to convert polemics into problems, and to press for answers.

In many communities, for example, a substantial and sometimes an overwhelming proportion of the people were *not* technically entitled to vote. Brown did not discuss some of these places, and the ones he did discuss were added to his evidence only with the special explanation that sometimes even the ineligible were admitted to the ballot box. But in the context of community such lapses would not necessarily invalidate his larger conclusions, nor would such *ad hoc* expedients be required; for the same imperatives impinged on towns where few were legally qualified as on the others, and the same results of wide political participation obtained because of the same sense that inclusiveness promoted peace while more rigorous methods threatened it. The town of Douglas, with only five qualified voters in its first years, flatly refused to be bound by a determination confined to those five, declaring its conviction "that the intent of no law can bind them to such ill consequences." Mendon, in its "infant state" in 1742, voted "to permit a considerable number of persons not qualified by law to vote . . . being induced thereto by an apprehension that it would be a means of preserving peace and unity amongst ourselves." Princeton, incorporated in 1760 with forty-three settlers but only fourteen eligible to vote according to provincial regulations, established a formal "agreement among themselves to overlook" those regulations, and the General Court upheld that agreement. "The poor freeholders" in the early days of Upton were also "allowed liberty to vote in town meeting," and it had produced "an encouraging harmony" in local affairs until 1746, when a few of the qualified voters, momentarily possessed a majority of the ten in town, sought to upset the customary arrangements and limit the franchise as the law required. The rest of the town at once protested that "such a strenuous method of proceeding would endanger the peace of the town" and begged the General Court "to prevent the dismal damages that may follow" therefrom. The Court did exactly as it was asked, and at the new meeting the town reverted to its old form: "everyone was admitted to vote, qualified or not." [6]

[The principle which governed such universalism was not deliberate democracy; it was merely a recognition that the community could not be governed solely by the qualified voters if they were too few in number. Such a situation was most likely to occur in new communities, but it was not limited to them] Middleton had been established for almost a quarter of a century when it was conceded that in the local elections of 1752 "there was double the number of votes to the lawful voters." In a variety of towns and at other times, requirements for the franchise were also ignored and admission of the unqualified acknowledged explicitly.[7] Thomas Hutchinson's wry lament that "anything with the appearance of a man" was allowed the vote may have been excessive, but it was not wholly fabricated.[8] And even towns whose political procedures were more regular resorted to universalism in cases of conflict or of major issues. Fitchburg, for instance, voted in 1767 that "every freholder be a votter in Chusing of a minestr," while twenty years earlier, in a bitterly contested election in Haverhill, "there was not any list of valuation read nor any list of non-voters nor any weighting of what name or nature whatsoever by which the selectmen did pretend to show who was qualified to vote in town affairs." [9]

The question of inclusiveness itself sometimes came before a town,

[6] Massachusetts Archives, CXV, 168, 169, 316–317, 319–320, 469–471, 864–865; CXVII, 647–649, 652; CXVIII, 734–735a, 762, State House, Boston; Francis E. Blake, *History of the Town of Princeton* (Princeton, Mass., 1915), I, 76–77.

[7] Mass. Archives, VIII, 279, for others see *ibid.*, 278; XLIX, 398–400; L, 20–22, 25–26, 85–88, 89–90; CXIII, 270; CXV, 36–37, 291; CXVI, 373–374; CXVII, 291–293, 302–305; CLXXXI, 23–24a.

[8] Brown, *Middle-Class Democracy*, 60.

[9] Walter A. Davis, comp., *The Old Records of the Town of Fitchburg Massachusetts 1764–1789* (Fitchburg, Mass., 1898), 39; Mass. Archives, VIII, 273.

not always without challenge but generally with a democratic outcome. Dudley, more than a decade after the incorporation of the town, voted "that all the freeholder of sd town should be voters by a graet majorytie and all agreed to it." In Needham in 1750 it was also "put to vote whether it be the mind of the town to allow all freeholders in town to vote for a moderator," and there too the vote carried in the affirmative. And that verdict for inclusion was not even as revealing as the method by which that verdict was reached, for in voting *whether* to include all in the election, Needham *did* include all in the procedural issue. Every man did vote on the question of whether every man was to be allowed to vote.[10]

Of course, absolute inclusiveness never prevailed in provincial Massachusetts — women could not vote at all, and neither could anyone under 21 — and property and residence qualifications, introduced in 1692, were probably adhered to as often as they were ignored, so that even the participation of adult males was something less than universal. It was an important part of Brown's achievement to show that, in general, it was not *very much* less than universal, but, by the nature of his research strategy, he could go no further than that. If we are to penetrate to particulars — if we are to ask who was excluded, and why, and why the suffrage standards were what they were — we must consider not only numbers but also the conditions of community.

The men who were not allowed legitimately to vote with their fellow townsmen were commonly tenants or the sons of voters; as Brown discovered, it was these two groups against which the property requirement primarily operated. But where the controversialists seek to *excuse* these exclusions, or to magnify them, a broader perspective allows one to *explain* them, for against these two groups sanctions were available that were far more effective than those of the generalized community. Stringent property qualifications were clearly self-defeating in a society where consensus was the engine of enforcement, but overly generous qualifications were equally unnecessary. Where some men, such as tenants and dependent sons, could be privately coerced, liberality on their behalf, from the standpoint of social control, would have meant the commission of a sin of superfluity.

Similarly, almost nothing but disadvantage could have accrued from a loose residence requirement enabling men not truly members of the community to participate in its decision-making process, since voting qualifications in provincial Massachusetts were connected to the concept of community, not the concept of democracy. The extensions and contractions of the franchise were significant to the townsmen of the eighteenth century primarily as a means of consolidating communal con-

---

[10] *Town Records of Dudley, Massachusetts, 1732–1754*, I (Pawtucket, R.I., 1893), 106; Mass. Archives, CXV, 616–617.

sensus. All those whose acquiescence in public action was necessary were included, and all those whose concurrence could be compelled otherwise or dispensed with were excluded, often very emphatically. Sixty-six citizens of Watertown, for example, petitioned against the allowance of a single unqualified voter in a 1757 election because he was "well known to belong to the town of Lincoln." In many towns such as Sudbury the town clerk "very carefully warned those that were not legally qualified not to vote and prayed the selectmen to be very careful and watchful that nobody voted that was not legally qualified." [11] Even in disputes over specific qualifications, both sides often agreed on the principle of exclusion of the unqualified; contention occurred only over the application of that principle.[12]

Consciousness of voting qualifications colored the conduct of other town affairs as well as elections, as indeed was natural since the meaning of the franchise went so far beyond mere electoral democracy. Protests by men recently arrived in a town could be discredited, as they were in Haverhill in 1748, without any reference to the justice of the protest itself, simply by stating that "many of their petitioners are not qualified to vote in town affairs as may be seen by the selectmen's list of voters, and some of them were never known to reside in town or did we ever hear of them before we saw their petition." Similarly, in the creation of new communities qualification for the franchise could be crucial. Inhabitants of Bridgewater resisted their own inclusion in a precinct proposed by thirty-seven men dwelling in their vicinity by pointing out that "there is not above eleven or twelve that are qualified to vote in town meetings as the law directs." Many towns in their corporate capacity made much the same plea when confronted with an appeal for separation from the community. As Worcester once noted in such a case, more than half the petitioners were "not voters and one is a single Indian." [13]

Such consciousness of qualifications sometimes appeared to be nothing more than an insistence on a "stake in society" in order to participate in the society's deliberations and decisions, but the stake-in-society concept, despite its popularity in the West and its convergence with certain conditions of public life in the province, was not precisely the notion which controlled those restrictions of the franchise which did persist after 1692. It was not out of any intrinsic attachment to that concept, but simply out of a fear that those without property were overly amenable to bribery or other such suasion, that the men of Massachusetts clung to

---

[11] Mass. Archives, CXVII, 302–305; XLIX, 361–362; see also *ibid.*, CXVII, 300, 306–307, 647–649; Jeremiah L. Hanaford, *History of Princeton* (Worcester, Mass., 1852), 23.

[12] See for example, Mass. Archives, CXV, 412–413, 463.

[13] *Ibid.*, 305–308, 144; "Early Records of the Town of Worcester," Worcester Society of Antiquity, *Collections* (Worcester, 1881–1882), II, no. 8, 42–43. See also, Mass. Archives, CXV, 392.

their voting qualifications.] As the Essex Result was to state the principle in 1778, "all the members of the state are qualified to make the election, unless they have not sufficient discretion, or are so situated as to have no wills of their own." [14] [Participation in community decisions was the pre-rogative of independent men, of *all* a town's independent men, but, ideally, *only* of those. Indeed, it was precisely because of their indepen-dence that they had to be accorded a vote, since only by their participation did they bind themselves to concur in the community's chosen course of action. The town meeting was an instrument for enforcement, not — at least not intentionally — a school for democracy.]

This logic competence governed the exclusion of women and children and also accounted for the antipathy to voting by tenants. The basis of the prohibitions which were insisted upon was never so much an objec-tion to poverty *per se* — the stake-in-society argument — as to the tenant's concomitant status of dependence, the pervasive assumption of which emerged clearly in a contested election in Haverhill in 1748. There the petitioners charged that a man had been "refused as a voter under pre-tense that he was a tenant and so not qualified, when the full reason was that he was a tenant to one of their [the selectmen's] opposers and so at all hazards to be suppressed," while another man, a tenant to one of the selectmen themselves, had been received as a voter though "rated at much less in the last year's taxes than he whom they refused." The protest was thus directed primarily against the abuses of the selectmen: that tenants would do as their landlords desired was simply taken for granted.[15] And naturally the same sort of asumption controlled the exclu-sion of sons still living with their parents. The voting age of twenty-one was the most rudimentary expression of this requirement of a will of one's own, but the legal age was not very firm at the edges. Like other laws of the province, it could not stand when it came up against local desires, and the age qualifications were often abrogated when unusual dependence or independence was demonstrable, as in the case of the eighteen-year-old who voted in a Sheffield election of 1751 because his father had died and he had become head of his family. As the town's elected representative could declare on that occasion, quite ignoring the legal age requirement, the lad "had a good right to vote, for his estate rested in him and that he was a town-born child and so was an inhab-itant." [16]

Of course, the townsmen of the eighteenth century placed no premium

[14] [Theophilus Parsons], *Result of the Convention of Delegates Holden at Ipswich* . . . (Newburyport, 1778), 28–29.

[15] Mass. Archives, CXV, 330–334, 412–413; CXVI, 276–277; CXVII, 84–86, 306–307; "Early Records of Worcester," Worc. Soc. Ant., *Coll.*, II, no. 6, 63.

[16] Mass. Archives, VIII, 278; for a comparable case in the opposite direction see *ibid.*, CXVI, 668–669. Another basis for exclusion was insanity. For a reveal-ing contretemps see *ibid.*, L, 85–88; CXVII, 295–297, 302–305.

on independence as such. Massachusetts townsmen were expected to be independent but not too independent; ultimately, they were supposed on their own to arrive at the same actions and commitments as their neighbors. Any *genuine* independence, excessive *or* insufficient, was denigrated if not altogether denied a place in the community. Thus, when a number of inhabitants of a gore of land near Charlton faced the threat of incorporation with the town, they submitted "one word of information" about the townsmen who had asked for that incorporation. The note said only:

Baptist signers	— 7
Churchmen	— 3
Tenants	— 4
Neither tenants nor freeholders but intruders upon other men's property	—15

The whole of the petitioners in Charlton consisting of 35 in number.

In other words, tenants were tainted, but so too were all others who were their own men, such as squatters and those who dared to differ in religion. In denigrating them, the inhabitants of the gore drew no distinctions: tenant and Baptist were equally offensive because equally outside of orthodoxy, beyond the confines of consensus.[17]

Ultimately almost *any* taint on membership in the homogeneous community was a potential basis for derogation. Some inhabitants of Rutland once even attempted to deny the validity of a town decision merely because many of its supporters were "such as were and are dissenters from the public worship of God in the old meeting-house." And though Rutland's religious orthodoxy was a bit exquisite even for eighteenth-century New England, it was so only in degree. For example, when Sutton opposed the erection of a new district out of parts of itself and several other towns in 1772, the town actually deducted the Anabaptists from the number of signatories to the application — Baptists simply did not count as full citizens. Worcester did the same thing and indeed went even further. Several of the signers of the petition for separation were not heads of families but mere "single persons, some of them transient ones," and so, said the town, were not to be "accounted as part of the number of families the petitioners say are within the limits of the proposed district." Whereas excessively reliable bonds confined the tenant, no reliable bonds at all attached a single man to the community, and either alternative evoked suspicion.[18]

[17] *Ibid.*, CXVII, 86, and see 84–85.
[18] *Ibid.*, CXV, 741–742; CXVIII, 613–616, 619; see also *ibid.*, CXVI, 276–277. And others found more reasons to discredit any who stood outside communal orthodoxy. See *ibid.*, CXV, 393–396, 412–413, 596.

Ultimately, however, the insistence on orthodoxy did not directly exclude any excessive number, and neither did the property and residence requirements disqualify any great proportion of the province's adult males. In the perspective of the English villages from which the New Englanders came, these very dimensions of disqualification may be better seen, in fact, as defining a broader qualification than had previously prevailed in English practice. Far more fundamentally, the criteria of exclusion were measures of the inclusiveness of the communities of early Massachusetts.

The most fundamental shift that had occurred was the one from property to residence as the irreducible basis of town citizenship. In England, several classes of property-holders were "technically termed inhabitants even though they dwelt in another town"; property defined political citizenship, and only those who held the requisite property in the community directed its affairs. In provincial Massachusetts such stake-in-society notions never prevailed for reasons that had little to do with any abstract attachment to democracy or antipathy to absentee ownership. They never prevailed because the point of the town meeting was not so much the raising of a revenue as it was political government, especially the maintenance of law and order. In Massachusetts it was necessary to act only on the individuals living in each town, and it was imperative to act upon all of them. Of course, taxation as well as residence provided the basis for the ballot in Massachusetts, but that was of a piece with the residence requirement. As early as 1638 "every inhabitant of a town was declared liable for his proportion of the town's charges," in sharp contrast to the towns of England where only a few were so taxed.[19]

The democracy of the Massachusetts towns was, then, a democracy despite itself, a democracy without democrats. But it was still, so far as anything yet said is concerned, a democracy, at least in the simple sense of a widely diffused franchise. Such democracy is admitted — indeed, required — in the analysis advanced above; the objection urged against the defenders of that democracy is not that they are wrong but that they are right for the wrong reasons, or for no reasons at all. When they examine electoral eligibility apart from its social setting and when they place franchise democracy at the center of provincial social organization instead of in the peripheral position it actually occupied, they do not condemn their findings to invalidity, only to sterility. They may be correct about the degree of diffusion of the vote, but they can go no further. Within their original terms, they cannot systematically study the

[19] Edward Channing, "Town and County Government in the English Colonies of North America," *Johns Hopkins University Studies in Historical and Political Science*, 2d Ser., II, no. 10 (1884), 12, 32.

purposes of participation, the relative importance of inclusiveness when it confronted competing values, the limits of eligibility and the reasons for them, or, more broadly, the particular texture of the electorate as against abstract statistics.

But if the analysis urged thus far has basically buttressed Brown's position by extending and explaining his statistics, that analysis also has another side. For when we see franchise democracy as a mere incident in the central quest for concord and concurrence among neighbors, we must also observe that the same concern for consensus which promoted wide participation also imposed very significant limitations on the democracy of the provincial community, limitations sufficiently serious to suggest that the democratic appellation itself may be anachronistic when applied to such a society.

For one thing, the ideal of "townsmen together" [20] implied the power of each town to control its own affairs, and that control not only extended to but also depended upon communal control of its membership. From the founding of the first towns communities retained the right to accept only those whom they wished, and that right persisted without challenge to the time of the Revolution. "Such whose dispositions do not suit us, whose society will be hurtful to us," were simply refused admission as enemies of harmony and homogeneity. Dedham's first covenant, "to keepe of from us all such, as ar contrarye minded. And receave onely such unto us as be such as may be probably of one harte," was typical. For inhabitancy was a matter of public rather than private concern, and among the original settlers it scarcely had to be argued that "if the place of our cohabitation be our own, then no man hath right to come in to us without our consent." [21] Consent meant the formal vote of the town or its selectmen, and none were admitted without one or the other. Not even inhabitants themselves could entertain outsiders — "strangers," they were called — without the permission of the town, and any who violated the rule were subject to penalties.[22] And of course the original thrust of congregational Puritan-

[20] The phrase is from Conrad M. Arensberg, "American Communities," *American Anthropologist*, LVII (1955), 1150. For affirmations of that ideal as a consummatory value see Mass. Archives, CXIII, 616–617; CIV, 645; CXV, 282–283; CXVI, 527–528; CXVII, 563–565; CLXXXI, 122b–122d.

[21] Sumner C. Powell, *Puritan Village* (Middletown, Conn., 1963), xviii; George L. Haskins, *Law and Authority in Early Massachusetts* (New York, 1960), 70; Josiah Benton, *Warning Out in New England* (Boston, 1911), 8. The early towns also forbade inhabitants to "sell or let their land or houses to strangers without the consent of the town"; see *ibid.*, 18, 19, 23, 87, and William Weeden, *Economic and Social History of New England, 1620–1789* (Boston, 1891), 57.

[22] Benton, *Warning Out*, 18, 33. And the fines were indeed established and enforced in the towns. See Myron Allen, *The History of Wenham* (Boston, 1860), 26, and Weeden, *Economic and Social History*, 79–80.

ism to lodge disciplinary powers with the individual churches rather than with bishops also aimed at more local control of the membership of the local community.[23]

Most of these practices continued unabated into the eighteenth century. Swansea's "foundation settlement" of 1667 provided that "if any person denied any particular in the said agreement they should not be admitted an inhabitant in said town," and half a century later seventy-eight townsmen reaffirmed their commitment to the ancestral covenant. Cotton Mather's manual of 1726, *Ratio Disciplinae Fratrum Nov-Anglorum* (Boston, 1726), described a process of "mutual Conferences" by which men came to "a good understanding" which might be subscribed to by any applicant. And even in the crisis of the dissolution of a church, as at Bellingham in 1747, the congregation could not simply disperse to the nearest convenient towns. Each of the congregants, for all that he had already met the tests of church membership and partaken of communion, had to be accepted anew into the nearby churches and approved by their towns, and in 1754 Sunderland claimed that this right of prior approval was "always customary." [24]

Another customary instrument for the stringent control of access to the town which was also sustained throughout the provincial era was the practice of "warning out." Under this aegis, anyone who did secure entry to the town and was then deemed undesirable could be warned and, if necessary, lawfully ejected from the community. Such a policy was, in some part, a device to escape undue expenses in the support of paupers, but it was also, and more importantly, the product of the powerful communitarian assumptions of the early settlers, and those assumptions did not decline in the eighteenth century. William Weeden found the invocation of warning procedures so common that "the actual occurrences hardly need particular mention," and he concluded that "the old restrictions on the admission of freemen to the municipality, and on the sale of land to outsiders, do not appear to have been relaxed generally" as late as the era immediately preceding the imperial crisis. Town records such as Worcester's were studded with such warnings, from the time of the town's founding to the time of the Revolution itself. In other towns, too, penalties were still imposed for violation of the rules of inhabitancy.[25]

[23] Morgan, *Visible Saints*, 10–12, 21.

[24] Mass. Archives, CXIII, 613–615; CXV, 268, 272, 276; XLIX, 380–383; Mather, *Ratio Disciplinae*, Pt. iii, 2. See also Mass. Archives, CXVI, 392–393; CXVII, 15–16. In one case, that of Medway, *ibid.*, XLIX, 380–383, such consideration was not accorded.

[25] Weeden, *Economic and Social History*, 519, 673; "Early Records of Worcester," Worc. Soc. Ant., *Coll.*, II, no. 6, 22–23, 102, 122–123; II, no. 8, 19, 27, 57–58, 128; IV, 28, 47, 67, 85, 99, 137, 147, 148, 202, 223. For penalties in

The result was that fundamental differences in values were rarely admitted within a town, while differences of race, nationality, or culture scarcely appeared east of the Hudson River before the Revolution. Massachusetts was more nearly restricted to white Anglo-Saxon Protestants than any other province in English America, with the possible exception of its New England neighbors, Connecticut and New Hampshire. Less than 1 per cent of the quarter of a million Germans who came to the English colonies between 1690 and 1770 came to New England, and the proportion of Irish, Scotch, and Scotch-Irish was little larger. There was no welcome whatsoever for French Catholics and very little encouragement, according to Governor Bellomont, even for the Huguenots.[26] Negroes never attained significant numbers at the Bay — by 1780 they accounted for only 2 per cent of the population of the province and a bare 1 per cent of all Negroes in the Confederation — and the Indians, who once were significant, were on their way to extinction well before the Revolution broke out.[27] Committed to a conception of the social order that precluded pluralism, the townsmen of Massachusetts never made a place for those who were not of their own kind. The community they desired was an enclave of common believers, and to the best of their ability they secured such a society, rooted not only in ethnic and cultural homogeneity but also in common moral and economic ideas and practices. Thus, the character of the community became a critical — and non-democratic — condition of provincial democracy; for a wide franchise could be ventured only after a society that sought harmony had been made safe for such democracy. In that society it was possible to let men vote precisely because so many men were not allowed entry in the first place.

Thus we can maintain the appearance of democracy only so long as we dwell on elections and elections alone, instead of the entire electoral process. As soon as we depart from that focus, the town meetings of Massachusetts fall short of any decent democratic standard. Wide participation did obtain, but it was premised on stringently controlled access

---

other towns, see *Town of Weston: Records of the First Precinct, 1746–1754 and of the Town, 1754–1803* (Boston, 1893), 61, 101, 108, 115, 126; Herman Mann, *Historical Annals of Dedham, from its Settlement in 1635 to 1847* (Dedham, Mass., 1847), 23, 25; Allen, *History of Wenham*, 26.

26 On the Germans and Scotch-Irish see Clarence Ver Steeg, *The Formative Years, 1607–1763* (New York, 1964), 167–168. On the Huguenots see Charles W. Baird, *History of the Huguenot Emigration to America* (New York, 1885), II, 251–253; G. Elmore Reaman, *The Trail of the Huguenots* . . . (London, 1964), 129.

27 On the Negro, Marvin Harris, *Patterns of Race in the Americas* (New York, 1964), 84. For some of the story of the extinction of the last Indian town in the province see Mass. Archives, CXVII, 690–691, 733–735.

to eligibility, so that open elections presupposed anterior constriction of the electorate. Similarly, most men could vote, but their voting was not designed to contribute to a decision among meaningful alternatives. The town meeting had one prime purpose, and it was not the provision of a neutral battleground for the clash of contending parties or interest groups. In fact, nothing could have been more remote from the minds of men who repeatedly affirmed, to the very end of the provincial period, that "harmony and unanimity" were what "they most heartily wish to enjoy in all their public concerns." Conflict occurred only rarely in these communities, where "prudent and amicable composition and agreement" were urged as preventives for "great and sharp disputes and contentions." When it did appear it was seen as an unnatural and undesirable deviation from the norm. Protests and contested elections almost invariably appealed to unity and concord as the values which had been violated; and in the absence of any socially sanctioned role for dissent, contention was generally surreptitious and scarcely ever sustained for long. The town meeting accordingly aimed at unanimity. Its function was the arrangement of agreement or, more often, the endorsement of agreements already arranged, and it existed for accommodation, not disputation.[28]

Yet democracy devoid of legitimate difference, dissent, and conflict is something less than democracy; and men who are finally to vote only as their neighbors vote have something less than the full range of democratic options. Government by mutual consent may have been a step in the direction of a deeper-going democracy, but it should not be confused with the real article. Democratic consent is predicated upon legitimate choice, while the town meetings of Massachusetts in the provincial era, called as they were to reach and register accords, were still in transition from assent to such consent. The evidence for such a conclusion exists in an abundance of votes from all over the province on all manner of matters "by the free and united consent of the whole" or "by a full and Unanimous Vote that they are Easie and satisfied With What they have Done." [29] Most men may have been eligible to vote, but their voting did not settle differences unless most men voted together. In fact, differences had no defined place in the society that voting could have settled, for that was not in the nature of town politics. Unanimity was expected ethically as well as empirically. Indeed, it was demanded as a matter of social decency, so that even the occasional cases of conflict were shaped by the canons of concord and consensus, with

---

[28] Mass. Archives, CXVIII, 707–712, 715–717. The theme is omnipresent in the records of the towns and of such conflicts as did occur. See Zuckerman, Massachusetts Town in the Eighteenth Century, especially chap. 3.

[29] Mass. Archives, CXVIII, 388–390; Weston Records, 11. See also Mass. Archives, CXVI, 446–447; CXVIII, 715–717; "Records of Worcester," Worc. Soc. Ant., Coll., II, no. 8, 43, 75; IV, 18, 173, 264–266.

towns pleading for the preservation of "peace and unanimity" as "the only occasion of our petitioning." [30]

This demand for unanimity found its ultimate expression in rather frequent denials of one of the most elementary axioms of democratic theory, the principle of majority rule. A mere majority often commanded scant authority at the local level and scarcely even certified decisions as legitimate. In communities which provided no regular place for minorities a simple majority was not necessarily sufficient to dictate social policy, and many men such as the petitioners from the old part of Berwick were prepared to say so quite explicitly. Since its settlement some eighty or ninety years earlier, that town had grown until by 1748 the inhabitants of the newer parts easily outnumbered the "ancient settlers" and wished to establish a new meetinghouse in a place which the inhabitants of the older parts conceived injurious to their interest. Those who lived in the newer parts of town had the votes, but the "ancient settlers" were icily unimpressed nonetheless. Injury could not be justified "merely because a major vote of the town is or may be obtained to do it," the petitioners protested. They would suffer "great hurt and grievance," and "for no other reason than this: a major vote to do it, which is all the reason they have for the same." Equity, on the other hand, required a "just regard" for the old part of town and its inhabitants. They "ought" to retain their privileges despite their loss of numerical preponderance. And that principle was no mere moral fabrication of a desperate minority. Six years earlier the Massachusetts General Court had endorsed exactly the same position in a similar challenge to the prerogatives of numerical power by the "ancient part" of another town, and in the Berwick controversy the town majority itself tacitly conceded the principle upon which the old quarter depended. Accusing the old quarter of "gross mis-representation," the rest of the town now maintained that there had been a disingenuous confusion of geography and population. There could be no question as to the physical location of the old town, but, as to its inhabitants, "the greatest part of the ancient settlers and maintainers of the ministry do live to the northward of the old meetinghouse and have always kept the same in times of difficulty and danger." The newer townsmen, then, did not deny that ancient settlers were entitled to special consideration; they simply denied that the inhabitants of the old quarter were in fact the ancient settlers.[31]

Antiquity restricted majoritarianism elsewhere as well in demands of old settlers and in determinations of the General Court. In Lancaster as in Berwick, for example, a "standing part" could cite efforts to disrupt the old order which had been rejected by the Court as unreasonable,

---

[30] Mass. Archives, L, 30–31; CXV, 479–480; CXVI, 709–710.
[31] *Ibid.*, CXV, 368–375, 377–378, 393–396.

"and now though they have obtained a vote from the town the case still remains equally unreasonable." In other towns, too, a majority changed nothing.[32] Consensus comprehended justice and history as well as the counting of a vote. In such a society a case could not be considered solely in its present aspects, as the original inhabitants of Lunenburg made quite clear. "What great discouragement must it needs give to any new settler," those old ones inquired,

> to begin a settlement and go through the difficulties thereof, which are well known to such as have ever engaged in such service, if when, so soon as ever they shall through the blessing of heaven upon their diligence and industry have arrived to live in some measure peaceably and comfortably, if then, after all fatigues and hardships undergone, to be cut to pieces and deprived of charter privileges and rights, and instead of peace and good harmony, contention and confusion introduced, there will be no telling what to trust to.[33]

Nor was history the only resort for the repudiation of a majority. Other men offered other arguments, and some scarcely deigned to argue at all. In a contested election in Haverhill, for example, one side simply denied any authority at all to a majority of the moment. It was, they said, nothing but the creature of "a few designing men who have artfully drawn in the multitude and engaged them in their own cause." That, they argued, was simply "oppression." The merchants of Salem similarly refused to accept the hazards of populistic politics, though their refusal was rather more articulate. The town meeting had enacted a tax schedule more advantageous to the farmers than to themselves, and the merchants answered that they felt no force in that action, because "the major part of those who were present were [farmers], and the vote then passed was properly their vote and not the vote of the whole body of the town." That legitimacy and obligation attached only to a vote of the whole community was simply assumed by the merchants, as they sought a subtle separation of a town ballot — sheer majoritarianism — from a "vote of the whole body of the town" — a notion akin to the general will — for which the consent of every part of the population was requisite.[34]

Disdain for direct democracy emerged even more explicitly and sweepingly in a petition from the west precinct of Bridgewater in 1738. The precinct faced the prospect of the loss of its northern part due to a town vote authorizing the northern inhabitants to seek separation as an inde-

[32] *Ibid.*, CXIV, 613–614; CXIII, 275–276; CXVI, 736–738.

[33] *Ibid.*, CXVII, 165–169. In this case, nonetheless, the General Court declined to accept the argument and thus afforded no special safeguard to the original settlers. For similar cases without the adverse action of the Court see *ibid.*, CXIV, 286–288; CXV, 729–730.

[34] *Ibid.*, 330–334, 596.

pendent town, and the precinct feared that the loss would be fatal. Accordingly, the parishioners prayed the General Court's intervention, and after briefly disputing the majority itself, the precinct allowed that, whether or not a majority in the town *had* been obtained, such a majority *could* be contrived. "We own it is easy for the two neighboring parishes joining with the petitioners to vote away our just rights and privileges and to lay heavy burdens upon us, which they would not be willing to touch with the ends of their fingers." Yet for all the formal validity of such a vote, the precinct would not have assented to it or felt it to be legitimate, "for we trust that your Excellency and Honors will not be governed by numbers but by reason and justice." Other men elsewhere urged the same argument; perhaps none caught the provincial paradox of legality without legitimacy any better than the precinct of Salem Village, soon to become the independent town of Danvers. After a recitation of the imposition it had suffered from the town of Salem for no reason but superior numbers, the village came to its indictment of the town: "we don't say but you have had a legal right to treat us so, but all judgment without mercy is tedious to the flesh." [35]

Typically in such cases, the defense against this indictment was not an invocation of majority rights but rather a denial of having employed them oppressively. Both sides, therefore, operated upon an identical assumption. One accused the other of taking advantage of its majority, the other retorted that it had done no such thing, but neither disputed the principle that majority disregard of a minority was indefensible. [36]

This principle was no mere pious protestation. In Kittery, for instance, the parent parish complained that the men who later became the third parish had "long kept us in very unhappy circumstances . . . counteracting us in all our proceedings" until finally "we were obliged to come into an agreement with them for dividing the then-lower parish of Kittery into two separate parishes," yet it was conceded on both sides that the old inhabitants enjoyed an easy numerical supremacy. Had they been disposed to employ it, almost any amount of "counteracting" could have been contained and ultimately quashed, so far as votes in public meeting were concerned. But the parish clearly did not rely upon simple majoritarian procedures. It was more than morality that made consensus imperative; it was also the incapacity for coercion without widespread consent. It was the same incapacity which shaped a hundred other accommodations and abnegations across the province, which enabled some "aggrieved brethren" in Rehoboth to force the resignation of a minister, which paralyzed the town of Upton in the relocation of its meetinghouse. "All are agreed that it should be removed or a new one built," a town

[35] *Ibid.*, CXIV, 244–246, 244a, 786–788; also CXVII, 463–465.
[36] *Ibid.*, CXV, 866, 872–875; CXVIII, 388–390; CLXXXI, 133–134, 139.

petition explained, "but cannot agree upon the place." In the absence of agreement they could see no way to act at all on their own account; there was never any thought of constructing a coalition within the town or contending for a majority.[37]

Ultimately almost every community in the province shared Upton's determination "to unite the people." Disputes, when they arose at all, were commonly concluded by "a full and amicable agreement" in which all parties "were in peace and fully satisfied," and the conflicts that did occur evoked no efforts at resolution in a majoritarian manner. "Mutual and general advantage" was the condition of town continuance in "one entire corporate body." [38] But that corporate ethos was something distant indeed from democracy, and electoral eligibility is, therefore, an unsatisfactory index even of political participation, let alone of any more meaningful democracy. Most men may have been able to vote in the eighteenth-century town, but the town's true politics were not transacted at the ballot box so much as at the tavern and all the other places, including the meeting itself, where men met and negotiated so that the vote might be a mere ratification, rather than a decision among significant alternatives. Alternatives were antithetical to the safe conduct of the community as it was conceived at the Bay, and so to cast a vote was only to participate in the consolidation of the community, not to make a choice among competing interests or ideals.

Accordingly, the claim for middle-class democracy in provincial Massachusetts simply cannot be sustained from the figures on electoral eligibility; relevant participation resided elsewhere than in the final, formal vote. And yet, ironically, local politics may have been democratic indeed, at least in the limited terms of political participation, since a politics of consensus required consultation with most of the inhabitants in order to assure accord. In little towns of two or three hundred adult males living in close, continuing contact, men may very well have shared widely a sense of the amenability of the political process to their own actions and attitudes, and the feeling of involvement may well have been quite general. But to find out we will have to go beyond counting heads or tallying the town treasurers' lists.

[37] *Ibid.*, CXV, 872–875; CXVI, 276–277; CXVIII, 207; George H. Tilton, *A History of Rehoboth, Massachusetts* (Boston, 1918), 106–107, 102.
[38] Mass. Archives, CXV, 461–462; CXVIII, 526, 707–712; see also Samuel A. Bates, ed., *Records of the Town of Braintree, 1640 to 1793* (Randolph, Mass., 1886), 69–70.

The Rattle of Rights and Privileges: Pennsylvania Politics, 1701–1709

GARY B. NASH

How shall we assess the popular political rhetoric of the early eighteenth century? Dare we conclude that the periodic demands for rights and privileges demonstrated a latent American preference for democratic government or, conversely, that they were merely a cynical electoral device used by ambitious politicians?

In this essay Gary Nash examines the decade in which Pennsylvania's political ideas sounded much like those of the Revolutionary era, as David Lloyd attempted to marshall the people of the colony against the proprietary government. Taken at face value, Lloyd's rhetoric was as extreme as any radical to be found in contemporary London, yet his opponents never doubted that he chose his words solely to advance his personal interests. Nash contends that, whatever Lloyd's motives, his rhetoric and choice of issues had the effect of democratizing Pennsylvania politics by attracting, for the first time, the participation of the lower classes. As a result, a new political style and leader emerged in a colony which had previously boasted an identity of interests among its religious, social, and political elites.

Nash bases his interpretation upon a statistical analysis of Pennsylvania society, which he finds to be remarkably unstratified and "middling." It seems that the combination of proprietary (and therefore somewhat alien) government and a relatively unstructured society permitted a dissident like Lloyd to politicize and organize a broadly based opposition to the administration. Thus Nash, like Zuckerman, suggests that politics cannot be fully understood apart from society.

For eight years, from late 1701 when Penn left his colony until December 1709 when James Logan embarked for England, Pennsylvania was caught in the crucible of political controversy. No element of government, whether Assembly, Council, governor, county court, provincial court, or proprietary agency, escaped unscathed in the cross fire of factional politics. Every component of constituted authority was challenged, deprecated, or called into question. Almost every institution of political and proprietary authority was scrutinized, found wanting, and, if it could not be altered, condemned. At moments — such as in 1703 and 1708 — government virtually ceased to function. Governors Hamilton and Evans gave up residency in Philadelphia, the courts lapsed for want of legislative backing, and the Council was reduced to a cypher.

In some measure this decade of strife was a response to particular developments in the early eighteenth century — Penn's tangled affairs in England, the economic dislocation caused by war, the rash behavior of Governor John Evans, and the personal feud between James Logan and David Lloyd. But at a more fundamental level, the political paralysis was simply the epitomization of tendencies imbedded in the Quaker experience in Pennsylvania since 1682. The embroidery of the early eighteenth-century political fabric depicted a variety of individual discontents, parochial issues, and emergent constitutional questions; but the warp and woof of the carpet was woven of strands tracing back to the previous decades. In this sense, the period from 1701 to 1710 represented no new departure in provincial politics, no embryonic drive to democratize political institutions anticipating the American Revolution, but the culmination of the response of first-generation Quakers to political responsibility.

Continued reluctance to accept constituted authority figured most prominently among the tendencies toward political instability in the colony. The aberrant behavior of many of the Quaker leaders in the 1680's, the open warfare against Blackwell, the Keithian controversy, and David Lloyd's campaigns of the eighteenth century were all a part of the pattern of defiance. Other colonies, it is true, were not free of the strife that gripped Pennsylvania; political faction and social disruption almost inevitably attended the rerooting and adaptation of English institutions in a wilderness environment. Robert Quary reported from Virginia in 1705 that he had never seen "such a soure temper'd people" in an assembly and warned that a "factious uneasy spirit" was common to all the plantations. Other governors sent home similar reports of churlish, disputatious persons, both in and out of power.[1] Though comparative quantification is hardly possible, one concludes that a behavior pattern common to all of the colonies was seen in Pennsylvania in somewhat magnified form. If antiauthoritarianism was residual in dissenting Englishmen transplanted to a frontier which in the early stages lacked well-established political institutions and social controls, it was seen in its most extreme form in Quaker Pennsylvania.

Conditions in Pennsylvania only intensified the antiauthoritarian cast of Quakerism. Penn, who alone possessed the charisma to stabilize the Quaker community, if it could be unified at all, was absent for all but a few years during the first three decades of the colony's existence. Ill-advised policies regarding land and proprietary revenues tended to split Pennsylvania society into contending and antagonistic groups, and, finally, to alienate even the closest of Penn's friends. Moreover, life in the "howling wilderness," as some called it, had a peculiar effect on the humor of men. Many, as they looked out from a modest farm in Bucks County or from an artisan's bench or merchant's wharf in Philadelphia, took a fierce pride in their accomplishments. They saw themselves as men who had endured for years the persecutions of petty authorities in England, suffered a long and hazardous ocean passage, toiled through droughts, epidemics, and fluctuating economic conditions, weathered religious controversy, and resisted Puritan governors, Anglican imperialists, and proprietary placemen. But withal, they had carved out a niche in the New World where men of humble station, as even the least optimistic would admit, had greater opportunity than England had ever promised. Pennsylvania was no place, William Markham said, for a man to learn breeding or polite language. "Conversation runs low," Logan complained in 1712; a learned man could hardly be found "for every 1000 miles of the Queen's Dominions." [2] But the average settler, if less educated and not so well read as his English counterpart, had more to show for his efforts.

Pride of this sort — a kind of crude nationalism — had as a corollary a hypersensitivity to criticism which sometimes bordered on cultural paranoia. Men were thin-skinned, quick to anger, and inclined to magnify the smallest issue which aroused their resentment. John Evans found

---

[1] Quary to the Board of Trade, Oct. 15, 1705, *CSP 1704–05,* #605. The colonial series of the *Calendar of State Papers* is filled with similar reports from royal officials and governors, which of course reflect something of the viewer as well as the viewed. Gov. Evans of Pennsylvania reported typically to the Board of Trade that "it is the great unhappiness of these parts of the world in Generall, to be too much divided in Opinions." Much skill would be required to "take off the Edge of some Men's unreasonable Anger," Evans concluded. Evans to the Board of Trade, May 30, 1704, *CSP 1704–05,* #359.

[2] Markham to Penn, April 27, 1697, *CSP 1697–98,* #76xiv; Logan to Thomas Goldney, July 3, 1712, Logan Letter Book (1712–1715), 27.

Pennsylvanians touchy beyond reason, given to enlarging the smallest issues into matters of great moment. Pride was "the national Infirmity," asserted James Logan, who on another occasion found "a general Infatuation gott amongst us, as if we were preparing for Destruction," and deemed that "we are generally in these parts too full of ourselves, and empty of sence to manage affairs of Importance." [3] Isaac Norris, one of those in Pennsylvania least given to hyperbole, found "a strange, unaccountable humour (almost a custom now) of straining and resenting everything, of creating monsters and then combating them." [4]

From easily aroused resentment, it was only a step to intractability. What Evans, Logan, and Norris noted in the early eighteenth century differed only in degree from what John Blackwell had described in the late 1680's when he concluded that the Pennsylvanians were temperamentally unfit for government. Nobody appreciated the colonial syndrome better than Penn himself. "There is an Excess of vanity," he wrote in 1705, "that is Apt to Creep in upon the people in power in America, who having got out of the Crowd, in which they were lost here . . . think nothing taller than themselves, but the Trees, and as if there were no After Superior Judgment to which they should be accountable." As an antidote to such self-importance, Penn suggested that the colonists take turns in revisiting England where they might "lose themselves again amongst the Crowds of so much more Considerable people." Their sense of proportion restored, Pennsylvanians might return to America "much more Discreet and Tractable and fit for Government." [5]

Also of great importance in the political dynamics of the early eighteenth century was the relatively unstructured character of the young society which made Penn's proprietary form of government seem painfully out of place and gave David Lloyd an ideal social milieu in which to make his appeals to the people. A rough profile of colonial society, which helps to illustrate this point, can be drawn from the provincial tax list of 1693 and the wills and inventories of estates for this era.[6]

Although they were not enumerated in the tax lists, Negroes, of course, occupied the lowest position in the social hierarchy. Since 1684,

[3] Evans to the Board of Trade, May 30, 1704, *CSP 1704–05*, #359; Logan to Hannah Penn, Oct. 28, 1715, Logan Letter Book (1712–1715), 352; Logan to Penn, Nov. 22, 1704, *Pennsylvania Archives*, 2nd Ser., VII, 15–16.

[4] Norris to Penn, Dec. 2, 1709, Norris Letter Book (1709–1716), 112.

[5] Penn to William Mompesson, Feb. 17, 1704/05, *Penn-Logan Correspondence*, I, 374–375.

[6] The tax list for the city and county of Philadelphia is in *PMHB*, 8 (1884), 85–105; for Bucks County in Bucks County Miscellaneous Papers, 1682–1772, foll. 17–23; for Chester County in Chester County Miscellaneous Papers, 1684–1847, fol. 17; for the Lower Counties in Miscellaneous Papers, Three Lower Counties, 1655–1805, foll. 25–33.

when a ship with 150 slaves had reached the colony, Negroes had arrived at Philadelphia and New Castle in small numbers. That 68 Negroes belonged to 19 individuals listed in the 198 inventories of estate probated at Philadelphia between 1683 and 1700 suggests that between 5 and 10 per cent of the colonists owned slaves at this time. By the early 1700's Negro slaves could be found on many of the larger farms in the colony and were numerous enough in Philadelphia to cause concern about their congregating in the streets.[7]

The indentured servants stood above the Negro slaves on the social ladder. In the early years of settlement such persons probably constituted about one-third of the population. But by 1700 almost all of those who had signed indentures as a means of obtaining passage to the New World had gained their freedom. Though other servants trickled into the colony during the 1680's and 1690's, it is likely that by the end of the century the proportion of indentured persons in the population had fallen considerably, possibly as low as 10 per cent.[8]

Free, white males who possessed little or no taxable property, either real or personal, composed a much larger group. In the country, these were men recently released from indentures, grown sons living at home, and agricultural laborers. In Philadelphia, they were often seamen and workers. As indicated in Table 1, more than half of the adult male population in the Lower Counties, where tobacco was cultivated on sizable farms, had no rateable estate. Land ownership was far more prevalent in the upper counties. Roughly four-fifths of the adult males in Chester County owned land; and for the upper counties as a whole only about one man in four paid only the head tax.

The generally roughhewn caste of rural society is further revealed by the predominance on the tax lists of men with modest estates. This was

[7] Edward R. Turner, *The Negro in Pennsylvania* (Washington, 1911), 1–3; Thomas E. Drake, *Quakers and Slavery in America* (New Haven, 1950), 1–33; Darold D. Wax, "Quaker Merchants and the Slave Trade in Colonial Pennsylvania," *PMHB*, 86 (1962), 143–159. The arrival of slaves in 1684 is recounted by Nicholas More in a letter to Penn, Dec. 1, 1684, Myers Collection, Box 2, #6, CCHS. The extent of slave ownership is based upon an analysis of wills given in Philadelphia Wills and Inventories, Book A (1682–1699); Book B (1699–1705), photostats at Genealogical Society of Pennsylvania. If inventories of estate were more commonly made for men of high economic standing, then the degree of slaveholding would be inflated. Fear of the sizable Negro population was expressed in 1702 when the Grand Jury of Philadelphia charged "the great abuse & The Ill Consiquence of the great multitude of Negroes who commonly meete togeither in a Riott & Tumultios manner on the first days of the weeke [Sundays]." Grand Jury Presentment, Sept. 18, 1702, Wallace Collection, Ancient Documents of Philadelphia, 11.

[8] Cheesman A. Herrick, *White Servitude in Pennsylvania* (Philadelphia, 1926), passim. The trend would be reversed with the great influx of Scotch-Irish and Germans after 1714.

Distribution of Taxable
TABLE 1   *Wealth in 1693*

Total value of taxable wealth	*Number of taxpayers in each bracket*				*Percentage of taxpayers in each bracket*			
Pounds	*Bucks County*	*Chester County*	*Phila. County*	*Phila. City*	*Bucks County*	*Chester County*	*Phila. County*	*Phila. City*
Unrated	63	52	109	75	42.0	18.5	32.4	21.4
1–50	37	179	99	80	24.6	63.7	29.5	22.9
51–100	35	42	92	109	24.2	15.0	27.4	31.1
101–200	12	6	30	43	7.8	2.1	8.9	12.3
201–500	2	2	6	31	1.4	.7	1.8	8.9
501–1,000	—	—	—	12	—	—	—	3.4
	149	281	336	350	100.0	100.0	100.0	100.0

	Kent County	*Sussex County*	*New Castle County*	*Kent County*	*Sussex County*	*New Castle County*
Unrated	67	107	167	42.6	56.3	62.5
1–50	—	—	2	—	—	.7
51–100	40	33	56	25.4	17.4	21.0
101–200	32	31	22	20.5	16.3	8.3
201–500	16	19	20	10.2	10.0	7.5
501–750	2	—	—	1.3	—	—
	157	190	267	100.0	100.0	100.0

particularly noticeable in Bucks, Chester, and Philadelphia counties. Almost two-thirds of the men with taxable wealth in Chester County, for example, had estates rated no higher than £50. Even more striking, only about one man in ten in the upper counties (excluding the city of Philadelphia) was assessed for more than £100. All such figures, of course, must be inflated somewhat to compensate for the common practice of undervaluing property for tax purposes. Even so, it is clear that the spectrum of wealth in the countryside was narrow. It appears that in the Lower Counties more accurate valuations were made. Again, however, the concentration of planters in the middle range of wealth is striking. Of 272 men with taxable estates, 214 (78.4 per cent) paid taxes on estates valued between £51 and £200. Even the wealthiest colonists boasted estates valued only a few hundred pounds higher than their middling neighbors. The estate of the richest man in the Lower Counties was rated at £750.

Added evidence of the colony's social structure can be gained by examining the wills and inventories of estate probated at Philadelphia between

1683 and 1702. Inventories of estate, which are extant for almost 60 per cent of the wills probated in the first two decades of settlement, as a rule reflect the true value of the deceased's real and personal property.[9] Generally, they may be taken as a more accurate gauge of individual wealth than the tax assessments. Even so, the inventories do not reveal a markedly different pattern of stratification. Again, one sees in the countryside a society of simple farmers struggling to make the transition from subsistence to commercial farming. In Chester County, where land-holding was most prevalent, 70 per cent of the inventories described assets worth no more than £250, including real property. In Bucks County the pattern was much the same. Typically, an inventory of £250 or less reveals a man who worked about a quarter of the 100 or 200 acres he had purchased, who lived in a crude two or three-room house worth no more than £25 or £30, and who owned, in addition, only an out-building or two, a dozen farm animals, and a meager assortment of implements and household goods. Richard Few, a Chester County yeo-man, who left an estate worth £256, may be taken as an example. All but about £60 of his estate was accounted for by his farm buildings and 197 acres of land of which only a part was under cultivation. Other than that, he possessed only some wearing apparel (£8), beds and bedding (£9), crude furniture and old lumber (£2), tools, utensils, and kitchen-ware (£4), two pair of oxen (£18), eleven swine and one bull (£9), and two cows and a calf (£9). Dozens of inventories tell a similar story.

Though the great majority of settlers owned a little more than the bare essentials of life, there were some whose standard of living was on the rise. In both Bucks and Chester counties, about one-fifth of the estates inventoried were valued between £251 and £500. Men in this category typically owned more land, usually 500 acres or more. But their inventories still portray a roughly textured life. More farm animals, a horse or two, some finished chairs, tables, and chests in the house, a bit of pewter or brassware in the kitchen, and an occasional piece of linen on the table was all that differentiated their existence from that of their

[9] The following discussion is based on an analysis of the inventories given in Philadelphia Wills and Inventories, Book A (1682–1699) and Book B (1699–1705). All values are given in Pennsylvania money, which, by 1700, could be converted to English sterling by subtracting one-third. It is difficult to determine whether the inventories are cross-sectional. Wills of laborers, husbandmen, and yeomen frequently lack inventories, but the same is true of some of the wealth-iest merchants and landowners — Andrew Robeson, Thomas Holme, Thomas Brassey, and Arthur Cooke, to cite just a few examples from this period. One suspects that the estates of lower-class individuals were less frequently inven-toried. Abstracts of all wills included in Books A and B are given in *Pennsylvania Genealogical Magazine*, 1 (1895), 45–84; 2 (1900), 7–33; 3 (1906), 12–37, 144–152, 245–254.

poorer neighbors. Usually it was the greater acreage they had under cultivation, not their style of life, that set them apart from men of lesser estates.

Only about 10 per cent of the country people could boast of estates worth £500 or more. In seventeenth-century Pennsylvania this signified a modest prosperity. Only at this level of wealth does one begin to find evidence in the inventories of occasional luxuries – the East India pillow case, fire dogs with brass heads, chair cushions, spice boxes, walnut chairs, silver buckles, and the like. That the mode of living began to change at about this level is also made apparent through the frequent mention of Negro slaves in inventories of £500 or more.

Because the city of Philadelphia had undergone commercial development, its social structure was somewhat different from that of the countryside. Numerous skilled craftsmen, shopkeepers, and even workers engaged in the rougher trades of a mercantile society swelled the middle class of society. One-quarter of the city dwellers were taxed for assets valued above £100, as opposed to about 10 per cent of the country folk (Table 1). Roughly one-fifth of the estates inventoried for residents of the city were valued between £250 and £500, and another fifth between £500 and £1,000 (Table 2). At the same time, a lesser number of shopkeepers and merchants attained a level of affluence rarely matched in the country. Men whose taxable assets exceeded £200 were uncommon outside of Philadelphia, while in the capital city 12.3 per cent of the white adult males fell into this category. In the upper counties not a single estate outside of Philadelphia was taxed at more than £400. But in the city, twenty-two individuals had property valued above £400 and four boasted estates assessed at £1,000 or more (Table 1). Similarly, the inventories of estate show that in the first two decades almost one Philadelphian in ten left an estate worth more than £1,000, whereas in the country such men were rarities (Table 2).

Among the prosperous, merchants predominated. Thomas Budd left an estate of £1,676. Philip Richards's estate was valued at £1,813, including three Negro slaves and land worth £1,260. James Claypoole left property worth £1,468, William Frampton, assets of £812, Robert Ewer, £865, and Arthur Cooke, £2,570. Well-to-do artisans were by no means uncommon. William Alloway, a tallow chandler, left an estate valued at £602; Nathaniel Harding, a basket maker, left £696; and there were many others like them. It was indicative of the high degree of mobility in Philadelphia that no man in the first twenty years of settlement died with a larger fortune than James Fox. Immigrating to Pennsylvania in 1686, Fox attempted to launch an enterprise for manufacturing woolens. When this failed, he moved to Philadelphia and started a bakery. Fox's operations flourished and by the time of his death in 1699 he was one

Distribution of
Inventoried Estates,
1683–1702

TABLE 2

Inventoried value of real and personal property	Number of inventoried estates in each wealth bracket			Percentage of inventoried estates in each wealth bracket		
Pounds	Bucks County	Chester County	Phila. City	Bucks County	Chester County	Phila. City
1–50	5	7	12	18.5	18.9	12.3
51–250	15	19	35	55.6	51.4	35.7
251–500	5	7	22	18.5	18.9	22.5
501–1,000	2	2	20	7.4	5.4	20.4
1,001–2,000	—	2	7	—	5.4	7.1
2,000 plus	—	—	2	—	—	2.0
	27	37	98	100.0	100.0	100.0

Inventoried value of real and personal property	Total value of inventoried estates in each wealth bracket			Percentage of total inventoried wealth in each wealth bracket		
Pounds	Bucks County	Chester County	Phila. City	Bucks County	Chester County	Phila. City
1–50	192	263	277	3.5	2.7	.7
51–250	1,864	2,536	4,756	33.9	25.7	11.2
251–500	2,316	2,456	7,664	42.1	24.9	18.1
501–1,000	1,132	1,688	13,471	20.5	17.2	31.7
1,001–2,000	—	2,905	10,899	—	29.5	25.7
2,000 plus	—	—	5,316	—	—	12.6
	5,504	9,848	42,383	100.0	100.0	100.0
Average Value of Inventoried Estates	204	266	427			

of the largest grain merchants and land speculators in the colony. His estate, valued at £2,746, included three white indentured servants, four Negro slaves, and real estate valued at £1,500.

Pennsylvania at the beginning of the eighteenth century, then, was still a society in the early stages of development. In the country many of the farms were beginning to produce surpluses for Philadelphia export market. But the small subsistence farm was typical, as was the unpretentious yeoman farmer. Everywhere outside of Philadelphia one saw a relatively undifferentiated society with only a handful of individuals standing above the common farmers and landless rural workers. In Philadelphia rapid growth had brought about a somewhat more complex social structure. Slowly, as the city took her place in the world of Atlantic commerce, the distance between rich and poor widened. As the city grew, it became more diverse and more stratified.[10] And yet even in Philadelphia clearly defined lines between economic classes were badly blurred and a distinctive upper class had not yet formed. The top and bottom layers of society, as they existed in England, were still largely unrepresented. Few could parade aristocratic pretensions. Even those merchants in the city who were later "Quaker grandees" were still a generation away from that status. James Logan warned a friend in 1713 that Pennsylvania was barren of "men of Parts & Learning," and cautioned that anyone who thought to take up a position of importance in Philadelphia should be "furnished with an Exteriour suited to take with the common humours of the Crowd." [11] Furthermore, mobility up and down the ladder of success was far greater than in the countryside. One observer in Philadelphia remarked that there were many who had come to the city penniless and were now "richer by several hundred pounds." Another citizen testified that some who had hardly been able to earn a living in England were well-to-do in Philadelphia.[12] Pennsylvania was a good place for a workingman "to gett a good living in," one commentator noted, but hardly a country in which to accumulate a great estate.[13]

Such a social setting offered David Lloyd ideal conditions in which to advertise his appeals against proprietary privilege and the authoritarian tactics employed by Penn's placemen. Conversely, this rough equality of condition made the work of James Logan and Penn's deputy governors for more difficult, for they were attempting to gain acceptance of proprietary prerogatives and to promote deferential attitudes in an environment where governors and governed lived much alike.

One further element in the political equation was the role played by individual eccentricities, the clash of personalities, and occasionally the intervention of sheer mischance. The importance of personalities in Pennsylvania may, in fact, have been amplified simply because men like Lloyd and Logan operated within a system where the respective powers

[10] The absence of tax lists for Philadelphia for more than fifty years after 1693 makes precise analysis of the changing social structure impossible. My conclusions are based on an analysis of wills for the first half of the eighteenth century and the incomplete tax lists of 1754 and 1756, given respectively in *Pennsylvania Genealogical Magazine*, 21 (1959), 161 ff, and 22 (1961), 10 ff.

[11] Logan to Josiah Martin, Aug. 4, 1713, Logan Letter Book (1712–1715), 131.

[12] Andreas Rudman to ——, 1700, *PMHB*, 84 (1960), 207; Gabriel Thomas, *An Historical and Geographical Account of Pensilvania and of West-Jersey*, 1698, in Myers, ed., *Narratives*, 327. See also Tolles, *Meeting House*, 114–115.

[13] Logan to Daniel Flexney, May 4, 1715, Logan Letter Book (1712–1715), 286.

of the various agencies of government were not precisely defined – a system which had been in flux since the initial Frame of 1682 was rejected by the first representative body convened in Pennsylvania.

It was Pennsylvania's peculiar fate that in the early eighteenth century the man best qualified to assume the role of political leader was also the one who took an almost perverse delight in battling prescriptive authority. David Lloyd was a gifted man, a brilliant orator and student of the law, a skilled advocate, and an unequaled legislative draughtsman and parliamentarian. But he was also proud, volatile, vindictive, and highly ambitious. After 1699, when Penn removed him from his public and proprietary offices at the demand of the Crown, he lapsed into a deeply revengeful mood and thereafter his resentment of Penn and all who supported him was boundless. All of the passion which in the mid-1690's he had directed against the King's officials in Pennsylvania, now found vent in an assault on the machinery of proprietary management. When his only child died in June 1701, a victim of shock or suffocation at the hands of a house servant who had locked the boy in a small closet, Lloyd sunk into a slough of despair which seems to have reinforced his view that the world was a hostile and unremitting place.[14] Embittered by his dismissal from office, shunned by the wealthier Quakers as a dangerous firebrand, and wounded by personal misfortune, Lloyd became the archetypical New World malcontent – fulminating against constituted authority, translating personal grievances into public causes, and conjuring up visions of encroaching and threatening forces which lay in wait of unwary and defenseless settlers.

Whether Lloyd's politics were personal rather than ideological is not an easy question to answer. Historians who look for tribunes of the people in the pre-Revolutionary period tend to stress Lloyd's unyielding commitment to democratic principles and his abiding faith in the people. Unwilling to probe the less accessible recesses of his mind, they have taken his political jeremiads at face value.[15] Men of the time, who did not know what epic events lay over the horizon, and whose problems were immediate and real rather than distant and historiographical, took a colder view of Lloyd. Evans, Gookin, and Logan frequently noted Lloyd's vindictiveness and believed that the Welshman was motivated far less by political principles than by the spirit of revenge and desire for power. Despite his smooth language and pretenses, Logan reported in

14 Lokken, David Lloyd, 95–96.
15 See, for example, Lokken, David Lloyd; H. Frank Eshelman, "The Constructive Genius of David Lloyd in Early Colonial Pennsylvania Legislation and Jurisprudence, 1686 to 1731," Pennsylvania Bar Association Reports, 16 (1910), 406–461; Burton A. Konkle, "David Lloyd and the First Half Century of Pennsylvania," unpublished manuscript at Friends Historical Library, Swarthmore College, Swarthmore, Pa.

1704, Lloyd "cannot sometimes conceal his resentment of thy taking, as he calls it, his bread from him, this expression he has several times dropped, overlooking his politics through the heat of his indignation." [16]

The objectivity of Logan and Penn's deputy governors is suspect, of course, since Lloyd was systematically attempting to reduce their power. But there is little in Lloyd's behavior during the early eighteenth century to discredit Logan's view. So intense was Lloyd's animosity toward Penn that he saw the proprietor's policies as premeditated attempts, dating back to the origins of settlement, to curtail colonial rights. To cast Penn in this light was to misunderstand the whole nature of proprietary politics. For although Penn often offended colonial sensibilities, he was neither vindictive, autocratic, nor hungry for power. It was stability and unity, he hungered for, along with a proprietary revenue. "There is some," Isaac Norris wrote aptly in a thinly veiled reference to Lloyd, "who by Linking [the] imaginery with the true Intrest of the Country therewith Couch & Cover their own Interests & disguise & do so perplex affairs as to . . . almost give the Honest and Undersigning to Dispair of any Reconciliation or progress to a Settlement." [17]

Lloyd's willingness to form almost any alliance which would further his ends provides another insight into the nature of his politics. After 1700, Lloyd openly recruited support among precisely the groups in Pennsylvania which he had so strenuously opposed in the 1690's — the King's officers in Pennsylvania, the Anglicans of Philadelphia and Chester, and the dissident Quakers who had followed Keith. Lloyd amazed Philadelphians in 1702 by accepting an appointment as deputy advocate of the vice-admiralty court at Philadelphia over which Robert Quary presided as judge.[18] It was Lloyd's mocking attack on Quary's court which had caused his removal from public office just three years before. Equally surprising was his alliance with John Moore, the Anglican advocate of Quary's court, for the purpose of enlarging the power of the Corporation of Philadelphia.

In the last analysis, there was no particular inconsistency between Lloyd's vendetta against Penn and his apparent promotion of "democratic" principles. Lloyd promoted the powers of the Assembly and the Corporation of Philadelphia because, as it happened, they were the only

---

[16] Logan to Penn, Oct. 3, 1704, *Penn-Logan Correspondence*, I, 323. For similar descriptions of Lloyd's vengefulness and emotionalism see Logan to William Penn, Jr., Sept. 25, 1700, Logan to Penn, Oct. 27, 1704 and July 27, 1706, *ibid.*, I, 18, 339–340, II, 142; Gov. Charles Gookin to Secretary of the Society for the Propagation of the Gospel, Aug. 27, 1709, Perry, ed., *History of the Church in Pennsylvania*, 50–52; Gov. John Evans to Council, April 12, 1709, *Minutes of Council*, II, 436.

[17] Norris to Penn, Feb. 13, 1704/05, Norris Letter Book (1704–1706), 21–22.

[18] Lokken, *David Lloyd*, 119.

centers of power in Pennsylvania beyond the reach of the proprietor — or the Crown if Penn should lose or sell his government. It was only good politics to dress his arguments in acceptable constitutional garb. Thus Lloyd took pains to invoke precedent whenever he could in arguing for the Assembly's privileges. If he sought a privilege for the legislature which Parliament enjoyed in England, he made much of the necessity of modeling colonial assemblies after the House of Commons.[19] Penn's deputies could play the same game, citing parliamentary precedent whenever Lloyd sought powers for the Assembly which were unknown in England.[20] It was precisely because antiproprietary rhetoric and constitutional arguments were mutually reinforcing that Lloyd could play the patriot in Pennsylvania while quenching his thirst for revenge and feeding his appetite for power.

Locked as they were in a struggle for power, it was almost inevitable that Lloyd and Logan should caricature each other's views. In Lloyd's mind, Logan took his rules of government from "Machiavel and those high flown statesmen." His "inclination to a despotic power" would lead to the oppression of the people, the violation of their charters, the denial of their rights, and, finally, to the elimination of all means of redress.[21] Logan, in short, was represented as a threat to all that Quakers had left England to escape. Conversely, Logan charged Lloyd with following a policy calculated to maim government in Pennsylvania permanently. It was Lloyd who, for all his lectures on English constitutional history, would have the Assembly invested with complete legislative power while reducing the Council to insignificance. What kind of constitutional precedent did that follow, asked Logan. Councils were deemed necessary in all governments, "from the most barbarous to the politest," especially in the crucial business of legislation. But Lloyd seemed to believe that England "never so truly knew liberty" as when the monarchy was overthrown more than a half century before. Logan, however, believed that those who now disturbed the equilibrium of government in Pennsylvania, like their predecessors in England during the Civil Wars, would perpetrate "the greatest grievance the nation has ever known." [22]

---

[19] *Minutes of Council*, II, 371; Lloyd, "The Speaker's Vindication . . . ," *Penn-Logan Correspondence*, II, 411. In 1709 the Assembly, again under Lloyd's leadership, gave its unanimous opinion "that 'twill be our great Happiness to follow the Queen's good example, and that of her Parliament, in the Administration at Home." *Votes of Assembly*, II, 832.

[20] Gov. John Evans accused Lloyd and his followers in the Assembly of attempting to "reverse the method of Govmt. according to our English Constitution, and Establish one more nearly resembling a republick in its stead." *Minutes of Council*, II, 325. See also, *ibid.*, II, 305–307, 309–310.

[21] Lloyd, "The Speaker's Vindication . . . ," *Penn-Logan Correspondence*, II, 408.

[22] Logan, "The Secretary's Justification . . . , *ibid.*, II, 365.

In actuality Logan was no lover of despotism and Lloyd no advocate of popular rule. Logan's political thought was consistent with the conventional Whig faith of the day in a balanced government which combined popular and aristocratic elements. As Penn's chief supporter and confidant in Pennsylvania, he sought to maximize the power of the Council, where Penn's conservative friends congregated, and to minimize the strengh of the Assembly, where the proprietor's enemies held sway. By the same token, Lloyd worked to enlarge the powers of that element of government which he controlled, while chipping away at instruments of government dominated by his opponents. In later, less vexed times, Lloyd too would acknowledge the wisdom of a government of counterbalancing powers. But in the confused and disorderly years of the early eighteenth century, circumstances required that both Logan and Lloyd act as if their political ideologies were poles apart. Obscured was the fact that both men were inheritors of the same political tradition. What passed for constitutional questions were in reality reflections of real and immediate problems. Both men might ransack the law books and historical texts in order to ground their position upon abstract theory and ancient precedents. But the problems over which they fought were not theoretical or philosophical but visible and palpable — issues which arose from particular conditions in Pennsylvania, from Penn's position in England, from bureaucratic activity at Whitehall, and from the international wars of Louis XIV. No amount of citing precedent and invoking ancient rights could obscure the fact that what both Logan and Lloyd sought in Pennsylvania was political supremacy.

Ironically, the interminable battle of words, the endless process of assertion and counterassertion, the taking of extreme positions for purposes of bargaining led both antagonists further afield than they wished to go. Logan grew increasingly distrustful of the people and came at last to doubt that they were capable of self-government.[23] By 1709 his misanthropy had hardened to the extent that he was inclined to question the good faith of any popular leader who opposed him. Pessimism distorted all his views. At the same time he came to believe that he alone could discern what was best for Pennsylvania. Lloyd followed a similar pattern, seeing only the worst in Logan, impugning the Secretary's motives at every turn, and convincing himself that Logan and Penn intended the destruction of representative government in Pennsylvania. As Isaac Norris

[23] The Quakers, Logan wrote in 1704, were "unfit for Government by themselves, and not much better with others." Logan to Penn, Nov. 22, 1704, *Pennsylvania Archives*, 2nd Ser., VII, 16. Even twenty years later Logan thought that the main source of trouble in Pennsylvania had been "in heaping things called Privileges (which no English subject ever had) on a People that neither knows how to use them nor how to be grateful for them." Logan to Hannah Penn, Jan. 1, 1725/26, Logan Letter Book (1702–1726), 288.

noted, government in Pennsylvania seemed incapable of reaching any middle ground "between arbitrary power and licentious popularity." [24]

In such a make-believe world, where hyperbole was the customary mode of argument and distrust the nearly universal attitude, words became more important than actions and points of ceremonial propriety took precedent over legislative proposals. Thus the Assembly of 1707 broke up over a question of whether or not the legislature was obliged to assemble when the Governor chose to address it. In 1709 a dispute over the Speaker's refusal to stand when addressing the Governor brought legislative proceedings to a halt. The Assembly, noted one of its members, showed less concern for considering "solids and substantials" than for indulging in windy debates "upon Everything that is said or done . . . always remonstrating, and valluing the last word highly." There was little hope of conducting business, given "the air of grandure and sacred care for the honor and Dignity of the house . . . and the Secret pride thereof . . . in the great pretenses to any professions of mean and Despicable thoughts of themselves." [25]

Though David Lloyd was more interested in shielding Pennsylvania from proprietary authority than in shifting the center of political gravity downward in the colony, his campaign against Penn and Logan had the latter rather than the former effect. In this sense, historians who have seen in Lloyd the spokesman of the people, and in his politics the democratization of Pennsylvania society, have fastened on an important truth, even if they misunderstood its causes and significance. For a radical shift in political power did occur in Pennsylvania after Penn's departure in 1701. It came neither as the planned result of Lloyd's policies nor as the fulfillment of his political beliefs, but rather as a side effect of the techniques he employed in battling traditional authority.

At the root of this inadvertent democratization was Lloyd's necessity to turn for political support to a segment of society which in England had been politically quiescent and in Pennsylvania had gradually been acquiring political awareness. To some extent, Pennsylvania had always had a high potential for "middle-class democracy." Society was relatively fluid and the incidence of land ownership among the humble was far greater in the New World than in the Old; expectations were higher and the distance between gentleman and husbandman was relatively slight.

Although Pennsylvanians crowded the middle of the economic and social spectrum in the period before 1720, the inherited traditions of deference and political acquiescence had not altogether disappeared. In the early years, county elections had usually served only to confirm such

---

[24] Norris to Penn, Oct. 11, 1704, Norris Letter Book (1704–1706), 2.
[25] Norris to Penn, Dec. 2, 1709, Norris Letter Book (1709–1716), 112.

candidates for the Council or Assembly as the leading men saw fit to propose. Poor roads, bad weather, and a general readiness to concede political power to the wealthier and better educated men in the province seems to have been the general rule. The comments of Phineas Pemberton to Penn in 1687 illustrate the point. Pemberton, a leading figure in Bucks County, related that one of the lesser county officeholders had "miscarried in several respects." The offender had been "dealt with" for his misdemeanors and would be excluded from the county court that year. So would another landowner, formerly a justice of the peace, but now out of favor. "William Beakes out [of office] last [year]," wrote Pemberton, "and intend [to] keep him so til he be better in our Country." [26] Even in 1700, though by that time the pattern had begun to change, only thirty freemen took the trouble to participate in the Bucks County election for the legislature.[27]

The importance of Lloyd's activities was that in his search for support he expanded the politically relevant strata of Pennsylvania society and drastically altered the social bases of political leadership.[28] As Lloyd was quick to see, the configuration of colonial values, which reflected English precedents in the early years, denied him the constituency he needed to wage his war against proprietary privilege. George Keith had faced the same problem a decade before. His answer had been to activate a part of the community that in a deferential society had rarely been heard from. Lloyd followed Keith's lead and carried his techniques a step farther. Like the Quaker apostate whom he had bitterly opposed, Lloyd pitched his appeal to the smaller country farmer, the city artisan, and the disaffected freeman — men whose economic or social expectations had not always been met under the existing leadership. Logan, for one, was well aware that Lloyd's success had much to do with his ability to capitalize on Keith's earlier work. By raking up the ashes of the Quaker controversy, Lloyd garnered the support of the common people who had joined the apostate in significant numbers in the 1690's.[29]

Aiding Lloyd in his quest to arouse the political consciousness of the lower classes were the election laws passed in 1700 and 1706 and the provisions of the Frame of 1701. Although none of these statutes altered

[26] Pemberton to Penn, April 3, 1687, Etting Collection, Pemberton Papers, I, 20.

[27] Penn to Logan, Sept. 8, 1701, *Penn-Logan Correspondence*, I, 54. This amounted to a turnout of between one-fourth and one-third of the electorate. The 1693 county tax list indicates 86 eligible voters; it is probable that by 1701 the number had increased to 100 or more.

[28] For a suggestive study of the functional relationship between social change and increased political participation see Karl Deutsch, "Social Mobilization and Political Development," *American Political Science Review*, 55 (1961), 493–514.

[29] Logan to Penn, Dec. 20, 1706, *Penn-Logan Correspondence*, II, 186–187; Logan, "The Secretary's Justification . . . ," *ibid.*, II, 381–382.

the electoral qualifications, which remained lenient, the manner of election underwent considerable revision. The 1700 election law initiated the
practice of publicizing writs of election — authorizations by the governor
for the holding of elections. Magistrates were required to read the writs
in "the capital town or most public places within their respective baili-
wicks" and post election notices upon a tree or house along the roads
leading from every precinct to the principal towns of each county. The
call to polls was also to be displayed on every county courthouse, church,
and meetinghouse in the province. Though seemingly innocuous, it was
an important encouragement to those, who, because of poor roads, distant polling places, or an ingrained sense of deference, had ordinarily
acquiesced to the political wisdom of the more experienced members of
the community. A second step was taken in 1701, when the secret ballot,
one of the Harringtonian devices incorporated in the Frame of 1683, was
abandoned. In its place, much to Penn's dismay, a complicated system
of oral voting was substituted. Both these measures were reenacted in
the election law passed in 1706. In Logan's judgment, both election laws
aided Lloyd in mobilizing the support of lesser men in Pennsylvania
against merchants and large landowners sympathetic to Penn. "We will
never obtain a good election," the Secretary wrote in 1709, "until the
recent voting law be replaced." [30]

The significance of David Lloyd's style of politics is clear if his supporters are compared with those of Thomas Lloyd, his seventeenth-century predecessor in the cause of antiproprietary reform. In terms of broad
objectives the two men differed little: both opposed Penn's control of the
judiciary, both viewed his land policy as inequitable and venal, both resented the power enjoyed by proprietary officeholders, both sought a
delimitation of proprietary prerogatives and an increase in provincial
autonomy. But whereas Thomas Lloyd had sought in the seventeenth
century to fashion an antiproprietary party from among the wealthier
Quakers — shopkeepers, merchants, and large landowners — David Lloyd
worked in the eighteenth century to politicize a mass of individuals who
were mixed in ethnic and religious background and who, with significant
exceptions, occupied lesser positions on the economic and social ladder.[31]

[30] Logan to Penn, Feb. 3, 1708/09, *ibid.*, II, 313. The election laws are in
Statutes of Pensylvania, II, 24–27, 212–221 . . . and *Votes of Assembly*, I,
389–390.

[31] Members of Lloyd's faction in the Assembly, though they owed their election mainly to their leader's mobilization of the colony's lower ranks, were themselves often men of considerable wealth. This was especially true of those elected
from the city and county of Philadelphia. Lloyd owned vast acreage in all three
counties of the province and lived handsomely on his fees as Pennsylvania's most
sought after lawyer. Griffith Jones and Joshua Carpenter were among the largest
property owners in Philadelphia; Joseph Wilcox and Francis Rawle did not lag
far behind them. The leading Lloydians in Chester and Bucks counties were less
prosperous, but could still be considered substantial farmers.

Thomas Lloyd's had been a revolt of the emerging Quaker Establishment — or at least a sizable portion of it. David Lloyd's was a revolt of
all those who resisted these uppermost Quakers: Anglicans, former Keithians, the Welsh, many of the younger Quakers, and farmers and city
artisans of all descriptions who had suffered from wartime economic
dislocation, resented proprietary taxes and quitrents, and suspected that
Penn had left them insecure in their property rights.

The pervasive feeling of alienation which distinguished David Lloyd's
followers is evident in James Logan's description of the "irretrievably
disaffected" Assembly of 1706.[32] In a letter to the proprietor, Logan
gave a group portrait of the incoming legislature: David Lloyd was "thy
Inveterate Revengefull Enemy"; Griffith Jones was "out of unity and
when he Traded, of a scandalous Character"; Joseph Wilcox and Francis
Rawle were leading Keithians; John Roberts and Robert Jones were "the
two most disaffected to thee that Cou'd be found among all the Welsh
being intirely D. Lloyd's Creatures"; Joshua Carpenter was "A Church-
man and thy sworne Enemy"; Samuel Levis had recently disavowed the
Society of Friends; John Swift, though formerly a Quaker, was now "an
obstinate Baptist"; William Paxton was "tolerably sensible but much
disaffected ever since 1701"; and Samuel Dark, though honest, was "much
disaffected since the reign of j[ohn] B[lackwell]." Others Logan described
as "simple honest weake men."

Though Logan could hardly be relied upon for total objectivity in
describing the Assembly, his analysis was accurate in important respects.
As in other years during this era, the House was largely composed of
Anglicans, former Keithians, other disillusioned Quakers, disaffected
Welshmen who represented a resentful ethnic minority, and Quakers
who were convinced by Lloyd's oratory and the depressing effects of the
war that Logan and those who inclined toward elitist politics in Pennsylvania served only the proprietor and themselves. Isaac Norris, whose
neutrality in the political warfare of the period made him a more reliable
commentator than either Lloyd or Logan, concluded that the political
distemper after 1701 was "fermented and Managed" by those who were
"Either professt or secritt enemies of the proprietor" and agreed with
Logan that "most of those Sticklers in assembly are Either Keithians or
such as Stand Loose from Friends." [33] Though he may not have known
it, Norris was describing a society in which social and religious leadership was no longer coincident with political leadership. In the 1680's and
1690's, the politics of discontent had involved staunch Quakers at the
top of the social ladder who sought to clog the machinery of proprietary

---

[32] Logan to Penn, ca. Oct. 1706 and June 12, 1706, *Penn-Logan Correspondence*, II, 119, 131.

[33] Norris to Joseph Pike, Feb. 18, 1709/10, Norris Letter Book (1709–1716),
132–133.

management so that they might themselves gain control of the "holy experiment." By contrast, the politics of discontent after Penn's departure in 1701 exemplified the reaction of various resentment-laden groups against all forms of authority, whether originating in proprietary policies, imperial regulation, or the attempt of Quaker worthies to monopolize political power.

One further characteristic distinguished the disaffected: on the whole they represented a second generation of Pennsylvanians. If one considers the ages of Logan and Lloyd, the two leading antagonists in the early eighteenth century, this fact would appear to be false: in 1705 Logan was thirty-one and Lloyd was forty-nine. But by and large the men who gathered in opposition to Lloyd were either Penn's personal friends or the last survivors of the first generation of Quakers who had joined the proprietor two decades before in the work of building a New Zion on the Delaware. Among them were Samuel Carpenter, John Goodson, Caleb Pusey, John Blunston, Samuel Finney, John Guest, Robert Assheton, Griffith Owen, Thomas Story, Joseph Growdon, William Mompesson, Nathaniel Newlin, Jeremiah Langhorne, and Edward Shippen. Many of them had followed Thomas Lloyd in the 1680's in attempting to limit Penn's power. But the Keithian schism and Penn's return in 1699 had reunited them with the proprietor. Clustered around Lloyd, by contrast, were many sons of First Purchasers — second generation Pennsylvanians such as John Roberts, Joseph Wilcox, Francis Rawle, Joseph Wood, William Hudson, and Robert Jones. Some of the old malcontents of the early days — William Biles and Griffith Jones, for example — also joined their ranks, as did Anglicans, Welshmen, and former Keithians of various ages. But it was the younger men to whom Logan referred when he wrote Penn of "that corrupted Generation here" which gave Lloyd such political strength. Similarly Logan complained that the "young forward novices and a few partisans of D. Lloyd" drowned out "the more sound and ancient Friends" at business meetings of the Society of Friends.[34]

Over this mixed lot of malcontents — a "Gallimaco fry," as Logan called it — David Lloyd held unchallengeable sway for almost a decade. He alone had the legal grasp, the legislative skill, the verbal capacity, and the fixity of purpose to lead a decade-long campaign against proprietary authority. Other men in Pennsylvania possessed legislative or legal skills during this period — Mompesson, Assheton, Guest, Logan, Carpenter, Pusey, Growdon, and others — but they rarely ran for seats in the Assembly. Unchallenged in the House, Lloyd found it easy to overawe those whose allegiance he did not already enjoy. The Welshman had a faculty of leading the assemblymen "out of their depth," Logan asserted in 1704; when this did not suffice, "his accomplices in the house drown

[34] Logan to Penn, Aug. 10, 1706, and June 28, 1707, *Penn-Logan Correspondence*, II, 147, 230.

all others with their noise." [35] Governors Evans and Gookin were both impressed with Lloyd's powers of persuasion. Honest men of good intentions were quickly won over by his arguments, wrote Evans, so that the whole Assembly vibrated with an "implacable & base malice" which really reflected the attitude only of Lloyd and his hard core of followers. The Assembly, wrote Gookin, was entirely governed by Lloyd — "one of those lawyers styled cunning," who did Penn all the harm in his power "under the pretence of reforming abuses." [36] The Council noted that many of the assemblymen could not fathom the complexities of Lloyd's bills for establishing courts, his arguments in behalf of legislative privileges, or his references to English law and parliamentary precedent. But Lloyd, using the difficult times to good advantage, convinced them of the necessity and legality of his program. The Lloydian leaders, concluded Isaac Norris, had "other Ends than what Is penetrated into by some pretty honest but not knowing men." [37]

In his more heated moments, Logan was wont to charge that Lloyd purposely induced "Knaves and fools" to run for the Assembly "that they might the easier be led by the Rattle of Rights and Privileges." But in calmer moods he recognized that most of the assemblymen were honest if plain men, who deferred to Lloyd's parliamentary knowledge, skill in drafting laws, and political fluency because they were untutored in the arts of government. It was the middle-class landowner or city artisan — hard hit by economic depression, apprehensive of the security of his land title, harassed by debts to city merchants, and disgusted by the impulsive actions of Governors Evans and Gookin — who was misled by the "artifices and smooth language" of David Lloyd.[38]

In expanding the politically relevant sector of society and in encouraging the common people to participate in government, Lloyd had introduced a style of politics in Pennsylvania which Penn and the original promoters of the colony had never anticipated. The proprietor had envisioned an annual gathering of the colony's most substantial men, who for eight or ten days would deliberate, much in the manner of the Quaker meeting, and pass such laws as were required for the common interest. Instead, government now seemed to consist of long verbal battles between the Assembly and the governor, extended legislative sessions which sometimes ran to seventy or eighty days a year, published remonstrances and accusatory letters to Penn, invective and recrimina-

[35] Logan to Penn, Oct. 3, and Oct. 27, 1704, *ibid.*, I, 323, 339.
[36] Evans to Gov. Charles Gookin and the Council, Apr. 12, 1709, *Minutes of Council*, II, 436; Gookin to Secretary of the Society for the Propagation of the Gospel, Aug. 27, 1709, Perry ed., *History of the Church in Pennsylvania*, 50–52.
[37] Council to Gookin, April 7, 1709, *Minutes of Council*, II, 439–441; Norris to Joseph Pike, Dec. 18, 1709/10, Norris Letter Book (1709–1716), 132–133.
[38] Logan to Penn, Nov. 22, 1704, *Pennsylvania Archives*, 2nd Ser., VII, 15; Logan to Penn, Oct. 3, 1704, *Penn-Logan Correspondence*, I, 323.

tion, and long harangues on the rights of the people and legislative bodies. Lloyd's ten-year outcry against proprietary prerogatives and upper-class privilege had infected the whole community, imparting a chronic feeling of resentment against authority of any kind.

Reminded repeatedly of their rights and encouraged to stand firm against unjust and oppressive external authorities, both proprietary and imperial, many colonists developed a deeply suspicious view of the world. Men who had been drawn together by ties of religion and background now looked warily at each other. The old sense of community had been lost. Penn could expect no support or affection from his colonists, Logan lamented, for "every man is for himself." [39] David Lloyd's supporters in the Assembly mirrored the changing popular attitude all too well. Determined to resist traditional sources of authority, they "filled a volume," as Robert Quary observed, with their remonstrances, resolutions, and votes on the rights and privileges of the people. "The infatuated people of this province," warned Logan, would scandalize the Society of Friends by their "ridiculous contending" for rights unknown to "others of the Queen's subjects." "In privileges," wrote Logan on another occasion, "they are for straining the strings till they break." [40]

Logan and Quary were not the only ones who thought the contagion of rights and privileges had become epidemic by dint of Lloyd's efforts. Governor Evans repeatedly complained that Lloyd had beguiled the Assembly into demanding privileges unheard of elsewhere in the English realm. "Through the Skill and artifice of Some Male Contents," wrote a Philadelphia Quaker, "Many narrow Tempers . . . have bin Greatly Enamored with the Name of priviledge and Affected with the Sound of Oppression." [41] When Evans denounced the "ill-grounded fury of a people drunk with wide notions of privileges," and warned that "the severest checks and reproofs from the authority att home" were necessary to tame the Pennsylvanians, he was only echoing sentiments frequently expressed by Penn over the years.[42]

To some extent, of course, the demand for wider privileges was grounded in the nature of colonial settlement. Penn had often admitted that the colonists rightly expected greater freedom in Pennsylvania than in England, that men did not uproot themselves, leave friends and relatives behind, and hazard a journey of 3,000 miles into a wilderness in

[39] Logan to Penn, May 28, 1706, *ibid.*, II, 129.

[40] Quary to the Board of Trade, June 28, 1707, *CSP 1706–08*, #1016; Logan to Penn, March 3, 1706/07, April 5, 1705, *Penn-Logan Correspondence*, II, 196, 11.

[41] Evans to the Board of Trade, Sept. 29, 1707, *CSP 1706–08*, #1126; *Minutes of Council*, II, 323–325; Samuel Preston to Penn, Nov. 28, 1710, Myers Collection, Box 2, #38, CCHS.

[42] Evans to the Board of Trade, Sept. 29, 1707, *CSP 1706–08*, #1126.

order to enjoy only the same privileges allowed in England.[43] But now, deftly led by David Lloyd and spurred on by the unfavorable conditions prevailing after Penn's return to England, the colonists had all but declared their independence from proprietary prerogatives and parliamentary restrictions. In their petitions and remonstrances, in their attempts to impeach proprietary officeholders, in their defiance of Penn's deputy governors, and in their refusal to pay taxes in support of either intercolonial defense or the proprietor in England, the colonists had reached a new proficiency in the science of antiauthoritarianism. Perhaps never in the first eighty years of colonial settlement in Pennsylvania was the spirit of defiance and alienation from established authority more visible and audible than during the decade of Lloyd's ascendancy. Even more certain is the fact that never in the colonial period were the uppermost members of society, to whom it was expected the generality would defer out of an inbred sense of the "natural degrees among men," less in control of the political process than in the years from 1701 to 1710. The balance of forces between the governor and Council on one hand and the Assembly on the other, between the proprietary and popular interest, was never more badly out of line. David Lloyd was no democrat in the modern sense of the word. Nevertheless his awakening of previously quiescent elements in Pennsylvania society, and his "Rattle of rights and Privileges" brought Pennsylvania as close to "middle-class democracy" in the first decade of the eighteenth century as it ever would be before the American Revolution.

[43] Penn to Charlewood Lawton, Aug. 18, 1701, Penn Letter Book (1699–1701), 111; also Penn to Robert Harley, 1701, Duke of Portland MSS, HMC, 15th Annual Report, Pt. IV, 31; and Penn to Board of Trade, April 22, 1700, Penn Letter Book (1699–1701), 24–29.

New York
Government and
Anglo-American
Politics

STANLEY N. KATZ

Federalism is not altogether a creation of the Philadelphia Convention of 1787, for colonial Americans were accustomed to being simultaneously subject to several different governments. Their primary frame of reference was indeed provincial, but the political histories of the colonies are generally written as though each colony had been self-contained. However, even though there was little in the way of English colonial policy beside the Navigation Acts, the colonists were conscious of participating in the larger but less structured arena of Anglo-American politics.

This brief analysis attempts to show how, for colonial politicians, the two principal systems were related in provincial New York. The royal governor was the obvious link between provincial and Anglo-American politics since he was an important officeholder in both systems. Groups of New Yorkers, both inside and outside the legislature, oriented themselves in relation to the governor's constitutional prerogatives and his informal power, especially patronage. Their behavior was also influenced by their knowledge that the course of provincial politics could be altered in a multitude of different ways by decisions taken, or not taken, by officials in London. If this argument is correct, the history of each colony must take into account its complex connections with English society and politics.

The haphazard recruitment of governors in England had an immediate effect on the practice of politics in America. As a New Yorker remarked during the Stamp Act crisis: "Government will never recover any Strength here, till it is in other hands, and in general will be loosing Ground as the Colonys increase, till other people are sent out to fill the most interesting Officers, than such as are fit for nothing at Home." [1] At the beginning of the eighteenth century, in the absence of formal party organization, the royal governor was the pivot of political life. Local politicians oriented their behavior in accordance with his preferences and foibles.

I

The governor of New York stood at the center of its governmental system, participating as he did in the executive, legislature, and judiciary.[2] His formal powers were considerable. As legislator he possessed an absolute veto over laws passed by the assembly, whose very existence depended upon his summoning it into being. As judge, he also exercised the power to pardon and chancery jurisdiction, and he acted with the council as the highest court of appeal in the province. As executive, he was the principal instrument for expression of the royal will and power in America and the military commander in chief. Cutting across his constitutional roles, moreover, were the powers of appointment and financial prerogatives which translated his legal authority into meaningful political terms. The governor appointed innumerable local officials as well as the principal governmental officers of Albany and New York City. He chose the members of the supreme court and exercised a *de facto* power to name the members of the provincial council, the naval officer, and the officers of the Independent Military Companies stationed at New York. This patronage was the governor's most important financial prerogative. At the same time, however, he shared with his council the power to grant the unsettled lands of the province, received numerous fees for performing governmental acts, and, especially in time of war, exercised considerable discretion in the distribution of military supply contracts.

The provincial council provided the institutional nucleus for the governor's local allies, both because of its political role and because seats at the council board were the most valuable sinecures in New York. The councillors were not, as the assembly pointed out early in the century, "another distinct state or Rank of People, in the Constitution . . .

---

[1] John Watts to Moses Franks, November 9, 1765 [New-York Historical Society, *Collections*], 1928, p. 399.
[2] For the powers of the governor, see Evarts B. Greene, *The Provincial Governor in the English Colonies of North America* (New York, 1898), passim, and Leonard W. Labaree, *Royal Government in America* (New York, 1958), pp. 92–133. For the structure of New York government generally, see Rex M. Naylor, "The Royal Prerogative in New York, 1691–1775," New York State Historical Association, *Quarterly Journal*, V (1924), pp. 221–255.

being all Commons." ³ They were appointed by the board of trade upon the recommendation of the governor as being "men of estate and ability, and not necessitous people or much in debt, . . . well affected to our government" and of "good life." ⁴ In short, the analogy to the house of lords will not do, for there was no necessary social distinction between councillors and assemblymen. The council was not, as ideally it should have been, a mobilization of the rich, wise, and just members of the community to help the governor to govern. Rather, the councillors were intended to be reliable supporters of the governor, and one of their functions was to bolster the administration against the encroachment of adverse political factions and the assembly.

The constitutional powers of the council were not extensive, but they were critical. It was an advisory board to the governor and the upper house of the colonial legislature. The advice and consent of the council were required for the calling, proroguing, and dissolving of assemblies, payment of public money, erection of courts of justice, granting of unsettled lands, and appointment to many offices.⁵ The council served with the governor as the highest court of appeal in New York, and it acted on its own as a legislature. It exercised little of the financial prerogative which was gradually bolstering the power of the assembly, but its functions were important enough to provide a rudimentary counterpoise to the increasingly aggressive lower house.⁶ Since councillors stood to gain from a strengthened royal prerogative, they were generally firm supporters of the administration and royal instructions even when they were not philosophical imperialists.

Only a few adherents of the governor could be provided with places on the New York council, however, because its membership fluctuated between seven and twelve. Even in this small body, a few places were taken up by professional officers of the crown (who could be counted on to support the governor anyway) and by English members who never came to America.⁷ Absenteeism and distance from New York City fre-

---

³ Quoted in H. Hale Bellot, "Council and Cabinet in the Mainland Colonies," Royal Historical Society, *Transactions*, 5th ser., V (1955), p. 168.

⁴ Charles W. Spencer, *Phases of Royal Government in New York, 1691–1719* (Columbus, O., 1905), p. 46; Charles Z. Lincoln, *The Constitutional History of New York* (Rochester, N.Y., 1906), I, 34.

⁵ Spencer, *Phases of Royal Government*, p. 52; Lincoln, *Constitutional History*, I, 443–447.

⁶ Spencer dates the transference of the dominant role from the council to the assembly during Hunter's administration (1709–1719), with "the imperious necessity for a working relation between the governor and the revenue-granting body." *Phases of Royal Government*, p. 96.

⁷ Examples of the former are Archibald Kennedy, George Clarke, and Richard Bradley. Examples of absentee membership are George Clarke, Jr., and Sir Peter Warren.

quently made it difficult even to achieve a quorum,[8] but the council nevertheless served as the symbolic rallying-point for the governor's faction. It was the patronage most ardently sought, and it played the double role of bringing men to the governor's side and serving as his foremost institutional ally.

The most rapidly changing institution in the New York political system was of course the assembly, whose power in regard to money bills afforded it a constantly expanding part in the control of public affairs.[9] This prerogative caused real concern among contemporary placeholders, such as Archibald Kennedy: "From an Assembly, if we value our Constitution, we have every Thing to dread; they have the purse on their Side, which greatly preponderates in the Balance, and will be doing . (I wish I could say fairly) what every other monied Person does; that is, turn it to their own particular Advantage." [10] Although the assembly steadily increased the sphere of its competency throughout the first half of the century, it did not achieve its majority until the onset of the Seven Year's War, when command of the disposition of men and money vastly strengthened its bargaining power, and when the internal affairs of the colonies finally captured the attention of English officials.

The assembly met for two brief sessions each year, spring and fall, to deal with appropriations and the minor legislation that constituted the bulk of its business. It was an intimate body, which gradually grew from a membership of twenty-two in 1698 to one of twenty-seven in 1769,[11] and thus it behaved quite differently from the large legislatures of the present day or even the English parliament of the eighteenth century. English constitutional experience was doubtless responsible for allowing the assembly to monopolize the power of the purse, which was the foundation of the emerging importance of the lower house. The assemblymen learned how to employ their financial prerogative against the executive by withholding passage of the appropriation bill in return for concessions from the governor. They also established the practice, even more damaging to royal government in America, of allotting salaries to individuals rather than to their offices, thereby acquiring "in

[8] James Alexander to Cadwallader Colden, April 14, 1729, NYHS *Colls.*, 1917, p. 278; Colden to Peter Collinson, January 10, 1761, *ibid.*, 1876, p. 56; John Watts to Monckton, October 11, 1764, *ibid.*, 1928, p. 298.

[9] For the traditional interpretation see Charles W. Spencer, "The Rise of the Assembly, 1691–1760," in Alexander C. Flick, ed., *History of the State of New York*, II (New York, 1933), pp. 151–198. A more sophisticated account of assembly development is Jack P. Greene, *The Quest for Power: The Lower Houses of Assembly in the Southern Royal Colonies, 1689–1776* (Chapel Hill, N.C., 1963).

[10] Archibald Kennedy, *Essay*, p. 17.

[11] For the assembly, see Spencer, *Phases of Royal Government*, pp. 70, 77; Lincoln, *Constitutional History*, I, 447–454.

effect the Nomination of all the Officers who are not immediately appointed by the King." [12]

New York governors were able to deal successfully with most legislatures for about forty years after the arrival of Governor Robert Hunter in 1710. The device they used was a system of barter pioneered by Hunter, whereby the assembly appropriated money for the governor's salary and crucial governmental and military expenditures in return for the governor's assent to acts that contravened his instructions, his acquiescence in appointments to provincial office, and, especially, his control of county patronage.[13] In this way the governor financed his operations and the leading assemblymen gained office, local power, and legislative freedom. From time to time, . . . governors were too loyal, proud, or inept to deal successfully with the increasing demands of the assembly, but until the onset of the great war for empire at mid-century the system generally worked to everyone's benefit.

Although the constitutional role and political effectiveness of the assembly were expanding throughout the eighteenth century, to speak of the "rise of the assembly" as the determining factor in colonial politics in this period it to distort its importance. Nor, except in the broadest sense, should the rise of the assembly in America be equated with the "winning of the initiative" by the house of commons, for the American development was inherently unselfconscious.[14] The New York assembly jealously guarded its privileges and strove to increase its power throughout the eighteenth century, but before mid-century its aggressiveness had no consistent ideological basis. Assemblymen sought to improve the position of the legislature for its own sake and for their own advantage, rather than in purposeful opposition to competitors within the colonial constitution. Indeed, the assembly's rivalry with the governor was frequently seen as a personal contest, an attitude derived largely from the primitive character of party organization. As Carl Becker noted: "there were no political parties; there were rather two centers of influence, and the only division that was permanent was that between the men who at any time were attached to the governor's interest and the men who made use of the assembly to thwart that interest." Furthermore, the governor's "interest" was inherently unstable: "there was no constant factor operating to hold any group of men to the governor's interest. Not being thoroughly identified with the colony, only while he was in a position to grant favors or insure the continuance of those already granted, could

---

[12] Colden to Secretary Popple, December 15, 1727, *New York Col. Docs.*, V, 844.

[13] Spencer, *Phases of Royal Government*, p. 155; Greene, Provincial *Governor*, p. 158.

[14] Wallace Notestein, *The Winning of the Initiative by the House of Commons* (London, 1924), Raleigh Lecture on History.

the governor hold individuals or factions, and the so-called popular party was likewise not a permanent group, but a residuum, as it were, composed at any time of those without the sphere of executive influence." [15] The political scene in eighteenth-century New York was therefore in a constant state of flux. True political parties had not yet emerged, and the stage was occupied by transitory factions formed about certain individuals, families, and issues, unable to develop the stable organizational mechanisms which would have rendered them self-perpetuating.

It is important at this point to remember that, although a considerable percentage of the adult male population of New York voted, a much smaller group participated in politics and exercised public office. This political elite was drawn from among the merchants and lawyers of New York City and Albany and the principal landholders of the Hudson Valley. It did not constitute an aristocracy, as Becker thought,[16] for access to the group was easily obtained, and newcomers to America and obscure New Yorkers freely participated in it. A few socially and economically prominent families remained dominant, however, families whose names still sound familiar — the Beekmans, DeLanceys, Livingstons, Morrises, Philipses, Schuylers, Van Rensselaers, and Van Cortlandts. Members of such families generally operated in unison, since the rewards of politics were considered familial rather than personal property. Likewise, intermarriage among the leading families created the binding ties of many political factions. The group was also united by economic interests, particularly those which arose from the fur trade, Hudson River Valley agriculture, and the mercantile life of New York City.

The power of great families was thus noticeable within the provincial ruling group, but by 1730 the bonds of family alliance which had characterized Leislerian New York were giving way to a more flexible system in which "interest often connects people who are entire strangers and it sometimes separates those who have the strongest natural connections." [17] The political elite thereafter played a multiple role. According to Becker: "The leaders within this class stood, as it were, between the governor and the assembly, using either as occasion demanded. When the governor was the real center of influence, with lands to grant or sinecures to offer, ambitious men with favors to ask turned to him and supported him. But with titles secure and position assured, their dependence upon the governor

[15] Carl L. Becker, *The History of Political Parties in the Province of New York* (Madison, Wis., 1960), pp. 7–8.

[16] *Ibid.*, pp. 8–10, 12–14.

[17] William Alexander to Robert Livingston, Jr. [?], March 1, 1756, in Livingston Rutherfurd, *Family Record and Events . . .* (New York, 1894), pp. 57–58. See also, Beverly McAnear, "Politics in Provincial New York, 1689–1761" (unpub. Ph.D. diss., Stanford, 1935), 954–955; Milton M. Klein, "Democracy and Politics in Colonial New York," *New York History*, XL (1959), 228.

decreased; and in the later period the leaders of the aristocracy in increasing numbers identified themselves with the assembly."[18] The leading politicians seldom acted together, however. Those New Yorkers favored by the governor's policies and patronage generally lent him their support, while the "outs" formed cliques against him, and attempted to use the assembly as a counterpoise to executive power. Neither group was stable, for men ceased to follow the governor when he treated them less well than they expected, and his opponents easily crossed into his camp after a bit of wooing. During any one administration, however, there was likely to be a fairly continuous division between the "outs" and the "ins," although of course there were frequently several different factions arrayed in opposition to the governor.

The assembly was composed of representatives from the several counties, New York City, Albany, Schenectady, a few smaller towns, and several of the great manors, such as Rensselaerswyck, Cortlandt Manor, and Livingston Manor. The leading families of the colony superintended the selection of candidates to stand for the legislature,[19] took the lead in securing election of these candidates, and controlled the assembly itself by means of their own votes and their influence over other representatives. To Cadwallader Colden's somewhat jaundiced eye, representation was scattered among "the owners of these extravagant Grants, the Merchants of New York, the principal of them strongly connected with the Owners of these great Tracts, by family Interest, and of Common Farmers, which last are Men easily deluded and led always with popular Arguments of Liberty and Privileges."[20] The merchants and landowners were indeed an interconnecting elite which had little difficulty in overcoming the numerical superiority of the "common farmers."[21] They acted, however, in a manner which does not fully accord either with Carl Becker's aristocratic interpretation of New York politics or with Milton Klein's democratic reading — opposing views which nevertheless agree that the lower house was the breeding ground of the American democratic tradition.[22]

[18] Becker, *Political Parties*, pp. 11–12.

[19] Carl L. Becker, "Nominations in Colonial New York," *American Historical Review*, VI (1900–1901), p. 265.

[20] Colden to Board of Trade, September 20, 1764, NYHS, *Colls.*, 1876, p. 363. See also Colden to Dr. John Mitchell, July 6, 1749, *ibid.*, 1935, p. 33.

[21] Charles W. Spencer, "Sectional Aspects of New York Provincial Politics," *Political Science Quarterly*, XXX (1915), pp. 423, 424.

[22] Carl L. Becker, "Growth of Revolutionary Parties and Methods in New York, 1765–1774," *American Historical Review*, VII (1901–1902), p. 57; Becker, *Political Parties*, pp. 5–22; Klein, "Democracy and Politics," pp. 223–240. George Chalmers was probably the first historian to find that the government of New York was "democratical," in 1714. Quoted in Greene, *Provincial Governor*, p. 194. For a general discussion of "democracy" in colonial America, see J. R. Pole, "Historians and the Problem of Early American Democracy," *American Historical Review*, LXVII (1962), pp. 626–646.

On the one hand, Becker exaggerates the degree to which an upper "social class" directly controlled New York politics until it was supplanted by popular masses using the techniques of modern political democracy. Klein, however, while correctly emphasizing the breadth of the franchise in colonial New York, overestimates the degree to which control of political activity was popularly based.

Klein admits that "the local aristocracy did occupy a commanding position in the colony's politics, and they continued to do so after independence," and he offers the explanation that: "Undoubtedly the landed aristocrats exercised great influence in the colony's politics, but their influence is better ascribed to voter illiteracy and indifference than to open balloting or the landlord-tenant relationship." [23] "Illiteracy" unquestionably played a part in restricting the popular basis of politics, but "indifference" was surely the prevailing temper. Contemporaries also caught the mood, as William Smith did when he remarked "that torpor which generally prevails when [the multitude] are uninfluenced by the arts and intrigues of the restless and designing sons of ambition." [24] "Deference" is probably an even better term than "indifference" to describe the behavior of an electorate which uncomplainingly forfeited its prerogatives of self-government to a few of its members.[25]

In the first part of the eigtheeenth century, New York political life was, as we have noted, more often based upon economic and family connections and interests than ideological concerns. This was also the case in mid-century England, where, to paraphrase the contemporary writer John Douglas, the infrequent occasions when the king's government could be overturned occurred when political opposition arose out of "an honest disapprobation of the public plan of government." [26] Ordinarily, however, opposition failed because the electorate recognized that it sprang from the disappointed ambitions of politicians. Voters therefore seldom believed that policy issues, rather than internecine struggles for power, were at stake. The public, as represented by a narrow electorate, was cynical and uninterested in the conduct of public affairs. The comparison between English and American politics in this regard is not exact, however, for on this side of the Atlantic, from the end of the seventeenth century the public accepted the reality and pertinence of political conflict. The American electorate was deferential and naïve rather than deferential and cynical.

For Americans, politics were primarily the concern of politicians, al-

---

[23] Klein, "Democracy and Politics," pp. 240, 232.
[24] Smith, *History*, II, 69.
[25] See Pole, "Early American Democracy," pp. 628–629, 642.
[26] John Douglas, *Seasonable Hints from an Honest Man* (1761), p. 7, quoted in Williams, *Eighteenth-Century Constitution*, p. 88. For English attitudes similar to those of America see Foord, *His Majesty's Opposition*, p. 238.

though the electorate occasionally took the rhetoric of public life at face value and reacted as though ideological issues were at stake. Essentially petty and self-interested opposition to governors by those members of the political elite who were out of favor therefore tended to take on a popular aspect, using the "popular Arguments of Liberty and Privilege." [27] The outs argued for access to power in the name of the people, and hence historians have traditionally referred to the conflict of the "court" party and the "popular" party. Once in office, however, the so-called popular leaders behaved no differently than had their erstwhile opponents, many of whom were now their allies. [28]

In New York, prior to the French and Indian War, local issues and the clash of personalities set the tone of public life. On a few occasions, such as in the Cosby administration, the public was genuinely aroused by broader issues and politicians took strong stands on principle. Even at these times, however, the underlying divisions seem to have been ephemeral, personal, and narrowly economic. Ideological Morrisites of the early 1730's, for instance, must have been horrified by the "courtly" conduct of their former leader when he became governor of New Jersey in 1738.

The keynote of politics in this period was flexibility. Governors came and went, and so did councillors. The assembly, although jealous of its prerogatives, responded freely to its fluctuating leadership. Power circulated widely among the ruling group. In many ways, then, New York politics mirrored the factionalism and confusion of early Georgian England. And to some extent, of course, New York responded directly to the English situation.

II

The Anglo-American nature of colonial politics has generally been neglected by historians, [29] although it is only from an Atlantic perspective that the intricacies of the characteristic political factionalism of the early years of the eighteenth century can clearly be seen. Royal governors and

[27] The phrase is Colden's: see above, n. 20. The best example of this phenomenon in early New York history is the public uproar during the Zenger trial of 1735. See Stanley N. Katz, ed., A Brief Narrative of the Case and Trial of John Peter Zenger (Cambridge, Mass., 1963), pp. 5–17.

[28] Note the behavior, to name the two most striking examples, of Lewis Morris as governor of New Jersey, and James DeLancey as lieutenant-governor of New York.

[29] More recently a broader approach has been taken by a number of colonial historians: Bernard Bailyn, The New England Merchants in the Seventeenth Century (Cambridge, Mass., 1955); Lawrence H. Leder, Robert Livingston, 1654–1728, and the Politics of Colonial New York (Chapel Hill, N.C., 1961); John A. Schutz, William Shirley: King's Governor of Massachusetts (Chapel Hill, N.C., 1961). "Anglo-American politics, 1675–1765" was the subject of the October 1966 session of the Conference on Early American History, the outgrowth of which is [Alison Gilbert Olson and Richard Maxwell Brown, Anglo-American Political Relations, 1675–1775 (New Brunswick, N.J., 1970)].

colonial politicians contended for the tangible rewards of place and power on this continent, but although the stakes of the game were in America, many of the best hands were not. Access to the principal jobs, favors, and policies sought by New York politicians more often than not lay through Whitehall rather than City Hall or Fort George. The powers of appointment and decision-making that were vested in the officers of state and imperial officials in England made a direct impact upon the conduct of politics in America.

Charles Andrews has observed that "the tendency to center colonial patronage in England" was a fundamental factor in "the growing centralization of the entire British system as we advance toward the climax of the Revolution." [30] Certainly this is so, although the process of centralization in itself was not as important as the growing necessity, after about 1750, to make appointments serve the needs of newly-formulated imperial policy. During the first half of the century, there were many sources of colonial patronage in England and there were no clearly formulated standards for its use, so that American posts could be distributed according to the pragmatic and self-interested canons of eighteenth-century English political life. Thus, in order to gain or retain their offices, Americans were obliged to enter into the politics of the mother country.

London was also the source of judicial, administrative, financial, military, and, occasionally, legislative activity that affected colonial life. The privy council was a court of last resort for major legal disputes as well as for questions of colonial policy. It resolved conflicts over land grants, as in the case of the Oblong, and displacements from office, as when Lewis Morris was replaced as chief justice, and disallowed colonial statutes.[31] The legal officers of the crown made decisions that changed the course of colonial politics, such as the 1735 opinion that the governor should not take part in the activities of the legislative council. The treasury, customs commissioners, admiralty, and other agencies were responsible for hundreds of decisions affecting New York: administering the navigation system, assigning military and civil officers, reimbursing Americans for imperial expenses, bringing business into the New World. Parliament was less likely to be involved with colonial administration prior to the Seven Years' War, but it was a factor in questions of trade and finance.[32]

For Englishmen holding colonial posts and ambitious colonists alike, then, the challenge of Anglo-American politics was to have "a good stake in the Hedge" [33] — to establish an influential English connection. Colo-

---

[30] Andrews, *Colonial Period*, IV, 187.

[31] . . . For the comparative rarity of disallowance of statutes see Russell, *Review . . . in Council*, p. 57n2.

[32] On the treasury, see Clark, *Rise of the British Treasury*; on the customs, see Thomas C. Barrow, *Trade & Empire: The British Customs in Colonial America, 1660–1775* (Cambridge, Mass., 1967).

[33] Quoted in Andrews, *Colonial Period*, IV, 309.

nials and English placemen sought out every avenue of approach to the great officers of state, members of the administrative boards and of parliament, as well as leaders of the military and the church. They appealed to formal organizations, such as the Protestant Dissenting Deputies, and informal groups, such as the American merchants resident in London.[34] They sought help in moments of crisis, but even more urgently, they tried to establish English connections that would spring to action of their own accord when they could be of service. For English placemen, who came to office through the interest of their friends and relatives, connections were already in existence and needed only to be tended and strengthened. For many Americans, however, especially when they were acting in opposition to such placemen, the problem was to establish contacts in an essentially alien ground, which, as a practitioner of the art complained, entailed "a pretty deal of pains." [35]

It was a complex, unsystematic business, which, in the first part of the century, was carried on largely without benefit of a formal colonial agency. New York employed no agent from 1730 to 1748, but even if it had he would not have solved the problem for most New Yorkers. The agent was, among other things, ill-paid and subject to the vicissitudes of assembly politics. Often he did act informally in behalf of an individual or faction, as George Bampfield did for the Livingstons and Robert Charles for James DeLancey, but since he was also ostensibly the agent of the whole colony (or, more accurately, the assembly) he had to take care whose personal interests he represented. There were, however, more compelling reasons for looking beyond the agent for a means of establishing a continuing personal contact in England. The most important was that it was difficult to find competent agents who were familiar enough with New York and loyal enough to their employers to be trusted with such weighty business. Moreover, the complexities of British politics were such that the formal representations to which an agent was likely to restrict himself were of little specific use to individual New Yorkers. In the words of Lewis Morris, "As to agents, unless the Court is dispos'd to do us service, no agent can do us much." [36]

[34] See, for instance, N. C. Hunt, *Two Early Political Associations: The Quakers and the Dissenting Deputies in the Age of Sir Robert Walpole* (Oxford, 1961); Bernard L. Manning, *The Protestant Dissenting Deputies*, ed. Ormerod Greenwood (Cambridge, Eng., 1952); Maurice W. Armstrong, "The Dissenting Deputies and the American Colonies," *Church History*, XXIX (1960), p. 316n6.

[35] Carl R. Woodward, *Ploughs and Politicks: Charles Read of New Jersey and His Notes on Agriculture, 1715–1774* (New Brunswick, N.J., 1941), p. 97.

[36] Lewis Morris to Mrs. Norris, May 14, 1742, *Governor Lewis Morris Papers*, p. 145. For the history of the New York agency, see Edward P. Lilly, *The Colonial Agents of New York and New Jersey* (Washington, 1936). For Morris' survey of potential New York agents, see his letter to James Alexander, February 25, 1736, Rutherfurd Collection, II, 177, NYHS.

Imperial placemen and New York politicians, faced with the need to protect or improve their positions in England, had therefore to establish personal channels of communication. Their efforts were of three (frequently concurrent) types: personal missions, the employment of private agents, and the mobilization of English friends and relatives in their behalf.

In moments of political crisis, the first instinct of English officials and American politicians who were losing their grasp in New York was to set off for London. There, they felt, it was possible to present their case more successfully than any English representative could. One of the first personal trips to England for political purposes was made by Lewis Morris in 1702 in order to wrest the government of New Jersey from the proprietors, although Robert Livingston had gone home as early as 1695 to claim reimbursement for his expenses in provisioning British troops during King William's War. Governor Hunter determined to return to England in 1719 when he received word of an organized attempt to secure disallowance of the most recent New York money bill. He was eager "that nothing may be resolved till I am brought Face to Face to answer these or any other men, as to what I Have done in my station," for he felt that only he could conduct an adequate defense: "I know not the objections but I forsee an inevitable necessity of my coming home for that very purpose for it is impossible to answer as one should at this distance or to instruct another." [37] When in 1725 Governor Burnet unwisely and unsuccessfully attempted to remove Stephen DeLancey from the political scene by questioning the validity of his citizenship, word traveled across the province that DeLancey was "Resolved to go for England if the Chief Justice gives his opinion that he is an alien." [38]

The best known of eighteenth-century New York political missions was of course that made by Lewis and Robert Hunter Morris in 1735, and recorded by the younger Morris in his diary,[39] but for a number of reasons it was also the last of its kind. A pamphleteer of 1714 had long before pointed out the inconvenience and inefficiency of such trips, noting "the great charge, vexation, and loss of time and damage to their Estates [of those] who are forced to take long and dangerous voyages." Such

[37] Robert Hunter to A. Philipse, August 15, 1718, *New York Col. Docs.*, V, 516.

[38] Philip Livingston to Robert Livingston, September 23, 1725, Livingston-Redmond Papers, Franklin Delano Roosevelt Library, Hyde Park, N.Y.; see also, William L. Sachse, *The Colonial American in Britain* (Madison, Wis., 1956), pp. 93–115, 132–153. For a typical letter of advice to an American in London, see [Lt. John Ormsby Donnellan,] "Advice to a Stranger in London, 1763," *Pennsylvania Magazine of History and Biography*, LXXIII (1949), 85–87.

[39] Beverly McAnear, ed., "R. H. Morris: An American in London, 1735–1736," *Pennsylvania Magazine of History and Biography*, LXIV (1940), pp. 164–217, 356–406. (Hereafter, R. H. Morris, "Diary.")

voyages were seldom successful: "Thus after two or three, sometimes four or five Years excessive charge and trouble, and severall long voyages from the other part of the World, the unhappy American Subjects are forced to bear their oppression." [40] The irrascible Lewis Morris failed in London and became extremely disgruntled when he considered the time, money, and effort he had expended there.[41] Henceforth, New Yorkers turned to methods of communication with England that did not require them to leave their local interests unprotected.

One alternative to private missions to England was the employment of private agents – personal representatives either sent from America or already resident in England. This technique was, of course, employed throughout the century, but it took on an added importance as the stakes of colonial politics grew higher with the onset of the imperial crisis. William Shirley, the experienced governor of Massachusetts, Robert Hunter Morris, veteran of his father's 1735 adventure and the ex-soldier John Catherwood, for example, were among other things the personal representatives of Governor Clinton when he was hard-pressed by the strong DeLancey connection at mid-century. Costs of transportation and maintenance in England were prohibitive, however, and colonials could afford representations in London only to a limited extent. It was also generally true that private agents, particularly Americans, stood outside the channels of English political power, and so were less useful as a "stake in the Hedge" than a continuing English connection.

Family connections were the strongest bonds to England a New Yorker could have, since they did not depend upon considerations of business or friendship that required reciprocity. As a leading New York politician put it in a letter to the English cousin who was his firmest supporter, "You will always find in me a gratefull mind, the only return can be made you from this quarter of the world." [42] It might, for instance, be argued that the DeLancey family's domination of New York politics at mid-century was a function of the strength of their family connection in England and a reflection of the failure of the Livingstons to establish such a relationship.[43] During the revolutionary crisis, conversely, when the English po-

[40] [Anon.,] *Of the American Plantations* (1714), in *Colonial Records of North Carolina*, II, 159.

[41] R. H. Morris, "Diary," pp. 213–214, 403.

[42] James DeLancey to John Heathcote, June 17, 1736, 1 ANC XI/B/5 "o," Lincolnshire Archives Committee, Lincoln, Eng.

[43] Controversy over the character of the DeLancey-Livingston rivalry has taken a new lease on life. See Roger Champagne, "Family Politics versus Constitutional Principles: The New York Assembly Elections of 1768 and 1769," *William and Mary Quarterly*, 3rd ser., XX (1963), pp. 57–79; Lawrence H. Leder, "The New York Elections of 1769: An Assault on Privilege," *Mississippi Valley Historical Review*, XLIX (1962–1963), pp. 675–682; Bernard Friedman, "The New York Assembly Elections of 1768 and 1769: The Disruption of Family Politics,"

litical situation became constricted by the requirements of imperial policy and the focus of American politics narrowed to this side of the Atlantic, the Livingstons had their day. Failing family, however, most New Yorkers nurtured any and all contacts they could muster. Cadwallader Colden, for instance, appealed to his old Scottish patron, the Marquis of Lothian, as well as his scientific correspondent, Peter Collinson.[44] The great task was simply to mobilize anyone with the slightest political influence in England.

The American governors generally had the strongest political interests in England, since it was through these connections that they were appointed. The same was true of many of the principal imperial placemen. If their influence in London had been sufficient to put them in office, it often remained strong enough to keep them there. One need only think of Clinton's relationship with Newcastle, Cosby's with Halifax and Newcastle, or George Clarke's with Blathwayt and Horatio Walpole to understand how hard it was for an opposition to displace them. American politicians had frequently to start from scratch in forming a connection, but it is characteristic of English politics at this time that there was sufficient mobility for even a rank outsider to work his way into the system.

The seeming triviality of the contest for English influence should not, however, obscure the importance of the long-range aims of Anglo-American politics. In contending for immediate objectives such as jobs, political favors, and changes of policy, colonists and imperial officials were really disputing the control of political power in New York. From a broader point of view, Anglo-American politics had two interconnected aspects: the demonstration of American power to impress imperial officials in England, and the display of English influence in order to maintain American political power.

Everyone active in colonial public life was continually aware of the scrutiny of English officials. Imperial administrators were seldom insistent upon the precise execution of detailed policies, but for a variety of reasons they were strongly committed to the maintenance of stability in colonial politics. Thus it was vital that the governor, when confronted with a vigorous colonial opposition, should convince his superiors at home that

---

New York History, XLVI (1965), pp. 3–24; Patricia U. Bonomi, "Political Patterns in Colonial New York City: The General Assembly Election of 1768," Political Science Quarterly, LXXXI (1966), pp. 432–447. For evidence that the Livingstons were not entirely insensitive to the need for English representation, see Robert Charles to Philip Livingston, August 31, 1742, Rutherfurd Collection, II, 207, NYHS.

[44] Lewis Morris to Marquis of Lothian, March 26, 1735, NYHS, Colls., 1918, pp. 126–127; Collinson to Colden, March 27, 1747, ibid., 1919, p. 369, and various other letters in NYHS Colden Papers and the British Museum Collinson Papers.

he was in control of the situation in America. When Lewis Morris was governor in New Jersey, for instance, his daughter warned him from England to maintain an orderly administration at all costs since, if he should "have any difference [he] would find no redress from hence, since they would leave [him] to fight it out" alone in New Jersey.[45] The governor had to restrain the assertive tendencies of the local assembly and use his domination of the council to demonstrate that he had local support. At the same time, of course, the opposition attempted to show the governor's incompetence to control the government of the colony in the hope that the English authorities would lose confidence in him and that he would be replaced, allowing a reallocation of offices and a redistribution of power.

Even more important, however, evidence of political influence in England was the prerequisite for political mastery in America, whether for the administration or for its opponents. For the governor and his adherents, the ins of colonial politics, signs of favor with the imperial administration provided a hedge against local political disaffection. So long as the governor's appointees and policies were confirmed in England, New Yorkers looked to him for places and favors. The New York governors were all intensely aware of this phenomenon, and George Clinton was virtually paranoid on the subject. As Cadwallader Colden explained the situation, Clinton decided against returning to England in 1749 because "The Faction had endeavour'd to persuade the people that the Governors conduct was so blamed that his friends could not support him and that the Chief Justice [James DeLancey] has a better Interest at Court than the Govr and had he gon people would have been confirm'd in this opinion . . . which was exceedingly strengthen'd by the Govrs not having been able to procure any thing directly from the ministry in vindication of his conduct."[46] New Yorkers were incredibly sensitive to the winds of political favor in England, and when the administration showed signs of having weaker English influence than its challengers (as was the case with Clinton and DeLancey in 1746), it was extremely difficult for the governor to retain control of the political situation in New York. Local families active in politics began to search out alternative sources of favor, the assembly increased its recalcitrance, and even the council was likely to waver. Thus the continuing contest for English attention was not simply a series of random private transactions, but a constant test of strength for the indications of imperial favor which were ultimately the determinants of political power in the royal colonies of America.

[45] Euphemia Norris to Lewis Morris, June 15, 1742, Morris Family Papers, R.U.L.
[46] Colden to John Catherwood, November 21, 1749, NYHS, *Colls.*, 1920, p. 159. See also, Clinton to R. H. Morris, November 28, 1751, R. H. Morris Papers, I, 33, New Jersey Historical Society, Newark, N.J.

New York politics were thus factional and Anglo-American. Within the colony, they were oriented around the governor, for it was to his instructions, patronage, and attitudes that local politicians and the assembly responded. Neither continuing lines of party organization nor consistent ideological divisions had yet emerged. At the same time, there was a direct involvement with English politics. Here again the governor provided the focal point, since he was the direct link not only to the prerogative of the crown but also to the king's ministers. His supporters sought to bolster his standing while those New Yorkers outside of his circle beseeched Whitehall to turn him out. Moreover, New Yorkers engaged in a perpetual competition for favor in London. Thus the interaction of two polycentric systems of politics intensified and complicated the characteristic public life of the royal colonies in America. The political history of New York in the early eighteenth century . . . is one of governors and factions contending for power in an Anglo-American context.

Jonathan Edwards and the Great Awakening

PERRY MILLER

Perry Miller believes that "social history" cannot adequately explain the Great Awakening of 1740. He notes that the "inexplicable outburst of neurotic energies" which marked the Awakening produced little other than increased religious controversy, and he rejects attempts to explain the event as the outgrowth of economic or social conflict.

Although Miller admits that the revival can be viewed as an aspect of eighteenth-century sociological change in western Europe, he thinks that it is more accurately interpreted as a crisis in the history of American culture. The Great Awakening was the logical outcome of the long series of Puritan attempts to increase the membership and restore the vitality of the New England churches. More specifically, it was the product of religious practice in the Connecticut Valley, where Solomon Stoddard and his grandson Jonathan Edwards laid particular stress upon the possibility of salvation for all the members of the community. If the doors of the church could be opened to all those who would come in, why should the unconverted not be excited into demanding admission?

Miller's interpretation thus makes the church the center of what was admittedly, at least on the surface, a religious revival. He argues that eighteenth-century Americans, as they revealed themselves in a time of crisis, were still essentially medieval and religious people, and that they chose a democratic theological solution to their social problems, rejecting at the same time the elitist philosophies of Europe and Boston. Miller's argument has recently been elaborated by Alan Heimert in Religion and the American Mind from the Great Awakening to the Revolution (*Cambridge, Mass., 1966*).

Miller mentions the Awakening in Pennsylvania, Virginia, and the Carolinas, but his interpretation is clearly based upon the history of New England. Can he really explain the revivals south of Connecticut using this evidence?

I

Although in the year 1740 some fairly flagrant scenes of emotional religion were being enacted in Boston, it was mainly in the Connecticut Valley that the frenzy raged and whence it spread like a pestilence to the civilized East. The Harvard faculty of that time would indeed have considered the Great Awakening a "crisis," because to them it threatened everything they meant by culture or religion or just common decency. It was a horrible business that should be suppressed and altogether forgotten. Certainly they would not have approved its being dignified as a starting point in a series of great American crises.

As far as they could see, it was nothing but an orgy of the emotions. They called it — in the lexicon of the Harvard faculty this word conveyed the utmost contempt — "enthusiasm." It was not a religious persuasion: it was an excitement of overstimulated passions that understandably slopped over into activities other than the ecclesiastical and increased the number of bastards in the Valley, where already there were too many. And above all, in the Valley lived their archenemy, the deliberate instigator of this crime, who not only fomented the frenzy but was so lost to shame that he brazenly defended it as a positive advance in American culture. To add insult to injury, he justified the Awakening by employing a science and a psychological conception with which nothing they had learned at Harvard had prepared them to cope.

It was certainly a weird performance. Edwards delivered his revival sermons – for example the goriest, the one at Enfield that goes by the title "Sinners in the Hands of an Angry God" and is all that most people nowadays associate with his name – to small audiences in country churches. In these rude structures (few towns had yet prospered enough to afford the Georgian churches of the later eighteenth century which are now the charm of the landscape) the people yelled and shrieked, they rolled in the aisles, they crowded up to the pulpit and begged him to stop, they cried for mercy. One who heard him described his method of preaching: he looked all the time at the bell rope (hanging down from the roof at the other end of the church) as though he would look it in two; he did not stoop to regard the screaming mass, much less to console them.

Of course, in a short time the opinion of the Harvard faculty appeared to be vindicated. In 1740 Edwards had writhing in the churches not only his own people but every congregation he spoke to, and he dominated the entire region. Ten years later he was exiled, thrown out of his church and town after a vicious squabble (the fight against him being instigated by certain of the first citizens, some of them his cousins, who by adroit propaganda mobilized "the people" against him), and no pulpit in New England would invite this terrifying figure. He had no choice but to escape to the frontier, as did so many misfits in American history. He went to Stockbridge, where he eked out his last years as a missionary to a lot of moth-eaten Indians. Because of the works he produced under these – shall we call them untoward? – circumstances, and because he was still the acknowledged leader of the revival movement, he was invited in 1758 to become president of the College of New Jersey (the present-day Princeton), but he died a few weeks after his inauguration, so that his life really belongs to the Connecticut Valley.

One may well ask what makes such a chronicle of frenzy and defeat a "crises" in American history. From the point of view of the social historian and still more from that of the sociologist it was a phenomenon of mass behavior, of which poor Mr. Edwards was the deluded victim. No sociologically trained historian will for a moment accept it on Edwards' terms – which were, simply, that it was an outpouring of the Spirit of God upon the land. And so why should we, today, mark it as a turning point in our history, especially since thereafter religious revivals became a part of the American social pattern, while our intellectual life developed, on the whole, apart from these vulgar eruptions? The answer is that this first occurrence did actually involve all the interests of the community, and the definitions that arose out of it were profoundly decisive and meaningful. In that perspective Jonathan Edwards, being the most acute definer of the terms on which the revival was conducted and the issues on which it went astray, should be regarded – even by the social historian – as a formulator of propositions that the American society, having been shaken by this experience, was henceforth consciously to observe.

There is not space enough here to survey the Awakening through the vast reaches of the South and the Middle Colonies, nor even to list the intricate consequences for the social ordering of New England. The splintering of the churches and the increase of sectarianism suggest one way in which Americans "responded" to this crisis, and the impulse it gave to education, most notably in the founding of Princeton, is another. Such discussions, however valuable, are external and statistical. We come to a deeper understanding of what this crisis meant by examining more closely a revelation or two from the most self-conscious – not to say the most literate – theorist of the Awakening.

The theme I would here isolate is one with which Edwards dealt only by indirection. He was skilled in the art of presenting ideas not so much by expounding as by vivifying them, and he achieved his ends not only by explicit statement but more often by a subtle shift in emphasis. In this case, it is entirely a matter of divining nuances. Nevertheless, the issue was present throughout the Awakening and, after the temporary manifestations had abated, on this proposition a revolution was found to have been wrought that is one of the enduring responses of the American mind to crisis.

I mean specifically what it did to the conception of the relation of the ruler – political or ecclesiastical – to the body politic. However, before we can pin down this somewhat illusive development, we are confronted with the problem of whether the Great Awakening is properly to be viewed as a peculiarly American phenomenon at all. It would be possible to write about it – as has been done – as merely one variant of a universal occurrence in Western culture. Between about 1730 and 1760 practically all of Western Europe was swept by some kind of religious emotionalism. It was present in Germany, Holland, Switzerland, and France, and in Catholic circles there was an analogous movement that can be interpreted as an outcropping of the same thing: this the textbooks call "Quietism." And most dramatically, it was present in England with the Wesleys, Whitefield, and Methodism.

Once this international viewpoint is assumed, the American outburst becomes merely one among many – a colonial one at that – and we hesitate to speak about it as a crisis in a history specifically American. What was at work throughout the Western world is fairly obvious: the upper or the educated classes were tired of the religious squabbling of the seventeenth century, and turned to the more pleasing and not at all contentious generalities of eighteenth-century rationalism; the spiritual hungers of the lower classes or of what, for shorthand purposes, we may call "ordinary" folk were not satisfied by Newtonian demonstrations that design in the universe proved the existence of God. Their aspirations finally found vent in the revivals, and in each country we may date the end of a Calvinist or scholastic or, in short, a theological era by the appearance of these movements, and thereupon mark what is by now called the era of Pietism or Evangelicalism.

In this frame of reference, the Great Awakening was only incidentally American. It is merely necessary to translate the European language into the local terminology to have an adequate account. In this phraseology, the Great Awakening in New England was an uprising of the common people who declared that what Harvard and Yale graduates were teaching was too academic. This sort of rebellion has subsequently proved so continuous that one can hardly speak of it as a crisis. It is rather a chronic state of affairs. And in this view of it, the uprising of 1740 belongs to the international history of the eighteenth century rather than to any account of forces at work only on this continent.

Told in this way, the story will be perfectly true. Because we talk so much today of the unity of Western European culture, maybe we ought to tell it in these terms, and then stop. But on the other hand there is a curiously double aspect to the business. If we forget about Germany and Holland and even England — if we examine in detail the local history of Virginia, Pennsylvania, and New England — we will find that a coherent narrative can be constructed out of the cultural developments in each particular area. This Awakening can be seen as the culmination of factors long at work in each society, and as constituting, in that sense, a veritable crisis in the indigenous civilization.

II

The church polity established in New England was what today we call congregational. This meant, to put it crudely, that a church was conceived as being composed of people who could certify before other people that they had a religious experience, that they were qualified to become what the founders called "visible saints." The founders were never so foolish as to suppose that everybody who pretended to be a saint *was a* saint, but they believed that a rough approximation of the membership to the covenant of grace could be worked out. A church was composed of the congregation, but these were only the professing Christians. The rest of the community were to be rigorously excluded; the civil magistrate would, of course, compel them to come to the church and listen to the sermon, collect from them a tax to support the preacher, but they could not be actual members. Those who qualified were supposed to have had something happen to them that made them capable — as the reprobate was not — of swearing to the covenant of the church. They were able, as the others were not, *physically* to perform the act.

The basic contention of the founders was that a church is based upon the covenant. Isolated individuals might be Christians in their heart of hearts, but a corporate body could not come into being unless there was this preliminary clasping of hands, this taking of the official oath in the open and before all the community, saying in effect: "We abide by this faith, by this covenant." In scholastic language, the congregation were the "matter" but the covenant was the "form" of the church. They objected above all things to the practice in England whereby churches were made by geography; that a lot of people, merely because they resided in Little Willingdon, should make the church of Little Willingdon, seemed to them blasphemy. That principle was mechanical and unreal; there was no spiritual participation in it — no covenant.

That was why they (or at any rate the leaders and the theorists) came to New England. On the voyage over, in 1630, John Winthrop said to them: "For wee must Consider that wee shall be as a Citty vppon a Hill, the eies of all people are vppon us." They had been attempting in England to lead a revolution; after the King's dismissal of Parliament in 1629 it looked as though there was no longer any hope of revolution there, and so they migrated to New England, to build the revolutionary city, where they could exhibit to Englishmen an England that would be as all England should be.

The essence of this conception was the covenant. As soon as they were disembarked, as soon as they could collect in one spot enough people to examine each other and acknowledge that each seemed visibly capable of taking the oath, they incorporated churches — in Boston, Charlestown, and Watertown, and, even in the first decade, in the Connecticut Valley. But we must always remember that even in those first days, when conviction was at its height, and among so highly selected and dedicated numbers as made up the Great Migration, only about one fifth of the population were found able, or could find themselves able, to take the covenant. The rest of them — with astonishingly few exceptions — accepted their exclusion from the churches, knowing that they were not "enabled" and praying for the grace that might yet empower them.

From that point on, the story may seem somewhat peculiar, but after a little scrutiny it becomes an old and a familiar one: it is what happens to a successful revolution. The New Englanders did not have to fight on the barricades or at Marston Moor; by the act of migrating, they *had* their revolution. Obeying the Biblical command to increase and multiply, they had children — hordes of them. Despite the high rate of infant mortality, numbers of these children grew up in New England knowing nothing, except by hearsay and rumor, of the struggles in Europe, never having lived amid the tensions of England. This second generation were, for the most part, good people; but they simply did not have — they could not have — the kind of emotional experience that made them ready to stand up before the whole community and say: "On Friday the 19th, I was smitten while plowing Deacon Jones's meadow; I fell to the earth, and I knew that the grace of God was upon me." They were honest people, and they found it difficult to romanticize about themselves — even when they desperately wanted to.

In 1662 the churches of New England convoked a synod and announced that the children of the primitive church members were included in the covenant by the promise of God to Abraham. This solution was called at the time the halfway covenant, and the very phrase itself is an instructive demonstration of the New Englanders' awareness that their revolution was no longer revolutionary. These children, they decided, must be treated as members of the church, although they had not had the kind of experience that qualified their fathers. They must be subject to discipline and censures, because the body of the saints must be preserved. But just in case the authorities might be mistaken, they compromised by giving to these children only a "halfway" status, which made them members but did not admit them to the Lord's Supper.

This provision can easily be described as a pathetic, where it is not a ridiculous, device. It becomes more comprehensible when we realize that it was an accommodation to the successful revolution. Second and third generations grow up inheritors of a revolution, but are not themselves revolutionaries.

For the moment, in the 1660's and 1670's, the compromise worked, but the situation got worse. For one thing, New England suffered in King Philip's War, when the male population was decimated. Then, in 1684, the charter of Massachusetts was revoked, and after 1691 the colony had to adjust itself to the notion that its governor was imposed by the royal whim, not by the election of the saints. Furthermore, after 1715 all the colonies were prospering economically; inevitably they became more and more concerned with earthly things — rum, land, furs. On the whole they remained a pious people. Could one go back to Boston of 1710 or 1720 — when the ministers were asserting that it was as profligate as Babylon — I am sure that one would find it, compared with modern Hollywood, a strict and moral community. Nevertheless, everybody was convinced that the cause of religion had declined. Something had to be done.

As early as the 1670's the ministers had found something they could do: they could work upon the halfway members. They could say to these hesitants: "You were baptized in this church, and if you will now come before the body and 'own' the covenant, then your children can in turn be baptized." Gradually a whole segment of doctrine was formulated that was not in the original theory — which made it possible to address these citizens who were neither outside the pale nor yet snugly inside, which told them that however dubious they might be as saints, visible or invisible, they yet had sufficient will power to perform the public act of "owning the covenant."

With the increasing pressures of the late seventeenth and early eighteenth centuries, the practice of owning the covenant gradually became a communal rite. It was not enough that the minister labored separately with John or Elizabeth to make an acknowledgement the next Sunday: a day was appointed when all the Johns and Elizabeths would come to church and do it in unison, the whole town looking on. It is not difficult to trace through the increasing reënactments of this ceremony a mounting crescendo of communal action that was, to say the least, wholly foreign to the original Puritanism. The theology of the founders conceived of man as single and alone, apart in a corner or in an empty field, wrestling with his sins; only after he had survived this experience in solitude could he walk into the church and by telling about it prove his right to the covenant. But this communal confession — with everybody doing it together, under the urgencies of an organized moment — this was something new, emerging so imperceptibly that nobody recognized it as an innovation (or rather I should say that some did, but they were shouted down) that by the turn of the century was rapidly becoming the focus for the ordering of the spiritual life of the town.

The grandfather of Jonathan Edwards, Solomon Stoddard, of Northampton, was the first man who openly extended the practice or renewal of covenant to those who had never been in it at all. In short, when these occasions arose, or when he could precipitate them, he simply took into the church and up to the Lord's Supper everyone who would or could come. He called the periods when the community responded en masse his "harvests," of which he had five: 1679, 1683, 1696, 1712, 1718. The Mathers attacked him for so completely letting down the bars, but in the Connecticut Valley his success was envied and imitated.

The Great Awakening of 1740, seen in the light of this development, was nothing more than an inevitable culmination. It was the point at which the method of owning the covenant became most widely and exultingly extended, in which the momentum of the appeal got out of hand, and the ministers, led by Jonathan Edwards, were forced by the logic of evolution not only to admit all those who would come, but to excite and to drive as many as possible, by such rhetorical stimulations as "Sinners in the Hands of an Angry God," into demanding entrance.

All of this, traced historically, seems natural enough. What 1740 did was present a number of leading citizens, like the Harvard faculty, with the results of a process that had been going on for decades but of which they were utterly unaware until the explosion. Then they found themselves trying to control it or censure it by standards that had in fact been

out of date for a century, although they had all that while professed
them. In this sense – which I regret to state has generally eluded the
social historian – the Great Awakening was a crisis in the New England
society.]

Professional patriots, especially those of New England descent, are
fond of celebrating the Puritans as the founders of the American tradition of rugged individualism, freedom of conscience, popular education,
and democracy. The Puritans were not rugged individualists; they did
indeed believe in education of a sort, but not in the "progressive" sense;
they abhorred freedom of conscience; and they did not believe at all in
democracy. They advertised again and again that their church polity was
not democratic. The fact that a church was founded on a covenant and
that the minister happened to be elected by the mass of the church –
this emphatically did not constitute a democracy. John Cotton made the
position of the founders crystal clear when he told Lord Say and Seal
that God never ordained democracy as a fit government for either church
or commonwealth; although at first sight one might suppose that a
congregational church was one, in that the people chose their governors,
the truth was that "the government is not a democracy, if it be administered, not by the people, but by the governors." He meant, in short, that
even though the people did select the person, the office was prescribed;
they did not define its functions, nor was it responsible to the will or the
whim of the electors. "In which respect it is, that church government is
iustly denied . . . to be democratical, though the people choose their
owne officers and rulers."

The conception ran through every department of the social thinking
of New England in the seventeenth century, and persisted in the eighteenth up to the very outbreak of the Awakening. The essence of it
always was that though officers may come into their office by the choice
of the people, nevertheless the definition of the function, dignity, and
prerogatives of the position does not depend upon the intentions or
wishes of the electorate, but upon an abstract, divinely given, absolute
prescription, which has nothing – in theory – to do with such practical
or utilitarian considerations as may, at the moment of the election, be at
work among the people.

The divine and immutable pattern of church government was set, once
and for all, in the New Testament; likewise, the principles of political
justice were given in an eternal and definitive form. The machinery by
which a particular man was chosen to fulfill these directives (as the
minister was elected by the vote of a congregation, or as John Winthrop
was made governor of the Massachusetts Bay Company by a vote of the
stockholders) was irrelevant. The existence of such machinery did not
mean that the elected officer was in any sense responsible to the electorate. He knew what was expected of him from an entirely other source

than their temporary passions; he knew what he, upon becoming such a being, should do — as such!

The classic statement, as is widely known, was the speech that John Winthrop delivered before the General Court on July 3, 1645. He informed the people that the liberty of the subject may sometimes include, as happily it did in Massachusetts, the privilege of selecting this or that person for office, but that it did not therefore mean the right to tell the officer what he should do once he was installed. The liberty that men enjoy in civil society, he said, "is the proper end and object of authority, and cannot subsist without it." It is not a liberty to do what you will, or to require the authority to do what you want: "It is a liberty to do that only which is good, just, and honest." Who defines the good, the just, and the honest? Obviously, the authority does.

In other words, the theory of early New England was basically medieval. Behind it lay the conception of an authoritative scheme of things, in which basic principles are set down once and for all, entirely antecedent to, and utterly without regard for, political experience. The formulation of social wisdom had nothing to do with the specific problems of any one society. It was not devised by a committee on ways and means. Policy was not to be arrived at by a discussion of strategy — for example (in modern terms), shouldn't we use the atomic bomb now? This sort of argument was unavailing, because the function of government was to maintain by authority that which was inherently — and definably — the true, just, and honest.

In Hartford, Connecticut, Samuel Stone, colleague of the great Thomas Hooker, summarized the argument by declaring that congregationalism meant a silent democracy in the face of a speaking aristocracy. There might be something which we call democracy in the form of the church, but the congregation had to keep silent when the minister spoke. And yet, for a hundred years after the death of Hooker, this strange alteration went on inside the institution. The official theory remained, down to the time of Edwards, that the spokesman for the society — be he governor or minister — told the society, by right divine, what it should or should not do, without any regard to its immediate interests, whether emotional or economic. He had laid upon him, in fact, the duty of forgetting such wisdom as he might have accumulated by living as a particular person in that very community or having shared the hopes and qualities of precisely these people.

What actually came about, through the device of renewing the covenant, was something that in fact completely contradicted the theory. (We must remember that the church was, during this century, not merely something "spiritual," but the institutional center of the organized life.) Instead of the minister standing in his pulpit, saying: "I speak; you keep quiet," he found himself, bit by bit, assuming the posture of pleading with the people: "Come, and speak up." He did not know what was happening. He began to find out only in the Great Awakening, when the people at last and multitudinously spoke up.

III

The greatness of Jonathan Edwards is that he understood what had happened. But note this carefully. He was not Thomas Jefferson: he did not preach democracy, and he had no interest whatsoever in any social revolution. He was the child of this aristocratic, medieval system; he was born to the purple, to ecclesiastical authority. Yet he was the man who hammered it home to the people that they *had* to speak up, or else they were lost.

Edwards was a Puritan and a Calvinist. He believed in predestination and original sin and all those dogmas which modern students hold to be outworn stuff until they get excited about them as slightly disguised by Franz Kafka. Edwards did not submit these doctrines to majority vote, and he did not put his theology to the test of utility. But none of this was, in his existing situation, an issue. Granting all that, the question he had to decide was: What does a man do who leads the people? Does he, in 1740, say with the Winthrop of 1645 that they submit to what he as an ontologist tells them is good, just, and honest?

What he realized (lesser leaders of the Awakening, like Gilbert Tennent, also grasped the point, but none with the fine precision of Edwards) was that a leader could no longer stand before the people giving them mathematically or logically impregnable postulates of the eternally good, just, and honest. That might work in 1640, or in Europe (where to an astonishing extent it still works), but it would not work in the American wilderness. By 1740 the leader had to get down amongst them, and bring them by actual participation into an experience that was no longer private and privileged, but social and communal.

In other words, Edwards carried to its ultimate implication – this constitutes his "relation to his times," which no purely social historian can begin to diagnose – that slowly forming tendency which had been steadily pressing through enlargements of the ceremonial owning of the covenant. He carried it so far that at last everybody could see what it really did mean. Then the Harvard faculty lifted their hands in horror – because this ritual, which they had thought was a segment of the cosmology of John Winthrop, was proved by Edwards' use to flow from entirely alien principles. For this reason, his own Yale disowned him.

IV

In the year 1748 Edwards' revolutionary effort – his leadership of the Awakening must be seen as a resumption of the revolutionary thrust that had been allowed to dwindle in the halfway covenant – was almost at an end. The opposition was mobilizing, and he knew, even before they did, that they would force him out. When the fight had only begun, his patron and friend, his one bulwark in the civil society, Colonel John Stoddard, chief of the militia and warden of the marches, died. There was now no civil power that could protect him against the hatred of the "river gods." Out of all New England, Stoddard had been really *the* outstanding magistrate in that tradition of aristocratic leadership which had begun with Winthrop and had been sustained through a massive succession. As was the custom in New England, the minister gave a funeral sermon; Edwards preached over the corpse of the town's greatest citizen — who happened, in this case, to be also his uncle and his protector. Those who were now certain, with Colonel Stoddard in the ground, that they could get Edwards' scalp were in the audience.

Edwards delivered a discourse that at first sight seems merely one more Puritan eulogy. He told the people that when great and good men like Stoddard are taken away, this is a frown of God's displeasure, which indicates that they ought to reform their vices. This much was sheer convention. But before he came, at the end, to the traditional berating of the populace, Edwards devoted the major part of his oration to an analysis of the function and meaning of authority.

It should be remembered that Winthrop had commenced the New England tradition by telling the people that they had the liberty to do only that which is in itself good, just, and honest; that their liberty was the proper end and object of authority thus defined; that the approbation of the people is no more than the machinery by which God calls certain people to the exercise of the designated powers. And it should also be borne in mind that these powers are given apart from any consideration of the social welfare, that they derive from ethical, theological — a priori — considerations.

Jonathan Edwards says that the supreme qualification of a ruler is that he be a man of "great ability for the management of public affairs." This is his first and basic definition! Let us follow his very words, underlining those which carry revolutionary significance. Rulers are men "of great *natural* abilities" who are versed in discerning "those things wherein the *public welfare or calamity consists*, and the proper *means* to avoid the one and promote the other." They must have lived among men long enough to discover how the mass of them disguise their motives, must have learned how to "unravel the false, subtle arguments and cunning sophistry that is often made use of to defend *iniquity*." They must be men who have improved their talents by — here are his great criteria — *study, learning, observation*, and *experience*. By these means they must have acquired "skill" in public affairs, "a great understanding of *men and things*, a great *knowledge of human nature*, and of the way of *accommodating* themselves to it." Men are qualified to be rulers if and when they have this "very extensive knowledge of men with whom they are concerned," and when also they have a full and particular understanding "of the *state and circumstances* of the country or people that they have the care of." These are the things — not scholastical articles — that make those in authority "fit" to be rulers!

Look closely at those words and phrases: skill, observation, men and things, state and circumstances — above all, experience! Is this the great Puritan revivalist? It is. And what is he saying, out of the revival? He is telling what in political terms the revival really meant: that the leader has the job of accommodating himself to the realities of human and, in any particular situation, of social, experience. No matter what he may have as an assured creed, as a dogma — no matter what he may be able to pronounce, in the terms of abstract theology, concerning predestination and original sin — as a public leader he must adapt himself to public welfare and calamity. He cannot trust himself to a priori rules of an eternal and uncircumstanced good, just, and honest. There are requirements imposed by the office; authority does indeed consist of propositions that pertain to it, but what are they? They are the need for knowing the people, the knack of properly manipulating and operating them, the wit to estimate their welfare, and the cunning to foresee what may become their calamity.

When we are dealing with so highly conscious an artist as Edwards, we not only are justified in submitting this crucial paragraph to close analysis, we are criminally obtuse if we do not. So it becomes significant to note what Edwards says immediately after his radically new definition of the ruler. Following his own logic, he is prepared at once to attack what, in the state and circumstances of the Connecticut Valley, constituted the primary iniquity, from which the greatest social calamity might be expected.

He says it without, as we might say, pulling punches: a ruler must, on these considerations of welfare, be unalterably opposed to all persons of "a mean spirit," to those "of a narrow, private spirit that may be found in little tricks and intrigues to promote their private interest, [who] will shamefully defile their hands to gain a few pounds, are not ashamed to hip and bite others, grind the faces of the poor, and screw upon their neighbors; and will take advantage of their authority or commission to line their own pockets with what is fraudulently taken or withheld from others." At the time he spoke, there sat before him the merchants, the sharp traders, the land speculators of Northampton; with the prompt publication of the sermon, his words reached similar gentlemen in the neighboring towns. Within two years, they hounded him out of his pulpit.

The more one studies Edwards, the more one finds that much of his preaching is his condemnation, in this language of welfare and calamity rather than of "morality," of the rising and now rampant businessmen of the Valley. It was Edwards' great perception — and possibly his greatest value for us today is precisely here — that the get-rich-quick schemes of his contemporaries were wrong not from the point of view of the eternal values but from that of the public welfare. The ruler, he said, must know the "theory" of government in such a way that it becomes "natural" to him, and he must apply the knowledge he has obtained by study and observation "to that business, so as to perform it most advantageously and effectually." Here he was, at the moment his protector was gone, when he knew that he was lost, telling those about to destroy him that the great man is he who leads the people by skill and experiential wisdom, and not by making money.

It is further revealing that, after Edwards had portrayed the ruler in this frame of utility and calculation, as he came to his fourth point, he then for the first time said that the authority ought to be a pious man, and only in his fifth and last did he suggest the desirability of a good family. For Winthrop these qualifications had been essentials of the office; for Edwards they were radically submitted to a criterion of utility. "It also contributes to the strength of a man in authority . . . when he is in such circumstances as give him advantage for the exercise of his strength, for the public good; as his being a person of honorable descent, of a distinguished education, his being a man of estate." But note — these are all "useful" because they "add to his strength, and increase his ability and advantage to serve his generation." They serve "in some respect" to make him more effective. It had never occurred to John Winthrop that the silent democracy should imagine for a moment that the elected ruler, in church or state, would be anyone but a pious, educated, honorably descended person, of adequate economic substance. Edwards (who was pious, educated, and very well descended, but not wealthy) says that in some respects these advantages are helps to efficiency.

From one point of view, then, this was what actually was at work inside the hysterical agonies of the Great Awakening. This is one thing they meant: the end of the reign over the New England and American mind of a European and scholastical conception of an authority put over men because men were incapable of recognizing their own welfare. This insight may assist us somewhat in comprehending why the pundits of Boston and Cambridge, all of whom were rational and tolerant and decent, shuddered with a horror that was deeper than mere dislike of the antics of the yokels. To some extent, they sensed that the religious screaming had implications in the realm of society, and those implications they — being businessmen and speculators, as were the plutocracy of Northampton — did not like.

Again, I would not claim too much for Edwards, and I have no design of inscribing him among the prophets of democracy or the New Deal. What he marks — and what he alone could make clear — is the crisis of the wilderness' Awakening, in which the social problem was taken out of the arcana of abstract morality and put into the arena of skill, observation, and accommodation. In this episode, the Americans were indeed participating in an international movement; even so, they came — or Edwards brought them — to sharper formulations of American experience. [What the Awakening really meant for Americans was not that they too were behaving like Dutchmen or Germans or Lancashire workmen, but that in the ecstasy of the revival they were discovering, especially on the frontier, where life was the toughest, that they rejected imported European philosophies of society. They were now of themselves prepared to contend that the guiding rule of this society will be its welfare, and the most valuable knowledge will be that which can say what threatens calamity for the state.]

The Great Awakening in Connecticut

RICHARD L. BUSHMAN

What happened to Puritanism in eighteenth-century New England? According to Richard Bushman, the religion retained its theological integrity, but it had to struggle against a dramatically transformed social situation. Prior to 1690 the settlers of Connecticut had been content to live within the context of law and order which implicitly bound state to church. The demands of their mundane existence did not seriously conflict with divine requirements. The economic expansion of the eighteenth century, however, created new problems as the pursuit of wealth created new social tensions and feelings of spiritual inadequacy. Men found it much harder to reconcile their inner convictions with their worldly ambitions.

Connecticut was thus prepared for the spiritual message of the Great Awakening, which emphasized the all-encompassing importance of God's grace. Men who had felt guilty when they subverted the laws of the colony were relieved to discover that they needed only to be bound by laws of conscience. For the revivalists and their supporters, the social order was no longer divine, and the Awakening therefore stimulated an entirely new attitude to the relations of man and the state.

> *Bushman links spiritual revolution to social change, for men's religious ideas cannot be kept separate from the pressures of daily life. Miller, on the contrary, argues that religious motivation was primary for eighteenth-century Americans. Do you think Bushman underestimates the determinative intellectual power of religion in Connecticut's Awakening?*

In 1721 an extraordinary number of conversions occurred in Windsor, Windham, and two parishes in Norwich. For the first time a rash of revivals occurred instead of individual instances spotted across the face of the colony at wide intervals in time. Another series, beginning in Northampton in 1735, followed the same pattern on a much larger scale. Religious excitement moved down the Connecticut Valley, eastward from the river into the back country, and in both directions along the coast.[1]

The conversion spirit spread rapidly because religious tension was high. Edwards said that news of the 1735 revival struck "like a flash of lightning, upon the hearts" of the people.[2] Throughout the decade ministers often had to comfort "*Souls in Distress under Inward Troubles.*"[3] Clap found this pastoral work the most difficult of his duties: "Persons are oftentimes under great Trouble and Distress of Mind," he wrote in 1732, "and sometimes brought almost to Despair."[4] A colleague in 1737 offered suggestions on the best method of leading persons under concern "thro' the Work of Humiliation . . . unto Christ."[5] The tide of conversions was already rising in 1740 when Whitefield visited New England.[6]

The need for an Awakening to heal society as well as to save men's souls was widely acknowledged. For eighty years the clergy had deplored the declension of piety. As vice, injustice, pride, contempt for authority, and contention in church and town became more prevalent, law after law was added to the books to restrain corruption but without appreciable effect. "There have been many Enquiries after the *Cause of our Ill State*," lamented the election sermon of 1734, "and after proper *Means* and

Reprinted by permission of the publishers from Richard L. Bushman, *From Puritan to Yankee*, Cambridge, Mass.: Harvard University Press, Copyright, 1967, by the President and Fellows of Harvard College.

[1] M. H. Mitchell, *Great Awakening*, 8–9; Larned, *Windham*, I, 330; B. Trumbull, *Connecticut*, II, 104.

[2] J. Edwards, *Works*, III, 234, 236.

[3] Marsh, *God's Fatherly Care*, 25.

[4] Clap, *Greatness*, 13.

[5] S. Whittelsey, *Sermon*, 9–10.

[6] For increasing conversions in 1739, see Orcutt, *New Milford*, 48–59; Cothren, *Woodbury*, 820–821; Norwich, "Fifth Congregational Church, Records," 59 ff.

Methods of Cure: Yea, and many *Attempts*, but alas, to how little purpose!" [7] Ministers pleaded with their congregations *"to awake out of Sleep."* [8] Privately they sought ways "to revive a Concern about religion." [9] Congregations fasted and prayed to humble themselves "before God Under the sense of Leaness and bareness . . . and to Implore the divine Graces to be poured out." [10] After the Windham revival in 1721, the pastor exclaimed, "Oh! that the same Good *Spirit from on High* were poured out upon the rest of the Country." [11] Hearing of Whitefield's success in the middle and southern colonies, several leading New England ministers invited him to visit and preach, and Governor Talcott gratefully welcomed him to Connecticut in 1740.[12]

For six weeks in September and October Whitefield toured New England, releasing a flood of religious emotions wherever he went. Along his route from Boston to Northampton, down the Connecticut Valley, and westward along the Sound hundreds were converted, and the itinerants Gilbert Tennent of New Jersey and James Davenport of Long Island continued the work through 1741 and 1742. Local ministers, adopting Whitefield's style of preaching, started revivals in their own congregations and aided neighboring pastors in theirs. The increase of admissions to full communion is a measure of the volume of religious experience.[13]

The revivals occurred throughout the colony. Even though some areas, such as the first parish in Fairfield, did not respond, religious activity flourished all around them. Coast and inland towns, new and old towns, towns in the east and in the west participated in the Awakening.[14] Although it was probably more intense in the east than in the west and on the coast and large rivers than inland, no area was immune to the contagion.

The Awakening affected people of all classes. One clergyman reported that men of "all orders and degrees, or all ages and characters" were converted.[15] Edwards marveled that "some that are wealthy, and of a fashion-

---

[7] Chauncey, *Faithful Ruler*, 49–50.

[8] Marsh, *God's Fatherly Care*, 22.

[9] Wadsworth, *Diary*, 20.

[10] Norwich, "First Congregational Church, Records," II, 19.

[11] E. Adams, *Sermon*, iv.

[12] B. Trumbull, *Connecticut*, II, 120.

[13] For example, *Records of the Congregational Church, Franklin*, 13–14; Lisbon, "Newent Congregational Church, Records," I, 26; Cothren, 820–821; Orcutt, *New Milford*, 48–49; Norwich, "Fifth Congregational Church, Records," 59 ff; C. Davis, *Wallingford*, 301; *First Congregational Church of Preston*, 134.

[14] Schenck, *Fairfield*, II, 131; *Bi-Centennial of Green's Farms*, 9; Fairfield, "First Congregational Church, Records," 7. For the location of revivals, B. Trumbull, *Connecticut*, II, 103–219; *Christian History*; Tracy, *Great Awakening*; Larned, *Windham*, I, 396, 431–432, 434, 444, 450, 464.

[15] Pemberton, *Duty*, 28.

able, gay education; some great beaus and fine ladies" cast off their vanities and humbled themselves.[16] In town after town leading citizens participated along with more common people. A comparison of the taxes of persons admitted to communion in two Norwich parishes from 1740 to 1743 with the taxes of the town as a whole shows that economically the new converts represented an almost exact cross-section of the population.[17]

The revivals Whitefield precipitated seemed to fulfill all the hopes placed in him. Vicious persons repented of their sins, inveterate absentees from worship returned, love for the minister waxed strong, contention in the town died away, and interest in worldly pursuits shifted to the scriptures and the state of one's soul. People could not get enough preaching: meetings were added to the regular schedule, and worshippers met privately to discuss religion. When the Hartford County Association in June 1741 urged ministers to hold extra meetings, preaching alternately for each other if necessary, it declared that the "awakening and Religious Concern, if duly cultivated and directed may have a very happy Influence to promote Religion and the Saving Conversion of Souls." [18]

A few ministers were dubious from the start, however, and their doubts steadily darkened into dislike. The news of enthusiasm on Long Island made Daniel Wadsworth, pastor of the first church in Hartford, uncomfortable even before Whitefield arrived. Upon seeing him in October 1740, Wadsworth was uncertain "what to think of the man and his Itinerant preachings," and by the following spring "irregularities and disorders" in the town worried him. In August 1741 the Hartford Association declared against itinerants and their unjust censures of other ministers. The clergy agreed that no weight was to be given to "those screachings, crying out, faintings and convulsions, which, sometimes attend the terrifying Language of some preachers," nor to the "Visions or visional discoveries by some of Late pretended to." The following month, after reports of Davenport's conduct had reached Hartford, Wadsworth concluded that "the great awakening etc. seems to be degenerating into Strife and faction." Itinerants had turned people "to disputes, debates and quarrels." "Steady christians and the most Judicious among ministers and people," he observed at the end of September 1741, "generally dislike these new things set afoot by these Itinerant preachers." [19] By the end of 1741 open opposition appeared to what had at first been considered to be a work of grace.

16 *Works*, III, 297.
17 B. Trumbull, *Connecticut*, II, 109; Gilman, *Historical Discourse*, 45; Larned, *Windham*, I, 397; "Norwich Town Rate"; *Records of the Congregational Church, Franklin*; *Manual of the First Congregational Church*.
18 Wadsworth, 66n.
19 Wadsworth, 49, 56, 66, 70n, 71, 72, 73.

At the request of several ministers, the Assembly in October 1741 underwrote the expenses of a general convention of ministers to stop the "unhappy misunderstandings and divisions" in the colony and to bring about "peace, love and charity." [20] Probably in response to the resolves of the clergy, the Assembly enacted a law in the spring of 1742 forbidding itinerants. Ministers were to obtain permission from the congregation and the pastor of a parish before preaching there. If a complaint was lodged against a pastor for preaching outside of his parish, the magistrates were not to enforce collection of his salary, and unordained persons and ministers without congregations or from other colonies were required to obtain permission before preaching. Realizing that one consociation might be more favorable to revival preachers or contentious individuals than another, the Assembly forbade any to advise or to license candidates to preach in the jurisdiction of another. Thus this act outlawed itineracy, the primary method of spreading the revival, and thereby officially denounced the Awakening. When Whitefield next visited Connecticut in 1744, most pulpits were closed to him.[21]

Conversions waned after 1743. Only sporadic and isolated revivals occurred in the next fifty years, and none was comparable in size to the Great Awakening. But the impact of the experience was felt long afterwards. The converted were new men, with new attitudes toward themselves, their religion, their neighbors, and their rulers in church and state. A psychological earthquake had reshaped the human landscape.

What had happened to prepare so large a portion of the population for this momentous change? What power was there in the words of a sermon to plunge a person into the blackest despair and then bring him out into light and joy, a new man? The answer lay in the revivalist's message. He told his listeners that they were enemies of God and certain to be damned. When sufficiently crushed by their sinfulness, they learned that good works would never save them but that God's free grace would. This idea lifted men from their misery and restored them to confidence in God's love. Men who had come to believe that they were damnably guilty were ready to rely on unconditional grace.

The peculiarities of the Puritan personality partly account for the listeners' conviction that they were worthy only of damnation and hence wholly dependent on God's favor. Hypersensitive to overbearing authority, and always afraid of its destructive power, Puritans instinctively resisted whenever it threatened — but not without guilt. Since they could not avoid conflicts, surrounded as they were by rulers and laws, they lived in

[20] *Conn. Recs.*, VIII, 438–439.
[21] *Conn. Recs.*, VIII, 454–457; Wadsworth, 130; B. Trumbull, *Connecticut*, II, 152.

the consciousness of multiple offenses. They did not separate earthly clashes with authority from sins against God, for they believed the rulers and laws derived their power from the heavens. With life so structured, deep feelings of guilt inevitably grew.

These tensions had existed long before 1740, but despite pleas from the clergy, conversions had been few. Not until 1721 were any appreciable number of men sufficiently overpowered by their own sinfulness to rely wholly on God's grace and be converted. Two conditions prepared men for conversion: an increased desire for material wealth that ministers called worldly pride or covetousness, and the growing frequency of clashes with authority entailed in the pursuit of wealth. Both were the results of economic expansion, and both were, in the Puritan mind, offenses against God.

The Puritans' feelings about wealth were ambiguous. Even the most pious associated it with a secure place in the community and divine approval, and everyone accorded great respect to rich men, numbering them among the rulers of society. Prosperity was a sign of good character: all were expected to practice industry and thrift, the virtues that brought the rewards of wealth. To some extent worldly success was a token of God's favor: none felt constrained to stint their efforts to prosper in their callings.

Yet the dangers of riches also were well known. The rich were prone to *"fall into Temptation,"* Cotton Mather warned, and be *drowned in Perdition."* "There is a venom in *Riches,"* he said, "disposing our depraved Hearts, to cast off their *Dependence on God."* [22] It was a maxim of the Jeremiads that "where a Selfish, Covetous spirit and Love of this world prevails, there the Love of God decayeth." [23] When Connecticut's first published poet, Roger Wolcott, occupied himself with the theme of the divine wrath visited on seekers of earthly honor and wealth, he explained that he might have chosen the path of pride himself, "but that I see Hells flashes folding through Eternities." In this world money answered everything but a guilty conscience. [24]

The contradiction in the prevailing attitudes toward wealth perplexed both the ministers and the people. Pastors complained that men excused avarice as justifiable enterprise. "They will plead in defense of a Worldly Covetous spirit, under the colour or specious pretence of Prudence, Diligence, Frugality, Necessity." [25] Cotton Mather lamented that even the farmer was grasped with worldliness, yet he turned away rebukes with the assertion that he was merely pursuing his calling as a husbandman. The

---

[22] C. Mather, *Agricola*, 59, 64.
[23] Russel, *Decay of Love*, 11.
[24] Wolcott, *Poetical Meditations*, 18, 12.
[25] Marsh, *Essay*, 15–17.

people could not distinguish respectable industry from covetousness: their ambitions drove them on year after year, while self-doubts were never far below the surface. Robert Keayne, the wealthy Boston merchant of the early period, built a fine fortune, but at great cost. When censured by the clergy for acting against the public good, he was crushed and, in a document written to clear himself of guilt, poured out the tensions he had long felt.[26]

Throughout the seventeenth century a few Puritans experienced Keayne's miseries, but the temptations of worldly pride were too remote to hurt the consciences of most. The opportunities for gain were largely inaccessible to ordinary men until after 1690, when economic expansion opened new prospects to many more farmers and merchants. Common men could take up a small trade or invest in a ship sailing to the West Indies, and land purchased in a new plantation doubled in value within a few years. The expansive economy of the early eighteenth century un-leashed ambitions restrained by the absence of opportunity. Everyone hoped to prosper; the demand for land banks and the 300 per cent in-crease in per capita indebtedness were measures of the eagerness for wealth.[27] An indentured farmhand in the 1740's complained that his master never spoke about religion: "His whole attention was taken up on the pursuits of the good things of this world; wealth was his supreme object. I am afraid gold was his God." [28]

In the midst of this economic growth, the ministers faithfully excori-ated the spreading worldliness. It was obvious, one minister wrote, "that the Heart of a People is gone off from God and gone after the Creature; that they are much more concerned about getting Land and Money and Stock, than they be about getting Religion revived." [29] "The Concern is not as heretofore to accommodate themselves as to the Worship of God," it was said in 1730, "but Where they can have most Land, and be under best advantages to get Money." [30] These accusations were put aside with the usual rationalizations, but so long as the ministers reminded men that riches cankered their souls, a grave uncertainty haunted everyone who pursued wealth.

The desire to prosper also precipitated clashes with law and authority, adding to accumulating guilt. With increasing frequency after 1690 people fought their rulers or balked at the laws, usually as a consequence of their ambition. Such friction wore away confidence as it convinced men inwardly of their own culpability.

Under more peaceful circumstances law and authority protected the

[26] C. Mather, *Agricola*, 71; Bailyn, "The Apologia of Robert Keayne."
[27] See Appendix III [in Bushman, *From Puritan to Yankee*].
[28] Bennett, "Solomon Mack," 631.
[29] Marsh, *Essay*, 15.
[30] Russel, 22.

Puritan from the asperities of his own doctrines. Taken seriously, Puritan theology kept men in unbearable suspense about their standing with God: He chose whom He would to be saved, and the rest were cast into the fires of hell. But the founding fathers had qualified this pure conception of divine sovereignty by stressing the authority vested in the social order. Since civil and ecclesiastical rulers were commissioned by God and the laws of society were an expression of His will, obedience to Connecticut's government was in effect obedience to divine government, and the good will of the rulers was an omen of God's good will. So long as man complied with the law and submitted to authority, he was safe from divine punishment.

After 1690, in their ambition to prosper, people disregarded the demands of social order. Nonproprietors contested the control of town lands with proprietors, and outlivers struggled with the leaders in the town center to obtain an independent parish. In the civil government settlers fought for a clear title to their lands and new traders for currency. Church members resisted the enlargement of the minister's power or demanded greater piety in his preaching. All these controversies pitted common men against rulers and the laws.

Under these circumstances the social order became a menace to peace of mind rather than a shield against divine wrath. Just as conformity gave an inward assurance of moral worth, so resistance, even in spirit, was blameworthy. Dissenters, in politics or economics as well as religion, could not oppose the community fathers whom God had set to rule without feeling guilty. Even when a move to the outlands or complaints about a minister's arrogance were well justified, the participants in the action feared that they sinned in resisting.

Few men in 1740 were outright rebels, for strong loyalties still bound almost all to their communities. By comparison to their forebears of 1690, however, this later generation was estranged. It could not comfort itself in the recollection of a life of conformity to the divinely sanctioned order. In part it was emboldened by the wealth it had sought and often gained, but that provided an unsteady support when the pursuit of riches was so often condemned. However hardened the contentious appeared, guilt generated by an undue love of wealth and by resistance to the social order had hollowed out their lives.

East of the Connecticut River, in the most rapidly expanding section of the colony, turmoil was greatest. Extravagant growth plunged the towns into strife over land titles, currency, and religion. The party battles loosened the social structure and alienated men from their social and religious leaders. Economic opportunity also aroused the hunger for land and commercial success. Here the revival was noticeably most intense. "Whatever be the reason," Ezra Stiles commented later, "the eastern part of Connecticut . . . are of a very mixt and uncertain character as to religion. Exhorters, Itinerants, Separate Meetings rose in that part." Around three-quarters of the separations between 1740 and 1755 occurred east of the Connecticut River. The greatest number in any town — four — were in Norwich, the commercial center of the east. Nearby towns — New London, Groton, Stonington, Lyme, Windham, and Preston — had similarly prospered, and a third of the separations in the colony took place in these towns and Norwich.[31] These departures, roughly measuring the fervor of the Awakening, were the outcome of the personal instability eastern men felt after a half-century of extraordinary expansion.

Before Whitefield arrived, ministers sensed the shaky state of their parishioners' confidence. One pastor noted the grave uncertainty of people under spiritual concern: "They want to know they shall be sure they believe, that they love God, that they are in the right way, are sincere and the like." [32] As the ministers recognized, an outward show usually covered somber doubts: reprobates disguised or fled from their real condition while inwardly they suffered from a consciousness of guilt.

Whitefield broke through this facade. Though he stood apart from the established clergy, he was accepted by them. He did not represent the repressive ministerial rule which entered so largely into the conflicts of the period but nevertheless came clothed with acknowledged authority. The revivals he started in the middle colonies also imbued him with a reputation of extraordinary power. "Hearing how god was with him every where as he came along," one awakened person later reported, "it solumnized my mind and put me in a trembling fear before he began to preach for he looked as if he was Cloathed with authority from the great god." [33] Besides, he was an impassioned and fluent preacher.

Whitefield moved his hearers because excessive worldliness and resistance to the divinely sanctioned social order had already undermined their confidence. He told men what they already knew subconsciously: that they had broken the law, that impulses beyond their control drove them to resist divine authority, and that outward observance did not signify loving and willing submission. Confronted with truth, his listeners admitted that they were "vile, unworthy, loathsom" wretches. "Hearing him preach," a converted man said, "gave me a heart wound. By gods blessing my old foundation was broken up and i saw that my righteousness would not save me." [34]

This confrontation of guilt, the first part of conversion, drove men to despair, but the revivalists did not leave their hearers there to suffer. By publicly identifying the sources of guilt and condemning them, the

---

[31] E. Stiles, *Extracts*, 299; Goen, *Revivalism and Separatism*, 302–309; cf. Brainerd, *Life*, 358.

[32] Wadsworth, 7.

[33] Quoted in G. Walker, *Some Aspects*, 91.

[34] G. Walker, *Some Aspects*, 91.

preachers also helped to heal the wounds they first inflicted. Converts were persuaded that by acknowledging and repudiating their old sins, they were no longer culpable. The reborn man was as joyful and loving when the process was completed as he was miserable at its start.

Converts were told, for instance, that wealth held no attractions for the saintly. The business of Christ's disciples, one preacher taught, "is not to hunt for Riches, and Honours, and Pleasures in this World, but to despise them, and deny themselves, and be ready to part with even all the lawful Pleasures and Comforts of the World at any Time." [35] In a dramatic gesture expressing a deep impulse, Davenport had his followers gather the symbols of worldliness — wigs, cloaks, hoods, gowns, rings, necklaces — into a heap and burn them.[36]

Converts responded eagerly, casting off with great relief their guilt-producing ambition. The pious David Brainerd spontaneously broke into poetry:

> Farewell, vain world; my soul can bid Adieu:
> My Saviour's taught me to abandon you.[37]

After Isaac Backus was converted, he felt that he "should not be troubled any more with covetousness. The earth and all that is therein appeared to be vanity." [38] His mother, also a convert, felt ready to "give up my name, estate, family, life and breath, freely to God." She would not relinquish her peace of soul "no, not to be in the most prosperous condition in temporal things that ever I was in." [39] For many the choice was to enjoy peace of soul or prosperity. The pursuit of wealth and an easy conscience were incompatible. Jonathan Edwards noted a temptation among converts to go to extremes and "to neglect worldly affairs too much." [40] They were unwilling to jeopardize their newfound peace by returning to worldliness.

The revivalists undermined the social order, the other main source of guilt, not by repudiating law and authority, but by denying them sanctifying power. Estrangement from rulers and the traditional patterns of life was demoralizing as long as the social order was considered divine, but Awakening preachers repeatedly denied that salvation came by following the law. No amount of covenant owning, Sabbath observance, moral rectitude, or obedience to rulers redeemed the soul. Praying, Bible study, and attendance at worship might result solely from worldly motives, to avoid disgrace or to pacify a guilty conscience. "Civility and external Acts belonging to Morality," one revivalist taught, "are no Part of the Essence of

---

[35] S. Williams, *Christ*, 70.
[36] Tracy, 248–249.
[37] *Life*, 82.
[38] I. Backus, "Account," 22–23.
[39] Denison, *Notes*, 28–29; Hovey, *Memoir*, 27–28.
[40] *Works*, III, 234–235; cf. 296–297.

the Religion of Christ." [41] Without grace, "tho men are adorn'd with many amiable qualities, and lead sober, regular, and to all appearance religious lives, yet they remain under the condemning sentence of the Law, and perish at last in a state of unsanctified nature." [42] Reborn men were expected to practice moral virtues, but their salvation was not at stake. Obedience brought no assurance of grace, and disobedience did not entail damnation. Though still driven to resist rulers or to depart from the approved pattern of community life, believers in the revival message felt little guilt.

In this fashion the Awakening cleared the air of tensions. Men admitted that they had lusted after wealth, condemned themselves for it, and afterwards walked with lighter hearts. They ended the long struggle with the social order by denying its power to save and hence to condemn. After a century of Puritan rule, law and authority were burdens too heavy to bear. All the anxiety they evoked was released when men grasped the idea that salvation came not by obedience to law.

In the converts' minds the escape from guilt was possible because of God's grace. The idea that the law could not condemn if God justified contained the deepest meaning of the Awakening. The rules and rulers, who governed both externally and in the conscience, had judged men and found them wanting until God out of His good grace suspended the sentence of damnation. The authority of Christ nullified earthly authority. Edwards said that converted men exulted that "God is self-sufficient, and infinitely above all dependence, and reigns over all." [43] In the inward struggle with guilt, God's infinite power overruled the older authority that had stood over every Puritan conscience, judging and condemning.

In that moment of grace the Awakening worked its revolution. Henceforth a personal relation with God governed reborn men who were empowered by faith to obey the God they knew personally above the divine will manifest in earthly law and authority. It was characteristic of the converted to "renounce all confidence in everything but Christ, and build all their hopes of happiness upon this unalterable Rock of Ages." [44] "I seemed to depend wholly on my dear Lord," Brainerd reported following his conversion. "God was so precious to my soul that the world with all its enjoyments was infinitely vile. I had no more value for the favor of men than for pebbles. The Lord was my ALL." [45] Though the old authority was still a substantial force in every life, it did not structure the identity of converts as much as their own bright picture of God.

Under the government of this personal, internal authority, converts ex-

---

[41] Frothingham, *Articles*, 8; S. Williams, *The Comfort*, 19–20; Tennent, *The Danger*, 4.

[42] Pemberton, *Knowledge*, 17.

[43] *Works*, III, 303.

[44] Pemberton, *Knowledge*, 9.

[45] *Life*, 84.

perienced a peace and joy unknown under earthly fathers and their old conscience. God's grace dissolved uncertainty and fear. The convert testified to the "sweet solace, rest and joy of soul," the image of God bestowed.[46] "The thought of having so great, so glorious, and excellent a Being for his Father, his Friend, and his Home, sets his heart at Ease from all his anxious Fears and Distresses." [47] The power to replace oppressive authority figures with faith in a loving God was the ultimate reason for the revivalists' success.

Thus the men affected by the Awakening possesed a new character, cleansed of guilt and joyful in the awareness of divine favor. Unfortunately for the social order, however, their personal redemption did not save society. In making peace with themselves, converts inwardly revolted against the old law and authority, and, as time was to show, they would eventually refuse to submit to a social order alien to their new identity. Conservative suspicions of the revival were confirmed when reborn men set out to create a new society compatible with the vision opened in the Great Awakening.

[46] J. Edwards, *Works*, III, 300.

[47] S. Williams, *The Comfort*, 15. Radicals carried this confidence to the point of asserting the new principle in them was perfection. "All Doubting in a Believer is sinful . . ." (Windham Consociation, *Result*, 7; cf. 18).

Popular Uprisings and Civil Authority in Eighteenth-Century America

PAULINE MAIER

The turbulence of twentieth-century America and the class-consciousness of the recent radical critique have tempted many historians to a new concern with the problem of disorder in colonial society. Although textbooks have traditionally referred to a few well-known outbreaks of mob violence, such as the New Jersey and New York land riots and the impressment riots which occurred in several places, they have ordinarily associated mobs with the supposedly democratic purposes of political disorder in the American Revolution.

> *Pauline Maier reminds us, however, that mob action was a relatively common aspect of colonial life. Furthermore, she argues, it was a quasi-legal form of political expression in an era when governments had at their disposal only the most primitive methods of social control. Mob action was a typically eighteenth-century European form of political behavior. It was not terribly violent, limited to very specific purposes, and extra-institutional rather than anti-institutional. Mobs expressed popular opinion in those areas where the ordinary forms of communication, such as legislatures, were incapable of acting. Their aims frequently coincided with the desires of officials, and they were recognized as an essential part of constitutional government in English political theory. Mob action was simply an accepted form of political action.*
>
> *Other scholars, Jesse Lemisch for example, disagree. They view riots as spontaneous expressions of lower-class discontent with the conditions of life, for they believe that the rioters represented a radically disaffected social group which played a vital role in precipitating the American Revolution. If one accepts this view, is there a sociological alternative to Mrs. Maier's explanation of the riots?*

It is only natural that the riots and civil turbulence of the past decade and a half have awakened a new interest in the history of American mobs. It should be emphasized, however, that scholarly attention to the subject has roots independent of contemporary events and founded in long-developing historiographical trends. George Rudé's studies of pre-industrial crowds in France and England, E. J. Hobsbawm's discussion of "archaic" social movements, and recent works linking eighteenth-century American thought with English revolutionary tradition have all, in different ways, inspired a new concern among historians with colonial uprisings.[1] This discovery of the early American mob promises to have a

Reprinted by permission from Pauline Maier, "Popular Uprisings and Civil Authority in Eighteenth-Century America," *William and Mary Quarterly*, 3d Ser., XXVII (1970), 3–35.

[1] See the following by George Rudé: *The Crowd in the French Revolution* (Oxford, 1959); "The London 'Mob' of the Eighteenth Century," *The Historical Journal*, II (1959), 1–18; *Wilkes and Liberty: A Social Study of 1763 to 1774* (Oxford, 1962); *The Crowd in History: A Study of Popular Disturbances in France and England, 1730–1848* (New York, 1964). See also E. J. Hobsbawm, *Primitive Rebels: Studies in Archaic Forms of Social Movement in the 19th and 20th Centuries* (New York, 1959), esp. "The City Mob," 108–125. For recent discussions of the colonial mob see: Bernard Bailyn, *Pamphlets of the American Revolution* (Cambridge, Mass., 1965), I, 581–584; Jesse Lemisch, "Jack Tar in

significant effect upon historical interpretation. Particularly affected are the Revolutionary struggle and the early decades of the new nation, when events often turned upon well-known popular insurrections.

Eighteenth-century uprisings were in some important ways different than those of today — different in themselves, but even more in the political context within which they occurred. As a result they carried different connotations for the American Revolutionaries than they do today. Not all eighteenth-century mobs simply defied the law: some used extralegal means to implement official demands or to enforce laws not otherwise enforceable, others in effect extended the law in urgent situations beyond its technical limits. Since leading eighteenth-century Americans had known many occasions on which mobs took on the defense of the public welfare, which was, after all, the stated purpose of government, they were less likely to deny popular upheavals all legitimacy than are modern leaders. While not advocating popular uprisings, they could still grant such incidents an established and necessary role in free societies, one that made them an integral and even respected element of the political order. These attitudes, and the tradition of colonial insurrection on which they drew, not only shaped political events of the Revolutionary era, but also lay behind many laws and civil procedures that were framed during the 1780's and 1790's, some of which still have a place in the American legal system.

I

Not all colonial uprisings were identical in character or significance. Some involved no more than disorderly vandalism or traditional brawls such as those that annually marked Pope's Day on November 5, particularly in New England. Occasional insurrections defied established laws and authorities in the name of isolated private interests alone — a set of Hartford County, Connecticut, landowners arose in 1722, for example, after a court decision imperiled their particular land titles. Still others — which are of interest here — took on a broader purpose, and defended the interests of their community in general where established

---

the Street: Merchant Seamen in the Politics of Revolutionary America," *William and Mary Quarterly*, 3d Ser., XXV (1968), 371–407; Gordon S. Wood, "A Note on Mobs in the American Revolution," *Wm. and Mary Qtly.*, 3d Ser., XXIII (1966), 635–642, and more recently Wood's *Creation of the American Republic, 1776–1787* (Chapel Hill, 1969), *passim*, but esp. 319–328. Wood offers an excellent analysis of the place of mobs and extralegal assemblies in the development of American constitutionalism. Hugh D. Graham and Ted R. Gurr, *Violence in America: Historical and Comparative Perspectives* (New York, 1969) primarily discusses uprisings of the 19th and 20th centuries, but see the chapters by Richard M. Brown, "Historical Patterns of Violence in America," 45–84, and "The American Vigilante Tradition," 154–226.

authorities failed to act.[2] This common characteristic linked otherwise
diverse rural uprisings in New Jersey and the Carolinas. The insurrec-
tionists' punishment of outlaws, their interposition to secure land titles or
prevent abuses at the hands of legal officials followed a frustration
with established institutions and a belief that justice and even security
had to be imposed by the people directly.[3] The earlier Virginia tobacco
insurrection also illustrates this common pattern well: Virginians began
tearing up young tobacco plants in 1682 only after Governor Thomas
Culpeper forced the quick adjournment of their assembly, which had
been called to curtail tobacco planting during an economic crisis. The
insurrections in Massachusetts a little over a century later represent a
variation on this theme. The insurgents in Worcester, Berkshire, Hampshire, Middlesex, and Bristol counties — often linked together as members
of "Shays's Rebellion" — forced the closing of civil courts, which threatened to send a major portion of the local population to debtors' prison,
only until a new legislature could remedy their pressing needs.[4]

This role of the mob as extralegal arm of the community's interest
emerged, too, in repeated uprisings that occurred within the more
densely settled coastal areas. The history of Boston, where by the mid-
eighteenth century "public order . . . prevailed to a greater degree than
anywhere else in England or America," is full of such incidents. During
the food shortage of 1710, after the governor rejected a petition from
the Boston selectmen calling for a temporary embargo on the exportation
of foodstuffs one heavily laden ship found its rudder cut away, and fifty
men sought to haul another outward bound vessel back to shore. Under

---

[2] Carl Bridenbaugh, *Cities in the Wilderness: The First Century of Urban
Life in America, 1625–1742* (New York, 1964), 70–71, 223–224, 382–384; and
Carl Bridenbaugh, *Cities in Revolt: Urban Life in America, 1743–1776* (New
York, 1964), 113–118; Charles J. Hoadly, ed., *The Public Records of the Colony
of Connecticut . . .* (Hartford, 1872), VI, 332–333, 341–348.

[3] See particularly Richard M. Brown, *The South Carolina Regulators* (Cambridge, Mass., 1963). There is no published study of the New Jersey land riots,
which lasted over a decade and were due above all to the protracted inability of
the royal government to settle land disputes stemming from conflicting proprietary grants made in the late 17th century. See, however, "A State of Facts concerning the Riots and Insurrections in New Jersey, and the Remedies Attempted
to Restore the Peace of the Province," William A. Whitehead *et al.*, eds.,
Archives of the State of New Jersey (Newark, 1883), VII, 207–226. On other
rural insurrections see Irving Mark, *Agrarian Conflicts in Colonial New York,
1711–1775* (New York, 1940), Chap. IV, V; Staughton Lynd, "The Tenant
Rising at Livingston Manor," *New-York Historical Society Quarterly*, XLVIII
(1964), 163–177; Matt Bushnell Jones, *Vermont in the Making, 1750–1777*
(Cambridge, Mass., 1939), Chap. XII, XIII; John R. Dunbar, ed., *The Paxton
Papers* (The Hague, 1957), esp. 3–51.

[4] Richard L. Morton, *Colonial Virginia* (Chapel Hill, 1960), I, 303–304;
Jonathan Smith, "The Depression of 1785 and Daniel Shays' Rebellion," *Wm.
and Mary Qtly.*, 3d Ser., V (1948), 86–87, 91.

similar circumstances Boston mobs again intervened to keep foodstuffs in the colony in 1713 and 1729. When there was some doubt a few years later whether or not the selectmen had the authority to seize a barn lying in the path of a proposed street, a group of townsmen, their faces blackened, levelled the structure and the road went through. Houses of ill fame were attacked by Boston mobs in 1734, 1737, and 1771; and in the late 1760's the *New York Gazette* claimed that mobs in Providence and Newport had taken on responsibility for "disciplining" unfaithful husbands. Meanwhile in New London, Connecticut, another mob prevented a radical religious sect, the Rogerenes, from disturbing normal Sunday services, "a practice they . . . [had] followed more or less for many years past; and which all the laws made in that government, and executed in the most judicious manner could not put a stop to." [5]

Threats of epidemic inspired particularly dramatic instances of this community oriented role of the mob. One revealing episode occurred in Massachusetts in 1773–1774. A smallpox hospital had been built on Essex Island near Marblehead "much against the will of the multitude" according to John Adams. "The patients were careless, some of them wantonly so; and others were suspected of designing to spread the smallpox in the town, which was full of people who had not passed through the distemper." In January 1774 patients from the hospital who tried to enter the town from unauthorized landing places were forcefully prevented from doing so; a hospital boat was burned; and four men suspected of stealing infected clothes from the hospital were tarred and feathered, then carted from Marblehead to Salem in a long cortege. The Marblehead town meeting finally won the proprietors' agreement to shut down the hospital; but after some twenty-two new cases of smallpox broke out in the town within a few days "apprehension became general," and some "Ruffians" in disguise hastened the hospital's demise by burning the nearly evacuated building. A military watch of forty men was needed for several nights to keep the peace in Marblehead.[6]

A similar episode occurred in Norfolk, Virginia, when a group of

[5] Bridenbaugh, *Cities in Revolt*, 114; Bridenbaugh, *Cities in the Wilderness*, 196, 383, 388–389; Edmund S. and Helen M. Morgan, *The Stamp Act Crisis*, rev. ed. (New York, 1963), 159; Anne Rowe Cunningham, ed., *Letters and Diary of John Rowe, Boston Merchant, 1759–1762, 1764–1779* (Boston, 1903), 218. On the marriage riots, see *New-York Gazette* (New York City), July 11, 1765 — and note, that when the reporter speaks of persons "concern'd" in such unlawful Enterprises" he clearly is referring to the husbands, not their "Disciplinarians." On the Rogerenes, see item in *Connecticut Gazette* (New Haven), Apr. 5, 1766, reprinted in Lawrence H. Gipson, *Jared Ingersoll* (New Haven, 1920), 195, n. 1.

[6] John Adams, "Novanglus," in Charles F. Adams, ed., *The Works of John Adams* (Boston, 1850–1856), IV, 76–77; Salem news of Jan. 25 and Feb. 1, 1774, in *Providence Gazette* (Rhode Island), Feb. 5, and Feb. 12, 1774.

wealthy residents decided to have their families inoculated for small-pox. Fears arose that the lesser disease brought on by the inoculations would spread and necessitate a general inoculation, which would cost "more money than is circulating in Norfolk" and ruin trade and commerce such that "the whole colony would feel the effects." Local magistrates said they could not interfere because "the law was silent in the matter." Public and private meetings then sought to negotiate the issue. Despite a hard-won agreement, however, the pro-inoculation faction persisted in its original plan. Then finally a mob drove the newly inoculated women and children on a five-mile forced march in darkness and rain to the common Pest House, a three-year old institution designed to isolate seamen and others, particularly Negroes, infected with small-pox.[7]

These local incidents indicate a willingness among many Americans to act outside the bounds of law, but they cannot be described as anti-authoritarian in any general sense. Sometimes in fact — as in the Boston bawdy house riot of 1734, or the Norfolk smallpox incident — local magistrates openly countenanced or participated in the mob's activities. Far from opposing established institutions, many supporters of Shays's Rebellion honored their leaders "by no less decisive marks of popular favor than elections to local offices of trust and authority." [8] It was above all the existence of such elections that forced local magistrates to reflect community feelings and so prevented their becoming the targets of insurrections. Certainly in New England, where the town meeting ruled, and to some extent in New York, where aldermen and councilmen were annually elected, this was true; yet even in Philadelphia, with its lethargic closed corporation, or Charleston, which lacked municipal institutions, authority was normally exerted by residents who had an immediate sense of local sentiment. Provincial governments were also for the most part kept alert to local feelings by their elected assemblies. Sometimes, of course, uprisings turned against domestic American institutions — as in Pennsylvania in 1764, when the "Paxton Boys" complained that the colony's Quaker assembly had failed to provide adequately for their defense against the Indians. But uprisings over local issues proved extra- ⟩

[7] Letter from "Friend to the Borough and county of Norfolk," in Purdie and Dixon's Virginia Gazette Postscript (Williamsburg), Sept. 8, 1768, which gives the fullest account. This letter answered an earlier letter from Norfolk, Aug. 6, 1768, available in Rind's Va. Gaz. Supplement (Wmsbg.), Aug. 25, 1768. See also letter of Cornelius Calvert in Purdie and Dixon's Va. Gaz. (Wmsbg.), Jan. 9, 1772. Divisions over the inoculation seemed to follow more general political lines. See Patrick Henderson, "Smallpox and Patriotism, The Norfolk Riots, 1768–1769," Virginia Magazine of History and Biography, LXXIII (1965), 413–424.

[8] James Madison to Thomas Jefferson, Mar. 19, 1787, in Julian P. Boyd, ed., The Papers of Thomas Jefferson (Princeton, 1950–), XI, 223.

institutional in character more often than they were anti-institutional; they served the community where no law existed, or intervened beyond what magistrates thought they could do officially to cope with a local problem.

[The case was different when imperial authority was involved. There legal authority emanated from a capital an ocean away, where the colonists had no integral voice in the formation of policy, where governmental decisions were based largely upon the reports of "king's men" and sought above all to promote the king's interests. When London's legal authority and local interest conflicted, efforts to implement the edicts of royal officials were often answered by uprisings, and it was not unusual in these cases for local magistrates to participate or openly sympathize with the insurgents] The colonial response to the White Pines Acts of 1722 and 1729 is one example. Enforcement of the acts was difficult in general because "the various elements of colonial society . . . seemed inclined to violate the pine laws — legislatures, lumbermen, and merchants were against them, and even the royal governors were divided." At Exeter, New Hampshire, in 1734 about thirty men prevented royal officials from putting the king's broad arrow on some seized boards; efforts to enforce the acts in Connecticut during the 1750's ended after a deputy of the surveyor-general was thrown in a pond and nearly drowned; five years later logs seized in Massachusetts and New Hampshire were either "rescued" or destroyed.[9] Two other imperial issues that provoked local American uprisings long before 1765 and continued to do so during the Revolutionary period were impressment and customs enforcement.

As early as 1743 the colonists' violent opposition to impressment was said to indicate a "Contempt of Government." Some captains had been mobbed, the Admiralty complained, "others emprisoned, and afterwards held to exorbitant Bail, and are now under Prosecutions carried on by Combination, and by joint Subscription towards the expense." Colonial governors, despite their offers, furnished captains with little real aid either to procure seamen or "even to protect them from the Rage and Insults of the People." Two days of severe rioting answered Commodore Charles Knowles's efforts to sweep Boston harbor for able-bodied men in November 1747. Again in 1764 when Rear Admiral Lord Alexander Colville sent out orders to "procure" men in principal harbors between Casco Bay and Cape Henlopen, mobs met the ships at every turn. When the *St. John* sent out a boat to seize a recently impressed deserter from a Newport wharf, a mob protected him, captured the boat's officer, and

---

[9] Bernhard Knollenberg, *Origin of the American Revolution: 1759–1776* (New York, 1965), 126, 129. See also, Robert G. Albion, *Forests and Sea Power* (Cambridge, Mass., 1926), 262–263, 265. Joseph J. Malone, *Pine Trees and Politics* (Seattle, 1964), includes less detail on the forceful resistance to the acts.

hurled stones at the crew; later fifty Newporters joined the colony's gunner at Fort George in opening fire on the king's ship itself. Under threat to her master the *Chaleur* was forced to release four fishermen seized off Long Island, and when that ship's captain went ashore at New York a mob seized his boat and burned it in the Fields. In the spring of 1765 after the *Maidstone* capped a six-month siege of Newport harbor by seizing "all the Men" out of a brigantine from Africa, a mob of about five hundred men similarly seized a ship's officer and burned one of her boats on the Common. Impressment also met mass resistance at Norfolk in 1767 and was a major cause of the famous *Liberty* riot at Boston in 1768.[10]

Like the impressment uprisings, which in most instances sought to protect or rescue men from the "press," customs incidents were aimed at impeding the customs service in enforcing British laws. Tactics varied, and although incidents occurred long before 1764 — in 1719, for example, Caleb Heathcote reported a "riotous and tumultuous" rescue of seized claret by Newporters — their frequency, like those of the impressment "riots," apparently increased after the Sugar Act was passed and customs enforcement efforts were tightened. The 1764 rescue of the *Rhoda* in Rhode Island preceded a theft in Dighton, Massachusetts, of the cargo from a newly seized vessel, the *Polly*, by a mob of some forty men with blackened faces. In 1766 again a mob stoned a customs official's home in Falmouth (Portland), Maine, while "Persons unknown and disguised" stole sugar and rum that had been impounded that morning. The intimidation of customs officials and of the particularly despised customs informers also enjoyed a long history. In 1701 the South Carolina attorney general publicly attacked an informer "and struck

[10] Admiralty to Gov. George Thomas, Sept. 26, 1743, in Samuel Hazard *et al.*, eds., *Pennsylvania Archives* (Philadelphia, 1852–1949), I, 639. For accounts of the Knowles riot, see Gov. William Shirley to Josiah Willard, Nov. 19, 1747, Shirley's Proclamation of Nov. 21, 1747, and his letter to the Board of Trade, Dec. 1, 1747, in Charles H. Lincoln, ed., *The Correspondence of William Shirley . . . 1731–1760* (New York, 1912), I, 406–419; see also Thomas Hutchinson, *History of the Province of Massachusetts Bay*, ed. Lawrence S. Mayo (Cambridge, Mass., 1936), II, 330–333; and *Reports of the Record Commissioners of Boston* (Boston, 1885), XIV, 127–130. David Lovejoy, *Rhode Island Politics and the American Revolution, 1760–1776* (Providence, 1958), 36–39, and on the *Maidstone* in particular see "O. G." in *Newport Mercury* (Rhode Island), June 10, 1765. Bridenbaugh, *Cities in Revolt*, 309–311; documents on the *St. John* episode in *Records of the Colony of Rhode Island and Providence Plantations* (Providence, 1856–1865), VI, 427–430. George G. Wolkins, "The Seizure of John Hancock's Sloop 'Liberty,'" Massachusetts Historical Society, *Proceedings* (1921–1923), LV, 239–284. See also Lemisch, "Jack Tar," *Wm. and Mary Qtly.*, 3d Ser., XXV (1968), 391–393; and Neil R. Stout, "Manning the Royal Navy in North America, 1763–1775," *American Neptune*, XXIII (1963), 179–181.

him several times, crying out, this is the Informer, this is he that will ruin the country." Similar assaults occurred decades later, in New Haven in 1766 and 1769, and New London in 1769, and were then often distinguished by their brutality. In 1771 a Providence tidesman, Jesse Saville, was seized, stripped, bound hand and foot, tarred and feathered, had dirt thrown in his face, then was beaten and "almost strangled." Even more thorough assaults upon two other Rhode Island tidesmen followed in July 1770 and upon Collector Charles Dudley in April 1771. Finally, customs vessels came under attack: the *St. John* was shelled at Newport in 1764 where the customs ship *Liberty* was sunk in 1769 — both episodes that served as prelude to the destruction of the *Gaspée* outside Providence in 1772.[11]

Such incidents were not confined to New England. Philadelphia witnessed some of the most savage attacks, and even the surveyor of Sassafras and Bohemia in Maryland — an office long a sinecure, since no ships entered or cleared in Sassafras or Bohemia — met with violence when he tried to execute his office in March 1775. After seizing two wagons of goods being carried overland from Maryland toward Duck Creek, Pennsylvania, the officer was overpowered by a "licentious mob" that kept shouting "Liberty and Duck Creek forever" as it went through the hours-long rituals of tarring and feathering him and threatening his life. And at Norfolk, Virginia, in the spring [of] 1766 an accused customs informer was tarred and feathered, pelted with stones and rotten eggs, and finally thrown in the sea where he nearly drowned. Even Georgia

---

11 Heathcote letter from Newport, Sept. 7, 1719, *Records of the Colony of Rhode Island*, IV, 259–260; Lovejoy, *Rhode Island Politics*, 35–39. There is an excellent summary of the *Polly* incident in Morgan, *Stamp Act Crisis*, 59, 64–67; and see also *Providence Gaz.* (R.I.), Apr. 27, 1765. On the Falmouth incident see the letter from the collector and comptroller of Falmouth, Aug. 19, 1766, Treasury Group 1, Class 453, Piece 182, Public Records Office. Hereafter cited as T. 1/453, 182. See also the account in Appendix I of Josiah Quincy, Jr., *Reports of the Cases Argued and Adjudged in the Superior Court of Judicature of the Province of Massachusetts Bay, between 1761 and 1772* (Boston, 1865), 446–447. W. Noel Sainsbury *et al.*, eds., *Calendar of State Papers, Colonial Series, America and the West Indies* (London, 1910), 1701, no. 1042, xi, a. A summary of one of the New Haven informer attacks is in Willard M. Wallace, *Traitorous Hero: The Life and Fortunes of Benedict Arnold* (New York, 1954), 20–23. Arnold's statement on the affair which he led is in Malcolm Decker, *Benedict Arnold, Son of the Havens* (Tarrytown, N.Y., 1932), 27–29. Gipson, in *Jared Ingersoll*, 277–278, relates the later incidents. For the New London informer attacks, see documents of July 1769 in T. 1/471. On the Saville affair see Saville to collector and comptroller of customs in Newport, May 18, 1769, T. 1/471, and *New York Journal* (New York City), July 6, 1769. On later Rhode Island incidents see Dudley and John Nicoll to governor of Rhode Island, Aug. 1, 1770, T. 1/471. Dudley to commissioners of customs at Boston, Newport, Apr. 11, 1771, T. 1/482. On the destruction of the *Liberty* see documents in T. 1/471, esp. comptroller and collector to the governor, July 21, 1769.

saw customs violence before independence, and one of the rare deaths resulting from a colonial riot occurred there in 1775.[12]

White Pines, impressment, and customs uprisings have attracted historians' attention because they opposed British authority and so seemed to presage the Revolution. In fact, however, they had much in common with many exclusively local uprisings. In each of the incidents violence was directed not so much against the "rich and powerful"[13] as against men who — as it was said after the Norfolk smallpox incident — "in every part of their conduct . . . acted very inconsistently as good neighbors or citizens." The effort remained one of safeguarding not the interests of isolated groups alone, but the community's safety and welfare. The White Pines Acts need not have provoked this opposition had they applied only to trees of potential use to the Navy, and had they been framed and executed with concern for colonial rights. But instead the acts reserved to the Crown all white pine trees including those "utterly unfit for masts, yards, or bowsprits," and prevented colonists from using them for building materials or lumber exportation even in regions where white pine constituted the principal forest growth. As a result the acts "operated so much against the convenience and even necessities of the inhabitants," Surveyor John Wentworth explained, that "it became almost a general interest of the country" to frustrate the acts' execution.

[12] On Philadelphia violence see William Sheppard to commissioners of customs, Apr. 21, 1769, T. 1/471; Deputy Collector at Philadelphia John Swift to commissioners of customs at Boston, Oct. 13, 1769, *ibid.*; and on a particularly brutal attack on the son of customsman John Hatton, see Deputy Collector John Swift to Boston customs commissioners, Nov. 15, 1770, and related documents in T. 1/476. See also Alfred S. Martin, "The King's Customs: Philadelphia, 1763–1774," *Wm. and Mary Qtly.*, 3d Ser., V (1948), 201–216. Documents on the Maryland episode are in T. 1/513, including the following: Richard Reeve to Grey Cooper, Apr. 19, 1775; extracts from a Council meeting, Mar. 16, 1775; deposition of Robert Stratford Byrne, surveyor of His Majesty's Customs at Sassafras and Bohemia, and Byrne to customs commissioners, Mar. 17, 1775. On the Virginia incident see William Smith to Jeremiah Morgan, Apr. 3, 1766, Colonial Office Group, Class 5, Piece 1331, 80, Public Record Office. Hereafter cited as C. O. 5/1331, 80. W. W. Abbot, *The Royal Governors of Georgia, 1754–1775* (Chapel Hill, 1959), 174–175. These customs riots remained generally separate from the more central intercolonial opposition to Britain that emerged in 1765. Isolated individuals like John Brown of Providence and Maximilian Calvert of Norfolk were involved in both the organized intercolonial Sons of Liberty and in leading mobs against customs functionaries or informers. These roles, however, for the most part were unconnected, that is, there was no radical program of customs obstruction *per se*. Outbreaks were above all local responses to random provocations and, at least before the Townshend duties, usually devoid of explicit ideological justifications.

[13] Hobsbawm, *Primitive Rebels*, 111. For a different effort to see class division as relevant in 18th century uprisings, see Lemisch, "Jack Tar," *Wm. and Mary Qtly.*, 3d Ser., XXV (1968), 387.

Impressment offered a more immediate effect, since the "press" could quickly cripple whole towns. Merchants and masters were affected as immediately as seamen: the targeted port, as Massachusetts' Governor William Shirley explained in 1747, was drained of mariners by both impressment itself and the flight of navigation to safer provinces, driving the wages for any remaining seamen upward. When the press was of long duration, moreover, or when it took place during a normally busy season, it could mean serious shortages of food or firewood for winter, and a general attrition of the commercial life that sustained all strata of society in trading towns. Commerce seemed even more directly attacked by British trade regulations, particularly by the proliferation of customs procedures in the mid-1760's that seemed to be in no American's interest, and by the Sugar Act with its virtual prohibition of the trade with the foreign West Indies that sustained the economies of colonies like Rhode Island. As a result even when only a limited contingent of sailors participated in a customs incident officials could suspect — as did the deputy collector at Philadelphia in 1770 — that the mass of citizens "in their Hearts" approved of it.[14]

Because the various uprisings discussed here grew out of concerns essential to wide sections of the community, the "rioters" were not necessarily confined to the seamen, servants, Negroes, and boys generally described as the staple components of the colonial mob. The uprising of Exeter, New Hampshire, townsmen against the king's surveyor of the woods in 1754 was organized by a member of the prominent Gillman family who was a mill owner and a militia officer. Members of the upper classes participated in Norfolk's smallpox uprising, and Cornelius Calvert, who was later attacked in a related incident, protested that leading members of the community, doctors and magistrates, had posted securities for the good behavior of the "Villains" convicted of mobbing him. Captain Jeremiah Morgan complained about the virtually universal participation of Norfolkers in an impressment incident of 1767, and "all the principal Gentlemen in Town" were supposedly present when a customs informer was tarred and feathered there in 1766. Merchant Benedict Arnold admitted leading a New Haven mob against an informer in 1766; New London merchants Joseph Packwood and Nathaniel Shaw commanded the mob that first accosted Captain William Reid the night the *Liberty* was destroyed at Newport in 1769, just as John Brown, a leading

14 "Friends to the borough and county of Norfolk," Purdie and Dixon's *Va. Gaz. Postscript.* (Wmsbg.), Sept. 8, 1768. Wentworth quoted in Knollenberg, *Origin of American Revolution*, 124–125. Lemisch, "Jack Tar," *Wm. and Mary Qtly.*, 3d Ser., XXV (1968), 383–385. Shirley to Duke of Newcastle, Dec. 31, 1747, in Lincoln, ed., *Shirley Correspondence*, I, 420–423. Dora Mae Clark, "The Impressment of Seamen in the American Colonies," *Essays in Colonial History Presented to Charles McLean Andrews* (New Haven, 1931), 199–200; John Swift to Boston customs commissioners, Nov. 15, 1770, T. 1/476.

Providence merchant, led that against the *Gaspée*. Charles Dudley reported in April 1771 that the men who beat him in Newport "did not come from the . . . lowest class of Men," but were "stiled Merchants and the Masters of their Vessels"; and again in 1775 Robert Stratford Byrne said many of his Maryland and Pennsylvania attackers were "from Appearance . . . Men of Property." It is interesting, too, that during Shays's Rebellion — so often considered a class uprising — "men who were of good property and owed not a shilling" were said to be "involved in the train of desperado's to suppress the courts." [15]

[Opposition to impressment and customs enforcement in itself was not, moreover, the only cause of the so-called impressment or customs "riots." The complete narratives of these incidents indicate again not only that the crowd acted to support local interests, but that it sometimes enforced the will of local magistrates by extralegal means.] Although British officials blamed the *St. John* incident upon that ship's customs and impressment activities, colonists insisted that the confrontation began when some sailors stole a few pigs and chickens from a local miller and the ship's crew refused to surrender the thieves to Newport officials. Two members of the Rhode Island council then ordered the gunner of Fort George to detain the schooner until the accused seamen were delivered to the sheriff, and "many People went over the Fort to assist the Gunner in the Discharge of his Duty." Only after this uprising did the ship's officers surrender the accused men.[16] Similarly, the 1747

---

[15] Malone, *White Pines*, 112. "Friends to the borough and county of Norfolk," Purdie and Dixon's *Va. Gaz. Postscrpt.* (Wmsbg.), Sept. 8, 1768; Calvert letter, *ibid.*, Jan. 9, 1772. Capt. Jeremiah Morgan, quoted in Lemisch, "Jack Tar," *Wm. and Mary Qtly.*, 3d Ser., XXV (1968), 391; and William Smith to Morgan, Apr. 3, 1766, C. O. 5/1331, 80. Decker, *Benedict Arnold*, 27–29; deposition of Capt. William Reid on the *Liberty* affair, July 21, 1769, T. 1/471; Ephraim Bowen's narrative on the *Gaspée* affair, *Records of the Colony of Rhode Island*, VII, 68–73; Charles Dudley to Boston customs commissioners, Apr. 11, 1771, T. 1/482, and deposition by Byrne, T. 1/513. Edward Carrington to Jefferson, June 9, 1787, Boyd, ed., *Jefferson Papers*, XI, 408; and see also Smith, "Depression of 1785," *Wm. and Mary Qtly.*, 3d Ser., V (1948), 88 — of the 21 men indicted for treason in Worcester during the court's April term 1787, 15 were "gentlemen" and only 6 "yeomen."

[16] Gov. Samuel Ward's report to the Treasury lords, Oct. 23, 1765, Ward Manuscripts, Box 1, fol. 58, Rhode Island Historical Society, Providence. See also deposition of Daniel Vaughn of Newport — Vaughn was the gunner at Fort George — July 8, 1764, Chalmers Papers, Rhode Island, fol. 41, New York Public Library, New York City. For British official accounts of the affair, see Lieut. Hill's version in James Munro, ed., *Acts of the Privy Council of England, Colonial Series* (London, 1912), VI, 374–376, and the report of John Robinson and John Nicoll to the customs commissioners, Aug. 30, 1765, Privy Council Group, Class I, Piece 51, Bundle 1 (53a), Public Record Office. Hill, whose report was drawn up soon after the incident, does not contradict Ward's narrative, but seems oblivious of any warrant-granting process on shore; Robinson and Nicoll — whose

Knowles impressment riot in Boston and the 1765 *Maidstone* impressment riot in Newport broke out after governor's request for the release of impressed seamen had gone unanswered, and only after the outbreaks of violence were the governor's requests honored. The crowd that first assembled on the night the *Liberty* was destroyed in Newport also began by demanding the allegedly drunken sailors who that afternoon had abused and shot at a colonial captain, Joseph Packwood, so they could be bound over to local magistrates for prosecution.[17]

In circumstances such as these, the "mob" often appeared only after the legal channels of redress had proven inadequate. The main thrust of the colonist's resistance to the White Pines Acts had always been made in their courts and legislatures. Violence broke out only in local situations where no alternative was available. Even the burning of the *Gaspée* in June 1772 was a last resort. Three months before the incident a group of prominent Providence citizens complained about the ship's wanton severity with all vessels along the coast and the colony's governor pressed their case with the fleet's admiral. The admiral, however, supported the *Gaspée*'s commander, Lieutenant William Dudingston; and thereafter, the *Providence Gazette* reported, Dudingston became "more haughty, insolent and intolerable, . . . personally ill treating every master and merchant of the vessels he boarded, stealing sheep, hogs, poultry, etc. from farmers round the bay, and cutting down their fruit and other trees for firewood." Redress from London was possible but time-consuming, and in the meantime Rhode Island was approaching what its governor called "the deepest calamity" as supplies of food and fuel were curtailed and prices, especially in Newport, rose steeply. It was significant that merchant John Brown finally led the Providence "mob" that seized the moment in June when the *Gaspée* ran aground near Warwick, for it was he who had spearheaded the effort in March 1772 to win redress through the normal channels of government.[18]

II

There was little that was distinctively American about the colonial insurrections. The uprisings over grain exportations during times of

---

report was drawn up over a year later, and in the midst of the Stamp Act turmoil — claimed that a recent customs seizure had precipitated the attack upon the *St. John*.

[17] On the Knowles and *Maidstone* incidents see above, n. 10. On the *Liberty* affair see documents in T. 1/471, esp. the deposition of Capt. William Reid, July 21, 1769, and that of John Carr, the second mate, who indicates that the mob soon forgot its scheme of delivering the crew members to the magistrates.

[18] Malone, *White Pines*, 8–9, and *passim*. *Records of the Colony of Rhode Island*, VII, 60, 62–63, 174–175, including the deposition of Dep. Gov. Darius Sessions, June 12, 1772, and Adm. Montagu to Gov. Wanton, Apr. 8, 1772. Also, Wanton to Hillsborough, June 16, 1772, and Ephraim Bowen's narrative, *ibid.*, 63–73, 90–92. *Providence Gaz.* (R.I.), Jan. 9, 1773.

dearth, the attacks on brothels, press gangs, royal forest officials, and customsmen, all had their counterparts in seventeenth- and eighteenth-century England. Even the Americans' hatred of the customs establishment mirrored the Englishman's traditional loathing of excise men. Like the customsmen in the colonies, they seemed to descend into localities armed with extraordinary prerogative powers. Often, too, English excisemen were "thugs and brutes who beat up their victims without compunction or stole or wrecked their property" and against whose extravagances little redress was possible through the law.[19]   Charges of an identical character were made in the colonies against customsmen and naval officials as well, particularly after 1763 when officers of the Royal Navy were commissioned as deputy members of the customs service,[20] and a history of such accusations lay behind many of the best-known waterfront insurrections. The Americans' complaints took on particular significance only because in the colonies those officials embodied the authority of a "foreign" power. Their arrogance and arbitrariness helped effect "an estrangement of the Affections of the People from the Authority under which they act," and eventually added an emotional element of anger against the Crown to a revolutionary conflict otherwise carried on in the language of law and right.[21]

The focused character of colonial uprisings also resembled those in England and even France where, Rudé has pointed out, crowds were remarkably single-minded and discriminating.[22] Targets were characteristically related to grievances: the Knowles rioters sought only the release of the impressed men; they set free a captured officer when assured he had nothing to do with the press, and refrained from burning a boat

[19] Max Beloff, *Public Order and Popular Disturbances, 1660–1714* (London, 1938), *passim*; Albion, *Forests and Sea Power*, 263; J. H. Plumb, *England in the Eighteenth Century* (Baltimore, 1961 [orig. publ., Oxford, 1950]), 66.

[20] See, for example, "A Pumkin" in the *New London Gazette* (Connecticut), May 14, 18, 1773; "O. G." in *Newport Merc.* (R.I.), June 10, 1765; *New London Gaz.* (Conn.), Sept. 22, 1769; complaints of Marylander David Bevan reprinted in Rind's *Va. Gaz.* (Wmsbg.), July 27, 1769, and *New London Gaz.* (Conn.), July 21, 1769. Stout, "Manning the Royal Navy," *American Neptune,* XXIII (1963), 174. For a similar accusation against a surveyor-general of the king's woods, see Albion, *Forests and Sea Power*, 262.

[21] Joseph Reed to the president of Congress, Oct. 21, 1779, in Hazard *et al.*, eds., *Pennsylvania Archives*, VII, 762. Five years earlier Reed had tried to impress upon Lord Dartmouth the importance of constraining Crown agents in the colonies if any reconciliation were to be made between Britain and the colonies. See his letter to Earl of Dartmouth, Apr. 4, 1774, in William B. Reed, *Life and Correspondence of Joseph Reed* (Philadelphia, 1847), I, 56–57. For a similar plea, again from a man close to the American Revolutionary leadership, see Stephen Sayre to Lord Dartmouth, Dec. 13, 1766, Dartmouth Papers, D 1778/2/258, William Salt Library, Stafford, England.

[22] Rudé, *Crowd in History*, 60, 253–254. The restraint exercised by 18th century mobs has often been commented upon. See, for example, Wood, "A Note on Mobs." *Wm. and Mary Qtly.*, 3d Ser., XXIII (1966), 636–637.

near Province House for fear the fire would spread. The Norfolk rioters, driven by fear of smallpox, forcefully isolated the inoculated persons where they would be least dangerous. Even the customs rioters vented their brutality on customs officers and informers alone, and the Shaysite "mobs" dispersed after closing the courts which promised most immediately to effect their ruin. So domesticated and controlled was the Boston mob that it refused to riot on Saturday and Sunday nights, which were considered holy by New Englanders.[23]

When colonists compared their mobs with those in the Mother Country they were struck only with the greater degree of restraint among Americans. "These People bear no Resemblance to an English Mob," John Jay wrote of the Shaysites in December 1786, "they are more temperate, cool and regular in their Conduct — they have hitherto abstained from Plunder, nor have they that I know of committed any outrages but such as the accomplishment of their Purpose made necessary." Similar comparisons were often repeated during the Revolutionary conflict, and were at least partially grounded in fact. When Londoners set out to "pull down" houses of ill fame in 1688, for example, the affair spread, prisons were opened, and disorder ended only when troops were called out. But when eighteenth-century Bostonians set out on the same task, there is no record that their destruction extended beyond the bordellos themselves. Even the violence of the customs riots — which contrast in that regard from other American incidents — can sometimes be explained by the presence of volatile foreign seamen. The attack on the son of customsman John Hatton, who was nearly killed in a Philadelphia riot, occurred, for example, when the city was crowded by over a thousand seamen. His attackers were apparently Irish crew members of a vessel he and his father had tried to seize off Cape May, and they were "set on," the Philadelphia collector speculated, by an Irish merchant in Philadelphia to whom the vessel was consigned. One of the most lethal riots in the history of colonial America, in which rioters killed five people, occurred in a small town near Norfolk, Virginia, and was significantly perpetrated entirely by British seamen who resisted the local inhabitants' efforts to reinstitute peace.[24] During and immediately

[23] Joseph Harrison's testimony in Wolkins, "Seizure of Handcock's Sloop 'Liberty,'" Mass. Hist. Soc., *Proceedings*, LV, 254.

[24] Jay to Jefferson, Dec. 14, 1786, Boyd, ed., *Jefferson Papers*, X, 597. Beloff, *Public Order*, 30. John Swift to Boston customs commissioners, Nov. 15, 1770, Gov. William Franklin's Proclamation, Nov. 17, 1770, and John Hatton to Boston custom commissioners, Nov. 20, 1770, T. 1/476. The last mentioned riot occurred in November 1762. A cartel ship from Havanna had stopped for repairs in October. On Nov. 21 a rumor spread that the Spaniards were murdering the inhabitants, which drew seamen from His Majesty's ship, *Arundel*, also in the harbor, into town, where the seamen drove the Spaniards into a house, set fire to it, and apparently intended to blow it up. A dignitary of the Spanish colonial

after the Revolutionary War some incidents occurred in which deaths are recorded; but contemporaries felt these were historical aberrations, caused by the "brutalizing" effect of the war itself. "Our citizens, from a habit of putting . . . [the British] to death, have reconciled their minds to the killing of each other," South Carolina Judge Aedanus Burke explained.[25]

To a large extent the pervasive restraint and virtual absence of bloodshed in American incidents can best be understood in terms of social and military circumstance. There was no large amorphous city in America comparable to London, where England's worst incidents occurred. More important, the casualties even in eighteenth-century British riots were rarely the work of rioters. No deaths were inflicted by the Wilkes, Anti-Irish, or "No Popery" mobs, and only single fatalities resulted from other upheavals such as the Porteous riots of 1736. "It was authority rather than the crowd that was conspicuous for its violence to life and limb": all 285 casualties of the Gordon riots, for example, were rioters.[26] Since a regular army was less at the ready for use against colonial mobs, casualty figures for American uprisings were naturally much reduced.

To some extent the general tendency toward a discriminating purposefulness was shared by mobs throughout western Europe, but within the British Empire the focused character of popular uprisings and also their persistence can be explained in part by the character of law enforcement procedures. There were no professional police forces in the eighteenth century. Instead the power of government depended traditionally upon institutions like the "hue and cry," by which the community in general rose to apprehend felons. In its original medieval form the "hue and cry" was a form of summary justice that resembled modern lynch law. More commonly by the eighteenth century magistrates turned to the *posse commitatus*, literally the "power of the country," and in practice all able-bodied men a sheriff might call upon to assist him. Where greater and more organized support was needed, magistrates could call out the militia.[27] Both the *posse* and the militia drew upon local men,

---

service, who had been a passenger on the cartel ship, was beaten and some money and valuables were stolen from him. Local men tried to quell the riot without success. It was eventually put down by militiamen from Norfolk. See "A Narrative of a Riot in Virginia in November 1762," T. 1/476.

[25] Burke and others to the same effect, quoted in Jerome J. Nadelhaft, The Revolutionary Era in South Carolina, 1775–1788 (unpubl. Ph.D. diss., University of Wisconsin, 1965), 151–152. See also account of the "Fort Wilson" riot of October 1779 in J. Thomas Scharf and Thompson Westcott, *History of Philadelphia, 1609–1884* (Philadelphia, 1884), I, 401–403.

[26] Rudé, *Crowd in History*, 255–257.

[27] On the "hue and cry" see Frederick Pollock and Frederic W. Maitland, *The History of English Law before the Time of Edward I* (Cambridge, Eng., 1968

including many of the same persons who made up the mob. This was particularly clear where these traditional mechanisms failed to function effectively. At Boston in September 1766 when customsmen contemplated breaking into the house of merchant Daniel Malcom to search for contraband goods, Sheriff Stephen Greenleaf threatened to call for support from members of the very crowd suspected of an intent to riot; and when someone suggested during the Stamp Act riots that the militia be raised Greenleaf was told it had already risen. This situation meant that mobs could naturally assume the manner of a lawful institution, acting by habit with relative restraint and responsibility. On the other hand, the militia institutionalized the practice of forcible popular coercion and so made the formation of extralegal mobs more natural that J. R. Western has called the militia "a relic of the bad old days," and hailed its passing as "a step towards . . . bringing civilization and humanity into our [English] political life." [28]

These law enforcement mechanisms left magistrates virtually helpless whenever a large segment of the population was immediately involved in the disorder, or when the community had a strong sympathy for the rioters. The Boston militia's failure to act in the Stamp Act riots, which was repeated in nearly all the North American colonies, recapitulated a similar refusal during the Knowles riot of 1747.[29] If the mob's sympathizers were confined to a single locality, the governor could try to call out the militias of surrounding areas, as Massachusetts Governor William Shirley began to do in 1747, and as, to some extent, Governor Francis Bernard attempted after the rescue of the *Polly* in 1765.[30] In the case of sudden uprisings, however, these peace-keeping mechanisms were at

---

[orig. publ., Cambridge, Eng., 1895]), II, 578–580, and William Blackstone, *Commentaries on the Laws of England* (Philadelphia, 1771), IV, 290–291. John Shy, *Toward Lexington: The Role of the British Army in the Coming of the American Revolution* (Princeton, 1965), 40. The English militia underwent a period of decay after 1670 but was revived in 1757. See J. R. Western, *The English Militia in the Eighteenth Century* (London, 1965).

[28] Greenleaf's deposition, T. 1/446; *Providence Gaz.* (R.I.), Aug. 24, 1765; Western, *English Militia*, 74.

[29] Gov. William Shirley explained the militia's failure to appear during the opening stages of the Knowles riot by citing the militiamen's opposition to impressment and consequent sympathy for the rioters. See his letter to the Lords of Trade, Dec. 1, 1747, in Lincoln, ed., *Shirley Correspondence*, I, 417–418. The English militia was also unreliable. It worked well against invasions and unpopular rebellions, but was less likely to support the government when official orders "clashed with the desires of the citizens" or when ordered to protect unpopular minorities. Sir Robert Wolpole believed "that if called on to suppress smuggling, protect the turnpikes, or enforce the gin act, the militia would take the wrong side." Western, *English Militia*, 72–73.

[30] Shirley to Josiah Willard, Nov. 19, 1747, Lincoln, ed., *Shirley Correspondence*, I, 407; Bernard's orders in *Providence Gaz.* (R.I.), Apr. 27, 1765.

best partially effective since they required time to assemble strength, which often made the effort wholly pointless.

When the disorder continued and the militia either failed to appear or proved insufficient, there was, of course, the army, which was used periodically in the eighteenth century against rioters in England and Scotland. Even in America peacetime garrisons tended to be placed where they might serve to maintain law and order. But since all Englishmen shared a fear of standing armies the deployment of troops had always to be a sensitive and carefully limited recourse] Military and civil spheres of authority were rigidly separated, as was clear to Lord Jeffery Amherst, who refused to use soldiers against antimilitary rioters during the Seven Years' War because that function was "entirely foreign to their command and belongs of right to none but the civil power." In fact troops could be used against British subjects, as in the suppression of civil disorder, only upon the request of local magistrates. This institutional inhibition carried, if anything, more weight in the colonies. There royal governors had quickly lost their right to declare martial law without consent of the provincial councils that were, again, usually filled with local men.[31]

For all practical purposes, then, when a large political unit such as an entire town or colony condoned an act of mass force, problems were raised "almost insoluble without rending the whole fabric of English law." Nor was the situation confined to the colonies. After describing England's institutions for keeping the peace under the later Stuarts, Max Beloff suggested that no technique for maintaining order was found until nineteenth-century reformers took on the task of reshaping urban government. Certainly by the 1770's no acceptable solution had been found — neither by any colonists, nor "anyone in London, Paris, or Rome, either," as Carl Bridenbaugh has put it. To even farsighted contemporaries like John Adams the weakness of authority was a fact of the social order that necessarily conditioned the way rulers could act. "It is vain to expect or hope to carry on government against the universal bent and genius of the people," he wrote, "we may whimper and whine as much as we will, but nature made it impossible when she made man." [32]

The mechanisms of enforcing public order were rendered even more fragile since the difference between legal and illegal applications of mass force was distinct in theory, but sometimes indistinguishable in practice. The English common law prohibited riot, defined as an uprising of three or more persons who performed what Blackstone called an "unlawful act of violence" for a private purpose. If the act was never carried out or

---

[31] Shy, *Toward Lexington*, 39–40, 44, 47, 74. Amherst, quoted in J. C. Long, *Lord Jeffery Amherst* (New York, 1933), 124.

[32] Shy, *Toward Lexington*, 44; Beloff, *Public Order*, 157–158; Bridenbaugh, *Cities in Revolt*, 297; C. F. Adams, ed., *Works of Adams*, IV, 74–75, V, 209.

attempted the offense became unlawful assembly; if some effort was made toward its execution, rout; and if the purpose of the uprising was public rather than private — tearing down whore houses, for example, or destroying all enclosures rather than just those personally affecting the insurgents — the offence became treason since it constituted a usurpation of the king's function, a "levying war against the King." The precise legal offence lay not so much in the purpose of the uprising as in its use of force and violence "wherein the Law does not allow the Use of such Force." Such unlawful assumptions of force were carefully distinguished by commentators upon the common law from other occasions on which the law authorized a use of force. It was, for example, legal for force to be used by a sheriff, constable, "or perhaps even . . . a private Person" who assembled "a competent Number of People, in Order with Force to suppress Rebels, or Enemies, or Rioters"; for a justice of the peace to raise the *posse* when opposed in detaining lands, or for Crown officers to raise "a Power as may effectually enable them to over-power any . . . Resistance" in the execution of the King's writs.[33]

In certain situations these distinctions offered at best a very uncertain guide as to who did or did not exert force lawfully. Should a *posse* employ more force than was necessary to overcome overt resistance, for example, its members acted illegally and were indictable for riot. And where established officials supported both sides in a confrontation, or where the legality of an act that officials were attempting to enforce was itself disputed, the decision as to who were or were not rioters seemed to depend upon the observer's point of view. Impressment is a good example. The colonists claimed that impressment was unlawful in North America under an act of 1708, while British authorities and some — but not all — spokesmen for the government held that the law had lapsed in 1713. The question was settled only in 1775, when Parliament finally repealed the "Sixth of Anne." Moreover, supposing impressment could indeed be carried on, were press warrants from provincial authorities still necessary? Royal instructions of 1697 had given royal governors the "sole power of impressing seamen in any of our plantations in America or in sight of them." Admittedly that clause was dropped in 1708, and a subsequent parliamentary act of 1746, which required the full consent of the governor and council before impressment could be carried on within their province, applied only to the West Indies. Nonetheless it seems that in 1764 the Lords of the Admiralty thought the requirement held throughout North America.[34] With the legality of impressment efforts

---

[33] The definition of the common law of riot most commonly cited — for example, by John Adams in the Massacre trials — was from William Hawkins, *A Treatise of the Pleas of the Crown* (London, 1716), I, 155–159. See also, Blackstone, *Commentaries*, IV, 146–147, and Edward Coke, *The Third Part of the Institutes of the Laws of England* (London, 1797), 176.

[34] Clark, "Impressment of Seamen," *Essays in Honor of Andrews*, 198–224;

so uncertain, especially when opposed by local authorities, it was possible to see the press gangs as "rioters" for trying *en masse* to perpetrate an unlawful act of violence. In that case the local townsmen who opposed them might be considered lawful defenders of the public welfare, acting much as they would in a *posse*. In 1770 John Adams cited opposition to press gangs who acted without warrants as an example of the lawful use of force; and when the sloop of war *Hornet* swept into Norfolk, Virginia, in September 1767 with a "bloody riotous plan . . . to impress seamen, without consulting the Mayor, or any other magistrate," the offense was charged to the pressmen. Roused by the watchman, who called out "*a riot by man of war's men*," the inhabitants rose to back the magistrates, and not only secured the release of the impressed men but also imprisoned ten members of the press gang. The ship's captain, on the other hand, condemned the townsmen as "Rioters." Ambiguity was present, too, in Newport's *St. John* clash, which involved both impressment and criminal action on the part of royal seamen and culminated with Newporters firing on the king's ship. The Privy Council in England promptly classified the incident as a riot, but the Rhode Island governor's report boldly maintained that "the people meant nothing but to assist [the magistrates] in apprehending the Offenders" on the vessel, and even suggested that "their Conduct be honored with his Majesty's royal Approbation." [35]

The enforcement of the White Pines Acts was similarly open to legal dispute. The acts seemed to violate both the Massachusetts and Connecticut charters; the meaning of provisions exempting trees growing within townships (act of 1722) and those which were "the property of private persons" (act of 1729) was contested, and royal officials tended to work on the basis of interpretations of the laws that Bernhard Knollenberg has called farfetched and, in one case, "utterly untenable." The Exeter, New Hampshire, "riot" of 1734, for example, answered an attempt of the surveyor to seize boards on the argument that the authorization to seize logs from allegedly illegally felled white pine trees in the act of 1722 included an authorization to seize processed lumber. As a result, Kollenberg concluded, although the surveyor's reports "give the impression that the New Englanders were an utterly lawless lot, . . . in many if not most cases they were standing for what they believed, with reason,

---

Stout, "Manning the Royal Navy," *American Neptune*, XXIII (1963), 178–179; and Leonard W. Labaree, ed., *Royal Instructions to British Colonial Governors, 1670–1776* (New York, 1935), I, 442–443.

[35] L. Kinvin Wroth and Hiller B. Zobel, eds., *Legal Papers of John Adams* (Cambridge, Mass., 1965), III, 253. Account of the Norfolk incident by George Abyvon, Sept. 5, 1767, in Purdie and Dixon's *Va. Gaz.* (Wmsbg.), Oct. 1, 1767. Capt. Morgan quoted in Lemisch, "Jack Tar," *Wm. and Mary Qtly.*, 3d Ser., XXV (1968), 391. Munro, ed., *Acts of the Privy Council, Colonial Series*, VI, 374; Gov. Samuel Ward to Treasury lords, Oct. 23, 1765, Ward MSS, Box 1, fol. 58.

were their legal and equitable rights in trees growing on their own lands." [36]

[Occasions open to such conflicting interpretations were rare. Most often even those who sympathized with the mob's motives condemned its use of force as illegal and unjustifiable. That ambiguous cases did arise, however, indicates that legitimacy and illegitimacy, *posses* and rioters, represented but poles of the same spectrum. And where a mob took upon itself the defense of the community, it benefited from a certain popular legitimacy even when the strict legality of its action was in doubt, particularly among a people taught that the legitimacy of law itself depended upon its defense of the public welfare.]

Whatever quasi-legal status mobs were accorded by local communities was reinforced, moreover, by formal political thought. "Riots and rebellions" were often calmly accepted as a constant and ever necessary element of free government. This acceptance depended, however, upon certain essential assumptions about popular uprisings. With words that could be drawn almost verbatim from John Locke or any other English author of similar convictions, colonial writers posited a continuing moderation and purposefulness on the part of the mob. "Tho' innocent Persons may sometimes suffer in popular Tumults," observed a 1768 writer in the *New York Journal*, "yet the general Resentment of the People is principally directed according to Justice, and the greatest Delinquent feels it most." Moreover, upheavals constituted only occasional interruptions in well-governed societies. "Good Laws and good Rulers will always be obey'd and respected"; "the Experience of all Ages proves, that Mankind are much more likely to submit to bad Laws and wicked Rulers, than to resist good ones." "Mobs and Tumults," it was often said, "never happen but thro' Oppression and a scandalous Abuse of Power." [37]

In the hands of Locke such remarks constituted relatively inert statements of fact. Colonial writers, however, often turned these pronounce-

[36] Knollenberg, *Origin of the Revolution*, 122–130; Albion, *Forests and Sea Power*, 255–258.

[37] *N.Y. Jour.* (N.Y.C.), Aug. 18, 1768 (the writer was allegedly drawing together arguments that had recently appeared in the British press); and *N.Y. Jour. Supplement* (N.Y.C.), Jan. 4, 1770. Note also that Jefferson accepted Shays's rebellion as a sign of health in American institutions only after he had been assured by men like Jay that the insurgents had acted purposely and moderately, and after he had concluded that the uprising represented no continuous threat to established government. "An insurrection in one of the 13. states in the course of 11. years that they have subsisted amounts to one in any particular state in 143 years, say a century and a half," he calculated. "This would not be near as many as has happened in every other government that has ever existed," and clearly posed no threat to the constitutional order as a whole. To David Hartley, July 2, 1787, Boyd, ed., *Jefferson Papers*, XI, 526.

ments on their heads such that observed instances of popular disorder became *prima facie* indictments of authority. In 1747, for example, New Jersey land rioters argued that "from their Numbers, Violences, and unlawful Actions" it was to be "inferred that . . . they are wronged and oppressed, or else they would never *rebell agt. the Laws.*" Always, a New York writer said in 1770, when "the People of any Government" become "turbulent and uneasy," it was above all "a certain Sign of Maladministration." Even when disorders were not directly levelled against government they provided "strong proofs that something is much amiss in the state" as William Samuel Johnson put it; that — in Samuel Adams's words — the "wheels of good government" were "somewhat clogged." Americans who used this argument against Britain in the 1760's continued to depend upon it two decades later when they reacted to Shays's Rebellion by seeking out the public "Disease" in their own independent governments that was indicated by the "Spirit of Licentiousness" in Massachusetts.[38]

Popular turbulence seemed to follow so naturally from inadequacies of government that uprisings were often described with similes from the physical world. In 1770 John Adams said that there were "Churchquakes and state-quakes in the moral and political world, as well as earthquakes, storms and tempests in the physical." Two years earlier a writer in the *New York Journal* likened popular tumults to "Thunder Gusts" which "commonly do more Good than Harm." Thomas Jefferson continued the imagery in the 1780's, particularly with his famous statement that he liked "a little rebellion now and then" for it was "like a storm in the atmosphere." It was, moreover, because of the "imperfection of all things in this world," including government, that Adams found it "vain to seek a government in all points free from a possibility of civil wars, tumults and seditions." That was "a blessing denied to this life and preserved to complete the felicity of the next." [39]

If popular uprisings occurred "in all governments at all times," they were nonetheless most able to break out in free governments. Tyrants imposed order and submission upon their subjects by force, thus dividing society, as Jefferson said, into wolves and sheep. Only under free govern-

---

[38] John Locke, *The Second Treatise of Government*, paragraphs 223–225. "A State of Facts Concerning the Riots . . . in New Jersey," *New Jersey Archives*, VII, 217. *N.Y. Jour., Supp.* (N.Y.C.), Jan. 4, 1770. Johnson to Wm. Pitkin, Apr. 29, 1768, Massachusetts Historical Society, *Collections*, 5th Ser., IX (1885), 275. Adams as "Determinus" in *Boston Gazette*, Aug. 8, 1768; and Harry A. Cushing, ed., *The Writing of Samuel Adams* (New York, 1904–1908), I, 237. Jay to Jefferson, Oct. 27, 1786, Boyd, ed., *Jefferson Papers*, X, 488.

[39] Wroth and Zobel, eds., *Adams Legal Papers*, III, 249–250; *N.Y. Jour. Supp.* (N.Y.C.), Aug. 18, 1768; Jefferson to Abigail Adams, Feb. 22, 1787, Boyd, ed., *Jefferson Papers*, XI, 174. C. F. Adams, ed., *Works of Adams*, IV, 77, 80 (quoting Algernon Sydney).

ments were the people "nervous," spirited, jealous of their rights, ready
to react against unjust provocations; and this being the case, popular
disorders could be interpreted as "Symptoms of a strong and healthy
Constitution" even while they indicated some lesser shortcoming in
administration. It would be futile, Josiah Quincy, Jr., said in 1770, to
expect "that pacific, timid, obsequious, and servile temper, so predominant in more despotic governments" from those who lived under free
British institutions. From "our happy constitution," he claimed, there
resulted as "very natural Effects" an "impatience of injuries, and a strong
resentment of insults." [40]

This popular impatience constituted an essential force in the maintenance of free institutions. "What country can preserve it's [*sic*] liberties
if their rulers are not warned from time to time that their people preserve
the spirit of resistance?" Jefferson asked in 1787. Occasional insurrections
were thus "an evil . . . productive of good": even those founded on
popular error tended to hold rulers "to the true principles of their institution" and generally provided "a medecine necessary for the sound
health of government." This meant that an aroused people had a role
not only in extreme situations, where revolution was requisite, but in
the normal course of free government. For that reason members of the
House of Lords could seriously argue — as A. J. P. Taylor has pointed
out — that "rioting is an essential part of our constitution"; and for that
reason, too, even Massachusetts's conservative Lieutenant Governor
Thomas Hutchinson could remark in 1768 that "mobs a sort of them at
least are constitutional." [41]

[40] Jefferson to Edward Carrington, Jan. 16, 1787, Boyd, ed., *Jefferson Papers*,
XI, 49, and Rev. James Madison to Jefferson, Mar. 28, 1787, *ibid.*, 252. Wroth
and Zobel, eds., *Adams Legal Papers*, III, 250. Quincy's address to the jury in
the soldiers' trial after the Boston Massacre in Josiah Quincy, *Memoir of the
Life of Josiah Quincy, Junior, of Massachusetts Bay, 1744–1775*, ed. Eliza Susan
Quincy, 3d ed. (Boston, 1875), 46. See also Massachusetts Assembly's similar
statement in its address to Gov. Hutchinson, Apr. 24, 1770, Hutchinson, *History
of Massachusetts Bay*, ed. Mayo, III, 365–366. This 18th century devotion to
political "jealousy" resembles the doctrine of "vigilance" that was defended by
19th century vigilante groups. See Graham and Gurr, *Violence in America*,
179–183.

[41] Jefferson to William Stephen Smith, Nov. 13, 1787, Boyd, ed., *Jefferson
Papers*, XII, 356, Jefferson to Carrington, Jan. 16, 1787, *ibid.*, XI, 49, Jefferson to
James Madison, Jan. 30, 1787, *ibid.*, 92–93. Taylor's remarks in "History of
Violence," *The Listener*, CXXIX (1968), 701. ("Members of the House of
Lords . . . said . . . if the people really don't like something, then they work
our carriages and tear off our wigs and throw stones through the windows of our
town-houses. And this is an essential thing to have if you are going to have a
free country.") Hutchinson to [John or Robert] Grant, July 27, 1768, Massachusetts Archives, XXVI, 317, State House, Boston. See also the related story
about John Selden, the famous 17th century lawyer, told to the House of Commons in Jan. 1775 by Lord Camden and recorded by Josiah Quincy, Jr., in the

III

[It was, finally, the interaction of this constitutional role of the mob with the written law that makes the story of eighteenth-century popular uprisings complexity itself.[42] If mobs were appreciated because they provided a check on power, it was always understood that, insofar as upheavals threatened "running to such excesses, as will overturn the whole system of government," "strong discouragements" had to be provided against them. For eighteenth-century Americans, like the English writers they admired, liberty demanded the rule of law.] In extreme situations where the rulers had clearly chosen arbitrary power over the limits of law, men like John Adams could prefer the risk of anarchy to continued submission because "anarchy can never last long, and tyranny may be perpetual," but only when "there was any hope that the fair order of liberty and a free constitution would arise out of it." This desire to maintain the orderly rule of law led legislatures in England and the colonies to pass antiriot statutes and to make strong efforts — in the words of a 1753 Massachusetts law — to discountenance "a mobbish temper and spirit in . . . the inhabitants" that would oppose "all government and order." [43]

[The problem of limiting mass violence was dealt with most intensely over a sustained period by the American Revolutionary leadership, which has perhaps suffered most from historians' earlier inattention to the history of colonial uprisings.] So long as it could be maintained — as it

---

"Journal of Josiah Quincy, Jun., During his Voyage and Residence in England from September 28th, 1774, to March 3d, 1775," Massachusetts Historical Society, *Proceedings*, L (1916–1917), 462–463. Selden was asked what lawbook contained the laws for resisting tyranny. He replied he did not know, "but I'll tell [you] what is most certain, that it has always been the custom of England — and the Custom of England is the *Law* of the *Land.*"

[42] On the developing distinction Americans drew between what was legal and constitutional, see Wood, *Creation of the American Republic*, 261–268.

[43] *N.Y. Jour. Supp.* (N.Y.C.), Jan. 4, 1770; Wroth and Zobel, eds., *Adams Legal Papers*, III, 250, and C. F. Adams, ed., *Works of Adams*, VI, 151. Adams's views were altered in 1815, *ibid.*, X, 181. It is noteworthy that the Boston town meeting condemned the Knowles rioters not simply for their method of opposing impressment but because they insulted the governor and the legislature, and the Massachusetts Assembly acted against the uprising only after Gov. Shirley had left Boston and events seemed to be "tending to the destruction of all government and order." Hutchinson, *History of Massachusetts Bay*, ed. Mayo, II, 332–333. *Acts and Resolves of the Province of Massachusetts Bay*, III, 647. (Chap. 18 of the Province laws, 1752–1753, "An Act for Further Preventing all Riotous, Tumultuous and Disorderly Assemblies or Companies or Persons. . . .") This act, which was inspired particularly by Pope's Day violence, was renewed after the Boston Massacre in 1770 even though the legislature refused to renew its main Riot Act of 1751. *Ibid.*, IV, 87.

was only fifteen years ago – that political mobs were "rare or unknown in America" before the 1760's, the Revolutionaries were implicitly credited with their creation. American patriots, Charles McLean Andrews wrote, were often "lawless men who were nothing more than agitators and demagogues" and who attracted a following from the riffraff of colonial society. It now seems clear that the mob drew on all elements of the population. More important, the Revolutionary leaders had no need to create mob support. Instead they were forced to work with a "permanent entity," a traditional crowd that exerted itself before, after, and even during the Revolutionary struggle over issues unrelated to the conflict with Britain, and that, as Hobsbawn has noted, characteristically aided the Revolutionary cause in the opening phases of conflict but was hard to discipline thereafter.[44]

In focusing popular exuberance the American leaders could work with long-established tendencies in the mob toward purposefulness and responsibility. In doing so they could, moreover, draw heavily upon the guidelines for direct action that had been defined by English radical writers since the seventeenth century. Extralegal action was justified only when all established avenues to redress had failed. It could not answer casual errors or private failings on the part of the magistrates, but had to await fundamental public abuses so egregious that the "whole people" turned against their rulers. Even then, it was held, opposition had to be measured so that no more force was exerted than was necessary for the public good. Following these principles colonial leaders sought by careful organization to avoid the excesses that first greeted the Stamp Act. Hutchinson's query after a crowd in Connecticut had forced the resignation of stampman Jared Ingersoll – whether "such a public regular assembly can be called a mob" – could with equal appropriateness have been repeated during the tea resistance, or in 1774 when Massachusetts *mandamus* councillors were forced to resign.[45]

From the first appearance of an organized resistance movement in 1765, moreover, efforts were made to support the legal magistrates such that, as John Adams said in 1774, government would have "as much vigor then as ever" except where its authority was specifically under

[44] Arthur M. Schlesinger, "Political Mobs and the American Revolution, 1765–1776," *Proceedings of the American Philosophical Society*, XCIX (1955), 246; Charles M. Andrews, *The Colonial Background of the American Revolution*, rev. ed. (New Haven, 1939), 176; Charles M. Andrews, "The Boston Merchants and the Non-Importation Movement," Colonial Society of Massachusetts, *Transactions*, XIX (1916–1917), 241; Hobsbawm, *Primitive Rebels*, 111, 123–124.

[45] Hutchinson to Thomas Pownall, [Sept. or Oct. 1765], Mass. Archives, XXVI, 157. Pauline Maier, From Resistance to Revolution: American Radicals and the Development of Intercolonial Opposition to Britain, 1765–1776 (unpubl. Ph.D. diss., Harvard University, 1968), I, 37–45, 72–215.

dispute. This concern for the maintenance of order and the general framework of law explains why the American Revolution was largely free from the "universal tumults and all the irregularities and violence of mobbish factions [that] naturally arise when legal authority ceases." It explains, too, why old revolutionaries like Samuel Adams or Christopher Gadsden disapproved of those popular conventions and committees that persisted after regular independent state governments were established in the 1770's. "Decency and Respect [are] due to Constitutional Authority," Samuel Adams said in 1784, "and those Men, who under any Pretence or by any Means whatever, would lessen the Weight of Government lawfully exercised must be Enemies to our happy Revolution and the Common Liberty." [46]

In normal circumstances the "strong discouragements" to dangerous disorder were provided by established legislatures. The measures enacted by them to deal with insurrections were shaped by the eighteenth-century understanding of civil uprisings. Since turbulence indicated above all some shortcoming in government, it was never to be met by increasing the authorities' power of suppression. The "weakness of authority" that was a function of its dependence upon popular support appeared to contemporary Americans as a continuing virtue of British institutions, as one reason why rulers could not simply dictate to their subjects and why Britain had for so long been hailed as one of the freest nations in Europe. It was "far less dangerous to the Freedom of a State" to allow "the laws to be trampled upon, by the licence among the rabble . . . than to dispence with their force by an act of power." Insurrections were to be answered by reform, by attacking the "Disease" — to use John Jay's term of 1786 — that lay behind them rather than by suppressing its "Symptoms." And ultimately, as William Samuel Johnson observed in 1768, "the only effectual way to prevent them is to govern with wisdom, justice, and moderation." [47]

In immediate crises, however, legislatures in both England and America resorted to special legislation that supplemented the common law prohibition of riot. The English Riot Act of 1714 was passed when disorder threatened to disrupt the accession of George I; a Connecticut act of

[46] C. F. Adams, ed., *Works of Adams*, IV, 51; Rev. Samuel Langdon's election sermon to third Massachusetts Provincial Congress, May 31, 1775, quoted in Richard Frothingham, *Life and Times of Joseph Warren* (Boston, 1865), 499; Samuel Adams to Noah Webster, Apr. 30, 1784, Cushing, ed., *Writings of Samuel Adams*, IV, 305–306. On Gadsden see Richard Walsh, *Charleston's Sons of Liberty* (Columbia, 1959), 87.

[47] N.Y. *Jour. Supp.* (N.Y.C.), Jan. 4, 1770; Jay to Jefferson, Oct. 27, 1786, Boyd, ed., *Jefferson Papers*, X, 488; Johnson to William Pitkin, July 23, 1768, Massachusetts Historical Society, *Collections*, 5th Ser., IX, 294–295.

1722 followed a rash of incidents over land title in Hartford County; the Massachusetts act of 1751 answered "several tumultuous assemblies" over the currency issue and another of 1786 was enacted at the time of Shays's Rebellion. The New Jersey legislature passed an act in 1747 during that colony's protracted land riots; Pennsylvania's Riot Act of 1764 was inspired by the Paxton Boys; North Carolina's of 1771 by the Regulators; New York's of 1774 by the "land wars" in Charlotte and Albany County.[48] Always the acts specified that the magistrates were to depend upon the *posse* in enforcing their provisions, and in North Carolina on the militia as well. They differed over the number of people who had to remain "unlawfully, riotously, and tumultuously assembled together, to the Disturbance of the Publick Peace" for one hour after the reading of a prescribed riot proclamation before becoming judicable under the act. Some colonies specified lesser punishments than the death penalty provided for in the English act, but the American statutes were not in general more "liberal" than the British. Two of them so violated elementary judicial rights that they were subsequently condemned — North Carolina's by Britain, and New York's act of 1774 by a later, Revolutionary state legislature.[49]

[In one important respect, however, the English Riot Act was reformed. Each colonial riot law, except that of Connecticut, was enacted for only one to three years, whereas the British law was perpetual. By this provision colonial legislators avoided the shortcoming which, it was said, was "more likely to introduce *arbitrary Power* than even an *Army* itself," because a perpetual riot act meant that "in all future time" by "reading a Proclamation" the Crown had the power "of hanging up their Subjects wholesale, or of picking out Those, to whom they have the greatest Dislike." If the death penalty was removed, the danger was less. When, therefore, riot acts without limit of time were finally enacted — as Connecticut had done in 1722, Massachusetts in 1786, New Jersey in 1797 — the punishments were considerably milder, providing, for example, for

---

[48] *The Statutes at Large* [of Great Britain] (London, 1786), V, 4–6; Hoadly, ed., *Public Records of Connecticut*, VI, 346–348 for the law, and see also 332–333, 341–348; Acts and Resolves of Massachusetts Bay, III, 544–546, for the Riot Act of 1751, and see also Hutchinson, *History of Massachusetts Bay*, ed. Mayo, III, 6–7; and *Acts and Laws of the Commonwealth of Massachusetts* (Boston, 1893), 87–88, for Act of 1786; "A State of Facts Concerning the Riots . . . in New Jersey," *N.J. Archives*, VII, 211–212, 221–222; *The Statutes at Large of Pennsylvania* . . . (n.p., 1899), VI, 325–328; William A. Saunders, ed., *The Colonial Records of North Carolina* (Raleigh, 1890), VIII, 481–486; *Laws of the Colony of New York in the Years 1774 and 1775* (Albany, 1888), 38–43.

[49] See additional instruction to Gov. Josiah Martin, Saunders, ed., *Colonial Records of North Carolina*, VIII, 515–516; and *Laws of the State of New York* (Albany, 1886), I, 20.

imprisonment not exceeding six months in Connecticut, one year in Massachusetts, and three years in New Jersey.[50]

[Riot legislation, it is true, was not the only recourse against insurgents, who throughout the eighteenth century could also be prosecuted for treason. The colonial and state riot acts suggest, nonetheless, that American legislators recognized the participants in civil insurrections as guilty of a crime peculiarly complicated because it had social benefits as well as damages] To some degree, it appears, they shared the idea expressed well by Jefferson in 1787: that "honest republican governors" should be "so mild in their punishments of rebellions, as not to discourage them too much." [51] Even in countering riots the legislators seemed as intent upon preventing any perversion of the forces of law and order by established authorities as with chastising the insurgents. Reform of the English Riot Act thus paralleled the abolition of constituent treasons — a traditional recourse against enemies of the Crown — in American state treason acts of the Revolutionary period and finally in Article III of the Federal Constitution.[52] From the same preoccupation, too, sprang the limitations placed upon the regular army provided for in the Constitution in part to assure the continuation of republican government guaranteed to the states by Article IV, Section IV. Just as the riot acts were for so long limited in duration, appropriations for the army were never to extend beyond two years (Article I, Section viii, 12); and the army could be used within a state against domestic violence only after application by the legislature or governor, if the legislature could not be convened (Article IV, Section iv).

[A continuing desire to control authority through popular action also underlay the declaration in the Second Amendment that "a well regulated Militia being necessary to the security of a free State," citizens were assured the "right . . . to keep and bear Arms." The militia was meant above all "to prevent the establishment of a standing army, the bane of liberty"; and the right to bear arms — taken in part from the English Bill of Rights of 1689 — was considered a standing threat to would-be tyrants. It embodied "a public allowance, under due restrictions, of the *natural right of resistance and self preservation*, when the sanctions of society and laws are found *insufficient* to restrain the *violence of oppression*." And on the basis of their eighteenth-century experience, Americans could consider that right to be "perfectly harmless. . . . If

[50] *The Craftsman* (London, 1731), VI, 263–264. Connecticut and Massachusetts laws cited in n. 45; and *Laws of the State of New Jersey* (Trenton, 1821), 279–281.

[51] Jefferson to Madison, Jan. 30, 1787, Boyd, ed., *Jefferson Papers*, XI, 93.

[52] See Bradley Chapin, "Colonial and Revolutionary Origins of the American Law of Treason," *Wm. and Mary Qtly.*, 3d Ser., XVII (1960), 3–21.

the government be equitable; if it be reasonable in its exactions; if proper attention be paid to the education of children in knowledge, and religion," Timothy Dwight declared, "few men will be disposed to use arms, unless for their amusement, and for the defence of themselves and their country." [53]

[The need felt to continue the eighteenth-century militia as a counterweight to government along with the efforts to outlaw rioting and to provide for the use of a standing army against domestic insurrections under carefully defined circumstances together illustrate the complex attitude toward peacekeeping that prevailed among the nation's founders. The rule of law had to be maintained, yet complete order was neither expected nor even desired when it could be purchased, it seemed, only at the cost of forcefully suppressing the spirit of a free people. The constant possibility of insurrection — as institutionalized in the militia — was to remain an element of the United States Constitution, just as it had played an essential role in Great Britain's]

This readiness to accept some degree of tumultuousness depended to a large degree upon the lawmakers' own experience with insurrections in the eighteenth century, when "disorder" was seldom anarchic and "rioters" often acted to defend law and justice rather than to oppose them. In the years after independence this toleration declined, in part because mass action took on new dimensions. Nineteenth-century mobs often resembled in outward form those of the previous century, but a new violence was added. Moreover, the literal assumption of popular rule in the years after Lexington taught many thoughtful Revolutionary partisans what was for them an unexpected lesson — that the people were "as capable of despotism as any prince," that "public liberty was no guarantee after all of private liberty." [54] With home rule secured, attention focused more exclusively upon minority rights, which mob action had always to some extent imperiled. And the danger that uprisings carried for individual freedom became ever more egregious as mobs shed their former restraint and burned Catholic convents, attacked nativist speakers, lynched Mormons, or destroyed the presses and threatened the lives of abolitionists.

Ultimately, however, changing attitudes toward popular uprisings turned upon fundamental transformations in the political perspective of Americans after 1776. Throughout the eighteenth century political institutions had been viewed as in a constant evolution: the colonies'

[53] Elbridge Gerry in Congressional debates, quoted in Irving Brant, *The Bill of Rights, Its Origin and Meaning* (Indianapolis, 1965), 486; Samuel Adams, quoting Blackstone, as "E. A." in *Boston Gaz.*, Feb. 27, 1769, and Cushing, ed., *Writings of Samuel Adams*, I, 317. Timothy Dwight, quoted in Daniel J. Boorstin, *The Americans: The Colonial Experience* (New York, 1958), 353.

[54] Wood, *Creation of the American Republic*, 410.

relationship with Britain and with each other, even the balance of power within the governments of various colonies, remained unsettled. Under such circumstances the imputations of governmental shortcoming that uprisings carried could easily be accepted and absorbed. [But after In-dependence, when the form and conduct of the Americans' governments were under their exclusive control, and when those governments repre-sented, moreover, an experiment in republicanism on which depended their own happiness and "that of generations unborn," Americans be-came less ready to endure domestic turbulence or accept its disturbing implications.] Some continued to argue that "distrust and dissatisfaction" on the part of the multitude were "always the consequence of tyranny or corruption." Others, however, began to see domestic turbulence not as indictments but as insults to government that were likely to discredit American republicanism in the eyes of European observers. "Mobs are a reproach to Free Governments," where all grievances could be legally redressed through the courts or the ballot box, it was argued in 1783. They originated there "not in Oppression, but in Licentiousness," an "ungovernable spirit" among the people. Under republican governments even that distrust of power colonists had found so necessary for liberty, and which uprisings seemed to manifest, could appear outmoded. "There is some consistency in being jealous of power in the hands of those who assume it by birth . . . and over whom we have no controul . . . as was the case with the Crown of England over America," another writer suggested. "But to be jealous of those whom we chuse, the instant we have chosen them" was absurd: perhaps in the transition from monarchy to republic Americans had "bastardized" their ideas by placing jealousy where confidence was more appropriate.[55] In short, the assumptions behind the Americans' earlier toleration of the mob were corroded in republican America. Old and new attitudes coexisted in the 1780's and even later. But the appropriateness of popular uprisings in the United States became increasingly in doubt after the Federal Constitution came to be seen as the final product of long-term institutional experimentation, "a momentous contribution to the history of politics" that rendered even that most glorious exertion of popular force, revolution itself, an obsolete resort for Americans.[56]

Yet this change must not be viewed exclusively as a product of America's distinctive Revolutionary achievement. J. H. Plumb has pointed

[55] Judge Aedanus Burke's Charge to the Grand Jury at Charleston, June 9, 1783, in *South-Carolina Gazette and General Advertiser* (Charleston), June 10, 1783; "A Patriot," *ibid.*, July 15, 1783; and "Another Patriot," *ibid.*, July 29, 1783; and on the relevance of jealousy of power, see a letter to Virginia in *ibid.*, Aug. 9, 1783. "Democratic Gentle-Touch," *Gazette of the State of South Carolina* (Charleston), May 13, 1784.

[56] Wood, *Creation of the American Republic*, 612–614.

out, that a century earlier, when England passed beyond her revolutionary era and progressed toward political "stability," radical ideology with its talk of resistance and revolution was gradually left behind. A commitment to peace and permanence emerged from decades of fundamental change. In America as in England this stability demanded that operative sovereignty, including the right finally to decide what was and was not in the community's interest, and which laws were and were not constitutional, be entrusted to established governmental institutions. The result was to minimize the role of the people at large, who had been the ultimate arbiters of those questions in English and American Revolutionary thought. Even law enforcement was to become the task primarily of professional agencies. As a result in time all popular upheavals alike became menacing efforts to "pluck up law and justice by the roots," and riot itself gradually became defined, as a purposeless act of anarchy, "a blind and misguided outburst of popular fury," of "undirected violence with no articulated goals." [57]

[57] J. H. Plumb, *The Origins of Political Stability, England 1675–1725* (Boston, 1967), xv, 187; John Adams on the leaders of Shays's Rebellion in a letter to Benjamin Hitchborn, Jan. 27, 1787, in C. F. Adams, ed., *Works of Adams*, IX, 551; modern definitions of riot in "Riot Control and the Use of Federal Troops," *Harvard Law Review*, LXXXI (1968), 643.

AMERICANS
IN THE
EIGHTEENTH
CENTURY

IV

Origins of the
Southern Labor
System

OSCAR AND MARY F. HANDLIN

As the title of this essay indicates, the Handlins take a broad institutional view of the origins of North American slavery. The problem, in their eyes, is very like that which faces the historian of the early colonial settlements: what was the impact of the New World environment on transplanted European institutions? They point out that slavery had no legal meaning in England, and that seventeenth-century Americans were accustomed to the idea of varying degrees of human unfreedom. When Negroes began to be imported from Africa in large numbers they were therefore simply considered servants of one sort or another. The question, then, is how the novel conception of chattel slavery as perpetual, heritable, and racial developed so rapidly in the eighteenth century, when Negro slaves became clearly distinguishable from all other types of servants?

The Handlins examine colonial legislation to discover the manner in which color became the legally significant feature of slave status, at the same time that other factors worked against social acceptance of the black as a human being. In the end, Negroes were treated in law as though they were nothing more than real property, and Southerners no longer had to worry about their human prerogatives. The rights of man did not pertain to property.

For the Handlins, slavery is a legal institution. They allude only briefly to "other developments which derogated the qualities of the Negro as a human being to establish his inferiority," for they clearly think that the creation of the new legal status is the critical process in the origins of slavery. Color, racial prejudice, and the economic requirements of staple agriculture seem almost accidental attributes of the system. The essays by Jordan and Sirmans suggest that the legal aspect is not so important as the Handlins contend.

In the bitter years before the Civil War, and after, men often turned to history for an explanation of the disastrous difference that divided the nation against itself. It seemed as if some fundamental fault must account for the tragedy that was impending or that had been realized; and it was tempting then to ascribe the troubles of the times to an original separateness between the sections that fought each other in 1861.

The last quarter century has banished from serious historical thinking the ancestral cavaliers and roundheads with whom the rebels and Yankees had peopled their past. But there is still an inclination to accept as present from the start a marked divergence in the character of the labor force, free whites in the North, Negro slaves in the South. Most commonly, the sources of that divergence are discovered in geography. In the temperate North, it is held, English ways were transposed intact. But the soil and climate of the South favored the production of staples, most efficiently raised under a regime of plantation slavery.

In this case, however, it is hardly proper to load nature with responsibility for human institutions. Tropical crops and climate persisted in the South after 1865 when its labor system changed, and they were there before it appeared.[1] Negro slavery was not spontaneously produced by heat, humidity, and tobacco. [An examination of the condition and status of seventeenth-century labor will show that slavery was not there from the start, that it was not simply imitated from elsewhere, and that it was not a response to any unique qualities in the Negro himself. It emerged rather from the adjustment to American conditions of traditional European institutions.]

By the latter half of the eighteenth century, slavery was a clearly defined status. It was

> that condition of a natural person, in which, by the operation of law, the application of his physical and mental powers depends . . . upon the will of another . . . and in which he is incapable . . . of . . . holding property [or any other rights] . . . except as the agent or instrument of another. In slavery, . . . the state, in ignoring the personality of the slave, . . . commits the control of his conduct . . . to the master, together with the power of transferring his authority to another.[2]

Thinking of slavery in that sense, the Englishmen of 1772 could boast

Reprinted by permission of Atlantic-Little, Brown and Co. from Oscar Handlin, *Race and Nationality in American Life*. Copyright 1950 by Oscar Handlin. This article originally appeared in the *William and Mary Quarterly*, 3d Ser., VII (1950), 199–222.

[1] See, in general, Lewis Cecil Gray, *History of Agriculture in the Southern United States to 1860* (New York, 1941), I, 302 ff.

[2] Summarized in John Codman Hurd, *Law of Freedom and Bondage in the United States* (Boston, 1858), I, 42, 43.

with Lord Mansfield that their country had never tolerated the institution; simply to touch the soil of England made men free.[3] But the distinction between slave and free that had become important by the eighteenth century was not a significant distinction at the opening of the
seventeenth century. In the earlier period, the antithesis of "free" was not
"slave" but unfree; and, within the condition of unfreedom, law and practice recognized several gradations.

The status that involved the most complete lack of freedom was
villeinage, a servile condition transmitted from father to son. The villein
was limited in the right to hold property or make contracts; he could be
bought and sold with the land he worked or without, and had "to do all
that that the Lord will him command"; while the lord could "rob, beat, and
chastise his Villain at his will." [4] It was true that the condition had almost
ceased to exist in England itself. But it persisted in Scotland well into the
eighteenth century. In law the conception remained important enough to
induce Coke in 1658/9 to give it a lengthy section; and the analogy with
villeinage served frequently to define the terms of other forms of servitude.[5]

For, law and practice in the seventeenth century comprehended other
forms of involuntary bondage. The essential attributes of villeinage were
fastened on many men not through heredity and ancient custom, as in the
case of the villein, but through poverty, crime, or mischance. A debtor, in
cases "where there is not sufficient distresse of goods" could be "sold at an
outcry." Conviction for vagrancy and vagabondage, even the mere absence
of a fixed occupation, exposed the free-born Englishman, at home or in
the colonies, to the danger that he might be bound over to the highest
bidder, his labor sold for a term. Miscreants who could not pay their fines
for a wide range of offenses were punished by servitude on "publick
works" or on the estates of individuals under conditions not far different
from those of villeinage. Such sentences, in the case of the graver felonies,
sometimes were for life.[6]

[3] William Blackstone, *Commentaries* . . . , edited by St. George Tucker
(Philadelphia, 1803), I, 126, 423. For Somerset's Case, see Hurd, *Law of Freedom and Bondage*, I, 189 ff.; also *ibid.*, I, 185 ff.

[4] [Thomas Blount], *Les Termes de la Ley; or, Certain Difficult and Obscure
Words and Terms of the Common Laws and Statutes . . . Explained* (London,
1685), 648–652; Hurd, *Law of Freedom and Bondage*, I, 136.

[5] Edward Coke, *First Part of the Institutes of the Laws of England; or, a Commentary upon Littleton* . . . , edited by Charles Butler (Philadelphia, 1853),
Bk. II, Ch. 11, Sections 172–212; James Paterson, *Commentaries on the Liberty
of the Subect and the . . . Security of the Person* (London, 1877), I, 492; Jacob
D. Wheeler, *Practical Treatise on the Law of Slavery . . .* (New York, 1837),
256, 257; Tucker's Appendix to Blackstone, *Commentaries*, I, 43n; Gray, *History of Agriculture*, I, 343 ff.

[6] See *Maryland Archives* (Baltimore, 1883 ff.), I, 69 (1638/9), 152 ff. (1642),
187 (1642), 192 (1642); William Waller Hening, *Statutes at Large Being a*

The sale by the head of a household of members of his family entailed a similar kind of involuntary servitude. A husband could thus dispose of his wife, and a father of his children. Indeed, reluctance to part with idle youngsters could bring on the intercession of the public authorities. So, in 1646, Virginia county commissioners were authorized to send to work in the public flaxhouse two youngsters from each county, kept at home by the "fond indulgence or perverse obstinacy" of their parents. Orphans, bastards, and the offspring of servants were similarly subject to disposal at the will of officials.[7]

Moreover servitude as an estate was not confined to those who fell into it against their wills. It also held many men who entered it by agreement or formal indenture, most commonly for a fixed span of years under conditions contracted for in advance, but occasionally for life, and frequently without definite statement of terms under the assumption that the custom of the country was definite enough.[8]

[Early modification in the laws regulating servitude did not, in England or the colonies, alter essentially the nature of the condition.[9] Whether voluntary or involuntary, the status did not involve substantially more freedom in law than villeinage.] It was not heritable; but servants could be bartered for a profit, sold to the highest bidder for the unpaid debts of their masters, and otherwise transferred like movable goods or chattels. Their capacity to hold property was narrowly limited as was their right to make contracts.[10] Furthermore, the master had extensive powers of discipline, enforced by physical chastisement or by extension of the term of service. Offenses against the state also brought on punishments different from those meted out to free men; with no property to be fined, the servants were whipped.[11] In every civic, social, and legal attribute, these victims of the turbulent displacements of the sixteenth and seventeenth centuries were set apart. Despised by every other order, without apparent means of rising to a more favored place, these men, and their children, and their children's children seemed mired in a hard, degraded life.[12] That they

---

Collection of all the Laws of Virginia . . . (New York, 1823 ff.), I, 117; Gray, *History of Agriculture*, I, 343; John H. Lefroy, *Memorials of the Discovery and Early Settlement of the Bermudas or Somers Islands, 1518–1685* (London, 1877), I, 127.

[7] See Hening, *Statutes*, I, 336; also Paterson, *Commentaries*, I, 495; Gray, *History of Agriculture*, I, 343; Susie M. Ames, *Studies of the Virginia Eastern Shore in the Seventeenth Century* (Richmond, 1940), 78 ff.; *infra*, 212.

[8] Paterson, *Commentaries*, I, 494; *infra*, 209.

[9] See Gray, *History of Agriculture*, I, 343 ff.

[10] *Maryland Archives*, I, 69 (1638/9); Hening, *Statutes*, I, 245, 253, 274, 439, 445; Ames, *Eastern Shore*, 77; *infra*, 214.

[11] See, for instance, Hening, *Statutes*, I, 167, 189, 192.

[12] Philip Alexander Bruce, *Institutional History of Virginia* . . . (New York, 1910), II, 614.

formed a numerous element in society was nothing to lighten their lot.

The condition of the first Negroes in the continental English colonies must be viewed within the perspective of these conceptions and realities of servitude. As Europeans penetrated the dark continent in search of gold and ivory, they developed incidentally the international trade in Blacks. The Dutch in particular found this an attractive means of breaking into the business of the Spanish colonies, estopped by the policy of their own government from adding freely to their supply of African labor. In the course of this exchange through the West Indies, especially through Curacao, occasional small lots were left along the coast between Virginia and Massachusetts.[13]

Through the first three-quarters of the seventeenth century, the Negroes, even in the South, were not numerous; nor were they particularly concentrated in any district.[14] They came into a society in which a large part of the population was to some degree unfree; indeed in Virginia under the Company almost everyone, even tenants and laborers, bore some sort of servile obligation.[15] The Negroes' lack of freedom was not unusual. These newcomers, like so many others, were accepted, bought and held, as kinds of servants.[16] They were certainly not well off. But their ill-fortune was of a sort they shared with men from England, Scotland, and Ireland, and with the unlucky aborigines held in captivity. Like the others, some Ne-

[13] See Elizabeth Donnan, ed., *Documents Illustrative of the History of the Slave Trade to America* (Washington, 1930 ff.), I, 83 ff., 105, 106, 151; Gray, *History of Agriculture*, I, 352.

[14] Philip Alexander Bruce, *Social Life of Virginia in the Seventeenth Century* (Richmond, 1907), 14; James M. Wright, *Free Negro in Maryland 1634–1860* (New York, 1921), 13.

[15] See Gray, *History of Agriculture*, I, 314 ff.

[16] This fact was first established by the work of James Curtis Ballagh, *History of Slavery in Virginia* (Baltimore, 1902), 9 ff., 28 ff. and John Henderson Russell, *Free Negro in Virginia 1619–1865* (Baltimore, 1913), 23 ff. Their conclusions were accepted by Ulrich B. Phillips, *American Negro Slavery* (New York, 1918), 75; although they ran counter to the position of Philip Alexander Bruce, *Economic History of Virginia in the Seventeenth Century* (New York, 1907), II, 52 ff. They were not seriously disputed until the appearance of Ames, *Eastern Shore*, 100 ff. Miss Ames's argument, accepted by Wesley Frank Craven, *Southern Colonies in the Seventeenth Century 1607–1689* (Baton Rouge, 1949), 402, rests on scattered references to "slaves" in the records. But these are never identified as Negroes; the reference is always to "slaves," to "Negroes or slaves," or to "Negroes and other slaves," just as there are many more frequent references to "Negroes and servants" (for the meaning of "slave" in these references, *see infra*, 204. Miss Ames also argues that the free Negroes referred to by Russell may have been manumitted. But unless she could prove — and she cannot — the Englishmen in Virginia had a previous conception of slavery as a legal status within which the Negro fell, it is much more logical to assume with Russell that these were servants who had completed their terms. For the same reasons we cannot accept the unsupported assumptions of Wright, *Free Negro in Maryland*, 21–23.

groes became free, that is, terminated their period of service. Some became artisans; a few became landowners and the masters of other men.[17] The status of Negroes was that of servants; and so they were identified and treated down to the 1660's.[18]

[The word, "slave" was, of course, used occasionally. It had no meaning in English law, but there was a significant colloquial usage. This was a general term of derogation] It served to express contempt; "O what a rogue and peasant slave am I," says Hamlet (Act II, Scene 2). It also described the low-born as contrasted with the gentry; of two hundred warriors, a sixteenth-century report said, eight were gentlemen, the rest slaves.[19] The implication of degradation was also transferred to the low kinds of labor; "In this hal," wrote More (1551), "all vyle seruice, all slauerie . . . is done by bondemen." [20]

[It was in this sense that Negro servants were sometimes called slaves.[21] But the same appellation was, in England, given to other non-English servants, — to a Russian, for instance.[22] In Europe and in the American colonies, the term was, at various times and places, applied indiscriminately to Indians, mulattoes, and mestizos, as well as to Negroes.[23] For that matter, it applied also to white Englishmen] It thus commonly described the servitude of child; so, the poor planters complained, "Our children, the parents dieinge" are held as "slaues or drudges" for the discharge of their parents' debts.[24] Penal servitude too was often referred to

[17] Marcus W. Jernegan, "Slavery and the Beginnings of Industrialism in the American Colonies," *American Historical Review*, XXV (1920), 227, 228; Ames, *Eastern Shore*, 106, 107.

[18] In such a work as [Nathaniel Butler], *Historye of the Bermudaes or Summer Islands*, edited by J. Henry Lefroy (London, 1882), for instance, the term "slave" is never applied to Negroes (see pp. 84, 99, 144, 146, 211, 219, 242). For disciplinary and revenue laws in Virginia that did not discriminate Negroes from other servants, see Hening, *Statutes*, I, 174, 198, 200, 243, 306 (1631–1645). For wills (1655–1664) in which "Lands goods & chattels cattle monys negroes English servts horses sheep household stuff" were all bequeathed together, see *Lancaster County Records*, Book 2, pp. 46, 61, 121, 283 (cited from Beverley Fleet, ed., *Virginia Colonial Abstracts* [Richmond, 1938 ff.]).

[19] *State Papers Henry VIII, Ireland*, II, 448; also III, 594 (under Sklaw); see also Shakespeare's *Coriolanus*, Act IV, Scene 5.

[20] Thomas More, *Utopia* (Oxford, 1895), 161, 221, 222.

[21] See Russell, *Free Negro*, 19.

[22] Paterson, *Commentaries*, I, 492.

[23] See Bruce, *Institutional History*, I, 673; Ames, *Eastern Shore*, 72 ff.; E. B. O'Callaghan, ed., *Documents Relative to the Colonial History of the State of New York* (Albany, 1856 ff.), III, 678.

[24] Butler, *Historye of the Bermudaes*, 295, 296. See also Lorenzo Johnston Greene, *Negro in Colonial New England 1620–1776* (New York, 1942), 19, *n.* 25; Arthur W. Calhoun, *Social History of the American Family* (Cleveland, 1917), I, 82; and also the evidence cited by Richard B. Morris, *Government and Labor in Early America* (New York, 1946), 339, 340.

as slavery; and the phrase, "slavish servant" turns up from time to time. Slavery had no meaning in law; at most it was a popular description of a low form of service.[25]

Yet in not much more than a half century after 1660 this term of deroga-tion was transformed into a fixed legal position. In a society characterized by many degrees of unfreedom, the Negro fell into a status novel to En-glish law, into an unknown condition toward which the colonists unstead-ily moved, slavery in its eighteenth- and nineteenth-century form. The available accounts do not explain this development because they assume that this form of slavery was known from the start.

Can it be said, for instance, that the seventeenth-century Englishman might have discovered elsewhere an established institution, the archetype of slavery as it was ultimately defined, which seemed more advantageous than the defined English customs for use in the New World? The inter-nationally recognized "slave trade" has been cited as such an institution.[26] But when one notes that the Company of Royal Adventurers referred to their cargo as "Negers," "Negro-Servants," "Servants . . . from Africa," or "Negro Person," but rarely as slaves, it is not so clear that it had in view some unique or different status.[27] And when one remembers that the transportation of Irish servants was also known as the "slave-trade," then it is clear that those who sold and those who bought the Negro, if they troubled to consider legal status at all, still thought of him simply as a low servant.[28]

Again, it has been assumed that Biblical and Roman law offered ade-quate precedent. But it did not seem so in the perspective of the contem-poraries of the first planters who saw in both the Biblical and Roman institutions simply the equivalents of their own familiar forms of servitude. King James's translators rendered the word, "bond-servant"; "slave" does not appear in their version.[29] And to Coke the Roman *servus* was no

---

[25] See Abbot Emerson Smith, *Colonists in Bondage* (Chapel Hill, 1947), 158, 186; *Maryland Archives*, I, 41; Gray, *History of Agriculture*, I, 359; Butler, *His-torye of the Bermudaes*, 295; Morris, *Government and Labor*, 346. Some of the earliest Negroes in Bermuda and Virginia seem thus to have been held as public servants, perhaps by analogy with penal servitude (Ballagh, *Slavery in Vir-ginia*, 29).

[26] See, for example, Craven, *Southern Colonies*, 219.

[27] Donnan, *Documents*, I, 128–131, 156, 158, 163, 164. For continued use of the term, "Negro Servants" by the Royal African Company, see *ibid.*, I, 195.

[28] John P. Prendergast, *Cromwellian Settlement of Ireland* (London, 1865), 53n, 238; Patrick Francis Moran, *Historical Sketch of the Persecutions Suffered by the Catholics of Ireland under the Rule of Cromwell and the Puritans* (Dub-lin, 1907), 343–346, 356, 363.

[29] See, for example, Genesis, XIV, 14, XXX, 43; Leviticus, XXV, 39–46; Exo-dus, XXI, 1–9, 16. See also the discussion by Roger Williams (1637), *Massa-chusetts Historical Society Collections*, Fourth Series, VI (1863), 212.

more than the villein ("and this is hee which the civilians call servus").[30]

Nor did the practice of contemporary Europeans fall outside the English conceptions of servitude. Since early in the fifteen century, the Portuguese had held Moors, white and black, in "slavery," at home, on the Atlantic islands, and in Brazil. Such servitude also existed in Spain and in Spanish America where Negroes were eagerly imported to supply the perennial shortage of labor in the Caribbean sugar islands and the Peruvian mines. But what was the status of such slaves? They had certain property rights, were capable of contracting marriages, and were assured of the integrity of their families. Once baptised it was almost a matter of course that they would become free; the right to manumission was practically a "contractual arrangement." And once free, they readily intermarried with their former masters. These were no chattels, devoid of personality. These were human beings whom chance had rendered unfree, a situation completely comprehensible within the degrees of unfreedom familiar to the English colonist. Indeed when Bodin wishes to illustrate the condition of such "slaves," he refers to servants and apprentices in England and Scotland.[31]

Finally, there is no basis for the assertion that such a colony as South Carolina simply adopted slavery from the French or British West Indies.[32] To begin with, the labor system of those places was not yet fully evolved.[33] Travelers from the mainland may have noted the advantages of Negro labor there; but they hardly thought of chattel slavery.[34] The Barbadian gentlemen who proposed to come to South Carolina in 1663 thought of bringing "Negros and other servants." They spoke of "slaves" as did other Englishmen, as a low form of servant; the "weaker" servants to whom the Concessions referred included "woemen children slaves." [35] Clearly American slavery was no direct imitation from Biblical or Roman or Spanish or Portuguese or West Indian models. Whatever connections

[30] Coke, *First Institute upon Littleton*, 116a, §172.

[31] I. [Jean] Bodin, *Six Bookes of a Commonweale*, translated by Richard Knolles (London, 1606), 33. For the Portuguese and Spanish situations, see Jose Antonio Saco, *Historia de la esclavitud desde los tiempos mas remotos hasta nuestros dias* (2d ed., Habana, 1937), III, 266–277; Donnan, *Documents*, I, 15, 16, 29 ff.; Frank Tannenbaum, *Slave and Citizen; the Negro in the Americas* (New York, 1947), 43 ff., 55; Gray, *History of Agriculture*, I, 110, 304–306; Marcus W. Jernegan, *Laboring and Dependent Classes in Colonial America, 1607–1783* (Chicago, 1931), 25.

[32] See, for example, Edward McCrady, *History of South Carolina under the Proprietary Government 1670–1719* (New York, 1897), 357; Gray, *History of Agriculture*, I, 322.

[33] See *infra, n.* 105.

[34] *Massachusetts Historical Society Collections*, Fourth Series, VI, 536 ff.

[35] *Collections of the South Carolina Historical Society*, V (1897), 11, 32, 42, 43.

existed were established in the eighteenth and nineteenth centuries when those who justified the emerging institution cast about for possible precedents wherever they might be found.

[If chattel slavery was not present from the start, nor adopted from elsewhere, it was also not a response to any inherent qualities that fitted the Negro for plantation labor] There has been a good deal of speculation as to the relative efficiency of free and slave, of Negro, white, and Indian, labor. Of necessity, estimates of which costs were higher, which risks — through mortality, escape, and rebellion — greater, are inconclusive.[36] What is conclusive is the fact that Virginia and Maryland planters did not think Negro labor more desirable. A preference for white servants persisted even on the islands.[37] But when the Barbadians could not get those, repeated representations in London made known their desire for Negroes.[38] No such demands came from the continental colonies.[39] [On the contrary the calls are for skilled white labor with the preference for those most like the first settlers and ranging down from Scots and Welsh to Irish, French, and Italians.[40] Least desired were the unskilled, utterly strange Negroes.[41]

It is quite clear in fact that as late as 1669 those who thought of large-scale agriculture assumed it would be manned not by Negroes but by white peasants under a condition of villeinage. John Locke's constitutions for South Carolina envisaged an hereditary group of servile "leetmen"; and Lord Shaftsbury's signory on Locke Island in 1674 actually attempted to put that scheme into practice.[42] If the holders of large estates in the

---

[36] For material relevant to these questions, see Lucien Peytraud, *L'Esclavage aux antilles françaises avant 1789* (Paris, 1897), 20 ff.; Gray, *History of Agriculture*, I, 362–370; Bruce, *Social Life*, 16; Ulrich B. Phillips, *Life and Labor in the Old South* (Boston, 1929), 23; Ralph B. Flanders, *Plantation Slavery in Georgia* (Chapel Hill, 1933), 9, 10; Ballagh, *Slavery in Virginia*, 51; Wright, *Free Negro in Maryland*, 21; E. Franklin Frazier, *Negro in the United States* (New York, 1949), 29 ff.; Donnan, *Documents*, I, 174.

[37] See C. S. S. Higham, *Development of the Leeward Islands under the Restoration 1660–1688* (Cambridge, 1921), 143, 165.

[38] Donnan, *Documents*, I, 91, 92, 115–118.

[39] Craven, *Southern Colonies*, 25. There is no evidence to support T. J. Wertenbaker's statement that the demand for Negro slaves remained active in Virginia after 1620 and that if England had early entered the slave trade, Virginia and Maryland "would have been from the first inundated with black workers." See *Planters of Colonial Virginia* (Princeton, 1922), 31, 125; *First Americans 1607–1690* (New York, 1929), 23.

[40] William Berkeley, *A Discourse & View of Virginia* (London, 1663), 4, 5, 7, 8; *Virginia Historical Register*, I, 63; Phillips, *Life and Labor*, 44; T. J. Wertenbaker, *Patrician and Plebeian in Virginia* (Charlottesville, Va., 1910), 137 ff.

[41] Ballagh, *Slavery in Virginia*, 14; McCrady, *South Carolina*, 383; Alexander S. Salley, Jr., ed., *Narratives of Early Carolina 1650–1708* (New York, 1910), 60.

[42] Locke also anticipated a lower form of labor to be performed by Negro slaves. But while the leetmen would be held only by the lords of manors, any

Chesapeake colonies expressed no wish for a Negro labor supply, they could hardly have planned to use black hands as a means of displacing white, whether as a concerted plot by restoration courtiers to set up a new social order in America,[43] or as a program for lowering costs.[44]

Yet the Negroes did cease to be servants and became slaves, ceased to be men in whom masters held a proprietary interest and became chattels, objects that were the property of their owners. In that transformation originated the southern labor system.

[Although the colonists assumed at the start that all servants would "fare alike in the colony," the social realities of their situation early gave rise to differences of treatment.[45] It is not necessary to resort to racialist assumptions to account for such measures; these were simply the reactions of immigrants lost to the stability and security of home and isolated in an immense wilderness in which threats from the unknown were all about them.] Like the millions who would follow, these immigrants longed in the strangeness for the company of familiar men and singled out to be welcomed those who were most like themselves. So the measures regulating settlement spoke specifically in this period of differential treatment for various groups. From time to time, regulations applied only to "those of our own nation," or to the French, the Dutch, the Italians, the Swiss, the Palatines, the Welsh, the Irish, or to combinations of the diverse nationalities drawn to these shores.[46]

In the same way the colonists became aware of the differences between themselves and the African immigrants. The rudeness of the Negroes' manners, the strangeness of their languages, the difficulty of communicating to them English notions of morality and proper behavior occasioned sporadic laws to regulate their conduct.[47] So, Bermuda's law to restrain the insolencies of Negroes "who are servents" (that is, their inclina-

---

freeman would have power to hold slaves. See John Locke, *First Set of the Fundamental Constitutions of South Carolina*, articles 22–26, 101 (a draft is in *Collections of the South Carolina Historical Society*, V, 93 ff.); also Gray, *History of Agriculture*, I, 323–325.

[43] William E. Dodd, "The Emergence of the First Social Order in the United States," *American Historical Review*, XL (1935), 226, 227.

[44] See Wertenbaker, *Planters*, 86 ff.; Wertenbaker, *Patrician*, 144 ff.; Wertenbaker, *First Americans*, 42 ff. In addition it might well be questioned whether large producers in a period of falling prices would have driven out the small producer who operated with little reference to conditions of prices and costs. See *Maryland Archives*, II, 45, 48 (1666); Gray, *History of Agriculture*, I, 231, 232, 276.

[45] Hening, *Statutes*, I, 117.

[46] See *Maryland Archives*, I, 328, 331, 332 (1651), III, 99 (1641), 222 (1648); Gray, *History of Agriculture*, I, 87, 88; Higham, *Leeward Islands*, 169 ff.

[47] See Bruce, *Social Life*, 139, 152; Bruce, *Institutional History*, I, 9.

tion to run off with the pigs of others) was the same in kind as the legislation that the Irish should "straggle not night or dai, as is too common
with them." [48] Until the 1660's the statutes on the Negroes were not at
all unique. Nor did they add up to a decided trend.[49]

But in the decade after 1660 far more significant differentiations with
regard to term of service, relationship to Christianity, and disposal of children, cut the Negro apart from all other servants and gave a new depth to
his bondage.

In the early part of the century duration of service was of only slight
importance. Certainly in England where labor was more plentiful than the
demand, expiration of a term had little meaning; the servant was free
only to enter upon another term, while the master had always the choice
of taking on the old or a new servitor. That situation obtained even in
America as long as starvation was a real possibility. In 1621, it was noted,
"vittles being scarce in the country noe man will tacke servants." [50] As
late as 1643 Lord Baltimore thought it better if possible to hire labor than
to risk the burden of supporting servants through a long period.[51] Under
such conditions the number of years specified in the indenture was not
important, and if a servant had no indenture the question was certainly
not likely to rise.[52]

That accounts for the early references to unlimited service. Thus
Sandys's plan for Virginia in 1618 spoke of tenants-at-half assigned to the
treasurer's office, to "belong to said office for ever." Again, those at Berkeley's Hundred were perpetual "after the manner of estates in England." [53]
Since perpetual in seventeenth-century law meant that which had "not
any set time expressly allotted for [its] . . . continuance," such provisions were not surprising.[54] [Nor was it surprising to find instances in the]

---

[48] Lefroy, *Memorials*, I, 308; Smith, *Colonists in Bondage*, 172. For the dangers of reading Negro law in isolation, see the exaggerated interpretation of the
act of 1623, Craven, *Southern Colonies*, 218.

[49] That there was no trend is evident from the fluctuations in naming Negroes
slaves or servants and in their right to bear arms. See Hening, *Statutes*, I, 226,
258, 292, 540; Bruce, *Institutional History*, II, 5 ff., 199 ff. For similar fluctuations with regard to Indians, see Hening, *Statutes*, I, 391, 518.

[50] Charles M. Andrews, *Colonial Period of American History* (New Haven,
1934 ff.), I, 137.

[51] *Maryland Archives*, III, 141. See also the later comment on the Barbados by
Berkeley, *Discourse*, 12; and the complaint of Thomas Cornwallis that the cost of
maintaining many servants was "never defrayed by their labor," *Maryland Archives*, I, 463.

[52] That the practice of simply renewing expired terms was common was shown
by its abuse by unscrupulous masters. See *infra*, n. 71, n. 78.

[53] Gray, *History of Agriculture*, I, 316, 318 ff.

[54] We have discussed the whole question in "Origins of the American Business
Corporation," *Journal of Economic History*, V (1945), 21 ff. See also Smith,
Colonists in Bondage, 108.

court records of Negroes who seemed to serve forever.[55] These were quite compatible with the possibility of ultimate freedom.]Thus a colored man bought in 1644 "as a Slave for Ever," nevertheless was held "to serve as other Christians servants do" and freed after a term.[56]

[The question of length of service became critical when the mounting value of labor eased the fear that servants would be a drain on "vittles" and raised the expectation of profit from their toil. Those eager to multiply the number of available hands by stimulating immigration had not only to overcome the reluctance of a prospective newcomer faced with the trials of a sea journey; they had also to counteract the widespread reports in England and Scotland that servants were harshly treated and bound in perpetual slavery.[57]

[To encourage immigration therefore, the colonies embarked upon a line of legislation designed to improve servants' conditions and to enlarge the prospect of a meaningful release, a release that was not the start of a new period of servitude, but of life as a freeman and landowner.[58] Thus Virginia, in 1642, discharged "publick tenants from their servitudes, who, like one sort of villians anciently in England" were attached to the lands of the governor; and later laws provided that no person was to "be adjudged to serve the collonie hereafter." [59] Most significant were the statutes which reassured prospective newcomers by setting limits to the terms of servants without indentures, in 1638/9 in Maryland, in 1642/3 in Virginia.[60] These acts seem to have applied only to voluntary immigrants "of our own nation." [61] The Irish and other aliens, less desirable, at first received longer terms.[62] But the realization that such discrimination retarded "the peopling of the country" led to an extension of the identical privilege to all Christians.[63]

But the Negro never profited from these enactments. Farthest removed from the English, least desired, he communicated with no friends

[55] Russell, *Free Negro*, 34.

[56] Helen Tunnicliff Catterall, *Judicial Cases Concerning American Slavery and the Negro* (Washington, 1926 ff.), I, 58.

[57] *Collections of the South Carolina Historical Society*, V, 152; Wertenbaker, *Planters*, 60; Higham, *Leeward Islands*, 169; Jeffrey R. Brackett, *Negro in Maryland* (Baltimore, 1889), 23.

[58] *Maryland Archives*, I, 52, 97 (1640).

[59] Hening, *Statutes*, I, 259, 459; Gray, *History of Agriculture*, I, 316, 346.

[60] *Maryland Archives*, I, 37, 80, 352 (1654); Hening, *Statutes*, I, 257.

[61] *Maryland Archives*, I, 80, 402–409 (1661), 453 (1662); Hening, *Statutes*, I, 411. The Maryland act specifically excluded "slaves."

[62] See Virginia acts of 1654/5 and 1657/8, Hening, *Statutes*, I, 411, 441, 471.

[63] *Ibid.*, I, 538, II, 113, 169, 297. The provision limiting the effectiveness of the act to Christians is not surprising in view of contemporary attitudes. See the act of the same year excluding Quakers, *ibid.*, I, 532. For later adjustments of term, see *Maryland Archives*, II, 147 (1666), 335 (1671).

who might be deterred from following. Since his coming was involuntary, nothing that happened to him would increase or decrease his numbers. To raise the status of Europeans by shortening their terms would ultimately increase the available hands by inducing their compatriots to emigrate; to reduce the Negro's term would produce an immediate loss and no ultimate gain. By midcentury the servitude of Negroes seems generally lengthier than that of whites; and thereafter the consciousness dawns that the Blacks will toil for the whole of their lives, not through any particular concern with their status but simply by contrast with those whose years of labor are limited by statute. The legal position of the Negro is, however, still uncertain; it takes legislative action to settle that.[64]

The Maryland House, complaining of that ambiguity, provoked the decisive measure; "All Negroes and other slaues," it was enacted, "shall serve Durante Vita." [65] Virginia reached the same end more tortuously. An act of 1661 had assumed, in imposing penalties on runaways, that *some* Negroes served for life.[66] The law of 1670 went further; "all servants not being christians" brought in by sea were declared slaves for life.[67]

But slavery for life was still tenuous as long as the slave could extricate himself by baptism. The fact that Negroes were heathens had formerly justified their bondage, since infidels were "perpetual" enemies of Christians.[68] It had followed that conversion was a way to freedom. Governor Archdale thus released the Spanish Indians captured to be sold as slaves to Jamaica when he learned they were Christians.[69] As labor rose in value this presumption dissipated the zeal of masters for proselytizing. So that they be "freed from this doubt" a series of laws between 1667 and 1671 laid down the rule that conversion alone did not lead to a release from servitude.[70] Thereafter manumission, which other servants could demand

[64] For an example of such uncertainty, see the case of "Degoe the négro servant" (Virginia, 1665), *Lancaster County Record Book*, Book 2, p. 337; also Craven, *Southern Colonies*, 219. It is instructive to note how that question was evaded by ninety-nine year terms in Bermuda as late as 1662. See Lefroy, *Memorials*, II, 166, 184.

[65] *Maryland Archives*, I, 526 ff., 533; Wright, *Free Negro in Maryland*, 21; Brackett, *Negro in Maryland*, 28.

[66] Hening, *Statutes*, II, 26, 116; Catterall, *Judicial Cases*, I, 59.

[67] Hening, *Statutes*, II, 283; it was reenacted more stringently in 1682, *ibid.*, II, 491. See also McCrady, *South Carolina*, 358.

[68] See Saco, *Historia de la esclavitud*, III, 158 ff.; Hurd, *Law of Freedom and Bondage*, I, 160; Donnan, *Documents*, I, 3, 4.

[69] John Archdale, *A New Description of the Province of Carolina* (1707), in Salley, *Narratives*, 300. For English law on the question, see Gray, *History of Agriculture*, I, 359.

[70] Catterall, *Judicial Cases*, I, 57; Hening, *Statutes*, II, 260; Locke, *Constitutions*, Article 101; *Maryland Archives*, I, 526, II, 265, 272; Ballagh, *Slavery in Virginia*, 46–48; Russell, *Free Negro*, 21; Wright, *Free Negro in Maryland*, 22; Hurd, *Law of Freedom and Bondage*, I, 210; Brackett, *Negro in Maryland*, 29.

by right at the end of their terms, in the case of Negroes lay entirely within the discretion of the master.[71]

[A difference in the status of the offspring of Negro and white servants followed inevitably from the differentiation in the length of their terms. The problem of disposing of the issue of servants was at first general. Bastardy, prevalent to begin with and more frequent as the century advanced, deprived the master of his women's work and subjected him to the risk of their death. Furthermore the parish was burdened with the support of the child. The usual procedure was to punish the offenders with fines or whippings and to compel the servant to serve beyond his time for the benefit of the parish and to recompense the injured master.[72]

The general rule ceased to apply once the Negro was bound for life, for there was no means of extending his servitude. The most the outraged master could get was the child, a minimal measure of justice, somewhat tempered by the trouble of rearing the infant to an age of usefulness.[73] The truly vexing problem was to decide on the proper course when one parent was free, for it was not certain whether the English law that the issue followed the state of the father would apply. Maryland, which adopted that rule in 1664, found that unscrupulous masters instigated intercourse between their Negro males and white females which not only gave them the offspring, but, to boot, the service of the woman for the life of her husband. The solution in Virginia which followed the precedent of the bastardy laws and had the issue follow the mother seemed preferable and ultimately was adopted in Maryland and elsewhere.[74]

[By the last quarter of the seventeenth century, one could distinguish clearly between the Negro slave who served for life and the servant for a period. But there was not yet a demarcation in personal terms: the servant was not yet a free man, nor the slave a chattel.] As late as 1686, the words slave and servant could still be conflated to an extent that indicated men conceived of them as extensions of the same condition. A Frenchman in

[71] For the feudal derivation of manumission, see Coke, *First Institute upon Littleton*, I, 137b, §204. For the application to servants see Bodin, *Six Bookes*, 33; Hening, *Statutes*, II, 115 (1661/2). The requirement for manumission of servants in Virginia, to some extent, seems to have become a means of protection against labor-starved masters who coerced their servants into new contracts just before the old expired. See Hening, *Statutes*, II, 388 (1676/7).

[72] *Maryland Archives*, I, 373 (1658), 428, 441 (1662); Hening, *Statutes*, I, 438, II, 114 (1661/2), 168 (1662), 298 (1672), III, 139; Bruce, *Institutional History*, I, 45–50, 85, 86; Calhoun, *American Family*, I, 314. Women were always punished more severely than men, not being eligible for benefit of clergy. See Blackstone, *Commentaries*, I, 445n.

[73] Ballagh, *Slavery in Virginia*, 38 ff.; Greene, *Negro in New England*, 290 ff.

[74] See Coke, *First Institute upon Littleton*, I, 123a, §187; *Maryland Archives*, I, 526–533; Wright, *Free Negro in Maryland*, 21, 22, 27; Wheeler, *Practical Treatise*, 3, 21; Russell, *Free Negro*, 19, 21; Greene, *Negro in New England*, 182 ff.

Virginia in that year noted, "There are degrees among the slaves brought here, for a Christian over 21 years of age cannot be held a slave more than five years, but the negroes and other infidels remain slaves all their lives." [75]

[It was the persistence of such conceptions that raised the fear that "noe free borne Christians will ever be induced to come over servants" without overwhelming assurance that there would be nothing slavish in their lot.] After all Pennsylvania and New York now gave the European newcomer a choice of destination.[76] In Virginia and Maryland there was a persistent effort to make immigration more attractive by further ameliorating the lot of European servants. The custom of the country undoubtedly moved more rapidly than the letter of the law. "Weake and Ignorant" juries on which former servants sat often decided cases against masters.[77] But even the letter of the law showed a noticeable decline in the use of the death penalty and in the power of masters over men. By 1705 in some colonies, white servants were no longer transferable; they could not be whipped without a court order; and they were protected against the avaricious unreasonable masters who attempted to force them into new contracts "some small tyme before the expiration of their tyme of service." [78]

[Meanwhile the condition of the Negro deteriorated. In these very years, a startling growth in numbers complicated the problem] The Royal African Company was, to some extent, responsible, though its operations in the mainland colonies formed only a very minor part of its business. But the opening of Africa to free trade in 1698 inundated Virginia, Maryland, and South Carolina with new slaves.[79] Under the pressure of policing these newcomers the regulation of Negroes actually grew harsher.

---

[75] [Durand], A Frenchman in Virginia Being the Memoirs of a Huguenot Refugee in 1686, edited by fairfax Harrison (Richmond, 1923), 95 ff. For laws conflating servant and slave, see Brackett, Negro in Maryland, 104. This contradicts the assumption of Catterall, Judicial Cases, I, 57, that the status of Negroes was completely fixed by 1667.

[76] The agitation against transportation of felons was also evidence of the desire to supply that assurance. See Maryland Archives, I, 464; Hening, Statutes, II, 509 ff., 515 (1670); Ballagh, Slavery in Virginia, 10; Phillips, Life and Labor, 25. The attractiveness of rival colonies may account for the low proportion of servants who took up land in Maryland. See Abbot Emerson Smith, "The Indentured Servant and Land Speculation in Seventeenth Century Maryland," American Historical Review, XL (1935), 467 ff.; Gray, History of Agriculture, I, 88, 348.

[77] See the complaint of Thomas Cornwallis, Maryland Archives, I, 463 ff.

[78] See Hening, Statutes, II, 117, 156, 157, 164 (1661/2), 388 (1676/7), 464 (1680); Maryland Archives, II, 30 (1666), 351 (1674); Smith, Colonists in Bondage, 110, 228, 233; Bruce, Economic History, II, 11 ff.

[79] See Donnan, Documents, I, 86, 87; Gray, History of Agriculture, I, 352–355; Bruce, Economic History, II, 85; Salley, Narratives, 204; Higham, Leeward Islands, 162 ff.; Craven, Southern Colonies, 401; Russell, Free Negro, 29; Hening, Statutes, II, 511 ff.

[The early laws against runaways, against drunkenness, against carrying arms or trading without permission had applied penalties as heavy as death to all servants, Negroes and whites.[80] But these regulations grew steadily less stringent in the case of white servants. On the other hand fear of the growing number of slaves, uneasy suspicion of plots and conspiracies, led to more stringent control of Negroes and a broad view of the master's power of discipline. Furthermore the emerging difference in treatment was calculated to create a real division of interest between Negroes on the one hand and whites on the other.] Servants who ran away in the company of slaves, for instances, were doubly punished, for the loss of their own time and for the time of the slaves, a provision that discouraged such joint ventures. Similarly Negroes, even when freed, retained some disciplinary links with their less fortunate fellows. The wardens continued to supervise their children, they were not capable of holding white servants, and serious restrictions limited the number of manumissions.[81]

The growth of the Negro population also heightened the old concern over sexual immorality and the conditions of marriage. The law had always recognized the interest of the lord in the marriage of his villein or neife and had frowned on the mixed marriage of free and unfree. Similarly it was inclined to hold that the marriage of any servant was a loss to the master, an "Enormious offense" productive of much detriment "against the law of God," and therefore dependent on the consent of the master.[82] [Mixed marriages of free men and servants were particularly frowned upon as complicating status and therefore limited by law.[83]]

There was no departure from these principles in the early cases of Negro-white relationship.[84] Even the complicated laws of Maryland in 1664 and the manner of their enactment revealed no change in attitude.

[80] See Hening, *Statutes*, I, 401, 440; *Maryland Archives*, I, 107 ff. (1641), 124 (1642), 193 (1642), 500 (1663); McCrady, *South Carolina*, 359.

[81] *Maryland Archives*, I, 249 (1649), 348 (1654), 451 (1662), 489 (1663), II, 146 (1666), 224 (1669), 298 (1671), 523 (1676); Hening, *Statutes*, II, 116, 118 (1661/2), 185, 195 (1663), 239 (1666), 266 (1668), 270, 273 (1669), 277, 280 (1670), 299 (1672), 481 (1680), 492 (1682), III, 86 ff., 102 (1691), 179 (1699), 210 (1701), 269, 276, 278 (1705); Thomas Cooper and David J. McCord, eds., *Statutes at Large of South Carolina* (Columbia, 1836 ff.), VII, 343 ff.; Brackett, *Negro in Maryland*, 91 ff.; Phillips, *Life and Labor*, 29; Russell, *Free Negro*, 10, 21, 51, 138 ff.; Bruce, *Social Life*, 138; Bruce, *Economic History*, II, 120 ff.; Ames, *Eastern Shore*, 99; also Addison E. Verrill, *Bermuda Islands* (New Haven, 1902), 148 ff.

[82] See Hening, *Statutes*, I, 252, 433, 438; *Maryland Archives*, I, 73, 97 (1638/9), 428, 442 ff. (1662), II, 396 (1674). For English law, see Coke, *First Institute upon Littleton*, 135b, 136a, §202; *ibid.*, 139b, 140a, §209.

[83] Hening, *Statutes*, II, 114 (1661/2); Jernegan, *Laboring and Dependent Classes*, 55, 180.

[84] Hening, *Statutes*, I, 146, 552.

The marriage of Blacks and whites was possible; what was important was the status of the partners and of their issue.[85] It was to guard against the complications of status that the laws after 1691 forbade "spurious" or illegitimate mixed marriages of the slave and the free and punished violations with heavy penalties.[86] Yet it was also significant that by then the prohibition was couched in terms, not simply of slave and free man, but of Negro and white. Here was evidence as in the policing regulations of an emerging demarkation.

The first settlers in Virginia had been concerned with the difficulty of preserving the solidarity of the group under the disruptive effects of migration. They had been enjoined to "keepe to themselves" not to "marry nor give in marriage to the heathen, that are uncircumcised." [87] But such resolutions were difficult to maintain and had gradually relaxed until the colonists included among "themselves" such groups as the Irish, once the objects of very general contempt. A common lot drew them together; and it was the absence of a common lot that drew these apart from the Negro. At the opening of the eighteenth century, the Black was not only set off by economic and legal status; he was "abominable," another order of man.

Yet the ban on intermarriage did not rest on any principle of white racial purity, for many men contemplated with equanimity the prospect of amalgamation with the Indians.[88] That did not happen, for the mass of Redmen were free to recede into the interior while those who remained sank into slavery as abject as that of the Blacks and intermarried with those whose fate they shared.[89]

Color then emerged as the token of the slave status; the trace of color became the race of slavery. It had not always been so; as late as the 1660's the law had not even a word to describe the children of mixed marriages. But two decades later, the term mulatto is used, and it serves, not as in Brazil, to whiten the Black, but to affiliate through the color tie the off-

[85] See *supra*, 354; Wright, *Free Negro in Maryland*, 28–31.

[86] Hening, *Statutes*, III, 86–87, 453 (1705); Brackett, *Negro in Maryland*, 32 ff., 195 ff.; Russell, *Free Negro*, 124; Craven, *Southern Colonies*, 402. For the use of "spurious" in the sense of illegitimate see the quotations, Calhoun, *American Family*, I, 42.

[87] *Ibid.*, I, 323.

[88] Almon W. Lauber, *Indian Slavery in Colonial Times* (New York, 1913), 252.

[89] See Hening, *Statutes*, I, 167, 192 (1631/2), 396, 415 (1655/6), 455, 456, 476 (1657/8), II, 340, 346 (1676); *Maryland Archives*, I, 250 (1649); Catterall, *Judicial Cases*, I, 69, 70; Lauber, *Indian Slavery*, 105–117, 205, 287; Brackett, *Negro in Maryland*, 13; Craven, *Southern Colonies*, 367 ff.; Ballagh, *Slavery in Virginia*, 34, 47–49; McCrady, *South Carolina*, 189, 478; Greene, *Negro in New England*, 198 ff.; Peytraud, *L'Esclavage*, 29; Gray, *History of Agriculture*, I, 361.

spring of a spurious union with his inherited slavery.[90] (The compiler of
the Virginia laws then takes the liberty of altering the texts to bring
earlier legislation into line with his own new notions.[91]) Ultimately the
complete judicial doctrine begins to show forth, a slave cannot be a white
man, and every man of color was descendent of a slave.[92]

The rising wall dividing the legal status of the slave from that of the
servant was buttressed by other developments which derogated the qualities of the Negro as a human being to establish his inferiority and thus
completed his separation from the white. The destruction of the black
mans' personality involved, for example, a peculiar style of designation. In
the seventeenth century many immigrants in addition to the Africans —
Swedes, Armenians, Jews — had brought no family names to America. By
the eighteenth all but the Negroes had acquired them. In the seventeenth
century, Indians and Negroes bore names that were either an approximation of their original ones or similar to those of their masters, — Diana,
Jane, Frank, Juno, Anne, Maria, Jenny. In the eighteenth century slaves
seem increasingly to receive classical or biblical appelations, by analogy
with Roman and Hebrew bondsmen.[93] Deprivation by statute and usage
of other civic rights, to vote, to testify, to bring suit, even if free, completed the process. And after 1700 appear the full slave codes, formal
recognition that the Negroes are not governed by the laws of other men.[94]

The identical steps that made the slave less a man made him more a
chattel. All servants had once been reckoned property of a sort; a runaway
was guilty of "Stealth of ones self." [95] Negroes were then no different
from others.[96] But every law that improved the condition of the white ser-

90 By 1705, a mulatto was a person with a Negro great grandparent. See Hening, *Statutes*, III, 252; also Ballagh, *Slavery in Virginia*, 44; Tannenbaum, *Slave
and Citizen*, 8.

91 See Hening, *Statutes*, II, iii, 170. For other alterations to insert "slave"
where it had not originally been, see *ibid.*, II, 283, 490.

92 Catterall, *Judicial Cases*, II, 269, 358; Wheeler, *Practical Treatise*, 5, 12.

93 *Lancaster County Record Book*, Book 2, p. 285; Catterall, *Judicial Cases*,
II, 7, 8; Greene, *Negro in New England*, 201; Calhoun, *American Family*, I, 190;
Bruce, *Institutional History*, I, 673.

94 No earlier laws covered the same ground. See *Maryland Archives*, II, 523 ff.
(1676); Hening, *Statutes*, III, 298, 447–453 (1705); *Statutes of South Carolina*,
VII, 343 ff.; Craven, *Southern Colonies*, 217; Morris, *Government and Labor*,
501; Russell, *Free Negro*, 117–119, 125 ff.

95 *Maryland Archives*, I, 72; Morris, *Government and Labor*, 432; Smith,
Colonists in Bondage, 234.

96 Thus the inclusion of the Negroes among the Virginia tithables was at first
a recognition of their status as personalities rather than as property. The tax was
not intended to be discriminatory, but to apply to all those who worked in the
fields, white and black. The first sign of discrimination was in 1668 when white
but not Negro women were exempt. See Hening, *Statutes*, I, 144, 241, 292, 356,

vant chipped away at the property element in his status. The growing emphasis upon the consent of the servant, upon the limits of his term, upon the obligations to him, and upon the conditional nature of his dependence, steadily converted the relationship from an ownership to a contractual basis. None of these considerations applied to the Negro; on the contrary considerations of consent and conditions disappeared from his life. What was left was his status as property, — in most cases a chattel though for special purposes real estate.[97]

To this development there was a striking parallel in the northern colonies. For none of the elements that conspired to create the slave were peculiar to the productive system of the South. The contact of dissimilar peoples in an economy in which labor was short and opportunity long was common to all American settlements. In New England and New York too there had early been an intense desire for cheap unfree hands, for "bond slaverie, villinage or Captivitie," whether it be white, Negro, or Indian.[98] As in the South, the growth in the number of Negroes had been slow until the end of the seventeenth century.[99] The Negroes were servants who, like other bondsmen, became free and owners of land. But there too, police regulations, the rules of marriage, and the development of status as property turned them into chattel slaves.[100]

A difference would emerge in the course of the eighteenth century, not so much in the cities or in the Narragansett region where there were substantial concentrations of Blacks, but in the rural districts where handfuls of Negroes were scattered under the easy oversight of town and church. There the slave would be treated as an individual, would become an equal, and acquire the rights of a human being. Men whose minds would be ever more preoccupied with conceptions of natural rights and

---

361, 454, II, 84, 170, 267, 296; Russell, *Free Negro*, 21; Bruce, *Institutional History*, II, 458, 546 ff. For other difficulties in treating Negroes as chattels see Hening, *Statutes*, II, 288.

[97] See *Maryland Archives*, II, 164 (1669); Hurd, *Law of Freedom and Bondage*, I, 179; Hening, *Statutes*, III, 333 (1705); Gray, *History of Agriculture*, I, 359; Brackett, *Negro in Maryland*, 28.

[98] *Massachusetts Historical Society Collections*, Fourth Series, VI, 64 ff.; Greene, *Negro in New England*, 63, 65, 125.

[99] *Ibid.*, 73 ff., 319.

[100] For an abstract of legislation, see Hurd, *Law of Freedom and Bondage*, I, 254–293. See also Greene, *Negro in New England*, 126–139, 169, 170, 178, 184, 208 ff.; George Elliott Howard, *History of Matrimonial Institutions* (Chicago, 1904), II, 225, 226; Calhoun, *American Family*, I, 65, 210; J. H. Franklin, *From Slavery to Freedom* (New York, 1947), 89–98; Ellis L. Raesly, *Portrait of New Netherland* (New York, 1945), 104, 161, 162.

personal dignity would find it difficult to except the Negro from their general rule.[101]

But by the time the same preoccupations would fire imaginations in the South, the society in which the slave lived would so have changed that he would derive no advantage from the eighteenth-century speculations on the nature of human rights. Slavery had emerged in a society in which the unit of active agriculture was small and growing smaller; even the few large estates were operated by sub-division among tenants.[102] After 1690, however, South Carolinians (and still later Georgians) turned from naval stores and the fur trade to the cultivation of rice, cotton, and indigo. In the production of these staples, which required substantial capital equipment, there was an advantage to large-scale operations. By then it was obvious which was the cheapest, most available, most exploitable labor supply. The immense profits from the tropical crops steadily sucked slaves in ever growing numbers into the plantation. With this extensive use, novel on the mainland, the price of slaves everywhere rose sharply, to the advantage of those who already held them. The prospect that the slave-owner would profit not only by the Negroes' labor, but also by the rise in their unit value and by their probable increase through breeding, accounted for the spread of the plantation to the older tobacco regions where large-scale production was not, as in the rice areas, necessarily an asset.[103]

The new social and economic context impressed indelibly on the Negro the peculiar quality of chattel with which he had been left, as other servants escaped the general degradation that had originally been the common portion of all. Not only did the concentration of slaves in large numbers call for more rigid discipline, not only did the organization of the plantation with its separate quarters, hierarchy of overseers, and absentee owners widen the gulf between black and white, but the involvement of the whole southern economy in plantation production created an effective interest against any change in status.[104]

Therein, the southern mainland colonies also differed from those in the West Indies where the same effective interest in keeping the black man debased was created without the prior definition of his status. The acutal condition of the Negro differed from island to island, reflecting variations

---

[101] Greene, *Negro in New England*, 86, 103 ff., 140; Calhoun, *American Family*, I, 82.

[102] See Ames, *Eastern Shore*, 16, 17, 30 ff., 37 ff.; McCrady, *South Carolina*, 189; Werkenbaker, *Planters*, 45, 52 ff.; Phillips, *Life and Labor*, 34; Craven, *Southern Colonies*, 210 ff.

[103] Flanders, *Plantation Slavery*, 20; Gray, *History of Agriculture*, I, 120, 278, 349.

[104] [Durand], *Frenchman in Virginia*, 112 ff.; Phillips, *Life and Labor*, 47; Salley, *Narratives*, 207, 208.

in the productive system, in the labor supply, and in economic trends. But with surprising uniformity, the printed statutes and legislative compilations show no concern with the problems of defining the nature of his servitude. The relevant laws deal entirely with policing, as in the case of servants.[105] A similar unconcern seems to have been characteristic of the French, for the most important aspects of the royal *Code noir* issued from Paris in 1685 were entirely disregarded.[106]

The failure to define status may have been due, in the islands which changed hands, to contact with the Spaniards and to the confusion attendent upon changes of sovereignty. More likely it grew out of the manner in which the Negroes were introduced. Places like the Barbados and St. Christopher's were at the start quite similar to Virginia and Maryland, societies of small farmers, with a labor force of indentured servants and *engagées*. The Negroes and the sugar plantation appeared there somewhat earlier than on the continent because the Dutch, English, and French African companies, anxious to use the islands as entrepots from which their cargoes would be re-exported to Latin America, advanced the credit not only for purchase of the Blacks, but also for sugar-making equipment. But the limited land of the islands meant that the plantation owner and the yeoman competed for the same acres, and in the unequal competition the farmer was ultimately displaced.[107]

The planter had no inveterate preference for the Negro, often expressed a desire for white labor. But the limits to the available land also prevented him from holding out the only inducements that would attract servants with a choice, – the prospect of landed freedom. From time to time desultory laws dealt with the term of service, but these showed no progression and had no consequences. The manumitted were free only to emigrate, if they could, or to hang about, hundreds of them "who have been out of their time for many years . . . [with] never a bit of fresh meat bestowed

[105] See *Montserrat Code of Laws from 1688 to 1788* (London, 1790), 8, 16, 38; *Acts of Assembly Passed in the Island of Nevis from 1664, to 1739, Inclusive* (London, 1740), 9, 10, 11, 17, 25, 28, 31, 37, 46, 75; *Acts of Assembly Passed in the Island of Barbadoes from 1648 to 1718* (London, 1721), 22, 101, 106, 137 ff.; *Acts, of Assembly Passed in the Island of Jamaica from the Year 1681 to the Year 1768, Inclusive* (Saint Jagoe de la Vesga, 1769), I, 1, 57; [Leslie], *New History of Jamaica* (2d ed., London, 1740), 204 ff., 217 ff. There seem to have been two minor exceptions. The question of slave status was implicitly touched on in the laws governing inheritance and the sale of property for debt (*Acts of Barbadoes*, 63, 147) and in early orders affecting term of service. See *Calendar of State Papers, Colonial*, I, 202; [William Duke], *Some Memoirs of the First Settlement of the Island of Barbados* . . . (Barbados, 1741), 19.

[106] Peytraud, *L'Esclavage*, 143 ff., 158 ff., 208 ff.

[107] See Peytraud, *L' Esclavage*, 13–17; Gray, *Southern Agriculture*, I, 303–309; Donnan, *Documents*, I, 92, 100, 108–111, 166, 197, 249 ff.; Vincent T. Harlow, *History of Barbados 1625–1685* (Oxford, 1926), 42.

on them nor a dram of rum." [108] The process of extending the rights of servants, which on the mainland was the means of defining the status of the slave, never took place on the islands.

The term, slave, in the West Indies was at the start as vague as in Virginia and Maryland; and when toward mid-century it narrowed down to the plantation Negroes as sugar took hold through the stimulus of the Africa traders, it does not seem to have comprehended more than the presumption of indefinite service.[109] To Europeans, any service on the islands continued to be slavery. For whatever distinctions might be drawn among various groups of them, the slavish servants remained slavish servants. All labor was depressed, Negro and white, "domineered over and used like dogs." That undoubtedly affected emigration from the islands, the decline of white population, the relationships of Blacks and whites, the ultimate connotation of the term slave, the similarities in practice to villeinage, the savage treatment by masters and equally savage revolts against them, the impact of eighteenth-century humanitarianism, and the direction of emancipation.[110]

[The distinctive qualities of the southern labor system were then not the simple products of the plantation. They were rather the complex outcome of a process by which the American environment broke down the traditional European conceptions of servitude. In that process the weight of the plantation had pinned down on the Negro the clearly-defined status of a chattel, a status left him as other elements in the population achieved their liberation. When, therefore, Southerners in the eighteenth century came to think of the nature of the rights of man they found it inconceivable that Negroes should participate in those rights. It was more in accord with the whole social setting to argue that the slaves could not share those rights because they were not fully men, or at least different kinds of men. In fact, to the extent that Southerners ceased to think in terms of the seventeenth-century degrees of freedom, to the extent that they thought of liberty as whole, natural, and inalienable, they were forced to conclude that the slave was wholly unfree, wholly lacking in personality, wholly a chattel.]

---

[108] Smith, *Colonists in Bondage*, 294.

[109] See Richard Ligon, *True & Exact History of the Island of Barbados . . .* (London, 1657), 43–47; [Charles C. de Rochefort], *History of the Caribby-Islands . . .* , translated by John Davies (London, 1666), 200 ff.

[110] Smith, *Colonists in Bondage*, 294. For examples of servant legislation, see *Acts of Barbadoes*, 22 ff., 80 ff., 145 ff., 150, 168, 204 ff. (1661–1703). See also Peytraud, *L'Esclavage*, 38, 135 ff.; Donnan, *Documents*, I, 97; Morris, *Government and Labor*, 503; Leslie, *New History of Jamaica*, 89, 148 ff.; Morgan Godwyn, *Negro's and Indian's Advocate* (London, 1680), 12 ff.; Frank W. Pitman, "Slavery on British West India Plantations in the Eighteenth Century," *Journal of Negro History*, XI (1926), 610 ff., 617; William L. Mathieson, *British Slavery and Its Abolition, 1823–1838* (London, 1926), 44, 50 ff.

Only a few, like St. George Tucker and Thomas Jefferson, perceived that here were the roots of a horrible tragedy that would some day destroy them all.[111]

[111] See the eloquent discussion in Tucker's appendix to Blackstone, *Commentaries*, I, 35 ff.

Enslavement of Negroes in America to 1700

WINTHROP D. JORDAN

Winthrop Jordan casts his net widely in search of the origins of Negro slavery in seventeenth-century America. While he admits that there was no such legal status in England, he argues that Englishmen were familiar with the conception of slavery as a condition of perpetual, absolute unfreedom and that contemporary Europe provided them with real examples of the practice. Jordan notes that slavery came into existence before the end of the seventeenth century everywhere in British North America, although the process varied greatly from the West Indian islands to New England to Virginia and Maryland. Unhindered by Puritan ideology or the "captivity" analogy, the Southern colonies provide an example of the gradual creation of a full-blown slave system. Southern blacks were treated differently from the start (and some may have served for life almost as soon), but by 1640 there is clear evidence of total enslavement and by the end of the century slaves were already treated more like property than men. Slave status and racial distaste worked together to create the "peculiar institution." Thus for Jordan, slavery resulted from social conditions in Europe and in the colonies, from the attitudes of the colonists, and from the experience of settling the New World. He believes that the legal structure of slavery did not reflect the conditions of its growth, since law so often lags behind social reality.

From the vantage point of the late eighteenth century, the question of the origins of slavery does not make very much difference, since on any account the results were the same. But for the historian of the colonial period the differences in interpretation are critical, for they reflect dramatically opposed views of social organization and human behavior in the first century of American life. To discover how men developed such a labor system is therefore to find out what is most basic about the way in which they lived.

At the start of English settlement in America, no one had in mind to establish the institution of Negro slavery. Yet in less than a century the foundations of a peculiar institution had been laid. The first Negroes landed in Virginia in 1619, though very, very little is known about their precise status during the next twenty years. Between 1640 and 1660 there is evidence of enslavement, and after 1660 slavery crystallized on the statute books of Maryland, Virginia, and other colonies. By 1700 when African Negroes began flooding into English America they were treated as somehow deserving a life and status radically different from English and other European settlers. . . . Englishmen in America had created a legal status [for Negroes] which ran counter to English law.

Unfortunately the details of this process can never be completely reconstructed; there is simply not enough evidence (and very little chance of more to come) to show precisely when and how and why Negroes came to be treated so differently from white men, though there is just enough to make historians differ as to its meaning. Concerning the first years of contact especially we have very little information as to what impression Negroes made upon English settlers: accordingly, we are left knowing less about the formative years than about later periods of American slavery. That those early years were crucial ones is obvious, for it was then that the cycle of Negro debasement began; once the Negro became fully the slave it is not hard to see why white men looked down upon him. Yet precisely because understanding the dynamics of these early years is so important to understanding the centuries which followed, it is necessary to bear with the less than satisfactory data and to attempt to reconstruct the course of debasement undergone by Negroes in seventeenth-century America. In order to comprehend it, we need first of all to examine certain social pressures generated by the American environment and how these pressures interacted with certain qualities of English social thought and law that existed on the eve of settlement, qualities

Reprinted by permission from Winthrop D. Jordan, *White over Black* (Chapel Hill: University of North Carolina Press for the Institute of Early American History and Culture, Williamsburg, Va., 1968), 44–82, 85–98.

that even then were being modified by examples set by England's rivals for empire in the New World.

1. The Necessities of a New World

When Englishmen crossed the Atlantic to settle in America, they were immediately subject to novel strains. In some settlements, notably James-town and Plymouth, the survival of the community was in question. An appalling proportion of people were dead within a year, from malnutri-tion, starvation, unconquerable diseases, bitter cold, oppressive heat, Indian attacks, murder, and suicide. The survivors were isolated from the world as they had known it, cut off from friends and family and the familiar sights and sounds and smells which have always told men who and where they are. A similar sense of isolation and disorientation was inevitable even in the settlements that did not suffer through a starving time. English settlers were surrounded by savages. They had to perform a round of daily tasks to which most were unaccustomed. They had under-gone the shock of detachment from home in order to set forth upon a dangerous voyage of from ten to thirteen weeks that ranged from un-pleasant to fatal and that seared into every passenger's memory the cease-lessly tossing distance that separated him from his old way of life.[1]

Life in America put great pressure upon the traditional social and economic controls that Englishmen assumed were to be exercised by civil and often ecclesiastical authority. Somehow the empty woods seemed to lead much more toward license than restraint. At the same time, by reaction, this unfettering resulted in an almost pathetic social conser-vatism, a yearning for the forms and symbols of the old familiar social order. When in 1618, for example, the Virginia Company wangled a knighthood for a newly appointed governor of the colony the objection from the settlers was not that this artificial elevation was inappropriate to wilderness conditions but that it did not go far enough to meet them; several planters petitioned that a governor of higher rank be sent. . . . English social forms were transplanted to America not simply because they were nice to have around but because without them the new settle-ment would have have fallen apart and English settlers would have be-come men of the forest, savage men devoid of civilization.

For the same reason, the communal goals that animated the settlement of the colonies acquired great functional importance in the wilderness; they served as antidotes to social and individual disintegration. The physi-cal hardships of settlement could never have been surmounted without the stiffened nerve and will engendered by commonly recognized if some-times unarticulated purposes. . . . For Englishmen planting in America

---

[1] There is an eloquent revivification by William Bradford, *Of Plymouth Plantation, 1620–1647*, ed. Samuel Eliot Morison (N.Y., 1952), 61–63.

. . . it was of the utmost importance to know that they were Englishmen, which was to say that they were educated (to a degree suitable to their station), Christian (of an appropriate Protestant variety), civilized, and (again to an appropriate degree) free men.

It was with personal freedom, of course, that wilderness conditions most suddenly reshaped English laws, assumptions, and practices. In America land was plentiful, labor scarce, and, as in all new colonies, a cash crop desperately needed. These economic conditions were to remain important for centuries; in general they tended to encourage greater geographical mobility, less specialization, higher rewards, and fewer restraints on the processes and products of labor. Supporting traditional assumptions and practices, however, was the need to retain them simply because they were familiar and because they served the vital function of maintaining and advancing orderly settlement. Throughout the seventeenth century there were pressures on traditional practices which similarly told in opposite directions.

In general men who invested capital in agriculture in America came under fewer customary and legal restraints than in England concerning what they did with their land and with the people who worked on it. On the other hand their activities were constrained by the economic necessity of producing cash crops for export, which narrowed their choice of how they could treat it. Men without capital could obtain land relatively easily: hence the shortage of labor and the notably blurred line between men who had capital and men who did not. Men and women in England faced a different situation. A significant amount of capital was required in order to get to America, and the greatest barrier to material advancement in America was the Atlantic Ocean.

Three major systems of labor emerged amid the interplay of these social and economic conditions in America. One, which was present from the beginning, was free wage labor, in which contractual arrangements rested upon a monetary nexus. Another, which was the last to appear, was chattel slavery, in which there were no contractual arrangements (except among owners). The third, which virtually coincided with first settlement in America, was temporary servitude, in which complex contractual arrangements gave shape to the entire system. It was this third system, indentured servitude, which permitted so many English settlers to cross the Atlantic barrier. Indentured servitude was linked to the development of chattel slavery in America, and its operation deserves closer examination.

A very sizable proportion of settlers in the English colonies came as indentured servants bound by contract to serve a master for a specified number of years, usually from four to seven or until age twenty-one, as repayment for their ocean passage. The time of service to which the servant bound himself was negotiable property, and he might be sold or conveyed from one master to another at any time up to the expiration of his indenture, at which point he became a free man. (Actually it was his *labor* which was owned and sold, not his *person*, though this distinction was neither important nor obvious at the time.) Custom and statute law regulated the relationship between servant and master. Obligation was reciprocal: the master undertook to feed and clothe and sometimes to educate his servant and to refrain from abusing him, while the servant was obliged to perform such work as his master set him and to obey his master in all things. This typical pattern, with a multitude of variations, was firmly established by mid-seventeenth century. In Virginia and Maryland, both the legal and actual conditions of servants seem to have improved considerably from the early years when servants had often been outrageously abused and sometimes forced to serve long terms. Beginning about 1640 the legislative assemblies of the two colonies passed numerous acts prescribing maximum terms of service and requiring masters to pay the customary "freedom dues" (clothing, provisions, and so forth) at the end of the servant's time.[2] This legislation may have been actuated partly by the need to attract more immigrants with guarantees of good treatment, in which case underpopulation in relation to level of technology and to natural resources in the English colonies may be said to have made for greater personal freedom. On the other hand, it may also have been a matter of protecting traditional freedoms threatened by this same fact of underpopulation which generated so powerful a need for labor which would not be transient and temporary. In this instance, very clearly, the imperatives enjoined by settlement in the wilderness interacted with previously acquired ideas concerning personal freedom. Indeed without some inquiry into Elizabethan thinking on that subject, it will remain impossible to comprehend why Englishmen became servants in the plantations, and Negroes slaves.

2. Freedom and Bondage in the English Tradition

Thinking about freedom and bondage in Tudor England was confused and self-contradictory. In a period of social dislocation there was considerable disagreement among contemporary observers as to what actually was going on and even as to what ought to be. Ideas about personal freedom tended to run both ahead of and behind actual social conditions. Both statute and common law were sometimes considerably more than a century out of phase with actual practice and with commonly held notions about servitude. Finally, ideas and practices were changing rapidly.

[2] William Waller Hening, ed., *The Statutes at Large Being a Collection of All the Laws of Virginia*, 13 vols. (Richmond, N.Y., and Phila., 1809–23), I, 257, 435, 439–42, II, 113–14, 240, 388, III, 447–62; *Archives of Maryland*, 69 vols. (Baltimore, 1883–), I, 53, 80, 352–53, 409–10, 428, 443–44, 453–54, 464, 469, II, 147–48, 335–36, 527.

It is possible, however, to identify certain important tenets of social thought that served as anchor points amid this chaos.

Englishmen lacked accurate methods of ascertaining what actually was happening to their social institutions, but they were not wrong in supposing that villenage, or "bondage" as they more often called it, had virtually disappeared in England. William Harrison put the matter most strenuously in 1577: "As for slaves and bondmen we have none, naie such is the privilege of our countrie by the especiall grace of God, and bountie of our princes, that if anie come hither from other realms, so soone as they set foot on land they become so free of condition as their masters, whereby all note of servile bondage is utterlie remooved from them." [3] Other observers were of the (correct) opinion that a few lingering vestiges — bondmen whom the progress of freedom had passed by — might still be found in the crannies of the decayed manorial system, but everyone agreed that such vestiges were anachronistic. In fact there were English men and women who were still "bond" in the mid-sixteenth century, but they were few in number and their status was much more a technicality than a condition. In the middle ages, being a villein had meant dependence upon the will of a feudal lord but by no means deprivation of all social and legal rights. In the thirteenth and fourteenth centuries villenage had decayed markedly, and it may be said not to have existed as a viable social institution in the second half of the sixteenth century.[4] Personal freedom had become the normal status of Englishmen. Most contemporaries welcomed this fact; indeed it was after about 1550 that there began to develop in England that preening consciousness of the peculiar glories of English liberties.

How had it all happened? Among those observers who tried to explain, there was agreement that Christianity was primarily responsible. They thought of villenage as a mitigation of ancient bond slavery and that the continuing trend to liberty was animated, as Sir Thomas Smith said in a famous passage, by the "perswasion . . . of Christians not to make nor keepe his brother in Christ, servile, bond and underling for ever unto him, as a beast rather than as a man." [5] They agreed also that the trend

[3] [Harrison], *Historicall Description of Britaine*, in *Holinshed's Chronicles*, I, 275.
[4] The best place to start on this complicated subject is Paul Vinagradof, *Villainage in England: Essays in English Mediaeval History* (Oxford, 1892). The least unsatisfactory studies of vestiges seem to be Alexander Savine, "Bondmen under the Tudors," Royal Historical Society, *Transactions*, 2d Ser., 17 (1903), 235–89; I. S. Leadam, "The Last Days of Bondage in England," *Law Quarterly Review*, 9 (1893), 348–65. William S. Holdsworth, *A History of English Law*, 3d ed., 12 vols. (Boston, 1923), III, 491–510, explodes the supposed distinction between villeins *regardant* and *gross*.
[5] Thomas Smith, *De Republica Anglorum: A Discourse on the Commonwealth of England*, ed. L. Alston (Cambridge, Eng., 1906), 133.

had been forwarded by the common law, in which the disposition was always, as the phrase went, *in favorem libertatis*, "in favor of liberty." Probably they were correct in both these suppositions, but the common law harbored certain inconsistencies as to freedom which may have had an important though imponderable effect upon the reappearance of slavery in English communities in the seventeenth century.

The accreted structure of the common law sometimes resulted in imperviousness to changing conditions. The first book of Lord Coke's great *Institutes of the Laws of England* (1628), for example, was an extended gloss upon Littleton's fifteenth-century treatise on *Tenures* and it repeatedly quoted the opinions of such famous authorities as Bracton, who had died in 1268. When Bracton had described villenage, English law had not yet fully diverged from the civil or Roman law, and villenage actually existed. Almost four hundred years later some legal authorities were still citing Bracton on villenage without even alluding to the fact that villenage no longer existed. The widely used legal dictionary, Cowell's *Interpreter* (1607 and later editions), quoted Bracton at length and declared that his words "expresse the nature of our villenage something aptly." [6] Anyone relying solely on Cowell's *Interpreter* would suppose that some Englishmen in the early seventeenth century were hereditary serfs. Thus while villenage was actually extinct, it lay unmistakably fossilized in the common law. Its survival in that rigid form must have reminded Englishmen that there existed a sharply differing alternative to personal liberty. It was in this vague way that villenage seems to have been related to the development of chattel slavery in America. Certainly villenage was not the forerunner of slavery, but its survival in the law books meant that a possibility which might have been foreclosed was not. Later, after Negro slavery had clearly emerged, English lawyers were inclined to think of slavery as being a New World version of the ancient tenure described by Bracton and Cowell and Coke.

That the common law was running centuries behind social practice was only one of several important factors complicating Tudor thought about the proper status of individuals in society. The social ferment of the sixteenth century resulted not only in the impalpable mood of control and subordination which seems to have affected English perception of Africans but also in the well-known strenuous efforts of Tudor governments to lay restrictions on elements in English society which seemed badly out of control. From at least the 1530's the countryside swarmed with vagrants, sturdy beggars, rogues, and vagabonds, with men who could but would not work. They committed all manner of crimes, the worst of

---

[6] Coke's section on villenage is Lib. II, cap. XI; see John Cowell, *The Interpreter: Or Booke Containing the Signification of Words* . . . (Cambridge, Eng., 1607), "villein."

which was remaining idle. It was an article of faith among Tudor commentators (before there were "Puritans" to help propound it) that idleness was the mother of all vice and the chief danger to a well-ordered state. Tudor statesmen valiantly attempted to suppress idleness by means of the famous vagrancy laws. . . . They assumed that everyone belonged in a specific social niche and that anyone failing to labor in the niche assigned to him by Providence must be compelled to do so by authority. . . .

. . . Tudor authorities gradually hammered out the legal framework of a labor system which permitted compulsion but which did not permit so total a loss of freedom as lifetime hereditary slavery. Apprenticeship seemed to them the ideal status, for apprenticeship provided a means of regulating the economy and of guiding youth into acceptable paths of honest industry. By 1600, many writers had come to think of other kinds of bound labor as inferior forms of apprenticeship, involving less of an educative functions, less permanence, and a less rigidly contractual basis. This tendency to reason from apprenticeship downward, rather than from penal service up, had the important effect of imparting some of the very strong contractualism in the master-apprentice relationship to less formal varieties of servitude. There were "indentured" servants in England prior to English settlement in America. Their written "indentures" gave visible evidence of the strong element of mutual obligation between master and servant: each retained a copy of the contract which was "indented" at the top so as to match the other.

As things turned out, it was indentured servitude which best met the requirements for settling in America. Of course there were other forms of bound labor which contributed to the process of settlement: many convicts were sent and many children abduced.[7] Yet among all the numerous varieties and degrees of non-freedom which existed in England, there was none which could have served as a well-formed model for the chattel slavery which developed in America. This is not to say, though, that slavery was an unheard-of novelty in Tudor England. On the contrary, "bond slavery" was a memory trace of long standing. Vague and confused as the concept of slavery was in the minds of Englishmen, it possessed certain fairly consistent connotations which were to help shape English perceptions of the way Europeans should properly treat the newly discovered peoples overseas.

3. The Concept of Slavery

At first glance, one is likely to see merely a fog of inconsistency and vagueness enveloping the terms *servant* and *slave* as they were used both

[7] The "standard" work on this subject unfortunately does not address itself to the problem of origins. Abbot Emerson Smith, *Colonists in Bondage: White Servitude and Convict Labor in America, 1607–1776* (Chapel Hill, 1947).

in England and in seventeenth-century America. When Hamlet declaims "O what a rogue and peasant slave am I," the term seems to have a certain elasticity. When Peter Heylyn defines it in 1627 as "that ignominious word, *slave*; whereby we use to call ignoble fellowes, and the more base sort of people," [8] the term seems useless as a key to a specific social status. And when we find in the American colonies a reference in 1665 to "Jacob a negro slave and servant to Nathaniel Utye," [9] it is tempting to regard slavery as having been in the first half of the seventeenth century merely a not very elevated sort of servitude.

In one sense it was, since the concept embodied in the terms *servitude, service,* and *servant* was widely embracive. *Servant* was more a generic term than *slave.* Slaves could be "servants" — as they were eventually and ironically to become in the ante-bellum South — but servants *should not* be "slaves." This injunction, which was common in England, suggests a measure of precision in the concept of slavery. In fact there was a large measure which merits closer inspection.

First of all, the "slave's" loss of freedom was complete. "Of all men which be destitute of libertie or freedome," explained Henry Swinburne in his *Briefe Treatise of Testaments and Last Willes* (1590), "the slave is in greatest subjection, for a slave is that person which is in servitude or bondage to an other, even against nature." "Even his children," moreover, ". . . are infected with the Leprosie of his father's bondage." . . . At law, much more clearly than in literary usage, "bond slavery" implied utter deprivation of liberty.

Slavery was also thought of as a perpetual condition. While it had not yet come invariably to mean lifetime labor, it was frequently thought of in those terms. Except sometimes in instances of punishment for crime, slavery was open ended; in contrast to servitude, it did not involve a definite term of years. Slavery was perpetual also in the sense that it was often thought of as hereditary. It was these dual aspects of perpetuity which were to assume such importance in America.

So much was slavery a complete loss of liberty that it seemed to Englishmen somehow akin to loss of humanity. No theme was more persistent than the claim that to treat a man as a slave was to treat him as a beast. Almost half a century after Sir Thomas Smith had made this connection a Puritan divine was condemning masters who used "their servants as slaves, or rather as beasts" while Captain John Smith was moaning about being captured by the Turks and "all sold for slaves, like beasts in a market-place." [10] No analogy could have better demonstrated how strongly Englishmen felt about total loss of personal freedom.

[8] *Hamlet,* II, ii; Heylyn, ΜΙΚΡΌΚΟΣΜΟΣ, 175.
[9] *Archives of Maryland,* XLIX, 489.
[10] William Gouge, *Of Domesticall Duties Eight Treatises* (London, 1622), 690; Edward Arber, ed., *Travels and Works of Captain John Smith* . . . , 2 vols. (Edinburgh, 1910), II, 853.

Certain prevalent assumptions about the origins of slavery paralleled this analogy at a different level of intellectual construction. Lawyers and divines alike assumed that slavery was impossible before the Fall, that it violated natural law, that it was instituted by positive human laws, and, more generally, that in various ways it was connected with sin. These ideas were as old as the church fathers and the Roman writers on natural law. In the social atmosphere of pre-Restoration England it was virtually inevitable that they should have been capsulated in the story of Ham. . . . Sir Edward Coke (himself scarcely a Puritan) declared, "This is assured, That Bondage or Servitude was first inflicted for dishonouring of Parents: For Cham the Father of Canaan . . . seeing the Nakedness of his Father Noah, and shewing it in Derision to his Brethren, was therefore punished in his Son Canaan with Bondage." [11]

The great jurist wrote this in earnest, but at least he did offer another description of slavery's genesis. In it he established what was perhaps the most important and widely acknowledged attribute of slavery: at the time of the Flood "all Things were common to all," but afterward, with the emergence of private property, there "arose battles"; "then it was ordained by Constitution of Nations . . . that he that was taken in Battle should remain Bond to his taker for ever, and he to do with him, all that should come of him, his Will and Pleasure, as with his Beast, or any other Cattle, to give, or to sell, or to kill." This final power, Coke noted, had since been taken away (owing to "the Cruelty of some Lords") and placed in the hands only of kings.[12] The animating rationale here was that captivity in war meant an end to a person's claim to life as a human being; by sparing the captive's life, the captor acquired virtually absolute power over the life of the man who had lost the power to control his own.

More than any other single quality, *captivity* differentiated slavery from servitude. Although there were other, subsidiary ways of becoming a slave, such as being born of slave parents, selling oneself into slavery, or being adjudged to slavery for crime, none of these were considered to explain the way slavery had originated. Slavery was a power relationship; servitude was a relationship of service. Men were "slaves" to the devil but "servants" of God. Men were "galley-slaves," not galley servants. Bondage had never existed in the county of Kent because Kent was "never van-

---

[11] *The Whole Works of the Right Rev. Jeremy Taylor* . . . , 10 vols. (London, 1850–54), X, 453; Sir Edward Coke, *The First Part of the Institutes of the Laws of England: or, a Commentary upon Littleton* . . . , 12th ed. (London, 1738), Lib. II, Cap. XI. For the long-standing assumption that slavery was brought about by man's sinfulness see R. W. and A. J. Carlyle, *A History of Medieval Political Theory in the West*, 6 vols. (Edinburgh and London, 1903–36), I, 116–24, II, 119–20.

[12] Coke, *Institutes*, Lib. II, Cap. XI.

quished by [William] the Conquerour, but yeelded it selfe by composition." [13]

This tendency to equate slavery with captivity had important ramifications. Warfare was usually waged against another people; captives were usually foreigners — "strangers" as they were termed. Until the emergence of nation-states in Europe, by far the most important category of strangers was the non-Christian. International warfare seemed above all a ceaseless struggle between Christians and Turks. Slavery, therefore, frequently appeared to rest upon the "perpetual enmity" which existed between Christians on the one hand and "infidels" and "pagans" on the other.[14] In the sixteenth and seventeenth centuries Englishmen at home could read scores of accounts concerning the miserable fate of Englishmen and other Christians taken into "captivity" by Turks and Moors and oppressed by the "verie worst manner of bondmanship and slaverie." [15] Clearly slavery was tinged by the religious disjunction.

Just as many commentators thought that the spirit of Christianity was responsible for the demise of bondage in England, many divines distinguished between ownership of Christian and of non-Christian servants. The Reverend William Gouge referred to "such servants as being strangers were bond-slaves, over whom masters had a more absolute power than others." The Reverend Henry Smith declared, "He which counteth his servant a slave, is in error: for there is difference betweene beleeving servants and infidell servants." [16] Implicit in every clerical discourse was the assumption that common brotherhood in Christ imparted a special quality to the master-servant relationship.

Slavery did not possess that quality, which made it fortunate that Englishmen did not enslave one another. As we have seen, however, Englishmen did possess a *concept* of slavery, formed by the clustering of several rough but not illogical equations. The slave was treated like a beast. Slavery was inseparable from the evil in men; it was God's punishment upon Ham's prurient disobedience. Enslavement was captivity, the loser's lot in a contest of power. Slaves were infidels or heathens.

On every count, Negroes qualified.

---

[13] William Lambard[e], *A Perambulation of Kent* . . . (London, 1576), 11. The notion of selling oneself into slavery was very much subsidiary and probably derived from the Old Testament. Isaac Mendelsohn, *Slavery in the Ancient Near East* . . . (N.Y., 1949), 18, points out that the Old Testament was the only ancient law code to mention voluntary slavery and self-sale.

[14] The phrases are from Michael Dalton, *The Countrey Justice* . . . (London, 1655), 191.

[15] *The Estate of Christians, Living under the Subjection of the Turke* . . . (London, 1595), 5.

[16] Gouge, *Domesticall Duties*, 663; *The Sermons of Master Henry Smith* . . . (London, 1607), 40.

4. The Practices of Portingals and Spanyards

Which is not to say that Englishmen were casting about for a people to enslave. What happened was that they found thrust before them not only instances of Negroes being taken into slavery but attractive opportunities for joining in that business. Englishmen actually were rather slow to seize these opportunities; on most of the sixteenth-century English voyages to West Africa there was no dealing in slaves. The notion that it was appropriate to do so seems to have been drawn chiefly from the example set by the Spanish and Portuguese.

Without inquiring into the reasons, it can be said that slavery had persisted since ancient times in the Iberian peninsula, that prior to the discoveries it was primarily a function of the religious wars against the Moors,[17] that Portuguese explorers pressing down the coast in the fifteenth century captured thousands of Negroes whom they carried back to Portugal as slaves, and that after 1500, Portuguese ships began supplying the Spanish and Portuguese settlements in America with Negro slaves. By 1550 European enslavement of Negroes was more than a century old, and Negro slavery had become a fixture of the New World.

For present purposes there is no need to inquire into the precise nature of this slavery except to point out that in actual practice it did fit the English concept of bond slavery. The question which needs answering pertains to contemporary English knowledge of what was going on. And the answer may be given concisely: Englishmen had easily at hand a great deal of not very precise information.

The news that Negroes were being carried off to forced labor in America was broadcast across the pages of the Hakluyt and Purchas collections. While only one account stated explicitly that Negroes "be their slaves during their life," it was clear that the Portuguese and Spaniards treated Negroes and frequently the Indians as "slaves."[18] This was the term customarily used by English voyagers and by translators of foreign . . . documents. Readers of a lament about the treatment of Indians in Brazil by an unnamed Portuguese could hardly mistake learning that slavery there was a clearly defined condition: Indians held "a title of free" but

[17] The complex situation is set forth by Charles Verlinden, *L'Esclavage dans L'Europe Médiévale. Vol. I, Péninsule Ibérique-France* (Brugge, 1955). The still prevalent state of enmity becomes clear in Franklin L. Baumer, "England, the Turk, and the Common Corps of Christendom," *American Historical Review*, 50 (1944–45), 26–48; Chew, *The Crescent and the Rose*.

[18] Hakluyt, *Principall Navigations* (1589), 572; see also the comment, "It is good traffiking with the people of Guinea, specialy with such as are not over ruled and opprest by the Portingales, which take the people, and make them slaves, for which they are hated," in *John Huigen van Linschoten. His Discours of Voyages into the Easte and West Indies . . .* , trans. William Phillip (London, [1598]), 198.

were treated as "slaves, all their lives," and when masters died the poor Indians "remaine in their wils with the name of free, but bound to serve their children perpetually . . . as if they were lawful slaves." . . . Repeatedly the language employed in these widely read books gave clear indication of how the Negro was involved. William Towrson was told by a Negro in 1556 "that the Portingals were bad men, and that they made them slaves, if they could take them, and would put yrons upon their legges." There were "rich trades" on that coast in Negroes "which be caried continually to the West Indies." The Portuguese in the Congo "have divers rich Commodities from this Kingdome, but the most important is every yeere about five thousand Slaves, which they transport from thence, and sell them at good round prices in . . . the West Indies." In the New World the Spaniards "buy many slaves to follow their husbandry" and had "Negros to worke in the mynes." . . .

Some Englishmen decided that there might be profit in supplying the Spanish with Negroes, despite the somewhat theoretical prohibition of foreigners from the Spanish dominions in the New World. John Hawkins was first; in the 1560's he made three voyages to Africa, the islands, and home. The first two were very successful; the third met disaster at San Juan de Ulua when the Spanish attacked his ships, took most of them, and turned the captured English seamen over to the Inquisition.[19] This famous incident . . . may have done something to discourage English slave trading in favor of other maritime activities. English vessels were not again active frequently in the slave trade until the next century.

As assiduously collected by Richard Hakluyt, the various accounts of the Hawkins voyages did not state explicitly that English seamen were making "slaves" of Negroes. They scarcely needed to do so. On the first voyage in 1562 Hawkins learned at the Canary Islands "that Negroes were very good merchandise in Hispaniola, and that store of Negroes might easily be had upon the coast of Guinea." At Sierra Leone Hawkins "got into his possession, partly by the sword, and partly by other meanes . . . 300. Negroes at the least." Thereupon, "with this praye" he sailed westwards where he "made vent of" the Negroes to the Spaniards. On his second voyage he was able to get hold of Negroes from one tribe which another tribe "tooke in the warres, as their slaves," and he attacked the town of Bymba where the "Portingals" told him "hee might gette a hundreth slaves." On the third voyage, in 1567, Hawkins agreed with an African chief to join in attacking another town "with promise, that as many Negroes as by these warres might be obtained, as well of his part as ours, should be at our pleasure." . . .

By the end of the first quarter of the seventeenth century it had be-

---

[19] Well told by Rayner Unwin, *The Defeat of John Hawkins: A Biography of His Third Slaving Voyage* (N.Y., 1960).

come abundantly evident in England that Negroes were being enslaved on an international scale. A century before, Leo Africanus had referred frequently to "Negro-slaves" in North Africa. By 1589 Negroes had become so pre-eminently "slaves" that Richard Hakluyt gratuitously referred to five Africans brought temporarily to England as "black slaves." [20] Readers of Hakluyt, Purchas, and other popular accounts were informed that the Dutch had "Blacks (which are Slaves)" in the East Indies; that Greeks ventured "into Arabia to steale Negroes"; that the "blacks of Mozambique" were frequently taken as "slaves" to India, and, according to George Sandys, that near Cairo merchants purchased "Negroes" (for "slavery") who came from the upper Nile and were "descended of *Chus*, the Sonne of cursed *Cham*; as are all of that complexion." [21]

As suggested by Sandys's remark, an equation had developed between African Negroes and slavery. Primarily, the associations were with the Portuguese and Spanish, with captivity, with buying and selling in Guinea and in America. . . . [Yet] there is no reason to suppose Englishmen eager to enslave Negroes, nor even to regard Richard Jobson eccentric in his response to a chief's offer to buy some "slaves": "I made answer, We were a people, who did not deale in any such commodities, neither did wee buy or sell one another, or any that had our owne shapes." [22] By the seventeenth century, after all, English prejudices as well as English law were *in favorem libertatis*.

When they came to settle in America, Englishmen found that things happened to liberty, some favorable, some not. Negroes became slaves, partly because there were social and economic necessities in America which called for some sort of bound, controlled labor. The Portuguese and Spanish had set an example, which, however rough in outline, proved to be, at very least, suggestive to Englishmen. It would be surprising if there had been a clear-cut line of influence from Latin to English slavery.[23]

[20] Leo Africanus, *The History and Description of Africa*, trans. Pory, ed. Brown, I, 76–77, II, 309, 482, III, 724, 780, 791, 835; Hakluyt, *Principall Navigations* (1589), 97.

[21] Purchas, *Purchas His Pilgrimes*, IV, 519; Hakluyt, *Principal Navigations*, V, 301–2; Burnell and Tiele, *Voyage of Linschoten*, I, 275; [George Sandys], *A Relation of a Journey Begun An: Dom: 1610 . . .* , 2d ed. (London, 1621), 136, which was reprinted by Purchas, *Purchas His Pilgrimes*, VI, 213.

[22] Jobson, *The Golden Trade*, ed. Kingsley, 112.

[23] The *clearest* instance of *direct* influence in America is probably the experience of Christopher Newport who was in Virginia five times between 1607 and 1611 and who had commanded a voyage in 1591 to the West Indies on which, as a member of his company reported, "wee tooke a Portugall ship . . . from Gunie . . . bound for Cartagena, wherein were 300. Negros young and olde." The English mariners took the prize to Puerto Rico and sent a Portuguese merchant ashore because "he hoped to help us to some money for his Negros there." Hakluyt, *Principal Navigations*, X, 184–85.

Elizabethans were not in the business of modeling themselves after Spaniards. Yet from about 1550, Englishmen were in such continual contact with the Spanish that they could hardly have failed to acquire the notion that Negroes could be enslaved. Precisely what slavery *meant*, of course, was a matter of English preconceptions patterning the information from overseas, but from the first, Englishmen tended to associate, in a diffuse way, Negroes with the Portuguese and Spanish. The term *negro* itself was incorporated into English from the Hispanic languages in mid-sixteenth century and *mulatto* a half century later. This is the more striking because a perfectly adequate term, identical in meaning to *negro*, already existed in English; of course *black* was used also, though not so commonly in the sixteenth century as later. . . .

By 1640 it was becoming apparent that in many of the new colonies overseas the English settlers had obtained Negroes and were holding them, frequently, as hereditary slaves for life. In considering the development of slavery in various groups of colonies [it is important to remember that the slave] status was at first distinguished from servitude more by duration than by onerousness; the key term in . . . many . . . early descriptions of the Negro's condition was *perpetual*. Negroes served "for ever" and so would their children. Englishmen did not do so. . . . Servitude, no matter how long, brutal, and involuntary, was not the same thing as perpetual slavery. Servitude comprehended alike the young apprentice, the orphan, the indentured servant, the redemptioner, the convicted debtor or criminal, the political prisoner, and, even, the Scottish and Irish captive of war who was sold as a "slave" to New England or Barbados. Yet none of these persons, no matter how miserably treated, served for life in the colonies, though of course many died before their term ended.[24] Hereditary lifetime service was restricted to Indians and Negroes. Among the various English colonies in the New World, this service known as "slavery" seems first to have developed in the international cockpit known as the Caribbean.

5. Enslavement: The West Indies

The Englishmen who settled the Caribbean colonies were not very different from those who went to Virginia, Bermuda, Maryland, or even New England. Their experience in the islands, however, was very different indeed. By 1640 there were roughly as many English in the little islands as on the American continent. A half century after the first settlements were established in the 1620's, the major islands — Barbados, St. Kitts and the other Leeward Islands — were overcrowded. Thousands of whites who had

[24] Smith, *Colonists in Bondage*, 171, said flatly that "there was never any such thing as perpetual slavery for any white man in any English colony." To my knowledge, he was correct.

been squeezed off the land by burgeoning sugar plantations migrated to other English colonies, including much larger Jamaica which had been captured from the Spanish in 1655. Their places were taken by Negro slaves who had been shipped to the islands, particularly after 1640, to meet an insatiable demand for labor which was cheap to maintain, easy to dragoon, and simple to replace when worked to death. Negroes outnumbered whites in Barbados as early as 1660. This rapid and thorough commitment to slavery placed white settlers under an ever-present danger of slave rebellion (the first rising came in 1638 on Providence Island), and whereas in the very early years authorities had rightly been fearful of white servant revolt, by the 1670's they were casting about desperately for means to attract white servants as protection against foreign and servile attack. Negro slavery matured hothouse fashion in the islands.

This compression of development was most clearly evident in the Puritan colony on the tiny island of Providence 150 miles off the coast of Central America, first settled in 1629 though not a going concern for several years. During the brief period before the Spanish snuffed out the colony in 1641 the settlers bought so many Negroes that white men were nearly outnumbered, and in England the Providence Company, apprehensive over possible Negro uprisings (with good reason as it turned out), drew up regulations for restricting the ratio of slaves to white men, "well knowing that if all men be left at Libty to buy as they please no man will take of English servants." [25] Not only were Negroes cheaper to maintain but it was felt that they could legitimately be treated in a different way from Englishmen — they could be held to service for life. At least this was the impression prevailing among officials of the Providence Company in London, for in 1638 they wrote Governor Nathaniel Butler and the Council, "We also think it reasonable that wheras the English servants are to answer XX [pounds of tobacco] per head the Negros being procured at Cheaper rates more easily kept as perpetuall servants should answer 40 [pounds of tobacco] per head. And the rather that the desire of English bodyes may be kept, we are depending upon them for the defence of the Island. We shall also expect that Negroes performe service in the publique works in double proporcon to the English." [26]

[25] Earl of Holland, John Pym, Robert Warwick, and others to Governor and Council, London, July 3, 1638, Box 9, bundle: 2d and last portion of List no. 3, *re* Royal African Co. and Slavery Matters, 17. Parish Transcripts, New-York Historical Society, New York City. For Providence, see Arthur P. Newton, *The Colonising Activities of the English Puritans: The Last Phase of the Elizabethan Struggle with Spain* (New Haven, 1914); for further details on early slavery in the English West Indies and New England, Winthrop D. Jordan, "The Influence of the West Indies on the Origins of New England Slavery," *William and Mary Quarterly*, 3d Ser., 18 (1961), 243–50.

[26] Earl of Holland and others to Governor and Council, July 3, 1638, Box 9, bundle: 2d and last portion of List no. 3, *re* Royal African Co. and Slavery Matters, 17, Parish Transcripts, N.-Y. Hist. Soc.

In Barbados this helpful idea that Negroes served for life seems to have existed even before they were purchased in large numbers. In 1627 the ship bearing the first eighty settlers captured a prize from which ten Negroes were seized, so white men and Negroes settled the island together.[27] Any doubt which may have existed as to the appropriate status of Negroes was dispelled in 1636 when Governor Henry Hawley and the Council resolved "that *Negroes* and *Indians*, that came here to be sold, should serve for Life, unless a Contract was before made to the contrary." [28] Europeans were not treated in this manner: in 1643 Governor Philip Bell set at liberty fifty Portuguese who had been captured in Brazil and then offered for sale to Barbadians by a Dutch ship. The Governor seems to have been shocked by the proposed sale of Christian white men.[29] In the 1650's several observers referred to the lifetime slavery of Negroes as if it were a matter of common knowledge. "Its the Custome for a Christian servant to serve foure yeares," one wrote at the beginning of the decade, "and then enjoy his freedome; and (which hee hath dearly earned) 10£ Ster. or the value of it in goods if his Master bee soe honest as to pay it; the Negros and Indians (of which latter there are but few here) they and the generation are Slaves to their owners to perpetuity." The widely read Richard Ligon wrote in 1657: "The Iland is divided into three sorts of men, *viz*. Masters, Servants, and slaves. The slaves and their posterity, being subject to their Masters for ever, are kept and preserv'd with greater care then the servants, who are theirs but for five yeers, according to the law of the Iland." [30] Finally, one Henry Whistler described the people of the island delightfully in 1655:

> The genterey heare doth live far better than ours doue in England: thay have most of them 100 or 2 or 3 of slaves apes whou they command as they pleas: hear they may say what they have is thayer oune: and they have that Libertie of contienc which wee soe long have in England foght for: But they doue abus it. This Island is inhabited with all sortes: with English, french, Duch, Scotes, Irish, Spaniards thay being Jues: with Ingones and miserabell Negors borne to perpetuall slavery thay and thayer seed: these Negors they doue alow as many wifes as thay will have, sume will have 3 or 4, according as they find thayer bodie abell: our English heare doth think a negor child the first day it is born to be worth 05[li], they cost them noething the bringing up, they goe all ways naked: some planters

---

[27] Vincent T. Harlow, *A History of Barbados, 1625–1685* (Oxford, 1926), 4.

[28] [William Duke], *Memoirs of the First Settlement of the Island of Barbados and Other the Carribee Islands, with the Succession of the Governors and Commanders in Chief of Barbados to the Year 1742* . . . (London, 1743), 20.

[29] Alan Burns, *History of the British West Indies* (London, 1954), 232n.

[30] "A Breife Description of the Ilande of Barbados," Vincent T. Harlow, ed., *Colonising Expeditions to the West Indies and Guiana, 1623–1667* (*Works Issued by the Hakluyt Soc.*, 2d Ser., 56 [1925]), 44–45; Richard Ligon, *A True and Exact History of the Island of Barbadoes* . . . (London, 1657), 43.

will have 30 more or les about 4 or 5 years ould: they sele them
from one to the other as we doue shepe. This Illand is the Dunghill
wharone England doth cast forth its rubidg: Rodgs and hors and
such like peopel are those which are gennerally Broght heare.[31]

Dunghill or no dunghill, Barbados was treating her Negroes as slaves for
life.

The rapid introduction of Negro slavery into the English islands was
accomplished without leaving any permanent trace of hesitation or misgivings. This was not the case in many of the continental colonies, both because different geographic and economic conditions prevailed there and
because these conditions permitted a more complete and successful transplantation of English ways and values. This difference was particularly
pronounced in New England, and it was therefore particularly ironic that
the treatment accorded Negroes in New England seems to have been
directly influenced by the West Indian model.

6. Enslavement: New England

. . . The question with New England slavery is not why it was weakly
rooted, but why it existed at all. No staple crop demanded regiments of
raw labor. That there was no compelling economic demand for Negroes
is evident in the numbers actually imported: economic exigencies scarcely
required establishment of a distinct status for only 3 per cent of the labor
force. Indentured servitude was adequate to New England's needs, and in
fact some Negroes became free servants rather than slaves. Why, then,
did New Englanders enslave Negroes, probably as early as 1638? Why
was it that the Puritans rather mindlessly (which was not their way)
accepted slavery for Negroes and Indians but not for white men?

The early appearance of slavery in New England may in part be explained by the provenance of the first Negroes imported. They were
brought by Captain William Peirce of the Salem ship *Desire* in 1638
from the Providence Island colony where Negroes were already being kept
as perpetual servants.[32] A minor traffic in Negroes and other products
developed between the two Puritan colonies, though evidently some of
the Negroes proved less than satisfactory, for Governor Butler was cautioned by the Providence Company to take special care of "the cannibal
negroes brought from New England." [33] After 1640 a brisk trade got
under way between New England and the other English islands, and

[31] "Extracts from Henry Whistler's Journal of the West India Expedition,"
Charles H. Firth, ed., *The Narrative of General Venables, with an Appendix of
Papers Relating to the Expedition to the West Indies and the Conquest of
Jamaica, 1654–1655* (London, 1900), 146.

[32] John Winthrop, *Winthrop's Journal: "History of New England," 1634–
1649*, ed. James K. Hosmer, 2 vols. (N.Y., 1908), I, 260.

[33] Newton, *Colonising Activities of the English Puritans*, 260–61.

Massachusetts vessels sometimes touched upon the West African coast before heading for the Caribbean. Trade with Barbados was particularly lively, and Massachusetts vessels carried Negroes to that bustling colony from Africa and the Cape Verde Islands. As John Winthrop gratefully described the salvation of New England's economy, "it pleased the Lord to open to us a trade with Barbados and other Islands in the West Indies." [34] These strange Negroes from the West Indies must surely have been accompanied by prevailing notions about their usual status. Ship masters who purchased perpetual service in Barbados would not have been likely to sell service for term in Boston. Then too, white settlers from the crowded islands migrated to New England, 1,200 from Barbados alone in the years 1643–47.[35]

No amount of contact with the West Indies could have by itself created Negro slavery in New England; settlers there had to be willing to accept the proposition. Because they were Englishmen, they were so prepared — and at the same time they were not. Characteristically, as Puritans, they officially codified this ambivalence in 1641 as follows: "there shall never be any bond-slavery, villenage or captivitie amongst us; unlesse it be lawful captives taken in just warrs, and such strangers as willingly sell themselves, or are solde to us: and such shall have the libertyes and christian usages which the law of God established in Israell concerning such persons doth morally require, provided, this exempts none from servitude who shall be judged thereto by Authoritie." [36] Here were the wishes of the General Court as expressed in the Massachusetts Body of Liberties, which is to say that as early as 1641 the Puritan settlers were seeking to guarantee in writing their own liberty without closing off the opportunity of taking it from others whom they identified with the Biblical term, "strangers." It was under the aegis of this concept that Theophilus Eaton, one of the founders of New Haven, seems to have owned Negroes before 1658 who were "servants forever or during his pleasure, according to Leviticus, 25: 45 and 46." [37] . . . Apart from this implication that bond slavery was reserved to those not partaking of true religion nor possessing proper nationality, the Body of Liberties expressly reserved the colony's right to enslave convicted criminals. For reasons not clear, this endorsement of an existing practice was followed almost immediately by discontinuance of its application to white men. The first instance of penal

[34] Winthrop, *Journal*, ed. Hosmer, II, 73–74, 328; Donnan, ed., *Documents of the Slave Trade*, III, 4–5, 6, 9, 10, 11–14.

[35] Harlow, *Barbados*, 340.

[36] Max Farrand, ed., *The Laws and Liberties of Massachusetts* (Cambridge, Mass., 1929), 4. See the very good discussion in George H. Moore, *Notes on the History of Slavery in Massachusetts* (N.Y., 1866).

[37] Simeon E. Baldwin, "Theophilus Eaton, First Governor of the Colony of New Haven," New Haven Colony Historical Society, *Papers*, 7 (1908), 31.

"slavery" in Massachusetts came in 1636, when an Indian was sentenced to "bee kept as a slave for life to worke, unles wee see further cause." Then in December 1638, ten months after the first Negroes arrived, the Quarter Court for the first time sentenced three white offenders to be "slaves" — a suggestive but perhaps meaningless coincidence. Having by June 1642 sentenced altogether some half dozen white men to "slavery" (and explicitly releasing several after less than a year) the Court stopped.[38] Slavery, as had been announced in the Body of Liberties, was to be only for "strangers."

The Body of Liberties made equally clear that captivity in a just war constituted legitimate grounds for slavery. The practice had begun during the first major conflict with the Indians, the Pequot War of 1637. Some of the Pequot captives had been shipped aboard the *Desire*, to Providence Island; accordingly, the first Negroes in New England arrived in exchange for men taken captive in a just war! That this provenance played an important role in shaping views about Negroes is suggested by the first recorded plea by an Englishman on the North American continent for the establishment of an African slave trade. Emanuel Downing, in a letter to his brother-in-law John Winthrop in 1645, described the advantages: "If upon a Just warre [with the Narragansett Indians] the Lord should deliver them into our hands, wee might easily have men woemen and children enough to exchange for Moores, which wilbe more gaynefull pilladge for us then wee conceive, for I doe not see how wee can thrive untill wee get into a stock of slaves sufficient to doe all our business, for our children's children will hardly see this great Continent filled with people, soe that our servants will still desire freedome to plant for themselves, not not stay but for verie great wages. And I suppose you know verie well how wee shall mayneteyne 20 Moores cheaper than one Englishe servant." [39]

These two facets of justifiable enslavement — punishment for crime and captivity in war — were closely related. Slavery as punishment probably derived from analogy with captivity, since presumably a king or magistrates could mercifully spare and enslave a man whose crime had forfeited his right to life. The analogy had not been worked out by commentators in England, but a fairly clear linkage between crime and captivity seems to have existed in the minds of New Englanders concerning Indian slavery. In 1644 the commissioners of the United Colonies meeting at New Haven decided, in light of the Indians' "proud affronts," "hostile prac-

---

[38] Nathaniel B. Shurtleff, ed., *Records of the Governor and Company of the Massachusetts Bay in New England*, 5 vols. in 6 (Boston, 1853–54), I, 181, 246; John Noble and John F. Cronin, eds., *Records of the Court of Assistants of the Colony of the Massachusetts Bay, 1630–1692*, 3 vols. (Boston, 1901–28), II, 78–79, 86, 90, 94, 97, 118.

[39] Donnan, ed., *Documents of the Slave Trade*, III, 8.

tices," and "protectinge or rescuinge of offenders," that magistrates might "send some convenient strength of English and, . . . seise and bring away" Indians from any "plantation of Indians" which persisted in this practice and, if no satisfaction was forthcoming, could deliver the "Indians seased . . . either to serve or be shipped out and exchanged for Negroes." [40] Captivity and criminal justice seemed to mean the same thing, slavery.

It would be wrong to suppose that all the Puritans' preconceived ideas about freedom and bondage worked in the same direction. While the concepts of difference in religion and of captivity worked against Indians and Negroes, certain Scriptural injunctions and English pride in liberty told in the opposite direction. In Massachusetts the magistrates demonstrated that they were not about to tolerate glaring breaches of "the Law of God established in Israel" even when the victims were Negroes. In 1646 the authorities arrested two mariners, James Smith and Thomas Keyser, who had carried two Negroes directly from Africa and sold them in Massachusetts. What distressed the General Court was that the Negroes had been obtained during a raid on an African village and that this "haynos and crying sinn of man stealing" had transpired on the Lord's Day. The General Court decided to free the unfortunate victims and ship them back to Africa, though the death penalty for the crime (clearly mandatory in Scripture) was not imposed.[41] More quietly than in this dramatic incident, Puritan authorities extended the same protections against maltreatment to Negroes and Indians as to white servants. . . .

. . . From the first, however, there were scattered signs that Negroes were regarded as different from English people not merely in their status as slaves. In 1639 Samuel Maverick of Noddles Island attempted, apparently rather clumsily, to breed two of his Negroes, or so an English visitor reported: "*Mr. Maverick* was desirous to have a breed of Negroes, and therefore seeing [that his "Negro woman"] would not yield by persuasions to company with a Negro young man he had in his house; he commanded him will'd she to go to bed to her which was no sooner done but she kickt him out again, this she took in high disdain beyond her slavery." In 1652 the Massachusetts General Court ordered that Scotsmen, Indians, and Negroes should train with the English in the

---

[40] Nathaniel B. Shurtleff and David Pulsifer, eds., *Records of the Colony of New Plymouth in New England*, 12 vols. (Boston, 1855–61), IX, 70–71. See also Ebenezer Hazard, comp., *Historical Collections; Consisting of State Papers, and Other Authentic Documents* . . . , 2 vols. (Phila., 1792–94), II, 63–64.

[41] Donnan, ed., *Documents of the Slave Trade*, III, 6–9. Exodus 21:16: "And he that stealeth a man, and selleth him, or if he be found in his hand, he shall surely be put to death." Compare with Deuteronomy 24:7: "If a man be found stealing any of his brethren of the children of Israel, and maketh merchandise of him, or selleth him; then that thief shall die; and thou shalt put evil away from among you."

militia, but four years later abruptly excluded Negroes, as did Connecticut in 1660.[42] Evidently Negroes, even free Negroes, were regarded as distinct from the English. They were, in New England where economic necessities were not sufficiently pressing to determine the decision, treated differently from other men.

7. Enslavement: Virginia and Maryland

In Virginia and Maryland the development of Negro slavery followed a very different course, for several reasons. Most obviously, geographic conditions and the intentions of the settlers quickly combined to produce a successful agricultural staple. The deep tidal rivers, the long growing season, the fertile soil, and the absence of strong communal spirit among the settlers opened the way. Ten years after settlers first landed at Jamestown they were on the way to proving, in the face of assertions to the contrary, that it was possible "to found an empire upon smoke." More than the miscellaneous productions of New England, tobacco required labor which was cheap but not temporary, mobile but not independent, and tireless rather than skilled. In the Chesapeake area more than anywhere to the northward, the shortage of labor and the abundance of land — the "frontier" — placed a premium on involuntary labor.

This need for labor played more directly upon these settlers' ideas about freedom and bondage than it did either in the West Indies or in New England. Perhaps it would be more accurate to say that settlers in Virginia (and in Maryland after settlement in 1634) made their decisions concerning Negroes while relatively virginal, relatively free from external influences and from firm preconceptions. Of all the important early English settlements, Virginia had the least contact with the Spanish, Portuguese, Dutch, and other English colonies. At the same time, the settlers of Virginia did not possess either the legal or Scriptural learning of the New England Puritans whose conception of the just war had opened the way to the enslavement of Indians. Slavery in the tobacco colonies did not begin as an adjunct of capacity; in marked contrast to the Puritan response to the Pequot War the settlers of Virginia did *not* generally react to the Indian massacre of 1622 with propositions for taking captives and selling them as "slaves." It was perhaps a correct measure of the conceptual atmosphere in Virginia that there was only one such proposition after the 1622 disaster and that that one was defective in precision as to how exactly one treated captive Indians.[43]

[42] John Josselyn, *An Account of Two Voyages to New-England* . . . , 2d ed. (London, 1675), reprinted in Massachusetts Historical Society, *Collections*, 3d Ser., 3 (1833), 231; Shurtleff, ed., *Records of Massachusetts Bay*, III, 268, 397, IV, Pt. i, 86, 257; *Acts and Resolves Mass.*, I, 130; Trumbull and Hoadly, eds., *Recs. Col. Conn.*, I, 349.

[43] Kingsbury, ed., *Recs. Virginia Company*, III, 672–73, 704–7.

In the absence, then, of these influences which obtained in other English colonies, slavery as it developed in Virginia and Maryland assumes a special interest and importance over and above the fact that Negro slavery was to become a vitally important institution there and, later, to the southwards. In the tobacco colonies it is possible to watch Negro slavery *develop*, not pop up full-grown overnight, and it is therefore possible to trace, very imperfectly, the development of the shadowy, unexamined rationale which supported it. The concept of Negro slavery there was neither borrowed from foreigners, nor extracted from books, nor invented out of whole cloth, nor extrapolated from sevitude, not generated by English reaction to Negroes as such, nor necessitated by the exigencies of the New World. Not any one of these made the Negro a slave, but all.

In rough outline, slavery's development in the tobacco colonies seems to have undergone three stages. Negroes first arrived in 1619, only a few days late for the meeting of the first representative assembly in America. John Rolfe described the event with the utmost unconcern: "About the last of August came in a dutch man of warre that sold us twenty Negars." [44] Negroes continued to trickle in slowly for the next half century; one report in 1649 estimated that there were three hundred among Virginia's population of fifteen thousand — about 2 per cent.[45] Long before there were more appreciable numbers, the development of slavery had, so far as we can tell, shifted gears. Prior to about 1640, there is very little evidence to show how Negroes were treated — though we will need to return to those first twenty years in a moment. After 1640 there is mounting evidence that some Negroes were in fact being treated as slaves, at least that they were being held in hereditary lifetime service. This is to say that the twin essences of slavery — the two kinds of perpetuity — first become evident during the twenty years prior to the beginning of legal formulation. After 1660 slavery was written into statute law. Negroes began to flood into the two colonies at the end of the seventeenth century. In 1705 Virginia produced a codification of laws applying to slaves.

Concerning the first of these stages, there is only one major historical certainty, and unfortunately it is the sort which historians find hardest to bear. There simply is not enough evidence to indicate with any certainty whether Negroes were treated like white servants or not. At least we can be confident, therefore, that the two most common assertions about the first Negroes — that they were slaves and that they were servants — are *unfounded*, though not necessarily incorrect. And what of the positive evidence?

Some of the first group bore Spanish names and presumably had

---

[44] Arber, ed., *Travels of John Smith*, II, 541.

[45] *A Perfect Description of Virginia* . . . (London, 1649), reprinted in Peter Force, ed., *Tracts* . . . , 4 vols. (N.Y., 1947), II, no. 8.

been baptized, which would mean they were at least nominally Christian, though of the Papist sort. They had been "sold" to the English; so had other Englishmen but not by the Dutch. Certainly these Negroes were not fully free, but many Englishmen were not. It can be said, though, that from the first in Virginia Negroes were set apart from white men by the word *Negroes*. The earliest Virginia census reports plainly distinguished Negroes from white men, often giving Negroes no personal name; in 1629 every commander of the several plantations was ordered to "take a generall muster of all the inhabitants men woemen and Children as well *Englishe* as Negroes." [46] A distinct name is not attached to a group unless it is regarded as distinct. It seems logical to suppose that this perception of the Negro as being distinct from the Englishman must have operated to debase his status rather than to raise it, for in the absence of countervailing social factors, the need for labor in the colonies usually told in the direction of non-freedom. There were few countervailing factors present, surely, in such instances as in 1629 when a group of Negroes were brought to Virginia freshly captured from a Portuguese vessel which had snatched them from Angola a few weeks earlier.[47] Given the context of English thought and experience sketched in this chapter, it seems probable that the Negro's status was not ever the same as that accorded the white servant. But we do not know for sure.

When the first fragmentary evidence appears about 1640 it becomes clear that *some* Negroes in both Virginia and Maryland were serving for life and some Negro children inheriting the same obligation.[48] Not all Negroes, certainly, for Nathaniel Littleton had released a Negro named Anthony Longoe from all service whatsoever in 1635, and after the mid-1640's the court records show that other Negroes were incontestably free and were accumulating property of their own. At least one Negro freeman, Anthony Johnson, himself owned a Negro. Some Negroes served only terms of usual length, but others were held for terms far longer than custom and statute permitted with white servants.[49] The first fairly clear indication that slavery was practiced in the tobacco colonies appears in 1639, when a Maryland statute declared that "all the Inhabitants of this Province being Christians (Slaves excepted) Shall have and enjoy all such

[46] Henry R. McIlwaine, ed., *Minutes of the Council and General Court of Colonial Virginia, 1622–1632, 1670–1676* (Richmond, 1924), 196. Lists and musters of 1624 and 1625 are in John C. Hotten, ed., *The Original Lists of Persons of Quality* . . . (N.Y., 1880), 169–265.

[47] Philip A. Bruce, *Economic History of Virginia in the Seventeenth Century* . . . , 2 vols. (N.Y., 1896), II, 73.

[48] Further details are in Winthrop D. Jordan, "Modern Tensions and the Origins of American Slavery," *Journal of Southern History*, 28 (1962), 18–30.

[49] Susie M. Ames, *Studies of the Virginia Eastern Shore in the Seventeenth Century* (Richmond, 1940), 99; John H. Russell, *The Free Negro in Virginia, 1619–1865* (Baltimore, 1913), 23–39; and his "Colored Freemen As Slave Owners in Virginia," *Journal of Negro History*, 1 (1916), 234–37.

rights liberties immunities priviledges and free customs within this Province as any naturall born subject of England." Another Maryland law passed the same year provided that "all persons being Christians (Slaves excepted)" over eighteen who were imported without indentures would serve for four years.[50] These laws make very little sense unless the term *slaves* meant Negroes and perhaps Indians.

The next year, 1640, the first definite indication of outright enslavement appears in Virginia. The General Court pronounced sentence on three servants who had been retaken after absconding to Maryland. Two of them, a Dutchman and a Scot, were ordered to serve their masters for one additional year and then the colony for three more, but "the third being a negro named John Punch shall serve his said master or his assigns for the time of his natural life here or else where." No white servant in any English colony, so far as is known, ever received a like sentence. Later the same month a Negro (possibly the same enterprising fellow) was again singled out from a group of recaptured runaways; six of the seven culprits were assigned additional time while the Negro was given none, presumably because he was already serving for life.[51]

After 1640, when surviving Virginia county court records began to mention Negroes, sales for life, often including any future progeny, were recorded in unmistakable language. In 1646 Francis Pott sold a Negro woman and boy to Stephen Charlton "to the use of him . . . forever." Similarly, six years later William Whittington sold to John Pott "one Negro girle named Jowan; aged about Ten yeares and with her Issue and produce duringe her (or either of them) for their Life tyme. And their Successors forever"; and a Maryland man in 1649 deeded two Negro men and a woman "and all their issue both male and Female." The executors of a New York County estate in 1647 disposed of eight Negroes — four men, two women, and two children — to Captain John Chisman "to have hold occupy posesse and injoy and every one of the afforementioned Negroes forever." [52] The will of Rowland Burnham of "Rapahanocke," made in 1657, dispensed his considerable number of Negroes and white servants in language which clearly differentiated between the two by specifying that the whites were to serve for their "full terme of tyme" and the Negroes "for ever." [53] Nothing in the will indicated that this distinction was exceptional or novel.

[50] *Archives Md.*, I, 41, 80, also 409, 453–54.

[51] "Decisions of the General Court," *Virginia Magazine of History and Biography*, 5 (1898), 236–37.

[52] For these four cases, Northampton County Deeds, Wills, etc., no. 4 (1651–54), 28 (misnumbered 29), 124, Virginia State Library, Richmond; *Archives Md.*, XLI, 261–62; York County Records, no. 2 (transcribed Wills and Deeds, 1645–49), 256–57, Va. State Lib.

[53] Lancaster County Loose Papers, Box of Wills, 1650–1719, Folder 1656–1659, Va. State Lib.

Further evidence that some Negroes were serving for life in this period lies in the prices paid for them. In many instances the valuations placed on Negroes (in estate inventories and bills of sale) were far higher than for white servants, even those servants with full terms yet to serve. Higher prices must have meant that Negroes were more highly valued because of their greater length of service. Negro women may have been especially prized, moreover, because their progeny could also be held perpetually. In 1643, for example, William Burdett's inventory listed eight servants, with the time each had still to serve, at valuations ranging from 400 to 1,100 pounds of tobacco, while a "very anntient" Negro was valued at 3,000 and an eight-year-old Negro girl at 2,000 pounds, with no time remaining indicated for either. . . . Similarly, the labor owned by James Stone in 1648 was evaluated as follows:

	lb tobo
Thomas Groves, 4 yeares to serve	1300
Francis Bomley for 6 yeares	1500
John Thackstone for 3 yeares	1300
Susan Davis for 3 yeares	1000
Emaniell a Negro man	2000
Roger Stone 3 yeares	1300
Mingo a Negro man	2000 [54]

. . . Besides setting a higher value on Negroes, these inventories failed to indicate the number of years they had still to serve, presumably because their service was for an unlimited time.

Where Negro women were involved, higher valuations probably reflected the facts that their issue were valuable and that they could be used for field work while white women generally were not. This latter discrimination between Negro and white women did not necessarily involve perpetual service, but it meant that Negroes were set apart in a way clearly not to their advantage. This was not the only instance in which Negroes were subjected to degrading distinctions not immediately and necessarily attached to the concept of slavery. Negroes were singled out for special treatment in several ways which suggest a generalized debasement of Negroes as a group. Significantly, the first indications of this debasement appeared at about the same time as the first indications of actual enslavement.

The distinction concerning field work is a case in point. It first appears on the written record in 1643, when Virginia almost pointedly endorsed it in a tax law. Previously, in 1629, tithable persons had been defined as "all those that worke in the ground of what qualitie or condition soever."

[54] York County Records, no. 2, 390, Va. State Lib.

The new law provided that *all* adult men were tithable and, in addition, *Negro* women. The same distinction was made twice again before 1660. Maryland adopted a similar policy beginning in 1654.[55] This official discrimination between Negro and other women was made by men who were accustomed to thinking of field work as being ordinarily the work of men rather than women. As John Hammond wrote in a 1656 tract defending the tobacco colonies, servant women were not put to work in the fields but in domestic employments, "yet som wenches that are nasty, and beastly and not fit to be so employed are put into the ground." [56] The essentially racial character of this discrimination stood out clearly in a law passed in 1668 at the time slavery was taking shape in the statute books:

> Whereas some doubts, have arisen whether negro women set free were still to be accompted tithable according to a former act, *It is declared by this grand assembly* that negro women, though permitted to enjoy their Freedome yet ought not in all respects to be admitted to a full fruition of the exemptions and impunities of the English, and are still lyable to payment of taxes.[57]

Virginia law set Negroes apart from all other groups in a second way by denying them the important right and obligation to bear arms. Few restraints could indicate more clearly the denial to Negroes of membership in the white community. This first foreshadowing of the slave codes came in 1640, at just the time when other indications first appeared that Negroes were subject to special treatment.[58]

---

[55] Hening, ed., *Statutes Va.*, I, 144, 242, 292, 454; *Archives Md.*, I, 342, II, 136, 399, 538–39, XIII, 538–39.

[56] John Hammond, *Leah and Rachel, or, the Two Fruitfull Sisters Virginia, and Mary-land: Their Present Condition, Impartially Stated and Related . . .* (London, 1656), 9.

[57] Hening, ed., *Statutes Va.*, II, 267.

[58] *Ibid.*, I, 226; for the same act in more detail, "Acts of General Assembly, Jan. 6, 1639–40," *Wm. and Mary Qtly.*, 2d Ser., 4 (1924), 147. In Bermuda, always closely connected with Virginia, the first prohibition of weapons to Negroes came in 1623, only seven years after the first Negro landed. The 1623 law was the first law anywhere in English specifically dealing with Negroes. After stressing the insolence of Negroes secretly carrying "cudgells and other weapons and working tools, very dangerous and not meete to be suffered to be carried by such vassalls," it prohibited (in addition to arms) Negroes going abroad at night, trespassing on other people's lands, and trading in tobacco without permission of their masters. Unfortunately the evidence concerning lifetime service for Negroes is much less definite in the scanty Bermuda sources than in those for Maryland and Virginia; the first known incident suggestive of the practice might reasonably be placed anywhere from 1631 to 1656. Later evidence shows Bermuda's slavery and proportion of Negroes similar to Virginia's, and it seems unlikely that the two colonies' early experience was radically different. Henry C. Wilkinson, *The Adventurers of Bermuda; A History of the Island from Its Discovery until*

Finally, an even more compelling sense of the separateness of Negroes was revealed in early reactions to sexual union between the races. Prior to 1660 the evidence concerning these reactions is equivocal, and it is not possible to tell whether repugnance for intermixture preceded legislative enactment of slavery. In 1630 an angry Virginia court sentenced "Hugh Davis to be soundly whipped, before an assembly of Negroes and others for abusing himself to the dishonor of God and shame of Christians, by defiling his body in lying with a negro," but it is possible that the "negro" may not have been female. With other instances of punishment for inter-racial union in the ensuing years, fornication rather than miscegenation may well have been the primary offense, though in 1651 a Maryland man sued someone who he claimed had said "that he had a black bastard in Virginia." . . . There may have been no racial feeling involved when in 1640 Robert Sweet, a gentleman, was compelled "to do penance in church according to laws of England, for getting a negroe woman with child and the woman whipt." [59] About 1650 a white man and a Negro woman were required to stand clad in white sheets before a congregation in lower Norfolk County for having had relations, but this punishment was sometimes used in cases of fornication between two whites.[60] A quarter century later in 1676, however, the emergence of distaste for racial intermixture was unmistakable. A contemporary account of Bacon's Rebellion caustically described one of the ringleaders, Richard Lawrence, as a person who had eclipsed his learning and abilities "in the darke imbraces of a Blackamoore, his slave: And that in so fond a Maner, . . . to the noe meane Scandle and affrunt of all the Vottrisses in or about towne." [61]

Such condemnation was not confined to polemics. In the early 1660's when slavery was gaining statutory recognition, the assemblies acted with full-throated indignation against miscegenation. These acts aimed at more than merely avoiding confusion of status. In 1662 Virginia declared that

---

the Dissolution of the Somers Island Company in 1684 (London, 1933), 114; J. H. Lefroy, comp., *Memorials of the Discovery and Early Settlement of the Bermudas or Somers Islands, 1515–1685* . . . , 2 vols. (London, 1877–79), I, 308–9, 505, 526–27, 633, 645, II, 34–35, 70. But Negroes were to be armed at times of alarm (*ibid.*, II, 242, 366, 380 [1666–73]): Bermuda was exposed to foreign attack.

[59] Hening, ed., *Statutes Va.*, I, 552; McIlwaine, ed., *Minutes Council Va.*, 477.

[60] Bruce, *Economic History of Va.*, II, 110.

[61] "The History of Bacon's and Ingram's Rebellion, 1676," in Charles M. Andrews, ed., *Narratives of the Insurrections, 1675–1690* (N.Y., 1915), 96. Cf. the will of John Fenwick (1683), *Documents Relating to the Colonial, Revolutionary and Post-Revolutionary History of the State of New Jersey* . . . [New Jersey Archives], 1st Ser. (Newark, etc., 1880–1949), XXIII, 162.

"if any christian shall committ Fornication with a negro man or woman, hee or shee soe offending" should pay double the usual fine. (The next year Bermuda prohibited all sexual relations between whites and Negroes.) Two years later Maryland banned interracial marriages: "forasmuch as divers freeborne English women forgettfull of their free Condicion and to the disgrace of our Nation doe intermarry with Negro Slaves by which alsoe divers suites may arise touching the Issue of such woemen and a great damage doth befall the Masters of such Negros for prevention whereof for deterring such freeborne women from such shamefull Matches," strong language indeed if "divers suites" had been the only problem. A Maryland act of 1681 described marriages of white women with Negroes as, among other things, "always to the Satisfaccion of theire Lascivious and Lustfull desires, and to the disgrace not only of the English butt allso of many other Christian Nations." When Virginia finally prohibited all interracial liaisons in 1691, the Assembly vigorously denounced miscegenation and its fruits as "that abominable mixture and spurious issue." [62]

From the surviving evidence, it appears that outright enslavement and these other forms of debasement appeared at about the same time in Maryland and Virginia. Indications of perpetual service, the very nub of slavery, coincided with indications that English settlers discriminated against Negro women, withheld arms from Negroes, and — though the timing is far less certain — reacted unfavorably to interracial sexual union. The coincidence suggests a mutual relationship between slavery and unfavorable assessment of Negroes. Rather than slavery causing "prejudice," or vice versa, they seem rather to have generated each other. Both were, after all, twin aspects of a general debasement of the Negro. Slavery and "prejudice" may have been equally cause and effect, continuously reacting upon each other, dynamically joining hands to hustle the Negro down the road to complete degradation. Much more than with the other English colonies, where the enslavement of Negroes was to some extent a borrowed practice, the available evidence for Maryland and Virginia points to less borrowing and to this kind of process: a mutually interactive growth of slavery and unfavorable assessment, with no cause for either which did not cause the other as well. If slavery caused prejudice, then invidious distinctions concerning working in the fields, bearing arms, and sexual union should have appeared *after* slavery's firm establishment. If

[62] Hening, ed., *Statutes Va.*, II, 170, III, 86–87; *Archives Md.*, I, 533–34,VII, 204; Lefroy, comp., *Memorials Bermudas*, II, 190 (a resolution, not a statute). Some evidence suggests miscegenation was not taken as seriously in 17th-century Bermuda as on the mainland: *ibid.*, I, 550, II, 30, 103, 141, 161, 228, 314.

prejudice caused slavery, then one would expect to find these lesser discriminations preceding the greater discrimination of outright enslavement. Taken as a whole, the evidence reveals a process of debasement of which hereditary lifetime service was an important but not the only part.

White servants did not suffer this debasement. Rather, their position improved, partly for the reason that they were not Negroes. By the early 1660's white men were loudly protesting against being made "slaves" in terms which strongly suggest that they considered slavery not as wrong but as inapplicable to themselves. The father of a Maryland apprentice petitioned in 1663 that "he Craves that his daughter may not be made a Slave a tearme soe Scandalous that if admitted to be the Condicon or tytle of the Apprentices in this Province will be soe distructive as noe free borne Christians will ever be induced to come over servants." [63] An Irish youth complained to a Maryland court in 1661 that he had been kidnapped and forced to sign for fifteen years, that he had already served six and a half years and was now twenty-one, and that eight and a half more years of service was "contrary to the lawes of God and man that a Christian Subject should be made a Slave." (The jury blandly compromised the dispute by deciding that he should serve only until age twenty-one, but that he was now only nineteen.) Free Negro servants were generally increasingly less able to defend themselves against this insidious kind of encroachment.[64] Increasingly, white men were more clearly free because Negroes had become so clearly slave.

Certainly it was the case in Maryland and Virginia that the legal enactment of Negro slavery followed social practice, rather than vice versa, and also that the assemblies were slower than in other English colonies to declare how Negroes could or should be treated. These two patterns in themselves suggest that slavery was less a matter of previous conception or external example in Maryland and Virginia than elsewhere.

The Virginia Assembly first showed itself incontrovertibly aware that Negroes were not serving in the same manner as English servants in 1660 when it declared "that for the future no servant comeing into the country without indentures, of what christian nation soever, shall serve longer then those of our own country, of the like age." In 1661 the Assembly indirectly provided statutory recognition that some Negroes served for life: "That in case any English servant shall run away in company with any negroes who are incapable of makeing satisfaction by addition of time," he must serve for the Negroes' lost time as well as his own. Maryland enacted a closely similar law in 1663 (possibly modeled on Virginia's)

[63] *Archives Md.*, I, 464.
[64] *Ibid.*, XLI, 476–78, XLIX, 123–24. Compare the contemporary difficulties of a Negro servant: William P. Palmer *et al.*, eds., *Calendar of Virginia State Papers* . . . , 11 vols. (Richmond, 1875–93), I, 9–10.

and in the following year, on the initiative of the lower house, came out with the categorical declaration that Negroes were to serve "Durante Vita." [65] During the next twenty-odd years a succession of acts in both colonies defined with increasing precision what sorts of persons might be treated as slaves.[66] Other acts dealt with the growing problem of slave control, and especially after 1690 slavery began to assume its now familiar character as a complete deprivation of all rights.[67] As early as 1669 the Virginia Assembly unabashedly enacted a brutal law which showed where the logic of perpetual servitude was inevitably tending. Unruly servants could be chastened by sentences to additional terms, but "WHEREAS the only law in force for the punishment of refractory servants resisting their master, mistris or overseer cannot be inflicted upon negroes, nor the obstinacy of many of them by other then violent meanes supprest," if a slave "by the extremity of the correction should chance to die" his master was not to be adjudged guilty of felony "since it cannot be presumed that prepensed malice (which alone makes murther Felony) should induce any man to destroy his owne estate." [68] Virginia planters felt they acted out of mounting necessity: there were disturbances among slaves in several areas in the early 1670's.[69]

By about 1700 the slave ships began spilling forth their black cargoes in greater and greater numbers. By that time, racial slavery and the necessary police powers had been written into law. By that time, too, slavery had lost all resemblance to a perpetual and hereditary version of English servitude, though service for life still seemed to contemporaries its most essential feature.[70] In the last quarter of the seventeenth century the trend was to treat Negroes more like property and less like men, to send them to the fields at younger ages, to deny them automatic existence as inherent members of the community, to tighten the bonds on their personal and civil freedom, and correspondingly to loosen the traditional restraints on

[65] Hening, ed., *Statutes Va.*, I, 539, II, 26; *Archives Md.*, I, 449, 489, 526, 533–34. The "any negroes who are incapable" suggests explicit recognition that some were free, but in several sources the law as re-enacted the next year included a comma between "negroes" and "who," as did the Maryland act of 1663. See *The Lawes of Virginia Now in Force: Collected out of the Assembly Records* . . . (London, 1662), 59.

[66] Hening, ed., *Statutes Va.*, II, 170, 270, 283, 490–91, III, 137–40, 447–48; *Archives Md.*, VII, 203–5, XIII, 546–49, XXII, 551–52.

[67] Especially Hening, ed., *Statutes Va.*, II, 270–71, 481–82, 493, III, 86, 102–3; *Archives Md.*, XIII, 451–53, XIX, 167, 193, XXII, 546–48, XXVI, 254–56.

[68] Hening, ed., *Statutes Va.*, II, 270; compare law for servants, I, 538, II, 118.
[69] *Ibid.*, II, 299.

[70] Robert Beverley, *The History and Present State of Virginia*, ed. Louis B. Wright (Chapel Hill, 1947), 271–72.

the master's freedom to deal with his human property as he saw fit.[71] In 1705 Virginia gathered up the random statutes of a whole generation and baled them into a "slave code" which would not have been out of place in the nineteenth century. . . .[72]

8. *The Un-English: Scots, Irish, and Indians*

In the minds of overseas Englishmen, slavery, the new tyranny, did not apply to any Europeans. Something about Negroes, and to lesser extent Indians, set them apart for drastic exploitation, oppression, and degradation. In order to discover why, it is useful to turn the problem inside out, to inquire why Englishmen in America did not treat any other peoples like Negroes. It is especially revealing to see how English settlers looked upon the Scotch (as they frequently called them) and the Irish, whom they often had opportunity and "reason" to enslave, and upon the Indians, whom they enslaved, though only, as it were, casually.

In the early years Englishmen treated the increasingly numerous settlers from other European countries, especially Scottish and Irish servants, with condescension and frequently with exploitive brutality. Englishmen seemed to regard their colonies as exclusively *English* preserves and to wish to protect English persons especially from the exploitation which inevitably accompanied settlement in the New World. In Barbados, for example, the assembly in 1661 denounced the kidnapping of youngsters for service in the colony in a law which applied only to "Children of the *English* Nation." [73] In 1650 Connecticut provided that debtors were not to "bee sould to any but of the English Nation." [74]

While Englishmen distinguished themselves from other peoples, they also distinguished *among* those different peoples who failed to be English. It seems almost as if Englishmen possessed a view of other peoples which placed the English nation at the center of widening concentric circles each of which contained a people more alien than the one inside it. On occasion these social distances left by Englishmen may be gauged with considerable precision, as in the sequence employed by the Committee for Trade and Foreign Plantations in a query to the governor of Connecticut in 1680: "What number of English, Scotch, Irish or Forreigners have . . . come yearly to . . . your Corporation. And also, what Blacks and Slaves have been brought in." Sometimes the English sense of dis-

---

[71] For illustration, Hening, ed., *Statutes Va.*, II, 288, 479–80 (Negro *children* taxed from age 12, white *boys* from 14), III, 102–3; *Archives Md.*, VII, 76 (county courts required to register births, marriages, burials of all "Except Negroes Indians and Molottos").

[72] Hening, ed., *Statutes Va.*, III, 447–62.

[73] Hening, ed., *Statutes Va.*, I, 161; *Acts of Assembly, Passed in the Island of Barbadoes, from 1648, to 1718* (London, 1721), 22.

[74] Trumbull and Hoadly, eds., *Recs. Col. Conn.*, I, 510.

tance seems to have been based upon a scale of values which would be thought of today in terms of nationality. When the Leeward Islands encouraged immigration of foreign Protestants the Assembly stipulated that the number of such aliens "shall not exceed the One Fourth of *English, Scotch, Irish, and Cariole* [Creole] Subjects." . . . Maryland placed a discrimatory duty on Irish servants while Virginia did the same with all servants not born in England or Wales.[75]

At other times, though, the sense of foreignness seems to have been explicitly religious, as instanced by Lord William Willoughby's letter from Barbados in 1667: "We have more than a good many Irish amongst us, therefore I am for the down right Scott, who I am certain will fight without a crucifix about his neck." [76] It is scarcely surprising that hostility toward the numerous Irish servants should have been especially strong, for they were doubly damned as foreign and Papist. Already, for Englishmen in the seventeenth century, the Irish were a special case, and it required more than an ocean voyage to alter this perception. . . .

As time went on Englishmen began to absorb the idea that their settlements in America were not going to remain exclusively English preserves. In 1671 Virginia began encouraging naturalization of legal aliens, so that they might enjoy "all such liberties, priviledges, immunities whatsoever, as a naturall borne Englishman is capable of," and Maryland accomplished the same end with private naturalization acts that frequently included a potpourri of French, Dutch, Swiss, Swedes, and so forth.[77]

The necessity of peopling the colonies transformed the long-standing urge to discriminate among non-English peoples into a necessity. Which of the non-English were sufficiently different and foreign to warrant treating as "perpetual servants"? The need to answer this question did not mean, of course, that upon arrival in America the colonists immediately jettisoned their sense of distance from those persons they did not actually enslave. They discriminated against Welshmen and Scotsmen who, while admittedly "the best servants," were typically the servants of Englishmen. There was a considerably stronger tendency to discriminate against Papist

---

[75] *Ibid.*, III, 293 (an inquiry also sent other governors); *Acts of Assembly, Passed in the Charibbee Leeward Islands, from 1690 to 1730* (London, 1734), 127; *Acts of Assembly, Passed in the Island of Jamaica; From 1681, to 1737, Inclusive* (London, 1738), 100; also *Montserrat Code of Laws: from 1668, to 1788* (London, 1790), 19; Hening, ed., *Statutes Va.*, III, 193; Thomas Bacon, ed., *Laws of Maryland at Large, 1637–1763* (Annapolis, 1765), 1715, chap. xxxvi, 1717, chap. x, 1732, chap. xxii. The Maryland laws aimed at Irish Papists.

[76] Willoughby quoted in C. S. S. Higham, *The Development of the Leeward Islands under the Restoration, 1660–1688; A Study of the Foundations of the Old Colonial System* (Cambridge, Eng., 1921), 170n.

[77] Hening, ed., *Statutes Va.*, II, 289–90, 464–65; for one of many in Maryland, *Archives Md.*, II, 205–6.

Irishmen, those "worst" servants, but never to make slaves of them.[78] And here lay the crucial difference. Even the Scottish prisoners taken by Cromwell at Worcester and Dunbar — captives in a just war! — were never treated as slaves in England or the colonies. Certainly the lot of those sent to Barbados was miserable, but it was a different lot from the African slave's. In New England they were quickly accommodated to the prevailing labor system, which was servitude. . . .

Indians too seemed radically different from Englishmen, far more so than any Europeans. They were enslaved, like Negroes, and so fell on the losing side of a crucial dividing line. It is easy to see why: whether considered in terms of complexion, religion, nationality, savagery, bestiality, or geographical location, Indians were more like Negroes than like Englishmen. Given this resemblance the essential problem becomes why Indian slavery never became an important institution in the colonies. Why did Indian slavery remain numerically insignificant and typically incidental in character? Why were Indian slaves valued at much lower prices than Negroes? Why were Indians, as a kind of people, treated like Negroes and yet at the same time very differently?

Certain obvious factors made for important differentiations in the minds of the English colonists. As was the case with first confrontations in America and Africa, the different contexts of confrontation made Englishmen more interested in converting and civilizing Indians than Negroes. That this campaign in America too frequently degenerated into military campaigns of extermination did nothing to eradicate the initial distinction. Entirely apart from English intentions, the culture of the American Indians probably meant that they were less readily enslavable than Africans. By comparison, they were less used to settled agriculture, and their own variety of slavery was probably even less similar to the chattel slavery which Englishmen practiced in America than was the domestic and political slavery of the West African cultures. But it was the transformation of English intentions in the wilderness which counted most heavily in the long run. The Bible and the treaty so often gave way to the clash of flintlock and tomahawk. The colonists' perceptions of the Indians came to be organized not only in pulpits and printshops but at the bloody cutting edge of the English thrust into the Indians' lands. Thus the most pressing and mundane circumstances worked to make Indians seem very different from Negroes. In the early years especially, Indians were in a position to mount murderous reprisals upon the English settlers, while the few scattered Negroes were not. When English-Indian relations did not turn upon sheer power they rested on diplomacy. In

---

[78] The designations are a prominent planter's, quoted in Higham, *Development of the Leeward Islands*, 169, also 170*n*.

many instances the colonists took assiduous precautions to prevent abuse of Indians belonging to friendly tribes. Most of the Indians enslaved by the English had their own tribal enemies to thank. It became a common practice to ship Indian slaves to the West Indies where they could be exchanged for slaves who had no compatriots lurking on the outskirts of English settlements.[79] In contrast, Negroes presented much less of a threat — at first.

Equally important, Negroes had to be dealt with as individuals — with supremely impartial anonymity, to be sure — rather than as nations. Englishmen wanted and had to live with their Negroes, as it were, side by side. Accordingly their impressions of Negroes were forged in the heat of continual, inescapable personal contacts. There were few pressures urging Englishmen to treat Indians as integral constituents in their society, which Negroes were whether Englishmen liked or not. At a distance the Indian could be viewed with greater detachment and his characteristics acknowledged and approached more coolly and more rationally. At a distance too, Indians could retain the quality of nationality, a quality which Englishmen admired in themselves and expected in other peoples. Under contrasting circumstances in America, the Negro nations tended to become Negro people.

Here lay the rudiments of certain shadowy but persistent themes in what turned out to be a multi-racial nation. Americans came to impute to the braves of the Indian "nations" an ungovernable individuality (which was perhaps not merited in such exaggerated degree) and at the same time to impart to Negroes all the qualities of an eminently governable sub-nation, in which African tribal distinctions were assumed to be of no consequence and individuality unaspired to. More immediately, the two more primitive peoples rapidly came to serve as two fixed points from which English settlers could triangulate their own position in America; the separate meanings of *Indian* and *Negro* helped define the meaning of living in America. The Indian became for Americans a symbol of their American experience; it was no mere luck of the toss that placed the profile of an American Indian rather than an American Negro on the famous old five-cent piece. Confronting the Indian in America was a testing experience, common to all the colonies. Conquering the Indian symbolized and personified the conquest of the American difficulties, the

[79] Hening, ed., *Statutes Va.*, II, 299. A good study of Indian slavery is needed, but see Almon Wheeler Lauber, *Indian Slavery in Colonial Times within the Present Limits of the United States* (N.Y., 1913). In 1627 some imported Carib Indians proved unsalable in Virginia and were turned over to the colony; the General Court decided that, since the Caribs had stolen goods, attempted murder, tried to run away to the Virginia Indians, and might prove the downfall of the whole colony, the best way to dispose of the problem was to hang them: McIlwaine, ed., *Minutes Council Va.*, 155.

surmounting of the wilderness. To push back the Indian was to prove the worth of one's own mission, to make straight in the desert a highway for civilization. With the Negro it was utterly different.

9. Racial Slavery: From Reasons to Rationale

And *difference*, surely, was the indispensable key to the degradation of Negroes in English America. In scanning the problem of *why* Negroes were enslaved in America, certain constant elements in a complex situation can be readily, if roughly, identified. It may be taken as given that there would have been no enslavement without economic need, that is, without persistent demand for labor in underpopulated colonies. Of crucial importance, too, was the fact that for cultural reasons Negroes were relatively helpless in the face of European aggressiveness and technology. In themselves, however, these two elements will not explain the enslavement of Indians and Negroes. The pressing exigency in America was labor, and Irish and English servants were available. Most of them would have been helpless to ward off outright enslavement if their masters had thought themselves privileged and able to enslave them. As a group, though, masters did not think themselves so empowered. Only with Indians and Negroes did Englishmen attempt so radical a deprivation of liberty — which brings the matter abruptly to the most difficult and imponderable question of all: what was it about Indians and Negroes which set them apart, which rendered them *different* from Englishmen, which made them special candidates for degradation?

To ask such questions is to inquire into the *content* of English attitudes, and unfortunately there is little evidence with which to build an answer. It may be said, however, that the heathen condition of the Negroes seemed of considerable importance to English settlers in America — more so than to English voyagers upon the coasts of Africa — and that heathenism was associated in some settlers' minds with the condition of slavery.[80] This is not to say that the colonists enslaved Negroes because they were heathens. . . .

---

[80] . . . Also John C. Hurd, *The Law of Freedom and Bondage in the United States*, 2 vols. (Boston, 1858–62), I, 159–60; Horne, *The Mirror of Justices*, ed. Robinson, 124; Marcus W. Jernegan, *Laboring and Dependent Classes in Colonial America, 1607–1783; Studies of the Economic, Educational, and Social Significance of Slaves, Servants, Apprentices, and Poor Folk* (Chicago, 1931), 24–26; Helen T. Catterall, ed., *Judicial Cases Concerning American Slavery and the Negro*, 5 vols. (Washington, 1926–37), I, 55n. Data in the following pages suggest this. The implication that slavery could last only during the heathen state is in Providence Company to Gov. Philip Bell, London, Apr. 20, 1635, Box 9, bundle: List no. 7, 2d portion, MS. relating to the Royal African Co. and Slavery matters, 43, Parish Transcripts, N.-Y. Hist. Soc.: ". . . a Groundless opinion that Christians may not lawfully keepe such persons in a state of Servitude during their strangeness from Christianity." In 1695 Gov. John Archdale of South Carolina prohibited sale of some Indians, captured by his own Indian allies, as slaves

The importance and persistence of the tradition which attached slavery to heathenism did not become evident in any positive assertions that heathens might be enslaved. It was not until the period of legal establishment of slavery after 1660 that the tradition became manifest at all, and even then there was no effort to place heathenism and slavery on a one-for-one relationship. Virginia's second statutory definition of a slave (1682), for example, awkwardly attempted to rest enslavement on religious difference while excluding from possible enslavement all heathens who were not Indian or Negro.[81] Despite such logical difficulties, the old European equation of slavery and religious difference did not rapidly vanish in America, for it cropped up repeatedly after 1660 in assertions that slaves by becoming Christian did not automatically become free. By about the end of the seventeenth century, Maryland, New York, Virginia, North and South Carolina, and New Jersey had all passed laws reassuring masters that conversion of their slaves did not necessitate manumission.[82] These acts were passed in response to occasional pleas that Christianity created a claim to freedom and to much more frequent assertions by men interested in converting Negroes that nothing could be accomplished if masters thought their slaves were about to be snatched from them by meddling missionaries.[83] This decision that the slave's religious condition had no relevance to his status as a slave (the only one possible if an already valuable economic institution was to be retained) strongly suggests that heathenism was an important component in the colonists' initial reaction to Negroes early in the century.

---

to the West Indies and freed them because they were Christians: John Archdale, *A New Description of That Fertile and Pleasant Province of Carolina . . .* (London, 1707), in Alexander S. Salley, Jr., ed., *Narratives of Early Carolina, 1650–1708* (N.Y., 1911), 300.

[81] Hening, ed., *Statutes Va.,* II, 490–92.

[82] *Archives Md.,* I, 526, 533 (1664), II, 272; "Duke's Laws," C. O. 5/1142, f. 33v., P.R.O., a portion of the section of "Bondslavery" omitted from the standard New York printed sources which reads "And also provided that This Law shall not extend to sett at Liberty Any Negroe or Indian Servant who shall turne Christian after he shall have been bought by Any Person." (This unpublished Crown Copyright material is reproduced by permission of the Controller of H. M. Stationery Office.) *The Colonial Laws of New York from the Year 1664 to the Revolution . . . ,* 5 vols. (Albany, 1894–96), I, 597–98 (1706); Hening, ed., *Statutes Va.,* II, 260 (1667); Saunders, ed., *Col. Recs. N.C.,* I, 204 (1670), II, 857; Cooper and McCord, eds., *Statutes S.C.,* VII, 343 (1691), 364–65; *Anno Regni Reginae Annae . . . Tertio;* [*The Acts Passed by the Second Assembly of New Jersey in December, 1704*] ([N.Y., 1704]), 20, an act which was disallowed for other reasons.

[83] For example, in 1652 a mulatto girl pleaded Christianity as the reason why she should not be "a perpetuall slave" (Lefroy, comp., *Memorials Bermudas,* II, 34–35, also 293–94), and in 1694 some Massachusetts ministers asked the governor and legislature to remove that "wel-knowne Discouragement" to conversion of slaves with a law denying that baptism necessitated freedom (*Acts and Resolves Mass.,* VII, 537).

Yet its importance can easily be overstressed. For one thing, some of the first Negroes in Virginia had been baptized before arrival. In the early years others were baptized in various colonies and became more than nominally Christian; a Negro woman joined the church in Dorchester, Massachusetts, as a full member in 1641.[84] With some Negroes becoming Christian and others not, there might have developed a caste differentiation along religious lines, yet there is no evidence to suggest that the colonists distinguished consistently between the Negroes they converted and those they did not. It was racial, not religious, slavery which developed in America.

Still, in the early years, the English settlers most frequently contrasted themselves with Negroes by the term *Christian*, though they also sometimes described themselves as *English*;[85] here the explicit religious distinction would seem to have lain at the core of English reaction. Yet the concept embodied by the term *Christian* embraced so much more meaning than was contained in specific doctrinal affirmations that it is scarcely possible to assume on the basis of this linguistic contrast that the colonists set Negroes apart because they were heathen. The historical experience of the English people in the sixteenth century had made for fusion of religion and nationality; the qualities of being English and Christian had become so inseparably blended that it seemed perfectly consistent to the Virginia Assembly in 1670 to declare that "noe negroe or Indian though baptised and enjoyned their owne Freedome shall be capable of any such purchase of christians, but yet not debarred from buying any of their owne nation." . . .

From the first, then, vis-à-vis the Negro the concept embedded in the term *Christian* seems to have conveyed much of the idea and feeling of *we* as against *they*: to be Christian was to be civilized rather than barbarous, English rather than African, white rather than black. The term *Christian* itself proved to have remarkable elasticity, for by the end of the seventeenth century it was being used to define a species of slavery which had altogether lost any connection with explicit religious difference. In the Virginia code of 1705, for example, the term sounded much more like a definition of race than of religion: "And for a further christian care and usage of all christian servants, Be it also enacted . . . That no negroes, mulattos, or Indians, although christians, or Jews, Moors, Mahometans, or other infidels, shall, at any time, purchase any christian servant, nor any other, except of their own complexion, or such as are declared slaves by this act." By this time "Christianity" had somehow become intimately and explicitly linked with "complexion." The 1705 statute de-

---

[84] Winthrop, *Journal*, ed. Hosmer, II, 26.

[85] These statements on prevailing word usage are based on a wide variety of sources, many of them cited in this chapter; some passages already quoted may serve to amplify the illustrations in the following paragraphs.

clared "That all servants imported and brought into this country, by sea or land, who were not christians in their native country, (except Turks and Moors in amity with her majesty, and others that can make due proof of their being free in England, or any other christian country, before they were shipped, in order to transportation hither) shall be accounted and be slaves, and as such be here bought and sold notwithstanding a conversion to christianity afterwards." [86] As late as 1753 the Virginia slave code anachronistically defined slavery in terms of religion when everyone knew that slavery had for generations been based on the racial and not the religious difference.[87]

It is worth making still closer scrutiny of the terminology which Englishmen employed when referring both to themselves and to the two peoples they enslaved, for this terminology affords the best single means of probing the content of their sense of difference. The terms *Indian* and *Negro* were both borrowed from the Hispanic languages, the one originally deriving from (mistaken) geographical locality and the other from human complexion. When referring to the Indians the English colonists either used that proper name or called them *savages*, a term which reflected primarily their view of Indians as uncivilized, or occasionally (in Maryland especially) *pagans*, which gave more explicit expression to the missionary urge. When they had reference to Indians the colonists occasionally spoke of themselves as *Christians* but after the early years almost always as *English*.

In significant contrast, the colonists referred to *Negroes* and by the eighteenth century to *blacks* and to *Africans*, but almost never to Negro *heathens* or *pagans* or *savages*. Most suggestive of all, there seems to have been something of a shift during the seventeenth century in the terminology which Englishmen in the colonies applied to themselves. From the initially most common term *Christian*, at mid-century there was a marked drift toward *English* and *free*. After about 1680, taking the colonies as a whole, a new term appeared — *white*.

So far as the weight of analysis may be imposed upon such terms, diminishing reliance upon *Christian* suggests a gradual muting of the specifically religious element in the Christian-Negro disjunction in favor of secular nationality: Negroes were, in 1667, "not in all respects to be admitted to a full fruition of the exemptions and impunities of the English." [88] As time went on, as some Negroes became assimilated to the

[86] *Ibid.*, III, 447–48 (1705), also 283, V, 547–48, VI, 356–57. Lingering aftereffects of the old concept cropped up as late as 1791, when *Negro* was still contradistinguished by *Christian:* Certificate of character of Negro Phill, Feb. 20, 1791, Character Certificates of Negroes, Papers of the Pennsylvania Abolition Society, Historical Society of Pennsylvania, Philadelphia.

[87] Hening, ed., *Statutes Va.*, VI, 356–57.

[88] *Ibid.*, II, 267.

English colonial culture, as more "raw Africans" arrived, and as increasing numbers of non-English Europeans were attracted to the colonies, the colonists turned increasingly to the striking physiognomic difference. By 1676 it was possible in Virginia to assail a man for "eclipsing" himself in the "darke imbraces of a Blackamoore" as if "Buty consisted all together in the Antiphety of Complections." In Maryland a revised law prohibiting miscegenation (1692) retained *white* and *English* but dropped the term *Christian* — a symptomatic modification. As early as 1664 a Bermuda statute (aimed, ironically, at protecting Negroes from brutal abandonment) required that the "last Master" of senile Negroes "provide for them such accomodations as shall be convenient for Creatures of that hue and colour untill their death." By the end of the seventeenth century dark complexion had become an independent rationale for enslavement: in 1709 Samuel Sewall noted in his diary that a "Spaniard" had petitioned the Massachusetts Council for freedom but that "Capt. Teat alledg's that all of that Color were Slaves." [89] Here was a barrier between "we" and "they" which was visible and permanent: the Negro could not become a white man. Not, at least, as yet.

What had occurred was not a change in the justification of slavery from religion to race. No such justifications were made. There seems to have been, within the unarticulated concept of the Negro as a different sort of person, a subtle but highly significant shift in emphasis. Consciousness of Negro's heathenism remained through the eighteenth and into the nineteenth and even the twentieth century, and an awareness, at very least, of his different appearance was present from the beginning. The shift was an alteration in emphasis within a single concept of difference rather than a development of a novel conceptualization. . . . Throughout the colonies the terms *Christian*, *free*, *English*, and *white* were for many years

[89] "History of Bacon's and Ingram's Rebellion," Andrews, ed., *Narratives of the Insurrections*, 96; *Archives Md.*, XIII, 546–49; Lefroy, comp., *Memorials Bermudas*, II, 216; *Diary of Samuel Sewall, 1674–1729* (Mass. Hist. Soc., *Collections*, 5th Ser. 5–7 [1878–82]), II, 248. In 1698 Gov. Francis Nicholson informed the Board of Trade that the "major part" of Negroes in Maryland spoke English: *Archives Md.*, XXIII, 499. For first use of "white" in statutes of various colonies, Bartlett, ed., *Recs. Col. R.I.*, I, 243 (1652); *Archives Md.*, VII, 204–5 (1681); Aaron Leaming and Jacob Spicer, eds., *The Grants, Concessions, and Original Constitutions of the Province of New Jersey . . .* , 2d ed. (Somerville, N.J., 1881), 236 (1683); *Col. Laws N.Y.*, I, 148 (1684); Cooper and McCord, eds., *Statutes S.C.*, VII, 343 (1691); Hening, ed., *Statutes Va.*, III, 86–87 (1691); *Acts of Assembly, Made and Enacted in the Bermuda or Summer-Islands, from 1690, to 1713–14* (London, 1719), 12–13 (1690 or 1691). West Indian assemblies used the term in the 1680's and 1690's, possibly earlier. Officials in England were using "whites" and "blacks" as early as 1670 in questionnaires to colonial governors: Hening, ed., *Statutes Va.*, II, 515; Trumbull and Hoadly, eds., *Recs. Col. Conn.*, III, 293.

employed indiscriminately as metonyms. A Maryland law of 1681 used all four terms in one short paragraph! [90]

Whatever the limitations of terminology as an index to thought and feeling, it seems likely that the colonists' initial sense of difference from the Negro was founded not on a single characteristic but on a congeries of qualities which, taken as a whole, seemed to set the Negro apart. Virtually every quality in the Negro invited pejorative feelings. What may have been his two most striking characteristics, his heathenism and his appearance, were probably prerequisite to his complete debasement. His heathenism alone could never have led to permanent enslavement since conversion easily wiped out that failing. If his appearance, his racial characteristics, meant nothing to the English settlers, it is difficult to see how slavery based on race ever emerged, how the concept of complexion as the mark of slavery ever entered the colonists' minds. Even if the colonists were most unfavorably struck by the Negro's color, though, blackness itself did not urge the complete debasement of slavery. Other qualities — the utter strangeness of his language, gestures, eating habits, and so on — certainly must have contributed to the colonists' sense that he was very different, perhaps disturbingly so. In Africa these qualities had for Englishmen added up to *savagery*; they were major components in that sense of *difference* which provided the mental margin absolutely requisite for placing the European on the deck of the slave ship and the Negro in the hold.

The available evidence (what little there is) suggests that for Englishmen settling in America, the specific religious difference was initially of greater importance than color, certainly of much greater relative importance than for the Englishmen who confronted Negroes in their African homeland. Perhaps Englishmen in Virginia, living uncomfortably close to nature under a hot sun and in almost daily contact with tawny Indians, found the Negro's color less arresting than they might have in other circumstances. Perhaps, too, these first Virginians sensed how inadequately they had reconstructed the institutions and practices of Christian piety in the wilderness; they would perhaps appear less as failures to themselves in this respect if compared to persons who as Christians were *totally* defective. In this connection they may be compared to their brethren in New England, where godliness appeared (at first) triumphantly to hold full sway; in New England there was distinctly less contrasting of Negroes on the basis of the religious disjunction and much more militant discussion of just wars. Perhaps, though, the Jamestown settlers were told in 1619 by the Dutch shipmaster that these "negars" were heathens and could be treated as such. We do not know. The available data will not bear all the weight that the really crucial questions impose.

[90] *Archives Md.*, VII, 204.

Of course once the cycle of degradation was fully under way, once slavery and racial discrimination were completely linked together, once the engine of oppression was in full operation, then there is no need to plead *ignoramus*. By the end of the seventeenth century in all the colonies of the English empire there was chattel racial slavery of a kind which would have seemed familiar to men living in the nineteenth century. No Elizabethan Englishman would have found it familiar, though certain strands of thought and feeling in Elizabethan England had intertwined with reports about the Spanish and Portuguese to engender a willingness on the part of English settlers in the New World to treat some men as suitable for private exploitation. During the seventeenth century New World conditions had exploited this predisposition and vastly enlarged it, so much so that English colonials of the eighteenth century were faced with full-blown slavery.

The Legal Status of the Slave in South Carolina, 1670–1740

M. EUGENE SIRMANS

This brief essay provides an opportunity to reconsider the origins of slavery by closely studying a single colony. Slavery in South Carolina, if Eugene Sirmans is correct, cannot be explained in terms of the Handlins' thesis. Rather [South Carolinian notions of slave status were derived from the West Indian experience of the early leaders of the colony, and the later practice of "mature" slavery preceded the development of its legal definition. Moreover, it was only the rapid increase in the black population and the outbreak of violent resistance to slavery which prompted South Carolina to define legally the already existing chattel slave system in 1740. Chattel slavery existed long before it was recognized at law.]

Sirmans's analysis and Jordan's essay perhaps combine to suggest that legal status alone does not explain the emergence of the Southern institution of slavery. They seem to believe that legal formulation follows rather than precipitates change.

Their clear implication is that social, political, and economic factors peculiar to the Southern colonies gave rise to the chattel slavery of the mid-eighteenth century. Do Sirmans and Jordan leave room for the view that legal history can make an important contribution to our understanding of colonial history? More important, do these three essays indicate that we need to know a great deal more about the black man's role in the origins of slavery?

The legal status of the negro slave was eventually the same in all the British colonies on the North American mainland, for by the middle of the eighteenth century the law in each of those colonies adjudged the slave to be his master's personal chattel. Despite their final unanimity the colonies arrived at chattel slavery on different roads. Following the trail pioneered by Virginia and Maryland, most provinces treated Negroes as perpetual servants for several decades prior to the legal adoption of chattel slavery. South Carolina took a somewhat different route. Before it made the Negro slave a chattel, it first experimented with other approaches to the legal problems involved.

In tracing the evolution of chattel slavery in South Carolina the colony's relationship with Barbados demands particular attention. Historians used to assume that immigrants to South Carolina from the West Indies "brought with them the slave code of those islands, especially that of Barbados,"[1] and that South Carolina copied its slave laws from those of Barbados. Some years ago this generalization was challenged by Oscar and Mary Handlin, who contended that South Carolina could not have borrowed its slavery customs from Barbados or any other island colony, because the "labor system of those places were not yet fully evolved" when South Carolina adopted its first slave laws and because statutory chattel slavery never existed in the islands.[2]

Throughout the history of Negro servitude in Barbados, the colonists there disliked specific legal definitions of slavery and preferred the institution to be defined by custom rather than by law. Consequently, their slave laws dealt with the control of slaves instead of their legal status. This enabled Barbados to impose upon the Negro the conditions of servi-

From M. Eugene Sirmans, "The Legal Status of the Slave in South Carolina, 1670–1740," *Journal of Southern History*, XXVIII (1962), 462–473. Copyright 1962 by the Southern Historical Association. Reprinted by permission of the Managing Editor.

[1] Edward McCrady, "Slavery in the Province of South Carolina, 1670–1770," in American Historical Association, *Report* (1895), 644.

[2] Oscar and Mary F. Handlin, "Origins of the Southern Labor System," *William and Mary Quarterly*, s. 3, VII (April 1950), 206.

tude desired by his master without English interference.[3] Nevertheless, Barbadians did develop a system of slavery – extralegal though it was – possibly as early as the 1630's, but certainly by the 1650's when one commentator observed, "They [Negroes] and the generation are Slaves to their owners to perpetuity." Barbadians of the time referred to Negroes as slaves, and slavery was the normal condition of Negroes. They served their masters for life, and Negro children inherited the status of their parents.[4] Custom, not law, defined the Negro's status. The system continued to be informal until 1668, when the assembly enacted a law defining slaves as real estate, or freehold property. Four years later the assembly amended the law by making the slave a personal chattel in payment of his master's debts. The laws of 1668 and 1672 were the colony's final words on the status of slaves. Thereafter, Barbados avoided further questions of legal status and passed only laws relating to police control, of which the most important was the comprehensive slave code of 1688.[5]

Barbados exerted its influence on South Carolina from the beginnings of the younger colony. A Barbadian, Sir John Colleton, was the prime mover in securing the proprietary charter for Carolina. Many of the first settlers were Barbadians, and the first Negroes in South Carolina came from Barbados. It would be reasonable to assume that the Barbadians brought their slavery practices with them, and the surviving evidence supports such an assumption. There may have been a Barbadian source even for the provision in John Locke's Fundamental Constitutions of Carolina that said, "Every freeman of Carolina, shall have absolute power and authority over his negro slaves. . . ." [6] Locke corresponded with Sir Peter Colleton, a proprietor and resident of Barbados,[7] and he may well have acquired his knowledge of slavery from this source.

South Carolina differentiated between white servants and Negroes

---

[3] *Ibid.*, 219–20; James Stephen, *The Slavery of the British West-India Colonies* . . . (2 vols., London, 1824–1830), I, 14–15.

[4] Winthrop D. Jordan, "The Influence of the West Indies on the Origins of New England Slavery," *William and Mary Quarterly*, s. 3, XVIII (April 1961), 248–50; the question is from "A Briefe Discription of the Ilande of Barbados" in Vincent T. Harlow (ed.), *Colonising Expeditions to the West Indies and Guiana, 1623–1667* (Hakluyt Society, *Works*, s. 2, No. 55 [London, 1925]), 44–45, quoted in Jordan, "The Influence of the West Indies on the Origins of New England Slavery," 249.

[5] Richard Hall (comp.), *Acts Passed in the Island of Barbados, from 1643, to 1762, Inclusive* (London, 1764), 64–65, 93–94, 112–21; Richard Hall, *An Abridgement of the Acts in Force, in the Island of Barbados, from 1643, to 1762, Inclusive* (London, 1764), 60; John Poyer, *The History of Barbados, from* . . . *1605, till* . . . *1801* (London, 1808), 132–33, 136–40.

[6] William L. Saunders (ed.), *The Colonial Records of North Carolina, 1662–1776* (10 vols., Raleigh, 1886–1890), I, 204.

[7] Maurice Cranston, *John Locke: A Biography* (New York, 1957), 120, 156.

from the first and treated the Negroes as slaves. For example, the Grand Council in 1672 and 1673 sentenced white servants to extra service as a punishment, but never Negroes, thus tacitly recognizing that Negroes already served for life.[8] In its first years South Carolina had but few persons who were subject to involuntary servitude. There was only a small number of Negroes and perhaps a slightly larger number of Indian captives, a group that always shared the Negro's status in South Carolina.[9] More important and more numerous than either were the white servants. The first laws relating to servitude therefore applied primarily to white servants, with provisions applying to Negroes and Indians added almost as an afterthought. Such laws were concerned only with the policing of the unfree population and made no explicit reference to legal status. Implicit in the laws, however, was a distinction between white servants and nonwhite slaves; the statutes followed the example of the Grand Council by providing extra service as punishment for white servants but never for Negroes or Indians.[10]

The first South Carolina law relating solely to slavery was passed by the assembly in 1690, a time when the government of the colony was under the control of a political faction headed by former Barbadians. The law of 1690 drew upon the Barbadian acts of 1668 and 1672 for its definition of slavery, retaining the meaning though not the wording of the Barbadian definition. The South Carolina statute provided that slaves "as to payment of debts, shall be deemed and taken as all other goods and chattels . . . and all negroes shall be accounted as freehold in all other cases whatsoever, and descend accordingly." In other words, except in payment of the master's debt, slaves were to be freehold property. Clauses relating to the policing of slaves came from earlier servant laws but with the addition of special controls for slaves. Slaves needed written permission to leave their masters' residences; slave-owners were required to make regular searches of slave quarters for weapons; and slaves who ran away or

[8] Grand Council Journals, January 10, October 8, 18, 1672, August 30, 1673, in South Carolina Historical Society, *Collections* (5 vols., Charleston, 1857–1897), V, 373–74, 413–14, 427. For other examples of differentiation between white servants and Negroes, see Alexander S. Salley (ed.), *Warrants for Land in South Carolina, 1672–1711* (3 vols., Columbia, 1910–1915), I, 55, 70, 94.

[9] Although South Carolina enslaved a large number of Indians, more than any other colony, their presence there did not exert a discernible influence on the legal development of slavery. The absence of such an influence may be explained by the fact that most of the captured Indians were immediately shipped out of the colony and sold in the West Indies. On this subject, see Almon Wheeler Lauber, *Indian Slavery in Colonial Times Within the Present Limits of the United States* (New York, 1913), 105–106, 240.

[10] Thomas Cooper and David J. McCord (eds.), *Statutes at Large of South Carolina* (14 vols., Columbia, 1836–1875), II, 22–23. This law is apparently a re-enactment of an earlier law of the same nature, see *ibid.*, II, v.

struck their masters faced severe penalties, among which were whipping, branding, slitting the nose, and emasculation.[11]

The unusual feature of the South Carolina act of 1690 was its definition of the slaves as freehold property. Freehold slavery was common in the Caribbean, whether the colony was English, French, Spanish, or Portuguese, but rare on the mainland. As freehold property the Negro enjoyed a higher legal status than he did as chattel, because freehold was a higher form of property than chattel. Freehold property was attached to a landed estate and could not be moved; its holder legally had a right only to its use and not absolute ownership. Freehold slavery thus implied that a master had a right to the slave's services rather than to the slave himself. On the other hand, chattels were defined as the owner's personal belongings which he could dispose of as he pleased. In short, freehold slavery attached the slave to land, like a serf, while chattel slavery attached him to a master, a condition unknown in English law and a uniquely North American development.[12]

The slave act of 1690, passed during the administration of the rebel governor, Seth Sothell, was disallowed by the proprietors along with all other laws passed during Sothell's governorship. South Carolina did not yet really need a slave law as slaveholding was not to become widespread until about five years later, when the colony began to produce a marketable staple that required a large labor force. After planters began to cultivate rice successfully and to demand cheap labor, the South Carolina assembly passed a new slave bill in 1696, a bill so comprehensive in its control of the slave's life as to deserve the designation of South Carolina's first slave code.

The assembly again borrowed from Barbados. The South Carolina law of 1696 was copied from the Barbados slave code of 1688. The assembly of South Carolina enacted verbatim the Barbadian statute's preamble and three fourths of its provisions for policing the slave population. As in the Barbadian law, the preamble to the South Carolina bill stated that special legislation was necessary to govern slaves, because Negroes had "barbarous, wild, savage Natures' and were "naturally prone and inclined" to "Disorders, Rapines, and Inhumanity." The South Carolina code reenacted the provisions of the act of 1690 relating to the control of slaves, and it added others from the Barbadian code on the prevention of slave

[11] *Ibid.*, VII, 343–47. On the political control of the colony by a Barbadian faction, see M. Eugene Sirmans, *Masters of Ashley Hall: A Biographical Study of the Bull Family of Colonial South Carolina, 1670–1737* (unpublished Ph.D. thesis, Princeton University, 1959), 68–69, 75–77.

[12] William Blackstone, *Commentaries on the Laws of England* (4 vols., London, 1765–1769), Bk. II, chs. 7, 24; "Chattels Personal" and "Freehold" in Giles Jacob, *The Law Dictionary*, T. E. Tomlins, ed. (2 vols., London, 1797); Stephen, *Slavery of British West-India Colonies*, I, 63–69.

crimes and the trial of miscreant slaves. A new clause, enacted by the South Carolina assembly in 1696, tried to eliminate potentially dangerous gatherings of slaves by directing the constables of Charles Town to break up slave assemblies on the Sabbath.[13]

Once again the most unusual part of the law was its definition of a slave. The law stated, "All Negroes, Mollatoes, and Indians which at any time heretofore have been bought and Sold or now are and taken to be or hereafter Shall be Bought and Sold are hereby made and declared they and their Children Slaves to all Intents and purposes." [14] This definition, which was solely the product of the South Carolina assembly, was unique in colonial America. Vague to the point of being cryptic, the definition followed the general policy of Barbados and other island colonies but went further. The purpose of the islanders in resting slavery upon custom instead of law had apparently been to obviate interference from authorities in England; perhaps the South Carolina legislators were seeking to achieve the same end. If so, they succeeded, for neither the proprietors nor the Crown intervened in the slave practices of South Carolina as long as the code of 1696 remained in force.

The simple but broad definition of slaves as "Slaves to all Intents and purposes" made custom the arbiter of slavery in South Carolina. The question remains, however, of just what that custom was. The surviving evidence that bears on this question is fragmentary and inconclusive, but it is all on one side. It indicates that it was the custom of South Carolina in the early eighteenth century to treat slaves as chattels. In a promotional tract of 1712, John Norris wrote, "When these people [Negroes] are thus bought, their Masters, or Owners, have then as good a Right to and title to them, during their lives, as a Man has here to a Horse or Ox, after he has bought them." [15] This sounds like chattel slavery. But Norris was only a pamphleteer and not a jurist or even an official of the colony. A more explicit statement by an official was offered in 1725 by Arthur Middleton, who was then acting governor of the colony. He said flatly that slaves "have been and are always deemed as goods and Chattels of their Masters." [16]

---

[13] Governor Archdale's Laws [1696] (South Carolina Archives, Columbia), fol. 60–66. David J. McCord omitted this law from his and Cooper's edition of the South Carolina statutes but included the re-enactment of it in 1712; see Cooper and McCord (eds.), *Statutes at Large of South Carolina*, VII, 352–65. This has led several historians to date the first passage of the law incorrectly as 1712; see, for example, McCrady, "Slavery in South Carolina," 645.

[14] Archdale's Laws, fol. 60.

[15] John Norris, *Profitable Advice for Rich and Poor* . . . (London, 1712), 17–18.

[16] Journal of the Council of South Carolina, September 10, 1725, Colonial Office Papers (Public Record Office, London; microfilm in Library of Congress), s. 5, CCCCXXVIII, fol. 108. The first historian of South Carolina, Alexander

The court records of a colony often provide the best indication of the slave's status, but some of the more important sets of South Carolina's judicial records offer few clues to the problem of status. The only provincial court of common pleas sat in Charles Town, and none of its records are extant for the period before 1733. No case that came before the court after that date involved the status of a Negro or Indian. The post-1733 records are only judgment books, so there is no way to tell whether slaves were attached by writs of ejectment or replevin, the first of which would indicate freehold slavery and the second, chattel slavery.[17] The records of the court of vice-admiralty contain the one surviving record of a court case involving in any way the status of Negroes, but it is an inconclusive one. In 1736 a sea captain found three Negroes adrift in a canoe off the coast of South Carolina. The court of vice-admiralty treated the Negroes as salvage and sold them at auction. The case does not prove that the court defined slaves as chattel property, because it might have treated freehold property the same way in the unlikely event that a house or a barn had been found adrift at open sea.[18]

Better evidence as to the slave's legal status is to be found in the colony's probate proceedings, the records of the Court of Chancery, and the records of slave sales. The probate proceedings are the only surviving judicial records in which the court system dealt regularly with slaves. When a will was probated, the governor — acting in his capacity of provincial ordinary — ordered an inventory of the decedent's personal estate. The inventories listed and evaluated all his personal chattels: his clothes, cattle, horses, hogs, furniture, china, even his chamber pots. The inventories included servants only very rarely and never listed real estate of any kind; they made no mention of lands, houses, warehouses, barns, or other buildings. [In other words, probate inventories included personal chattels but not freehold property or, except rarely, servants. The inventories always included the decedent's slaves, which strongly suggests that in probate proceedings slaves were considered chattels rather than real estate or servants of some kind.] The practice of listing slaves with personal chattels began as early as 1693 and continued as long as slavery

---

Hewatt, misquoted Middleton and gave the statement an entirely different meaning; he quoted Middleton as saying, "Negroes were real property, such as houses and land, in Carolina." See Hewatt's *An Historical Account of the Rise and Progress of the Colonies of South Carolina and Georgia* (2 vols., London, 1779), in B. R. Carroll (ed.), *Historical Collections of South Carolina* (2 vols., New York, 1836), I, 270–71. Hewatt's misquotation has been widely accepted as accurate; see, for example, David D. Wallace, *The History of South Carolina* (4 vols., New York, 1934), I, 375.

[17] Records of the Court of Common Pleas: Judgment Books, 1733–1791 (South Carolina Archives).

[18] South Carolina Admiralty Records, 1716–1763 (Federal Records Center, East Point, Ga.), C (1736–38), 146–62; D (1738–47), 19.

existed in South Carolina.[19] That it was the custom to treat slaves as chattels is confirmed by records of the Chancery Court. In three different cases involving the divisions of estates, the only ones of their kind to come before the Chancery Court before 1740, the court classified slaves with the decedent's personal goods, not with his real estate.[20] The legal form used by South Carolinians to sell Negroes provides additional confirmation that slaves were treated as chattels by custom long before they were defined as such by law. Slaves were transferred from one owner to another by indenture; land was always sold by lease and release.[21] The available evidence, then, indicates that under the vague definition of slavery in the code of 1696 South Carolinians began treating their slaves as personal chattels nearly half a century before the code of 1740 formally inaugurated chattel slavery.

The assembly made no basic changes in the slave code until 1740, although it re-enacted the original law three times and amended it twice after 1696.[22] Believing that "if negroes are well used, they never run" away, South Carolinians did not enforce the harsher police provisions of this code of 1696.[23] Most slave owners chose to deal gently with their bondsmen, but they did not trust them. They feared a slave insurrection, and with good reason. Small groups of Negroes initiated slave revolts in 1714 and 1720, but their masters managed to put down both outbursts before they became general.[24] Meanwhile, as the production of rice and

[19] Wills, Inventories of Estate, and Miscellaneous Records [title varies], 1671–1868 (office of judge of probate court, Charleston, S.C.). I have found only two inventories out of more than 200 for the period 1693–1740 that listed freehold property of any kind. A total of 25 white servants appear in the inventories prior to 1740; see Warren B. Smith, *White Servitude in Colonial South Carolina* (Columbia, 1961), 135–36.

[20] Anne King Gregorie (ed.), *Records of the Court of Chancery of South Carolina, 1671–1779* (Washington, 1950), 278–80, 383–85.

[21] Mesne Conveyances, 1719–1800 (office of register of mesne conveyances, Charleston).

[22] Cooper and McCord (eds.), *Statutes at Large of South Carolina*, VII, 352–96.

[23] *Manuscripts of the Earl of Egmont: Diary of Viscount Percival, Afterwards First Earl of Egmont, 1730–1747* (Historical Manuscripts Commission, *Sixteenth Report* [3 vols., London, 1920–1923]), III, 201. See also Francis LeJau to Secretary, Society for the Propagation of the Gospel, June 30, 1707, in Frank J. Klingberg (ed.), *The Carolina Chronicle of Dr. Francis LeJau, 1706–1717* (Berkeley, 1956), 26–27; William Bull, Jr., to the Earl of Hillsborough, November 30, 1770, Records in the British Public Record Office Relating to South Carolina, 1711–1782 (South Carolina Archives), XXXII, 382; Hewatt, *Historical Account*, in Carroll (ed.), *Collections*, I, 349–50; and Howell M. Henry, *The Police Control of the Slave in South Carolina* (Emory, Va., 1914).

[24] LeJau to Secretary, S.P.G., January 22, 1714, in Klingberg (ed.) *LeJau Chronicle*, 136–37; Francis Varnod to same, January 10, 1722, Manuscripts of the Society for the Propagation of the Gospel (office of the Society for the Propagation of the Gospel, London; transcripts and microfilm, Library of Con-

other crops expanded, the number of slaves in the colony increased, and after 1708 the population of South Carolina included more Negroes than whites. In 1730 the colony entered into a period of unprecedented prosperity, and planters began to import slaves at the rate of 2,500 a year. After a decade of this high rate of importation, Negroes outnumbered whites by 39,000 to 20,000.[25] The flow of slaves into South Carolina was so great that in 1738 a Georgian commented, "Our Neighbours at Charles Town, I hear have their Belly-full of 'em. . . ." [26]

[The rapid influx of Negroes into South Carolina after 1730 helped to produce a crisis in the institution of slavery. The ever-growing number of slaves made it impossible for slave owners to continue the traditionally indulgent treatment of their slaves and at the same time maintain discipline among them. Enforcement of the slave code, never efficient, became almost nonexistent, and owners lost control of their slaves.] As many as two hundred Negroes sometimes engaged in drinking parties in Charles Town, while many slaves openly defied the law by buying and selling goods in the Charles Town market.[27] Then [in 1738 the Spanish governor of Florida stirred up South Carolina's Negroes by publishing a royal edict that promised freedom to all English slaves who made good their escape to St. Augustine.] Spain and England were approaching war, and the edict attempted to forestall English aggression on the southern frontier by encouraging slave unrest and exploiting South Carolina's fears of its slave population. Publication of the edict was followed by several successful escapes by parties of runaways from South Carolina and an unknown number of abortive attempts. News of the escapes, combined with lax enforcement of slave laws, made many whites believe that a general slave insurrection could begin at any moment.[28]

---

gress), s. A, XVII, 171; Richard Ludlam to Secretary, July 2, 1722, *ibid.*, XVIII, 83.

[25] Governor and Council to Proprietors, September 17, 1708, in *Records in the British Public Record Office Relating to South Carolina, 1663–1710* (5 vols., Atlanta and Columbia, 1928–1947), V, 203; J. H. Easterby (ed.), *The Colonial Records of South Carolina: The Journal of the Commons House of Assembly, 1736–1750* (9 vols., Columbia, 1951–1962), 1741–1742, 460 (March 3, 1742); E. B. Greene and V. D. Harrington, *American Population Before the Federal Census of 1790* (New York, 1932), 174; Elizabeth Donnan, "The Slave Trade into South Carolina Before the Revolution," *American Historical Review*, XXXIII (July 1928), 807.

[26] William Stephens to the Trustees of Georgia, January 19, 1738, in Allen D. Candler (ed.), *The Colonial Records of the State of Georgia, 1732–1782* (26 vols., Atlanta, 1904–1916), XXII, pt. 1, 76.

[27] Charles Town *South-Carolina Gazette*, October 28, 1732; Presentments of the Grand Jury, March 20, 1735, Records in the British P.R.O. Relating to S.C., XVII, 304.

[28] Journal of the Upper House, 1721–1773 (South Carolina Archives), VII, 142–43 (January 19, 1739); William Bull, Sr., to the Duke of Newcastle, May 9, 1739, Records in the British P.R.O. Relating to S.C., XX, 40–41.

The assembly of South Carolina ignored all the signs of warning and acted as if it were blind to the dangers of unrest among the slaves. It clung to the old laws and passed no corrective legislation, other than an ineffective patrol law, and it failed to meet the challenge of the Spanish edict.[29] The assembly was more concerned with conventional politics. The council and Commons House were entangled in a prolonged struggle for control of the purse, and every attempt to relieve the crisis growing out of the slavery situation fell a victim to that struggle.[30]

The insurrection that had been brewing finally broke out on Sunday, September 9, 1739, although in fact it was less an insurrection than an attempt by slaves to fight their way to St. Augustine. The trouble started on Saturday night when about twenty slaves, led by a Negro named Jemmy, broke into a warehouse near the Stono river and armed themselves with guns, ammunition, and other military supplies. The armed slaves killed ten whites and burned several houses on Sunday morning. Then, with flags flying, drums beating, and shouts of "liberty," about sixty slaves set out to march to St. Augustine. Lieutenant Governor William Bull, who had escaped the initial outburst only by fast riding, called out the militia, which caught the fleeing slaves at four o'clock that afternoon. The Negroes fought bravely, but the militia outnumbered them, and many of the Negroes had drunk too much rum. By sunset the insurrection had ended, with forty Negroes and twenty whites dead.[31]

Two other abortive uprisings followed the Stono insurrection, but the assembly remained preoccupied with its internal struggles.[32] It was not until May 1740 that the Commons and council agreed on a new slave code, one which represented a new departure in South Carolina's slave laws. The law defined slaves as personal chattels. This was the first precise definition of slavery since the disallowed act of 1690; slavery no longer rested upon custom but upon law. Thus, in 1740, South Carolina definitely and finally abandoned its Barbadian traditions of slavery and set the institution upon the legal foundations developed in other English mainland colonies.

In other respects, the slave code of 1740 was more consistent with the practices of the institution in South Carolina. The assembly sought to

[29] Cooper and McCord (eds.), *Statutes at Large of South Carolina*, III, 395–99, 456–61; Easterby (ed.), *Commons Journal*, 1736–1739, 604, 673 (January 24, March 16, 1739).

[30] See for example Easterby (ed.), *Commons Journal*, 1736–1739, 362, 547, 681, 707 (December 13, 1737, March 22, 1738, April 2, May 30, 1739).

[31] "An Account of the Negroe Insurrection in South Carolina," in Candler (ed.), *Colonial Records of Georgia*, XXII, pt. 2, 232–36. See also William Bull, Sr., to the Board of Trade, October 5, 1739, Records in the British P.R.O. Relating to S.C., XX, 179–80.

[32] Petition of Assembly, July 26, 1740, *ibid.*, 300–301; Easterby (ed.), *Commons Journal*, 1739–1741, 324, 327 (May 2, 1740).

maintain the tradition of kind treatment of slaves by enacting provisions designed to keep "the owners and other persons having the care and government of slaves" from "exercising too great rigour and cruelty over them." The law forbade masters to work their slaves on Sunday or more than fourteen or fifteen hours a day during the week. Owners were required to provide sufficient food and clothing. If a white were accused of killing or maiming a slave he was to face a jury trial, and, if found guilty, he could be fined up to £100 sterling. A second and equally traditional goal of the slave code was to make sure that the slave "be kept in due subjection and obedience." The assembly re-enacted all the old provisions regulating the slave's conduct and added new ones. The law outlawed all assemblies of slaves, forbade the sale of alcohol to them, and prohibited them from learning to write.[33] At the same time it passed the new slave code, the assembly strengthened the patrol system by vesting responsibility for it in the militia. It also tried to reduce the number of Negroes being shipped to the colony by raising the import duty.[34]

The new slave code was permitted to go into effect despite some opposition in England, where the Crown's legal advisers seemed suddenly aware of chattel slavery. In 1748 the Board of Trade's legal counsel, Mathew Lamb, recommended disallowance of the South Carolina code on the grounds that the colonial law conflicted with an act of Parliament of 1732 designed to help English merchants recover debts in the colonies. One of the provisions of this act directed that slaves be treated as real estate in the recovery of colonial debts. Lamb considered that the act sanctioned freehold slavery but not chattel slavery. The Board of Trade, however, took no action on the South Carolina slave code, and the code remained in force, although three years later the Board secured the disallowance of a Virginia law because it defined slaves as chattels.[35] The Crown's permissive treatment of the code of 1740 may well have been due to the intercession of Charles Town merchants, who often owned slaves and who enjoyed considerable influence with the Board of Trade.

[In South Carolina the slave code of 1740 worked well. It seemed to have found the balance between kindness and discipline required to keep slaves in good order, for there were no further slave rebellions in the colonial period.] A few changes in the law were found necessary, but they

[33] The slave code of 1740 is in Cooper and McCord (eds.), *Statutes at Large of South Carolina*, VII, 397–417.

[34] *Ibid.*, III, 556–73.

[35] Mathew Lamb to Board of Trade, November 2, 1748, Records in the British P.R.O. Relating to S.C., XXIII, 261; Leo F. Stock (ed.), *Proceedings and Debates of the British Parliaments Respecting North America, 1542–1754* (5 vols., Washington, 1924–1941), IV, 150; James Curtis Ballagh, *A History of Slavery in Virginia* (Baltimore, 1902), 63–68; Gerald Montgomery West, *The Status of the Negro in Virginia During the Colonial Period* (New York, [1889?]), II, 27–32.

were minor. For example, the assembly had to amend the patrol law, but by 1750 the patrols functioned efficiently.[36] In some other instances, the assembly found provisions of the 1740 law too severe on the slaves and either amended the law accordingly or else permitted it to be ignored. Most notably, it allowed the Society for the Propagation of the Gospel to operate a grammar school for fifty to sixty Negro boys in Charles Town.[37]

[Thus did South Carolina evolve chattel slavery in a manner unique among American colonies. In the seventeenth century it imported the slave pattern of Barbados in piecemeal fashion, adopting first the Barbadian definition of a slave as freehold property and then the comprehensive Barbadian slave code. It was under South Carolina's own deliberately vague definition of a slave, however, that South Carolinians developed chattel slavery without benefit of legislative action and without interference from England. Not until after the slave insurrections of 1739 did the colonists completely abandon the Barbadian approach to slavery and write chattel slavery into law.]

Summary

[36] Cooper and McCord (eds.), *Statutes at Large of South Carolina*, III, 681–85; Klaus G. Loewald and others (trans. and eds.), "Johann Martin Bolzius Answers a Questionnaire on Carolina and Georgia," *William and Mary Quarterly*, s. 3, XIV (April 1957), 234.

[37] Cooper and McCord (eds.), *Statutes at Large of South Carolina*, VII, 420–25; James Glen to Board of Trade, January 29, 1752, Records in the British P.R.O. Relating to S.C., XXV, 7–8; Robert Smith to Secretary, S.P.G., July 25, 1759, Manuscripts of the S.P.G., s. B, V, No. 252.

The Legal Transformation: The Bench and Bar of Eighteenth-Century Massachusetts

JOHN M. MURRIN

John Murrin's hypothesis is that the American colonies experienced a rapid and pervasive Anglicization during the middle of the eighteenth century. They became self-consciously English and rejected the customary patterns of life which had evolved in the first century of settlement. The legal profession in Massachusetts illustrates this process. Puritan Massachusetts had rejected lawyers as a matter of principle, although a small group of practitioners had come into existence by the early eighteenth century. The number of lawyers then began to increase rapidly when it became evident that the law was a stepping-stone to royal patronage, political preferment, and prestige. By mid-century the bar had become highly professionalized. Lawyers banded together to maintain standards, limit the number of practitioners, and enhance their social standing. They modeled themselves after the English bar in every way possible, adopting robes and wigs and the complex hierarchy of legal statuses in England.

The paradox, as Murrin points out, is that such a highly Anglicized profession should have provided so many revolutionary leaders and statesmen of a new nation. He analyzes the membership of the Massachusetts bar to determine what motivated men in determining their allegiance during the American Revolution and concludes that, ironically, the very Anglicization of colonial America gave the Revolution its peculiar character.

Murrin suggests a number of intriguing questions about the quality of life in colonial America. To what extent was American society "provincial"? Why should the process of Anglicization have taken so long to begin? What is the role of professionalization (of lawyers, doctors, and ministers) in social development? How important were educational institutions in the transmission of culture from the Old World to the New, from older generations to younger? What is the impact of the legal profession upon the conduct of politics?

Between 1686 and 1702 the court system of Massachusetts was altered drastically. The Dominion of New England imposed unwanted changes on the colony from outside which Massachusetts repudiated during the Glorious Revolution. Yet in a series of legislative enactments between 1692 and 1702, the General Court adopted practically the entire court system of the hated Dominion. Colonial courts designed to implement

A revised and expanded version of this essay will appear in John M. Murrin, *Anglicizing an American Colony: The Transformation of Provincial Massachusetts*, to be published by the Oxford University Press. It originally appeared as "Anglicizing an American Colony: The Transformation of Provincial Massachusetts" (Unpubl. Ph.D. diss., Yale University, 1966).

Puritan or "American" law yielded to a simplified and rationalized structure of English common law courts. Trial by jury, which Puritan magistrates had all but eliminated in criminal cases involving non-capital
offenses, revived under steady royal pressure during the first generation under the new charter. In a very real sense, the ghost of Sir Edmund Andros
triumphed where the man himself had failed.

This transformation of the courts within a fifteen-year period was a
momentous event in New England history. Yet by itself the court system
was merely a framework or a shell within which human beings could
function from one day to the next. The legal revolution of the eighteenth
century had to go much farther before it could mean much at all. It had
to touch the lives and minds and hearts of the men pleading before the
courts and passing judgment within them. This task was as difficult as it
was fundamental. Unlike the court system, it could not be enacted by
statute, and it would take much longer than fifteen years to achieve. But
it too was done. By the eve of the Revolution, the judges and lawyers of
Massachusetts were more self-consciously English than they had ever
been before.

I

The Puritans never allowed their reverence for law to betray them into
respect for lawyers, men who profited by the distress of others and who
found occupational reasons for encouraging disputes, and hence litigation,
within the community. Article 26 of the Body of Liberties of 1641 prohibited anyone from accepting a fee to assist another in court.[1] A few
years later the General Court unenthusiastically conceded that lawyers,
like physicians, were not the sole cause of the evils they tried to cure.
Thus the legislature omitted this restriction from the Code of 1648, but
in 1663 it again displayed its old suspicion by barring from a seat in the
legislature any person "who is an usual and Common Attorney in any
Inferior Court." [2] This provision indicates that some people did practice
law in seventeenth-century Massachusetts, but only in 1673 did the General Court formally concede their power to do so.[3] Partly because of this
hostility, the men who became lawyers before 1686 achieved the full ob-
scurity which the Puritans thought they deserved.[4]

---

[1] *The Colonial Laws of Massachusetts. Reprinted from the Edition of 1660,
with the Supplements to 1672. Containing also, the Body of Liberties of 1641,*
ed. William H. Whitmore (Boston, 1889), 39.

[2] *Ibid.,* 224.

[3] *The Colonial Laws of Massachusetts. Reprinted from the Edition of 1672,
with the Supplements through 1686,* ed. William H. Whitmore (Boston, 1887),
211.

[4] For some account of these men, see *Records of the Suffolk County Court,
1671–1680,* ed. Zechariah Chafee, Jr., Part I, in CSM, *Publications,* XXIX

Again the major break with tradition came during the brief rule of Dudley and Andros. In 1686 the new Superior Court or governor's council conceded to attorneys, not just the right to exist, but even a kind of professional status as officers of the court when it initiated the practice of licensing them.[5] Soon a qualified professional arrived from New York only to remind the province how pleasant things had been without him. The man "drives all before him," observed the chief architect of the Dominion, Edward Randolph; "he also takes extravagant fees, and for want of more [lawyers] the country cannot avoid coming to him, so that we had better be quite without them than not to have more." [6]

Yet this change became permanent under the new charter. The various acts establishing courts between 1692 and 1699 grudgingly yielded a place for lawyers within the judicial system.[7] When these laws were disallowed, the General Court finally responded in 1701 with a statute devoted exclusively to attorneys.[8] While one clause permitted plaintiff or defendant either to plead his own cause or to accept "the assistance of such other person as he shall procure," another revealed through the low fees it established the province's continuing distrust of the whole profession. In Massachusetts, so long as the General Court would have its way, attorneys would exist for the welfare of other clients, not clients for the enrichment of their attorneys.

The heart of this statute was the attorney's oath. "You shall do no falsehood nor consent to any to be done in the court," the wary legislators made him swear,

> and if you know of any to be done you shall give knowledge thereof to the justices of the court, or some of them, that it may be reformed. You shall not wittingly and willingly promote, sue or procure to be sued any false or unlawful suit, nor give aid or consent to the same. You shall delay no man for lucre or malice, but

---

(1933), xxiii–xxvii. [See list of abbreviations at end of essay. — Ed.] A more recent but less enlightening account is Anton-Hermann Chroust, *The Rise of the Legal Profession in America* (Norman, Okla., 1965), I, 55–108, which concentrates overwhelmingly on the seventeenth century without any noticeable effort to understand what the Puritans were trying to do.

[5] *Laws of New Hampshire Including Public and Private Acts and Resolves and the Royal Commissions and Instructions, with Historical and Descriptive Notes, and an Appendix,* ed. A. S. Batchellor (Manchester, N.H., 1904–22), I, 105.

[6] Edward Randolph to John Povey, January 24, 1687/88, in *Edward Randolph; Including his Letters and Official Papers from the New England, Middle, and Southern Colonies in America, with Other Documents Relating Chiefly to the Vacating of the Royal Charter of Massachusetts Bay, 1676–1703,* ed. Robert N. Toppan and A. T. S. Goodrick, in Prince Society, *Publications* (Boston, 1898–1909), IV, 198.

[7] *A & R,* I, 75 (1692–93, c. 33, s. 13), 185 (1694–95, c. 17, s. 3), 287 (1697, c. 9, s. 11), 374 (1699–1700, c. 4, s. 6).

[8] *Ibid.,* 467 (1701–02, c. 7).

you shall use yourselfe in the office of an attorney within the court according to the best of your learning and discretion, and with all good fidelity as well to the court as to your clients. So help you God.

This ill-concealed hostility to the lawyer's profession seems to indicate a Puritan origin for the oath. But in fact the General Court had simply modified the oath prescribed by Dudley fifteen years before,[9] which in turn was a direct copy of the standard English oath adopted in 1403.[10] Prejudice against lawyers was powerful in England too, but there the legal corps was sufficiently entrenched within the social system to thrive despite these obstacles.[11]

This was not so in Massachusetts. An old profession can survive community prejudice far more readily than a new profession can establish itself against the same obstacle. Yet in 1708 the General Court reluctantly acknowledged the importance of an attorney to his client when it forbade anyone to employ more than two attorneys in one case, "that the adverse party may have liberty to retain others of them to assist him, upon his tender of the establish'd fee, which," the legislators added sourly, "they may not refuse." [12]

II

Not surprisingly the provincial bar grew slowly under these accumulated discouragements. Before 1706 three sons of Massachusetts did journey to the Inns of Court to study law, but when they returned to the province they all sought the prestige of the bench rather than the strife of the bar.[13] They knew what were doing. When a gentleman like Charles Story displayed his legal attainments too lavishly before a York County

9 *Laws of New Hampshire*, I, 123–24.

10 Charles Warren, *A History of the American Bar* (Boston, 1911), 26; Chroust, *Rise of the Legal Profession*, I, 85.

11 Under Cromwell the Nomination Parliament undertook to "new model" the law. It hoped, explained one spokesman, to make the laws "easy, plain and short" by reducing them "into the bigness of a pocket book" — roughly what Puritan Massachusetts had already accomplished. Samuel Rawson Gardiner, *History of the Commonwealth and Protectorate, 1649–1656*, new edn. (New York, 1903), II, 302, n. 3. The scheme was never completed. Even the requirements that all court proceedings be in English lapsed with the Restoration, to be revived only in 1730 over the opposition of most judges. Yet despite Puritan prejudice against the legal profession, lawyers rendered considerable service to the Puritan Revolution. See William Haller, *Liberty and Reformation in the Puritan Revolution* (New York, 1955), 69–78.

12 A & R, I, 622 (1708–09, c. 3, s. 2).

13 See generally, E. Alfred Jones, *American Members of the Inns of Court* (London, 1924). The three were Benjamin Lynde, Paul Dudley and William Dudley. Paul Dudley first became attorney general rather than a judge (a position he finally obtained in 1718), but his identification was clearly with the bench rather than the bar even though he occasionally argued important cases as a private attorney.

court, he quickly learned that New England juries had their own standard of legal propriety which made few allowances for the refinements of accurate pleading.[14]

For a generation after the Glorious Revolution, the best trained lawyers in Massachusetts earned their livings primarily from other sources than the actual practice of law. Story soon became provincial secretary of New Hampshire. Paul Dudley returned from the Inner Temple to become attorney general under his father. Benjamin Lynde, a product of the Middle Temple, remained a Salem merchant until appointed to the Superior Court.[15] The obscure but talented Henry Turner of Braintree was primarily an apothecary.[16]

Consequently the regular practice of law fell to a host of "pettifoggers" whose conduct easily confirmed the province's direct fears that life for the lawyers would mean death for the law. In Hampshire County, an ex-tailor, Cornelius Jones, outraged the court with his unmatched talent for postponing the execution of justice.[17] In York County, the few regular attorneys were in some cases barely literate.[18] The apothecary Henry Turner was probably a pettifogger at first who somehow transcended the limitations of his peers.

Lack of numbers among the skilled and lack of skill among the numbers who practiced law left a vacuum which gentlemen amateurs often filled in individual cases, perhaps most often as favors for their friends. A few ministers accepted occasional cases for members of their congregations.[19] Gentlemen such as John Walley or Inferior Court judges, such as Nathaniel Byfield, Elisha Cooke, Jr., or Jonathan Remington, often appeared before provincial courts.[20] Paul Dudley's services, when he was not

[14] *Province and Court Records of Maine*, Vol. IV, ed. Neal W. Allen, Jr. (Portland, 1958), lxiv–lxvi.

[15] Lynde (H.C., 1686); Dudley (H.C., 1690).

[16] Wait Winthrop lists a "Mr. Turner" as his third choice for a lawyer in 1714, behind Paul Dudley and Jonathan Remington. To John Winthrop, May 14, 1714, MHS, *Collections*, 6th ser., V, 293n. This was probably the Henry Turner, "apothecary," who handled five cases before Justice John Quincy on September 16, 1734. Quincy, Braintree Cases, 1716–1758, Quincy Mss (MHS).

[17] George Bliss, *Address to the Members of the Bar of the Counties of Hampshire, Franklin and Hampden, at their annual Meeting at Northampton, September, 1826* (Springfield, 1827), 20–21.

[18] *Province and Court Records of Maine*, IV, ed. Allen, lxiv–lxviii.

[19] E.g., Joseph Lord (H.C., 1691); John Avery (H.C., 1706); and Samuel Phillips (H. C., 1708), who disliked lawyers.

[20] For Walley, see *Boston Gazette*, April 10–17, 1721, p. 4/2. See Byfield's accounts as attorney for Mrs. John Leverett and Mrs. Denison, 1725 to 1727, photostat collection (MHS). Remington (H.C., 1696) and Cooke (H.C., 1697). Cooke frequently defended the timber interests before Byfield's Court of Vice-Admiralty. See Joseph J. Malone, *Pine Trees and Politics: The Naval Stores and Forest Policy in Colonial New England, 1691–1775* (Seattle, 1964), 108.

occupied as attorney general, were frequently requested. Wait Winthrop, at least, considered him the foremost attorney in New England.[21]

Only in the Boston area did standards noticeably improve during the first generation under the new charter, doubtless because the expanding commercial life of the capital created a genuine need for specialized legal talents. One newcomer under Andros, Thomas Newton, had apparently read law in an attorney's office in England. When Boston overthrew Andros, Newton fled to New York where he became crown prosecutor in the notorious Leisler-Milbourne trial of 1691.[22] When Phips and the new charter reached Boston the following spring, Newton hastened back to Massachusetts just in time to display similar talents as prosecutor in the still more notorious witch trials in Salem, arguing successfully for the admission of spectral evidence.[23] Probably realizing that he had no important competition in Boston, he decided to stay, even when his zeal for the Navigation Acts cost him the office of attorney general, which he failed to regain despite persistent efforts.[24] When the New Yorker William Atwood became judge of vice-admiralty in 1701, he appointed Newton his resident deputy in Boston, a post which lasted about a year. Under Dudley, Newton eventually became comptroller of the customs for Boston, but disappointed in his quest for higher office, he joined the Matherian opposition of 1706–1708 until Dudley forced him to an abject apology before the entire Council.[25] During these years he once again displayed his remarkable genius for crushing the rights of the accused through the way he assisted the prosecuting during the Quelch piracy trial of 1705.[26] Yet before his death in 1721 he had accumulated the largest law library in New England.[27]

---

[21] Wait Winthrop to John Winthrop, May 14, 1714, MHS, *Collections*, 6th ser., V (1892), 293n.

[22] For the trial and execution, see Jerome R. Reich, *Jacob Leisler's Rebellion: A Study of Democracy in New York, 1664–1720* (Chicago, 1953), pp. 117–25; and "Records of the Trials of Jacob Leisler and His Associates," ed. Lawrence H. Leder, New York Historical Society, *Quarterly*, XXXVI (1952), 431–57.

[23] Chroust, *The Rise of the Legal Profession in America*, I, 87, and 126. I have found no direct evidence on this point. Chroust provides no source for his statement, but his account of Newton rests heavily on the sketch by Paul M. Hamlin and Charles E. Baker (See below, n. 24), which mentions only spectral evidence and which cites in turn an irrelevant letter by Newton in Charles W. Upham, *Salem Witchcraft* . . . (Boston, 1867), II, 255. Yet the attribution is plausible. Only Newton knew enough law to override the contrary precedents cited by the clergy.

[24] *The Supreme Court of Judicature of the Province of New York, 1691–1704*, ed. Paul M. Hamlin and Charles E. Baker (New York, 1959), III, 143–47 is the best account of Newton's career.

[25] Sewall, *Diary*, II, 202.

[26] See A & R, VIII, 391–93.

[27] Justin Windsor et al., *The Memorial History of Boston Including Suffolk County, Massachusetts. 1638–1880* (Boston, 1882–32), II, 428.

Newton, in short, became the first professional lawyer in Massachusetts simply by default. He constantly sought a better position but could never quite get it. When Paul Dudley returned from England in 1702, Newton was the best attorney in Boston — more of a commentary on Boston than on Newton. His only serious competition came from Anthony Checkley, James Menzies and John Valentine. But Checkley, a native Bostonian who died in 1708, was occupied as attorney general throughout the 1690's.[28] Menzies, brother of the John Menzies who later became judge of vice-admiralty, was a Scottish immigrant on the prowl for a government job. He served Governor Dudley in various capacities in Rhode Island and Connecticut after 1702.[29] In 1705 he provided an able defense for the accused pirate, John Quelch.[30] Apparently he tried without success to build a law practice in New Hampshire under the friendly auspices of Lieutenant-Governor John Usher.[31] Unable to obtain the position he sought, he went back to England in 1708, to return to Boston eight years later as register of his brother's Court of Vice-Admiralty.[32]

Only Valentine joined Newton as a full-time lawyer and even this situation lasted only until Newton once again became a part-time attorney when he finally obtained the comptrollership of the customs. By contrast, New York City, though much smaller than Boston, had eight qualified lawyers in 1702 and gained six more in the next two years.[33]

Like Newton, Valentine was an English immigrant, born in 1653. He probably migrated to Boston with his father, who was admitted a freeman in 1675 but who eventually went back to England.[34] Valentine's early years remain quite obscure. By 1700 he was a common lawyer, which means that he had probably failed in some other occupation, if only because men do not normally change careers in their forties. By Massachu-

---

[28] The fullest account of Checkley is still James Savage, *A Genealogical Dictionary of the First Settlers of New England, Showing Three Generations of Those who Came before May, 1692, on the Basis of Farmer's Register* (Boston, 1860–62), I, 369.

[29] *CSP, Amer.*, 1702, p. 577, No. 935; *ibid.*, pp. 659 (No. 1422), 663–67 (No. 1424).

[30] See *A & R*, VIII, 391–93. He received £20 for his efforts. *Ibid.*, 395, 396.

[31] He had been practicing in New Hampshire at least as early as 1701 and had apparently been in New England since the early 1690's. *Documents and Records relating to the Province of New-Hampshire*, ed. Nathaniel Bouton *et al.* (Manchester, N.H., 1867–1943), II, 517, 551–52, 559, 560; III, 121–23; Usher to the Board of Trade, March 6 and 15, 1707/08, *CSP, Amer.*, 1706–08, 691, 706–7 (Nos. 1381, 1397).

[32] Same to same, March 6, 1707/08, *ibid.*, 691 (No. 1381).

[33] *The Supreme Court of Judicature of the Province of New York*, ed. Hamlin and Baker, I, 108.

[34] Henry Wilder Foote, *Annals of King's Chapel, From the Puritan Age of New England to the Present Day* (Boston, 1882), I, 247–48.

setts standards he became an outstanding lawyer, rising to the office of attorney general in 1718.

As if to confirm their pariah status and Puritan forebodings about the incompatibility of the legal profession with the New England Way, both Newton and Valentine became prominent members of King's Chapel.[35] Checkley too was an Anglican,[36] while Menzies was probably a Presbyterian.[37] Puritans might refuse to profit from disputes within the commonwealth, but outsiders felt no such misgivings. Ominously, Valentine was the first man to work his way into high office through the unholy practice of law. His unbearable haughtiness soon infuriated a Boston town meeting during a heated election.[38] But then, as a wonderful confirmation of all that the province suspected, his suicide in 1724 dramatically demonstrated to wavering Puritans the evils begotten by a life at the bar.[39]

Significantly, every talented attorney in this period — Story, Dudley, Lynde, Checkley, Newton and Valentine — at one time or another held appointive office under the crown. Just as the crown was the primary engine for transforming the court system of New England, so too would it elevate the bench and bar.

III

If Newton and Valentine improved the standards of their profession in Boston, both were dead by 1724, and they had trained no successors. At most they had created a demand for competent attorneys, a demand which still had to be filled from outside. But already another transformation had occurred, a development which was considerably more important for both bench and bar. For only after the training of judges had improved could the standards of the bar rise accordingly. And by 1720 the governors, through a series of intelligent appointments, had transformed the character of the Superior Court.

None of the five original judges of the Superior Court in 1692 had received any formal legal training. During the witch trials, four of them betrayed slight knowledge of the law of evidence and no concern whatever

[35] See *ibid.*, II, 603, 605.

[36] *Ibid.*, I, 89.

[37] His brother John was a Presbyterian who worshipped sometimes with the Anglicans and sometimes with the Congregationalists. *Ibid.*, I, 396.

[38] *Reflections upon Reflections: Or, More News from Robinson Cruso's Island, in a Dialogue Between a Country Representative and a Boston Gentleman, July 12, 1720.* (Boston, 1720), reprinted in *Colonial Currency Reprints*, ed. Andrew McFarland Davis, in Prince Society, *Publications*, II (1911), 115–16, and 123–24n. Valentine, claimed the author, demonstrated to Boston's satisfaction "that Lawyer and Liar are syñonimous Terms." *Ibid.*, 116.

[39] Sewall, *Diary*, III, 330–31; Jeremiah Bumstead's Diary, in *NEHGR*, XV (1861), 200; *BNL*, February 13, 1723/24.

that the court had been illegally constituted from the start.[40] Only Stoughton and Sewall were college graduates. These two, plus Thomas Danforth and John Richards, had all served as magistrates under the first charter, while Wait Winthrop had belonged only to the Dominion Council.

The appointees between 1692 and 1718 were better qualified. Of twelve newcomers, four lacked previous judicial experience, but all four were Harvard graduates. Of the remaining eight, two were Harvard graduates, two had attended Harvard without graduating, three had sat on the county courts for nine to twenty years, and the other had been a Plymouth magistrate from 1684 to 1686.

A standard of apprenticeship was slowly emerging. The ideal, typified by Paul Dudley, was a college graduate with years of legal experience, in his case as attorney general rather than as county judge. Otherwise these two criteria fought each other for predominance. Apparently around 1720 education was more important than experience, marking a sharp change from 1692. The appointment of Addington Davenport in 1715 and Edmund Quincy in 1718, both college graduates with no judicial experience, indicated that the governors would willingly bypass experienced county judges who lacked formal education.

When Samuel Sewall succeeded Wait Winthrop as chief justice in 1718, the Superior Court embarked on a decade of unprecedented stability. No one died or resigned until Sewall retired in 1728. His colleagues included Benjamin Lynde (since 1712) and Paul Dudley (from 1718), both products of the Inns of Court. Because Sewall by 1718 had had twenty-six years in which to master English law on the bench, the three together constituted a well-trained majority for the next ten years.[41] They set a standard of professional competence which the court maintained at least until 1760, when new problems arose.[42] Lynde succeeded Sewall as chief justice in 1728, and Dudley replaced Lynde in 1745. When he died in 1752, his successor was Stephen Sewall, a nephew of Samuel who had used his time as Harvard tutor to study English law in depth. He achieved such renown for his mastery of the subject that Governor Belcher appointed him directly to the Superior Court in 1739.[43]

The quality of associate justices, and also of Inferior Court judges, im-

---

[40] The charter vested the power of creating courts in the General Court, but the court of oyer and terminer which sat at Salem was created by the unilateral action of the governor, Sir William Phips. Thomas Hutchinson, *The History of the Colony and Province of Massachusetts-Bay*, ed. Lawrence Shaw Mayo (Cambridge, Mass., 1936), II, 37.

[41] The fullest study of Sewall is Ola Elizabeth Winslow, *Samuel Sewall of Boston* (New York, 1964), which unfortunately is weak on his judicial career. But see Chp. 9. See also, T. B. Strandness, *Samuel Sewall: A Puritan Portrait* (East Lansing, 1967), 78–94.

[42] See below, section VII.

[43] Stephen Sewall (H.C., 1731).

proved markedly during the same period. Of seventeen appointees to the Superior Court between 1728 and the Revolution, only two, John Cushing II and John Cushing III of Scituate, were not college graduates. But the elder Cushing served twenty-eight years on the Plymouth Inferior Court before his elevation in 1728, and his son spent ten years on the same body before his promotion in 1748. Despite his lack of college training, he displayed a definite familiarity with Coke.[44] After 1748, every appointee to the Superior Court was a Harvard graduate.

But college education was rarely a sufficient qualification after 1728. Of the fifteen college graduates appointed between then and the Revolution, only two, Stephen Sewall and Richard Saltonstall, had not served an apprenticeship on a county court before their elevation, a defect for which only Saltonstall had not compensated. The remaining thirteen plus the two Cushings averaged twelve years of apprenticeship before their elevation to the Superior Court. And of the thirteen judges who sat longer than three years on the Superior Court, five would have done credit to the judiciary anywhere in the Empire.[45]

Simultaneously the third provincial graduate of the Inns of Court, William Dudley, boosted the standards of the Suffolk Common Pleas throughout his sixteen years on the bench.[46] Across the Charles, Jonathan Remington did the same for Middlesex after 1715 until his advancement to the Superior Court in 1733.[47]

During the second generation under the new charter, the hierarchy of courts and judges became firmly established. Increasingly the standard for advancement became both a college education and previous service on the county level. Just as the undistinguished reality of 1692 had yielded to the ideal of Paul Dudley by 1718, so the ideal of 1718 slowly became the distinguished reality of 1760.

IV

Any body of trained judges will make exacting demands upon the bar. In the case of provincial Massachusetts, this response followed quickly. John Read, an ex-clergyman who had already built a considerable practice in Connecticut, moved to Boston around 1720 where he soon stood preeminent in the profession, after the deaths of Newton (1721) and Valentine (1724).[48] Three other newcomers arrived from Britain between 1716

[44] See John Cushing to William Cushing, March 25, 1762, quoted in Clifford K. Shipton, *Biographical Sketches of Those Who Attended Harvard College* . . . (Boston, 1933–   ), XIII, 28.

[45] In the order of their appointment, Jonathan Remington, Stephen Sewall, Benjamin Lynde, Jr., Chambers Russell, and Edmund Trowbridge.

[46] (H.C., 1704).

[47] (H.C., 1696).

[48] Read (H.C., 1697).

and 1730. Two possessed thorough legal training, Robert Auchmuty at the Middle Temple and William Shirley at the Inner Temple.[49] Auchmuty arrived with Governor Shute in November 1716, and within a few months he passed "with all to be very able in his profession &c." [50] He apparently inaugurated the practice of accepting understudies in his office, for within a decade he had trained another British immigrant, William Bollan, who built a considerable practice for himself before Shirley's arrival in 1730.[51] Between them, these four engrossed most of the province's legal business in the Superior Court by the early 1730's.[52]

Together the three Britons conclusively demonstrated that a man could open a spectacular career for himself through the practice of law despite the low fees established by the General Court. Auchmuty became judge of vice-admiralty in 1733. Shirley rose to governor within eleven years of his arrival, and Bollan later retired to a profitable mercantile career in England where he served as provincial agent under his father-in-law, Governor Shirley.

Like Newton and Valentine before them, the newcomers were all Anglicans. Even John Read, originally a Congregationalist minister, became a vestryman in King's Chapel.[53] The lawyers were still outsiders, though not freebooters like Thomas Newton. They still sought government appointments, higher ones than Newton or Valentine had dreamed of. But they were no longer pariahs, and consequently they could menace the New England Way more directly than ever. As Shirley, Auchmuty, and Bollan dramatically proved, the conscientious practice of law was now a highway to royal favor and patronage.

[Accordingly, Massachusetts men began reaching for the opportunities which the new profession offered. In the 1730's, despite the success of the outsiders, the bar still lacked the respectability of the church or the medical profession. This declining social stigma remained powerful enough to deter scions of the provincial elite from a legal career, unless like Jonathan Belcher, Jr., they could attend the Inns of Court, or like

---

[49] Annette Townsend, *The Auchmuty Family of Scotland and America* (New York, 1932), 1–21; John A. Schutz, *William Shirley, King's Governor of Massachusetts* (Chapel Hill, 1961), Chp. 1. Both are sketched in *DAB*.

[50] John Nelson to John Eastwicke, April 20, 1717, *Lloyd Papers* (New-York Historical Society, *Collections*, LIX–LX, 1926–27), I, 215.

[51] See the sketch in *DAB*, which is corrected by Malcolm Freiberg, "William Bollan, Agent of Massachusetts," *More Books*, XXIII (1948), *passim*, especially 44–45.

[52] Of 254 cases in 1734–35, attorneys are listed for 188, and these four men handled a total of 141, doubtless with considerable overlapping. Schutz, *Shirley*, 11, n. 18.

[53] Foote, *King's Chapel*, II, 604, 606.

Stephan Sewall, they could move directly to the bench untainted with an advocate's experience.[54]

Instead those who invaded the new profession came almost exclusively from undistinguished families. Most of their parents expected them to take a quiet pastorate in rural New England, to judge from the number who considered the ministry before veering towards the law.[55] The number of these defectors increased rapidly in the 1730's, declined sharply during the Great Awakening, and then rose steadily from the late 1740's until the Revolution. Occasionally piety had its revenge, as when Joshua Eaton deserted his practice at Worcester in 1743, denounced the whole profession as a snare to the godly, and became a New Light preacher.[56] Even in John Adam's day, the choice between ministry and bar was quite agonizing.[57] But significantly, more and more youths somehow wrestled their Puritan consciences into the law at the expense of the church, rather than the other way around. In the concrete sense of young men choosing what to do with their lives, the rise of the bar was the secular counterpart for the decline of the New England Way.

The prototype of these young adventurers was Jeremiah Gridley who, after graduating from Harvard, dabbled with school teaching, theology, and journalism before concentrating his great mental powers upon the law.[58] He was still sufficiently orthodox to become a founder of Boston's West Church in 1737, but he reacted strongly against the Great Awakening a few years later. In 1748 he joined St. John's Lodge in Boston, and seven years later he was elected Grand Master of the Masons of North

[54] Belcher (H.C., 1728), who never returned to New England to practice; Sewall (H.C., 1731).

[55] For example, among the eleven Harvard graduates between 1731 and 1735 who eventually became lawyers, the choice of a legal career was for eight of them a negative response to a career in the church. Six (Henry Hale, 1731; William Skinner, 1731; Timothy Ruggles, 1732; Joshua Eaton, 1735; Oliver Fletcher, 1735; Samuel Swift, 1735) contemplated the ministry before switching to law. One (Otis Little, 1731) became an Anglican a few years after graduation, and another (Thomas Ward, 1733) was already a Rhode Island Baptist. A ninth graduate (David Gorham, 1733) defended a theological thesis for his master's degree, a normal sign that one was studying for the ministry. But apparently he had planned a business career from the start. Of the remaining two, Samuel White (1731) switched from medicine, but apparently Daniel Lewis (1734) had preferred the law all the time, for he defended a legal master's thesis. On the other hand, even if he had contemplated the ministry as an undergraduate, the records would not show it. Statistics about defection from the ministry probably reveal a minimum, not a maximum.

[56] (H.C., 1735).

[57] A check of Yale graduates in the 1750's shows that many lawyers originally planned a ministerial career.

[58] (H.C., 1725).

America, an organization which strongly attracted irreligious artisans, such as young Benjamin Franklin. Although Gridley maintained his membership in the Congregational Church, his death in 1767 prompted scandalous rumors among both New Lights and Old Lights about the lack of piety with which he faced his Maker.[59]

Gridley began to practice law in the mid-1730's. After Shirley and Auchmuty abandoned the profession for more lucrative appointments, he had no peer at the bar. In the next generation a parade of legal luminaries emerged from a period of tutelage in his Boston office. Gridley trained Benjamin Prat, who eventually became chief justice of New York. He drilled the elder Oxenbridge Thacher, the younger James Otis and William Cushing, one of the original appointees to the United States Supreme Court. To John Adams, who had done his legal apprenticeship at Worcester, Gridley gave the run of his library and a store of free advice.[60]

During these years Gridley's main competitor was Edmund Trowbridge, also of humble parentage, though a Cambridge Goffe by adoption.[61] Unlike Gridley, Trowbridge apparently planned a legal career from his college days, for he defended a legal thesis for his master's degree at Harvard. Doubtless he realized that legal training would have been quite useful to his foster grandfather, who had squandered the Goffe estate in a storm of ill-conceived litigation. Trowbridge harvested a crop of young attorneys which nearly equalled Gridley's, for it included James Putnam, Francis Dana, Theophilus Parsons, Rufus King and Harrison Gray Otis.[62]

Soon joining Gridley and Trowbridge at the Boston bar were two other bright young men, Benjamin Kent and Benjamin Prat. Kent turned to the law only after a spectacular heresy trial which prompted his dismissal from his Marlborough pastorate in 1735.[63] At about the same time, Prat, physically deformed through a childhood accident, accepted a Hopkins scholarship at Harvard to prepare for the ministry. He not only lost interest in his original calling, but eventually he became an open skeptic.[64]

[59] For the New Light rumors, see John Adams, *Diary and Autobiography of John Adams,* ed. Lyman Butterfield (Cambridge, Mass., 1961), II, 38. For the Old Light version, see Charles Chauncy to Ezra Stiles, September 26, 1767, *Extracts from the Itineraries and other Miscellanies of Ezra Stiles, D.D., LL.D., 1755–1794, with a Selection from his Correspondence,* ed. Franklin B. Dexter (New Haven, 1916), pp. 443–45.

[60] Prat (H.C., 1737); Otis (H.C., 1743); Thacher (H.C., 1738); and Cushing (H.C., 1751). See also, Adams *Diary,* ed. Butterfield, I, 54–55, 56, 199; III, 270–73.

[61] (H.C., 1728).

[62] Putnam (H.C., 1746); Dana (H.C., 1762); Parsons (H.C., 1769); King (H.C., 1777); and Otis (H.C., 1783). For brief sketches of the last four, see *DAB.*

[63] Kent (H.C., 1727). Cf., Conrad Wright, *The Beginnings of Unitarianism in America* (Boston, 1955), 22–23.

[64] Prat (H.C., 1737).

His scoffing at the afterlife infuriated young John Adams almost as much as did Kent's frivolous mockery of religious conviction, denominational loyalty, and popular education — all that New England cherished most.[65] Significantly, Kent carried this light-hearted attitude into King's Chapel.

Rightly suspicious of this heterodox quartet, Massachusetts reluctantly accepted them anyway. Trowbridge, the most respectable of the four, eventually became an associate justice of the Superior Court. Between 1757 and 1759, Prat became the first professional lawyer to serve more than one term in the House of Representatives for Boston before he moved on to the chief-justiceship of New York Province. In 1755 Gridley finally won election to the house from Brookline, serving four terms before his death. Only Kent, the arch-heretic, escaped high office until the Revolution, when for a brief period he served as attorney general.

The arrival of these four men marked the permanent establishment of the legal profession in Massachusetts. The province needed lawyers regardless of their social and religious disqualifications. By 1740, the New England Way was directly threatened by the old English lawyers it once had tried to ban entirely.

V

Of course not everyone succeeded who ventured into the law. Those who sought careers outside Boston still confronted serious obstacles. Some either went bankrupt, like Jonathan Loring at Marlborough, or took to drink, like John Sparhawk at Plymouth.[66] A number turned to soldiering when the French wars seemed to provide wider opportunities.[67] Still others continued the old practice of augmenting their income by adding a sideline — a government office when they could get one, or perhaps school teaching or even tavern keeping when they could not.[68] But a growing number in the out-towns, like John Chipman at Marblehead, found their profession adequate to their needs, if not lucrative. Undoubtedly they took increasing comfort in the growing prestige which the bar was wringing from a hostile community.[69]

By 1750 the nucleus of a bar existed in every county in the province, except on the islands of Nantucket and Martha's Vineyard. Everywhere the impetus had come from Harvard, except in Hampshire where Yale's

[65] Adams, *Diary*, ed. Butterfield, I, 152–53, 346–47; II, 50.
[66] Loring (H.C., 1738); Sparhawk (H.C., 1723).
[67] Peter Prescott (H.C., 1730); Otis Little (H.C., 1731); Timothy Ruggles (H.C., 1732).
[68] John Sturgis (H.C., 1723); Robert Eliot Gerrish (H.C., 1730); Daniel Lewis (H.C., 1734); Timothy Ruggles (H.C., 1732); Oliver Fletcher (H.C., 1735).
[69] Chipman (H.C., 1738). For an example of this continuing prejudice, see *The Lawyer's Pedigree* (Boston, 1755), which nicely blends the anti-papal, anti-prelatical and anti-lawyer biases into one ballad.

Phineas Lyman opened an office in Suffield.[70] Before that town seceded to Connecticut in 1749, he trained two other Yale graduates, John Worthington of Springfield and Joseph Hawley of Northampton.[71] In succeeding years these two, both of whom collected respectable law libraries, received into their studies a widening stream of graduates, mostly from Yale, and sprinkled them throughout the towns of Berkshire, Hampshire and even Worcester counties.[72]

Everywhere the story was similar. From Kittery in Maine to Barnstable on Cape Cod, midst the commercial breezes of Boston, Charlestown and Salem or the lordly air breathed by the Connecticut "river gods," a strange new man, the lawyer, had convinced the community that it needed his services and that he should have its respect.

[Unlike their predecessors in the era of Newton and Valentine, the generation of Auchmuty, Gridley, Trowbridge and Lyman made careful provision for the future. By the 1740's a college education and several years of apprenticeship in the office of an established attorney, if not yet mandatory requirements, were rapidly becoming normal procedure for the practice of law.] Newton and Valentine had nearly carried the profession off with them when they died. No similar danger remained by 1750.

If this achievement was impressive, the steady advance of the next twenty years was phenomenal. The Harvard and Yale classes of 1730 through 1738 contributed seventeen lawyers to Massachusetts. The next nine classes, piously seduced by the Great Awakening, added only nine. But beginning with the class of 1748, the number of graduates who entered the law increased with each three-year period through 1765, reaching a peak of twenty in the last three years alone. The pace definitely slackened in the next four years and then fell off altogether as the Revolution approached. Yet if the two colleges had produced fifty-one Massachusetts lawyers between 1730 and 1759, they added at least fifty more in the next ten years alone. By 1770 the cycle was complete. Only one Yale and two Harvard graduates in that year became Massachusetts lawyers. The disruption of royal government, the Toryism of many lawyers and the closure of the courts for long periods during the Revolution made a legal career inordinately hazardous until the restoration of peace permitted renewed growth in the 1780's.[73]

Just before the collapse of royal government in 1774, perhaps eighty to ninety lawyers were practicing in Massachusetts. At the same date, the

---

[70] (Y.C., 1738). Apparently the first lawyer on Martha's Vineyard was Jonathan Allen (H.C., 1757), and he did not practice full-time.

[71] Worthington (Y.C., 1740); Hawley (Y.C., 1742). Cf., E. Francis Brown, "The Law Career of Major Joseph Hawley," *NEQ*, IV (1931), 482–508.

[72] See Bliss, *Address to the Hampshire Bar*, 34–39.

[73] See Section IX.

province had about four hundred Congregational clergymen.[74] In other words, the legal profession had grown to a fifth the size of the established ministry, whereas even a generation earlier any comparison between the two would have been ludicrous. Right down to independence and beyond, English law continued to erode the New England Way. The men who practiced it for a living rejected the ministry and flirted with Anglicanism, or worse still, with deism and skepticism.[75]

VI

Yet size alone barely illustrates the remarkable growth which the bar experienced in the generation before independence. Perhaps even more important were its expanding prestige and its increasing solidarity.

No longer did leading families spurn the profession. James Otis, Jr., sporting one of the most illustrious pedigrees from old Plymouth Colony, began to practice in 1748.[76] He was soon followed by William Pynchon, William Cushing, Abel Willard, Pelham Winslow, the Bristol County Leonards, the Worcester Chandlers, and even a Dudley, a Sewall, two Quincys, and an Oliver.[77] Doubtless a few, such as Jonathan Sewall, hoped to recoup the sliding fortunes of their families through the practice of law, which by 1750 was yielding about £750 per annum to a man like

---

[74] The figures for attorneys are minimal. By another method, I get a total of about one hundred. After computing the ratio between barristers and attorneys in the five counties for which I have complete information (Suffolk, Hampshire, Worcester, Berkshire and York), I have projected it against the number of barristers in the remaining five counties (Essex, Middlesex, Plymouth, Barnstable and Bristol) to obtain a rough idea of the number of attorneys. But even by raw count, I get over eighty practicing lawyers on the eve of independence.

[75] See Edmund S. Morgan, *The Gentle Puritan: A Life of Ezra Stiles, 1727–1795* (New Haven, 1962), pp. 93, 113, 414–15.

[76] An outstanding study is John J. Waters, Jr., *The Otis Family in Provincial and Revolutionary, Massachusetts* (Chapel Hill, 1968), esp. 61–161. See also Otis (H.C., 1743) for Shipton's unsympathetic sketch which offsets William Tudor's *The Life of James Otis of Massachusetts* (Boston, 1823). See also, Ellen E. Brennan, "James Otis: Recreant and Patriot," *NEQ.* XII (1939), 691–725. Otis's grandfather and great-grandfather had served a total of thirty-one terms on the Council between 1708 and 1756. His father, James, Sr., would be elected for the first of thirteen times (to be negatived four times) in 1762. In the three counties of old Plymouth Colony, only John Cushing II and John Cushing III had done better. They amassed fifty-one terms between them and both sat on the Superior Court, while their Boston cousins frequently won election to both houses after 1720.

[77] Pynchon (H.C., 1743); Cushing (H.C., 1751); Willard (H.C., 1752); Winslow (H.C., 1753); George Leonard (H.C., 1748); Daniel Leonard (H.C., 1760); Rufus Chandler (H.C., 1766); Jonathan Sewall (H.C., 1748); Samuel Sewell (H.C., 1761); Samuel Quincy (H.C., 1754); Daniel Oliver (H.C., 1762). On the Chandlers and Leonards, see Adams, *Diary*, ed. Butterfield, I, 2n, 227.

Benjamin Prat.[78] Some, like Daniel Oliver, probably considered the bar as a step to public office.[79] Still others must have hoped to rise through the bar to the bench itself. Several discovered that the legal profession could vault them from the aristocracy of a small rural town to the highest social circles of the seaboard. Thus James Otis, Jr., jumped from Barnstable to Boston, and William Pynchon moved from Springfield to Salem.[80]

There were other signs of creeping respectability. Before 1730, many gentlemen felt qualified to practice law on the side without bothering to study it. A generation later, gentlemen were beginning to study it with no intention of practicing it.[81] And if Gridley's contemporaries finally attained public office in their old age, their successors did much better. Most of them received commissions as justices of the peace, unless the governor distrusted their politics. Many of them moved quickly into the house. In 1748, Worthington began his first of twenty terms in the house for Springfield, and Hawley began his first of twelve for Northampton in 1754. Chambers Russell won election for three different towns, including commercial Charlestown.[82] Timothy Ruggles, after serving a term for Rochester in 1736, won election for Hardwicke in 1754 and served fourteen more terms through 1770.

Boston remained a tougher problem. It had elected John Read for a single term in 1738, but then it returned no lawyers to any of its four seats for nearly twenty years, even though the best lawyers in the province practiced in the capital. Then Boston elected Prat for three consecutive terms beginning in 1757. In 1761, James Otis, Jr., won his first of ten elections. Oxenbridge Thacher came next in 1763 and was followed by John Adams in 1765.

Significantly, Read, Prat, Otis and Adams were all outsiders from country towns, crashing the preserve of the Hutchinsons, Cushings and Hancocks. Only Thacher was a native Bostonian whose father had also

[78] Shipton, *Harvard Graduates*, X, 229, citing *Herald of Freedom*, February 2, 1790, 1/1.

[79] H.C., 1762. See E. Alfred Jones, *The Loyalists of Massachusetts, Their Memorials, Petitions and Claims* (London, 1930), 222; James H. Stark, *The Loyalists of Massachusetts and the Other Side of the American Revolution* (Boston, 1907), 189–90. Daniel was the son of Lieutenant-Governor (formerly Secretary) Andrew Oliver (H.C., 1724), and the nephew of Chief Justice Peter Oliver (H.C., 1730).

[80] Pynchon (H.C., 1743). Undoubtedly the move was more important for Otis than for Pynchon.

[81] E.g., Royall Tyler (H.C., 1743); Thomas Oliver (H.C., 1753); William Browne (H.C., 1775).

[82] Russell sat in the house for Concord (1740), for Charlestown (1744–45), for Concord again (1750–52), and for Lincoln (1754–57, 1761, 1763–65). He also sat on the Council for two terms (1759–60).

sat in the house. If Boston would not provide native lawyers for the voters, the voters would find their own lawyers for Boston.

This movement of lawyers into politics was a significant event in itself, and it occurred within a remarkably short period, roughly the ten years after 1754. In that decade the lawyers appeared in force from country towns, conquered Boston, and even moved near the pinnacle of provincial politics. Between 1759 and 1765, the house elected three different Speakers — all of them lawyers — before Thomas Cushing III returned the office to his own family. Two years later Governor Bernard promoted the second Massachusetts-trained lawyer to the Superior Court, a trend which within twenty years would be a fixed rule.[83] In other words, the domination of local politics by lawyers had its beginnings, at least in Massachusetts, less than a generation before the Revolution, which lawyers would largely shape and define.

When Gridley and Trowbridge turned to the law in the 1730's, they had only the example of a few British immigrants to follow, and they could hardly have predicted the degree of success awaiting them or the social precedents they would set. But by 1760 their example was available to everyone else. One acute observer, a young Harvard graduate, brought together all the contradictory tensions, anxieties and aspirations which for a whole generation had been propelling men into the law. After finishing college, he taught school and studied for the ministry. "Let us look upon a lawyer," he wrote contemptuously to a friend in early 1756:

> In the beginning of life we see him fumbling and raking amidst the rubbish of writs, indictments, pleas, ejectments, enfiefed, illatebration and one thousand other *lignum vitae* words which have neither harmony nor meaning. When he gets into business, he often foments more quarrels than he composes, and enriches himself at the expense of impoverishing others more honest and deserving than himself.

After this eloquent distillation of a century of New England prejudice against lawyers, his conclusion was obvious, for "the noise and fume of Courts and the labour of inquiring into and pleading dry and difficult cases have very few charms in my eyes." [84]

But was it that simple? Not in 1756. "I now resolve for the future,"

---

[83] The first was Chambers Russell in 1752, and the second was Edmund Trowbridge in 1767. Between 1783 and 1824, only two nonlawyers were appointed to the court. William Sullivan, *An Address to the Members of the Bar of Suffolk, Mass. at their stated Meeting on the First Tuesday of March, 1824* (Boston, 1825), 41–42.

[84] Quoted in Warren, *A History of the American Bar*, 79–80.

this same young man promised himself that summer, "never to say an ill naturd Thing, concerning Ministers or the ministerial Profession, never to say an envious Thing concerning Governors, Judges, Ministers, Clerks, Sheriffs, Lawyers, or any other honorable or Lucrative offices or officers." A month later he decided differently and contracted to study law in Worcester. "My Inclination I think was to preach," he pondered intro-spectively. "However that would not do. But [now] I set out with firm Resolutions I think never to commit any meanness or injustice in the Practice of Law. The Study and Practice of Law," he had to assure him-self, "does not dissolve the obligations of morality or of Religion. And altho the Reason of my quitting Divinity was my Opinion concerning some disputed Points," he finally admitted, "I hope I shall not give reason of offense to any in that Profession by imprudent Warmth." Yet only a few months later he asserted that most sermons make "no sense at all." By comparison, "How greatly elevated, above common People, and above Divines is this Lawyer," he announced after listening to Benjamin Prat. Finally in the summer of 1759 he acknowledged his lifetime goal — "to make a figure to be useful, and respectable" as a provincial lawyer.

This agonizing rejection of New England churches in favor of English law did not drive this man towards a royal governorship or even towards Toryism. Instead it vaulted John Adams towards the presidency of the United States. He too had to become painfully more English before he could help to create a new American nation.[85]

Even if the growing respectability of the law attracted an increasing number of men from the provincial elite, the profession still remained an avenue of upward mobility for less exalted individuals. Adams craved fame, integrity and respectability, and he won more than he ever sought. He was not alone. Thanks to the Revolution, others such as John Lowell, Timothy Pickering, Theodore Sedgwick and Theophilus Parsons could soar to the top, not simply of a small province within an enormous Em-pire, but of an entire new nation which needed their specialized talents and which gladly paid them the social respect for which they all yearned. Ironically, without the assistance of English courts and English law, they would never have been equipped for their role.[86]

VII

Soon the bar demonstrated that its growing self-consciousness would keep pace with its heightened prestige. With no difficulty at all, it found two targets against which to uncoil the taut spring of its adolescent pride. First it challenged the bench itself. Then it assaulted the amorphous band of

[85] Adams, *Diary*, ed. Butterfield, I, 37, 42–43, 73, 107.
[86] Lowell (H.C., 1760); Pickering (H.C., 1763); Sedgwick (Y.C., 1765). For sketches, see *DAB*.

"pettifoggers" or semi-professionals who in earlier days had swarmed into the void created by the lack of trained attorneys.

If the original impetus to a trained bar had come from a highly qualified bench, by 1760 the lawyers had clearly outstripped the judges. By 1730 the judges had evolved fairly rigid requirements of education and experience. Thirty years later the bar had done the same with one major improvement. A lawyer's education, unlike a judge's, included the intensive and systematic study of the law itself. Consequently many lawyers knew a good deal more than some judges about English law, and they betrayed no embarrassment in revealing this fact to the public. The occasion for an open dispute arose when Chief Justice Stephen Sewall died in September 1760, leaving to the new provincial governor, Francis Bernard, the delicate task of appointing a successor.

From the arrival of the second charter until 1760, every chief justice of the Superior Court had come from a leading provincial family. But beginning with the appointment of Samuel Sewall in 1718, each chief justice could also claim a college education, a thorough grounding in the law, and a lengthy apprenticeship as associate justice. Of the current associate justices, only Benjamin Lynde II of Salem possessed all the requirements. A Harvard graduate, the son of a chief justice, and an associate justice himself for fourteen years, he was the obvious choice. Among the other judges, only Chambers Russell could have mustered serious pretensions to the office, but apparently no one thought of him anyway. The Russells of Charlestown hardly compared with the Sewalls, the Lyndes or the Hutchinsons in the social hierarchy of the province.

The bar expected Lynde's advancement, but if Bernard ever offered him the post — and there is no evidence that he did — the judge declined. Lynde was a political supporter of Lieutenant-Governor Thomas Hutchinson who desired the office for himself because, as he put it, the chief justiceship "was an employment which nothing but a diffidence of his qualifications for it would render unwelcome to him." [87] While Hutchinson wrestled successfully with these scruples, the governor did nothing for weeks. His hesitation threw the whole question wide open.

Or so people thought. Two men benignly offered their services, not necessarily as chief justice, but at least as associate justice should anyone on the court be prompted to the first position. One, General William Brattle of Cambridge, was an eccentric semi-professional soldier, physician, attorney and county judge who possessed both the necessary lineage and the Harvard degrees, but not much legal experience. The other, James Otis, Sr., was a competent attorney with a large practice in Barnstable County who had been promised a position on the court by Governor Shir-

---

[87] Peter Orlando Hutchinson, *The Diary and Letters of His Excellency Thomas Hutchinson, Esq. . . . .* (London, 1883–86), I, 64–66.

ley. But if he could claim adequate legal experience for promotion to the court, he lacked a liberal education. Doubtless he considered his ancestry as illustrious as Hutchinson's, but on this point he encountered the inveterate Massachusetts prejudice against Plymouth families.[88] None of the leading members of the bar — Gridley, Trowbridge, Prat, Kent and Thacher — had the family qualifications, except possibly Trowbridge who had been adopted by a Goffe. On the other hand, the attorneys who did have the necessary pedigree were all far too young for the position.

Recognizing a dismal problem, Bernard found an appropriately dismal solution. To the chief justiceship he appointed Hutchinson, whose family was perhaps the most exalted in the province and whose education included both Harvard degrees. But his judicial experience above the level of probate judge consisted of only six years on the Suffolk Inferior Court, and he had never made any attempt to practice law. While either Brattle or Otis would have settled for an associate justiceship, Hutchinson would not, lest the lieutenant-governor be outranked on the court on which he sat.[89]

Hutchinson placidly violated two venerable traditions. He became the first person in nearly sixty years to move directly into the chief justiceship without any previous service on the court. And he became the first lieutenant-governor since William Stoughton to sit on the bench at all. Stoughton, at least, had possessed two plausible excuses. He had been ranking associate justice under Andros and was the logical choice for promotion to the chief justiceship in 1692. Second, his two offices had not accumulated separate traditions at the time of his appointment.

In other words, Hutchinson's political aspirations had blocked Lynde to create the problem in the first place. Bernard then had to choose between insulting the best provincial families or the provincial bar. He selected the bar, though apparently with the backing of some of its older members.[90]

If the unconcealed wrath of Brattle and the Otises drew its vigor from disappointed ambition, their charge of office-grabbing and nepotism had one redeeming element: it was true.[91] It also gave the younger members

[88] See Clifford K. Shipton, "Yᵉ Mystery of Yᵉ Ages Solved, or, how Placing Worked at Colonial Harvard & Yale," *Harvard Alumni Bulletin*, LVII (1954–55), 262–63. For the Otis family in particular, see above, n. 76.

[89] Hutchinson (H.C., 1727). For a near contemporary analysis of this struggle, see Edmund Trowbridge to William Bollan, July 15, 1762, MHS, *Collections*, LXXIV (1918), 66. A recent analysis by John J. Waters, Jr., and John A. Schutz reaches many of the conclusions suggested above. See their "Patterns of Massachusetts Colonial Politics: the Writs of Assistance and the Rivalry between the Otis and Hutchinson Families," *WMQ*, 3rd Ser., XXIV (1967), 543–67.

[90] So Hutchinson claimed, at any rate. Hutchinson, *History*, ed. Mayo, III, 63.

[91] See generally, Ellen E. Brennan, *Plural Office-Holding in Massachusetts*,

of the bar a splendid occasion to display their exuberant self-confidence. If "the Superior Court could not be tolerably filled by any Gentleman from the Bar, or elsewhere, without [Hutchinson's condescending] . . . to take upon him the Office of Chief Justice, in Addition to the Rest of his lucrative Places," snarled the younger Otis, "he is highly to be praised for his disinterested Benevolence to an otherwise sinking Province." [92] Take "all the superiour Judges and every Inferiour Judge in the Province, and put them all together," he told the House in one fiery speech, "and they would not make one half of a Common Lawyer." [93] John Adams decided that this claim was quite excessive, but he also drafted an essay which he never published, setting forth the need of all judges for rigorous legal training.[94] Joseph Hawley and Oxenbridge Thacher both joined the assault.[95] Naturally the government resisted these attacks. "How can the Bar expect Protection from the Court," complained Judge Peter Oliver to John Adams, "if the Bar endeavours to bring the Court into Contempt[?]" [96]

Announcing that he "would set the Province in a flame," the younger Otis went into systematic opposition with his father, then Speaker of the House, and General Brattle, then a member of the Council. For the next five years they kept Boston in an uproar and the House almost evenly divided.[97]

Thus began the famous "opening round of the Revolution" — a demand, not to get out of the empire, but to get into one of its highest offices.

1760–1780 (Chapel Hill, 1945). Hutchinson was related by marriage to Andrew Oliver (H.C., 1724), who was Province Secretary, and to Andrew's brother Peter (H.C., 1730), who was already an associate justice of the Superior Court. Hutchinson himself combined more offices than anyone else in the province. He was simultaneously lieutenant-governor, chief justice, councillor, and judge of probate for Suffolk County. Professor Shipton in his sketch of Hutchinson (H.C., 1727) tries to refute the charges of office-grabbing, but he is not very successful. Plural office-holding and family alliances were both established practices, he argues. Many lieutenant-governors had also been chief justices, he asserts, citing Stoughton's example which, in fact, was unique. Shipton also insists that Hutchinson retained his office as probate judge for philanthropic reasons whereas Hutchinson himself acknowledged the importance of the income he derived from that post. See Bernhard Knollenberg's review of Shipton, in *WMQ*, 3rd Ser., X (1953), at 118.

[92] *Boston Gazatte*, April 4, 1763, 1/1.

[93] Adams, *Diary*, ed. Butterfield, I, 225.

[94] *Ibid*., pp. 225, 167–68.

[95] *Peter Oliver's Origin & Progress of the American Rebellion; A Tory View*, ed. Douglass Adair and John A. Schutz (San Marino, 1961), 28–29; Brennan, *Plural Office-Holding*, 41–47.

[96] Adams, *Diary*, ed. Butterfield, I, 225.

[97] Still the fullest account of this struggle is John C. Miller, *Sam Adams, Pioneer in Propaganda* (Boston, 1936), Chp. 2.

VIII

[The fight over the chief justiceship seriously divided bench and bar. Hutchinson badly needed some issue which would reunite both groups under his own leadership. He soon found an appropriate victim in the pettifoggers still loitering on the fringes of the legal profession].

Until mid-century, many persons with no college education or formal apprenticeship had sought legal careers. Some, like the elder James Otis or Elisha Bisby of Pembroke, had won their positions early enough to escape the coming wrath of the professionals.[98] After 1750 such success was extremely rare. It might come to a talented person willing to build his practice in an obscure corner of the province, like James Sullivan in Maine.[99] Or it might flow to someone of incredible dexterity, like Captain Ebenezer Thayer of Braintree. John Adams ransacked his vocabulary in vain search of appellations sufficiently dishonorable to epitomize his townsman, Thayer. Bankruptcy had rewarded the other three Braintree residents who had foully sought to better themselves through pettifoggery, noted Adams with glee, and he lamented that no similar fate would overtake Thayer, who had assured himself of ample routine business from people who could suppy it.[100]

Had the pettifoggers encountered no enemy more dangerous than the spleen of Adams, they might have continued to thrive. Not Adams, but Chief Justice Hutchinson decreed otherwise, for he desperately needed the support of the bar. [In 1762 Hutchinson decided to cloak the entire profession in exterior dignity by requiring distinct gowns for judges, barristers and attorneys.[101] He also decided to give substance to these different ranks by importing their English prototypes]. The lawyers en-

[98] For Otis, Sr. (1702–78), see Waters, *Otis Family*, 61–109. Bisby (or Bisbee) was a self-trained lawyer who practiced in Plymouth, Suffolk, and Worcester counties. He was the first lawyer to win regular election to the house, sitting for twelve of the fourteen terms between 1725 and 1736, when he withdrew in mid-year because of ill health. He was succeeded by Daniel Lewis (H.C., 1734), a lawyer whom he had trained. Little else survives in print about Bisby, known to folklore as "the honest lawyer," save that he speculated in Maine lands and died in 1737. See *NEHGR*, X (1856), 65; XVII (1863), 164; L (1896), 192; and, IV (1850), 99. See also, *JHR*, XIV, 64, 79; and Joseph Willard, *An Address to the Members of the Bar of Worcester County, Massachusetts, October 2, 1829* (Lancaster, 1830), 42.

[99] See *DAB*.

[100] Adams, *Diary*, ed. Butterfield, I, 71, 132–33, 135–58. The Thayers, father and son, won uninterrupted election to the house from Braintree between 1760 and 1774. In 1761 Adams drafted a letter to the newspapers, which he never published, outlining his own version of how the elder Thayer managed to get elected, chiefly by courting the tavern interest. *Ibid.*, 205–06.

[101] The regulations went into effect in August term, 1762. Josiah Quincy, *Reports of Cases Argued and Adjudged in the Superior Court of Judicature of the Province of Massachusetts Bay between 1761 and 1772* . . . , ed. Samuel M. Quincy (Boston, 1865), 35.

thusiastically joined the campaign. Even in the 1750's, the county bar had assumed the right to recommend new attorneys to the court.[102] Now in each county the lawyers organized a formal bar association which promptly accepted the English ranking system by establishing minimum requirements for attorneys and barristers.

According to the new standards, a man needed a liberal arts education or its equivalent and three years' apprenticeship with a recognized barrister before he could ask the bar to recommend him to the county court as an attorney. Even then he could practice only in the Inferior Court for the next two years, after which, again subject to the recommendation of the bar, he could be promoted to attorney in the Superior Court. Finally after two more years he could be raised to barrister, the only rank entitled to plead before the Superior Court.[103] The title of barrister might have been used occasionally in Massachusetts as early as 1700, but never before had its privileges been rigorously defined.[104]

[Mere precautions against future pettifoggers were insufficient. The bar took deliberate action against all lingering examples of this species when it resolved that its members would not participate in any case which a non-member presumed to bring before the court.[105]

Discounting the antecedents of the 1750's, these regulations originated with the Suffolk bar around 1763.[106] Essex formally adopted them in 1767.[107] They were then re-enacted with several amendments by the re-

---

[102] Note the procedure when John Adams was admitted in 1758, *Diary*, ed. Butterfield, I, 54, 58–59.

[103] See John Adams's "Record-Book of the Suffolk Bar," MHS, *Proceedings*, XIX (1881–82), 150.

[104] Massachusetts lore credits the title to Thomas Newton around 1700, but I have found no contemporary evidence supporting the claim, nor have Paul Hamlin and Charles Baker, *The Supreme Court of Judicature of the Province of New York, 1691–1704*, III, 143–47.

[105] The bar adopted four rules aimed at excluding pettifoggers and offered them to the court in February 1763. But the younger Otis opposed the rules so vehemently that the court postponed the matter until April, when presumably they were adopted, to judge from subsequent practice. The bar was enraged with Otis. "He made the Motion at first to get some of these Under strappers into his service," charged Adams. "He could not bear that Q[uincy] and Auch[muty] should have Underworkers and he none. And he objected to the Rules, to save his Popularity, with the Constables, Justices Story and Rudock &c. and Pettyfoggers of the Town, and with the Pettyfoggers that he uses as Tools and Mirmidons in the House." Adams, *Diary*, ed. Butterfield, I, 235–36.

[106] *Ibid.*, 235–36. Possibly Suffolk had a still earlier set of rules. In 1757 the Worcester Inferior Court, rather than the bar, adopted a rule limiting who could appear before it as an attorney. Worcester was not likely to take the lead in this matter and could well have been following Suffolk's example. Willard, *Address to the Worcester Bar*, 41.

[107] For the Essex bar, see William D. Northend, "Address before the Essex Bar Association," *EIHC*, XXII (1885), 161–76; XXIII (1886), 17–35; and also Northend and Edward P. George, *Memorials of the Essex Bar Association and*

constituted Suffolk Bar Association in 1770, by which time they had been dispersed to the out-counties.[108] The records of these other associations have not survived, but an analysis of the men practicing there in the fifteen years before independence indicates that similar rules must have been in force everywhere.

And indeed, the rules were enforced. In this period the Suffolk Bar flatly rejected the only applicant who lacked a college education.[109] Even college graduates had to seek the bar's permission before they could begin to study with a barrister. Apparently promotion was not automatic, either. Just before independence, the bar contained forty-six barristers and perhaps forty or more attorneys. Obviously some of the attorneys had served their minimal period without being promoted.[110]

These accumulated developments consciously and effectively shaped the bar along English lines. At the top of the profession stood the judges, corresponding to their English counterparts but lacking the additional title of "sergeant-at-law." [111] Next came the barristers and then the attorneys,

---

Brief Biographical Notices of Some of the Distinguished Members of the Essex Bar prior to the Formation of the Association (Salem, 1900). Neither work equals Bliss for Hampshire and Berkshire or Willard for Worcester. For the Essex rules of 1768, see "Record-Book of the Suffolk Bar," 146–47, 149–50.

108 *Ibid.*, 149–50. For Hampshire County, see Bliss, *Address to the Hampshire Bar*, 23–28.

109 William Lithgow, July 1772. "Record-Book of the Suffolk Bar," 150–51. After 1762 two persons who lacked college degrees were created barristers. One was Andrew Cazneau of Boston (1738–92), son of a Boston taverner. Boston Record Commission, *Report*, XXIV, 232, 241; XX, 251. Possibly he was educated in some college outside New England, or perhaps he won an exemption from the rules. In any case he had probably begun to practice before 1763 when the bar rules went into effect, for he was admitted as an attorney before the Superior Court in 1765 and as a barrister two years later. The other exception was James Sullivan in Maine, a remote area with few lawyers and few college graduates.

110 David Gorman (H.C., 1733); Oliver Fletcher (H.C., 1735); Samuel Sewall (H.C., 1761); Thomas Danforth (H.C., 1762); Jonothan Ashley (Y.C., 1758); Woodbridge Little (Y.C., 1760); David Ingersoll (Y.C., 1761); Samuel Field (Y.C., 1762); William Billings (Y.C., 1765); Apollos Leonard (Y.C., 1765); Timothy Langdon (H.C., 1765). The only attorney recommended by the bar for promotion to barrister whom the Superior Court rejected was Josiah Quincy (H.C., 1763). Because the court's motives were blatantly political, Quincy retaliated by pleading a case before it anyway, thus daring the court to stop him. The court did not dare. Quincy, *Reports*, ed. Quincy, 317.

111 Originally the sergeants were a class of lawyers attached to the Common Pleas from whom all judges were chosen. But by the eighteenth century the title had become honorary, not substantive. Sir William Searle Holdsworth, *A History of English Law* (London, 1903–66), VI, 474–78; Sir William Blackstone, *Commentaries on the Laws of England*, 11th edn. (London, 1791), III, 25–29 (Bk. 3, Chp. 3); Warren, *History of the American Bar*, 23. Thus of the Thirteen Colonies, only New Jersey adopted this rank. *Ibid.*, 113.

two ranks directly imported from the mother country with one significant difference. In Britain these titles denoted permanent ranks within the profession. A man might be either attorney or barrister through his entire career.[112] By contrast the rank of attorney in Massachusetts was a normal first step to the higher rank of barrister, though a permanent corps of attorneys might have been arising by the 1770's. In any case the presumption of mobility still distinguished the province from Great Britain.

A second difference was really a corollary of the first. By the eighteenth century, England had evolved separate methods for training attorneys and barristers. An attorney learned his profession through apprenticeship and was admitted to practice by the courts, but a barrister, who alone could plead in court, studied for three years at one of the Inns and was admitted to practice by the Inn itself. Attorneys were always officers of the courts, but barristers remained members of their Inns.[113]

To some extent, the use of the term "barrister" in Massachusetts reflected a provincial inflation of titles. If Massachusetts barristers copied the function of their English models, they did not undergo the same training. By this standard they were simply attorneys with seven years of apprenticeship instead of three. Their formal education did not differ from that of attorneys, a lack which only the establishment of professional law schools could have remedied. County bar associations did provide inadequate substitutes for the Inns, and Jeremy Gridley created an informal society, the Sodalitas, to promote the professional study of law.[114] But by the time the young republic began to establish law schools in the 1790's, the Revolution had already undercut the ideal of England's privileged, hierarchical bar. Consequently these schools produced, not barristers, but American "lawyers."

Similarly, colonial barristers remained officers of the courts, like English attorneys, again because no Inns existed to which they could belong instead. Ultimately the bar association and the bar examination would provide American substitutes for the English Inns. But even before the Revolution, Massachusetts arranged an institutional compromise — a typical New World amalgam of several Old World originals. Through this arrangement the court appointed barristers only upon the recommendation of the bar. Had Massachusetts established a law school before independence, the gap between attorneys and barristers would have widened enormously. But because law schools came only after the Revolution and shared its ideological condemnation of privilege, the effect was just the reverse. Even so, right up to 1776 the trend in Massachusetts was clearly towards increased differentiation between barristers and attorneys.

[112] For eighteenth century practice, see Blackstone, *Commentaries*, III, 25–29.
[113] Holdsworth, *A History of English Law*, VI, 432–36.
[114] Adams, *Diary*, ed. Butterfield, I, 251–55; III, 285–86.

No longer officially recognized as part of the profession were the remaining pettifoggers, struggling to keep alive beneath the vast superstructure erected by Hutchinson and the bar. By the 1760's these men could not plead in court on either the county or province level. They were reduced to the lowly function of drafting legal documents and scraping up business for established lawyers like the younger Auchmuty or Samuel Quincy, who together controlled a swarm of them. [Partly through competition but mostly through organized institutional pressure, the amateurs had been channelled into occupational lines strikingly similar to those of an English "solicitor." [115]

Still the bar was not satisfied. In 1770 the Maine Association, where competition with pettifoggers was probably more serious than elsewhere, voted not to participate in any case in which the *writs* had been drafted by anyone other than a recognized attorney.[116] Already the General Court had deprived sheriffs of this function.[117] But this resolve threatened, not just pettifoggers and sheriffs, but also respectable justices of the peace like Enoch Freeman of Falmouth (Portland), who normally added about £20 to his annual income through routine business of this kind.[118] Freeman protested vigorously, but the dispute lost its fire when public attention suddenly turned to the weighty events following the Boston Tea Party.[119] Doubtless because this controversial measure could alienate every justice in the province, the other counties carefully avoided Maine's example.

[Between 1760 and 1775, the Massachusetts bar consciously restructured itself along English lines. Significantly, a revolutionary movement which was defined and largely dominated by lawyers exploded, not while the profession groped towards something uniquely American, but precisely when it was more belligerently English than it had ever been before]

IX

[The relationship between the rise of the bar and the Revolution is one of the strangest paradoxes of early American history. On the one hand most lawyers were Tories. On the other hand, those who were Patriots won

---

[115] *Ibid.*, I, 236. Two reasons probably prevented anyone from suggesting the title of solicitor. First in England solicitors were formally attached to the Court of Chancery, not the common law courts. Second, the bar was trying to downgrade the pettifoggers, not dignify them with a formal title. Demand for the title would have had to come from the pettifoggers themselves, which might have occurred once they had acquiesced in their new roles, but not before.

[116] William Willis, *The History of Portland from its First Settlement with Notices of the Neighbouring Towns, and of the Changes of Government in Maine* (Portland, 1833), II, 210–11.

[117] *A & R*, IV, 174–75 (1758–59, c. 14).

[118] In 1758–59, Freeman filed twenty-eight writs for April term, fourteen for October and eleven for January. His price per writ was eight shillings, which thus netted him £21.4.0. Willis, *Portland*, II, 210 n. 2.

[119] *Ibid.*, pp. 210–11.

control of the movement and gave it consistent intellectual goals. In 1765 the professional lawyer was the intellectual mainstay of the Patriot opposition to the Stamp Act. A decade later he was indispensable to both sides. The greatest Whig-Tory debate in New England did not pit a lawyer against a layman. It matched two lawyers against each other, John Adams and Daniel Leonard.[120]

In 1774 forty-seven barristers were practicing law in Massachusetts, among whom the politics of all but one are ascertainable. Of the forty-six, only fifteen were confirmed Patriots and four were "reluctant Patriots." Nineteen were avowed Tories, of whom seventeen became refugees during the Revolutionary War. Eight others were Tory sympathizers. In other words, 37 per cent of the forty-six barristers fled the province rather than compromise their loyalty to the crown. Altogether thirty-one barristers, or 67 per cent, had serious misgivings about the Revolutionary movement, though fourteen of them managed to remain in the province as Tories, Tory sympathizers, or reluctant Patriots.

A significant correlation appears between a barrister's age and his political leanings. Those who finished college before 1740 divided evenly between Whigs and Tories. No graduate before 1742 became a Tory refugee, probably because the thought of beginning a new career elsewhere was unbearable to an older man. Most Loyalists finished college during the "Tory" administrations of Governors Shirley and Bernard. Most Whigs graduated either before Shirley or under Thomas Pownall, the "Patriot" governor. Until 1765, younger men showed pronounced Tory leanings, a clear reflection of the growing power and attraction of the crown between 1741 and 1765.

After 1765 this trend reversed. If one counts both attorneys and barristers of known political leanings, Tories outnumbered Whigs thirteen to seven in the college classes from 1761 to 1765. But among those graduating between 1766 and 1772, Patriots outstripped Loyalists eleven to five. Quite possibly the pronounced Toryism of most young lawyers was a major reason for the sharp decline in new recruits to the profession after the Stamp Act crisis. Certainly the Stamp Act itself is the key to the remarkable shift towards Whiggery among the young men who did venture into the profession after 1765. After 1775, of course, new barristers were bound to be Whigs. All eight appointed during and after the Revolutionary War were Patriots who had begun to practice in the last years of the royal regime.[121]

---

[120] John Adams and Daniel Leonard, *Novanglus and Massachusettensis; or Political Essays, published in the Years 1774 and 1775, on the Principal Points of Controversy, between Great Britain and her Colonies* . . . (Boston, 1813), which mistakenly identifies Massachusettensis as Jonathan Sewall, another Tory lawyer.

[121] See Edmund S. and Helen M. Morgan, *The Stamp Act Crisis, Prologue to Revolution* (Chapel Hill, 1953). The eight were Caleb Strong (H.C., 1764),

[In other words, lawyers over fifty-five years of age in 1774 were likely to choose either side. Most of those under thirty became Patriots. But the crown won and held the loyalties of most lawyers between those age limits, which accounted for the vast majority of the lawyers in the province. Like their English counterparts,[122] most Massachusetts lawyers could not reconcile systematic opposition to royal government with their own devotion to English law acquired in a lifetime's practice in sympathetic royal courts. The lawyers owed their growing prestige to the support of the crown. Without this encouragement, their prestige might wane or even vanish, as indeed the Shaysites hoped it would in the 1780's when they lustily revived the ancient New England prejudice against the whole legal fraternity.[123]]

Similarly a squabble for place, however furious, could keep the province in turmoil for only a limited period, even when that place happened to be the chief justiceship of the Superior Court. This quarrel could not wean the majority of the bar from their loyalty to the crown, to which they owned a great deal of their success. Hutchinson guessed correctly when he sought to placate the bar by offering it more exalted privileges than it had yet possessed. In similar manner he calmed the elder Otis in 1764 by granting him the chief justiceship of the Barnstable Inferior Court of Common Pleas. Even the younger Otis showed fitful signs of softening, especially after his followers suffered serious losses in the provincial election of May 1765.[124] He too might well have deserted the opposition for the government had not the Stamp Act undercut Bernard's entire administration a few months later.[125]

Benjamin Hichborn (H.C., 1768), William Tudor (H.C., 1769), Theophilus Parsons (H.C., 1769), William Wetmore (H.C., 1770), Perez Morton (H.C., 1771), Levi Lincoln (H.C., 1772), and John Sullivan.

[122] English lawyers voted conservatively throughout the eighteenth century until for some reason many of them supported parliamentary reform in 1785. Ian R. Christie, *Wilkes, Wyvill and Reform: The Parliamentary Reform Movement in British Politics, 1760–1785* (London, 1962), 219.

[123] See Bliss, *Address to the Hampshire Bar*, 52–53; Marion L. Starkey, *A Little Rebellion* (New York, 1955), pp. 15–18 and *passim*. We want "no more courts, nor sheriffs, nor collectors, nor lawyers . . . ," announced one Shaysite. *Ibid.*, 15. Such prejudices were common and quite pronounced, throughout the Republic during the generation after the Revolution, largely because of the Tory sympathies of most pre-Revolutionary lawyers. Warren, *A History of the American Bar*, 211–39. But, like its counterpart in seventeenth century England, the American bar was sufficiently entrenched by 1776 to grow rapidly despite these prejudices.

[124] In a test vote on February 1, 1765, the house by a margin of forty-two to forty-one granted Hutchinson an extra £40. In the May elections, only four affirmatives were not returned, as against nine negatives — a serious loss in a house so closely divided. *JHR, 1764–1765,* 205–06.

[125] For the political aftermath of the Stamp Act in Massachusetts, see Miller, *Sam Adams,* Chp. 5, and Waters, *Otis Family,* Chp. 7.

The universal unpopularity of the Stamp Act changed everything. Throughout the colonies its major opponents were nearly all lawyers — Otis in Boston, the "Triumvirate" in New York, John Dickinson in Philadelphia, Patrick Henry in Virginia and Daniel Dulany in Maryland.[126] Hence after 1765 new lawyers imitated, not the youthful Tory majority of the profession, but the confident and articulate though small Patriot minority, which became enormously powerful in the next ten years.

This escalation in the importance of the lawyer was by no means peculiar to Massachusetts. It was general throughout the thirteen colonies. Twenty-five of fifty-six signers of the Declaration of Independence were lawyers. So were thirty-one of the fifty-five delegates to the Constitutional Convention.[127] A thorough knowledge of the English constitution and English law provided the colonists with an intellectual basis for unity until they could manufacture their own nationalism to take its place. Without the common heritage of English law, the Carolinians, Virginians, Pennsylvanians, New Yorkers and Yankees who assembled in continental congresses after 1774 would have found embarrassingly little in common to talk about, much less agree upon. They might have revolted; they would hardly have united. Until independence generated its own revolutionary substitute, England remained the only common denominator among Americans, who in other respects differed from each other far more radically than they differed from Great Britain.[128]

126 For the Triumvirate, see Dorothy R. Dillon, *The New York Triumvirate; A Study of the Legal and Political Careers of William Livingston, John Morin Scott and William Smith, Jr.*, (New York, 1949). The major writings of Otis, Dulany and Dickinson in this crisis are collected in *Pamphlets of the American Revolution*, ed. Bernard Bailyn (Cambridge, Mass., 1965–   ), I. Patrick Henry, unlike the above six, was a lawyer by profession but hardly by training. See Robert D. Meade, *Patrick Henry, Patriot in the Making* (Philadelphia, 1957), esp. Chp. 7. Of the major pamphleteers of 1765, only Stephen Hopkins of Rhode Island was not a lawyer, but even he had been chief justice of his colony.

127 Daniel J. Boorstin, *The Americans: The Colonial Experience* (New York, 1958), 205.

128 I do not mean to deny the existence of a self-conscious American nationalism such as Irving Brant has discovered before the Declaration of Independence. See *James Madison: The Virginia Revolutionist* (Indianapolis, 1941), 370–400. I do claim that the *content* of this nationalism rested heavily upon a common understanding of English law and English constitutionalism. Significantly, most prominent American nationalists were either born or educated outside the thirteen colonies. Forrest McDonald, *E Pluribus Unum: The Formation of the American Republic, 1776–1790* (Boston, 1965), 5. Even Madison, though he never ventured abroad, was educated at the College of New Jersey well outside Virginia, and there he began to acquire his nationalist ideas. Thus if colonial nationalism helped to procure independence, independence in turn badly weakened American nationalism by severing it from its English moorings. This nationalism drooped sadly after 1776 just when the republic most needed a

X

The radicalism of lawyers such as John Adams guaranteed that the Massachusetts bar would survive the Revolution, despite the Toryism of most lawyers, the closure of the courts during much of the war, and the violent hostility of the Shaysites in western Massachusetts where the Tory leanings of the bar had been unusually pronounced.[129]

[But the bar did not survive unchanged, in Masachusetts or elsewhere. Those colonies which had relied on the English Inns of Court for their supply of lawyers found this source cut off after 1776. South Carolina, which probably possessed the most talented colonial bar on the eve of independence, had never developed a method of training lawyers locally.] Consequently one generation later, young John C. Calhoun had to journey to Connecticut to obtain both the collegiate and the legal education which he could not get at home.[130] Massachusetts and Connecticut, which had never relied significantly on the Inns of Court, were less shaken by the Revolution. They continued to produce their own lawyers much as they had been doing since 1730. There the bar lost heavily through Tory defection, but Harvard, Yale, the apprenticeship system and eventually Judge Tappan Reeve's Law School at Litchfield more than restored the loss before 1800.[131]

---

strong central government to hold back the British. This decline has obviously puzzled Brant who, in his discussion of Thomas Burke's state-sovereignty clause in the Articles of Confederation, solves the problem by refusing to acknowledge its existence. *Ibid.*, pp. 383–84. If my analysis is correct, then the main problem is to explain the transformation from a constitutional English to a revolutionary American nationalism between 1774 and 1789. So far the most penetrating suggestions have come from Stanley Elkins and Eric McKitrick, "The Founding Fathers, Young Men of the Revolution," *Political Science Quarterly*, LXXVI (1961), 181–216; from Max Savelle, "Nationalism and other Loyalties in the American Revolution," *AHR*, LXVII (1961–62), 901–23; and from Paul A. Varg, "The Advent of Nationalism, 1758–1776," *American Quarterly*, XVI (1964), 169–81.

[129] For example, of eight lawyers practicing in Worcester County just before independence, seven became Tories. In Hampshire and Berkshire, perhaps two-thirds of twenty or more went Tory. Willard, *Address to the Worcester Bar, passim*; Bliss, *Address to the Hampshire Bar, passim*.

[130] South Carolina took seventy-four lawyers from the Inns of Court, Virginia forty-nine and Maryland twenty-nine. Pennsylvania got twenty-three and New York twenty-one. Jones, *American Members of the Inns of Court*, xxviii–xxix. By 1774, the Inns were quite irrelevant to the growth of the Massachusetts and Connecticut bars. Pennsylvania, New York, and to a lesser extent Virginia, had already developed alternate methods of training their own lawyers, though they still used the Inns of Court. But the South Carolina bar could not possibly compensate for its complete dependence on the Inns. See generally, Warren, *A History of the American Bar, passim*.

[131] My statistics for the post-Revolutionary period are fragmentary. In Suffolk

Virginia stood somewhere between these extremes. Although the colony still relied upon the Inns of Court right up to Independence, it had already begun to produce its own lawyers. After 1760 George Wythe assumed the role that Gridley and Trowbridge had undertaken in Massachusetts over twenty years before. His apprentices included Thomas Jefferson, John Marshall, James Monroe and, for a brief period, James Madison. In 1780 the College of William and Mary awarded him the first professorship of law to be created in an American college. But in effect, Virginia remained about a generation behind Massachusetts in its legal standards when Independence cut off the colony from the Inns of Court. Patrick Henry is an accurate index of the difference. With almost no legal education, he won appointment to the Virginia bar after a battle with his examiners. The Massachusetts bar would have dismissed him as another pettifogger.[132]

[One result of these differences has become permanent. In terms of overall quality, the New England-New York-Pennsylvania bar rapidly outstripped the legal profession in the plantation colonies between 1775 and 1800, and the South has never caught up. In the staple colonies, imitation of English ways was a surface habit, a valuable luxury imposed upon a social framework which continued to differ radically from that of Great Britain. In the South, most lawyers were also plantation owners. The Revolution forced them to choose between an older American ideal and a newer English pattern. They chose the older, if indeed they had a real choice, and they have never recovered from the loss. By contrast, in New England the re-creation of English standards had been built deeply into the institutional fabric of the whole society. The region had adopted new English ways as a dynamic substitute for the New England Way. To get English lawyers, the region did not have to import them from the Inns of Court. It could produce them for itself.]

Yet after the Revolution it did not produce them in quite the same way. After 1784 the Superior Court appointed no new barristers. Even the title died altogether shortly after 1800. In the same period judges

---

County, 127 new men were admitted to the bar between 1784 and 1812, and by 1824 the county had 116 lawyers. Sullivan, *Address to the Suffolk Bar*, 49–50. In Hampshire the bar had risen to 14 by 1786, though this did not yet compensate for Tory defections. Bliss, *Address to the Hampshire Bar*, 66. By 1820, Connecticut had 216 lawyers and New York over 2000, according to Timothy Dwight. Quoted in Dixon Ryan Fox, *Yankees and Yorkers* (New York, 1940), 19. If Dwight was correct, the growth in New York after 1800 was astounding. Compare Fox, *The Decline of Aristocracy in the Politics of New York, 1801–1840*, ed. Robert V. Remini (New York: Torchbook edn., 1965), pp. 11–17.

[132] Warren, *A History of the American Bar*, esp. 47, 343–45; Meade, *Patrick Henry*, Chp. 7, esp. 96–97.

gradually dropped their great wigs and ostentatious robes for plainer garb, better suited to simple republicans.[133]

[Just as radical English lawyers largely shaped the Revolution, so the Revolution reshaped the Massachusetts bar in accordance with ideals it generated between 1775 and 1789. After independence the American bar developed, not in the direction of England's privileged hierarchy, but away from it and towards the common lawyers of the nineteenth century who differed from one another, not by rank, but by area of specialization. Like the Revolution itself, the bar recognized and encouraged the triumph of equality over privilege.]

This change has prompted American historians, led by Daniel Boorstin, to announce that England's hierarchical profession could never have survived in pragmatic America anyway.[134] The evidence suggests quite a different interpretation. The trend of the whole eighteenth century was not towards the common lawyer of the nineteenth, but away from the uncommon lawyer of the seventeenth and towards England's hierarchical model instead. By 1770 this model was firmly established in Massachusetts, and it was getting measurably stronger every year. It finally yielded, not to the incurably pragmatic spirit of old America, but to the shockingly new spirit of 1776.

The Revolution utterly reversed the trend of the whole previous century — one very good reason for calling it a revolution. A unique American bar did not create the Revolution. Rather, English lawyers dominated a Revolution which rapidly created a new American bar.

ABBREVIATIONS

A & R	*The Acts and Resolves, Public and Private, of the Province of Massachusetts Bay* . . . , 21 Vols. (Boston, 1869–1922.)
AHR	*American Historical Review* (since 1895).
BNL	*Boston News-Letter* (1704–1776).

[133] Sullivan, *Address to the Suffolk Bar*, 45–46; Willis, *Portland*, II, 207, n. 3. Cf., Bliss, *Address to the Hampshire Bar*, pp. 30–31. See the anecdote about William Cushing who provided unintentional amusement for the youngsters of New York City in 1789 when he walked through the streets in his great wig. He quickly discarded it. James D. Hopkins, *An Address to the Members of the Cumberland Bar* (Portland, 1833), 45.

[134] Boorstin, *The Americans: The Colonial Experience*, 195–205. Boorstin's portrait of the "lay lawyer," though accurate for about 1730, is highly inappropriate for any later period because it does not consider the transformation of the bar in the forty or fifty years before independence. In effect, Boorstin plots a straight line to connect the early eighteenth century with the nineteenth, and he assumes — like nearly all writers on the period — that whatever deviated from this "norm" must have been exotic, ephemeral and therefore inconsequential.

CSM, *Publications*	*Publications of the Colonial Society of Massachusetts* (since 1895).
CSP, Amer.	*Calendar of State Papers, Colonial Series, America and West Indies* (London, since 1860). Volumes are indicated by the dates they cover.
DAB	*Dictionary of American Biography.*
EIHC	*Essex Institute Historical Collections* (since 1859).
H.C.	This notation, followed by a date, indicates a graduate of Harvard College in the class of that year. A sketch of the person is available in John Langdon Sibley and Clifford K. Shipton, *Biographical Sketches of Those Who Attended Harvard College . . . ,* 14 Vols. to date (Boston, 1883–), which is organized alphabetically by class. The series has reached the class of 1760.
JHR	*Journals of the House of Representatives of Massachusetts.* This abbreviation, followed by a volume number, indicates the reprint edition published by the Massachusetts Historical Society, 37 Vols. to date (Boston, 1919–). The same abbreviation, followed by dates indicates the original edition.
MHS	Massachusetts Historical Society. This notation indicates the location of specific manuscript collections.
MHS, *Collections*	*Collections of the Massachusetts Historical Society* (since 1792).
NEHGR	*New England Historical and Genealogical Register* (since 1847).
NEQ	*New England Quarterly* (since 1928).
Sewall, *Diary*	*The Diary of Samuel Sewall,* 3 Vols. in *Collections of the Massachusetts Historical Society,* fifth series, V–VII (Boston, 1878–82).
WMQ, 3rd Ser.	*William and Mary Quarterly,* third series (since 1944).
Y.C.	This notation followed by a date indicates a graduate of Yale College in the class of that year. A sketch of that person is available in Franklin B. Dexter, *Biographical Sketches of the Graduates of Yale College . . . ,* 6 Vols. (New York, 1885–1912), which is organized alphabetically by class.

Economic
Development
and Social Structure
in Colonial Boston

JAMES A. HENRETTA

*In this essay, James A. Henretta explores the relationship be-
tween economic development and the structure of society in
pre-Revolutionary Boston, Massachusetts. He appropriates the
economist's concept of "growth" and asks a relatively new historical question: What is the impact of economic growth
upon social organization?*

 *Henretta argues that Boston underwent a steady transforma-
tion from an agricultural, land-based society to a maritime,
commercial society. This process was significantly advanced by
the end of the seventeenth century. Using the tax list of 1687,
Henretta asserts that wealth was fairly evenly distributed in
Boston at that time, but that various conditions of social dependency characterized the community.*

 *As the economy developed in the eighteenth century, so-
ciety became more fluid and dependency decreased, but the
distribution of wealth fell radically out of balance. As the
influence of the propertied classes proliferated, society became
more rigidly stratified. Henretta finds, on the basis of the tax
list of 1771, that "merchant princes" and "proletarians" were
the most notable figures of late eighteenth-century Boston
society.*

A distinctly urban social structure developed in Boston in the 150 years
between the settlement of the town and the American Revolution. The
expansion of trade and industry after 1650 unleashed powerful economic
forces which first distorted, then destroyed, the social homoegeneity and
cohesiveness of the early village community. All aspects of town life were
affected by Boston's involvement in the dynamic, competitive world of
Atlantic commerce. The disruptive pressure of rapid economic growth,
sustained for over a century, made the social appearance of the town more

 Reprinted by permission from James A. Henretta, "Economic Development
and Social Structure in Colonial Boston," *William and Mary Quarterly*, 3d Ser.,
XXII (1965), 75–92.

diverse, more complex, more modern — increasingly different from that of the rest of New England. The magnitude of the change in Boston's social composition and structure may be deduced from an analysis and comparison of the tax lists for 1687 and 1771. Containing a wealth of information on property ownership in the community, these lists make it possible to block out, in quantitative terms, variations in the size and influence of economic groups and to trace the change in the distribution of the resources of the community among them.[1]

The transformation of Boston from a land-based society to a maritime center was neither sudden nor uniform. In the last decade of the seventeenth century, a large part of the land of its broad peninsula was still cultivated by small farmers. Only a small fraction was laid out in regular streets and even less was densely settled. The north end alone showed considerable change from the middle of the century when almost every house had a large lot and garden. Here, the later-comers — the mariners, craftsmen, and traders who had raised the population to six thousand by 1690 — were crowded together along the waterfront.[2] Here, too, in the series of docks and shipyards which jutted out from the shore line, were tangible manifestations of the commercial activity which had made the small town the largest owner of shipping and the principal port of the English colonies. Over 40 per cent of the carrying capacity of all colonial-owned shipping was in Boston hands.[3]

Dependence on mercantile endeavor rather than argricultural enterprise had by 1690 greatly affected the extent of property ownership. Boston no longer had the universal ownership of real estate characteristic of rural Massachusetts to the end of the colonial period. The tax list for 1687 contained the names of 188 polls, 14 per cent of the adult male population, who were neither owners of taxable property of any kind nor "dependents" in a household assessed for the property tax.[4] Holding no real

---

[1] "Tax List and Schedules — 1687," in *First Report of the Record Commissioners of the City of Boston, 1876* (Boston, 1876), 91–133; "Tax and Valuation Lists — 1771," in Massachusetts Archives, CXXXII, 92–147, State House, Boston.

[2] The tax list for 1687 shows 80 polls with holdings of five acres or more within the town limits. For the size and location of most Boston real estate holdings from 1630 to 1645 see the "Book of Possessions" (and "Appendix"), *The Second Report of the Record Commissioners of the City of Boston*, 2d ed. (Boston, 1881) and also the detailed property maps compiled by George Lamb, *Series of Plans of Boston . . . 1630–1635–1640–1645* (Boston, 1905).

[3] Curtis Nettels, "The Economic Relations of Boston, Philadelphia, and New York, 1680–1715," *Journal of Economic and Business History*, III (1930–31), 185–215.

[4] In 1771, in Concord, Middlesex County, only 26 of 396 polls (6.5 per cent) were without taxable property; in Easton, Bristol County, 26 of 261 (10 per cent); and in Hadley, Hampshire County, 8 of 157 polls (5.1 per cent). Mass. Archives, CXXXII, 199–210, 269–274, 251–254.

estate, owning no merchandise or investments which would yield an income, these men constituted the "propertyless" segment of the community and were liable only for the head tax which fell equally upon all men above the age of sixteen.[5] Many in this group were young men, laborers and seamen, attracted by the commercial prosperity of the town and hoping to save enough from their wages to buy or rent a shop, to invest in the tools of an artisan, or to find a start in trade. John Erving, a poor Scotch sailor whose grandson in 1771 was one of the richest men in Boston, was only one propertyless man who rose quickly to a position of wealth and influence.[6]

But many of these 188 men did not acquire either taxable property or an established place in the social order of Boston. Only sixty-four, or 35 per cent, were inhabitants of the town eight years later. By way of contrast, 45 per cent of the polls assessed from two to seven pounds on the tax list, 65 per cent of those with property valued from eight to twenty pounds, and 73 per cent of those with estates in excess of twenty pounds were present in 1695. There was a direct relation between permanence of residence and economic condition. Even in an expanding and diversifying economic environment, the best opportunities for advancement rested with those who could draw upon long-standing connections, upon the credit facilities of friends and neighbors, and upon political influence. It was precisely these personal contacts which were denied to the propertyless.[7]

A second, distinct element in the social order consisted of the dependents of property owners. Though propertyless themselves, these dependents — grown sons living at home, apprentices, and indentured servants — were linked more closely to the town as members of a tax-paying household unit than were the 188 "unattached" men without taxable estates. Two hundred and twelve men, nearly one sixth of the adult male population of Boston, were classified as dependents in 1687. The pervasiveness of the dependency relationship attested not only to the cohesiveness of

[5] William H. Whitmore, ed., *The Colonial Laws of Massachusetts. Reprinted from the Edition of 1672, with the Supplements through 1686* (Boston, 1887), 22–23; Edwin R. A. Seligman, "The Income Tax in the American Colonies and States," *Political Science Quarterly*, X (1895), 221–247.

[6] Clifford K. Shipton, *Sibley's Harvard Graduates*, XII (Boston, 1962), 152–156. For other examples of mercantile success, see Bernard Bailyn, *The New England Merchants in the Seventeenth Century* (Cambridge, Mass., 1955), 192–197.

[7] Mobility and residence data were determined by comparing the names on the tax list of 1687 with those of a list of the inhabitants of Boston in 1695 in the *First Report of the Record Commissioners*, 158–170. While the death rate was higher among the poorer sections of the population, this alone does not explain the variation in permanence of residence. See John B. Blake, *Public Health in the Town of Boston, 1630–1882* (Cambridge, Mass., 1959), chap. 6.

the family unit but also to the continuing vitality of the apprenticeship and indenture system at the close of the seventeenth century.

Yet even the dependency relationship, traditionally an effective means of alleviating unemployment and preventing the appearance of unattached propertyless laborers, was subjected to severe pressure by the expansion of the economy. An urgent demand for labor, itself the cause of short indentures, prompted servants to strike out on their own as soon as possible. They became the laborers or semiskilled craftsmen of the town, while the sons of the family eventually assumed control of their father's business and a share of the economic resources of the community.[8]

The propertied section of the population in 1687 was composed of 1,036 individuals who were taxed on their real estate or their income from trade. The less-skilled craftsmen, 521 men engaged in the rougher trades of a waterfront society, formed the bottom stratum of the taxable population in this pre-industrial age. These carpenters, shipwrights, blacksmiths, shopkeepers owned only 12 per cent of the taxable wealth of the town.[9] Few of these artisans and laborers had investments in shipping or in merchandise. A small store or house, or a small farm in the south end of Boston, accounted for their assessment of two to seven pounds on the tax list. (Table 3, p. 465)

Between these craftsmen and shopkeepers and the traders and merchants who constituted the economic elite of the town was a middle group of 275 property owners with taxable assets valued from eight to twenty pounds. Affluent artisans employing two or three workers, ambitious shopkeepers with investments in commerce, and entrepreneurial-minded sea masters with various maritime interests, bulked large in this center portion of the economic order. Of the 275, 180 owned real estate assessed at seven pounds or less and were boosted into the third quarter of the distribution of wealth by their holdings of merchandise and shares in shipping. (Table 3) The remaining ninety-five possessed real estate rated at eight pounds or more and, in addition, held various investments in trade. Making up about 25 per cent of the propertied population, this middle group controlled 22 per cent of the taxable wealth in Boston in 1687. Half as numerous as the lowest group of property owners, these men possessed almost double the amount of taxable assets. (Table 1, p. 463)

Merchants with large investments in English and West Indian trade and individuals engaged in the ancillary industries of shipbuilding and

---

[8] See Samuel McKee, Jr., *Labor in Colonial New York, 1664–1776* (New York, 1935), chaps. 2, 3; also, Richard B. Morris, *Government and Labor in Early America* (New York, 1946), 147–149.

[9] The lower 50 per cent of the property owners is treated as a whole as Tables 1 and 2 and Chart A, below, indicate that the proportion of wealth held by this section of the population is approximately the same in 1687 and 1771.

distilling made up the top quarter of the taxable population in 1687. With taxable estates ranging from twenty to 170 pounds, this commercial group controlled 66 per cent of the town's wealth. But economic development had been too rapid, too uneven and incomplete, to allow the emergence of a well-defined merchant class endowed with a common outlook and clearly distinguished from the rest of the society. Only eighty-five of these men, one third of the wealthiest group in the community, owned dwellings valued at as much as twenty pounds. The majority held landed property valued at ten pounds, only a few pounds greater than that of the middle group of property holders.[10] The merchants had not shared equally in the accumulated fund of capital and experience which had accrued after fifty years of maritime activity. Profits had flowed to those whose daring initiative and initial resources had begun the exploitation of the lucrative colonial market. By 1687, the upper 15 per cent of the property owners held 52 per cent of the taxable assets of the town, while the fifty individuals who composed the highest 5 per cent of the taxable population accounted for more than 25 per cent of the wealth. (Table 1)

By the end of the seventeenth century widespread involvement in commerce had effected a shift in the locus of social and political respectability in Boston and distinguished it from the surrounding communities. Five of the nine selectmen chosen by the town in 1687 were sea captains.[11] This was more than deference to those accustomed to command. With total estates of £83, £29, £33, £33, and £24, Captains Elisha Hutchinson, John Fairweather, Theophilus Frary, Timothy Prout, and Daniel Turell were among the wealthiest 20 per cent of the population.[12] Still, achievement in trade was not the only index of respectability. Henry Eames, George Cable, Isaac Goose, and Elnathan Lyon, the men appointed by the town to inspect the condition of the streets and roads, had the greater part of their wealth, £105 of £130, invested in land and livestock.[13] And the presence of Deacon Henry Allen among the selectmen provided a tangible indication of the continuing influence of the church.

These legacies of an isolated religious society and a stable agricultural economy disappeared in the wake of the rapid growth which continued unabated until the midlle of the eighteenth century. In the fifty years

[10] See Table 3; and Edwin L. Bynner, "Topography and Landmarks of the Provincial Period," in Justin Winsor, ed., *The Memorial History of Boston . . . ,* II (Boston, 1881), chap. 17; Bailyn, *New England Merchants,* chaps. 6, 7; Nettels, "Economic Relations," 185–200.

[11] Robert Francis Seybolt, *The Town Officials of Colonial Boston, 1634–1775* (Cambridge, Mass., 1939), 74.

[12] *First Report of the Record Commissioners,* 99, 116, 126, 99, 95; Table 1, below.

[13] Seybolt, *Town Officials,* 74; *First Report of the Record Commissioners,* 98, 109, 127, 109; Bailyn, *New England Merchants,* chaps. 6, 7.

after 1690, the population of the town increased from 6,000 to 16,000. The farms of the south end vanished and the central business district became crowded. In the populous north end, buildings which had once housed seven people suddenly began to hold nine or ten.[14] Accompanying this physical expansion of Boston was a diversification of economic endeavor. By 1742, the town led all the colonial cities in the production of export furniture and shoes, although master craftsmen continued to carry on most industry on a small scale geared to local needs. Prosperity and expansion continued to be rooted, not in the productive capacity or geographic position of the town, but in the ability of the Boston merchants to compete successfully in the highly competitive mercantile world.[15]

After 1750, the economic health of the Massachusetts seaport was jeopardized as New York and Philadelphia merchants, exploiting the rich productive lands at their backs and capitalizing upon their prime geographic position in the West Indian and southern coasting trade, diverted a significant portion of European trade from the New England traders. Without increasing returns from the lucrative "carrying" trade, Boston merchants could no longer subsidize the work of the shopkeepers, craftsmen, and laborers who supplied and maintained the commercial fleet. By 1760, the population of Boston had dropped to 15,000 persons, a level it did not exceed until after the Revolution.[16]

The essential continuity of maritime enterprise in Boston from the late seventeenth to the mid-eighteenth century concealed the emergence of a new type of social system. After a certain point increases in the scale and extent of commercial endeavor produced a new, and more fluid, social order. The development of the economic system subjected the family, the basic social unit, to severe pressures. The fundamental link between one generation and another, the ability of the father to train his offspring for their life's work, was endangered by a process of change which rendered obsolete many of the skills and assumptions of the older,

---

[14] Clifford K. Shipton, "Immigration to New England, 1680–1740," *The Journal of Political Economy*, XLIV (1936), 225–238; Boston's population was 9,000 in 1710; 13,000 in 1730; 16,382 in 1742; 15,731 in 1752; and 15,520 in 1771. Lemuel Shattuck, *Report to the Committee of the City Council Appointed to Obtain the Census of Boston for the Year 1845* (Boston, 1846), 3–5. In 1687 there were 850 houses for 6,000 people or 7.05 persons per house. "Tax Lists and Schedules — 1687." The average number of persons per house in 1742 was 9.53; in 1771, 8.47. Shattuck, *Census of Boston*, 54.

[15] Samuel Eliot Morison, "The Commerce of Boston on the Eve of the Revolution," in American Antiquarian Society, *Proceedings*, New Ser., XXXII (Worcester, 1922), 24–51.

[16] See the table of entries and clearances in 1773 for the major colonial ports, *ibid.*, 28. By 1760 Philadelphia had 23,750 inhabitants and New York 18,000. Carl Bridenbaugh, *Cities in Revolt, Urban Life in America, 1743–1776* (New York, 1955), 5.

land-oriented generation and opened the prospect of success in new fields and new places. The well-known departure of Benjamin Franklin from his indenture to his brother was but one bright piece in the shifting mosaic of colonial life.

The traditional family unit had lost much of its cohesiveness by the third quarter of the eighteenth century. The Boston tax lists for 1771 indicate that dependents of property owners accounted for only 10 per cent of the adult male population as opposed to 16 per cent eighty-five years earlier. Increasingly children left their homes at an earlier age to seek their own way in the world.

A second factor in the trend away from dependency status was the decline in the availability of indentured servants during the eighteenth century. Fewer than 250 of 2,380 persons entering Boston from 1764 to 1768 were classified as indentured servants.[17] These were scarcely enough to replace those whose indentures expired. More and more, the labor force had to be recruited from the ranks of "unattached" workers who bartered their services for wages in a market economy.[18]

This laboring force consisted of the nondependent, propertyless workers of the community, now twice as numerous relative to the rest of the population as they had been a century before. In 1687, 14 per cent of the total number of adult males were without taxable property; by the eve of the Revolution, the propertyless accounted for 29 per cent. The social consequences of this increase was manifold. For every wage earner who competed in the economy as an autonomous entity at the end of the seventeenth century, there were four in 1771; for every man who slept in the back of a shop, in a tavern, or in a rented room in 1687, there were four in the later period. The population of Boston had doubled, but the number of propertyless men had increased fourfold.

The adult males without property, however, did not form a single

---

[17] Compiled from "Port Arrivals — Immigrants," in Record Commissioners of the City of Boston, *A Volume of Records Relating to the Early History of Boston* (Boston, 1900), 254–312. See, also, Mildred Campbell, "English Emigration on the Eve of the American Revolution," *American Historical Review*, LXI (1955–56), 1–20.

[18] For most of the 18th century, Negro slaves compensated for the lack of white servants. From 150 in 1690, the number of Negroes rose to 1,100 in a population of 13,000 in 1730. In that year, they made up 8.4 per cent of the population; in 1742, 8.4 per cent; in 1752, 9.7 per cent; but only 5.5 per cent in 1765. Computed from data in Shattuck, *Census of Boston*, 4–5, 43. The 1771 tax list indicates that only 17 of 318 Negro "servants for life" were held by persons whose property holdings placed them in the lower 50 per cent of the distribution of taxable wealth; 70 by individuals in the third quarter of the economic scale; and 231 or 72.6 per cent by the wealthiest 25 per cent of the population. A somewhat different picture is presented by Robert E. Brown, *Middle-Class Democracy and the Revolution in Massachusetts, 1691–1780* (Ithaca, 1955), 19; and McKee, *Labor in Colonial New York*, 171.

unified class, a monolithic body of landless proletarians. Rather, the bottom of society consisted of a congeries of social and occupational groups with a highly transient maritime element at one end of the spectrum and a more stable and respected artisan segment at the other. Although they held no taxable property, hard-working and reputable craftsmen who had established a permanent residence in Boston participated in the town meeting and were elected to unpaid minor offices. In March 1771, for instance, John Dyer was selected by the people of the town as "Fence Viewer" for the following year. Yet according to the tax and valuation lists compiled less than six months later, Dyer was without taxable property.[19] At the same town meeting, four carpenters, Joseph Ballard, Joseph Edmunds, Benjamin Page, and Joseph Butler, none of whom was listed as an owner of taxable property on the valuation lists, were chosen as "Measurers of Boards." [20] That propertyless men should be selected for public office indicates that the concept of a "stake in society," which provided the theoretical underpinning for membership in the community of colonial Boston, was interpreted in the widest possible sense. Yet it was this very conception of the social order which was becoming anachronistic under the pressure of economic development. For how could the growing number of propertyless men be integrated into a social order based in the first instance on the principle that only those having a tangible interest in the town or a definite family link to the society would be truly interested in the welfare of the community? [21]

Changes no less significant had taken place within the ranks of the propertied groups. By the third quarter of the eighteenth century, lines of economic division and marks of social status were crystalizing as Boston approached economic maturity. Present to some degree in all aspects of town life, these distinctions were very apparent in dwelling arrangements. In 1687, 85 per cent of Boston real estate holdings had been assessed within a narrow range of two to ten pounds; by the seventh decade of the eighteenth century, the same spectrum ran from twelve to two hundred pounds. (Table 3) Gradations in housing were finer in 1771 and had social connotations which were hardly conceivable in the more primitive and more egalitarian society of the seventeenth century. This sense of distinctiveness was reinforced by geographic distribution. Affluent members of the community who had not transferred their residence to Roxbury, Cambridge, or Milton built in the spacious environs of the south and west ends. A strict segregation of the social groups was lacking; yet the milieu of the previous century, the interaction of merchant, trader,

[19] Seybolt, *Town Officials*, 341; "Tax and Valuation Lists — 1771," ward 1. Dyer apparently paid rent for part of a house assesed at £20.

[20] Seybolt, *Town Officials*, 340–341; "Tax and Valuation Lists — 1771," wards 1 and 2.

[21] For a different view, see Brown, *Middle-Class Democracy*, 28–30, 79–95.

artisan, and laborer in a waterfront community, had all but disappeared.[22]

The increasing differences between the social and economic groups within the New England seaport stemmed in part from the fact that craftsmen, laborers, and small shopkeepers had failed to maintain their realtive position in the economic order. In the eighty-five years from 1687 to 1771, the share of the taxable wealth of the community controlled by the lower half of the propertied population declined from 12 to 10 per cent. (Table 2, p. 464) If these men lived better at the end of the century than at the beginning, it was not because the economic development of Boston had effected a redistribution of wealth in favor of the laboring classes but because the long period of commercial prosperity had raised the purchasing power of every social group.

The decline in the economic distinctiveness of the middle group of property holders, the third quarter of the taxable population in the distribution of wealth, is even more significant. In 1771, these well-to-do artisans, shopkeepers, and traders (rising land values had eliminated the farmers and economic maturity the versatile merchant-sea captain) owned only 12½ per cent of the taxable wealth, a very substantial decrease from the 21 per cent held in 1687. These men lived considerably better than their counterparts in the seventeenth century; many owned homes and possessed furnishings rarely matched by the most elegant dwellings of the earlier period. But in relation to the other parts of the social order, their economic position had deteriorated drastically. This smaller middle group had been assessed for taxable estates twice as large as the bottom 50 per cent in 1687; by 1771 the assets of the two groups were equal.

On the other hand, the wealthiest 25 per cent of the taxable population by 1771 controlled 78 per cent of the assessed wealth of Boston. This represented a gain of 12 per cent from the end of the seventeenth century. An equally important shift had taken place within this elite portion of the population. In 1687, the richest 15 per cent of the taxpayers held 52 per cent of the taxable property, while the top 5 per cent owned 26.8 per cent. Eighty-five years later, the percentages were 65.9 and 44.1. (Tables 1 and 2 and Chart A)

Certain long-term economic developments accounted for the disappearance of a distinct middle group of property owners and the accumulation of wealth among a limited portion of the population. The scarcity of capital in a relatively underdeveloped economic system, one in which barter transactions were often necessary because of the lack of currency, required that the savings of all members of the society be tapped in the interest of economic expansion. The prospect of rapid commercial success and the high return on capital invested in mercantile activity attracted the small investor. During the first decade of the eighteenth century,

[22] Walter Muir Whitehill, *Boston, A Topographical History* (Cambridge, Mass., 1959), chaps. 1–3; Bridenbaugh, *Cities in Revolt*, 25.

nearly one of every three adult males in Boston was involved directly in trade, owning at least part of a vessel. In 1698 alone, 261 people held shares in a seagoing vessel.[23] Trade had become "not so much a way of life as a way of making money; not a social condition but an economic activity." [24] This widespread ownership of mercantile wealth resulted in the creation of a distinct economic "middle class" by the last decades of the seventeenth century.

A reflection of a discrete stage of economic growth, the involvement of disparate occupational and social groups in commerce was fleeting and transitory. It lasted only as long as the economy of the New England seaport remained underdeveloped, without large amounts of available capital. The increase in the wealth and resources of the town during the first half of the eighteenth century prompted a growing specialization of economic function; it was no longer necessary to rely on the investments of the less affluent members of the community for an expansion of commerce. This change was slow, almost imperceptible; but by 1771 the result was obvious. In that year, less than 5 per cent of the taxable population of Boston held shares in shipping of ten tons or more, even though the tonnage owned by the town was almost double that of 1698. Few men had investments of less than fifty tons; the average owner held 112 tons. By way of contrast, the average holding at the end of the seventeenth century had been about twenty-five tons.[25] Moreover, on the eve of the Revolution ownership of shipping was concentrated among the wealthiest men of the community. Ninety per cent of the tonnage of Boston in 1771 was in the hands of those whose other assets placed them in the top quarter of the population.[26] With the increase in the wealth of the town had come a great increase in the number of propertyless men and a bifocalization of the property owners into (1) a large amorphous body of shopkeepers, artisans, and laborers with holdings primarily in real estate and (2) a smaller, somewhat more closely defined segment of the population with extensive commercial investments as well as elegant residences and personal possessions.

A similar trend was evident in other phases of town life. In the transi-

---

[23] Bernard and Lotte Bailyn, *Massachusetts Shipping, 1697–1714, A Statistical Study* (Cambridge, Mass., 1959), 56, 79 (Table II).

[24] Bailyn, *New England Merchants*, 194.

[25] In 1771, Bostonians owned 10,396 tons of taxable shipping; the town's tonnage was 6,443 in 1698. See Bailyn and Bailyn, *Massachusetts Shipping*, 79 (Table II).

[26] Only 2.3 per cent of the 8,898 tons of shipping for which the owners are known was held by individuals in the bottom half of the distribution of wealth (estates of £100 or less in Table 2); 5.9 per cent more by those with estates valued from £100 to £200; and an additional 19 per cent by persons with wealth of £200 to £500. 73 per cent of Boston's shipping was held by the wealthiest 12 per cent of the propertied population, those with estates in excess of £500. See Table 2.

tional decades of the late seventeenth and early eighteenth century, the fluidity inherent in the primitive commercial system had produced a certain vagueness in the connotations of social and economic status. Over 10 per cent of the adult males in Boston designated themselves as "merchants" on the shipping registers of the period from 1698 to 1714, indicating not only the decline in the distinctiveness of a title traditionally limited to a carefully defined part of the community but also the feeling that any man could easily ascend the mercantile ladder. Economic opportunity was so evident, so promising, that the social demarcations of the more stable maritime communities of England seemed incongruous.[27] By the sixth decade of the eighteenth century, however, rank and order were supplanting the earlier chaos as successful families tightened their control of trade. The founding in 1763 of a "Merchants Club" with 146 members was a dramatic indication that occupations and titles were regaining some of their traditional distinctiveness and meaning.[28]

An economic profile of the 146 men who composed this self-constituted elite is revealing. Of those whose names appeared on the tax and valuation lists of 1771, only five had estates which placed them in the bottom three quarters of the distribution of wealth. Twenty-one were assessed for taxable property in excess of £1,500 and were thus in the top 1 per cent of the economic scale. The taxable assets of the rest averaged £650, an amount which put them among the wealthiest 15 per cent of the population.

That 146 men, 6½ per cent of the adult male population, were considered eligible for membership in a formal society of merchants indicates, however, that mercantile activity was not dominated by a narrow oligarchy. The range of wealth among the members of the top quarter of the propertied population was so great and the difference of social background so large as to preclude the creation of a monolithic class or guild with shared interests and beliefs.

Yet the influence of this segment of society was pervasive. By the third quarter of the eighteenth century, an integrated economic and political hierarchy based on mercantile wealth had emerged in Boston to replace the lack of social stratification of the early part of the century and the archaic distinctions of power and prestige of the religious community of the seventeenth century. All of the important offices of the town government, those with functions vital to the existence and prosperity of the town, were lodged firmly in the hands of a broad elite, entry into

---

[27] Bailyn and Bailyn, *Massachusetts Shipping*, 57–58.

[28] "Society for the Encouraging of Trade and Commerce Within the Province of Massachusetts Bay," Ezekiel Price Papers, Massachusetts Historical Society, Boston. See also, Charles M. Andrews, "The Boston Merchants and the Non-Importation Movement," in Colonial Society of Massachusetts, *Publications*, XIX (Boston, 1918), 159–259.

which was conditioned by commercial achievement and family background. The representatives to the General Court and the selectmen were the leaders of the town in economic endeavor as well as in political acumen. John Hancock's taxable wealth totaled £18,000; James Otis was assessed at £2,040, while Colonel Joseph Jackson had property valued at £1,288. Other levels of the administrative system were reserved for those whose business skills or reputation provided the necessary qualifications. Samuel Abbot, John Barrett, Benjamin Dolbeare, John Gore, William Phillips, William White, and William Whitewell, Overseers of the Poor in 1771, had taxable estates of £815, £5,520, £850, £1,747, £5,771, £1,953, and £1,502 respectively. All were among the wealthiest 7 per cent of the property owners; and Barrett and Phillips were two of the most respected merchants of the town. John Scollay, a distiller with an estate of £320, and Captain Benjamin Waldo, a shipmaster assessed at £500, who were among those chosen as "Firewards" in 1771, might in an earlier period have been dominant in town affairs; by the seventh decade of the century, in a mature economic environment, the merchant prince had replaced the man of action at the apex of the social order.

Gradations continued to the bottom of the scale. Different social and occupational levels of the population were tapped as the dignity and responsibility of the position demanded. It was not by accident that the estates of the town assessors, Jonathan Brown, Moses Deshon, and John Kneeland, were £208, £200, and £342. Or that those of the "Cullers of Staves," Henry Lucas, Thomas Knox, and Caleb Hayden, totaled £120, £144, and £156. The assumption of a graded social, economic, and political scale neatly calibrated so as to indicate the relation of each individual to the whole was the basic principle upon which the functioning of town-meeting "democracy" depended. William Crafts, with a taxable estate of £80, was elected "Fence Viewer." Half this amount qualified William Barrett to be "Measurer of Coal Baskets," while Henry Allen and John Bulfinch, "Measurers of Boards," was assessed at £80 and £48. The design was nearly perfect, the correlation between town office and social and economic position almost exact.[29]

As in 1687, the distribution of political power and influence in Boston conformed to the standards and gradations of a wider, more inclusive hierarchy of status, one which purported to include the entire social order within the bounds of its authority. But the lines of force which had emerged on the eve of the American Revolution radiated from different economic and social groups than those of eighty-five years before, and now failed to encompass a significant portion of the population. The weakening of the "extended" family unit and the appearance of a large body of autonomous wage earners, "proletarians" in condition if not in con-

[29] Seybolt, *Town Officials*, 339–343; "Tax and Valuation Lists — 1771."

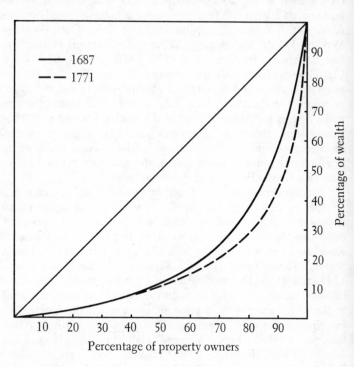

*Lorenz Curves Showing
the Distribution of Wealth
in Boston in 1687 and 1771
(Drawn from data in Tables
1 and 2)*

CHART A

sciousness, had introduced elements of mobility and diversity into the bottom part of society. Equally significant had been the growing inequality of the distribution of wealth among the propertied segment of the community, notably the greater exclusiveness and predominance of a mercantile "elite." Society had become more stratified and unequal. Influential groups, increasingly different from the small property owners who constituted the center portion of the community, had arisen at either end of the spectrum. Creations of the century-long development of a maritime economy in an urban setting, these "merchant princes" and "proletarians" stood out as the salient characteristics of a new social order.

Distribution of Assessed
Taxable Wealth in
Boston in 1687 *

TABLE 1

Total value of taxable wealth	Number of taxpayers in each wealth bracket	Total wealth in each wealth bracket	Cumulative total of wealth	Cumulative total of taxpayers	Cumulative percentage of taxpayers	Cumulative percentage of wealth
£ 1	0	£ 0	£ 0	0	0.0%	0.0%
2	152	304	304	152	14.6	1.8
3	51	153	457	203	19.5	2.7
4	169	676	1,133	372	35.9	6.8
5	33	165	1,298	405	39.0	7.8
6	97	582	1,880	502	48.5	11.3
7	19	133	2,013	521	50.2	12.1
8	43	344	2,357	564	54.4	14.2
9	22	198	2,555	586	56.6	15.4
10	45	450	3,005	631	60.9	18.1
11	17	187	3,192	648	62.5	19.2
12	30	360	3,552	678	65.4	21.4
13	13	169	3,721	691	66.6	22.4
14	12	168	3,889	703	67.9	23.4
15	22	330	4,219	725	69.9	25.4
16	21	336	4,555	746	72.0	27.5
17	1	17	4,572	747	72.0	27.6
18	18	324	4,896	765	73.8	29.5
19	1	19	4,915	766	73.9	29.6
20	30	600	5,515	796	76.8	33.2
21–25	41	972	6,487	837	80.7	39.0
26–30	48	1,367	7,854	885	85.4	47.3
31–35	29	971	8,825	914	88.2	53.1
36–40	21	819	9,644	935	90.2	58.1
41–45	19	828	10,472	954	92.1	63.1
46–50	16	781	11,253	970	93.6	67.8
51–60	16	897	12,150	986	95.1	73.2
61–70	19	1,245	13,395	1,005	97.0	80.7
71–80	7	509	13,904	1,012	97.8	83.8
81–90	3	253	14,157	1,015	97.9	85.3
91–100	7	670	14,827	1,022	98.6	89.3
100–	14	1,764	16,591	1,036	100.0	100.0

*Money values are those of 1687. Many of the assessments fall at regular five pound intervals and must be considered as an estimate of the economic position of the individual. No attempt was made to compensate for systematic overvaluation or undervaluation inasmuch as the analysis measures relative wealth. The utility of a relative presentation of wealth (or income) is that it can be compared to another relative distribution without regard to absolute monetary values. See Mary Jean Bowman, "A Graphical Analysis of Personal Income Distribution in the United States," *American Economic Review*, XXXV (1944–45), 607–628, and Horst Mendershausen, *Changes in Income Distribution during the Great Depression* (New York, 1946).

Distribution of Assessed Taxable Wealth in
TABLE 2   Boston in 1771 *

Total value of taxable wealth	Number of tax- payers in each wealth bracket	Total wealth in each wealth bracket	Cumu- lative total of wealth	Cumu- lative total of tax- payers	Cumu- lative per- centage of tax- payers	Cumu- lative per- centage of wealth
£ 3–30	78	£1,562	£1,562	78	5.0%	0.3%
31–40	86	2,996	4,558	164	10.6	0.9
41–50	112	5,378	9,936	276	17.9	2.2
51–60	74	4,398	14,334	350	22.6	3.5
61–70	33	3,122	17,456	383	24.7	3.8
71–80	165	12,864	30,320	548	35.4	6.5
81–90	24	2,048	32,368	572	36.9	7.0
91–100	142	13,684	46,052	714	46.1	10.0
101–110	14	494	46,546	728	47.1	10.1
111–120	149	17,844	64,390	877	56.7	13.9
121–130	20	2,570	66,960	897	58.0	14.5
131–140	26	4,600	71,560	923	59.7	15.5
141–150	20	2,698	74,258	943	60.9	16.1
151–160	88	14,048	88,306	1,031	66.6	19.1
161–170	11	1,846	90,152	1,042	67.4	19.6
171–180	18	3,128	93,280	1,060	68.6	20.3
181–190	10	1,888	95,168	1,070	69.2	20.7
191–200	47	9,368	104,536	1,117	72.2	22.7
201–300	126	31,097	135,633	1,243	80.4	29.4
301–400	60	21,799	157,432	1,303	84.2	34.1
401–500	58	24,947	182,379	1,361	88.0	39.6
501–600	14	7,841	190,220	1,375	88.9	41.3
601–700	24	15,531	205,751	1,399	90.4	44.6
701–800	26	19,518	225,269	1,425	92.2	48.9
801–900	20	17,020	242,289	1,445	93.4	52.6
901–1,000	16	15,328	257,617	1,461	95.4	55.9
1,001– 1,500	41	48,364	305,963	1,502	97.1	66.4
1,501– 5,000	37	85,326	391,289	1,539	99.5	84.9
5,001–	7	69,204	460,493	1,546	100.0	100.0

* The extant tax list is not complete. In ward 3, there are two pages and 69 polls missing; in ward 7, one page and 24 polls; in ward 12, an unknown number of pages and 225 polls. Only the total number of polls (224) is known for ward 11. The missing entries amount to 558, or 19.3 per cent of the total number of polls on the tax list. Internal evidence (the totals for all wards are known) suggests the absent material is completely random. Nevertheless, it should be remembered that this table represents an 80 per cent sample.

The value of shipping investments and of "servants for life" was not included in the computation of the table as it was impossible to determine the assessor's valuation. For the law regulating the assessment, see *The Acts and Resolves, Public and Private, of the Province of the Massachusetts Bay* . . . , IV (Boston, 1881), 985–987. Money values are those of 1771.

Real Estate Ownership in
Boston in 1687 and 1771 *

TABLE 3

	1687			1771	
Assessed total value of real estate	Number of owners	Cumulative total of owners	Assessed annual worth of real estate	Number of owners	Cumulative total of owners
£1	0	0	£1	0	0
2	168	168	2	1	1
3	75	243	3	9	10
4	203	446	4	49	59
5	85	531	5	22	81
6	167	698	6	79	160
7	3	701	7	0	160
8	54	755	8	115	275
9	2	757	9	3	278
10	107	864	10	91	369
11	0	864	11	4	373
12	24	888	12	43	416
13	0	888	13	163	579
14	3	891	14	10	589
15	25	916	15	3	592
16	8	924	16	148	740
17	0	924	17	6	746
18	7	930	18	7	753
19	1	931	19	5	758
20	46	932	20	236	994
21–30	25	1,003	21–25	41	1,035
31–40	11	1,014	26–30	163	1,198
41–50	2	1,016	31–35	93	1,291
			36–40	92	1,383
			41–45	5	1,388
			46–50	42	1,430
			51–60	32	1,462
			61–70	10	1,472
			71–80	9	1,481
			81–90	3	1,484
			91–100	3	1,487

* The assessed annual worth of real estate in the 1771 valuation must be multiplied by six to give the total property value.

Land, Population and the Evolution of New England Society, 1630–1790; and an Afterthought

KENNETH LOCKRIDGE

Kenneth Lockridge here attempts to synthesize recent contributions to colonial social history, especially those of demographic historians. He finds an increasing body of proof that eighteenth-century America was not the expansive, open society we have traditionally assumed it to be. Two types of evidence lead to this conclusion: on the one hand, the population of towns grew much faster than their ability to make unsettled lands available to residents; on the other, Americans were reluctant to emigrate from the towns of their birth. The combination of rising numbers of inhabitants and an almost constant quantity of arable lands resulted in conditions of land shortage, overcrowding, economic hardship, and social stratification by the late eighteenth century.

As Lockridge admits in his Afterthought, his hypothesis will remain unproven until more local, demographic, and economic studies have been made. But if the "overcrowding" notion has any substance at all, it indicates that we shall have to revise our views of colonial social organization and process dramatically. There may be grounds, for instance, to conclude that an alternative explanation of Murrin's "Anglicization" may be that there occurred a pronounced reversion to more European conditions of limited landholding, class antagonism and social tension in the eighteenth century. Whatever future research may show, this essay joins the others in this volume to indicate that historians are in the midst of a rigorous reexamination of early American social development, and that the techniques of contemporary social analysis can be employed in the task.

I

Was early America an overcrowded society? Though the idea seems absurd on the face of it, there is evidence in its favor.

American society began with a few men set down in the midst of a vast and fruitful wilderness. From this beginning until late in the nineteenth century there was no time at which the country was without a frontier in the literal sense of the word. Whatever it was or whatever it has meant to those seeking the origins of the American character, the frontier has had one meaning upon which all men, colonial speculators, genteel visitors from abroad and modern historians alike, could agree. That meaning is room. Land was always available. If some did not take it up or if others found themselves holding bad land, still others, millions and generations of others who might never have had the opportunity had they lived in another country, did take up acres of good land and throve on those acres.

Yet at first Americans moved only slowly out into the wilderness. For most of the two hundred years preceding 1800 they clustered near the eastern coastline. Particularly in the later eighteenth century, even as Daniel Boone and Ethan Allen led settlers into what were to become the states of Kentucky and Vermont, a variety of circumstances held most would-be settlers back of the Appalachian mountains. Behind the mountains, this side of the war zones of the interior, there had developed by the end of the eighteenth century a society in some respects old, stable, concentrated.

Some historians have been led to reflect on the precocious maturity of late colonial and early national society and to weigh the possibility that the society might have become less than comfortable for some of its inhabitants.[1] But the prevailing tendency has been to treat early American society as a relatively fixed conception, trimmed at either end by periods of "settlement" and "early nationhood," a conception in which the powerful influence of the frontier and the widespread existence of opportunity are not seriously questioned.[2] Certainly no historian has yet come to grips

World Copyright: The Past and Present Society, Corpus Christi College, Oxford. This article is reprinted with the permission of the Society and the author from *Past and Present*, a Journal *of Historical Studies*, No. 39, April 1968.

[1] Rowland Berthoff, "The American Social Order: A Conservative Hypothesis," *Amer. Hist. Rev.*, LXV (April, 1960), pp. 495–514, particularly p. 501; see also, Lois Kimball Mathews, *The Expansion of New England* (Boston, 1909), and Percy Wells Bidwell and John I. Falconer, *History of Agriculture in the Northern United States, 1620–1860* (Washington, 1925).

[2] Stuart Bruchey, *The Roots of American Economic Growth, 1607–1861* (New York, 1965); though sensitive to hints of change, Bruchey is forced by sheer lack of evidence to accept the prevailing assumptions of continuity and opportunity. Jackson Turner Main, *The Social Structure of Revolutionary America* (Princeton,

with the quantitative problems posed by the maturation and relative containment of early American society. What does it signify that, by 1790, Americans were not entirely a new or a restless people, or that some counties in Virginia or Maryland and some towns in New England could trace their histories back through a century and a half? How much had the conditions of life changed with time? Was it everywhere, always, necessarily, the America of room and opportunity?

Land and time must be the touchstones of any enquiry into the social evolution of early America: land because the economy was overwhelmingly agricultural and because land has been both the symbol and the essence of American opportunity; time because there was so much of it, so much time in which evolution might have taken place. How much land was available to the typical farmer and how were this and other characteristics of the society changing with time? As a beginning, these questions will be asked of early New England at large and in particular of the agricultural towns of eastern Massachusetts in the years 1630–1790.[3]

II

The only authoritative work on agriculture in colonial New England is a *History of Agriculture in the Northern United States, 1620–1860* by P. W. Bidwell and J. I. Falconer. In discussing the average area of land holdings in early seventeenth century New England they offer a figure of 25 to 50 acres. But, as the authors freely admit, the evidence from which this figure is drawn is extremely weak. Nearly every one of the several hundred cases upon which they base their estimate is rendered valueless by the circumstances under which it was recorded.[4] But, if casting doubt on

---

1965), has made the first systematic attempt to study the structure of early American society. Main's conception is fundamentally static, covering only the decades encompassing the Revolution (1760s–1780s), but he is the first to recognize the need for further, long-range studies.

[3] The questions at hand could just as well be put to the southern colonies. See Robert E. and B. Katherine Brown, *Virginia 1705–1786: Democracy or Aristocracy?* (East Lansing, 1964). The Browns assert that room and opportunity were prevailing characteristics, but no long-range statistical studies exist which would either support or weaken their view. As will be seen, there are indications that a contrary argument could be offered.

[4] Percy Wells Bidwell and John I. Falconer, *History of Agriculture in the Northern United States 1620–1860* (Washington, 1925), pp. 37–8, 53–4. Two major flaws may be noted. In the cases drawn from the towns of Dorchester, Hartford and New Haven, the acreage-per-individual is merely that granted in a single public division of town land. As is well known and as will become evident below, a settler in most early towns could expect roughly three to ten such divisions to be made during his lifetime. Secondly, the figures for several towns on Long Island are only for taxable land. In the Long Island towns the figures "do not include pasture land which was largely held in common" and which was a major component of a man's land-rights. Had this been included, the average

the 25–50 acre figure of Bidwell and Falconer is a simple matter, putting a new estimate in its place is not so simple. The best source of information on landholdings in these years should be the public records of land grants made by the various towns.[5] These would show how much land the typical early settler could expect to receive in his lifetime.[6] The trouble with using New England town records as a source is that few are precise in recording the number and area of dividends granted. In spite of this difficulty, enough bits and pieces of evidence exist to replace Bidwell and Falconer's several hundred suspect cases with several hundred other, better examples. Drawn chiefly from the records of older communities in eastern Massachusetts, these cases show that the usual early settler received a good deal more than 25 to 50 acres.

A thorough investigation has been made of the system of land allotment in Dedham, Massachusetts.[7] Complete records of land acquisitions both public and private can be compiled for thirty-two of the first fifty men to settle in the town. They averaged no less than 210 acres apiece in grants and purchases during lifetimes which ended between 1650 and 1690. From the record of public land divisions alone (of which there were from ten to thirteen between the founding of Dedham in 1636 and the year 1660) it is clear that *any* man in town by 1640 and still alive in 1660 could have expected town grants of between 100 and 200 acres. Some men who died before 1660 and missed the large divisions of the 1650s received less than this, but others who lived long and prominent lives were granted public lands up to a total of 400 acres. Since the divisions continued into the first decade of the eighteenth century, the second generation likewise drew large totals of land. Altogether, there were not fewer than 200 individuals each of whom lived for more than three dec-

---

acreage would have been "much larger." This circumstance may also have prevailed near Boston; in any event Muddy River was an area assigned to Boston's poor — hardly a fair test-area!

[5] The early estate inventories are unreliable.

[6] He might sell these lands as fast as they were granted him but on the other hand he might buy more land privately. Neither action, given a fairly self-contained local land market, would affect the average area of landholdings per man.

[7] Published town records have been cross-checked against manuscript land records in the Town Hall. Samples of each of the first two generations have been taken and their wills, inventories and deeds co-ordinated with the local records. A full exposition of the methods and results of this work may be found in K. A. Lockridge, *Dedham, 1636–1736: The Anatomy of a Puritan Utopia* (unpublished Ph.D. dissertation. Princeton University, 1965). See also the *Early Records of the Town of Dedham* (Dedham, 1866–1936), I–VI, ed. Don Gleason Hill (I–V) and Julius H. Tuttle (VI). The deeds are in manuscript in the Dedham Historical Society and in the Registry of Deeds in the Suffolk County Courthouse in Boston. There is no indication that more than a very few (if any) landless adult males have escaped inclusion in the averages.

ades as an adult in the town between 1636 and 1690. The typical man among them received an average of 150 acres from the common lands of Dedham.

The records of neighboring Watertown include land records which give a complete survey of landholdings in the 1630s.[8] For the 160 men listed at this time the average landholding was 126 acres. This average may exclude a few unlisted men who held no land, but it also excludes whatever lands those who were listed held in other towns or were granted in the several subsequent general divisions. Specifically, it does not take cognizance of the fact that the men who held only tiny "homelots" when this record was made were soon after granted farms of respectable acreage. With Dedham, Watertown gives from 300 to 400 cases averaging from 125 to 150 acres.

In six other towns of the immediate region there are indications that the seventeenth-century settlers found that America had plenty of land to offer. Medfield split off from Dedham in 1651; during the first two decades of its existence it made at least six general divisions of land. A man who lived in the town for these two decades would have received roughly 150 acres. The division of 1659 alone ranged from 50 to 150 acres per man.[9] A recent study of Sudbury, Massachusetts implies that any men who lived in that town from its founding in 1638 until 1658 must have been granted approximately 150 acres apiece.[10] The original proprietors of Milford, near Dedham in south-eastern Massachusetts, resolved in 1662 "that the divisions of land . . . shall be by these ensuing rules: that to one hundred pounds estate be granted one hundred and fifty acres of land." Since an estate of twice one hundred pounds was average, the forty original proprietor-settlers must have planned on very large individual holdings.[11] The fifty-five founders of Billerica, north of Cambridge, started off with 115 acres each.[12] A survey of the sixty men living in one section of Concord, Massachusetts in 1665 revealed that each of them

8 *Watertown Records* (Watertown, 1894–1939), I–VIII. Volumes I and II have been used. The editorial warnings on the use of these records have been observed.

9 William S. Tilden, *History of the Town of Medfield, Massachusetts* (Boston, 1887); and inventories and wills for the period in the Suffolk County Courthouse.

10 Sumner Chilton Powell, *Puritan Village* (Middletown, Connecticut, 1963), pp. 118, 122, 191, and Plate xi. The 130-acre farms spoken of on page 191 are the chief component of the total. Sudbury is north of Dedham, a few miles east of Boston. Nearby Marlborough, in deliberately retarding the process of division and keeping most land in common for some time (see Charles Hudson, *History of the Town of Marlborough* [Boston, 1862]) seems to have been the exception to the rule set by Watertown and Sudbury.

11 A. Ballou, *History of the Town of Milford* (Boston, 1882), pp. 5, 33; also inventories for Suffolk County.

12 Henry Hazen, *History of Billerica, Massachusetts* (Boston, 1883).

held on the average 250 acres.[13] In nearby Andover, "four successive divisions of town land [between 1646 and 1662], together with additional divisions of meadow and swampland, provided each of the inhabitants with at least one hundred acres of land for farming, and as much as six hundred acres." [14] With the information from Dedham and Watertown, these references make it seem that an estimate of 150 acres for the typical early inhabitant of an eastern Massachusetts town is a reasonable figure. Scattered evidence from early communities elsewhere in New England reenforces this assumption.[15]

In 1786 the Revolution was over. America was now an independent nation. Dedham had been founded exactly a century and a half before; Watertown was older still; Milford, Medfield and the other towns not quite so old. By 1786 Dedham was a town of some 2,000 souls; Watertown had grown more slowly but contained nearly 1,000 inhabitants; there were more than 775 persons in Medfield, close to 1,500 in Billerica, nearly 2,000 in Concord and more than 2,000 in Sudbury.[16] These were no longer tiny villages, but were now towns of a respectable population for an agricultural society. In 1786 the Commonwealth of Massachusetts enacted a law which required every community in the state to complete a detailed questionnaire on the basis of which taxes were to be assessed. Among other items to be filled in were the number of male polls (males over sixteen) and the acreage of every type of land within the town. This last is of the utmost importance. Included under it were "tillage," "En-

[13] Lemuel Shattuck, *History of the Town of Concord* (Boston, 1835), pp. 36–7.

[14] Philip J. Greven, Jr. "Family Structure in Seventeenth-Century Andover, Massachusetts," *William and Mary Quarterly*, 3rd Ser., XXIII (1966), pp. 234–56.

[15] To the evidence of Massachusetts' towns should be added that of Rehoboth, then a part of Plymouth Colony. Here there were some fifteen divisions of land between 1643 and 1713. Richard Le Baron Bowen, *Early Rehoboth* (Rehoboth, 1945–50), 4 vols., IV, pp. 1–21. Another bit of evidence on early land holdings may be drawn from Bidwell and Falconer, one of whose larger samples was based upon the records of New Haven in Connecticut. There 123 persons were found to have averaged a mere 44 acres each. But, as has been pointed out, a single division accounted for the acreage held by these individuals. A few pages later, in another context, the authors reveal that a second division in New Haven in the very same year had the effect of raising the average holding to 110 acres; Bidwell and Falconer, *History of Agriculture*, pp. 37, 54. In nearby Milford, Connecticut, there were four divisions in addition to an initial distribution of homelots between the founding of the town in 1639 and 1657. The process of division continued through the seventeenth century, including a large division ranging from roughly 50 to 200 acres in 1687; Leonard W. Labaree, *Milford, Connecticut, the Early Development of a Town as Shown in its Land Records* (New Haven, 1933), no. 13 in a series of pamphlets sponsored by the Tercentenary Commission of the State of Connecticut.

[16] E. V. Greene and V. Harrington, *American Population before the Federal Census of 1790* (New York, 1932), pp. 19–40.

lish upland and mowing," "fresh meadow," "saltmarsh," "pasture," "woodlands," "other unimproved land," and "unimprovable land." No type of land was left out. By dividing the number of adult males in a given town (polls minus a quarter yields a rough estimate of the number of males over twenty-one) [17] into the total acreage of the town, one may arrive at the average number of acres per man.[18]

[In what had been the "Puritan Village" of Sudbury, there were now 56 acres for each man, and in Medfield and Dedham 44 and 38 acres respectively. Even though town lands and worn lands are indiscriminately included, this represents a shrinkage to less than one-third of the land-holdings of the first generation] The shrinkage was greater in Watertown, where the average had fallen to a mere 17 acres per man — less than one-seventh of what it had been in the 1630s! But whether one-third or one-seventh, the change was substantial in each of these old towns. The same might be said of all the towns of the area, almost without exception. The truth is that for the whole of Suffolk County the land area per adult male now averaged no more than 43 acres. If the average rose to 71 acres in Chelsea, it fell to 22 acres next door in Roxbury; if to the south in Wrentham the imaginary "typical" man had 70 acres, to the east in Hingham he had but 32 acres.[19]

[17] By comparing information available in volumes i and vi of the *Early records of . . . Dedham*, it is possible to find out how many males included in the typical tax list were not of age; K. A. Lockridge, "The Population of Dedham, Massachusetts, 1636–1736," *Econ. Hist. Rev.*, 2nd Ser., XIX (1966), pp. 318–44. The estimate that one-fourth of all males over 16 years of age were in the 16–21 group is a conservative one, judging from an article by James A. Henretta on the "Social Structure of Colonial Boston," *William and Mary Quarterly*, 3rd Ser., XXII (1965), pp. 75–92.

[18] The discussion which follows is based upon uncatalogued documents in the Archives of the State of Massachusetts. They are in microfilm in volume clxiii. The resultant figures do not include lands held in other towns, but what evidence exists argues that it was not usual for a man to hold more than trifling amounts of land in towns other than his own. Further, the results make no distinction between good and worn land. Since over a century of rather unsophisticated New World farming must have produced worn land in many towns, an acre in 1786 was likely to have been less productive than an acre in 1636. Lockridge, *Dedham*, chaps. vi and vii; the Suffolk inventories also bear out this assertion. Finally, residual public (town) lands seem to be included in the total, though these were not in the possession of individual farmers. Subsequent computer analysis of the 1786 lists by Professor Van Beck Hall of the University of Pittsburgh indicates that the estimates derived here are in every respect conservative and that the *arable* land per adult male in the older areas of Massachusetts probably fell below five acres. Professor Hall is now engaged in work which will make these revealing documents yield a full picture of the economy and society of Massachusetts at the end of the eighteenth century.

[19] The narrowness of the range from top to bottom is significant. The average of 43 acres for Suffolk County was not produced by a few impossibly crowded towns pulling down the average of a more comfortable, well-endowed majority.

If time and the growth that time brought were essential factors in the decrease in the average area of landholdings, the oldest towns in the county should have had the lowest average acreages per man. This was exactly the situation. Twelve towns of Suffolk County were founded between 1630 and 1673.[20] In 1786, their adult males would have had but 37 acres apiece had all the land in these towns been parcelled out equally. The seven newer towns founded between 1705 and 1739 contained in 1786 some 55 acres for every adult male residing within their bounds — an average holding significantly above that found in the older towns, if still substantially below the average of the first generation of New England farmers.[21] Moreover, there is evidence that pressure on the land supply was most severe in the older towns. "Woodlands" and "unimproved" lands totalled 25 acres per man in the towns begun since 1705 but only 13 acres in those begun before 1673. The older towns had half as much uncultivated land per capita because the need for farm land had become most intense in these towns and was pushing men to put poor land under the plough.

More sharply diminished landholdings and a greater cultivation of marginal lands in the older towns are two indications of a mounting pressure on the land supply. A third index is the level of land prices. If there

---

The figures for each town begin with Roxbury's 22 acres and rise through averages of 25, 32, 32, 36, 38, 42, 44, 44, 47, 51, 52, 60, 68 and 70 acres to the peak of 71. As the years passed many of the inventories of estates on file in the Suffolk County Courthouse became quite specific as to landholdings. A sample of 300 of these for the years 1765–75 confirms the average-landholding figure derived from the assessment lists of 1786. The average rural estate included 65 acres of land. There are good reasons why this earlier figure is a little above the 43 acres average of 1786. For one thing, these are acreages at death. A man is likely to have held more land at the end of his life than he held on the average throughout that life. There is a second way in which they reflect success. Though there are inventories for men who held no land whatsoever (and 17 per cent of the 300 had no land at death, confirming the indications of the assessment lists that the suffrage could not possibly have been above 90 per cent), inventories for servants and paupers who had virtually no real or personal estate are extremely rare — almost nonexistent. Evidence will be presented below to show that such persons must have existed. Their exclusion from the sample of inventories naturally raises the average landholdings attributed to those who were included. With these adjustments made, it may be seen that the inventories describe much the same situation with regard to landholdings as was described in the town assessment lists of 1786. And, as would be expected, the inventories of estates from the older towns tend to include less land than those based on estates in towns more recently established.

[20] Watertown is included as one of the twelve, though it later came under the jurisdiction of Middlesex County. As it was only the eleventh largest of the nineteen towns considered, its inclusion does not greatly weight the results.

[21] Brookline, Needham, Medway, Bellingham, Walpole, Stoughton and Chelsea. No towns were incorporated between 1673 and 1705.

was a disproportionate demand for land, land prices, and probably food prices as well, should have risen more than the prices of most other commodities through the colonial period. A perusal of hundreds of inventories of estates for all of the rural towns of Suffolk County in the years 1660–1760 reveals that land values easily doubled and often tripled over the century throughout the region. By contrast, there was a remarkable long-term stability in items of personal estate, such as furniture, tools, and even clothing. Though a systematic enquiry might refine this contrast, it seems to have been a general phenomenon.

A similar decline in average landholdings may have prevailed elsewhere in New England, and may elsewhere have reached the point at which many towns were becoming "crowded," with waste land turned to crops and the cost of land soaring. A striking study of one particular Connecticut town follows the fortunes of local families through three generations, from 1740 to 1800. Family lands were divided and divided again to accommodate the increasing numbers of young men in the families, young men who did not seem to want to try their fortunes elsewhere. Ultimately, in Kent, Connecticut, "economic opportunity, which had been exceptionally bright from 1740 to 1777, was darkened . . . by the pressure of population . . . against a limited supply of land." [22] Speaking of the whole of late eighteenth century Connecticut, Albert Laverne Olson observed, "Contemporaries were well aware of the decline of Connecticut agriculture and the exhaustion of its soil." It was plain to several of these observers that the population, which had grown fourfold from 1715 to 1756, had become too great for the countryside to support. Land values were rising sharply and marginal lands were being turned into farmlands. [23]

The "why" of the process, whether in eastern Massachusetts or in Connecticut, is fairly obvious. In Suffolk County as in Kent, Connecticut the pressure of population against a limited supply of land was the critical mechanism. Boston and a few suburbs aside, Suffolk County was a predominantly agricultural area. Farmers, "yeoman" or "husbandman" or "gentleman" farmers were the solid main stock of inhabitants. [24] Land was the essence of life throughout the region; a sufficiency of land was a

[22] Charles S. Grant, *Democracy in the Connecticut Frontier Town of Kent* (New York, 1961), p. 170.

[23] Albert Laverne Olson, *Agricultural Economy and the Population in Eighteenth Century Connecticut* (New Haven, 1935), no. 40 in a series of pamphlets sponsored by the Tercentenary Commission of the State of Connecticut.

[24] See Lockridge, *Dedham, 1636–1736*. Also, wills and inventories of estates for all of Suffolk and parts of Middlesex and Essex Counties may be found in the Probate Office of the Suffolk County Courthouse in Boston; several thousand of these have been surveyed. For one example, of 142 men who died in Suffolk County towns outside Boston from 1750 to 1759, 71 per cent were "yeomen" or "husbandmen," and roughly a third of the remaining 29 per cent held over half of their estates in the form of land.

vital concern of the great majority of men. Yet, despite the simultaneous settlement of scores of towns to the west, the estimates of the population of eastern Massachusetts reveal the same inexorable growth which was characteristic of Connecticut.[25] Up until 1765, and for most towns even after, an increase of from one to five per cent a year was a normal condition of life. Accompanying this growth, again as in Connecticut, was a pattern of inheritance in which partible descent dominated. Virtually no men left their lands intact to any one son. A double share of the whole estate for the eldest son with equal shares going to all other children (sons and daughters alike) was the standard set by the law for cases of intestacy. Even the minority of men who left wills followed this standard with very few deviations. Since emigration was not sufficient to relieve the situation, the consequence was a process of division and re-division of landholdings.

The process was a product of the fundamental conditions of existence in New England, and its operation could be perceived long before its effects became serious. As early as 1721, "Amicus Patriae" observed that "many of our old towns are too full of inhabitants for husbandry; many of them living upon small shares of land, and generally all are husbandmen . . . . And also many of our people are slow in marrying for want of settlements: . . . ." [26] Had "Amicus Patriae" returned in 1790, he might well have redoubled his lamentations.

[There is a paradox involved in considering that thousands of farmers in late eighteenth-century New England held on the average little over 40 acres of land apiece. It is the paradox of a land full of opportunity and with room to spare which in practice was coming to support an agricultural society reminiscent of that in the old, more limited nations of Europe.] Nor is this just so much verbiage. The English yeoman of the previous century had farmed lands ranging in area from 25 to 200 acres.[27] In

---

[25] See E. V. Greene and V. Harrington, *American Population Before the Federal Census of 1790.* One of these eastern towns, Dedham, has been studied as a demographic test case, and confirms the broad outlines above. The curve of Dedham's population follows that of the colony as a whole, rising slowly in the seventeenth century, surging and hesitating between 1690 and 1730, rising steadily thereafter — but never declining. Growth of a little less than three per cent a year was average. Natural increase seems to have accounted for the growth, as immigration was negligible until 1736 and probably thereafter. As in Kent, there was no general exodus to new western towns, though the population rose from less than 400 in 1645 to nearly 2,000 in 1765. K. A. Lockridge, "The Population of Dedham, Massachusetts, 1636–1736."

[26] A. P. (John Wise?), *A Word of Comfort to a Melancholy Country* (Boston, 1721), in A. M. Davis, ed., *Colonial Currency Reprints,* II (Boston, 1911), p. 189.

[27] Mildred Campbell, *The English Yeoman Under Elizabeth and the Early Stuarts* (New Haven, 1942), pp. 74–100. A remarkably similar process of crowding was experienced in this same period by the English village of Wigston Magna; see W. G. Hoskins, *The Midland Peasant* (London, 1957).

terms of land, many "yeomen" or "husbandmen" in this section of late eighteenth-century America were not perceptibly better off as a result of the long-ago emigration of their great-great-grandfathers.[28] In terms of the future, in terms of the sons of these American farmers and of the amount of land which each son could hope to inherit, America was no longer the land of opportunity.

III

Further evidence drawn from eastern Massachusetts brings to light the possibility that the process which was causing the decrease in average landholdings might have been accompanied by, and perhaps have been leading to, alterations in the structure of the society.

A study of the distribution of estates from the agricultural villages of Suffolk County has been undertaken to see if the pattern in which wealth was distributed in the society could have been changing with time.[29] For the several years on either side of 1660, 300 inventories have been distributed according to their size in £100 increments and the same has been done for 310 inventories from the years adjoining 1765. A process of economic polarization was under way. In 1660 there were only 13 of 300 men whose estates surpassed £900 and only three of these were worth more than £1,500. By 1765 there were 54 out of 310 men worth more than £900 and 19 of them had estates which ranged above £1,500, averaging £2,200. The average estate in 1660 was worth £315; the average in 1765 was £525. This difference came about not because of any long-term inflation or because of any true increase in the individual wealth of most men (land prices went up, but landholdings fell); it is the huge estates of the fifty-four rich men which caused nearly all of the increased size of the "average" estate in the sample of 1765! If there were more very rich men, there were also more distinctly poor individuals among those sampled in 1765. In 1660, fifty-seven men had left estates worth less than £100. In 1765, in spite of the greater aggregate wealth represented in this later sample, seventy-two men had estates in the lowest category. Moreover, the distance between the poor and the rest of society was growing. In 1660 the better-off 80 per cent of the sample had an average wealth 7.6 times as great as the average wealth of the lowest 20 per cent. By 1765 the bulk of society had estates which averaged 13.75 times the size of

---

[28] For hints of similar changes in the southern colonies, see V. J. Wyckoff, "The Sizes of Plantations in Seventeenth-Century Maryland," *Maryland Historical Magazine*, XXXII (1937), pp. 331–9; and Jackson T. Main, "The Hundred," *William and Mary Quarterly*, 3rd Ser., XI (1955), pp. 354–84.

[29] The inventories of these estates may be found in the Probate Office in the Suffolk County Courthouse in Boston. The sample taken represents over 50 per cent of the existing inventories for the towns studied in the years for which the sample was taken.

the estates of the poorest one-fifth. Not only were the rich becoming more numerous and relatively more rich, but the poor were becoming more numerous and relatively poorer.

Before 1700, it had been rare for an inhabitant of a Suffolk County town to call himself "gentleman" or "Esquire" when the time came for him to write his will. This, too, changed as America approached the revolution and in one more small way this change hints at an evolving society. For by the 1750s no less than 12.5 per cent of some 150 men from the farming towns had appropriated these titles of distinction. This becomes more impressive when one considers that the corresponding figure for the great metropolis of Boston was only 13.5 per cent.[30] Perhaps some sort of landed gentry was arising here in the hallowed home of the New England yeoman!

An American pauper class may also have been developing at the same time and for the same reasons. In Dedham the number of vagabonds warned out of town increased sixfold in the first three decades of the eighteenth century, reaching the point where three strangers had to be moved along in the typical year.[31] There was a parallel increase in Watertown.[32] In Rehoboth, the warnings-out increased steadily from one a year (1724–33) to 3.8 (1734–43) to 4.5 (1744–53) to 6.25 (1754–7) – where the record ends.[33] In all three towns in the previous century it had been an unusual year which had seen the selectmen have to bestir themselves to ask anyone to move along. By the middle 1700s the wandering poor had become a part of the landscape in this part of New England.

If the town of Dedham has been cited from time to time as an example, it is because this is the only town in the immediate area for which an intensive analysis has been made.[34] Though that analysis has been carried in detail only to 1736, it has uncovered more bits and pieces of evidence indicating social change. Almost every development thus far suggested may be seen in microcosm in Dedham. To run through these quickly. The population grew steadily and few sons emigrated. "Worn land" appears in the inventories of Dedham estates after 1700. In the tax assessment surveys of the 1760s, 70s, and 80s a rich "loaner class" appears in the town, men with large amounts out at interest, men for whom very few seventeenth-century counterparts can be found to have existed. Not only do the numbers of vagabonds warned out increase but the numbers of indigenous poor also rise sharply after 1700. After 1710 the collective

[30] This is based on a study of 350 wills in connection with an investigation into charitable bequests. The wills are in the Suffolk County Probate Office.
[31] Lockridge, *Dedham*, 98; the figures are from the *Early Records of . . . Dedham*, vols. III–VI.
[32] *Watertown Records*, vols. I and II.
[33] Bowen, *Rehoboth*, II, pp. 139 ff.
[34] Lockridge, *Dedham*.

and very English term "the poor" comes into use in this town; contributions are taken under this heading almost yearly. As in the 610 Suffolk inventories, so in Dedham the pyramid of wealth derived from tax and proprietors' lists changes in such a way as to put a greater percentage of men in the lower brackets. The numbers of men with no taxable land increase from less than 5 per cent around 1700 to 12 per cent by 1736. Not fully developed in 1736, projected over another half-century these trends must have had a powerful effect on the nature of life in Dedham. Similar trends most certainly had a great effect on the society of Kent, Connecticut.[35]

In all of this there is (as there is in the study of Kent) an assumption of some degree of cause-and-effect relationship between the process which was causing a shrinkage in landholdings and these indications of social polarization — the two together going to make up what has been labelled an "overcrowded" society. Various linkages are possible. The most obvious would run as follows. In the intensifying competition for land, some men would lose out through ill luck or a lack of business sense. Since competition would be pushing land prices up, a loser would find recovery ever more difficult, a family with little land would have a hard time acquiring more. By the same token those men and families who somehow had acquired large amounts of land would prosper as its value rose with rising demand. In such a process, the pressure would be greater at the lower end of the spectrum. There the continuing division by inheritance would reduce ever greater numbers of young men to dependence upon other sources of income, sources from which to supplement the insufficient profits from their small plots of land, sources which might or might not be available.

IV

Clearly there were evolutionary patterns present within the society of early New England, patterns which reflect most significantly on the direction in which that society was heading. To repeat the hypothesis, the trends which existed in New England were essentially those first isolated in Kent by Charles Grant.[36]

> Economic opportunity, bright in 1751, had turned relatively dark by 1796 . . . society, predominantly middle class in 1751, included a growing class of propertyless men by 1796 . . . increased poverty stemmed from the pressure of a population swollen by a fantastic birthrate against a limited amount of land.

[35] Grant, in *Kent*, observes that a similar evolutionary process had created an agricultural "proletariat" by 1800: *Kent*, p. 97. Main's *Social Structure of Revolutionary America* confirms these indications. Using tax lists and inventories from many towns, he finds that at least 20 per cent of men in late eighteenth-century New England lived a marginal existence, with little, if any, land.

[36] The following excerpts are from Grant, *Kent*, pp. 83–103.

[A finite supply of land and a growing population, a population notably reluctant to emigrate, were combining to fragment and reduce landholdings, bringing marginal lands increasingly into cultivation and raising land prices. Ultimately, the collision of land and population may have been polarizing the structure of society, creating an agricultural "proletariat" and perhaps even a corresponding rural "gentry."] As it was in Kent, so, our evidence has suggested, it could have been throughout much of eastern Massachusetts and implicitly throughout much of New England.

What might such a process mean for our understanding of the history of early America? Charles Grant saw one of the major implications of the process which had turned his "frontier town" of Kent into a crowded and poverty-stricken backwater within fifty years. Since 1955 Robert E. Brown has been insisting that colonial society can best be characterized as a "middle-class democracy." He depicts a prosperous, satisfied society in which room and opportunity were available to nearly all, a society in which land and wealth were distributed widely and in which the suffrage was accordingly broad (since the suffrage was tied to a property qualification). The era of the American Revolution, in Brown's view, involved little internal social antagonism. The colonists simply defended their "middle-class democracy," by throwing off British rule and writing the Federal Constitution.[37] Brown musters impressive evidence to support his analysis of the society, yet his critics and other analysts of the society have found scattered evidence to the contrary, evidence which argues for poverty, for a relative lack of opportunity, for a narrower suffrage than he claims prevailed, and for bitter social conflicts in the Revolutionary era.[38] The real issue, as Grant perceived, may not be "who is right?" but "from what period of time does each side draw its evidence?" Thus:

> If Kent were established as typical, then Brown's "middle-class democracy" would be characteristic of the early stages of a new settlement . . . On the other hand, Brown's prosperity would disappear, and the depressed conditions described by a Nettels or an Adams would creep in [together with a reduction in the numbers of men qualified to vote] at a later date. Such conditions . . . would emerge mainly from the pressure of population on a limited supply of land.[39]

In short, as the century wears on Brown's thesis loses validity. In so far as the level of the suffrage is one (and to Brown the chief) element in

[37] Robert E. Brown, *Middle Class Democracy and the Revolution in Massachusetts* (Ithaca, 1955); see also Robert E. and B. Katherine Brown, *Virginia 1705–1786* (cited above, note 3).

[38] See James Truslow Adams, *Provincial Society* (New York, 1948); Curtis P. Nettels, *Roots of American Civilization* (New York, 1940); and Robert Taylor's review of Brown's book on Massachusetts in the *Mississippi Valley Hist. Rev.*, LXIII (1956).

[39] Grant, *Kent*, pp. 102–3.

political democracy, the overcrowding which was becoming a part of the social evolution of so many New England towns must have contributed to a reduction in democratic expression in the society by the time of the American Revolution or shortly after. As the numbers of landless or near-landless men rose, the numbers of men qualified to participate in the political process fell. The men of the Suffolk County town of Dorchester demonstrated their awareness of the political dimensions of the social change which was taking place when, in objecting to the suffrage qualifications written into the Massachusetts Constitution of 1780, they observed that even a low property qualification "infringes upon the Rights and Liberties of a number of useful and Respectable members of Society; which number we believe is daily increasing and possibly may increase in such proportion that one half the people of this Commonwealth will have no choice in any branch of the General Court." [40]

But the most important issue is not whether social changes were reducing the level of the suffrage in early America. Even when *Kent* appeared in 1961, most historians were a bit weary of the battle over Brown's definition of political "democracy." Most were and are more occupied with political democracy as a matter of social attitudes and political traditions than as the difference between a suffrage of 90 per cent and one of 60 per cent.[41] What is of greatest consequence is not that the society was becoming less "democratic" in the sense of a narrowing suffrage, but that it was becoming less "middle-class." Brown treated eighteenth-century colonial society as relatively static, but the evolutionary hypothesis derived from Kent and from eastern Massachusetts shows the flaw in this conception and points to a society moving from decades of rosy "middle-class" existence toward years of economic polarization and potential class conflict.

Further, the evolutionary patterns which threatened to erode the "middle-class" society described by Brown may have shaped the thinking of many of America's Revolutionary leaders. Recent work suggests that a number of American clergymen and politicians of the later eighteenth century were dissatisfied with the condition of their society. That society

[40] Massachusetts Archives, CCLXXVII, p. 67; quoted in Robert J. Taylor ed., *Massachusetts, Colony to Commonwealth* (Chapel Hill, 1961), p. 155.

[41] J. R. Pole, "Historians and the Problem of Early American Democracy," *Amer. Hist. Rev.*, LXVII (1962), pp. 626–646. (It might, however, be noted that the reduction in the suffrage caused by "overcrowding" might have been as great as the difference between a suffrage of 90 per cent and one of 60 per cent. The tax surveys of 1786 reveal that at least 20 per cent of the men in the towns of Suffolk County had not enough real or personal property to qualify as voters. See also Grant, *Kent*, p. 140 for evidence of a similar decline.) It is only fair to add that Brown himself has broadened his definition of "democracy" and increased the subtlety of his argument; see Brown, *Virginia*.

was certainly not as stratified, oppressive and corrupt as the society of England had become, but it seemed to some men that it was moving in that direction. The fear of a gradual "Europeanization" of American society, a fear given ground by the tendencies outlined here, probably lent a special energy to their Revolutionary rhetoric. Thus, the leaders of the Revolution adopted Enlightenment ideas with such speed and fervor not merely because these ideas described the egalitarian, "middle-class" society which was the distinctive feature of life in the American colonies, but also because independence and the reforms engendered by Enlightenment ideas would guarantee that happy society against the changes which even then were bringing it closer to the Old World model. The radical ideas of European intellectuals would restore and protect, as well as "complete, formalize, systematize and symbolize," the unique American social order which was the pride of the Revolutionary generation.[42]

If the evolutionary hypothesis advanced here poses problems for one controversialist, it resurrects another. Frederick Jackson Turner was convinced that the frontier — and by this he meant above all the expansive frontier of the nineteenth century — had a great rôle in shaping an energetic, egalitarian and optimistic American character. His speculations have lent energy to several generations of undergraduate lecture courses, but they have most often served as targets for historians who have been more cautious if usually less interesting.[43] Most of these critics have attacked Turner on the basis that conditions on the frontier either were not what he said they were or did not have the effect on men that he claimed they did, or both. A question which might better be asked is: Where would we have been without Turner's frontier? The trend to an overcrowded society sketched in the previous pages throws a new light on this question. Without the emigration that followed 1790, New England society would have become ever more crowded at a rapid rate. If already by 1790 many towns were experiencing an excessive demand for land and the attendant consequences of that demand, what would conditions have been twenty or

---

[42] The relevant works are Alan Heimert, *Religion and the American Mind from the Great Awakening to the Revolution* (Cambridge, Massachusetts, 1966); and Gordon S. Wood, "Republicanism as Revolutionary Ideology" (paper delivered at the Organization of American Historians meeting in Chicago in April, 1967) and "Rhetoric and Reality in the American Revolution," *William and Mary Quarterly*, 3rd Ser., XXIII (1966). The view that Enlightenment ideas served chiefly to "complete, formalize, systematize and symbolize" the American national spirit is that of Bernard Bailyn, "Political Experience and Enlightenment Ideas in Eighteenth Century America," *Amer. Hist. Rev.*, LXVII (1962), p. 351; Bailyn's analysis rests in large part upon an acceptance of Brown's thesis.

[43] Among those both cautious and interesting have been Paul W. Gates, "Frontier Estate Builders and Farm Laborers," *The Frontier in Perspective* (Madison, Wisconsin, 1957), pp. 143–63; and Page Smith, *As a City upon a Hill: the Town in American History* (New York, 1966).

Turner

thirty years later? [The most important point to make about the mass
exodus to the frontier of the nineteenth century may be that it rescued
America as the land of mobility and opportunity at a time when it was
beginning to lack both and was beginning to undergo major social
changes as a result.[44]

V

Regardless of one's view of the evidence and speculations presented here,
it should be clear that historians' understanding of the evolution of early
American society is not at all adequate.

For example, a decline in landholdings, even if it was general, need not
have meant an overcrowded society. There are at least four interrelated
propositions whose validity would render a substantial decline in landholdings meaningless in terms of "negative" social and economic effects.
The validity of several of these propositions would open the possibility
that any decline in landholdings could actually have been accompanied
by an improvement in productivity and in the overall social and economic
situation – the evidence offered above notwithstanding. First, agricultural
methods might have improved to a substantial degree and, in company
with the more favorable man-land ratio which could have resulted from a
decrease in the land-area per man, this improvement would have meant
that 40-odd acres in 1786 were far more productive than 150-odd acres
circa 1660. Second, better transportation coupled with the growth of
urban areas might have so improved the market situation that a given
quantity of agricultural produce in 1786 was worth more than that same
quantity *circa* 1660. Third, non-farm occupations (presumably crafts and
manufacturing) might have increased in the period under consideration,
offering lucrative alternatives to men who chose to or had to leave the
land. Finally, 40-odd acres, even though it included "worn" or waste
lands, might still have been ample with which to support a large family.
The point which must be made is that there is available virtually no evidence in favor of any of these propositions – probably because they are
not valid, but also and most significantly because no one has cared to try
to find the evidence. What evidence does exist argues that propositions
one, two, and probably three are not valid.[45] The only enquiry into the

44 The hypothesis likewise reflects on the background of the exodus of 1790–
1830. If conditions were tending in the directions depicted, it may be that the
waves of New Englanders heading west after 1790 were more "pushed" west by
the difficulties of life in Old New England than "pulled" west by the attraction
of better land. Lois Mathews felt that this was the case, but even she does not
seem to have realized how great the difficulties caused by a dense population
might have become by 1790: *Expansion of New England*, pp. 99 ff.

45 Bruchey's basic argument, in his *Roots of American Economic Growth*,
rests on the substantial invalidity of propositions one, two, and possibly of proposition three, in the period preceding 1790. Bidwell and Falconer, in their *History*

question of subsistence sets the total landholdings required for the support of a farm family at between 40 and 89 acres,[46] indicating that Suffolk County had reached a critical point by 1786.

Papers calling for "further study" have become one of the clichés of the historical profession. Yet the unavoidable conclusion is that the impact of this paper must reside not so much in its evidence and speculations as in a long list of specific questions. Was the decline in landholdings general? Was it always accompanied by the use of marginal lands and by a relative rise in the price of land? [47] How much of the land farmed in the late eighteenth century was "worn" land? Was there an improvement in agricultural techniques and in the man-land ratio? Was there an improvement in access to markets? [48] Did non-farm occupations offer alternate sources of income? [49] Why did sons not leave the crowded towns, towns like Kent, Connecticut and Watertown, Massachusetts, to take advantage of the room which the frontier seemed to offer? Was it fear of Indians or the traditional inertia of rural society or something not yet considered? [50] Was 40 acres enough to support a large family, and exactly how large were families in this period? [51] Was the distribution of wealth in the society changing with time? How reliable are inventories of estates in determining this? Are tax lists better sources for this purpose? Did the numbers of vagabonds and paupers increase with time? Was the increase, if any, greater than the mere rise in population would account for? Did the appropriation of titles of social distinction increase similarly? Who appropriated these titles and why? How did all these

---

of Agriculture, pp. 84 ff., 142, are skeptical about proposition one and have little to say about propositions two and three.

[46] Grant, Kent, pp. 36–8. Only a fraction of this total would be under cultivation — the rest serving as woodlot and pasture or lying fallow, but being nonetheless essential.

[47] For the theoretical basis of the study of differential price increases, see E. Phelps-Brown and S. Hopkins, "Wage-Rates and Prices: Evidence for Population Pressure in the Sixteenth Century," Economica, VII (1967).

[48] Inventories of estates could provide answers to these questions, since they list tools, crops as well as debts and credits resulting from commercial transactions. They also list "worn" lands in many instances.

[49] It would be possible to do a long-term census based on records of land transactions in the Registries of Deeds in each county. Men's occupations and ranks are listed with great consistency in these documents.

[50] See Grant, Kent, p. 102; Lockridge, "The Population of Dedham"; Greven, "Family Structure in Andover" for various explanations of inertia. This is an essential question, since, as this enquiry shows, the real problem may have been not so much the lack of a viable frontier as the relative failure to take advantage of that frontier.

[51] On the uses of historical demography, American scholars could learn a great deal from the work of their French and English colleagues. See E. A. Wrigley, ed., An Introduction to English Historical Demography (London, 1966).

factors come together in the history of a single town? The studies of Kent, Connecticut and Dedham, Massachusetts are the only long-term local case histories presently available. We need more of them.[52] Finally, what were the attitudes of thoughtful men of the time regarding the state of their society? Was there a universal awareness of change?

Until this work is begun, the irritating hypothesis that much of New England was becoming seriously "overcrowded" by 1790 will have to stand. Instead of being the land of opportunity, this part of America was rapidly becoming more and more an old world society; old world in the sense of the size of farms, old world in the sense of an increasingly wide and articulated social hierarchy, old world in that "the poor" were ever present and in increasing numbers. The word "becoming" is carefully selected. The fact of independence and the egalitarian ideas broadcast by the Revolution, together with the great exodus to the west after 1790, quickly made it ridiculous to speak of this or any part of America as an old world society. Yet this had been the tendency in much of New England for decades. Had it been allowed, by some miraculous suspension of subsequent events, to continue unchecked — who can say what might have been the result? This part of America might soon have come to resemble the Anglicized society dreamed of by some arch-Federalists more than the vigorous, expansive society which has since been a characteristic feature of our national history.

[52] At the Iowa University Conference on Early American History in March of 1967, Professor John M. Bumstead of Simon Fraser University (now of McMaster University) delivered a paper on "Religion, Finance, and Democracy in Massachusetts; the Town of Norton as a Case Study"; Norton, like Kent, Connecticut was a relatively new town which within three generations began to experience many of the characteristic difficulties of overcrowding; here, as elsewhere, there was a reluctance to emigrate. A recent and excellent study of Andover, Massachusetts (Philip Greven, Jr., "Family Structure in . . . Andover," "Four Generations: a Study of Family Structure, Inheritance, and Mobility in Andover, Massachusetts, 1630–1750" [Ph.D. dissertation, Harvard University, 1965]) confirms the trends depicted here, but also supports the possibility that these trends may have called forth a contemporaneous response. Emigration increased during the third and fourth generations, while the use of partible inheritance declined. When and where such responses operated, they could have done much to mitigate the effects of the trend to overcrowding.

Afterthought, 1970

Since 1968 two more studies of New England towns have come to my attention while one cited in the article has been completed. All confirm the broad outlines of the "overcrowding" hypothesis. These are: John Waters's work on Barnstable, Massachusetts included in his book on the Otis family; [1] Maris Vinovskis's unpublished Harvard University seminar paper on Chelsea, Massachusetts; [2] and Philip Greven's book-length investigation of Andover, Massachusetts. [3] So the weight of the evidence is still on the side of an evolutionary perspective which points to growing social problems.

Criticisms to date have not been individually as specific nor collectively as wide-ranging as the article deserves. But, whether implicitly incorporated in new evidence or explicitly put as direct challenges, they have forced some extensions of my ideas. These might be worth mentioning.

Emigration from the towns did in fact increase significantly during the third or fourth generation, and with the emergence of a trend to primogeniture, it probably eased somewhat the pressures of a growing population. Philip Greven's superb book on Andover and Edward M. Cook's research into Dedham's later history have convinced me of this. [4] More significant, however, is the fact that in Andover as in the Suffolk towns emigration was not enough to halt the process leading to social polarization. For those who stayed on within the town the future remained in doubt, as I had anticipated.

How many remained in the dubious context of aging towns and how many joined the movement to fresher pastures? This is the larger question posed anew by Greven's book. An answer of sorts may be found in the well-known 1765 Census of Massachusetts and Maine. Over half the population of this area lived in towns more than ninety years old, towns which had grown through three and a half generations and which by the indications of every study to date must have been facing the consequences of insufficient land. This figure takes on greater impact when one considers that in 1700 no towns were ninety years old hence none of the populace lived in towns likely to be "overcrowded." Despite the ensuing foundation of several score new towns on untilled land, the proportion of persons living in old towns grew to 50 per cent over the next half century.

---

[1] John Waters, *The Otis Family* (Chapel Hill, 1969).
[2] Maris Vinovskis, "Chelsea, Massachusetts," unpubl. seminar paper, Harvard University, 1968.
[3] Philip Greven, Jr., *Four Generations* (Ithaca, 1970).
[4] Edward M. Cook, Jr., "Social Behavior and Changing Values in Dedham, Mass., 1700–1775," *William and Mary Quarterly*, 3rd. Ser., XXVII (1970).

[Counterbalancing the emergence of the legendary American frontier was a trend to social maturation which embraced an ever larger share of the whole society and which in its magnitude and implications was at least as important]

Greven considers the fate of those who left. Many of the few whose lives can be followed did well for themselves, but the rest are in a sort of historical limbo. What is clear is that leaving for newer areas involved an unknown blend of opportunity and desperation, of enthusiasm and trauma, of success and failure. The rapid evolution of Kent and Norton into overcrowded towns leads one to wonder how good were the prospects for the emigrants' posterity.

Many readers have suggested that those who stayed more than compensated for the shortage of land by undertaking cash crop farming or entering artisan occupations. This brings up an almost infinitely complex series of questions and potential replies. To begin with, I have already expressed skepticism concerning any significant degree of economic development during the latter half of the eighteenth century. A recent article by Bruce Steiner tends to confirm the consequent assumption that, whether they changed their occupational labels or not, most surplus young men who remained in their native towns simply hung on in the form of disguised unemployment or overt pauperism. Unless present knowledge about the standard of living represented by a given tax assessment or estate inventory is radically wrong, Steiner's remarkable collection of information opens the possibility that as much as one-fifth of the population was hard put to support itself. This degree of impoverishment would raise further problems not only for those who believe substantial economic development took place but also for anyone who would argue that the productivity of land increased irrespective of other trends.[5]

[5] Bruce Steiner, "New England Anglicanism: A Genteel Faith?" *ibid*. Steiner's evidence not only suggests that by the second half of the eighteenth century significant numbers of men had been reduced to a slightly above minimal standard of living by means of declining landholdings-per-capita in a context of no offsetting increase in either the productivity of land or in alternative sources of income, but also tends implicitly to confirm Charles Grant's estimate that under these conditions upwards of 40 acres was needed to support a family at such a level. For more explicit support of this latter assumption, see James T. Lemon, "Household Consumption in Eighteenth Century America . . . ," *Agricultural History*, XL (1967).

Under such circumstances, by the way, one should not be surprised to find an increase in credit activity (loans) and in occupational specialization. These certainly took place in overcrowded Russian and Pakistani villages — probably also in New England towns — and they reflect only the increasing precariousness of the local farmers' situation, the extortive credit-monopoly of the local land speculators, and the desperate struggle of marginal farmers to find an ecological niche. Loans and occupational specialization, in such a context, should *not* necessarily be taken as signs of economic development.

I would now admit that there was some sort of development in the commercial sector of the economy, hence a limited degree of meaningful occupational shift. This most plausibly originated with increases in per capita agricultural exports which enabled some men to maintain their incomes despite landholdings whose output was otherwise marginal. (By specializing in selling such high-demand products as meat or hides or perhaps in taking employment with other farmers specializing in market agriculture, men might have obtained the cash with which to supplement their home-grown foodstuffs by purchasing other goods, particularly produce from neighboring towns more removed from access to urban markets.) But how many persons did in fact benefit from such changes? How many lived in or near towns accessible to markets, and within these areas what segments of the society actually profited to an extent that enabled them to maintain or raise their standards of living? Most of all, what were the social and political implications of a movement from the traditional independence of semi-subsistence farming toward complete dependence on the vagaries of the commercial world? Such a half-wanted but half-forced substitute for the traditional way could have seemed undesirable to some of those involved. It certainly seems to have worried a number of idealogues who believed in the moral superiority of the self-reliant yeoman. One could even go so far as to argue that impending commercialization was a trauma uniquely severe in the American society of the period and fundamental to the Revolution. So all in all commercial development is not to be regarded as an automatic solution to any of the problems raised by the "overcrowding" hypothesis.

Unsatisfied by these parries a few economists have observed that a model could be constructed opposite in all its effects to my own. What can I say? This is a logical possibility which holds forth to every scholar a delightful promise of an understanding that reverses much existing evidence and fits as much new evidence into a satisfying explanation.[6] More subtly, they insist that a fully articulated model of the economic mechanisms at the core of the "overcrowding" hypothesis might reveal unforeseen logical consequences either inconsistent with the evidence or antithetical to my conclusions or both. Again I agree, and urge the econometricians to their task.

The nub of the economists' discontent seems to lie in this matter of definitions. They tend to construe "overcrowding" in the strict sense of a crisis of subsistence affecting a majority of the society. Such an extreme definition would make me their ally in challenging my own article, and the fault is mine for leaving the way open to this construction. I was

---

[6] The only remote approximation of an explicit alternative model now in print will be found in Eric Jones, "Agricultural Origins of Industry," *Past and Present*, No. 40 (1968). The article is stimulating, but evidence is lacking that the model applies to New England before 1790.

using "overcrowding" in a more allusive sense to encompass: (1) the mechanism operating in older primarily eastern towns by which population growth within a fixed supply of land whose productivity is if anything dwindling leads to an average landholding approaching that insufficient to support a family; (2) the indicated economic and social consequences of this mechanism between 1760 and 1790, to wit an actual crisis of subsistence for a small but significant (as much as 10 per cent) and growing proportion of the inhabitants of these towns, a prospective crisis of subsistence or at least of comfort of varying degrees of immediacy for present and future generations, causing varying intensities of economic and psychological difficulty for a wider circle of men around the acutely impoverished core, a spreading polarization of relative and probably of absolute wealth, and increasing disenfranchisement, to which I might now add rising emigration and limited commercialization which do no more than slow the process while bringing social traumas of their own; and (3) the political consequences of the erosion in so many influential towns of a tradition of nearly universal economic sufficiency and moderately wide political participation, to which I would now add the political consequences of all of the various efforts men made to adjust to the problems posed by population pressure. Thus, the term "overcrowding" was at once an economic, a social, and implicitly a political term. If the economists would prefer, I would be willing to speak of their part of the whole in terms of "population pressure" which in lieu of sufficient viable alternatives was reducing the standard of living of an ever larger proportion of men within towns embracing from a quarter to a half of the population. But this is only part of a larger historical point which entails such unquantifiable issues as a man's reaction to the uncertain future facing his sons.

These technical probings have reminded me that every good hypothesis ought to predict evidence beyond that on which it is based. For the demographers, this could take the form of a prediction that they will find some sort of birth control coming into increasing use in the period from 1740 to 1780 — whether artificial, natural, or as delayed marriage. The use should be greatest in the communities where the crowding is most severe. An increase in illegitimacy might be anticipated as well, similarly differentiated.

Several historians have entered skeptical points in the historical journals. Here I refer the reader to an article by Gary Nash and James Lemon in the 1968 *Journal of Social History* [7] and to an extended discussion of opportunity by P. M. G. Harris in volume III of *Perspectives in*

[7] James Lemon and Gary Nash, "The Distribution of Wealth in Eighteenth-Century America," *Journal of Social History*, II (1968).

American History.[8] Their ideas are worth considering in any eventual synthesis, especially Harris's insights into generational variations in opportunity, though his misconstruction of my argument and claims to have refuted it should be examined carefully. In addition, for a rather extreme working out of the assumption that there was essentially *no* change of *any* sort on the local level, and for a very persuasive argument in favor of the continuity of certain essential social and political traits, see Michael Zuckerman's *Peaceable Kingdoms.*[9]

But it is not only new evidence and blunt criticisms that have led me to extend my thought. The spur which has pushed me farthest has been the question silently renewed by Richard L. Bushman's *Puritan To Yankee:* in what sense was the society which had evolved in eighteenth-century New England truly "American" and in what sense "European"? [10]

This depends, of course, on how one defines the evolution of the society. In this instance that is obvious. *In every town which has thus far been subjected to long-term study* the passage of time erodes an early period of stability and ample sufficiency. By the advent of the fourth generation, after the increase of the native population over a span of perhaps ninety years, the size of the average landholding is shrinking toward the subsistence level, land prices are up, poverty and landlessness are rising, the nucleus of a local landed gentry has formed, and sons are beginning to abandon the towns of their fathers and grandfathers. In one sense the emigrants are beginning or reviving an American tradition by finding opportunity in mobility, but in another sense they are men driven by their own numbers to abandon a village no longer adequate to their needs, driven to venture out into less rich, less known lands and into new relationships. Leaving their fate aside, the fact is that not enough men leave the towns to ease entirely the problems facing those who stay. These problems are augmented after 1750 in Massachusetts by a deflation which sharply reduced the numbers eligible for the franchise.

But what to make of this reaffirmed evidence is another matter. For as I have pointed out elsewhere the whole process could be viewed as a mere return to social normalcy or a sort of anglicization.[11] Perhaps the geographic mobility of the fourth generation in New England had only become equivalent to that of its counterpart across the Atlantic. Unquestionably both internal migrations arose in some sense from desperation

[8] P. M. G. Harris, "The Social Origins of American Leaders," *Perspectives in American History,* III (1969).

[9] Michael Zuckerman, *Peaceable Kingdoms* (New York, 1970).

[10] Richard L. Bushman, *From Puritan to Yankee* (Cambridge, Mass., 1967); see also the review essay by Kenneth Lockridge in *History and Theory,* VIII (1969).

[11] *Ibid.* [But compare the slightly different use of "Anglicization" in the essay above by John Murrin, pp. 415–449.—Ed.]

while both also offered opportunity — America chiefly the opportunity of new if rocky land, England primarily the opportunities of a diversified economy. The increase in the price of land, in pauperism, in a proto-gentry class, could be seen in the same light. New England had merely got over an unusually spacious, simple, and stable past and begun to be-come a western equivalent to the mother society which had spawned it.

Yet if this is so, how do we explain the American Revolution? As a sort of Civil War between equivalently "normal" societies, stemming per-haps from nothing more than a newly conscious sense of American cul-tural and constitutional uniqueness, followed by a working out of the political implications of our new sense of national identity? Yes, to some extent. And we could go one short step farther by calling forth a more inclusive version of an idea raised in the original article: the idea that Americans, with their wide tradition of independent subsistence farming, viewed the changes here subsumed under anglicization *not* as a normaliza-tion but as an undesirable return to "European" complexities. But more, might we not also stress the rapid *pace* of the return to this normal social diversity? From an isolated, closely knit, largely subsistence society of self-governing and self-supporting communes, much of rural New England was somewhat suddenly entering a period of insufficient land, of social divergencies, of forced migration, of speculation as a necessity, of pressure for commercialization — *too suddenly for a society whose majority* had for more than two generations lived in hermetic corporate security. The strain was bound to tell, most logically in a certain popular paranoia which ran through the Revolution from beginning to end. Other results were an increase in internal conflicts and ultimately an articulate demo-cratic ideology which accepted conflict as a norm.[12]

We can broaden this last argument by applying the concept of "social mobilization." What was taking place was a process in which "major clusters of social, economic and psychological commitments are eroded or broken and people become available for new patterns of socialization and behavior [especially political behavior]." These are the general terms of a model for the political effects of social change in developing nation's created by Karl Deutsch.[13] The model fits eighteenth-century New En-gland, especially in a modified version [14] in which population pressure in an essentially static economy leads to changes subsumed under the heading of social mobilization and these lead to growing demands on an estab-lished political system, demands which could culminate in revolution, re-

---

[12] See Thomas Barrow, "The American Revolution as a Colonial War for Independence," *William and Mary Quarterly*, 3rd. Ser., XXV (1968), for a parallel and not inconsistent interpretation.

[13] Karl W. Deutsch, "Social Mobilization and Political Development," *American Political Science Review*, LV (1961).

[14] *Ibid.*, 499.

form, or both. It implies that on the eve of the Revolution this part of America was going through a mild and rather backhand version of an unsettling process encountered by modernizing areas today.[15]

To be sure, great and fundamental continuities ran through the history of New England from the seventeenth century well into the nineteenth, as Michael Zuckerman sees and I agree. But it is an accepted cliché that no revolution, social or political, ever really revolutionizes. My present point is only that insofar as there was social change it would seem useful to regard it not only through the immediate perspective of the deprivations consequent on "overcrowding," but also through the whole range of wider perspectives from mere "normalization" or "anglicization" through "Europeanization" to "social mobilization." Together these put a less exclusive emphasis on the economic prospects in the older towns by bringing into the picture the concomitant rises in migration and *perhaps* in commercialization, indeed all the consequences of social maturation in New England. Social mobilization in particular goes beyond the old requirement of a direct link between impending "overcrowding" and revolutionary agitation for reform by positing a more generalized malaise which could more pervasively have affected the political history of the era. Each of these views contains something of the truth of the relationship between social change and the American Revolution. Needless to say, I would tend to stress a combination of the fear of "Europeanization" with the tensions consequent on a mildly mobilized society.

These, however, are still gross simplifications of the interpretive avenues leading from the issue of "overcrowding." For now the thing to do, as the original article urged, is to go back to the evidence and build a structure of hard data and rigorous analysis.

[15] See Gordon Wood, *The Creation of the American Republic, 1776–1787* (Chapel Hill, 1969), for indirect evidence of such unsettlement.